THE POLITICS OF THE POLICE

THE POLITICS OF THE POLICE

Fifth Edition

BENJAMIN BOWLING

Professor of Criminology and Criminal Justice
King's College London

ROBERT REINER

Emeritus Professor of Criminology
The London School of Economics and Political Science

JAMES SHEPTYCKI

Professor of Criminology
York University, Toronto, Canada

OXFORD

UNIVERSITY PRESS

OXFORD
UNIVERSITY PRESS

Great Clarendon Street, Oxford, OX2 6DP,
United Kingdom

Oxford University Press is a department of the University of Oxford.
It furthers the University's objective of excellence in research, scholarship,
and education by publishing worldwide. Oxford is a registered trade mark of
Oxford University Press in the UK and in certain other countries

Second edition 1992
Third edition 2000
Fourth edition 2010

Impression: 1

Published in the United States of America by Oxford University Press
198 Madison Avenue, New York, NY 10016, United States of America

British Library Cataloguing in Publication Data
Data available

Library of Congress Control Number: 2019937524

ISBN 978–0–19–876925–5

Printed in Great Britain by
Bell & Bain Ltd., Glasgow

For the next generations:
Samson, Johannes, and Frederik
Liam and Nadia
Toby, Charlotte, Ben, Jacob, and Ezra

EPIGRAPHS

He who lets himself in for politics, that is, for power and force as means, contracts with diabolical powers and for his action it is not true that good can follow only from good and evil only from evil, but that often the opposite is true. Anyone who fails to see this is, indeed, a political infant.

Max Weber, 'Politics as a Vocation'

If the Lord does not guard the city, the watchman keeps watch in vain.

Psalm 127

What is good? . . . Only to do justice, and to love mercy, and to walk humbly with your God.

Micah, VI, v:8

The romance of the police force is . . . the whole romance of man. It is based on the fact that morality is the most dark and daring of conspiracies. It reminds us that the whole noiseless and unnoticeable police management by which we are ruled and protected is only a successful knight-errantry.

G. K. Chesterton, *The Defendant*

CONTENTS

PART II HISTORY

PART III SOCIAL RESEARCH ON CONTEMPORARY
POLICING PRACTICE AND IMAGERY

PART IV LAW AND POLITICS

PREFACE TO THE FIFTH EDITION

The core argument of this book is that policing is inherently and inescapably a political activity. However the word politics is defined—as the theory and practice of governing, organizing control over a human community, or the social relationships that allow some people to have power over others—it is integral to the practice of policing and to the institution of the police.

Policing is the aspect of social control that is directed at identifying and rectifying conflict. It uses surveillance and emergency response to problems, underpinned by the authority and capacity to deploy coercive force to 'overpower resistance to an attempted solution in the native habitat of the problem' (Bittner 1970: 40). The police have developed in modern societies as the specialist organization charged with the maintenance of order. Policing is the sharp edge of governance, the point at which law—as an abstract system of rules—becomes the concrete physical experience of being ruled. At the heart of the police task, therefore, are two fundamental paradoxes, encapsulated in the quotations in the frontispiece.

The first paradox is that the police use physical force—a morally dubious means—to preserve peace, order, and tranquility. The patrolling officer's toolkit includes handcuffs, an extendable baton and firearm, taser, or pepper spray backed up with legal tools that permit the use of force and intrusion into private life. In divided and complex societies, there is unlikely to be agreement about the borderline between order and oppression. One side's reasonable and necessary force is the other's unjust tyranny. The resolution of the perpetual scandal caused by the deployment of the 'diabolical powers' of the police is resolved by the rhetorical claim that the police represent the democratic will of the people and the rule of law. This, of course, is always qualified by the inequalities and conflicts generated in complex market societies.

The second paradox is that not all that is policing lies with the police. Although the police stand as romantic symbols of crime control—'knights errant' ever ready to protect against threats—the sources of order and community safety lie, to a large extent, beyond the ambit of the police in the political economy and culture of society. To the extent that these provide most people with meaningful and rewarding lives, conflict, crime, and disorder will be relatively infrequent. Subtle, informal social controls, and policing processes embedded in other institutions, regulate most potential deviance. Consequently, the police appear more successful the less they are actually necessary.

The politics of the police in a just society should therefore be geared towards enhancing informal social control and minimizing the need to resort to police intervention so that—when they do respond to occurrences of crime and disorder—their intervention is fair, effective, legitimate, and experienced as just. This assertion gives rise to a wide range of questions that are covered in this book: the role and function of the police in democratic societies; the meaning of justice, fairness, effectiveness, and legitimacy; how best to ensure that police power can be held accountable to the people that it purports to serve; and about the nature of the political processes that govern policing.

*　*　*

Along with everything else, the politics of policing has transformed since the first edition of this book in 1984. In the year made infamous by Orwell, the Cold War was still raging, the Soviet Union was intact, Hong Kong was a British colony, and the construction of the Channel Tunnel had not yet begun. In that year, Apple produced the Macintosh, the first commercially successful personal computer, and DNA fingerprinting was discovered. There was no internet, mobile phones, digital cameras, or outdoor video surveillance. Police records were made with ink pens on index cards or sheets of paper stored in filing cabinets. Today, the police world is fully computerized. All voice calls to the police are digitally recorded and every item of information is captured in a computer file. Every police officer carries a smartphone, and all will soon have a video camera attached to their uniform. Many police patrol cars have on-board computers with video recording equipment and automatic number-plate readers. All are potentially connected to globally searchable databases holding millions of records. Interpol's stolen and lost travel documents database, for example, is checked more than seven million times per day. The past thirty-five years have witnessed the spread of information technology, the globalization of the financial system, the growth of global mobility of goods, services, and people, and increases in inequality within and between countries.

It will become clear in the pages of this book that many fundamental aspects of policing—including the paradoxes referred to earlier—remain unchanged. However, the far-reaching transformations just alluded to inevitably shape police policy, the resultant relationships between police and public, and the politics of police accountability in new ways. The challenge is to understand both the deeply rooted historical continuities that are integral to policing, and how these take shape in contemporary networked society.

In this fifth edition, three authors have joined together to take a broad geographical and historical view of the politics of the police, understood in the context of globalization and the rapidly changing policing scene. Private policing has grown into a major global corporate security industry. At the same time, the structure of public policing has shifted with internal diversification and specialization, and the rise of global, regional, and national policing bodies such as Interpol, Europol, and the National Crime Agency. Transnational networks connecting operational police officers around the world, which were a novelty in the 1980s, are now ubiquitous, extensive, and crucial to understanding contemporary policing. There is closer cooperation with other members of the wider policing family such as immigration, customs, security and secret intelligence services, and the military.

As everywhere else, information technology has shaped the nature of policing and representations of the police in the mass media. While the police have long been a staple of print and broadcast news, novels, films and television, in recent years they have featured extensively in 'reality television' and have an pervasive presence on social media platforms such as Facebook, Instagram, and Twitter. As is now clear, digital media, information communication technologies, and algorithmic analysis are an integral part of contemporary policing.

As we show in these pages, for more than two centuries, political battles have raged in many countries of the world over the nature and breadth of the policing task, its underpinning political ideology, limits to the power and autonomy of the police, the role of the police in crime control, and the extent to which the police are seen as legitimate or oppressive. Some historical moments are characterized as periods of consensus, such as the postwar 'golden age' of British policing. Other eras are conflict-ridden such as 1960s USA and 1980s Britain, both of which were characterized by political battles over the police and widespread rioting and public disorder often resulting in serious injury and death. The 'law and order' consensus of the 1990s between police and political elites in Britain and the USA was also a global one, with the ideas shared around the world that 'zero tolerance', 'intelligence-led', and 'community policing' models held the promise of crime reduction, efficiency, and improvements in the quality of service.

The competitive conflict to deliver policing solutions for crime and insecurity overlooks its wider social context. This is bracketed out as the focus narrows to 'what works in policing', and the pursuit of magic-bullet strategies that hold out the empty promise of a technical solution to the problems of crime and disorder. The international comparative analysis of the history of policing in this book shows that, while police strategy is important, the successful legitimation of the British police in the nineteenth and early twentieth centuries depended upon the wider social process of increasing social inclusion and the spread of citizenship. The subsequent evident declines in effectiveness and legitimacy since the late 1960s were only superficially due to failures of police policy and tactics. The key changes were in the wider social context, above all in the shift to neo-liberal, free-market economic policies, with a reversal of the general (if slow, spasmodic, and uneven) trend to increasing social equality and solidarity that had prevailed in Europe from the eighteenth century (with major historical regressions punctuating that trajectory, above all in the 1930s and early 1940s). Interdependent with the recent transformations of political economy and social structure, there has developed a neo-liberal mentality, characterized by an increasingly individualistic, and social-Darwinist celebration of the survival of the fittest. Social theorists have referred to it variously as post-modernity, late-modernity, and liquid-modernity. Regardless of terminology, policing an ever-more multicultural and fragmented social terrain, riven by the inequality and divisions engendered by neo-liberal economics, has become an increasingly fraught enterprise.

Sometimes the police stand alone in these debates, but more frequently the ideas are framed in the language of partnership with local government and other agencies. The emphasis is on evidence-led policing, joined up strategies, monitoring and evaluation, performance targets, more business-like policing for continuous improvement in efficiency and effectiveness. The problems of race and gender discrimination, corruption, and abuse have dogged policing everywhere throughout its history. Allegations of excessive use of force recur with dispiriting regularity. News media frequently highlight police scandals. Sometimes this concerns the police failure to respond effectively to the needs of victimized groups. At other times, those very same people experience over-policing when police respond in an overly aggressive manner. In many parts of the world, communities assert that they are over-policed and under-protected.

Most of the politics of policing is local. Debates about how quickly the police turn up when they are called in an emergency, the extent of crime in general, and responses to particular kinds of crime (especially serious violence such as gun and knife crime) tend to focus on how well the police are doing locally. And in many places, the structures of police governance are focused on locality, whether this is the British shire constabulary, a North American municipal police department or county sheriff, or a local police division of one of the European or Australian state police agencies. Yet, concerns about national and international security also beg questions of the police in cases of terrorism, transnational organized crime, money laundering, and cybercrime. In recent years there have even been rare, but serious, state-sponsored chemical attacks.

In the first decades of the new millennium, the heat of debate about security and policing was intensified by the fears engendered by tragic terror attacks. The iconic 9/11 destruction of the World Trade Center in 2001 was followed by the bombings on trains in Madrid in 2004 and the London underground in 2005, the attack on the Bataclan in Paris of 2015, the Brussels bombings and Nice lorry attacks in 2016 to name just a few of the atrocities in cities around the world. The fear of terrorist violence has come on top of continuing concerns about more routine forms of crime and disorder, ratcheted up by an ever-more ferocious tabloid press. In this volatile and contradictory political maelstrom, issues of police malpractice and injustice have been frequently subordinated by the clamour for toughness, while the *contra* social movements, symbolized by Black Lives Matter, Occupy Wall Street, Eco-Activism, and the like, multiply.

The 2008 financial crisis had complex effects on the politics of the police. Many commentators predicted that there would be an immediate upsurge of crime as a consequence of the 'credit crunch' and the cuts in public spending resulting from the politics and policy of austerity. However, the anticipated crime spike failed to materialize. By most measures, and in all categories, formal measures of crime, which had already been falling across Europe and North America since the mid-1990s, continued to do so for another seven years until around 2015. This decline occurred even as police budgets tightened and police numbers fell. After that time, recorded crime increased, along with significant public anxiety about crime levels in many places across Europe and North America. As we argue in this book, crime will always flourish in the absence of the social democratic, welfarist, and Keynesian policies which provide the social security that is the necessary underpinning of public safety. The rise and fall of crime rates is a complex matter, but the actual social ills that they are symptomatic of cannot be solved by policing alone.

The past last three or four decades have been a time of historical transformation. Social and economic inequality and exclusion increased sharply and rapidly from the 1970s, reversing a slow, halting, and uneven process towards human rights, social solidarity, and justice envisaged by Enlightenment thinkers more than two centuries previously. The populist political reactions to the attendant dramatic rise of crime and disorder were increasingly punitive and harsh. Policing became pressured to have zero tolerance of the socially marginal and outsiders. The war of all-against-all that is inherent in laissez-faire economics enjoins people to become ever-more ruthlessly assertive defenders of purely individual interest. In short, the three pillars of the good life identified by the prophet Micah—justice, mercy, and humility—have been undermined. With the conditions of civility eroded, 'the watchman keeps watch in vain'. Good policing may help to preserve social order: it cannot produce it. Yet increasingly this is what is being demanded of the police. As the epigraph from Raymond Chandler puts it, policing is at best symptom-relief like aspirin. It cannot substantially reduce our social tumours, let alone eradicate them. And it always leaves unwelcome secondaries.

*   *   *

Earlier editions of this book acknowledged intellectual debts to a host of scholars who have helped us to understand policing. In the thirty-five years since the first edition of this book the field of policing research has grown beyond the capacity of even dedicated specialists to keep abreast of. In 1979 Simon Holdaway edited a collection of papers, entitled *The British Police*, that claimed to include contributions from almost all the researchers then active in the field. In recent years not only has Tim Newburn published two editions of a *Handbook of Policing* challenging the bookbinder's art at nearly 1,000 pages, and including thirty chapters by specialists on a large range of aspects of policing, he accompanied this by a similar-sized volume of forty-five *Key Readings*! That these invaluable encyclopaedic ventures do not exhaust the contemporary field even in Britain is shown by the fact that there is also a burgeoning library of 'handbooks' of similar proportions, for example *The Oxford Handbook of Police and Policing* and *The Handbook of Knowledge-Based Policing* as well as many others. This means that listing the individual scholars who have inspired all the editions would now exhaust our word allowance. Eighty-five people were listed in the preface to the third edition and eager readers are referred to that. We owe them and many others very much for their inspiration and support over the years. In the preparation of this fifth edition we have also benefited additionally from research assistance from Jake Longhorn, Charline Kopf, and Lila Beesley, and valuable comments from Coretta Phillips, Estelle Marks, Maurice Punch, Conor O'Reilly, Matthew Light, Michael Mann, Michelle Bonner, Fabien Jobard, Christian Mouhanna, Kira Vrist Rønn, and Benoit Dupont.

As with all writers, our most profound debts are personal. Our respective families have given us great support and shown remarkable patience as we have endeavoured to update this book and make it as accurate and relevant as possible. Our grown-up children and toddling grandchildren—to whom this book is dedicated—have stimulated us with fresh ideas and encouragement. The original impetus and inspiration for this book, and all else, we owe to our parents. As the Book of Proverbs (1:8) enjoins, 'hear, my son, the moral instruction of your father and forsake not the law of thy mother'.

Ben Bowling, Robert Reiner, and James Sheptycki
December 2018

NEW TO THIS EDITION

The fifth edition of *The Politics of the Police* offers a considerable extension of the range of coverage of empirical and theoretical issues. It builds upon the previous editions' political economy of primarily British policing with several entirely new chapters and considerable rewriting of the others. The main aim is to encompass a much wider global and transnational scope, and reflect the growing diversity of policing forms. The new chapters are on: 'Theories and Models of Police and Policing'; 'Out of the Blue: The Establishment and Diffusion of the Modern Police from the French Revolution to the Twentieth Century'; 'Below, Beyond, and Above the Police: Pluralization of Policing'; 'The Politics of Global Policing'. The chapter on media and policing has been entirely rewritten, moving beyond a focus on the content of representations of policing to encompass analysis of the significance of media technologies themselves, as implied by its new title: 'Police and Media'. The chapter on the police role, justice, and effectiveness has been split into two new completely revised chapters: 'The Police Role, Function and Effects' and 'A Fair Cop? Policing and Social Justice?' The chapters on theory and research on policing, the development and legitimation of British policing, cop cultures, police powers and accountability, and histories of the future have all been considerably revised and updated.

PART I

POLICING: THEORY AND RESEARCH

1

WATCHING THE WATCHERS: THEORY AND RESEARCH IN POLICING STUDIES

INTRODUCTION

The academic study of policing is just about sixty years old, venerable enough to seem an ancient edifice to most of the growing numbers pursuing police research today, but still young by comparison with most disciplines. This chapter offers a broad introduction to the study of policing. It begins with a discussion of the concepts of police and policing, and their long-term evolution. Following that, it reviews the development of police research. Finally, the vexed conceptual relationship between policing and politics will be probed.

WHO ARE THE 'POLICE'? WHAT IS 'POLICING'?

Most research on the police has been concerned with immediate policy matters. Researchers have assumed a taken-for-granted, common-sense notion of the police and their proper functions. A particular modern conception has tacitly been taken as inevitable. The police are identified as a body of people patrolling public places in blue uniforms, with a broad mandate of crime control, order maintenance, and some social service and specialist functions (such as detective work or motorway policing). Anyone living in a modern society has this intuitive notion of what the police are. However, understanding the nature and role of policing, especially over a broader span of space and time, requires conceptual exploration of the taken-for-granted idea of police.

Modern societies are characterized by what can be termed 'police fetishism', which conceives of a time-bound human product—the police institution—as if it was an eternal entity. It tacitly presumes that the police are a functional prerequisite of social order and that without a police force chaos would ensue. This is an unwarranted ideological assumption. In fact, many societies have existed without a formal police force of any kind, and certainly without the present model. The police contribution to crime control and order maintenance is debatable (see Chapter 5).

It is important to distinguish between the ideas of 'police' and 'policing'. 'Police' refers to a particular kind of social institution, while 'policing' implies a set of processes with specific social functions. 'Police' are not found in every society, and police organizations and personnel can have a variety of shifting forms. 'Policing', however, *is* arguably a necessity in any social order, which may be carried out by a number of different processes and institutional arrangements. A state-organized specialist 'police' organization of the modern kind is only one example of policing.

SOCIAL CONTROL

The idea of policing is an aspect of the more general concept of social control. Social control is itself a complex and much-debated notion. In some theories social control is seen broadly as everything that contributes to the reproduction of social order. This makes the concept all-encompassing, virtually coterminous with society. It would include all aspects of the formation of a culture and the socialization of the individuals who are its bearers.

The problem with this broad concept of social control is its amorphousness. It fails to distinguish the specificity of what are ordinarily understood to be control processes: that they are essentially reactive, intended to prevent or respond to threats to social order. As Stan Cohen acerbically expressed it, this broad usage is 'a Mickey Mouse concept', and the term should be restricted to 'the organized ways in which society responds to behaviour and people it regards as deviant, problematic, worrying, threatening, troublesome or undesirable' (Cohen 1985: 1–2).

The idea of social control may be evaluated positively or negatively, according to different political interests and positions. In conservative versions of functionalist sociology, social control was seen as the necessary bulwark of a consensus underpinning social order. Ensuring adequate control mechanisms in the face of deviance or disintegration was a functional prerequisite of any society, although it was especially hard to accomplish in rapidly changing modern societies.

The development since the 1960s of critical perspectives within criminology changed the moral evaluation of social control institutions. From being seen as a necessary protection against deviance, social control came to be regarded as *producing* deviance through labelling and stigmatization (Becker 1963). Social control agents were seen as oppressors to be questioned and opposed (Becker 1967). More structuralist or Marxist versions of critical criminology saw these simple reversals of moral blame as merely making social control agents 'fall-guys' for the inexorable working of a wider hierarchy of power and privilege (McBarnet 1979). All radical analyses see social control at least in part as the oppressive maintenance of the privileged position of dominant groups. More complex critiques, however, see social control and policing as inextricably intertwining the maintenance of universally beneficial general order *and* particular structures of social dominance: the police produce 'parking tickets' *and* 'class repression' (Marenin 1982).

THE IDEA OF POLICING

Policing connotes a specific aspect of social control: the activities aimed at preserving the security of a particular social order, and social order in general. That order may be regarded as based on a consensus of interests, or a (manifest and/or latent) conflict of interests between social groups differentially placed in a hierarchy of advantage, or a complex intertwining of the two.

Policing may be *aimed* at securing social order, but its effectiveness is always debatable. Policing does not encompass *all* activities directed at achieving social order. What is specific to policing is the operation of surveillance, coupled with the threat of sanctions for deviance—either immediately or by initiating penal processes. The most familiar such system is of course the one denoted by the modern sense of police: regular uniformed patrol of public space, coupled with *post hoc* investigation of reported or discovered crime or disorder. As will be seen later (especially in Chapters 7 and 9), although beat patrol of streets remains a mainstay of police organizations, a variety of other police institutions have proliferated in the last half century.

THE IDEA OF POLICE

Policing thus defined may be carried out by a diverse array of people and techniques. Indeed, the term 'police' itself carried a broader connotation in early modern times (Rawlings 2008; Zedner 2006; see also Chapter 2 of this book). This was exemplified by the 'science of police', which was a broad international movement in the eighteenth and early nineteenth centuries, aimed at maintaining and promoting the 'happiness' of populations (Radzinowicz 1956; Reiner 1988; Pasquino 1991; McMullan 1996, 1998; Garland 1996, 1997; Neocleous 2000; Dubber 2005; Dubber and Valverde 2006).

Policing may be done by a variety of agents: professionals employed by the state in an organization with an omnibus policing mandate—the archetypal modern idea of the police—or by state agencies with primarily other purposes, such as the Civil Nuclear Constabulary, parks constabularies, the British Transport Police, and other 'hybrid' policing bodies (Johnston 1992a and 1992b). In addition to local police forces, today's public police include the National Crime Agency, Europol, Interpol, and the United Nations Police (Bowling and Sheptycki 2015a). Policing may be carried out by professionals employed by specialist private policing firms—contract security—or security employees of an organization whose main business is something else—in-house security (Shearing and Stenning 1987; Jones and Newburn 2006; Button 2016; Abrahamsen and Leander 2016). Patrols may be carried out by bodies without the full status, powers, equipment, or training of the core state police, such as Police Community Support Officers (Crawford *et al.* 2005). Policing functions may be performed by citizens in a voluntary capacity within state police organizations, such as the Special Constabulary (Bullock and Millie 2017; Leon 2017), in association with the state police, such as neighbourhood watch schemes (McConville and Shepherd 1992), or in completely independent bodies, such as many vigilante bodies which have flourished at many times and places (Johnston 1996). Policing functions may be carried out by state bodies with other prime functions, such as the army, or by employees (state or private) as an adjunct of their main job (such as concierges or bus conductors). Policing may be carried out by technology, such as CCTV cameras (Sheptycki 2000d; Goold 2004, 2009; Norris and McCahill 2006). Policing may be designed into the architecture and furniture of streets and buildings, as epitomized by Mike Davis's celebrated example of the bum-proof bench (Davis 1990). All these policing strategies are proliferating today, even though it is the state agency with the omnibus mandate of order maintenance that is popularly understood by the label 'the police'.

THE EVOLUTION OF POLICING

Until modern times, policing functions were carried out primarily as a by-product of other social relationships, and by citizen 'volunteers' or private employees. Anthropological studies show that many pre-literate societies have existed without any formalized system of social control or policing. A cross-cultural study of the relationship between legal evolution and societal complexity in a sample of fifty-one pre-industrial societies found that 'elements of legal organisation emerge in a sequence, such that each constitutes a necessary condition for the next' (Schwartz and Miller 1964: 160). Police in the sense of a 'specialized armed force used partially or wholly for norm enforcement' were found in only twenty of the fifty-one societies in the sample (ibid.: 161). These were almost all societies that were sufficiently economically developed to have monetary systems, and with a high degree of specialization including full-time priests, teachers, and official functionaries of various kinds. Police appear 'only in association with a substantial degree of division of labour' (ibid.: 166) and are usually preceded by other elements of a developed legal system like mediation and damages.

Specialized policing institutions emerge in relatively complex societies, but they are not a straightforward reflex of a burgeoning division of labour. Specialist police forces develop hand in hand with social inequality and hierarchy. They are a means for the emergence and protection of more centralized and dominant class and state systems. The development of specialized police 'is linked to economic specialization and differential access to resources that occur in the transition from a kinship- to a class-dominated society' (Robinson and Scaglion 1987: 109). During this transition, communal policing forms are converted in incremental stages to state-dominated ones, which begin to function as agents of class control in addition to more general social control (Robinson, et al. 1994). The complex and contradictory function of contemporary police, simultaneously embodying the quest for general and stratified order—'parking tickets' as well as 'class repression' (Marenin 1982)—is thus inscribed in their birth process.

British and other Anglosphere police ideologies rest upon the myth of a fundamental distinction between their model of community-based policing and alien, 'Continental', European, and other state-controlled systems. The varying modern models of police and their origins will be traced in more detail in Chapters 2 and 3. Conventional histories of the British police attempt to trace a direct lineage between ancient tribal forms of collective self-policing and contemporary cops and bobbies. Such claims have been characterized aptly as 'ideology as history' (Robinson 1979). It is true that many European systems of police did develop more overtly as instruments of state control (Chapman 1970). Critical histories, however, emphasize the relationship between modern police development and the shifting structures of class and state in Britain, as well as the USA and other common law systems. The supposedly benign 'British model' was in any case for home consumption only. A more militaristic and coercive model was, from the outset, exported to the colonies, including Ireland (Brogden 1987; Palmer 1988; Anderson and Killingray 1991, 1992; Sinclair 2006; Mulcahy 2013).

Conventional histories of British policing also downplay the role of covert 'high policing' methods (Brodeur 1983). Yet it is clear that from the earliest times the police collected secret intelligence, conducted surveillance, ran informers, and worked undercover; they continue to do so today (Gill and Phythian 2018). Indeed, there is good evidence that covert policing is a normal part of everyday operational practice in Britain today (Loftus 2019).

Although contemporary patterns of police vary considerably in detail, they have tended to converge increasingly around fundamentally similar organizational and cultural lines, without the qualitative distinctions of the kind implied in traditional British police ideology. This has been facilitated by the emergence of a new international body of technocratic police experts who are responsible for the diffusion of fashions in police thinking around the globe, as witnessed by the continued enthusiasm for 'community policing' strategies (Skolnick and Bayley 1988; Fielding 2002; Skogan 2006; Brogden and Nijhar 2005).

POLICE: FUNCTION OR FORCE?

Around the world, police organizations label themselves as some variant of either 'force' or 'service', and there has been much debate about which better characterizes the police role. Police commonly claim their mission as being 'to serve and protect' or similar social contributions that are both indispensable and benign. It is problematic, however, to define contemporary police mainly in terms of their supposed function (Klockars 1985). The police are called upon routinely to perform a bewildering miscellany of tasks, from controlling traffic to terrorism, from collaring criminals to cats that stray (Bittner 1970, 1974; Brodeur 2007). This has been a commonplace finding of empirical police research from the outset (Chapter 5).

The uniting feature of the tasks that come to be seen as policework is not that they are aspects of a particular social function, whether it be crime control, surveillance, crime detection, social service, order maintenance, or political repression. Rather it is that policing tasks arise in emergencies, usually with an element of at least potential social conflict. The police may invoke their legal powers to handle the situation, but more commonly they resort to a variety of ways and means to keep the peace without invoking the law or initiating legal proceedings. Nonetheless, underlying all their tactics for peacekeeping is their bottom-line power to wield legal sanctions, ultimately the use of legitimate force and intrusive surveillance. 'A benign bobby . . . still brings to the situation a uniform, a truncheon, and a battery of resource charges . . . which can be employed when appeasement fails and fists start flying' (Punch 1979b: 116).

The distinctiveness of the police lies not in their performance of a specific social function, but in being the specialist repositories for the state's monopolization of legitimate force and capacity for covert surveillance within a specific territory (Brodeur 1983, 2010). This does not imply that all policing is about the use of force or intrusion into privacy. On the contrary, 'good' policing has often been seen as the craft of handling trouble without resort to coercion, usually by skillful verbal tactics (Muir 1977; Bayley and Bittner 1984).

The police are not the only people who can use legitimate force. This remains the right (and in some circumstances the moral duty) of every citizen. There are many occupations in which the potential for the legitimate use of force may arise with a fair degree of frequency, for example workers in the health or social services handling disturbed patients, or public transport staff dealing with disorder. However, they are not 'equipped, entitled and required to deal with every exigency in which force may have to be used' (Bittner 1974: 35). Indeed, other workers are likely to 'call the cops' at the earliest opportunity in troublesome situations and use legitimate force themselves only as a stopgap emergency measure.

The police are also not the only people who have legal powers to conduct intrusive surveillance. Background checks, secret filming, voice recording, monitoring phone calls, and internet covert observation by informers or undercover operatives can all be done by private companies for profit (Gill and Phythian 2018). Many other public and private organizations gather intelligence on suspicious people and activities, including domestic and overseas secret intelligence agencies, local and central government departments (e.g. environment), the military, and corporations (ibid.). But it is the police who have the capacity for surveillance that combines with power to use coercive force in responding to a wide range of social problems and situations. The ability to coerce and intrude into privacy are the core features of policework, its occupational culture, the working environment, and 'the police métier'.

To sum up, 'policing' is an aspect of social control which occurs universally, in all social situations in which there is the potential for conflict, deviance, or disorder. The 'police'—a specialized body of people given primary formal responsibility for legitimate force and intrusive surveillance—is a feature only of relatively complex societies. The police have developed in particular with the rise of modern state forms (see Chapters 2 to 4). They have been 'domestic missionaries' in the historical endeavours of centralized states to propagate and protect a dominant conception of peace and propriety throughout their territories (Storch 1976).

This is not to say, however, that they have been mere tools of the state, faithfully carrying out tasks determined from above. Whether this is regarded as legitimate or not, all police forces have been characterized by discretion exercised by the lowest ranks in the organization, necessitated by the basic nature of policework as dispersed surveillance and control. The determination of policework in practice is achieved by the interplay of a variety of processes and pressures, and is problematically related to formal policies determined at the top (Chapter 11).

Many of these features of modern police organizations are currently under great challenge, and policing is undergoing profound changes in what many commentators have interpreted as a fundamentally new stage of social development. Policing has been a focus of political controversy since the mid-twentieth century, and this has been a factor generating the development of a burgeoning body of research and theoretical analysis.

THE DEVELOPMENT OF POLICING RESEARCH

Empirical research on the police originated in Britain and the USA during the early 1960s. The impetus for this came from the politics of criminal justice as well as theoretical developments in criminology, sociology, and law. The underlying context was rising concern about crime and disorder, and a growing public questioning of authority. The police became increasingly visible, controversial, and politicized in response to these tensions and pressures. Many academics have been motivated primarily by the intellectual project of advancing the analysis of policing as a mode of control and governance. Nonetheless the politicization of law and order since the 1960s has shaped the trajectory of police research (Reiner 1989, 1992a; Jones, Newburn, and Reiner 2017). More recently empirical police research has also spread to many parts of the non-Anglophone world (Marks 2005; Ungar 2011; Fassin 2013, 2017; O'Reilly 2017; Nogala *et al.* 2017).

SOURCES OF POLICE RESEARCH

Police research has emanated from a variety of sources. These include: academic institutions, official government-related bodies, think-tanks and pressure groups, journalists, and policing organizations themselves.

Academic research

From the 1960s to the 1980s most police research was carried out by academics, in a variety of disciplines including criminology, sociology, social policy, law, history, psychology, and economics. Policing research is a mainstay of the many centres for criminology and criminal justice that have burgeoned around the world. Academic and professional police research journals have proliferated. Textbooks and monographs on policing are being published at such a pace that it is no longer possible even for specialists in the field to keep up.

Official police research

The greatest volume of police research today no longer emanates from academe. There has been a rapid growth of research by policy-making bodies and by the police themselves. During the 1980s, for example, the British Home Office Research Unit became increasingly concerned with policing matters. Local government bodies have also sponsored police research. In the 1980s several radical Labour local authorities established police-monitoring groups which collected information on a regular basis about police practices and policy and financed outside research projects by academics. Since the 1980s, local and central government authorities became involved in police research in a rather different way. The new model of research, conducted in conjunction with the police, is policy oriented, directed at achieving the most effective and efficient crime reduction policies. Similar trajectories have been followed in the USA, Canada, Australia, and many other countries (Skogan and Frydl 2004; Ratcliffe 2018).

Perhaps the most significant growth point in official police research is by the police themselves (Brown 1996). Since the 1980s a large number of graduates have joined police services, and many serving officers are taking degrees on a seconded or part-time basis (Sklansky 2006; Lee and Punch 2006; Brunger, Tong, and Martin 2016). Many officers acquired the skills for conducting research. Occasionally research projects begun by serving police officers as students have resulted in influential publications (Holdaway 1983; Young 1991, 1993 are early examples). A significant number of former police officers have become academic specialists in police research (e.g. Waddington 1994, 1999b; Neyroud 2016). In Britain much of this police-based research is associated with the College of Policing established in 2012 as the hub of a professionalization agenda (Brown 2014: Part V).

Think-tanks and independent research organizations

Independent research organizations, notably the British and American Police Foundations, have made significant contributions to policing research. The US Police Foundation is a national, independent non-profit organization. It was founded in 1970 by the Ford Foundation, but is now funded by a mix of private and governmental sources. Its 'mission is to advance policing through innovation and science' (www.policefoundation.org). It carried out some seminal evaluative studies, notably the Kansas City Preventive Patrol Experiment and the Newark Foot Patrol Experiment (discussed in Chapter 5), pioneering the now flourishing approach of experimental field research (Braga and Weisburd 2010; Sherman 2013). The UK Police Foundation is a politically independent registered charity established in 1979 with no core government funding. Although it has firm establishment roots (Prince Charles was its first president), it has succeeded in maintaining a quality of critical independence and objectivity in its work. Its mission is 'developing knowledge and understanding of policing and crime reduction, while challenging the police service and the government to improve policing for the benefit of the public' (www.police-foundation.org.uk).

In addition to these independent research organizations, several pressure groups and politically aligned think-tanks have generated influential research-based work on the police. In Britain they include Liberty (formerly the National Council for Civil Liberties) which, as well as producing regular reviews of new legislation and policy developments, has financed work by academics through its research arm, the Civil Liberties Trust (formerly the Cobden Trust). Other organizations concerned with the human rights and civil liberties aspects of policing include the Centre for Crime and Justice Studies, Statewatch, and StopWatch. US counterparts include the Brennan Center, the American Civil Liberties Union (ACLU) and Cop Watch. Other examples of police research by politically oriented think-tanks include studies of police accountability by the centre left-oriented Institute for Public Policy Research (Reiner and Spencer 1993), and work by Conservative-leaning bodies, such as the Institute of Economic Affairs (Dennis 1998), Centre for Social Justice, and the Policy Exchange (Loveday 2006). As policing has emerged as a matter for global research and engagement, international non-governmental organizations such as Human Rights Watch, Amnesty International, the Open Society Foundation and Forensic Architecture have also produced extensive research on policing matters.

Journalists

Since the beginnings of police research in the early 1960s, studies by journalists have made significant contributions to analysis and debate. These include Whitaker 1964; Laurie 1970; Cox et al. 1977; and Graef 1989. The hallmark of many of the best journalistic studies has been the ability to probe aspects of police malpractice that academics have seldom dealt with. An important example in the past decade is the work of investigative journalists who brought to light serious malpractice in the field of undercover policing (e.g. Lewis and Evans 2014). Collaboration between academics and journalists in understanding aspects of policework, such as riot policing, have also developed in recent years (Lewis et al. 2011).

CHANGING AGENDAS OF POLICE RESEARCH

The focal concerns of policing research have varied over time, related closely to the changing politics of criminal justice. The development of police research has gone through various stages, which have been referred to as: consensus, controversy, conflict, and contradiction (Reiner 1989, 1992a). The contradictory stage now seems to have resolved into a period in which research is dominated by a clear (though not unchallenged) crime control agenda (Reiner and Newburn 2007). Much of this is focused on formulating and evaluating strategies in conjunction with police and governmental agencies for crime reduction. Experimental techniques have become an increasingly influential, albeit not unquestioned, model. At the same time, police research has burgeoned to provide empirical data and theories about a range of hitherto unexplored topics such as police custody areas (Skinns 2019), covert policing (Loftus 2019), together with well-established examination of police leadership (Reiner 1991), public order policing (Waddington 1994), and has developed a tradition of methodologically rigorous research based on interviews, ethnographic observation, and document analysis using innovative visual methods (Rowe 2018).

The first empirical research on policing by a British academic was Michael Banton's *The Policeman in the Community* (Banton 1964; for recent analyses of this, see McLaughlin 2007: chap. 2; Reiner 2015). Like almost all writing on the police at that time, it was framed within a celebratory mode, and assumed a harmonious view of British society. Its premise that 'it can be instructive to analyse institutions that are working well in order to see if anything can be learned from their success' (Banton 1964: vii) exemplified the *consensus* stage of police research.

During the *controversy* stage of police research that developed in the later 1960s, policing was beset by a flurry of problems, ultimately resulting from growing divisions and declining deference in society generally (see Chapter 4). Reflecting these tensions, an increasing number of academic researchers began working on the police. The key theoretical influences were symbolic interactionism and the labelling perspective, which saw policing as an important process in shaping (rather than merely reacting to) the pattern of deviance through the exercise of discretion (Cain 1973; Chatterton 1976, 1979, 1983; Holdaway 1983; Manning 1979, 1997; Punch 1979a, 1979b; Shearing 1981b, 1984; Ericson 1982, 1993). The introduction to Simon Holdaway's 1979 collection of essays on the British police, which includes examples of most of the research then being conducted, sums up accurately the focal concern: 'the lower ranks of the service control their own work situation and such control may well shield highly questionable practices' (Holdaway 1979: 12).

Research tended to be critical of police practice, whatever its institutional base. While academics, journalists, and pressure groups were concerned primarily with police deviance, official government research pointed out the limitations of policing as a means of controlling crime, reflecting a more general 'nothing works' mood (Clarke and Hough 1980, 1984; Morris and Heal 1981).

The issues examined in the controversy stage linked directly to the key focus of the *conflict* stage of police research in the late 1970s: accountability—who controls policing? This indicated the increasing politicization of policing analysed in Chapter 4. It also reflected the growth of radical criminology. Many academic studies of the police in this period were explicitly Marxist (e.g. Hall *et al.* 1978; Brogden 1982; Bernstein *et al.* 1982;

Jefferson and Grimshaw 1984; Scraton 1985; Grimshaw and Jefferson 1987). Uniting all the various causes of concern and controversy was a critique of the inadequacy of existing mechanisms for holding the police to account, whether as individuals through the complaints process or the courts, or force policy and operations as a whole through the institutions of police governance (see Chapter 11).

By the late 1980s a new stage of debate and research on policing was emerging, in which a number of *contradictory* tendencies seemed to be in competition. The key theme was the growth of an avowed 'realism' across the political spectrum. Most marked in this country was the new 'left realism' advocated by Jock Young and others (Lea and Young 1984; Kinsey, Lea, and Young 1986). This contrasted itself with what it called the 'administrative criminology' of governmental criminal justice policy-making institutions, and the 'new right' realism associated most clearly with James Q. Wilson in the USA (Wilson 1975). Although these variants embodied vastly different political and theoretical assumptions, they shared a similar trope of 'realism'.

The espousal of 'realism' reflected wider developments in both criminological theory and criminal justice politics. In criminology it was part of a more general turn away from grand theory. The momentum was towards research of a policy-oriented and managerialist kind. The common premise was that crime was a serious problem above all for the poorer and weaker sections of society, and research should be directed primarily at developing concrete, immediately practicable tactics for crime control.

Police research came increasingly to focus on the search for what works in effective crime control practice, monitoring, and evaluating the policing initiatives that proliferated in the search for greater effectiveness. These innovations have been credited with contributing to crime reduction since the 1990s, although the extent is debatable (Reiner 2016b: 164–85). At the harder end of crime control tactics, the much-touted 'zero tolerance' approach, rooted in the idea of 'broken windows' developed by James Q. Wilson and George Kelling (1982), has been popularly seen as the basis of the New York 'miracle' of rapidly declining violence and crime in the 1990s, although these claims are highly questionable (see Chapter 5).

This was paralleled by a new, 'second order', political consensus about law and order which emerged in the 1990s (Downes and Morgan 2007; Reiner 2007: chap. 5). During the 1970s the political parties had become polarized over law and order. In the 1980s the police basked in a honeymoon period with the Thatcher and Reagan governments. They were a special case with regard to the drive for 'value for money' and cuts in public expenditure, a loyal police being seen as essential to defeat the 'enemy within' in the shape of militant trade unionism and other resistance to the economically polarizing consequences of free-market economics. Liberal and left parties were successfully stigmatized as anti-law and order, because of their social democratic interpretations of crime and disorder as—at least in part—produced by economic inequality and social exclusion, and because of their civil libertarian concerns.

During the 1990s, following Clinton's Presidential campaign in 1991–2, and Tony Blair's tenure as Shadow Home Secretary in 1992–4, there emerged a new cross-party consensus on law and order, based on shared commitment to toughness in the war against crime. There was renewed faith in the efficacy of policing and punishment. The overriding priority for the police had to be crime control. This was spearheaded in Britain by the mid-1990s Conservative policy package embodied in the 1993 White

Paper on Police Reform, the 1993 Sheehy Report on pay and career structures, and the 1994 Police and Magistrates' Courts Act. These were aimed at creating a 'business-like' police, constrained by market disciplines to achieve efficient and economic delivery of their primary objective, 'catching criminals' (as the White Paper put it).

New Labour left this reform package intact, although it gave it a spin in a more sophisticated direction with the 1998 Crime and Disorder Act, and its programme for crime reduction through partnership and evidence-led implementation and evaluation. The promise of a research-based strategy was rapidly dashed by the relentless drive for short-term results (Maguire 2004; Hope 2004), and the proliferation of headline catching initiatives to deal with immediate crises (Newburn and Reiner 2007). However, the search for evidence-based policing strategies has continued and is deeply embedded in a professionalization agenda across the Western world.

The driving paradigm for most police research now is clearly *crime control*. In the USA and Britain there is a resuscitated belief among policy-makers and some researchers that policing is a key element in crime control, not only through broader community strategies but through tougher, more directed patrol and detective work. There was explicit rejection of the earlier 'nothing works' pessimism (Sherman 1992a; Bayley 1998; Bratton 1998; Weisburd and Neyroud 2013). In this new intelligence-driven, crime control paradigm, research figures in an integral way. Policy-oriented research is no longer just a matter of *post hoc* evaluation of police initiatives, although the quantity and sophistication of evaluation has (debatably) grown (Cohen 1997; Brodeur 1998; Skogan and Frydl 2004; Skogan 2004; Gravelle and Rogers 2014; Brunger and Tong 2016).

Detailed crime analysis and the tailoring of specific local policing responses in conjunction with other agencies were at the heart of the problem-oriented and intelligence-led approaches which the New Labour government promoted, albeit with mixed evidence of success (Maguire 2008; Tilley 2008; Cope 2008; James 2013, 2016). These require an ongoing research capacity within police forces, as well as closer collaboration with policy-oriented researchers outside. The failure of public confidence in the police to rise as crime rates fell from around the mid-1990s stimulated a particular policy concern with reducing fear as well as crime itself, focused on 'reassurance policing' programmes (Hough 2003; Millie and Herrington 2005).

Four important things changed in the two decades between 1995 and 2015. First, crime fell in most categories including homicide. Second, spending on the police, which had risen continuously since 1979, slowed in 2003 and then faced cuts from around 2010. Third, the 'zero tolerance' approach to policing espoused by New Labour was condemned by the Conservative Party as an ineffective and authoritarian abuse of human rights and civil liberties. From the election of a coalition government in 2010, the use of police powers was significantly reigned-in (see Chapter 5). There was a brief period in which crime was not much of a public policy issue, police legitimacy was relatively high while resources and powers were reduced in the name of a tight public purse and austerity for the state agencies. In 2016, crime rose significantly and by 2018 there was something approaching a full-blown crisis for the police, who were accused of failing to meet public demand. Debates rage about police numbers, tactics, and effectiveness and still the question of the role of police in crime control remained vexed. For many years, critical and theoretical work was eclipsed by pragmatic policy-oriented police research on crime control.

We might characterize the current phase of police research as its *diversity* or *plural* phase. The 'omnibus' mandate of the police is now well established, and as soon as an empirical researcher finds themselves in the field, they are inevitably drawn to ask questions beyond 'Do the police control crime?'. Other starting points include: Are the police fair? Do they provide a good all-purpose emergency service? Do the police do a good job of looking after people in custody? Empirical studies have explored a range of police specialisms including covert operations, public order, traffic policing, immigration policing, police custody suites, transnational policing, overseas peace building, and policing tourist resorts and Disneyland. Researchers have grasped the distinction between police and policing, and are developing interesting lines of inquiry in institutions within the 'wider police family'. The inquisitive researcher asks questions about how the organization functions and how its practices are shaped by things like politics, law, culture, and technology. Information communication devices—mobile phones and networked computers using increasingly complex algorithmic models are playing a major role in policing and being examined by police researchers. Historical research has provided a clearer understanding of the development of the police in local and colonial contexts. There are extensive international comparisons and examinations of local, regional, and global policing organizations. The current phase of police research is also methodologically diverse with many following venerable traditions in ethnography, long interviews, detailed case histories, historical, transnational, and comparative studies.

Meanwhile, critical and theoretical work have not disappeared, in Britain or elsewhere. Indeed, new academic work has been stimulated by instances of the abuse of police power and broader inquiry into controversial police practices. Prominent among these is the systematic research on US policing following a series of notorious shootings of unarmed black men and controversy over police stop and search practices (see Chapter 5). The research chimes with the Black Lives Matter movement and some scholarly work links directly with the political movements (e.g. Davis 2017). In the UK, scholarly research on the increasing use, normalization even, of covert policing (Loftus 2019; Gill and Pythian 2018) has coincided with the 'SpyCops' scandal. Seeking to make sense of the growing diversity of empirical evidence, a body of theoretical work has probed the impact of changes in political economy, culture, and society, variously characterized as post or late modernity, risk society, globalization, and neo-liberalism. These will be reviewed in the concluding chapter (Chapter 12).

Police research and theoretical analyses of policing are addressed to a number of fundamental and inter-related questions, which will be considered in more detail in later chapters focusing on each issue (and of course other chapters address them too):

(1) What is policing? (Chapters 1, 2).

(2) Who is involved in policing? (Chapters 1, 7, 9)

(3) What do the police actually do? (Chapter 5).

(4) What are the means and powers of policing? (Chapter 11).

(5) What social functions do they achieve? (Chapters 1, 5).

(6) How does policing impact on different groups? (Chapter 6).

(7) How may the powers and practices of policing be legitimated? (Chapters 4, 10, 11).

(8) By whom are the police themselves policed, by what means, and to what ends? (Chapter 11).

(9) How can the developing purposes and practices of policing be understood? (Chapters 2, 3, 4, 8).

POLITICS AND POLICING

The group of words, police, policy, polity, politics, politic, political, politician is a good example of delicate distinctions

Maitland 1885: 105.

Most police officers stoutly maintain that policing and politics do not mix. Chief officers regularly declaim on the political neutrality of the police service (Reiner and O'Connor 2015). As shown in Chapter 4, an important ingredient of the legitimation of the British police was their supposed non-partisanship. This notion of the political neutrality or independence of the police cannot withstand serious consideration. It rests on an untenably narrow conception of 'the political', restricting it to partisan conflict (Amatrudo 2009: chap. 4). In a broader sense, all relationships which have a power dimension are political, so policing is inherently and inescapably political.

As argued earlier, their specific role in the maintenance of order is as specialists in coercion. The craft of successful policing is to be able to minimize the use of force, but it remains the specialist resource of the police, their distinctive role in the political order. In this sense, the police are at the heart of the state's functioning, and political analysis in general tends to underplay the significance of policing as source and symbol of the quality of a political civilization.

The control of overtly political behaviour is the task of the specifically political police, or 'high policing' (Bunyan 1977; Brodeur 1983, 1999, 2010; Marx 1988; Hoogenboom 1991, 2010; Gill 1994; Mazower 1997; Huggins 1998; Sheptycki 2000b, 2007c; van Dijk et al. 2015: chap. 2; Gill and Phythian 2018). A characteristic of the British police tradition is the attempted unification in the same organization of the 'high policing' function of regulating explicit political dissidence with the 'low policing' task of routine law enforcement and street-level order maintenance. In most other countries there is a greater degree of organizational separation, although the Special Branch developed in the late nineteenth century as a separate, specifically political, unit within the police in Britain (Porter 1987). The 'high policing' tactics have always been underplayed in Britain, but it is clear not only that they are, in fact, part of the British tradition but that the use of covert tactics now extends far beyond political policing to include terrorism and radicalization, cybercrime, serious organized crime, and money laundering but also relatively mundane neighbourhood crime. Covert policing is now very much normal practice (Loftus 2019).

Chief officers are most concerned to claim that the police are not involved in partisan politics, but impartially enforce the law. Yet, of course police officers engage politically on matters such as police resources and priorities (lobbying government, speaking to the media, and so on) and always have done so.

The narrower claim to impartial enforcement is sustainable only in small part, if at all. A distinction must be made between partisanship in intent and in impact. In a society that is divided on class, ethnic, gender, and other dimensions of inequality, the impact of laws, even if they are formulated and enforced impartially and in a universalist manner, will reproduce those social divisions. This is the point encapsulated in Anatole France's celebrated aphorism about 'The majestic equality of the law, which forbids the rich as well as the poor to sleep under bridges, to beg in the streets, and to steal bread' (*Le Lys Rouge*, Paris, 1894).

In practice, of course, the inequalities of social power are likely to have an impact on the processes of legislation and administration of justice, so that the law itself may deviate from formal impartiality. For both these reasons the impact of law and its enforcement in an unequal society will be objectively political even in the narrower sense of partisanship, favouring some groups at the expense of others. 'The rich get rich, and the poor get prison' (Reiman 2004)—and they also get more criminal victimization and the hard end of police power. Policing bears down most heavily on the most marginal and least powerful groups in our society, who are in effect denied the full status of citizenship (Waddington, 1999b) and become 'police property' (Lee 1981), especially at times of economic or political conflict or crisis (Hall *et al.* 1978; Crowther 2000a, 2000b). In addition, there is plentiful evidence in many places and times of overt partisanship, with disproportionate surveillance and control of groups on the left rather than the right of the political spectrum (Lipset 1969; Skolnick 1969; Fassin 2013: chap. 6; Deflem 2016; Vitale 2017: chap. 10; Evans 2018).[1]

The British police tradition has to a large measure eschewed overt partisanship. The constitutional structure within which it operates, autonomous of direct control by elected authorities, is intended to preserve this. Moreover, it must be emphasized that, while policing is inherently political and indeed partisan in reproducing social inequalities, at the same time it preserves the minimal conditions of civilized and stable social existence from which all groups benefit, albeit differentially.

However, if policing is an inherently political activity, it does not follow that it usually appears as such. Policing may be inescapably political, but it need not be *politicized*, that is, the centre of overt political controversy about its manner, tactics, or mode of operation and organization. Like riding a bike, policing is the sort of activity that is thought about mainly when the wheel comes off. When things are running smoothly it tends to be a socially invisible, undiscussed and, routine.

This book explores the de facto politics of policing in terms of its uneven social impact (Chapter 6), the political ideology of police officers and the political role of the police in popular ideology (Chapters 8 and 10), and the politicization of the police, their involvement in overt political conflict (Parts II and IV). As Chapter 4 shows, the British police were established in the face of acute political opposition, and this is largely true of other policing models too (Chapters 2 and 3). To gain acceptance, the architects of the British policing tradition constructed an image, organization, and strategy which were intended to win over the various strands of political opposition, as did the big city US police (Miller 1999). Over the first century

[1] 'https://www.theguardian.com/uk-news/2018/oct/15/undercover-police-spies-infiltrated-uk-leftwing-groups-for-decades?';https://www.theguardian.com/uk-news/ng-interactive/2018/oct/15/uk-political-groups-spied-on-undercover-police-list?

and a quarter of its existence the police in England and Wales were largely successful in accomplishing their depoliticization, and came to be seen as legitimate by the mass of the population.

It should be stressed, however, that there are inherent limits to police legitimation in any society. Since policing is centrally concerned with the resolution of conflicts, ultimately dependent on the capacity to use force, there is in most police actions someone who is being policed against. In this sense the police are inherently dealers in and dispensers of evil and can never command universal love.

For policing to be accepted as legitimate, it is not necessary that all groups or individuals in a society agree with the substantive content or direction of specific police operations. It means at minimum only that the broad mass of the population, and possibly even some of those who are policed against, accept the authority, the lawful right, of the police to act as they do, even if disagreeing with or regretting some specific actions (Jackson *et al.* 2014). Of course, in conditions of relative social harmony, acceptance of judicious policing may be a lot more wholehearted. But as policing is inherently an activity concerned with the ordering of conflict, 'policing by consent' cannot imply complete and universal approval. To suggest otherwise is dangerous in that it raises expectations which can never be realized. This is the inherent limit to all the fashionable notions of 'community policing', despite this becoming the 'rhetorical giant' (Manning 1997: 11) of police reform talk around the world. As Waddington (1999b: 223) sums it up trenchantly, '"community policing" is an oxymoron, for if the police could serve the *whole* community there would be little point in having a police at all'.

The politics of policing at the end of the second decade of the twenty-first century exhibits a number of paradoxes. Despite many years of criticism and loss of legitimacy the police remain pivotal—at least symbolically—to a crucial policy concern of the public: crime. There is now bipartisan consensus around a fundamentally 'law and order' definition of the issue, and of the police role. However, there is fierce partisan conflict over specific strategies and over who can deliver the best results. Policing and crime control are scarcely debated in principled ways, but are fiercely contested at a pragmatic level.

The competing arguments and strategies will be evaluated in the light of the substantial body of evidence about police culture, operations, and images that is reviewed in Part III. Arguably, however, all the reform initiatives of recent years have been vitiated by a failure to reject the 'law and order' framework, and to recognize the inherent limitations of policing. They have been fatally damaged by neo-liberal government economic policies which aggravated unemployment and exclusion, especially among the young and ethnic minorities, creating problems of policing a new and growing underclass (Crowther 2000a, 2000b; Reiner 2007, 2011, 2016b). The problems reflect broader structural changes in political economy and culture, often referred to in a broad-brush way as 'globalization', which limit the scope of action of national governments. The emergence of transnational policing is related to anxieties about the capacity of the nation state to deal with transnational criminality, but must be understood within the architecture of the transnational state system more generally (see Chapter 9). However, the divisive and unsettling consequences of neo-liberal globalization have become manifest since credit crunched in 2007, and brought economic collapse and 'austerity policies' with consequences that continue to fester. The social, economic, and cultural transformations since the 1970s have multiplied the problems facing the police, as we explore in this book.

Between the 1960s and 1980s the police were pigs in the middle of sharply polarizing political debate. In Britain, they were the darlings of the Tories and in conflict with Labour-controlled police authorities, to which the national Labour Party threatened to make them more accountable. Gone were the halcyon days of consensus, when the police stood above the party fray as beloved totems of the nation. By the early 1990s the police stood at a lower ebb in public trust and esteem than at any time since they were established in the nineteenth century. They had been rocked by scandals revealing gross miscarriages of justice. At the same time the police appeared less able to protect people from criminal victimization, which was rising at record speed, and seemingly unable to reassure an ever-more fearful public.

By the mid-1990s the configuration had changed again. Seeking to be 'tough on crime and tough on the causes of crime', New Labour courted the police assiduously, while the Tories sought to apply tough 'businesslike' market-based rigours to their management and accountability.

There was good news and bad news for the police. The good news was the return of a degree of consensus about policing, and about their symbolic importance to a vital objective for any government. This was reflected in a stabilization of public confidence in the police, following pronounced decline up to the early 1990s.

The bad news was the new consensus view that the police were failing badly on almost every front, and in need of drastic reform. It was increasingly apparent that the police felt trapped in a time warp. They were intent on reform. However, the impact of reforms on public perceptions of the police was continuously being undercut by scandalous revelations, as well as unrealistic expectations of performance and probity built up in the bygone era when the lid was shut tight on scandals.

In response to all these problems, police and government pursued a number of reform strategies at a bewilderingly accelerating pace, and competing ones have been on offer. Police thinking at policy-making levels is a bricolage of different themes originating at different times in response to the crisis of the moment. In Britain there remain echoes of the 1981 Scarman philosophy emphasizing peacekeeping and consensus, which were reinforced by the 1999 MacPherson report on the Stephen Lawrence case. These pointed towards 'community' and 'problem-solving' policing approaches that spread from the USA worldwide. These are intertwined with facets of management theory, the 'quality of service' language of consumerism, and bytes of business speak. However, these softer tones have been threatened increasingly by a renewed enthusiasm for tough policing, embodied above all in the much-debated notion of 'zero tolerance', and vastly exacerbated by the terror attacks of the 2000s around the world. Research evidence on covert policing and public revelations about wrongdoing in the use of police spies also raises questions about police ethics in 'high policing', and how these can be reconciled with Peel's words: 'God forbid that he should mean to countenance a system of espionage.'[2] This was a 'direct rejection' of surveillance powers 'exemplified in the public mind by the French police' and seen as the antithesis of the British model (Ashworth and Zedner 2014).

This book analyses how the police got to their present situation, and what research on their working suggests about the prospects of success for the reforms being pursued.

---

[2] *Parliamentary Debates VII, 803*, cited by Emsley (1996: 25).

SPOILER ALERT: The verdict is not encouraging. The effects of neo-liberal, free-market economic policies have increased social division, poverty, and injustice. The frustration and anger to which injustice gives rise are the bitter fruits with which the police must cope. Even if the 'golden age' of consensus policing (symbolized by Dixon of Dock Green or Dragnet) ever existed, we cannot return to it (Chapter 10). The more pragmatic but attainable target is to achieve public recognition for doing 'dirty work' (Hughes 1961) as professionally, efficiently, and impartially as it can be done in an ever-more fragmented and divided society. Whether even that can be achieved must be doubtful in a period of massive social transformation, generating profound disloca-tion and insecurity. The success of their efforts, as at the birth of modern policing in the early nineteenth century, depends largely on wider questions of political economy and culture: can the malign consequences of neo-liberalism be reversed? Can the long march towards inclusive social democratic citizenship be restored?

2

THEORIES AND MODELS OF POLICE AND POLICING

INTRODUCTION

The politics of the police and policing is complicated, made all the more so by the seemingly confusing number of models and theories used to talk about the subject. The task of this chapter is to organize thinking in this domain around a number of specifiable theoretical standpoints. The literature can get quite confusing because of the plethora of models on offer which tend to operate at entirely different levels of abstraction (Mawby 1991, 1999; Mawby and Wright 2008). Politicians, police chiefs, and scholars often propound models of policing advocating particular policing methods, styles, and supporting norms and values. Police chiefs and policy-makers especially promulgate policing models as prototypes to be followed or imitated. Sometimes an explicitly architectural metaphor is used to describe a picture of good policing. Getting to grips with the theoretical standpoints that help to form our abstract models of the police and policing is an essential first step in confronting the politics of the police.

What is a model? A model is not the real thing. For the purposes of the present discussion we can say that the notion has two relevant meanings. A model may be a representation of something and it is an example to follow. For instance a model of the Eiffel Tower is not the Eiffel Tower, it is a figure that looks like the real Eiffel Tower with the major exception of its scale which (presumably) is smaller than the original. When architects want to promote a building project, they make models in the hope that their ideas will be made real. However, modelling is a different proposition when what is being modelled is a total abstraction. Consider the concept of 'intelligence-led policing'. There are a variety of models of the 'intelligence cycle' (James 2013, 2016; Ratcliffe 2009, 2016). Empirical research has shown that police organization is, of necessity, chaotic and fluid (Jackall 1997, 2005; Manning 2003; Manning 2010; Sheptycki 2017b). Drawing a picture of the 'model intelligence cycle' is a useful fiction for police practitioners because it helps them to make sense of the interminable flow of events in operational policing, but sometimes it can be institutionally reified and become a mechanistic straitjacket (Aepli et al. 2011; Gill 1998; Phythian 2013; Sheptycki 2004b). Intelligence-led policing (ILP) is an attempt (usually made by police practitioners in the first instance) to model police organization so that it can be presented as scientific, rational 'knowledge work' (Ericson 1994; Ericson and Shearing 1986). It is one way to theorize about policing practice among many. Should we buy it? Is it an example to follow?

Theorists use many different kinds of models for talking about the politics of police. The reason there are so many is that, unlike the particular example of the Eiffel Tower, the 'strange word police' is an abstraction. The word 'police' may be used to denote seemingly real things—like Scotland Yard, FBI HQ at Quantico, Europol, and the rest. But these institutions are, in important respects, symbolic ideas and both the institutions and their symbolic representations change over time. This leads to great difficulties and the huge plethora of theories and models available in the literature on police and policing is therefore difficult to synthesize. One major problem is that, once we have adopted a theory or a model—'police subcultural theory' or the 'colonial model', for example—we tend to treat the concepts as real things. That is, we reify our concepts. Reification is a fallacious form of reasoning summed up in the common-sense aphorism 'the map is not the territory'. The concept (police subculture or colonial policing) is not the phenomenon it purports to describe. The task is to develop a sophisticated enough language for theorizing about the police and policing that does not encourage this fallacy of misplaced concreteness and is useful in thinking about the political issues at stake.

In what follows we will outline seven different ideal-type theoretical standpoints. These ideal-types are not mutually exclusive and are sometimes only tacit in theoretical thinking. Each of our headings encapsulates a style of thought about policing and the politics involved. There is not a single paradigm concerning the police, in the classic Kuhnian sense of a scientific community labouring under the conditions of 'normal science' (although some might wish it were so, e.g. Sherman 2011/2015). Neither is there one model, or set of models, that the police can be reduced to. Rather, typically scholars in the field flexibly mobilize theory in an effort to think through the dynamic, shifting, and problematic complexities of policing power. Our headings reflect an interdisciplinary field of enquiry made up of partially autonomous language communities and provide a sense of order to the multifaceted problematic of the politics of the police.

The following subsections sketch out a variety of theories and models for thinking about the politics of policing:

1. Police and Legality: Crime-Control and Due Process

2. Policing Functions: High Policing and Low Policing

3. Styles of Police: Police Force and Police Service

4. Explaining Police Behaviour: Organizational Structure and Officer Discretion

5. Police, People, and Community: State, Market, and Civil Society

6. Police Knowledge Work: *Post hoc* and Pre Cog—Investigation and Intelligence

7. Politics of Police: Democratic, Authoritarian, and Totalitarian Policing

Foreshadowing our conclusions, we can say at the outset that the myriad problems inherent in the politics of the police are manifest in a potentially endless variety of unique circumstances and can in no way be settled with the rhetorical invocation of the 'rule of law'. The desire to make police problems concrete by specifying models that can be manipulated by formal rules runs up against the difficult facts of human agency, interpretation, and conflict over meaning. Over the past thirty years there has been a parade of theoretical models—community-oriented policing, problem-oriented policing, zero-tolerance policing, hotspots policing, etc.—each of which has promised better policing because of better regulations, more training, and superior management technology.

The politics of policing in the twenty-first century exhibits a number of paradoxes and antinomies. Despite years of criticism and loss of legitimacy the police remain pivotal—at least symbolically—to public concerns about crime and security. If there has been a failure in the politics of the police over this time, it has been because of the widely held expectation that with sufficient 'law and order' social problems can be policed. We cannot arrest our way out of the problems of 'knife crime' and the 'opioid crisis' any more than we can arrest our way out of the problem of 'white-collar crime', because the foundational issues in the politics of the police lie in the political economy and culture. The theoretical standpoints we outline below can be flexibly combined and re-combined to give a critical appreciation of the present situation, one which is unfortunately dominated by massive social transformations, profound dislocations, and seemingly insurmountable insecurities. From the birth of modern policing until now, the politics of the police has always been conflicted and it remains to be seen if the current malign consequences of global neo-liberal hegemony can be reversed and the long march of inclusive social democratic citizenship for all people be restored.

POLICE AND LEGALITY:
CRIME CONTROL AND DUE PROCESS

Socio-legal theories concerning legality and policing are very important in the politics of the police. Police are, in this way of thinking, somehow beholden to law. Herbert Packer's classic essay *Two Models of Criminal Process*, initially published in 1968, counter-posed two normative models underlying the process of apprehension, screening, and adjudication of crime phenomena, one which valued crime control and the other which valued the rules of the game. This foundational thinking gave 'operational content to a complex system of values underlying the criminal law' (Packer 1971: 211). Skolnick's *Justice without Trial* (1966) and Goldstein's and Goldstein's (1971) *Crime, Law and Society* capture the crux of the matter: police officer discretion whether or not to invoke the law.

Joseph Goldstein observed that total enforcement against every legal infraction was inhibited by constitutional legality and due process restrictions. He also thought that, after abiding by those restrictions, full enforcement of the law was a sociological impossibility due to the limitations of institutional resources. Police law enforcement is therefore inevitably *selective* law enforcement. The initial concern was with 'low visibility decisions' in the criminal process about whether or not to invoke the law (Goldstein 1960; Goldstein and Goldstein 1971: 153). This way of thinking about the politics of police has long been an important constituent in socio-legal thinking more generally (Feeley 2001). It reveals law as a form of instrumental reason, wherein 'due process is for crime control' (McBarnet 1981) and it raises difficult normative and political questions that are impossible to answer exclusively within the terms of legal discourse (Cotterrell 1992: 196–200).

In *The Case for the Prosecution*, the authors note that police use their legal powers for purposes other than obtaining convictions:

> The police use the law as a control device. The aims of stops and arrests are often not to enforce the law per se, but to secure broader objectives: the imposition of order, the assertion of authority, the acquisition of information. (McConville, Sanders, and Leng 1991: 16)

In other words, 'the law' is a tool that police use discretionarily and is an instrument of sociological engineering (Feeley 2001: 178). The law is made up, or socially constructed, by legal architects, legal engineers, and legal technicians (Ericson 1983: 2). The paradox is that, whereas the public rhetoric concerning the rule of law connotes the values of fairness and equality, the actual deployment of legal tools by police (and any other agent of governance) enacts the 'constitution of legal inequality' (Ericson 1983).

Socio-legal thinking about the politics of the police can be arranged between two poles, one conservative the other more radical. According to David J. Smith, police discretion is 'irreducible' (Smith 1997). That is to say, in order to be recognizable as 'the police', they must be able to make decisions based on available evidence about emergent, conflictual, or otherwise socially troublesome situations and intervene authoritatively by representing what they do in legal terms. In this regard, legal tools are enabling (Ericson 1982). Police use legal tools 'skillfully to make the complex simple and to make the ambiguous definite in justifying a particular course of action [thus] . . . a situation with many possible interpretations, each with many possibilities for investigation, is transformed into one interpretation and one course of action that is routinely accepted by all parties concerned. The glass menagerie of social life remains intact; social order is reproduced' (ibid.: 194).

More conservative thinkers argue that it is 'inevitable that the police will use the law as a resource to pursue the objectives that are proper to them' (Smith 1997: 343). Thus, 'due process values can only be sustained if it is recognized that crime control is a "high purpose" and that the police have a legitimate job to do' (ibid.: 344). More radical thinking suggests that law enforcement is often a matter of class repression. Observing that street-level police officers make distinctions between the deserving public and 'the scum', Shearing (1981b) averred that what he called 'liberal social control', and what conservatives call the rule of law, is an institutional hypocrisy. He argued that at the macroscopic level, liberal democracy promises legal equality, but subterranean processes in the maintenance of power ensure that social conflicts manifest at the micro-level become pretexts that legitimate the work necessary to reproduce capitalist relations of domination.

Police and other legal actors use legal tools to symbolize, represent, justify, and undertake action. This model for thinking about the politics of policing in society addresses, in one way or another, the ideological role of law as an instrument useful in legitimating action aimed at reproducing social order and institutionally making crime (Ericson 1981, 1982). Socio-legal theory emphasizes the place of law in the politics of the police. Police are street corner politicians with a legal remit (Muir 1977).

POLICING FUNCTIONS:
HIGH POLICING AND LOW POLICING

The conceptual distinction between high and low policing has been enormously important analytically for theorizing the politics of the police. The most elemental definition is that 'high policing' concerns 'the control of overtly political behavior' whereas 'low policing' is 'routine law enforcement and street-level order maintenance' (Reiner 1985: 2). Not all policing can be called political, neither can any policing not be called political, and this difficult ambiguity renders police practice inherently conflictual. 'A political police is not so much an instrument for the protection of society as a form of political activity through the medium of police' (Radzinowcz 1956: 572). High policing 'reaches out for potential threats in a systematic attempt to preserve the distribution of power in a given society' (Brodeur 1983: 513). Further, 'it can refer to police interventions in the struggles taking place inside society over the possession and exercise of state power' (ibid.: 507).

Private agencies are involved in multifarious ways in high policing (Brodeur 2007; Ellison and O'Reilly 2006) and there is also transnational high policing that takes place above the level of particular states (Anderson *et al.* 1995; Bowling and Sheptycki 2012; Brodeur 2010). In general, high policing is concerned with the promotion of the *status quo* and acts in the particular interests of political, social, and economic elites. High policing 'aims to control by storing intelligence' (Brodeur 1983: 513), which casts a critical light on 'intelligence-led policing', 'smart policing', policing with 'big data', and the like (cf. Ratcliffe 2009; Sanders and Sheptycki 2017). High policing is 'greatly enhanced by exhaustively charting the physical and social space' and aims to 'increase the scope and precision of surveillance' (Brodeur 2010: 513). Moreover, high policing fights dirty. It makes extensive use of covert agents and paid informers, and 'the use of common criminals to crush political deviance is a regular tactic of high policing' (ibid.: 514). High policing 'is not a piecemeal endeavour; it is relentless and implies systematic continuity' (ibid.: 518). It focuses on the processing of information in order to be able to forecast future events and, where feasible, avert or shape them. High policing is central to the reproduction of social order.

What of low policing? It is describable 'as a forceful reaction to conspicuous signs of disorder, whether or not of a criminal nature'. The Peelian notions of uniformed, high visibility, primarily preventive policing called 'low policing' (Brodeur 1983: 512). Social order cannot exist without low policing. Whereas high policing aims particularly to secure the integrity of the state and the interests of political, economic, and social elites who have the greatest access to power within it, low policing is undertaken with concern for the general interest and is of benefit to almost everybody in the social order (Bowling and Sheptycki 2012: 16). The correspondence between high policing and the particular interest, on the one hand, and between low policing and general social interest, on the other, demonstrates that 'the police, a priori, are neither repressive nor deserving of support as defenders of a universal consensus on the public good' (Marenin 1982: 259).

The challenge of policing in democracies is to, in one sense, 'keep it low' and ensure that it is directed at maintaining order in the sense of a general social peace with minimal repressiveness and partiality on behalf of specific (elite) interests (cf. Reiner, in Brogden *et al.* 1986: 104). To be sure, political, economic, and social elites may be motivated to provide low policing services in order to maintain a population capable of engaging in the competitive relations required in the international system of states, and the systemic insecurity provides a further pretext and logic for high policing (Bowling and Sheptycki 2012: 15). Far from being a simple dyad, high policing and low policing are as isomorphic as a Möbius ribbon (cf. Bigo 2001). The distinction between high and low policing helps to make sense of the politics of the police, but they are not reducible to these terms.

STYLES OF POLICE: POLICE FORCE AND POLICE SERVICE

When it comes to the general social order, it is impossible to think about the politics of the police without considering the twin tropes of 'force' and 'service'. These two terms are intertwined in the historical roots of the police idea which once pertained to all aspects of urban governance (see Chapter 3). Both contemporary and historical scholarship confirms the lasting importance of police social service capacities (Gilling 2007; Landau 1996; Marquis 1992, 2016; Punch and Naylor 1973; Waddington 1999b: 4–20). Contemporary scholarship regarding police crime prevention and community capacity building (Skogan 2006; Tilley and Sidebottom 2017) and the policing of 'vulnerable populations' (Morabito 2014) also reflect a concern with the performance of police service. On the other hand, academic work on police use-of-force, especially its mis-use and the governance of its mis-use, is voluminous (e.g. Dunham and Alpert 2015: especially 162–80, 517–30, 532–47, 548–66, 567–83; Punch 2010).

It is interesting to examine the formal names of common police agencies to see how these concerns are signalled. For example, in the UK there is the London Metropolitan Police Service, the Greater Manchester Police, and the Durham Constabulary, as well as the Police Service for Northern Ireland and the Police Service of Scotland. In Australia a partial list would include the Australian Federal Police, the New South Wales Police Force, and the Australian Border Force. Most cities in Canada have police services, whereas in the United States most cities have police departments. The motto of the Los Angeles Police Department emblazoned on its patrol cars is *To Protect and Serve*. The motto of the Toronto Police Service is *To Serve and Protect*. These examples from three Anglo-American jurisdictions indicate something about intertwined ideas of force and service in formal conceptions of policing. Sometimes force is a service, which is why people 'call the cops' in situations like the 'family beef' and because of 'neighbourhood conflict'.

French scholarship reveals other interesting dimensions in thinking about police force and service. Two words '*sûreté* and *sécurité*—safety and security—strongly pervade the common language relating to '*les flics*'. Revolutionary France in the eighteenth century established, in the first attempt at a declaration of human rights, that 'the goal of any political association is the preservation of the natural and imprescriptible rights of man. These rights are freedom, property, safety (*sûreté*) and resistance to oppression'. (*Déclaration de Droits de l'Homme et du Citoyen de 1789 Art. 2*—'*Le but de toute association politique est la conservation des droits naturels et imprescribtibles de l'Homme. Ces droits sont la liberté, la propriété, la sûreté et la résistance à l'oppression*'). At one time the term *sûreté* connoted a sense of communal safety. Etymologically distinct from *sécurité*, initially it had strong democratic associations. In 1812 Eugéne François Vidocq established the *Sûreté*, a special squad of detectives modelled on Napoleon's political police, in order to undertake 'more effective' criminal detective work. Although the *Sûreté* are famous for dramatic decreases in crime, due to the fact that Vidocq was formerly a criminal and most of the people under his command had extensive criminal records, they are also what gave the word *sûreté* more than a whiff of sulphur.

In the contemporary period the famously tough CRS act as the 'riot squad' of the *Police Nationale*. CRS stands for *Compagnies Républicaines de Sécuritié*—and its reputation for brutality has similarly helped to taint the word *sécuritié* in relation to talk about '*les flics*'—that is, 'the cops'. Just like their Anglo-American counterparts, scholars of French policing have long recognized the difficult particularities of police use-of-force as well as its contrasting and concomitant services to society (Anderson 2011; Monjardet 1996; Mouhanna 2008, 2009; Jobard and Maillard 2015: especially chap. 6). As elsewhere, police in France are a tainted occupation and evidence suggests that French police recruits are socialized on the basis of a crime fighting dogma that emphasizes dangerousness enacted in a hostile and mistrustful environment (Cassan 2010; Fassin 2013).

While local cultural contexts may differ from time to time and place to place, both force and service remain modal concerns in the politics of policing in democracies. This can lead to certain antinomies when police are observed to use non-democratic means ostensibly in order to preserve the conditions of democracy, a contradiction that cannot, by definition, happen in a Police State.

Since Egon Bittner's original theoretical pronouncements, the use-of-force has loomed large in definitions of the police (Brodeur 2010: 105–6). According to this view, the police are 'the fire it takes to fight fire' (Bittner 1970/1990: 96). While the limitation of police use-of-force to its minimum is recurrently stressed in Bittner's work (1970/1990: 187, 190, 1974/1990: 262), the notion of 'minimum use-of-force' has been criticized as being a vague yet pervasive standard in discussion of democratic policing (Manning 2010).

Mawby and Wright reviewed the scholarly literature concerning 'debates over whether the police are primarily a police "force" or a police service delivering care or control' (Mawby and Wright 2008: 240). They point out that 'preservation of public tranquility' is an important goal for police and that even public order policing includes aspects of both force and service, concluding that 'police combine both roles and it is a balance between the two that at times comes into conflict' (ibid.).

Extensive research efforts have been devoted to the subject of police use-of-force (e.g. Alpert and Dunham 2004; Skolnick and Fyfe 1993; Stenning *et al.* 2009). Research has revealed how the hardening of use-of-force in the context of policing political protest has amplified protest tactics and led to a 'crisis in control' (Wood 2014). Because police are involved in disaster preparedness and emergency response, service requirements inevitably form part of their mandate in circumstances where public order is in question. Egon Bittner provides a fitting image that captures the essence of this in his essay 'Florence Nightingale in Pursuit of Willie Sutton: A Theory of Police':

> As long as there will be fools who can insist that their comfort and pleasure take precedence over the needs of firemen for space in fighting a fire, and who will not move to make room, so long will there be a need for policemen. (Bittner 1980: 137)

EXPLAINING POLICE BEHAVIOUR: ORGANIZATIONAL STRUCTURE AND OFFICER DISCRETION

The apparent recalcitrance of the frontline police occupational subculture to conform to managerial efforts to impose organizational and structural models onto their work routines is a recurring theme in the literature (Chan 1997; Loftus 2010; Sklansky 2008: 53–7, 145–51). Similar issues can be found in classic criminological theory too. Important ideas concerning differential association, differential learning, and differential opportunity arising from the work of Edwin Sutherland and the subcultural theorists all point to the relationship between individuals and the social structures in which they find opportunities to act (Downes, Rock, and McLaughlin, 2016: especially chap. 6). These are examples of a larger sociological issue, that being the relationship between social structure and individual human agency theorized by Anthony Giddens under the heading of structuration theory (Giddens 1986).

Most research on the police has been concerned with the activities of frontline uniformed police agents and 'the internal diversity of the public police forces has been far from adequately explored' (Brodeur 2010: 9). As a result, a great deal of the theorizing about police culture has been narrowly construed. The structure-agency problematic in police institutions is often simplified into a two-sided conflict between 'street cops and management cops' (Reuss-Ianni 1983).

Nonetheless, the widening understanding of the police division of labour (Maguire 2003) has extended theoretical understanding of the complex relationships between individual police agents and the institutional structures within which they work. Work in this vein has been extensive, so much so that critical scholars have sometimes mistaken this way of thinking as being the totality of the subject field (e.g. Neocleous 2006: 17). It is useful to recognize at the outset that, even if only at an unconscious level, much of the literature reviewed in this book is infused with theories concerning the socio-structural peculiarities of police agency.

Since so much thinking about the politics of the police at least implicitly mobilizes this kind of thinking, it is interesting and useful to step back and consider its parameters. Here we can distinguish between 'police culture' or police culture imaginary—the set of attitudes, beliefs, norms, and values characterizing the system of meaning at the level of the society as a whole—and the 'police subculture'—the set of attitudes, beliefs, norms, and values arising out of participation in the police occupation. Thinking in this manner provides a set of theoretical stepping-stones from the macro-level to the more micro-level of social action. This is not yet a conventional distinction in the literature, but it is useful shorthand for distinguishing between the external and internal differences in cultural awareness of police organization.

Research concerned to illuminate the backstage areas reserved for police institutional insiders is central to a fully rounded politics of policing (e.g. Grimshaw and Jefferson 1987; Waddington 1999a). Other scholarship is more concerned to explore broader questions regarding generalized cultural symbols shaping the politics of the police in the public sphere (e.g. Manning 2003; Loader and Mulcahy 2003). The general culture of policing is substantially shaped by media representations (see Chapter 10).

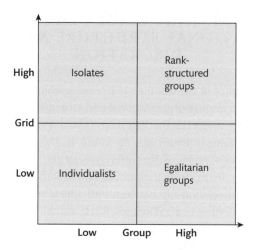

Figure 2.1 General grid-group diagram

People tend to imagine the police organization in monolithic terms—a 'police ma-chine'. For most outsiders, the notion of 'police subculture' is equally monolithic. In order to challenge these habits of thinking at the outset, it is useful to briefly consider one standpoint from which organized human behaviour has been conceptualized. Grid-group analysis is one of the most widely used heuristic devices in social science (Douglas 1999). Used imaginatively, it can help to demonstrate the complexity of the police occupation and it can provide clues about the internal and external politics of policing. In very simple terms, the approach identifies two axes along which two di-mensions of human organization can be said to lie, as shown in Figure 2.1.

The horizontal axis is a continuum of group affinity, from weaker to stronger. Along the vertical axis lies a continuum of grid organization—that is, regulatory, bureaucratic, and administrative structures, also ranged from weaker to stronger. The group dimension reflects upon the degree to which an individual's situation is controlled by group membership. Individuals accept constraints on behaviour by the mere fact of group belonging, which in the police occupation is often reckoned to be quite high on the scale. For a group to be said to exist there will be some collective influencing to signal group loyalty which may vary in strength.

The grid dimension reflects upon the degree of formal organizational structure influencing the individual's situation, which again may be lesser or greater. The police are supposedly a 'totalizing institution' with a 'chain of command'. However, in defining the 'bureaucracy problem' in *Varieties of Police Behavior*, J. Q. Wilson observed that 'the police department has the special property . . . that within it discretion increases as one moves *down* the hierarchy' (Wilson 1968: 7 emphasis in the original), and showed that the strength of grid orientation within the police organization is variable.

This four-fold typology can be used to classify a range of studies. For example it can be used to discuss public order policing as compared with the work of homicide detectives and others working in special squads. In the former instance, studies have revealed how public order police units are subject to the intense demands of group work while simultaneously subject to intense grid supervision (Jefferson 1990;

Waddington 1994). The work of special squads is more insulated from grid supervision because high group solidarity can facilitate the mobilization of management methods to protect group autonomy (Jackall 1997, 2005).

Formally speaking, there are relatively few positions within the police division of labour which are low on both the grid and group axes (bottom left quadrant of Figure 2.1). Positions classifiable as low on group and grid may be at risk of 'going rogue'. Formal examples of such positions might include police dog handlers, forensic investigators, and others who have highly specialized skill sets and who work relatively independently. The proverbial 'burned out uniform carrier' who has been assigned to desk duty in the Police Library might be another one. Lastly, positions classed in the top left-hand corner of the diagram, those who are relatively low on group solidarity but who register as high on the grid axis, are characteristic of mid- and upper level management. Among senior police commanders, status competition and risk aversion affect the strength of group affiliation and grid supervision (Reiner 1991).

Using the grid-group diagram as a heuristic device is one way of illustrating the internal complexity of police institutions and provides clues as to the diversity of their occupational subculture(s). Theories concerning police culture and subculture have been highly influential on thinking about the regulation of police conduct (Punch 1985; Brodeur 1998).

The relationship between the structures of policing and the individual agency of police actors has been very important in the understanding of the relationship between police and the law. Numerous studies have shown that, while legality and rules are set with the expectation that they establish parameters, opportunities, and constraints for police action, they are simultaneously useful as presentational rules that give an acceptable appearance to policework (Black 1976, 1980; Henry and Smith 2017; Moskos 2008; Smith and Gray 1985).

Among other things, thinking about the relationship between the occupational structures of the police and their scope for individual agency suggests that the rule-tightening approach to police reform is predicated on a mechanistic understanding of the relationship between the occupational and institutional structures of the profession, and between individual agency and group action. Unfortunately, because of the tendency to reify police culture, this theoretical approach sometimes returns thinking to a monolithic and homogenizing view.

POLICE, PEOPLE, AND COMMUNITY: STATE, MARKET, AND CIVIL SOCIETY

Political sociologists, political theorists, sociologists, and others thinking about the politics of the police sometimes speak in monolithic terms about institutions such as 'the state' and 'the police', large institutions which are often then counterpoised against similarly monolithic conceptions of 'society' and 'community'. Often a chief concern in democratic societies is with the legitimacy of the state or with police legitimacy. We need these larger conceptions for thinking about the politics of the police because they help to raise the level of consideration above the level of street corner politics and the everyday reproduction of social order to a more strategic one. As long as the adoption of this theoretical standpoint does not end up reifying its central categories to the detriment of other ways of examining the subject, it provides an essential vantage point of consideration.

Most empirical studies of police are at micro-level, rooted in individual psychological or the small-scale occupational culture. These tend to emphasis reform remedies like improved training. Some studies look at meso-level variables, for example in departmental organization or police-community relations, and they tend to focus on remedies in law and policy. These are in turn theoretically structured by macro-level variables linking the political economy and cultural spheres. At this level of abstraction we are thinking in terms of the relationship between state and civil society or perhaps police and community. In so-called democratic states 'the citizen' in 'the community' is endowed with practical reason and is capable of moral judgement, and is the bearer of political, economic, social, and cultural rights. As such, 'those who do not govern are the sources and justification, not just the subjects, of political authority and [are] the ultimate judges about how and whom should exercise that authority and its consequent powers' (O'Donnell 2010: 208).

Serious questions have been asked about the relationship between the state and society. Political scientists, historians, and criminologists have all exhibited curiosity about the effects of the modern state on changing rates of crime over time (Eisner 2001, 2003: especially 127–30; Gurr *et al.* 1977; Pratt 2014). A pattern of declining statistical rates of homicide took place across Europe from the fifteenth century until the end of the nineteenth century. Beginning in southern England and the Low Countries, spreading outward to Scandinavia and unevenly across France, the Germanies, southward to Italy, the Iberian Peninsula, and the Balkans, this civilizing trend has been discerned. Was this perhaps a social pattern arising out of the process of modern state-building, or perhaps it was the other way around and societal trends enabled the building of the modern state?

More recently, dramatic changes in statistical crime rates have presented many challenges to criminologists and raised questions about the extent to which police and state policies have affected these trends (Tonry 2014; Reiner 2016b: 104–27). While the legitimacy of some states and some police agencies is sometimes judged by reference to crime trends and other measures, the converse is that in some instances states and their police agencies have been understood to be serious criminal actors causing great social harm in communities they exploit (Green and Ward 2004; Ross 2017). States (and by extension the police) may be 'necessary virtues' in civilizing societies, but in de-civilizing societies they are not often virtuous (cf. Loader and Walker 2006, 2007).

Drawing on Weberian ideas, a 'building block model' of the state is sometimes conjured up. Such theoretical models of the state picture it as a series of inter-connected boxes on an organization chart, for instance linking: the Treasury, Ministry of Foreign Affairs, Ministry of the Interior, Ministry of Defence, etc. Organograms of this type are useful, but prone to reification, thereby discounting individual human agency (O'Donnell 2010). Federal states have multiple tiers of governance at municipal, provincial, and federal levels and, coupled with the transnational level of governance, the building block model of the state can end up looking like a complicated stack of boxes of which the police are just one kind (Bowling and Sheptycki 2012).

Such tidy theoretical models of states have been troubled by the advent of the 'networked society', (Castells 1996/2000), the 'death of the social' (Rose 1996; O'Malley 1999), and other manifestations of 'post-modernity' that signal the dissolution of the modern state and the social order upon which it depends (Reiner 1992b; Murphy 1998; O'Malley 1997; Sheptycki 1995). Some theorists now think of the relationship between policing and society as being the accomplishment of networks of private and public actors who collaborate in the inter-institutional governance of security (Johnston and Shearing 2003). Connectedly, observing the complex inter-institutional connectivity of police organizations themselves, theorists have begun to think of 'the police' not strictly as a hierarchical order like a stack of boxes, but rather in terms of a web of relations or networks of communicative action (e.g. Brodeur 2010; Giacomantonio 2014, 2015).

Theories depict the police 'surveillance assemblage' as developing like a rhizome defining and shaping the social order (Bauman and Lyon 2007; Haggerty and Ericson 2003). International relations theorists have also adjusted their thinking and now depict the transnational system in terms of networks of actors inhabiting a variety of institutional sites that comprise a complex machinery of governance for a cosmopolitan social order (Held and McGrew 2007; Slaughter 2004). In the context of the hollowing out of the welfare state under conditions of global neo-liberalism, scholars have begun to think about the politics of policing in terms of hybrid security governance and the 'securitization of society' (e.g. Schuilenburg 2015).

Theoretical questions about how best to picture the relationship between state and society, and police and community have implications for how we can imagine the role of law and the possibility of police democratic accountability. Power is discernibly moving away to the democratically uncontrolled global (and in many ways extraterritorial) space beyond the classic state. The ability of police to undertake purposive action remains, as always, highly localized. The seeming absence of democratic political control makes policing power into a source of profound uncertainty, potentially untamable by historically constituted legal and political means. With the hollowing of the state, policing functions (along with many other attributes of state governance) become subject to notoriously capricious and inherently unpredictable market forces and private initiative substitutes for public policy (Bauman 2013: 2; Ericson 2007; Young 1999, 2007, 2011).

A perennial theoretical problem, therefore, is how to describe the governance of security and insecurity that exist empirically at the micro- and meso-levels—interactions between police, people, and community—and connect it to macro-level thinking about states, markets, and civil society where issues of political legitimacy are resolved.

POLICE KNOWLEDGE WORK: *POST HOC* AND PRE COG—INVESTIGATION AND INTELLIGENCE

As will be shown in detail in Chapter 3, since the inception of the modern police idea in the late eighteenth century, policing practice has been concerned to govern the past with an eye to the future. That is, the modern police have always been inscribed with the potential to investigate past wrongs in order to prevent future harms to the social order. However, the future orientation of modern policing was historically limited to things like maintaining emergency preparedness for when things did go wrong and preventing crime and disorder from occurring by maintaining in the present a visible deterrent and the appearance of constant surveillance in public places. Some of the first police research focused on the activity of urban police car patrol and viewed policing as primarily reactive, as emphasized through the notion of 'fire-brigade policing' (Clarke and Hough 1984; Reiner 2012c; Holdaway 1983: 121).

Police investigation and intelligence gathering can be proactive, reactive, or retrospective (Aepli *et al.* 2011; Gill 1998; James 2013, 2016; Phythian 2013; Ratcliffe 2016). Police information processing and 'knowledge work' extend the temporal dimensions of control both forwards and backwards in time (Brodeur 2010: 199–205; Newburn, Williamson, and Wright 2007). There is a fundamental distinction in police 'knowledge work' between 'intelligence'—which consists of information at a pre-investigative phase—and 'investigation'—which is geared to the job of producing forensic information that is suitable for presentation as evidence in a public court of law (Innes 2003; Travers and Manzo 1997; McCulloch and Wilson 2016: 94–7; Sheptycki 2004). The former exists in the backstage areas of the police institution and has a 'projected internal career'; the latter has a 'projected external career' and is information intended for public exhibition in one or more forums (Sheptycki 2017c: 290–1). This dividing line raises difficult questions regarding accountability and oversight in police decision-making.

A considerable proportion of policework is information-gathering enabled by techniques including covert surveillance, tasked criminal informants, 'bugging' and visual surveillance devices, CCTV, financial tracking capabilities, and a vast range of computer facilities, packages, and databases (Billingsley *et al.* 2000; Maguire 2000; Maguire and John 1995; McCue 2014; Peterson 2005). Enormous quantities of information—dirty data—exists at the pre-investigative stage. This information forms an important part of the basis of institutional decision-making in tactical priority and strategic agenda setting (Ratcliffe 2009: 194).

The amount of information in police hands frequently 'outstrips the organizational capacity to act upon it' (Innes and Sheptycki 2004: 13). An important feature of police decisions based upon intelligence therefore is that, due to a variety of internal technical, social, and structural factors, they may result in no action and hence are invisible to any external agent (Giacomantonio 2015; Hughes and Jackson 2004; Sanders and Henderson 2013). Since these decisions are made in backstage areas of police organizations that are protected by conventions surrounding covert information handling, and concomitant concerns to protect personal privacy, national security, and the details of operational policing, they largely escape the purview of external legal accountability (Fijnaut and Marx 1995; Delpeuch and Ross 2016; Dunnighan and Norris 1999).

Even in European jurisdictions that emphasizes the place of the judiciary in the orchestration of police enquiries, there exists a 'grey zone' where the information in police hands—police intelligence—is not yet considered a forensic object capable of juridical objectification, that is, 'investigative evidence' (Aepli *et al.* 2011; Devroe *et al.* 2012; Fyfe, Gundhus, and Rønn 2017; Rønn 2012).

Traditional sources of police intelligence information are now supplemented by a variety of other kinds of 'open source' intelligence—including information in new social media and through commercial data providers. 'Big Data analytics' are a means to augment intelligence processes and analytical products (Chan and Moses 2017;

Ratcliffe 2016: 11). In effect, traditional police surveillance practice has been amplified and transformed. Intelligence analysis—constituted as formal 'objective' risk scores and threat measurements—now shapes individual discretionary police assessments of risks and threats.

In the contemporary period, data are used to predict or forecast future events and the automation of police information systems makes possible systematic surveillance of far larger numbers of people with fewer personnel resources. Notably, the threshold for inclusion in the surveillant assemblage is low (Bauman and Lyon 2007). Even in police databases themselves, the tendency to record as 'persons of interest' individuals who are merely associated with others who may have a criminal record of some sort has been observed and documented.

New techniques and technologies facilitating database policing make feasible system surveillance across multiple institutions. Critical observers have remarked that the growth of policing with predictive analytics promotes social exclusion and inequality. Proponents argue that the efficiency gains brought about by these technological innovations result in improved police service delivery (Brayne 2017; Ericson 2007; Manning 2010; Sanders, Christensen, and Weston 2015).

The future orientation of police knowledge work has only recently come under scrutiny and consideration (Amicelle *et al.* 2017; Chan and Moses 2017; McCue 2014; Peterson 2005; Sanders and Sheptycki 2017). Future-oriented policing aims at 'pre-crime', that is, 'substantive coercive state interventions [are] targeted at non-imminent crimes' (McCulloch and Wilson 2016: 5; Zedner 2007). Phenomena defined as pre-crimes constitute a growing category for policework as 'more behaviors and groups are deemed threats warranting pre-emption' (McCulloch and Wilson 2016: 5). Pre-crime 'embraces a dark vision of the future by anticipating worst-case scenarios and acting as if they were foregone conclusions' (ibid.: 142). An example of this would be a report in the *Daily Telegraph* in March 2010 suggesting that terrorists might resort to packing explosives into women's breast implants in order to carry out an attack on a civilian airliner (Blake 2010), thereby providing further justification for airport 'security theatre' (Maguire and Fussey 2016).

The notion that sustains this manner of thinking—the precautionary principle—seems neutral and sensible enough on first consideration, but according to McCulloch and Wilson it undermines fundamental social values such as trust, justice, and fairness (McCulloch and Wilson 2016: 5–6). As a result of the recent rise to prominence of this way of thinking in the politics of the police, enormous state and corporate resources are now expended to secure the future practices. It turns out, 'can incubate harmful activity and become part of the problem rather than the solution' (Ericson 2007: 154).

The intelligence-led policing model exhibits a constant danger of creating self-fulfilling prophecies since acting against predicted futures may in fact create the conditions and harmful situations that are the pretext of security practices (Norris 2016; Fyfe, Gundhus, and Rønn 2017). Moreover, since an important feature of police intelligence operations is to 'disrupt' potential future events (and not traditional criminal case construction) the publicly knowable evidentiary basis of police action is often opaque and incomplete (Innes and Sheptycki 2004: 3).

The police continue to investigate past crimes, but as they move increasingly towards predictive modes of thinking they become even more central to defining and ranking what counts as crime and disorder. Close observers have recognized that this is a far from objective process (Vestby 2018: 280).

In the contemporary period, this model of understanding policework—which directs thinking onto a temporal continuum of perception from past to future crime, and from police investigative practices to police intelligence practices—exposes the politics of policing in different ways and raises questions about the role of law in police governance. The digitization of data and surveillance has extended the power of police investigative and intelligence practice dramatically, and with it the power of police to define the past, present, and future seems more inviolable than previously.

Predictive policing at street level, mass ambient surveillance, and biometric surveillance, coupled with the ability to marshall a range of legal instruments beyond mere criminal law ones, raise significant issues concerning the scope of authorities' surveillance and coercive order-maintenance powers (Ball, Haggerty, and Lyon 2012: 420–2; Joh 2014; Jochelson *et al.* 2017).

POLITICS OF POLICE: DEMOCRATIC, AUTHORITARIAN, AND TOTALITARIAN POLICING

The majority of scholarship concerning the politics of policing and society is concerned with happenings in a relatively few countries broadly recognized as democratic (Brown 2014; Newburn, Williamson, and Wright 2007; Reisig and Kane 2014). It is difficult enough to undertake a first-hand observational study of police violence in a city like Gary Indiana, as William Westley did in his landmark study of the 1950s (Westley 1970). Since then many sociological studies have been done in democratic countries and most of the theorizing about the politics of the police stands on this empirical base (e.g. Bayley and Stenning 2016; but see Hinton and Newburn 2008).

At least implicitly but often explicitly, academic and scholarly approaches to the politics of police and society have had an abiding concern to foster some sense of democratic legitimacy (Loader and Walker 2007; Manning 2010; Sklansky 2008). As Bayley put it in the context of his early observations of police and political development in India, the police affect democracy and democracy affects policing by shaping how police are able to undertake their functions, how those functions are defined, and how the police are treated as personnel (1969: 409–10).

Thinking about policing and the idea of democracy has coalesced around a suite of features, notably equity of service, police responsiveness to citizen demand, modes of redress for police malpractice and malfeasance, and citizen participation in policy setting (Jones, Newburn, and Smith 1996). Critics observe that policy-oriented thinking is shaped by managerial criteria that tend to reaffirm existing police practice at the expense of community empowerment and capacity building (Manning 2010: 10). Police managerialism with a democratic face, critics charge, merely serves to promote social division and intolerance (McLaughlin 2007: 96). At its best, democratic police research provides an auto-critique of the empirical practices that make its own discourse possible.

Studying other kinds of policing regimes is more often the work of historians or political scientists (e.g. Bonner et al. 2018; Chapman 1970; Liang 1992; Raeff 1983; Mazower 1997;

Tipton 1990). What is the difference between authoritarian policing and totalitarian policing? What is the difference between colonial policing and imperialist policing? These questions are important to consider in thinking about the politics of the police because, at a certain level of abstraction, these terms mean something in relation to each other. In other words, we understand democratic police in relation to other kinds of policing.

The conventional distinction between the so-called 'Westminster model' of policing and the 'Dublin model' is one illustration. The former designates the form of parliamentary democratic policing established in England from 1829. The latter refers to the colonial police administered from Dublin Castle from about 1812. Totalitarian policing can be distinguished from authoritarian policing on the basis of the degree to which the political ideology is more or less totalizing. Historical Police States like that of Nazi Germany or Stalinist Russia would thereby provide examples of totalitarian policing. In slight contrast, authoritarian states like that of France under the Bonapartes are typically more concerned with the maintenance of state power than the total control of the social basis of that power (Mazower 1997).

Imperialist policing is part and parcel of any foreign adventure that either a totalitarian or authoritarian state might venture into and is thereby distinguishable from colonial policing which has historically emanated from democratic and capitalist societies. Contemporary critics of policing in these same countries sometimes argue that supposed democratic policing is 'internal colonialism' and they also draw attention to the police excesses of 'settler colonialism', thereby emphasizing the authoritarian tendencies underlying it (Correia and Wall 2018; Veracini 2010; Weizman 2012).

The difficulty faced in the contemporary period is the changing morphology of governance as the modern international system of states—framed by notions of national sovereign independence (Bayley 1975)—is transformed by the technological rise of the networked society (Castells 1996/2000). In this context, transnational police interconnectivity (both formal and informal) has the potential to 'reach deep' into the local 'human terrain' (Bayer 2010: 86–7), and significantly shape the opportunities for open forums of social engagement upon which democracy rests (Bayley 2006). Notably, promotion of the 'rule of law', rather than democratic political accountability and control, provides the means to work around the 'crushing parochialism and bureaucratic constraints' that seemingly hinder transnational policing and security efforts (Bayer 2010: 142).

Policing on the basis of a 'whole earth overt intelligence resource' (ibid.) and with the habits of *dirigiste* rule of law carries within it the seeds of a global authoritarian policing system (Bowling and Sheptycki 2012: 19). The inter-depedence of policing in the transnational state system, and the structural relations with global capital, raise questions about democratic accountability. Local democratic accountability structures might provide ideological cover that legitimates state violence while preserving a myth of governmental benevolence (Goldsmith and Lewis 2000; Seigel 2018).

In trying to visualize contemporary shifts along these dimensions, Ericson (2007) suggests sharply contrasting images of the Leviathan. The first is taken from the frontispiece of Hobbes' famous treatise on the form and power of a government of the commonwealth. Abraham Bosse's etching that forms the frontispiece of that book dramatically captures this idea of Leviathan: a crowned giant, whose body is actually composed of many human figures (the body politic), rising up from the landscape clutching a sword and a staff of office beneath a quotation from the Book of Job (41:25—*Non est potestas Super Terram quae Comparetur ei*—There is no power on Earth but him). The picture presents a theory of the social contract and the state. The sovereign appears protective and benevolent. Beneath the body politic of Leviathan are ranged the products of collective endeavour, a prosperous land of undulating hills, rivers, farms, roads, and a citadel. Underpinning this landscape are depicted the nascent liberal institutions and technologies imagined to constitute this orderly state of certainty (Ericson 2007: 35). It is commonplace in democratic theory to counterpoise the supposed authoritarianism of Hobbes with the more liberal democratic views of John Locke and the radical views of the social contract found in Rousseau.

Ericson instead contrasts the Hobbesian Leviathan with the Leviathan of the biblical 'social imaginary'. Ericson observed the authoritarian conservative forces of the seventeenth century who opposed Hobbes' views invoked this emblem and suggested that it is more apt for the present age as well. This is an altogether different Leviathan, 'a monstrous body that leaves only death and destruction in its wake . . . this imaginary signifies catastrophe and the need for precaution at all costs' (ibid.: 32). As the Leviathan of the biblical social imaginary supplants the alternative view based on some notion of a social contract, the politics of policing are tarnished and begin to unravel, as selected populations are criminalized in ways that create terror, insecurity, injustice, and diminishing prosperity.

THINKING THEORETICALLY ABOUT THE POLITICS OF THE POLICE

The foregoing explorations outline important currents in theoretical thinking about problems in the politics of policing. They are not mutually exclusive, tightly defined, or closed off. Under each of our headings was explored a set of interconnected language games derived from the literature reflecting on the multifaceted politics of police and policing. In most theorizing about the subject the ideas just described operate in concert and are sometimes consciously worked through, while at other times they are only fragmentarily, or partially, even unconsciously, interpolated into thinking. They are loosely connected and can be combined into different thought styles that give shape and coherence to thinking about the politics of the police.

Since Saussure and Wittgenstein first precipitated the 'linguistic turn', scholars have long understood that all phenomena can be understood as being constituted through language in a system of meaning wherein words (signs) are held together by chains of syntagmatic and associative relations (Harris 1988). The ideas outlined under the seven headings just explored offer an invitation to the reader to imaginatively, critically, and flexibly engage with the politics of the police.

The police métier is a theoretical constant that lends overall coherence to the multiple ways of combining concerns enumerated in the previous sections. Manning refers to the métier in terms of a set of habits and assumptions focused on the trope of 'crime' that envisions only the need to control, deter, and punish the visible and known contestants (Manning 2010: 217). The modern police métier has evolved around the empirical practices of tracking, surveillance, keeping watch, and unending vigilance, and it remains ready to apply force, up to and including fatal force, in pursuit of organizational goals of 'reproducing order', 'making crime', policing the 'risk society' and 'governing insecurity' (Ericson 1981, 1982, 2007; Ericson and Haggerty 1997). Manning argued that the theatrical core of the métier lies in the work of police patrol officers and that the occurrence of crime and disorder—'the incident'—is its 'sacred center' (Manning 2010). Obviously the work of police patrol is a very important part of the police division of labour but, as we will argue throughout this book, there is more to police practice than merely police patrol and crime control. The métier is a useful idea because it focuses attention on what is unique to police, but it widens out from the Bittnerian focus on police use-of-force to take account of the control potential of surveillance and thereby comes closer to a more complete theorization of the phenomenon (Brodeur 2010).

It would be remiss of us at this point not to say something about how we ourselves think through these theoretical ideas. First, we would again emphasize the importance of not reifying the abstract analytical categories by which we are seeking to understand the politics and practices of the police. The complex theoretical language we have outlined here is necessary if we are going to raise thinking above the level of utter condemnation or unbridled admiration. As long as words like 'police occupational culture', 'high policing', or 'intelligence-led policing' are not concretized and are merely used as sensitizing concepts by which to explore the empirical manifestations of police practice and the politics involved, they can help to provide theoretical stepping stones from the micro-level of everyday interaction to more macro-levels of consideration.

Of necessity, research on what the police do is often grounded at a micro-level where individual psychological or the social-psychology of the small group is most evident. In turn, organizational studies of police departments and institutions can expose concerns at a figurative meso-level of social order. When thinking about the politics of the police we inevitably return to a macro-level thinking about the political economy and cultural spheres. At this level of abstraction we can see the problems inherent in trying to foster an antimony like 'democratic policing', and because policing is both global and local, the problems need attending at all levels. It remains to be seen how societal leaders in all walks of life might breath life into the dry bones of democracy. Regardless of the outcome, there will still be the police.

PART II

HISTORY

3

OUT OF THE BLUE: THE ESTABLISHMENT AND DIFFUSION OF THE MODERN POLICE FROM THE FRENCH REVOLUTION TO THE TWENTIETH CENTURY

INTRODUCTION

The modern police can be found on all the continents where there are human societies but it was not always this way. The task of this chapter is to provide an outline of the historical development of the modern police, from inception prior to the French Revolution until more recent times. Building on the work of historical sociologists and others, in this chapter we will advance the view that the modern police ought to be understood as an institutional mainstay of the modern state system (e.g. Hobden and John 2002; Mann 1993). The international state system that first grew up in Europe following the Treaty of Westphalia of 1648, and which came to its global apotheosis sometime in the twentieth century, provided the institutional framework upon which the practices of modern governance (including those of the police) were made possible.

A considerable vein of scholarship can be identified which traces these developments (e.g. Anderson and Killingray 1991, 1992; Andreas and Nadelmann 2008; Bayley 1975; Deflem 2002; Emsley 1999, 2007, 2011, 2014; Jaschke *et al.* 2007; Lane 1992; Liang 1992; Marquis 2016; Miller 1999; Monkkonen 1981; Mazower 1997; Palmer 1988; Raeff 1983; Stead 1983; Tilly 1975, 1985). Today policing is a particular aspect of governance that relies on vigilance, surveillance, and a constant watch backed up by the ability to employ force legitimately in the service of the existing socio-legal order based in an international system of states. This manifests paradoxes in democratic jurisdictions where the means of policing appear at odds with political values, raising a host of questions about the police in relation to power and law, political accountability, perceptions of justice, fairness, and human rights. A historical awareness is vital to understanding how the sociological phenomenon of the police came to be a global force to be reckoned with.

There is a family resemblance between the police in different countries revolving around the police métier, those special attributes of policing that make it a distinct aspect of governance. Obviously governmental practice in different states around the world is not homogeneous, and there is likewise variation in how the police fit in with local practices of social ordering. However, with the imposition of the global international state system the modern police have everywhere, and to varying degrees, come to be the depositories of legitimate force in 'the law' (Brodeur 2010: 106–10; Cotterrell 1989: 62–3, 1992: 246–7). Additionally, modern police hold a dual capacity which is both past and future oriented, by which the present is managed so as to reproduce as nearly as possible the existing social order despite exigencies that may intrude upon that order (Pasquino 1991).

The means by which the police reproduce social order involve a variety of instruments of coercion and also of surveillance, because fundamentally the police métier concerns both enforcement of the law and keeping watch. This is not an essentialist claim about the police, but rather a sensitizing notion that draws attention to two specific and interrelated facets of police practice enacted rather differently in different types of social order. The coordination of surveillance and the use of force in the maintenance of social order are not the same in contemporary Brazil, Russia, India, or South Africa, and the family resemblance we see in the police in these different jurisdictions calls into question any essentialist claims about the historical phenomenon of the police.

At the same time, the notion of the police métier identifies relevant empirical reference points that make cross-national and historical comparison possible. In any given social order, the practices of police agencies are organized around various surveillance and coercive means, and it is possible and useful to trace the historical development and spread of these as the modern international state system of governance evolved and spread across the world.

The discussion in this chapter unfolds under five headings. First we will consider policing in Europe prior to the French Revolution and describe the modern systems of European police that emerged in the wake of the Napoleonic Empire. We will then briefly contrast this with a consideration of the evolution of the police under the common law in England up until the early nineteenth century. Next we will outline the independent evolution of the American police tradition in the USA from independence up until the time of the First World War. After that we will look at how European colonial and imperial expansion spread police practices to other countries around the world. Lastly, we will look briefly at a few examples of places where, independent of expanding European power, efforts to build modern police institutions also occurred.

The diffusion of modern police practice around the world was complex and contingent. Interwoven into these historical developments were cross-cutting political language games that eventually crystalized into a number of recognizable models for thinking about the politics of the police (i.e. democratic, authoritarian, colonial). Contemporary concerns about the relationship between democratic and totalitarian policing, high and low policing, between police force and service, and the role of law in policing practice did not spring fully formed into political language. Rather they had to evolve as the discourse of modern governance replaced traditional ways of social ordering based on feudal and other pre-capitalist social relations.

This chapter will cast light on the historical development of the police métier, and with it the political language of modern policing. As will be seen, police practices are manifest in situations of social conflict over power relations, and these are exhibited on different geographical scales from the parochial to the global. If, as Walter Benjamin put it, the police are an all-pervasive and yet somehow 'ghostly presence in the life of civilized states', then only by dragging them closer to the world historical centre stage can the politics of contemporary policing be made properly meaningful (Benjamin 1996: 243–4, 287).

THE EMERGENCE OF MODERN POLICE IN EUROPE

The first step in the historical emergence of the modern police was undertaken in Paris prior to the French Revolution. In 1666 the French King, Louis XIV, created by decree the first office of the Lieutenant General of the Police of Paris. This was partly an expression of the supposed Divine Right of Kings—as sovereign over the territory and population of France, the King asserted control. It was also a response to the growing social pressures attributable to living in large cities.

In the seventeenth century, Paris was the first European city since ancient times to approach a population of one million inhabitants, but the city had grown up without any planning. There was no sewage system or street lighting and no systematic way to fight fires: public health problems were rampant. The well-off were insulated from the poor and destitute by private retainers, but the overall life of the metropolis was marred by the increasingly unhealthy, anomic, and fetid environment (see Anderson 2011; Bayley 1975; Cameron 1977; 1981; Emsley 1999, 2011; Neocleous 1998; Stead 1957, 1983; Robisheaux 1973).

Contemporaneous with the first thinkers of the European Enlightenment tradition, such as Beccaria (1738–94), Voltaire (1696–1778), Kant (1724–1804), and Adam Smith (1738–94), was the German political economist Johann Heinrich Gottlob von Justi (1717–71). He was appointed Director of Police for the city of Göttingen in 1755, from which position he articulated a 'science of police' that was heard everywhere in Europe (Jaschke *et al.* 2007: 31–2). Another important early figure in defining the practices of police was Joesph von Sonnenfels (1732–1817) who was a professor of political science at the University of Vienna from 1763.

Among other things, Sonnenfels was influential in outlawing the practice of judicial torture. He first defined the police saying: 'police is a science to establish and manage the internal security of the state' (quoted in Axtmann 1992: 46–7). All across Europe there ranged a wide discussion about the practice and politics of the police, enriched by (among others) Adam Smith's *Lectures on Justice, Police, Revenue and Arms* (1762–3), Patrick Colquhoun's *Treatise on the Police of the Metropolis* (1796), Johann von Justi's *Polizeiwissenschaft* (1756), Joseph von Sonnenfels' *Grundsätze der Policey* (1765–7), and Nicolas Delemare's four-volume treatise *Traité de la Police* (1705–38) (Jaschke *et al.* 2007: 48–9). All shared a common focus on governance and how best to organize police surveillance and control over populations and territory in order to maximize 'happiness' in a 'state of prosperity' (Pasquino 1991).

Prior to the French Revolution, policing in Europe was largely a private affair and the privileges of rank and position largely determined social impositions of policing power. The overthrow of the *Ancien Régime* and the coming into being of recognizably modern states at the beginning of the nineteenth century accelerated the development of police as the guarantors of social order and social peace on behalf of 'the people' and 'the nation'. Article 12 of the 1789 French Declaration of the Rights of Man and the Citizen, the precursor to modern human rights doctrine, states that the 'guarantee of the rights of man and of the citizen necessitates a public force [i.e. a police force]: this force is thus instituted for the advantage of all and not for the particular utility of those to whom it is confided' (quoted in Brodeur 2010: 51).

Almost from the very outset police practice was understood to have two aspects. First, it was concerned with the promotion of public safety (*cura promovendi salutem*) and, second, also with the prevention of future ills (*cura advertendi mala futura*). Initially the police undertook every aspect of city governance from fire-fighting to street lighting. The etymology of that 'strange word police' (Radzinowicz 1956) reveals a great deal about modern politics. The ancient Greek term *polis* (from which is derived a number of words including cosmopolitan and metropolitan, but also others such as policy and politics, and of course the word 'police') signalled a broad concern with all aspects of governance of cities and urban spaces (Pasquino 1991). The Latin term *politia* meant the state, and in Roman law the Prefect of a City was empowered by the emperor to issue statutes concerning public order, buildings, fire, sanitation, religion, assembly, health, morality, prostitutes, beggars, and foreigners (Emsley 1983: 2).

After Europe entered the age of Enlightenment, prevailing ideological and legal assumptions entailed the building of police institutions seen as integral to the formation of the modern state (Axtmann 1992). For von Justi, 'police' comprised all activities concerned with the promotion of the common welfare and he argued that, in order for the state to do that successfully, it was necessary to curb the power and influence of all social groups and the political estates since conflicts within these destabilize the community as a whole.

Making use of the sensitizing 'high-low' distinction, we can see that, in addition to having a temporal dimension and a desire to control the future, from very early on European policing was both high policing—that is, concerned with the integrity of the state and its power elite—and with low policing—the promotion of general welfare. Low policing included everything from maintenance of street lighting and clean streets, aiming at dirt and darkness, and was central to the state's claims to legitimacy (Stead 1983: 16).

The concern to avert future ills accompanied a shift in the meaning of police as the synonym for good governance generally towards a conceptualization of the police as an organizational force charged with maintaining public order and safety, and with preventing and investigating unlawful activities (Axtmann 1992: 48). In that regard, police under the absolutist monarchs of the *Ancien Régime* (e.g. Maria Teresa, Joseph II, King Louis XIV) had recourse to an impressive array of legal powers, including checking compulsory identity papers, enforcing sumptuary laws, regulating begging, controlling workhouses, and regulating guilds and labour markets.

The gradual dissociation of the police from responsibility for the all-encompassing notion of *bonum commune* and the consequent narrowing of the concept took place as states became functionally differentiated. Matters regarding street lighting, supervision of town markets, sanitation, and fire were separated off from matters concerning beggars, perpetrators of common crimes, and other unwanted individuals. Systems of secret police spying were common and were to maintain the integrity of the state as a system of governance on the grounds that, as Kant maintained, the *salus publica* (public health) required a legal constitution that guaranteed every person's freedom within law.

This is the prototypical understanding of the police. The police act on the basis of legal instruments that enable social engineering and social ordering in order to create a context within which all citizens can pursue their individual happiness by whatever means. The caveat is that the police are there to ensure that the pursuit of individual happiness does not impair the general lawful freedom and rights of others.

To a considerable extent, the birth of the modern came in the wake of Napoleon's conquest of Europe and his defeat (Johnson 1991; Thomson 1957/1990). The establishment of the London Metropolitan Police came in the aftermath of the Napoleonic wars and it thereby established the archetype of liberal democratic policing in contradistinction to the authoritarianism of 'continental policing' (Emsley 2011). In France, Napoleon Bonaparte re-established the modus operandi of the modern police after a period of revolutionary terror, installing a centralized and rationalized bureaucracy for policing that was dispersed and integrated into civil society. The police system was centralized and segmented. The secret police were under the control of Joseph Fouché, the 'man Napoleon feared' (Arnold, 1979; Forsell 1928/2018). Departmental prefects and town mayors had police powers in their localities and were answerable to Napoleon through the Minister of the Interior.

Napoleon encouraged independence on the part of Adrien de Moncey (the Inspector-General of the Gendarmerie), of Louis Dubois (the first Prefect of Police in Paris), and of General Anne-Jean Savary (chief of military intelligence), thereby ensuring his own dominance over all of them (Emsley 1983: 34). However authoritarian Napoleonic policing was, it was also wedded to Enlightenment ideas of rationality and humanitarianism and the new legal code was in the Beccarian tradition, thereby featuring an end to arbitrary punishment and torture. Certain but humane punishment became the responsibility of public officials acting, in theory at least, on behalf of the sovereign people (Emsley 1983: 35).

The system combined the hierarchical organizational principles and administrative rationality of the military together with legal rationality and complex communications networks for the purposes of gathering intelligence and disseminating official government pronouncements. It was an important archetype in thinking about modern governance.

'The police' wrote Fouché to the Duke of Wellington in 1816, 'is a political magistracy which, apart from its special functions, should co-operate by methods, irregular perhaps, but just, legitimate and benevolent, in augmenting the effectiveness of every measure of government' (quoted in Brodeur 2010: 48). In many respects the variegated police system that was established across Europe during and immediately following the Napoleonic period remained in place for the next hundred years (cf. Stead 1983: 53).

During the early modern period, as the technological and destructive power of armies grew, they became less useful for internal pacification. The invention of modern police institutions (very often as direct off-shoots of the military) allowed the newly emerging modern states to ensure a modicum of social order without unleashing the killing power of the military on civilian populations. The police-military distinction was crucial to the basic logic of *raison d' état*. However, European countries did not evolve to be precisely the same. 'By fitting diverse situations into a Procrustean bed, loss of empirical richness is assured' (Bayley 1975: 329).

The modern police in Europe developed resemblances because state-making was intertwined in the co-development of one interlocking system of states (Tilly 1985; Liang 1992: 8–9). Nonetheless, there was considerable variety (Emsley 2011). Notably, Prussian absolutism (and later German absolutism) did not mimic French centralization. 'The codification of laws and ordinances', Marc Raeff observed of the Germanies prior to unification, 'marked the culminating effort of the well-ordered police state', positive law embodied in the police was the instrument for social, economic, and political elites in Germany to maintain stability and order during a period of rapid transformation (Raeff 1983: 151). Prior to unification in 1871, a German Police Union flourished between 1851 and 1866 to facilitate information exchange and cooperation in the suppression of political dissent (Deflem 2002).

German cities were policed by municipal authorities and the countryside was effectively policed by the Junker class through a system of landed estates in the old feudal manner. After 1871, while Berlin assumed responsibility for taxation, war, and foreign policy, the constituent states and cities retained authority over the regulation of internal affairs and the Police Union network was superseded by similar structures under national German auspices.

In France, and beginning with Paris in 1667, *lieutenants-general de la police* held police authority in major cities and towns, while in the countryside and villages the *Maréchausée* assured the King's Peace. The momentousness of the French Revolution did nothing to change the essential outlines of the system, only changing *lieutenants-general* to *commissaires* and the *Maréchausée* to the *Gendarmerie*.

After the failed revolutionary events of 1848, police in Belgium, the Netherlands, and Switzerland evolved along highly decentralized lines and were left largely under local authority. In the Scandinavian countries, which were extremely poor and backward up until the First World War and where one in three persons was an alcoholic in the nineteenth century, the police were largely dispersed through hundreds of autonomous city, town, or district agencies that remained effectively under local control (Bayley 1975; Hörqvist 2016; Pratt 2014).

After 1848, the Emperor Franz Joseph of Austria also established a Gendarmerie along French lines, initially as a direct adjunct of the army. By 1867 a highly centralized yet segmented system of policing existed throughout the length and breadth of the multi-ethnic Austro-Hungarian Empire, a system geared towards maintaining the structures of the Empire's governance by suppression of democratic ethno-nationalist impulses welling up from below (Liang 1992; Mann 1993: 500–4).

Governance on the Iberian Peninsula, where Spain and Portugal had been unified states since the fifteenth century European voyages of discovery, was reflective of the patrimonial sensibilities and police and social order were again different. In Spain, prior to the establishment of the Guardia Civil in 1844, social order was chiefly maintained through the medieval system of *Santa Hermandad* (the 'Holy Brotherhood'); a semi-corrupt country-wide protection racket which had the backing of the Holy See and the local Spanish aristocratic elites.

The *Santa Hermandad* occupied a power position between the central Spanish state and the local interests of the towns and provinces and could be depended on to raises taxes for its own operations and to maintain the status quo. The Guardia Civil that replaced it remained in place in its essential aspects until the post-Franco period in the late twentieth century; its chief mission as a highly mobile force was the pacification of restive, regional, ethno-national, and class-based aspirations (Shubert 2003: 94–8, 104–6, 177–81, 250). The Guardia Civil was torn evenly apart into two opposing factions during the Civil War and was reconstituted along more military lines by Franco afterwards.

In Portugal there has been a unified body of state police since the establishment of the Royal Guard of the Police in 1801, which again has remained remarkably stable in its essential aspects throughout the Fascist period in the twentieth century, but in this instance the infrastructure of the state was insubstantial. Most social ordering was given over to landed elites who were able to use traditional religious beliefs, patrimonial obligations, and the traditional *Latifundia* system to control the rural population in the absence of formal state institutions, and the Gendarmerie itself was a quite limited institution (Trindade 2013: 44–60). Perhaps more than any other European country, police presence in Portugal was a matter of 'internal colonialism' (Cerezales 2013).

In both Iberian countries, as in most other places in southern and eastern Europe, religious observance remained an essential component underpinning social ordering and, to the extent that it existed, formal state-based policing was largely concerned with maintaining territorial domination and extracting taxes. Political organization on the Iberian and Italian peninsulas involved a web of personal connections and accommodations between various local political, economic, and social elites, and informal politics and clientalism persisted long after the consolidation of modern state apparatus in the region (Hopkin 2012: 198). The rationale of clientalism and patronage continued to exist in southern Europe long after formal democratization took place (Magone 2003: 11). This had fundamental consequences for the local cultures of policing.

In Italy the history of the *Carabinieri* is longer than that of the country itself, dating its establishment by the House of Savoy in the Kingdom of Piedmont to 1802. A highly militarized police force, one of its chief roles, apart from suppression of dissent and tax collection, was preventing desertion from the army itself. The unification of Italy began in earnest with the establishment of a Civil Code (modelled along Napoleonic lines) in 1865 and formally culminated in national unification in 1871, but this did little to change the social order of patrimonialism, the attitude of amoral familialism, and the importance of *notabili* in securing political and economic life at all levels from the small local village to the new national state.

In contrast, the process of national state unification in Germany was preceded by 'police union' within the German Confederation that united most of the Rhineland and Prussia within a network of trade, industry, and cultural connections in which policing was devolved to local authorities (Deflem 2002: 52–3). Italian unification, especially of 'the south', including the cities of Palermo and Naples, was more a matter of successful European power politics and the application of force to subjugate a population that the Piedmontese, Lombards, and other northern Italians (who led the drive to national unification) considered to be corrupt, barbaric, and uncivilized (Moe 2006: 156–83). Italy ended up with two separate national police structures. The *Carabinieri* continued in its role of enforcing state presence across the Italian peninsula but was eventually confined to policing the countryside. As of 1848, a 'National Guard (*Guardia Nazionale*) recruited primarily from among the middle classes' and, reconfigured in 1852 as the Public Security Guards (*Guardi di Pubblica Sicurezza*) answerable to the Ministry of Interior, assumed the tasks of policing in the larger cities. This two-fold centralized system of police was cemented in rivalry and conflict between the differing military and a civilian ethos (Dunnage 1997: 2–3).

Beginning in the seventeenth century, with France leading the way, the social order of Europe revolutionized itself out of its feudal form and the birth of the modern began. Gradually there crystallized a system of modern states. Across continental Europe there evolved a common police métier concerned to organize the internal order of states. The police métier was a crucial aspect of governance concerned with the surveillance of territories and populations. Police social ordering is the *sine qua non* of positive law, undertaken with legal power tools which also define the jurisdictions in which the politics of the police take place. Police give force to law (Cotterrell 1992: 272–7). For better and for worse, by the nineteenth century the modern police—along with other inventions like the passport (Torpey 2000)—had been firmly established as fundamental elements in an unfolding international system of governance.

Before going on to discuss the early emergence of modern policing in England, a pivotal development in the global spread of the modern police, an interesting generalization regarding the differences in the relationship between police and society can be derived from the foregoing historical description and is worth pointing to. If an imaginary line were to be drawn across Europe dividing the Protestant north from the Catholic south it would not map on to the divide in police culture, neither does language itself provide the declension of cultural meaning attributed to the police in different places. As it emerged in Europe, the state system was a patchwork quilt of legal jurisdictions and where the culture of patrimony lingered and the logic of the ideal-typical Weberian state was thereby stultified, the relations between the police and the communities in which they were embedded were more characterized by tradition, informalism, and distain or disregard for the positive law of the state.

When English parliamentarians debated the pros and cons of establishing a police for the metropolis of London in the eighteenth and early nineteenth century, they made bold rhetorical claims about English liberty and the oppressive nature of 'continental policing'. On the cusp of the Industrial Revolution and already a self-proclaimed great power, the evolving British state was no less a part of the emerging international system of states. The nineteenth-century English jurisprudence of John Austin and A.V. Dicey reflects 'a change in the nature of law itself' (Cotterrell 1989: 123).

The emerging international system of states was characteristic of modernity and with it came the modern police métier. In the next section we will say more about the evolution of the police in the context of the common law tradition because this has had specific consequences concerning the cultural understanding of legality and the politics of the police not only in the UK, but also globally.

POLICE AND THE ENGLISH
COMMON LAW TRADITION

With the largest navy, the smallest nobility, and an aversion to standing armies, Britain differed in important respects from its great power rivals on the continent (Emsley 1999, 2007; Hobsbawm 1988; Johnson 1991; Liang 1992). Being an island nation, with sea-faring naval power and access to global trade, it also had no land borders to patrol and consequently no need for border sentries and regiments who would be suitable for easy conversion to low-intensity pacification when the need arose (Mann 1993: 409).

In London and elsewhere in England during the eighteenth century policing was done through a patchwork system of constables appointed and segmentally controlled by local notables, supplemented by private means (Armitage 1932). Social, political, and economic elites lived in splendid isolation, protected from the dangerous classes by privilege, servants, and armed retainers. If trouble escalated beyond the resources of the constables, if traditions of law enforcement were insufficient and the barriers of class privilege broke down, the only recourse was the army, and the gentry militias (the volunteers and the yeomanry) (Mann 1993: 407–9).

The Marxist historian E.P. Thompson acknowledged the deeply held cultural importance of legality in the early politics of law enforcement prior to the establishment of the modern police in England (Thompson 1975: 261–8). Historically in the British context, domestic social control was less invested in military means of repression and more so in social ordering through administration and arbitration through courts of law.

Nonetheless, military repression was not uncommon, a major occurrence being the Gordon riots of 1780 when 285 people were officially recorded as being killed (Mann 1993: 408). Reith documents an exchange of letters in 1819, only a few years after Bonaparte's final defeat at Waterloo, between the Duke of Wellington and Sir John Byng, commander of troops in the north (Reith 1948: 20–1). Wellington wrote to Byng:

> As long as no misfortune happens to them [the troops], the mischief will be confined to plunder and a little murder, and will not be irretrievable; but it is impossible to see how far it will go if the mob shall in any instance get the better of the troops . . . expose no detachments in a populous town to the danger of being disarmed, insulted or destroyed. It is much better that a town be plundered and even some lives lost, than that the whole country should be exposed to the danger which would result from the success of the mob against even a small detachment of troops.

Byng replied:

> I have always fought against the dispersion of my force in trivial detachments; it is quite impossible to defeat the disaffected if they rise, and to protect at the same time any town from plunder; that resistance should be made by the inhabitants . . . but I am sorry to say the general remark from manufacturers in and near Manchester has been that government is bound to protect them and their property.

The year 1819 was the year of the Peterloo Massacre and a full decade before the establishment of the London Metropolitan Police.

The interaction between legal means and the technical capacities of the military and the evolving police constabulary is illustrated in Vogler's historical account *Reading the Riot Act* (1991). Vogler presents a subtle and complex picture of the relations between class factions and segments of the state apparatus, between the constabulary, the magistracy, and the military in responding to civil disorder. Under the terms of the infamous Riot Act of 1715 a local magistrate was to read aloud a proclamation ordering a crowd to disperse. If the mob failed to do so within the hour the law allowed them to be attacked and killed with impunity.

For example, Vogler presents a case study of the 1831 Bristol riot focusing particular attention on the class background of the local Tory magistrates who were 'West India aristocracy' and had earned their fortunes from slavery. By that year, those fortunes were in decline and the local Tory magistrates, who also dominated the city corporation, were at odds with other citizens of wealth and aspiration who owed their fortunes to other forms of trade and who associated with the Liberals in politics. The rioters in question were incensed at the anti-reform tactics of the Recorder of Bristol and initially vented their wrath on corporation (i.e. public) property. So long as the disorder remained limited in this way, neither the 'respectable classes' generally, nor the military detachments stationed in the city were inclined to respond to the appeals of the magistrates. After the mob attacked private property, opinions changed and citizens flocked to join the constabulary and help to suppress the riot. Once order was restored pressure was put on central authorities by local Liberals to depose the sitting magistrates. Not only did Parliament respond positively to these demands, it also, if only half-heartedly, prosecuted them for negligence.

Vogler's history of public order policing in the early modern period serves to illustrate the general point that the modern police in Britain were forged between the hammer of new rising bourgeois class expectation and the anvil of an already existing traditional culture of control. It also shows that the law was viewed as a common resource and was not merely an instrument of state power.

The early history of modern policing in England suggests that notions of the 'rule of law' evolved out of common law not as an abstract 'command of the sovereign', but rather a *sui generis* synthesis of customary right and the logic of authoritative governance that in theory allowed access to legal tools to any who could manage to afford them. At the beginning of the modern age, London was faced with problems similar to those of Paris (perhaps even more so due to its size and the accelerated pace of the Industrial Revolution in Britain) and the English were driven to similar answers concerning social order as the French. Consequently, the British evolved and consolidated the modern police métier within a distinctive socio-legal tradition.

The British police evolved chiefly as a form of urban governance. With the advent of the London Metropolitan Police in 1829 the ambit of the police métier was narrowed. Police were a branch of the criminal justice system purveying offenders to judicial powers and the term 'the police' came to refer almost exclusively to a body of 'stout men in blue coats' strictly focused on the provision of security, the prevention and detection of crime, and the preservation of social peace (Brodeur 2010: 62–5). This was to have considerable resonance globally, as we shall show elsewhere in this book, and we will explore the British case in more detail in Chapter 4. Next we need to turn attention to the development of the police in the USA, because there things evolved differently and the culture of American policing had tremendous influence on the development of the international system.

POLICE AND THE AMERICAN FRONTIER: FROM COLONIAL SETTLEMENT TO THE FIRST WORLD WAR

Arguably no other country has done more to shape the development of modern police than the USA. The surface of emergence for American policing was first laid during the Colonial period when a mixture of traditional religious institutional means and penal ones were the primary pillars of social order (Isenberg 2016). In the early American colonies oppression of indigenous cultures and the legal institutions of human servitude were just as oppressive as the feudal systems of Europe.

Despite the rhetoric, the social order of the American colonies on the brink of the War of Independence in 1776 was as inegalitarian as European ones (Mann 1993: 137–49). After independence, and even more indisposed to the idea of a strong central government and standing army than their erstwhile British foes, the new American power elite drafted a constitutional order that left the central state divided by a separation of powers and weak in terms of infrastructural capacity. Most governance was devolved to local states, including matters relating to education, health, family, law, most public works, police, and the administration of the poor (ibid.: 159). The largely lawless unfolding vistas of American manifest destiny gave rise to the vigilante tradition amid frontier violence and the continuing efforts to enforce racial exclusion of African Americans (Brown 1969; Frantz 1969; Graham and Gurr 1969; Silberman 1978).

Up to the close of the western frontier in 1898, there was a central state and a military, and local states and municipalities provided some governmental services, but the American state was 'born puny' (Mann 1993: 159). At every level and in every aspect of American governance, capacity, and expenditure were weak in comparison to those of Europe (ibid.: 369). Although the Federal Marshal's Service was established in the wake of the revolutionary War of Independence in 1789—with an initial complement of twelve officers—it was not until the twentieth century that the federal government developed a significant policing capacity under the rubric of 'law enforcement'.

The state apparatus did maintain coercive capacity, an army to kill indigenous people and assist the slave patrol, a national guard to help private security providers break up strikes and control urban riots (ibid.: 407), but there was relatively little in the way of public provision for policing. Indeed, until the early twentieth century, private police—notably under the auspices of the Pinkerton Detective Agency—performed the majority of policing in the context of labour disputes, draft riots, and other occasions when working-class elements required disciplining (Brodeur 2010: 73–4, 266–7). Private policing of this sort was large scale, and involved the use of covert surveillance against and violent confrontations with organized labour.

The diffusion of big city policing in the USA in the nineteenth century—Boston (1837), New York (1844), Philadelphia (1844), San Francisco (1849), Chicago (1855), and Los Angeles (1869)—developed in the context of the expanding 'wild' western frontier. The American vigilante tradition was exacerbated by the conditions of the Civil War (1861–65), slavery was followed by decades of 'Jim Crow' segregation, and from the 1870s onwards there 'was massive and continuous' repression of labour organization (Mann 1993: 407). When the western frontier was finally closed in 1898, the modern American police tradition had been established along significantly different lines from any of the European continental states. It differed even from the English tradition from which it was spawned (Miller 1999).

On the one hand was the British 'old world' liberal democratic police officer epitomizing *impersonal* authority; an agent appointed by the responsible rulers of representative government for the public good and with the consent of the governed functioning according to common law. According to Miller, in the more culturally heterogeneous cities of the USA, where capitalist economic relations governed social life, the democratic American cop's authority was *personal*. Before the professional era of police in the USA, the police métier was different because democracy in America was suspicious of officialdom and did not like uniforms.

So personalized was the American cop, Miller records, that in 1857 division house captains encouraged their men to arm themselves with pistols and that revolvers had become standard equipment by the late 1860s, although they were not formally authorized as such until the Fenian scare of 1867–8 (Miller 1999: 50, 115). Despite these cultural differences, the rapid growth of cities and the consequent disorder gave rise to a similar demand for modern police in the USA as in the cities of Europe (Lane 1992; Monkkonen 1981, 1992).

The diffusion of the modern municipal police was 'a part of the growth of urban service bureaucracies' (Monkkonen 1981: 55). During the last half of the nineteenth century American urban administrations began to provide a growing range of services—police, fire, health, and sewerage—which had previously been provided on an entrepreneurial basis. Any one of several precipitants—a riot, or a series of serious crimes, or some other perceived major occurrence of disorder—might lead to the adoption of the system of police inspired by the example of London (ibid.).

Brodeur contends that police in the USA were a distortion of what was happening in Britain, that American police were less centralized, more discretionary, and more heavily armed than their British counterparts (Brodeur 2010: 72). Moreover, there was a significant interpenetration of public and private policing from the last half of the nineteenth century onwards (ibid.: 73). American policing under both public and private auspices, Brodeur shows, was significantly involved in the covert policing of labour radicals, breaking strikes by violence, and political policing (ibid.: 73–4). Unlike high policing in the absolutist states of Europe, in the American context it was also both privatized and decentralized.

According to Monkkonen, by 1920 the police in American cities had undergone two significant periods of innovation. The first was a shift to standardized uniformed police with a locally based, centralized hierarchical command structure. As Mokkonen puts it 'the importance of hierarchy came, not from the central exercise of power downward, but from the flow of information upward to one place. The very organizational shape of the new police helped them to provide informational order to otherwise fragmented cities' (Monkkonen 1981: 149).

During the second transformation, city police departments shed many of the general service functions and became more specialized in crime-related work (ibid.: 150). The stripping away of welfare functions from policing echoed the consolidation of the police métier in Europe one hundred or so years previously. The American police métier was much the same as in other places, surveillance and the ability to muster coercive force, but it had a particular cultural inflection (Bayley 1992). Accompanying these organizational shifts was a change in the meaning of the 'dangerous class', which went from signifying the poor, the criminal, and the homeless infirm to signifying the unemployed and 'revolutionaries' (Monkkonen 1981: 150).

Miller, Monkkonen, and Brodeur all agree that the police in the USA acted with much greater discretion and more often with greater use of force than their British or European counterparts. Because the targets of police oppression were migrants to the burgeoning cities (poor white trash and black former slaves), police 'had unconditional majority backing' (ibid.: 72). Historically entrenched heavy-handedness meant police were negatively viewed by the people they traditionally targeted but it also 'hindered their legitimacy for the whole population they claimed to protect' (ibid.). Like police in Europe and Britain, the American police métier was also future oriented and this 'ideology provided motivation for subverting any person or group perceived as potential offenders . . . the prevention mission . . . was irreconcilable with Anglo-American notions of civil liberty [and] destined to keep the police involved in criminal activity themselves in efforts to prevent crime' (ibid.: 158–9).

By the dawn of the twentieth century, police in the USA marched to the tune of crime control deliberately conceived in non-local terms, ultimately paving the way for the Federal Bureau of Investigation. This was part of the second transformation of the police in the USA creating a national police communication network thereby transforming the police into 'quasi-military social control agents' (Monkkonen 1981: 157). After its founding in 1893, the National Chiefs of Police Union quickly morphed into the International Association of Chiefs of Police, a nation-wide professional communications infrastructure, and by the 1890s the USA had a central bureau of criminal identification as well (ibid.: 158). This bureau mutated into the Bureau of Investigation in 1908, and some years after J. Edgar Hoover took the helm in 1924, it eventually became the Federal Bureau of Investigation in 1932.

Geller and Morris (1992) describe a historical process in three stages that explains the eventual emergence of the American system of law enforcement. In the first stage, prior to the Civil War, the federal state had negligible influence on policing which developed by the 1890s, as we have already seen, into a patchwork quilt consisting of thousands of local and municipal police departments, linked in a nation-wide communications network. According to Geller and Morris, during the second phase of police development, US federal law enforcement gradually began to influence local policing activities. The third phase they describe commenced just prior to the First World War and continued throughout the twentieth century. During the initial phases the institutional precursors of federal law agencies which later became the Federal Bureau of Investigation, the Federal Bureau of Narcotics (later Drug Enforcement Administration), and the Bureau of Firearms, Alcohol and Tobacco, gradually formed separate networks of control along narrowly defined enforcement parameters that spanned the USA and extended abroad (Andreas and Nadelmann 2008). During the third phase federal US regulatory functions advanced to touch on most aspects of the single market underpinning American industry, commerce, and society.

The American version of the modern police métier was established by the time Raymond Fosdick published his two books—*European Police Systems* (1915) and *American Police Systems* (1920)—and commenced the first course on the subject taught at

Harvard in 1916.[1] The American police and law enforcement system evolved to expand internationally as an interpenetrated public and private networked structure and it had already begun to do so before the First World War (Nadelmann 1993).

COLONIAL POLICE

British colonial policing was closely intertwined with domestic policing (Godfrey and Dunstall 2012). Stanley Palmer's magisterial *Police and Protest in England and Ireland 1780–1850* shows the deep inter-connectedness in the development of the police in the two jurisdictions (Palmer 1988). Robert Peel, the son of a wealthy textile manufacturer, entered politics at the age of 21 as an MP for the proprietorial borough of Cashel, Tipperary in Ireland. The Duke of Wellington was a close personal friend. As Chief Secretary for Ireland he steered the Peace Preservation Act (1814) through Parliament, establishing the Royal Irish Constabulary. Peel was Home Secretary from 1822 until 1827 and again from 1828 until 1830, during which time he worked on simplifying the criminal law, ridding it of 'the bloody code', and later nursed the Metropolitan Police Improvement Bill through Parliament in 1829.

Throughout his tenure he promoted the notion of modern preventive policing as the necessary corollary to the paring back of capital and corporal punishments that characterized criminal justice under the old regime (Emsley 1983: 59–61). Orthodox histories of British policing present a sharp polarity between the Royal Irish Constabulary and the London Metropolitan Police (the so-called Dublin and Westminster models), arguing that the latter represented the rationalizing, civilizing, Benthamite march of progress (Critchley 1970, 1978; Reith 1938, 1948; Tobias 1972). Revisionist police historians initially tended to counter with the parochial criticism that the British police were 'domestic missionaries' who were received as a 'plague of blue locusts' by the English working class (Ignatieff 1979; Storch 1975, 1976) and an 'ideological reaction' by the British elite to a demand for order in domestic civil society (Silver 1967, 1971). Brogden (1987) added to the revisionist critique, arguing that a 'filial relationship' existed between the London Metropolitan Police, the Royal Irish Constabulary, and all other British colonial police constabularies to come. This family resemblance was, according to Brogden, based on the widely held assumption that all British police throughout the empire drew on the same body of common law police powers.

The emergent system of modern British policing cannot be separated from the era in which it developed, the time of global *Pax Britannica* (1815–1914) when the UK became globally hegemonic and the 'world policeman' (Johnson 1991: 286–354). Anderson and Killingray's two volumes—*Policing the Empire: Government, Authority, and Control, 1830–1940*, and *Policing and Decolonisation: Politics, Nationalism, and the Police, 1917–65*—trace the arc of this development, and they document the marked variation in police practice across the empire (Anderson and Killingray 1991, 1992). According to them, there evolved many 'mutant strains' of English common law (Anderson and Killingray 1991: 5) and the local imposition of colonial policing in the different jurisdictions depended on the political and discretionary choices made by commanding officers.

---

[1] 'Police Course at Harvard; Raymond Fosdick Invited to Become First Instructor', *New York Times*, 28 October 1916, 12 (no byline).

Nevertheless, the core of the police métier—watchful vigilance backed up with the threat or use of force—remained regardless (Emsley 2014; Emsley and Shpayer-Makov 2006: 200–5). Historical scholarship concerning American colonial adventures in Latin America, the Philippines, and elsewhere also reveals colonial police as more than a 'blunt instrument for physical coercion', identifying 'its role as a panopticon, sweeping the shadows for sensitive information with spies or surveillance' (McCoy 2009: 47; see also Boot 2002).

A distinction should be drawn between 'exploitation colonialism' and 'settler colonialism', although there was often an admixture of the two in any particular colonial jurisdiction (Veracini 2010). With the latter, the colonial power intends to establish an outpost of the central metropole, populating it with colonists, and displacing the local indigenous population in order to do so. Obvious examples of this are Australia, Canada, and New Zealand, but other places—notably South Africa and Kenya—experienced the implantation of pockets of settler colonialism (Anderson and Killingray 1991; Finnane 1994; Ford 2010; Hill 1995; Marquis 2016; Neal 1991; Richards 2008).

Colonies of exploitation involve lesser numbers of colonialists in proportion to local indigenous inhabitants and the intent is not settlement as such, but rather exploitation of trade opportunities, the local population, and natural resources for extraction and the benefit of the metropolitan centre (Agozino 2003, 2004; Altbeker 2005; Anderson and Killingray 1991; Beek et al. 2017; Brogden and Shearing 1993; Deflem 1994; Hills 2000; Levy and Hagan 2006; Marks 2005; Mullins and Rothe 2008: especially 71–7). The Indian Raj, and trade concessions in China, the French colonies of Indochina, the Belgian Congo, and the Dutch trading colonies of the East Indies are clearly distinguishable from the colonies of settlement in this respect.

Colonies of settlement and of exploitation evolved along different trajectories that are underscored by the differential impositions of colonial police. The post-colonial era saw a relatively rapid retreat of European colonial police power from most colonies of exploitation, but the institutional remnants of policing were more marked in the colonies of settlement (Cole 1999: 89; Lin 2007; Veracini 2010). The imposition of colonial rule and the historical legacies of colonial exploitation are present in contemporary police donor assistance (Bonner et al. 2018; Chevigny 1995; Ellison and Pino 2012; Goldsmith and Sheptycki 2007; Huggins 1998; O'Reilly 2017; Machold 2018; Sinclair 2006).

Evidence suggests that there are qualitative differences between common law and civil law impositions in the aftermath of colonial rule, with the former being more disposed to legality and providing for 'the rule of law' (Joireman, 2001), however, the latter also exhibited considerable variation (Daniels, Trebilcock, and Carson 2011).

Of all the historically contingent outcomes relating to the development of modern policing, the attempted abolition of slavery is the most remarkable. The British were not the first to outlaw slavery, because actually Denmark did so in 1802, but it was British insistence that assured a clause pursuing the same end was included in the treaties signed at the Congress of Vienna in 1814 following the first major defeat of Napoleon. For the first time in written human history a society sought to universally outlaw slavery (Johnson 1991: 323; Oldfield 1998). In 1830 it was abolished throughout the British Empire. Law backed by the might and global reach of the Royal Navy made the abolition of the slave trade de facto the first 'global prohibition regime' (Nadelmann 1990).

In the USA as of 1830, opinion on the institution of slavery was split: south of latitude 36°30′ it was considered legal and moral, whereas to the north it was neither. It was not until the Civil War was fought and settled after 1865 that the institution of slavery was legally ended in the USA, but in the Americas latitude 36°30′ remained an enduring symbolic boundary south of which the legacy of slavery long lingered.

The British Admiralty took policing the high seas to suppress the slave trade very seriously. All the same, the Royal Navy's primary duty was to secure the seas and oceans for shipping and trade. Globally the trade in commodities like pepper and spices, tea, coffee, and opium was incredibly lucrative. In-shore and coastal piracy was endemic throughout the Indian Ocean, the Persian Gulf, the Malacca Straits, the Dutch East Indies, the Philippine archipelago, and the West Caribbean. The pirates pursued by the Royal Navy were not swashbuckling sons of the Metropole and blue-eyed Blackbeards. They were mostly non-European local 'Big Men', opportunistically feeding off the sea trade routes. Similar patterns of coastal piracy emerged in the same regions at the end of the twentieth century (Vagg 1995).

The situation in the south Atlantic during the nineteenth century was criminogenic, as historians studying the slave trade routes there have determined (Curto 2004; Curto and Lovejoy 2004). The slaves bought in Africa for shipment to the sugar plantations of South America were paid for with alcohol made from the sugar produced on the plantations, with the profits flowing back to Europe. Actually, the slave trade between South America and Africa was approximately ten times bigger than what went on in the north Atlantic. Portugal continued to exert control over the coast around São Paulo da Assunção de Loanda (now Luanda) until 1975. Although other Europeans countries did not have significant military naval power, some did have significant merchant navies. Dutch, Spanish, Portuguese, Italian, and other sea-faring and trading nations continued to sail in pursuit of capitalist trade opportunities and benefited from the guarantees offered by the Royal Navy.

So much of this history has yet to be written and there is scant evidence to say how effective this global policing power actually was. One general lesson we know from the history of colonial policing is that it is, like policing more generally, Janus faced. The history of colonial domination is replete with reprehensible conduct by imperial power. But arguably by the end of the Victorian era humanity was measurably closer to the ideals of universal human rights first articulated during the fall of the *Ancien Régime*. However, any such advance was far from assured.

OTHER EXAMPLES OF MODERN POLICE INSTITUTION BUILDING

A common defect of theorizing about the police is a tendency towards Anglo-American centrism. Because of the historical importance of the USA and the UK in establishing and spreading modern police institutions globally (as well as their academic study), this is not surprising. However, it is a distorted view because the unfolding of the state system, complete with its logic of 'internal security' (police) and 'international insecurity' (military), was not simply the unfolding of power structures emanating from the emerging centres of global capitalism.

During the period we are interested in other countries developed, or tried to develop, their own endogenous forms of modern policing. It is useful for a more complete picture of the historical development of the modern police to include at least some discussion of these other cases. This is especially important because these alternative trajectories in the development of the police occurred in different socio-legal and political-cultural conditions. Understanding something of the history of these alternative trajectories in the development of the modern police is crucial for how we theorize contemporary global policing.

We have chosen four examples to illustrate the point that the police métier—the organization of surveillance and coercive power in the governance of social order—has emerged in widely different political and cultural conditions. These examples are of a 'faltering', a 'failed', a 'renascent', and a 'recrudescent' policing tradition, those being respectively the cases of Iran, Japan, China, and Russia.

The following sketches are provisional. Our goal is to show that the politics of the police is global as well as local. Existing scholarship provides some broader insights into policing and the socio-historical foundations of the global system of states. The cases show both similarities and differences. Local attempts to create modern police institutions were shaped by geo-political rivalry in the international system of states.

IRAN

Efforts to establish a modern system of police in what is now the country of Iran were first undertaken by the Shahs of the Qjar dynasty, beginning in 1879. The Qjars brought in expert foreign consultants from Austria, France, and Sweden at different times in the attempt to bring order not only to the capital, Tehran, but also in an effort to extend governance capacity over a wider territory.

These efforts were confounded, first because the internal conditions of the country which were based on feudal relations to the land and, in large swaths of territory, still given over to communities of migrant herders organized along tribal lines. Second, they were stultified due to the pressures of Russia from the north (begun by Peter the Great in 1722) and from the USA and Great Britain in the south. In 1922 the Qjars were overthrown by an officer of the cavalry, Reza Pahlavi, who established a dynasty in his name. In a highly symbolic move, Reza Shah had the ancient walls of Tehran taken down and also promoted standards of western dress for both men and women; the clash of modernity and traditionalism had begun in Iran. Pahlavi introduced compulsory two-year military service for all 18-year-old males, he established two police schools in 1936 and a centralized Department of Police Education in 1947.

The emerging modern state of Iran was a multi-ethnic society. Social order was traditionally the product of the mosque and the bazaar, the former the traditional seat of religious and ideological power, the latter the traditional seat of economic power. Formally there were several police institutions, the Royal Gendarmerie, the National Police, the *Shahrbani* (various city police), and SAVAK (the 'high police', created in 1957). Thinking in terms of the high-low distinction, formally at the local level the Iranian police hardly penetrated the social fabric, except in terms of low-level corruption and bribe taking. Famously, the police in Tehran have never been able to bring order to the traffic on the roads.

With the support of British and American interests in the region, Reza Shah's son, Mohammad Reza Pahlavi, took the throne in 1947. There was a brief attempt by indigenous Iranian elites to reform the state along democratic nationalist lines leading to the election of Mohammad Mosaddegh, who was Prime Minister from 1951–3. His attempt to nationalize the oil industry was foiled by Anglo-American meddling and the Pahlavi dynasty was reinstalled, thus thwarting what could have been Iran's transition to a multi-ethnic democratic society. Instead, the ruling '400 families' were largely reduced to a comprador class, culturally divorced from the masses. The degree of alienation helps to explain why elite consensus crumbled so readily in 1979. Under the Pahlavi regime, the high policing capacity of the state was over-developed and, under CIA tutelage, exclusively aimed at the communist Tudeh Party of Iran with which it waged a violent struggle.

Until the revolution which overthrew the regime in 1979, the first modern police system in Iran most strongly resembled the Bonapartist one. The political and cultural resistance of traditional religious leaders to the pressures of modernization came as a complete surprise and religious conservatism (not communism) captured the revolutionary moment, establishing an Islamic Republic of Iran. Subsequently policing in Iran has continued to adapt modern police technologies. In 1992 the Disciplinary Force of the Islamic Republic of Iran (answerable to the Ministry of the Interior) was created, by merging the existing city police with the remnants of the Gendarmerie and the Islamic Revolutionary Committees that had sprung up from the revolution.

In a country where both adultery and homosexuality are considered criminal acts, the police métier appears as a specific cultural form, but the modern police of contemporary Iran respond to a list of duties that are otherwise familiar: homicide, smuggling, tax evasion, and robbery as well as political crimes and road traffic enforcement. Domestic high policing in Iran in the contemporary period aims to contain the grass roots 'Green Movement', which has led to significant public demonstrations and demands for democratic reform put down by heavy-handed policing (Ansari 2003; Golkar 2011; Graham 1980; Wardak and Sheptycki 2005; Zamani and Jordan 1989).

JAPAN

The Japanese case unfolded differently and with a different outcome. Japan's first contact with Europeans dates from the end of the sixteenth century, but the Tokugawa Shogunate expelled all foreigners in 1634 and uniquely Japanese feudal relations stabilized during the subsequent Edo period in which the hierarchy of social order was held in place by the traditional code of *bushido*. Society was policed by the *samurai*, a hereditary class with a complex internal hierarchy numbering about 4 to 5 per cent of a total population estimated to have been about 30 million, ruled by an elite class of aristocratic clans called the *daimyo*. When US Admiral Perry sailed into Edo (Tokyo) Bay in 1853 demanding open trade, the Japanese power elite responded with the restoration of the Meji dynasty, subsequent to which modern state-building began in earnest and Japanese feudalism gave way to Japanese militarism and nationalism.

By 1885, under the tutelage of foreign advisers from Prussia, there emerged a system of widely dispersed police sub-stations and call boxes, the precursors to the celebrated *Koban* system of contemporary Japan. State surveillance was deeply embedded in localities. The German legal principle of *Rechtsstaatsprinzip*, which is usually interpreted in English to refer to the rule of law and due process, was translated as meaning rule by law. Uniformed police were highly visible and entwined in the fabric of communities. Officers were selected on the basis of a minimum height requirement (that they be taller than average) and an age requirement (that they be of sufficient age to gain respect and trust from the public) and were required to be young enough to be fit for police duties. They were supposed to uphold general social peace, investigate crime, and provide other aspects of social service, but they were officials of the state, not servants of the people. They were told to be kind and courteous, were not to compromise justice or harm the dignity of the police institution, and needed to use discretion wisely.

The chief targets of high policing were the *tenkôsha* (revolutionary Marxist cells). Created in 1911, the political police were called the *Tokkô* but Japanese police had been performing political functions continuously since the Tokugawa period. Institutional longevity and tradition was considered important to the legitimacy of the police. Policing in Japan depended heavily on ideological persuasion and combined both administrative and criminal legal instruments in maintaining social order. Tipton (1990) argued that the twentieth-century Japanese Police State that entered World War Two resembled its nineteenth-century French Bonapartist counterpart.

This indigenous police system came to an abrupt end in 1945, after which the country was fully integrated into the circuits of global neo-liberal capitalist exchange, and a new legal constitution and a police system modelled on American lines was installed. One paradoxical outcome of this was that the Yakuza (traditional Japanese organized criminality) were incorporated into the fabric of postwar Japanese social ordering, ensuring decades of right-wing political ascendency in the country (Kaplan and Dubro 2012: 41–4).

The Japanese attempt to foster a distinctive, indigenous modern police tradition might be considered a failure. Nevertheless, the importance of the cultural code of *bushido* and the consequent network of duties and obligations it inscribes remain important in Japanese society and inflect the Japanese police métier which, in spite of important cultural differences, is recognizably similar to its counterparts in Europe and North America (Bayley 1976, 1991; Ellis, Hamai, and Williamson 2008; Miyazawa 1992; Thomas 1996/2014; Tipton 1990).

CHINA

The modern history of police in China did not commence until relatively late in the twentieth century. China's initial contact with European modernity occurred in a period of declining state capacity and before the end of the nineteenth century its existing system of governance had all but collapsed. Modern Chinese state-making and the police system that went with it did not begin until after the Communist Revolution in the period 1949–54. During this period policing in China was totalitarian in character and focused on political control rather than crime in the usual sense of the word. Police criminal law enforcement became central to the police métier in China during the so-called 'strike hard' campaigns (*yandas*) of the 1980s.

Before that time, during the Maoist period, crime did not officially exist and the practices of social control were ideologically determined by the Communist Party of China. The renascent police power of China has pretensions to authoritarian control rather than totalitarian control, but the research literature reveals that police capacity in China is actually quite weak, undermined by corruption and entangled in organized crime. There is a veneer of legality and the language of due process is evident in official pronouncements but, because of the impact of the Cultural Revolution, police have no grass roots connections within communities.

In China, police combine administrative and criminal legal instruments in order to rule *by* law. Decrees are obeyed when they have to be and ignored when they can be. In the absence of the compliance that a legal order based on trust can achieve, local police in China have the reputation of being petty, violent, and corrupt tyrants. Accelerating from the 1990s onwards, the introduction of market relations and accompanying tremendous migrations from the countryside to the cities increased social disorder and the demand for policing. At the same time opportunities for police collusion with organized crime in the burgeoning markets for sex and drugs increased significantly. The legitimacy of state police was further undermined by abuse of power at every level. Policy negligence with regard to environmental degradation and other systematic crimes of the powerful undermined the legitimacy of governance, even while state efforts to control the population and exert control over a wider territory intensified.

Chinese crime statistics systematically inflate the image of police success and diminish evidence of social problems they cannot address. In the major cities, there is a considerable economic middle class with a stake in conformity who respond positively to the crime control messages of the 'strike hard' campaigns which are targeted at a range of suitable enemies—rural riff-raff, migrant workers, the young unemployed. The intensification of state violence as the means to control crime and enforce social order has been accompanied by an intensification of criminal violence, and organized crime involving state-agents in China is more virulent than ever. High policing and heavy-handed policing are especially hard felt by ethnic minorities in the country, notably the Uyghurs and Tibetans, but ethnic Chinese people who do not properly conform to political expectations, for example the spiritual practitioners of Falun Gong, are no less vulnerable to police abuse.

The police métier in China is undergirded by a high degree of technological sophistication and the organization of surveillance and police coercive force is extensive. The contemporary political culture of China has been shaped by a blend of capitalist ideology and selective adoption of traditional Confucian dogma, but the reality more accurately reflects Charles Tilly's pithy notion that state-making is an organized crime racket (Bakken 2000, 2005; Dillon 2012; Jones 2004; Kaiming 1985; Keith and Lin 2005; McConville 2011; Sheptycki 2008a; Trevaskes 2007; Tilly 1985).

RUSSIA

Efforts to establish a modern 'well-ordered police state' in Russia are usually dated from the time of Peter the Great, who ruled Russia as Tsar between 1682 and 1725. He built on the political and cultural foundations of an even older police tradition dating from the time of Ivan Grozny—which can be translated either as Ivan 'the Great' or Ivan 'the Terrible'. Sometime around 1565 Tsar Ivan created the *oprichniki*, a secret police organization, to enforce his rule. Although this institution did not survive his dynasty, it made a lasting political and cultural impression because its reign of terror lasted years and consumed thousands of lives.

The recrudescence of this culture of policing was again manifest in the political policing organized by Lavrentiy Pavlovich Beria, head of the NKVD under Joseph Stalin. During the eighteenth century the Romanovs, both Catherine and Peter the Great, ruled by the Divine Right of Kings, but most social ordering took place on the landed feudal estates and, except for the high policing functions needed for dynastic stability, Russian policing never displayed the pretence that it was undertaken for the general well-being of all.

In the nineteenth century, during the reign of Tsar Alexander I, the Ministry of the Interior (MVD) was established, transforming an archaic authoritarianism into a more modern kind. The police structure he created had three tiers and consolidated the modus operandi of the modern Russian police métier. At the bottom, the most numerous, were the ordinary police based in the regions, districts, and villages. Known for graft, abuse of authority, and corruption, these police were the visible foundation of social order and could be organized to police in the event of political disruptions. At the mid-level was the *Korpus Zhandarmov*, a gendarmerie offshoot of the military. As well as operating in support of the ordinary police when needed, they served as political police in charge of investigation, prevention and suppression of crimes, political surveillance, and the internal system of exile. The third level was the secret political police, a part of the MVD continually undergoing administrative refinement and resultant name changes but which is generally known as the *Okhrana*.

The secret police used every manner of covert policing, informant cultivation, and intelligence gathering in the attempted surveillance of all political activity. In Russia prior to the Revolution in 1917, policing was rule by law. As Count Benckendorff, at one time chief of the *Okhrana* put it: 'Laws are written for subjects, not for the authorities' (quoted in Johnson 1991: 837).

With only rather superficial alterations in the detail, titles, offices and acronyms, the organizational logic of this basic structure was recreated in the aftermath of the Revolution and remains fundamental to Russian policing up to today. Contemporary Russia is characterized by considerable criminality and corruption and policing frequently disregards notions of human rights and procedural fairness while engaging in corrupt and criminal practices. In that context, ideological commitment to abstract notions of the nation substitute as the basis of police legitimacy. After the dissolution of the Soviet Union in 1991, the Russian police system reconsolidated and in the 'post-Soviet space' there developed an archipelago of interlocking and conflicting Police States (Daly 2018; Fukuyama 2012; Johnson 1991; Raeff 1975; Robinson 1967; Slade and Light 2015).

These four outline case study examples hardly scratch the surface of the histories they uncover. However, they are sufficient to illustrate the point that the police métier—the orchestration of surveillance and coercion in the maintenance of social order—is manifest differently according to the socio-legal, political, and cultural traditions in which it is embedded.

Summation

The point of view established here is that the politics of the police should not only be understood in relation to the parochial circumstances in which most policing takes place, but also there needs to be recognition that, since the modern police developed in the context of the evolving international system of states, a more global outlook is salutary (Mazower 1997). Looked at this way, the dominance of certain socio-legal ideologies of legality vis-à-vis the police (concerning human rights and due process, for example) cannot be assumed.

SUMMARY AND CONCLUSION

This chapter has provided a series of historical sketches describing a narrative of modern world police history from prior to the French Revolution up to the twentieth century. With such a lot of ground to cover in a short space, this historical overview may seem teleological, a 'just so' story of an unfolding logic that makes modern policing in all its manifestations seem inevitable. The police are a manifestation of social conflict over power relations and every historical turn is contingent.

Despite any artificiality involved in historical summation on this scale, it is important and useful to shine a spotlight on the police as crucial historical actors because, since modern times, police institutions have become integral to social ordering, social controlling, and the living law. The politics of the modern police needs to be read against this broader historical background so as to derive a more complete perspective for theorizing the phenomenon (Brodeur 2010: 9–12). Read alongside other accounts of world, social, political, and economic history the particular history of the modern police might lead to more general conclusions. In terms of the politics of the police developed in this book there are a number of suggestive points that can be made.

First, there are some thoughts concerning the pragmatic issues of due process, transparency and accountability. This is a central preoccupation of socio-legal scholarship and this sketch has shown that, looked at from the historical long view and on a worldwide basis, most often police institutions have been built in the absence of such concerns. Indeed, looked at critically and from a world perspective, the best that can be made is a situation of rule *with* law where all social actors as a matter of principle have equal access to all the legal tools involved in the governance of the personal, political, economic, and social fields. Policing chiefly concerns social control and the reproduction of existing social order, and its proponents—especially in Europe and North America—often profess an extraordinary regard for the interests of society as a whole through piecemeal social engineering by 'rule of law'.

The theoretically sensitizing and multi-dimensional distinction between high and low policing reveals antinomies (Brodeur 2010: 38). High policing in general is something that social, political, and economic elites do to ensure the order of their supremacy. Low policing is that kind of policing that raises the general level of prosperity. Conservative elites like to argue that existing arrangements are in the interests of everybody, but clearly sometimes the luxuriant view from the Palace has come at great cost to the labouring poor, and sometimes the gulf between high and low police functions is so great that the legitimacy of such claims has been found wanting. Perhaps it is better to say that policing is inherently political, since it involves the reproduction of power relations and the exercise of power, and yet the citizens of Tehran might ask: 'what is so political about the enforcement of the rules of road traffic safety?' In this regard, not all policing could be called political, nor could no policing (i.e. lawlessness) be called not political, as the American vigilante tradition reveals.

Understanding of police culture is often limited to thinking about the Anglo-American situation (Cockcroft 2013). The notion of 'police culture' on its own cannot help to convey the complexities of the world politics of the modern police because they are manifest in so many different political contexts. The classic sociological questions about the relationship between social structure and human agency remain relevant but clearly more flexible and refined theoretical tools than the broad brush of 'police culture' are needed.

Contemporary and growing interest in the anthropology of the police recognizes the broader surface of emergence upon which police institutions and practices are made manifest (Fassin 2017; Garriott 2013). In our understanding of the police, the métier—surveillance of territories and populations and the social ordering thereof whether by persuasive or, when need be, coercive means—remains definitionally constant. Police subcultures evolve on the basis of working through the métier in different and specific local contexts in which police practice is made manifest, making for the complex world of the politics of the police.

That is why all police subcultures share at least some familial resemblance. With respect to notions of legality, political consent, and other cultural norms, not all police subcultural traditions exhibit the same concerns. The constancy of the métier amid the fluidity of political, economic, and social change helps to account for the quite startling differences in the disposition of homicide detectives in contemporary São Paulo and in Sussex (see Willis 2015: 5–6, 153–5; Innes 2003).

Use of force is central to all theories of the police (Brodeur 2010: 105–6; 136–8). The provision of police services also seems central to their institutional legitimacy. Sometimes force is a service, but for whom? Even with colonial policing the social service role can be made a central plank in achieving policing ends and policing can sometimes be fashioned for the benefit of general well-being and not merely the comfort of the well-off. As the Japanese example shows, even authoritarian police systems can rely very heavily on persuasion as well as repressive means. In most instances, modern police institutions have spread by a complex process of institutional diffusion and, as the American example shows, over time these organizations can form dense multi-level networks with public-private interactions happening at each tier.

However, policing institutions were built in the context of modern state-making and the formation of the international state system. State sovereignty and state jurisdiction—with armies 'pointing out' and police engaged in internal ordering and pacification—shaped the practices of policing at a geo-political level. Not only did police institutions spread across the globe as a result of colonialism of the European powers, they were also made manifest in what was called great power rivalry.

Everyday interactions between police and people are shaped by local cultural understandings of the broader meaning of the state-society relation. The patrimonial states of Latin America exhibit their own manifestations of the police métier. Where states are authoritarian or totalitarian (or try to be), rule is by decree and it is a rule *by* law system. As the contrasting examples of Japan and Iran illustrate, the high policing strategy of governance and rule by law can more or less penetrate the fabric of social life, while the relative success of low policing measures, rather than the intensity of high policing ones, often provides the hard test of police legitimacy.

Contemporary scholarship on the politics of the police expresses the interconnected concerns about police militarization and the policing of 'pre-crime' (e.g. Ericson 2007; Haggerty and Ericson 1999; McCulloch 2001; Zedner 2007), and what this history demonstrates is that none of these concerns are new. What is new are the media and technologies available in the twenty-first century, but it is striking to think that when looked at from this level of sociological abstraction the patterns of policing were transnational and plural from the outset and largely advanced with scant regard for the democratic governance of security (cf. Walker 2012; Loader and Walker 2007; Wood and Dupont 2006). The point has already been made but is worth emphasizing, the manifold problems inherent in the politics of the police are manifest in a potentially endless variety of unique circumstances and can in no way be settled with the rhetorical invocation of the 'rule of law'. Human discretion is the *sine qua non* of living law and the history of modern police up until the twentieth century reveals the democratic-republican slogan: 'an empire of laws, not of men' is an empire for all that.[2]

We conclude this chapter with two final thoughts, the first somewhat hopeful, the second rather dire. The hopeful thought springs from the observations regarding the project to abolish slavery during the *Pax Britannica* of the mid-nineteenth century. The political success of William Wilberforce in Great Britain was contingent on the democratic politics of the day. This social-political movement need not have won, but it did and it had global ramifications. While it did not install the Enlightenment vision put forth by Kant in *Perpetual Peace* (1795) or the universal conditions for human rights set forth in the 1789 French Declaration of the Rights of Man and the Citizen, it brought humanity marginally closer to them.

This symbolizes on a global scale the more general point that policing is Janus faced: it concerns both class repression and general crime control, mixes elements of high and low policing (Brodeur 2010), and has implications for both the particular well-being of social elites and the general well-being of the social order upon which they depend. Despite contemporary fears about the present trajectories of world history, observing this contingent historical fact gives pause for hope.

The second thought concerns the stubborn presence of brutal *raison d' état*, notably manifest in the *longue durée* of the Russian police tradition and the emerging versions of modern police systems in China and Iran. Police States are not monolithic entities, but in the conflictual political arithmetic of the international system of states they can seem to be. A fully rounded theory of the politics of the police cannot limit itself to experiences in democracies (Bayley and Stenning 2016), it has to extend to the international system of states as a whole.

In making the distinction between police and the military, Brodeur emphasizes that the conventional metaphor of the 'thin-blue line' is misguided because 'battle waged across lines of combat is characteristic of military operations, not policing' (Brodeur 2010: 179). His theory of policing (along with many others in the western academy) emphasizes minimal force, which is inconsistent with the destructive capabilities of troops trained for combat. In the absence of a democratic basis where all have equal access to be able to participate in rule with law, police power can degenerate into power for its own sake.

The Russian and Chinese examples are not the only ones that empirically ground Foucault's extreme cynicism in saying that: 'Since the population is nothing more than what the state takes care of for its own sake, of course, the state is entitled to slaughter it, if necessary' (Foucault 1994: 416). The perennial choice, it would seem, is either a social democratic police or barbarism (Reiner 2012a, 2012b).

---

[2] Referring to John Adams, *Thoughts on Government* (1776).

4

LEARNING THE BLUES: THE ESTABLISHMENT AND LEGITIMATION OF PROFESSIONAL POLICING IN BRITAIN 1829–2018

INTRODUCTION

The history of British policing is of more than parochial significance. It was the earliest attempt to establish a state-organized police force in a country that prided itself on being a liberal representative democracy, albeit with a very limited franchise initially. The creation of the police in Britain aroused deep opposition, so its pioneers were concerned to cultivate widespread popular legitimacy. For some time in the twentieth century this project was so successful that many countries saw the British model as a template. This chapter will analyse the origins of modern police in Britain, and how a substantial degree of legitimacy was achieved. (For a more detailed treatment cf. Reiner 2010c: chaps 3 and 4.)

PART I: THE BIRTH OF THE BLUES: THE ESTABLISHMENT OF PROFESSIONAL POLICING IN BRITAIN 1829–56

As shown in Chapter 1, while *policing* is a universal feature of social relations, specialized *police* institutions are not. Formal police organizations are associated with social complexity, inequality, and the development of modern states. The establishment of the British police was a protracted, painful struggle, against bitter resistance.

INTERPRETATIONS OF POLICE HISTORY

Traditional accounts of the development of policing in Britain reflected palpably conservative assumptions. In this 'cop-sided' perspective the police were seen as inevitable, and unequivocally beneficent—a cornerstone of national pride, embodying English pragmatic genius in response to fearsome threats to social order and civilized existence. Initial opposition to the police was attributable to vested interests, malevolence, or blinkered obscurantism, and rapidly dissipated when the benefits of a benign police institution became apparent.

The 'cop-sided' view of police history was challenged in the 1970s by a Marxist-inspired revisionist account. In this the police were seen as a means of maintaining the dominance of ruling elites over the working-class majority. This revisionist interpretation was a 'lop-sided' antithesis, reversing the biases of the 'cop-sided' thesis. We suggest a more complex, nuanced picture, a 'neo-Reithian' synthesis, based on the answers to ten fundamental questions about the development of British policing.

What was the source of the need for a new police?

The 'cop-sided' view sees the professional police as a rational response to the twin pressures of urban and industrial revolution, which posed new problems of order. By contrast, revisionism stressed that industrialization and urbanization occurred within a specifically capitalist framework. Crime and disorder are not hard and unequivocal categories, but defined variously by different political viewpoints. At the root of the new problem of order was accentuated class division and conflict, associated with the rise of capitalism.

The rapid growth of large cities involved the development of much greater segregation between classes. The poor areas may have generated more crime as a consequence of anonymity, demoralization, and despair, although this is hard to know for sure. Whatever the objective trends, the upper-class perception of routine crime altered. Crime came to signify a deeper threat to the social order, stemming from the 'dangerous classes', the rapidly proliferating urban poor.

The meaning of collective disorder also changed. Until the early nineteenth century, riotous protest was a mutually understood means whereby the politically unrepresented masses communicated grievances to the ruling elite—'bargaining by riot' (Hobsbawm 1959). But with the spread of industrial capitalism riot came to be regarded as a fundamental threat to the social and political order.

Capitalism required a tighter disciplining of hitherto loosely regulated aspects of social relations. The development of a formally 'free' labour market meant that the traditional practice of workers retaining some of the produce they handled had to be replaced by the 'cash nexus'. Payment in kind was redefined as theft. This was part of a broader pattern of change whereby a 'moral economy', in which prices and relationships were seen as subject to traditional conceptions of justice, was replaced by a pure market economy, governed only by the impersonal laws of supply and demand (Thompson 1971).

The new mechanized conditions of factory production also required that formally free labour be subject to tighter discipline, to fit the rhythms and regimentation of capitalist organization. The police officer became a 'domestic missionary' (Storch 1976), charged with converting the folkways and mores of savage street dwellers to respectability and decency. The industrial bourgeoisie and their property were more exposed to crime and disorder than the landed gentry, as they were less embedded in traditional social networks of paternalistic personalized authority.

Both the traditionalist thesis and the revisionist antithesis contain valid elements that can be incorporated into a neo-Reithian synthesis. A fundamental complexity is that police have an inextricably dual function. They handle troubles derived both from the problems of *any* industrial society *and* from its specifically capitalist form. Orthodoxy neglects the role of the police in conflicts generated by inequality and injustice. But revisionism minimizes the aspects of policing safeguarding universal interests in social order and protection. Interpersonal offending and political conflict are engendered by the pressures of industrialization and urbanization whatever the social framework, but in early nineteenth-century England they were constituted by class conflict as capitalism established itself. With the decline of Marxist perspectives in the academy during the heyday of neo-liberal hegemony the significance of class inequalities in shaping policing has been sidelined.

What was wrong with the old policing arrangements?

During the eighteenth century the punitiveness of the criminal code was increasingly seen as counter-productive. It made victims reluctant to prosecute, and juries loath to convict. That certainty of punishment was a more effective deterrent than severity became axiomatic in Beccaria's 'classical' criminology, and the arguments for police reform proposed by Henry and John Fielding, Patrick Colquhoun, and Jeremy Bentham.

The key agents of the 'old' policing system, the constables, watchmen, and amateur justices, were widely lampooned by eighteenth- and nineteenth-century advocates of police reform. The London nightwatchmen were said to be 'contemptible, dissolute and drunken buffoons who shuffled along the darkened streets after sunset . . . and thus warned the criminal of their approach' (Critchley 1978: 30). Those who were not ineffective were represented as corrupt, milking their offices for rewards. Thief-takers became thief-makers.

The revisionists discerned upper-class snobbery in the traditional knockabout humour at the expense of the old police (Brogden 1982: 53). What was represented by respectable contemporaries as inefficiency or corruption may have masked fears that working-class police drawn from the local community could not be depended upon by manufacturers for controlling industrial disputes. Similar motives stimulated the later American establishment of state police forces, and the 'professionalization' of city forces in the late nineteenth and early twentieth centuries (Robinson 1978).

Contrary to the view of contemporary reformers and orthodox police historians that eighteenth-century criminal justice was an antiquated mess, revisionists argued it maintained the stability of the old hierarchical social order. Its rules and rituals emphasized the majesty and terror of the law, the 'Bloody Code' (Thompson 1975; Gatrell 1994; Linebaugh 2006). This was combined with strict adherence to legality, so the system symbolized impartial and formal justice. Less than half of the people condemned to death were executed, the nub of the utilitarian reformers' criticism that severe nominal punishments, which were unlikely to be carried out, became counter-productive. Revisionists turned this argument on its head. The moral bonds built up between superiors and subordinates by the process of interceding to seek mercy cemented a social order based on personal ties. In the end the rulers gained most from their own mercy. 'The private manipulation of the law by the wealthy and powerful . . . made it possible to govern eighteenth-century England without a police force' (Hay 1975: 52–6).

The old institutions of suppressing riot became counter-productive, revisionists claimed. The militia was politically unreliable, as those selected often employed deputies, who would be drawn from the same social strata as rioters. This motivated the establishment of a 'bureaucratic police system that . . . seemed to separate the assertion of "constitutional" authority from that of social and economic dominance' (Silver 1967.: 11–12).

The new manufacturing urban bourgeoisie lacked certain protections against the 'dangerous classes' which the rural gentry enjoyed: the ecological safeguards of large estates, and the services of private retainers. Manufacturing capital took the form of movable merchandise and machinery, much more vulnerable to theft or damage.

More recent research qualifies both sides of the debate. Neither the old constables nor the watchmen were as ineffective or corrupt as painted by orthodoxy). Eighteenth-century developments in policing, such as the Bow Street Runners or the Thames River Police, achieved a degree of preventive and investigative competence that was not evidently inferior to the subsequent Peelian police (Styles 1983; Beattie 2006, 2007).

In sum, eighteenth-century criminal justice was diverse and discretionary, but not as ineffective as orthodoxy suggested. Nor was it the unilateral weapon of the ruling class portrayed by revisionism. The establishment of the new police was not due to the patent breakdown or inadequacy of the old.

What were the motives for police reform?

Fear of crime was a main motif of police reformers. Patrick Colquhoun, a London stipendiary magistrate, attempted in his 1795 *Treatise on the Police of the Metropolis* to quantify the number of criminals and the amount of loss they engendered. In 1810 the government began publishing annual figures of indictable committals for trial in England and Wales, which showed an apparently inexorable increase. Home Secretary Robert Peel relied heavily on these statistics in the parliamentary debate before the 1829 Metropolitan Police Act. Colquhoun and other police reformers waxed loquacious about moral decay, which was also seen as an economic and political threat (Dodsworth 2007).

The role of politically motivated disorder in the creation of the new police was downplayed by the orthodox view. The notorious 1819 Peterloo Massacre (the brutal suppression by magistrates, cavalry, and yeomanry of a large but peaceful demonstration in St Peter's Field, Manchester, in support of parliamentary reform) got the briefest of mentions in Reith (1956: 122), and was assimilated to the 'crime industry'.

The motives for establishing the new police were reversed in the revisionist account. The basic driver was disorder produced by capitalist development. This disrupted existing social networks, destroyed moral communities, replaced personal bonds by the cash nexus, and caused widespread deprivation and demoralization. The crime statistics which began to be published in the early nineteenth-century registered an upward trend, but revisionists questioned how far this was a genuine increase in criminality, and how much was due to changed sensitivities, penal reform, and the availability of police, leading to a greater propensity to prosecute offences (King 2006).

However, revisionists saw the crucial reason for the creation of the new police as neither crime control, moral discipline, nor riot control per se. It was the need for a force that could stabilize relations between conflicting social classes. The police were charged with an 'omnibus mandate' of regulating all facets of working-class life (Storch 1976).

The motive stressed by Home Secretary Peel for his 1829 Metropolitan Police Bill was fear of rising crime. But there were those even in the parliamentary debates who challenged the validity of his figures (Philips 1980: 179–80). By the time of the debates on the 1839 and 1856 Police Bills opponents proposed the counter-argument that police reformers were using rising crime statistics to justify the extension of a preventive police, the efficacy of which was called into question by those very figures (Watts-Miller 1987: 43–7). On the other hand, the revisionist notion of 'social' crime as proto-political protest is also hard to sustain. Most offences were 'prosaic and undramatic'.

The same qualifications must be levelled at the thesis that fear of political and social disorder was the primary motive for police reform. The disorders associated with Chartism were certainly at the forefront of the debates leading to the 1839 County Police Act. But fears for the survival of the social order, even at the height of Chartist agitation, were not sufficient to overcome the traditional miserliness of over half of the counties of England and Wales, which refused to utilize the possibility of establishing a rural constabulary allowed by the 1839 Act (Philips and Storch 1999).

Monkkonen has made similar points about the parallel thesis that American city police were a straightforward response to rising crime or political and class conflict: 'If each city had adopted a uniformed police only after a riot, changing crime rate, or the need for a new kind of class-control agency, many places would not today have a uniformed police' (Monkkonen 1981: 57). Rather, 'growth of uniformed urban police forces should be seen simply as a part of the growth of urban service bureaucrats' (ibid.: 55). The establishment of the English and Welsh provincial police was a similar process of gradual and uneven diffusion of models of rationalized urban administration.

The police reformers certainly perceived threats of crime and disorder, but influential sections of the elite did not share this panic. The entrepreneurial activities of the reformers themselves played a large part in the setting up of the new police throughout Britain. It was neither an automatic reflex of urbanization nor industrial capitalism.

Who opposed the new police?

Six parliamentary committees between 1812 and 1822 considered London's policing arrangements but recommended against a new police. The orthodox historians' only explanation of this was to impugn the intelligence and integrity of the opponents of police reform. Much resistance to the police was couched in rhetoric drawing on the supposed traditional liberties of Englishmen, epitomized by the 1822 Committee Report: 'It is difficult to reconcile an effective system of police, with that perfect freedom of action and exemption from interference, which are the great privileges and blessings of society in this country.' Reith saw the opposition in a sinister light: 'It was the efforts of gangsterdom alone . . . which frustrated for nearly a century every attempt to end the menace of crime and disorder by creating police' (Reith 1943: 12).

The source of ruling-class opposition was a distinct sector of the class, the landed gentry. They did not need to support a public police out of rate-payers' money, when their own security was adequately protected by private means. They could rely on 'large numbers of personal servants to guard their plate and their wives' (Hay 1975: 59). The gentry could expatiate high-mindedly on the threat to traditional liberties posed by the importation of French, Russian, or Prussian influenced policing schemes, and scoff at the evidence of mere larceny assembled by Colquhoun and Peel. But if initially opposition to the police came from the landed gentry, this evaporated as the threat of Chartism grew.

The deepest opposition to the new police was from the labouring masses. The prime arenas for working-class opposition to the police were collective disorder and small-scale street conflicts. Anti-police riots regularly followed the coming of the 'plague of blue locusts' to northern working-class communities (Storch 1975: 94).

How long did opposition to the police last?

The opposition of the masses, clearly virulent in the early 1830s, was depicted by the cop-sided interpretation as rapidly evaporating once the worth of the new police became apparent. At first pamphlets circulated attacking 'Peel's bloody gang'. During fighting in 1833 between the police and a meeting of the National Political Union, a PC Culley was fatally stabbed. The inquest jury returned a verdict of 'justifiable homicide'. This clearly indicated the strength of popular opposition to the police, but the conventional view has it that after a parliamentary inquiry, 'public opinion . . . veered in favour of the police' (Critchley 1978: 55). In the orthodox view, opposition to the police may have been nasty and brutish, but it was blessedly short.

The revisionists, however, trace a line of intermittent overt hostility, and continuous latent conflict, right down to contemporary protest and disorder. While police relations between the regularly employed, respectable, and organized sections of the working class were not characterized by regular open conflict, approval was tentative and brittle.

Nonetheless there is clear evidence of growing acquiescence with the police among a broad section of the working class, as well as the middle class. This was partly because their 'service' activities stitched a velvet glove of superficial acquiescence over the reality of an iron fist of repression (Emsley 1983: 146–7, 158–9).

The incursion of the new police into working-class leisure activities, and the use of the police to control strikes, caused considerable disgruntlement. But a significant proportion of prosecutions at quarter sessions was brought by unskilled working-class people. Many accepted the basic legitimacy of laws protecting property (Emsley 1983: 158–60). Working-class attitudes to the law and its enforcement were complex and ambivalent, and varied between different times and places.

Some radical leaders, and the emerging 'respectable' working-class strata, welcomed control of 'the most dissolute and abandoned' habits of the rougher elements, seen as a threat to the political and social advance of the whole class (Emsley 1983: 157–8). 'From opposing the very idea of a policed society, radical critics had come to judge the police by those abstract standards laid down by the system's pioneers' (Field 1981: 59).

What was new about the 'new police'?

The orthodox histories argued both that the 'new' police was a novel creation in terms of efficiency and integrity, *and* that it had roots in ancient traditions of communal self-policing.

The 'newness' consisted of the institution of a bureaucratic organization of professionals, rationally administering a policy of 'preventive policing' through regular patrols. 'Newness' was also emphasized by the high standards of entry and discipline established by Peel and the two commissioners he appointed, Colonel Charles Rowan (of the Light Brigade) and Richard Mayne, a barrister.

On the other hand, the force's ancient origins in communal self-policing and the continuity of the office of constable were also stressed. Reith saw the police as 'directly traceable to the dawn of European history, and to the customs of the Aryan tribes of the Continent whom their leaders made responsible for securing the observance of tribal laws' (Reith 1943: 14).

To the revisionists, the novelty of the 'new' police was neither efficiency nor integrity. Ineffectiveness, indiscipline, and corruption remain endemic among modern police officers. The 'new' police were a bureaucratically organized force charged with a mandate to 'prevent' crime by regular patrol and surveillance, especially of the denizens of the 'dangerous classes'—St James's was to be guarded by watching St Giles. Spasmodic law enforcement dependent upon private initiative was replaced by continuous state policing, financed by the public purse. Particularistic traditions of personal deference were displaced by impersonal authority, legitimated by values of legal rationality and universalism.

Revisionists rebutted the orthodox mythology of fundamental continuity between the modern constable and antique traditions of tribal self-policing. The police were a 'new engine of power and authority' (Philips 1980), legally mandated to ensure the discipline required by industrial capitalism.

By the time of the debates preceding the 1856 Act, the argument was about the costs and control of the professional police, not the principle itself. But the 'new' police were not a sharp break towards a professional police with a significantly higher calibre than the old constables. Peel's explicit policy of not recruiting people with 'the rank, habits or station of gentlemen' meant that the social status of the intake was similar to the old constabulary. Many studies document the very high turnover rates in the first decades of the new police, due to dismissals for drunkenness or other peccadilloes, and through rapid resignation from a disciplined and demanding job (Steedman 1984; Shpayer-Makov 2002). There was not a revolutionary change towards a powerful system of surveillance, whether for protection *or* oppression of the population, although this did evolve during the twentieth century.

What was the social impact of the new police?

In the orthodox account, the social impact of the police was unequivocally benign: solving the problem of order. '3000 unarmed policemen, cautiously feeling their way against a hostile public, brought peace and security to London in place of the turmoil and lawlessness of centuries' (Critchley 1978: 55–6).

In the revisionist account, by contrast, modern professional policing created a 'policed society'. 'Central power exercises potentially violent supervision over the population by bureaucratic means widely diffused throughout civil society in small and discretionary operations that are capable of rapid concentration' (Silver 1967: 8). The net result was the penetration of society by the political and moral authority of the dominant strata, the construction of an essentially manipulated consensus.

The new police spearheaded a move to a more centralized social order, in which the state penetrated the depths of society. Acting as advance scouts of the state implied some integration with the policed, and the police painted a surface gloss of serenity over the volatile conflicts of capitalism.

In the longer term, the police were associated with a general increase in the orderliness and pacification of Victorian society. From the 1850s until the First World War 'the war against criminal disorder was palpably being won by the State, and contemporaries knew it' (Gatrell 1980: 240–1). However, the statistical evidence for falling crime in the late nineteenth century is debatable. It is arguable that the figures were manipulated to suit the joint interests of police and government in creating an appearance of order and pacification (Taylor 1998a, 1998b, 1999).

Other authors, while broadly concurring with the conventional picture of declining crime, are sceptical about the precise contribution of the police to this (Emsley 1983: chap. 7). The prime way in which the police affected law enforcement was not through technical efficacy in apprehending criminals, but by symbolizing a functioning legal order. 'While policemen were not the ultimate answer to theft and disorder which they and many reformers claimed (and continue to claim), they became the placebo of property' (Emsley 1983: 162).

The police were also a factor in declining disorder. Obviously riot did not disappear, and in some periods political and industrial conflict intensified, as in the 1880s or immediately before the First World War. On occasion the police *aggravated* disorder by provocation or poor tactics (Bailey 1981: 94–125). But the degree of collective violence tended to decline secularly, as much because of changes in crowd behaviour as police effectiveness. In sum, while their initial impact on anything but the marginal illegalities of the casual street economy was small, the police were implicated in a broader process of pacification of Victorian society, although the weight of their distinctive contribution is impossible to state precisely.

Who gained from the new police?

Orthodox historians claimed universal benefits were achieved by the police, emphasizing the special gains of the poor and working class. Police were the guardians of the weak against the strong, 'designed to stand between the powerful and the weak, to prevent oppression, danger and crime' (Lee 1901: xxx). The masses not only came to be protected from criminal victimization, but were prevented from sinking into crime themselves through the 'moral improvement of the labouring classes by the exercise of supervision and restraint' (Radzinowicz 1956: 233; Dodsworth 2007).

Revisionism stood on its head the orthodox conception of universal benefits from policing. The bourgeoisie gained most from the new police, who protected their property, safeguarded their security, and stabilized the social order on which their power and position were based.

The middle and upper classes certainly gained a sense of security, which many contemporaries gratefully expressed. Many began to take the police for granted, as they became socially invisible public servants. Cynics saw the PC as a mere 'fool in blue' who did nothing but walk about, and wondered if he was worth his weight in higher rates (Steedman 1984: 6–7, 142–5).

In the third quarter of the nineteenth century, the notion of policework as a distinctive career, with a specific ideology of service, professional identity, and craft skills, emerged (Steedman 1984: chap. 8; Klein 2001; Shpayer-Makov 2002; Lawrence 2003). Policework began to hold out an opportunity for social mobility to some working-class men.

Who controlled the police?

It was a central claim of the orthodox histories that English police power was only the crystallized power of the people. Reith emphasized 'the historic tradition that the police are the public and that the public are the police' (Reith 1956: 287).

A measure of central direction over provincial policing arrangements marched on steadily from the 1835 Municipal Corporations Act (which required all boroughs to institute police forces). It was opposed by a continuing strain of rhetoric, denouncing each step as a sinister French, Russian, or Venetian (but at any rate distinctly Continental) usurpation of the traditional English rights of self-government. In the end, the 1856 Act expressed a rough balance between the continuing responsibilities of local government and justices, and a measure of central government supervision. This was exercised through the establishment of a Home Office Inspectorate of Constabulary, which had to certify a force as efficient before it could qualify for a new Exchequer grant of 25 per cent of the cost of pay and clothing. This proved to be a wedge with which the Home Office was able to introduce more central direction, and chief constables to construct a large measure of autonomy from local control. The final ingredient in popular control of the police was the 'deliberate policy to recruit men "who had not the rank, habits or station of gentlemen" . . . the police was to be a homogeneous and democratic body, in tune with the people, understanding the people, belonging to the people, and drawing its strength from the people' (Critchley 1978: 52).

Revisionists rejected the orthodox claim that 'the people' control the police. The Home Secretary nominally controlled the Metropolitan Police as its police authority, but from early on commissioners were conceded discretion to determine the conduct of the force. However, the relationship between the Home Office and the commissioner continued to be ill-defined (Bailey 1981: 94–125).

Much debate among revisionists concerned the degree of control of police by local elites in the counties (through the magistracy) and in boroughs (through the Watch Committee). The two positions on these issues reflected wider theoretical differences between an 'instrumentalist' conception of the police as 'tools' of the dominant class, and a 'structuralist' account of policing as a function of the political economy.

Storch suggested an instrumentalist view when he attributed the 'implantation of a modern police in the industrial districts of Northern England' to 'a new consensus among the propertied classes that it was necessary to create a professional, bureaucratically organized lever of urban discipline' (Storch 1975: 86).

The structuralist account was put most clearly by Brogden (1982), arguing that chief constables achieved a large measure of autonomy very early on after the establishment of the new police. This was true not only of county forces, whose chief constables had overt control over policing, but also of boroughs, where chief constables were supposed to be under the direction of the Watch Committee. In the case of Liverpool, Brogden found that the head constable began to show a measure of independence from the Watch Committee soon after the force was established, and by the end of the century had achieved 'considerable latitude of decision-making'. Brogden referred to the 1890 Watch Committee instruction to Head Constable Captain Nott-Bower to 'proceed against all brothels'. This order has usually been invoked to demonstrate Watch Committee control. Brogden argued that the episode meant the opposite. Not only was it an isolated occurrence, but the chief constable could within a year revert to the old approach because the strict prosecution policy had such damaging effects on trade (Brogden 1982: 69). However, while the revisionists argued about the precise relations of local elite and police chief, and of both to the political economy, they were united in denying the orthodox claim that the new police were subject to popular control.

The working class had no direct influence on Watch Committees until the slow extension of the franchise to them. It was perhaps no coincidence that by that time Watch Committees had lost much of their power over the increasingly autonomous chief constables. The middle class had some degree of influence over Watch Committees, depending on the local political balance.

Nominally chief constables had the authority to control police policy and administration in the counties, but as the magistracy chose men with a social standing which ensured a harmony of outlook, the gentry viewpoint dominated (Wall 1998). However, during the 1870s chief constables in both counties and boroughs began to assert a greater measure of professional independence. This was facilitated by legislative changes conferring on the police more duties directly from national government, as well as more powers and resources (Steedman 1984: 53–5, 62–3, chap. 10).

In sum, the orthodox view has no foundation for the claim that the 'people' controlled the police. The new police became increasingly autonomous of local government, formalized in the 1920s as the doctrine of 'constabulary independence' (see Chapter 11).

What model of historical explanation underlies orthodox police history?

The orthodox histories operated with a model of explanation which was teleological and unilinear. The order maintenance requirements of an industrialized, liberal-democratic society urged on the progressive realization of the police idea. But police development was not just the product of impersonal forces. The structural problems of industrialism and urbanization constituted merely 'the demand for order'. The supply of appropriate ideas and institutions to satisfy the requirements for order without eroding traditional liberties came from 'far-sighted' reformers, perspicacious 'pioneers of policing', like the Fieldings, Colquhoun, Peel, Rowan, and Mayne (Stead 1977). However, the 'correct' ideas of these great men (as well as the 'false' notions of the opposition) were essentially epiphenomenal. At most they oiled (or spoked) the wheels of development and speeded (or retarded) its progress.

The pattern of development was portrayed as 'unilinear', that is, it had one clear direction, and despite temporary setbacks never departed from this trajectory. The irresistible force of industrialization and its control problems, meeting the immovable object of stubborn English commitment to liberty, could result in only one outcome: the British bobby. The implicit explanation of police development was that the model which ultimately emerged (in stages, to be sure) best met the conflicting demands of order and liberty.

Revisionism, crystallizing in the 1970s and 80s, was an unequivocal advance, specifying precise social bases of political conflict around the police, and relating policing to a wider context. However, it embodied opposite distortions to the orthodox account—a lop-sided rebuttal of cop-sided history.

While the orthodox view has been usefully analysed as 'ideology as history' (Robinson 1979), and revisionism undeniably exposed its shortfalls as history, this does not dispose of it as ideology. The Reithian Police Principles, supposedly derived from those originally formulated by Sir Robert Peel in 1829 (Lentz and Chaires 2007), may not be or ever have been realized in practice. But as an aspiration for what a police force should be like they ought not to be dismissed too readily. A police force with the Reithian ethic as an institutional ideal to which obeisance is paid is preferable to one which is not committed explicitly to the 'transmuting of crude physical force . . . into the force . . . of public recognition' (Reith 1956: 286).

The revisionist account was itself largely teleological and unilinear. In the instrumentalist variant, the ruling class was induced to establish the police by the perceived 'fit' between the police and the control requirements of capitalism. In the structuralist version there was the same notion of an inexorable drive along only one possible trajectory. The working-class resistance which revisionists celebrated was nonetheless doomed to romantic failure. The ideas of the opposition (laudable) or the proponents of police reform (oppressive) were ultimately epiphenomenal. The real dynamic was the unfolding requirements of capital. To the idealist dialectic of orthodoxy, revisionism counter-posed a similarly deterministic materialist dialectic.

Revisionism constituted an unequivocal advance in understanding of the emergence of the new police, locating it in a broader analysis of the class and power structure of the eighteenth and nineteenth centuries. However, revisionism opposed the orthodox uncritical consensus model with a one-sided conflict perspective. Just as the orthodox historians dismissed hostility to the police as malevolent or misguided, so too the revisionists, regarded any apparent working-class consent to policing as manipulated, a brittle skin over a bubbling volcano. To the revisionists, conflict between police and working class in a capitalist society had structural roots, so superficial social integration could be only an artificially constructed, temporary truce.

Both the orthodox and revisionist approaches assumed a 'fit' between the type of police system and the control requirements of an industrial or capitalist society. It was those conditions, not of their own making, which called into being the actions of the men who made their own history by creating a new police force. The ultimate question is whether a complex modern industrial society could exist without some sort of police force, in the minimal sense of a body of people mandated to intervene in situations potentially requiring the exercise of legitimate force. This is an essentially metaphysical issue, dependent upon conceptions of human nature, the 'iron laws' of social interaction and organization (if any), views of morality, justice, and even deeper matters of ultimate ends, meaning, and the nature of being—the province of religious belief.

Anthropological evidence clearly documents small-scale societies without specialist police, and police institutions have complex conditions of emergence. Nonetheless it seems utopian to suppose that we could do without a police force in any conceivable large-scale and complex industrial social order, whether or not it was capitalist. Policing is Janus faced, reproducing simultaneously the conditions of existence of complex social coexistence, 'general order', *and* of specific patterns of inequality and hierarchy, 'special order', 'parking tickets and class repression' (Marenin 1982). But, even if some police force is necessary in the last analysis, it does not follow that alternative lines of development were or are impossible.

Is it conceivable that Peel might not have been able to pilot the 1829 Act so skilfully through Parliament? After all, most histories do express surprise that, following so many decades of opposition, the Act was eventually passed as smoothly as it was. It may be granted that the metropolis would eventually have needed a new police. But by the time that eventuality materialized, perhaps the reformed Parliament would have taken a different view of making the Home Secretary the police authority? Perhaps it would have wanted to include a measure of local elected representation for the police authority—no taxation without representation.

CONCLUSION: A NEO-REITHIAN–REVISIONIST SYNTHESIS

All historians of the emergence of professional policing in Britain have shown that it was surrounded by acute political conflict. While not securing the quick and relatively painless passage into acceptance suggested by the Reithians, the police did gain increasing acquiescence from substantial sections of the working class, not only as a result of 'soft' service activities, but in their 'hard' law enforcement functions. This anchored consent in substantial benefits and cooperation, not mere ideological manipulation. The police succeeded in acquiring this degree of legitimacy, in which they were no longer widely seen as a politically oppressive force, by a combination of specific strategies which gave the British police a unique character, implanting them firmly in national mythology. The success of these policies was enabled by the wider spread of citizenship in terms of civil, political, and socio-economic rights. The processes by which the comparatively benign British policing tradition was constructed in the century after their controversial introduction, the manner of their legitimation and depoliticization, will be analysed next.

PART II: POLICE LEGITIMATION 1856–2018: CONSTRUCTION, DECONSTRUCTION, RECONSTRUCTION

Modern British police came into being as a deeply contested institution, yet by the middle of the twentieth century had become a key component of national identity. The second part of the chapter analyses the construction of British police legitimacy. Challenges to it re-emerged in the latter half of the twentieth century, as 'law and order' became deeply politicized with the ascendancy of neo-liberal political economy (Reiner 2007). Since the 1990s the police in Britain have seemed to move on to a different stage as a new consensus developed, accepting the politics of 'tough' law and order in the context of a profound restructuring of state, society, and culture (Morgan and Smith 2017). This pragmatic and precarious 'post-legitimacy' is ever-more fragile with the continuing disruption of neo-liberal hegemony since the 2007–8 economic crisis.

The police are a Teflon service: they have survived all manner of scandal and controversy to remain a powerful political and cultural force—more so than any other governmental institution in an increasingly neo-liberal, privatized world that has 'hollowed out' the state. However, they are now only one element in an array of competing policing services, and are subject to increasingly rigorous audit. At a tactical level policing policy has never been more fiercely controversial. But the deeper issues of legitimacy which were struggled over for more than two centuries—the contribution of the police to the shaping of the fundamental structure of power and advantage in society—have largely been bracketed out of debate.

FROM CRUSHERS TO BOBBIES: THE DEPOLITICIZATION OF THE POLICE 1856–1959

Analysing police legitimacy

The British police were established in the face of massive opposition. Working-class resentment lived on for at least a century, expressed in sporadic physical violence and a stream of derogatory epithets: 'Crushers', 'Peel's Bloody Gang', 'Blue Locusts', 'Jenny Darbies', 'Blue Drones'. Yet by the 1950s the police had become lionized by the broad spectrum of opinion. In no other country has the police force been such a symbol of national pride (Loader and Mulcahy 2003).

Many contemporary statements testify to the almost universal acceptance the police had attained. A pioneering sociological study of the police began with the 'idea that it can be instructive to analyse institutions that are working well in order to see if anything can be learned from their success' (Banton 1964: vii). The fictional character PC George Dixon, who first appeared in the 1950 film *The Blue Lamp*, and was subsequently resurrected for a long-running TV series, embodied the quintessential beloved British bobby. He still stands as a regularly evoked ideal (Leishman and Mason 2003; McLaughlin 2005; Reiner 2008: 320–1). The relative social harmony and consensus of the mid-twentieth century, symbolized by the Battle of Britain and the Festival of Britain, was also the finest hour of the British bobby myth.

By the end of the 1950s there were indications of increasing tension. Recorded crime was rising at a rate described by the chief inspector of constabulary as an 'upsurge', 1958 saw race riots in Notting Hill and Nottingham, and there was growing police anxiety about their relations with the 'law-abiding', but increasingly car-owning, public.

Some relatively minor incidents led to the 1959 establishment of a Royal Commission to review the constitutional position of the police. Significantly, the Royal Commission's national opinion survey found 'an overwhelming vote of confidence in the police'. Paradoxically, however, this may well have shrouded considerable malpractice and corruption, indicated by the evidence of oral histories in poor areas, and some police memoirs (Mark 1978; Cohen 1979; Daley 1986; Brogden 1991; Weinberger 1995).

Legitimacy and 'policing by consent'

The Royal Commission on the Police's Report (1962) was criticized for neglecting aspects of their own survey data which called into question the optimistic overall summary (Whitaker 1964: 151–7). However, the survey shows no evidence of variation *by social class* in attitudes to the police, indicating that middle-class veneration had trickled down the social structure (Shaw and Williamson 1972).

There are conceptual ambiguities in the much-debated notion of policing by consent. Policing is an inherently conflict-ridden enterprise. As discussed in Chapter 1, the distinctive resource of the police is the potential use of legitimate force. Policework is thus 'a tainted occupation . . . ambivalently feared and admired, and no amount of public relations work can entirely abolish the sense that there is something of the dragon in the dragon-slayer' (Bittner 1970: 6–7).

If there were universal consensus about norms, values, and appropriate modes of social behaviour there would be no need for a police force. In most situations there is somebody being policed *against*, whose assent to policing is bound to be brittle. At best they may utter a grudging 'It's a fair cop, guv' in the time-honoured tradition of British gangster movies. Those who are frequently at the receiving end of police authority are unlikely to give more consent than a sullen acceptance of de facto power. Realistically, 'policing by consent' cannot mean universal love of the police, but that those at the sharp end of police practices do not extend resentment of specific actions into a withdrawal of legitimacy from the institution of policing per se. Contemporary research shows that legitimacy is partly dependent on the extent to which policing is seen as conducted in a procedurally fair way (Tyler 2004), and is asymmetrically more sensitive to 'bad' than 'good' experience of policework (Skogan 2006). Above all, however, it is dependent on wider images of the social order (Smith 2007a, 2007b; Bradford 2016). Legitimation is higher among those who have no direct experience of police than those who do, whether as suspects, victims, witnesses, or recipients of services.

By the 1950s 'policing by consent' had been achieved in Britain to the maximal degree it may be attainable. The police enjoyed the wholehearted approval of the majority of the population who did not experience the coercive exercise of police powers, and de facto acceptance of the legitimacy of the institution by those who did. Police *power*, that is, the capacity to inflict legal sanctions including force, had been transmuted into authority, power which is accepted as at least minimally legitimate (Beetham 1991).

The construction of consent

The achievement of consensus policing in Britain was mutually interdependent with a wider process of pacification of social relations. It was crucially intertwined with the incorporation of the working class, the main source of initial hostility to the new police, into the political and economic institutions of British society. Peelian architects of the benign and dignified English police image shaped their policies in the light of the bitter opposition to the very existence of the police. They encouraged a low-profile, legalistic stance precisely in the teeth of the acute political conflict and deep divisions of early nineteenth-century English society, not as an expression of underlying harmony.

In the USA by contrast, a more free-wheeling and aggressive style of policing evolved, because American society was in large part a property-owning democracy (Miller 1999). Popular participation in government meant confidence that control of the police could be entrusted to the political process, rather than legal rules and regulations.

The policy choices made by the creators of the British police were central to the force becoming accepted. But these policy-makers acted in conditions of class resistance and political conflict not of their own making. There were eight Peelian policies which were crucial for engineering consent in the face of initial opposition.

Police policy and legitimation

Bureaucratic organization

The basis of the 'new' police was the establishment of a full-time force of professional police officers, organized into a bureaucratic hierarchy. This contrasted with the previous motley assortment of entrepreneurial thief-takers and amateur volunteers. Entry and promotion were meritocratic, especially after 1856 and the introduction of a minimal element of standardization through the Inspectorate of Constabulary. Training began to be taken seriously after the 1919–20 reports of the Desborough Committee, appointed following the 1918 and 1919 police strikes in London and Liverpool.

Rowan and Mayne elaborated a strict set of rules and regulations for the Met governing dress, deportment, and discipline, and the prescribed demeanour for dealing with the public. These were inculcated during drill and training, and enforced by sanctions for disobedience.

Although never realized completely, the image of policemen as disciplined professionals was constructed. An 1856 article in the *London Quarterly Review* summed it up: 'Amid the bustle of Piccadilly or the roar of Oxford Street, P.C.X. 59 stalks along, an institution rather than a man' (Miller 1999: 15).

The rule of law

The way in which the police maintained order and enforced law was itself supposed to be governed by legalistic procedures. The nineteenth-century London 'police courts' were fiercely concerned to maintain their role as independent regulators of the legality of police conduct (Davis 1984: 332). The commissioners realized that subjection to legal regulation was a major factor legitimating police authority (Miller 1999: 4–12, 56–66, 94).

Minimal force

Police forces generally claim to use as little force as necessary, but the British tradition stands out for its eschewal of arms (Waddington and Wright 2008: 466). With characteristic forthrightness, in a television interview Sir Robert Mark, commissioner of the Met, articulated their crowd control strategy thus: 'The real art of policing a free society or a democracy is to win by appearing to lose.' Their secret weapon was not water cannon, tear gas, or rubber bullets, but public sympathy. To this end, he claimed, the Metropolitan Police had trained an especially comely horse—the 'Brigitte Bardot' of police horses—to collapse, feigning death, at a word of command. This was guaranteed to win the support of the animal-loving British public.

Rowan and Mayne limited constables' weapons to the truncheon, carried concealed until 1863. On specific dangerous assignments selected officers might carry a pistol or a cutlass, but each drawing of a weapon was closely scrutinized. The army was available as the ultimate backup, and was used on many occasions in the nineteenth and early twentieth centuries. But gradually the non-lethally-armed police became the sole means of riot control. Paradoxically, one of the last occasions troops acted in a public order role was in 1919 during the Liverpool police strike.

Although they have never acted with kid gloves, the British police developed a tradition of containing industrial disputes and political demonstrations with minimum force when contrasted with other countries. There have been periods of intensified conflict, with complaints of police brutality and right-wing bias. The most notable were a series of clashes between police and the organized unemployed of 'Outcast London' in the late 1880s, bitter industrial disputes immediately before and after the First World War, and conflicts between the police and the unemployed movement and anti-Fascist demonstrators in the 1930s (Morgan 1987; Weinberger 1991). Nonetheless Geary (1985) documents declining levels of violence between police and pickets in industrial conflicts between the 1890s and the 1970s, arguing that these changed from resembling a war to something like a sporting contest.

Non-partisanship

When the 'new' police force was established working-class leaders saw it as a thoroughly political spy agency, 'the minion and paid servant of the Government' (*Poor Man's Guardian*, 11 October 1830: 3).

Crucial to legitimating the police was an image of non-partisanship. The police were insulated from direct political control, and police authorities (the Home Secretary, local watch, and standing joint committees) largely abstained from interventions in operational policy. It was not until the 1920s, though, that this discreet stance began to be transmuted explicitly into a notion of constabulary independence from policy guidance, which would have been considered 'so unconstitutional as to be absurd' in the nineteenth century (Marshall 1965: 31).

Police officers were denied the vote until 1887. This tradition dies hard. In an article celebrating the 150th anniversary of the Metropolitan Police, the then commissioner, Sir David McNee, wrote: 'I no longer exercise my right to vote . . . Police officers must be men and women of the middle, bound only by the rule of law' (McNee 1979: 25). Insistence on suppressing indications of partisanship softened the initial conception of the police as a tool of government oppression. An 1864 article in *Chambers's Magazine* said the police, 'know nothing of politics; the man in blue preserves his neutral tint . . . the good old cause of order is the only side the policeman supports' (Miller 1999: 13).

Accountability

Although the police were not controlled by any elected body, they were seen as accountable in two ways. First, the legality of police action was reviewable by the courts. Second, the police were purported to be accountable through an almost mystical process of identification with the British people, not the state: 'the police are the public and the public are the police' (Reith 1956: 287). The recruitment policies of the police (including chief officers since the Second World War) were attuned to this principle, drawing upon manual working-class backgrounds representative of the mass of the people (Wall 1998; Klein 2001; Shpayer-Makov 2002).

The service role

The notion of the friendly bobby was summed up for modern ears by the cliché: 'If you want to know the time, ask a policeman.' The meaning was rather different in the nineteenth century. 'The popular catchphrase . . . reflected not so much the confidence of the Victorians in the reliability of the police, as their assumption that any policeman who did not quickly . . . win . . . a watch from the pockets of a drunken reveller was unnaturally honest or dull' (Rolph 1962: 52).

Nineteenth-century police carried out a range of tasks wider than law enforcement and order maintenance. Some were formal duties, such as inspecting weights and measures, others were informal, such as knocking people up early in the morning for work (Emsley 1983: 158–9). These were often regarded as unwelcome 'extraneous' burdens (Steedman 1984: 53–4). But the 'service' role played some part in securing police legitimation.

Preventive policing

The primacy of prevention over detection was emphasized in Peel's celebrated instructions to the Metropolitan Police (cited in Critchley 1978: 52–3):

> It should be understood at the outset, that the object to be attained is the prevention of crime . . . The security of person and property . . . will thus be better effected than by the detection and punishment of the offender after he has succeeded in committing crime.

The practical implementation of this principle meant primarily uniform beat patrol, a 'scarecrow function'. This was also aimed at allaying fears of the abominable French experience of undercover police spies.

Hostility to the idea of plain clothes police delayed the formation of detective branches for many years. In 1842 the Met secured the Home Secretary's approval for a detective branch of six men, and ultimately a separate Criminal Investigation Department (Emsley 1996: 72–3). By the 1880s the police had become sufficiently well accepted for the formation of a specifically political unit, initially to deal with Fenian terrorism, later the Special Branch (Porter 1987).

Police effectiveness

How effective the police actually were in crime control remains debatable (Gatrell 1980, 1990), but certainly the appearance of success in crime-fighting was cultivated. In the 1860s there was a moral panic in the respectable classes about a new 'crime wave', fuelled by anxiety about a supposed epidemic of garrottings. Conservative critics campaigned for the police to be 'armed with preventive powers similar to those exercised by the Continental police'. This was precisely what working-class spokesmen feared. *Reynolds's Weekly Newspaper* claimed that: 'The Government proposes converting the English Peeler into a species of continental policeman . . . the mouchard, or spy.'

Gradually, however, the bulk of the working class became reconciled to the criminal justice system. A sizeable proportion of the work of the police courts comprised prosecutions and summonses for theft and assault brought by working-class men and women (J. Davis 1984: 321). Slowly, the new police were inserting themselves into working-class life, not only as an intrusive controlling apparatus, but also as a potential means of redress. 'Street by street, the police negotiated a complex, shifting, largely unspoken "contract"' (Ignatieff 1979: 444–5). But as long as the masses felt excluded from political and economic participation, their acquiescence to policing remained fragile and grudging.

The social context of police legitimation

The all-important factor which facilitated the legitimation of the police was not any aspect of policing, but the changing social, economic, and political context. The working class, the main structurally rooted source of opposition to the police, gradually, unevenly, and incompletely came to be incorporated as citizens into the political, social, and economic institutions of British society (Marshall 1950; Reiner 2010a).

The process of incorporation had very clear limits. It enabled the bulk of the working class to share in the growth of the economy. However, class inequality remained in proportionate terms virtually unaltered, and has widened substantially since the neo-liberal resuscitation of free market economics in the late 1970s (Reiner 2007: 95–114, 2016a: 178).

Nonetheless, the wide gulf between Disraeli's 'two nations', which was sharply manifest in the mid-nineteenth century as the new police came into being, had become blurred by the 1950s, the high point of police legitimation. The first century of Peel's police transformed them from a widely hated institution to the embodiment of legitimate authority, enforcing the rule of law on behalf of the broad mass of society rather than any partisan interest.

FROM PLODS TO PIGS: THE POLITICIZATION OF THE POLICE 1959–92

From a position of almost complete invisibility as a political issue, after 1959 policing became a babble of scandalous revelation, controversy, and competing agendas for reform. The tacit contract between police and public, so delicately drawn between the 1850s and 1950s, began to fray. Evidence mounted of an increasing haemorrhage of public confidence in the police. Fully 83 per cent of the national sample surveyed in 1959 for the Royal Commission on the Police said they had 'a great deal of respect for the police'. In 1989 a Mori poll for *Newsnight* asked the same question. The proportion having 'a great deal of respect' for the police had slumped to 43 per cent.

The 1960 Royal Commission on the Police was the outcome of a series of *causes célèbres* which in retrospect seem pretty small beer (Bottoms and Stevenson 1990). After 1955 the crime statistics began to rise inexorably each year, heralding 'a crime wave unparalleled in modern times' (Critchley 1978: 254). The teddy-boys and beatniks of the mid-1950s created new 'folk devils' and presaged perennial moral panic about shifting styles of youth culture (Cohen 1972; Pearson 1983). Future concerns about public order policing were signalled by the launching of CND and the Aldermaston marches in 1957.

The immediate trigger for the Royal Commission, however, was a Whitehall farce. In December 1958 Brian Rix the comedy star was stopped for speeding by a PC. An obscure argument and mutual assault allegations provoked a parliamentary debate, in which the Home Secretary indicated his intention to institute a Royal Commission on the Police.

Its proposals on accountability and complaints, embodied in the Police Act 1964, had the net effect of empowering the Home Office and chief constables at the expense of local police authorities (Reiner 1991). Despite its inadequacies, the Police Act 1964 constituted a settlement which was generally accepted for a time.

This was aided by the transformation of police organization in the mid-1960s, with the motorized Unit Beat System. The emphasis was on technology and managerial professionalism to win 'the fight against crime'. 'The "British Bobby" was recast as the tough, dashing, formidable (but still brave and honest) "Crime-Buster"' (Chibnall 1977: 71).

Given the now universal bad press accorded the 'fire-brigade' policing that the Unit Beat System heralded, it is salutary to recall that its birth was greeted with general acclaim. It was intended simultaneously to bolster efficiency, improve relations with the public, and advance the constable's lot. In practice, the system soon frustrated these hopes, partly because of shortage of manpower to implement it properly, but primarily because an action-centred perspective on policing was accentuated by the technology of fast cars, sirens, and flashing blue lights.

By the end of the 1960s the growth of the counter-culture, and police clashes with anti-Vietnam War and anti-apartheid demonstrators, heralded a renewed politicization of policing. In 1970, the Police Federation chairman announced to the annual conference: 'We have been eyeball to eyeball with the fanatics, the lunatics and the hooligans.' Later that year, the Federation magazine drew attention to the institution of a 'Pig of the Month' contest in *Frendz*, an underground newspaper.

> Should we be upset? Not at all. The pig has made a notable contribution to our national well-being over the centuries. . . In America, they say P-I-G stands for Pride, Integrity and Guts. (*Police*, September 1970: 6)

What processes were transforming the police image from plod to pig? All the factors that produced the earlier depoliticization of policing had question marks placed against them after 1959, as social and economic changes had the unintended effect of reversing them.

Policing policies and de-legitimation

Bureaucratic organization?

Recruitment, training, and discipline. Standards of entry and training, though much higher than in the nineteenth century, had not kept up with general improvements. The poor educational standards of recruits—and in particular the shortage of graduates—which the Royal Commission had lamented, remained a concern. Despite increasing attention to training, there were still many complaints that it was inadequate for the complex needs of modern society. The old emphasis on drill and discipline was eroded to match changing social fashions and attract recruits (Reiner 1978a: 186–94).

There have been many attempts worldwide since the 1960s to raise police educational and training standards (Stanislas 2015). Significant results were not achieved in the UK until the 1980s, when following the 1978 Edmund-Davies pay award the intake of graduates accelerated sharply. Changes occurred in recruit training, largely following from the 1981 *Scarman Report* (Bryant *et al.* 2014; Fielding 2018). Despite the merit of these developments, they did not prevent an erosion of public confidence in police professional standards.

Corruption scandals. The image of the police force as a disciplined, impersonal bureaucracy came to be dented by a series of Scotland Yard corruption scandals that rocked it after 1969 (Cox *et al.* 1977). Since then the police have experienced a repeated cycle of scandal and reform (Sherman 1978; Punch 2009).

The Times' revelations in November 1969 were a bombshell with lasting reverberations. What was most shocking was the unmasking of an institutionalized network of corruption, the so-called 'firm within a firm'.

During the mid-1970s there were two more major corruption scandals at the Met, one involving the Drug Squad, the other the Obscene Publications Squad. Both led to the imprisonment of several senior detectives. Home Secretary Reginald Maudling's answer was to appoint as commissioner an 'outsider', Robert Mark, who had been assistant commissioner since 1967 but had previously served entirely in provincial forces.

Mark introduced a dramatic strategy of associated reforms, clearly seeing the excision of the 'cancer' at the Yard as the price of its continued independence (Mark 1978: chaps 7–10). As a result of this new climate some five hundred policemen left the force, many in anticipation of being investigated.

The resilience of corruption at the Yard was shown by new revelations in 1978 of alleged involvement of detectives in major armed robberies (Ball *et al.* 1979). The commissioner, Sir David McNee, set up Operation Countryman under the direction of the Dorset chief constable, Arthur Hambleton. Hambleton and his team claimed on several occasions that their work was sabotaged by corrupt Yard pressure. The Countryman investigations cast doubt on any idea that endemic corruption in the Yard detective squads had been eliminated. Three centuries' experience of thief-taking suggests that criminal investigation operates perennially on the borderline of legality. Rule-bending justified initially by a sincere determination to 'crack down' on serious crime becomes the 'invitational edge' of the kind of wholesale predatory wrongdoing revealed in the 1970s (Manning and Redlinger 1977).

The explosion of corruption scandals was the product of the dangers inherent in detective methods, coupled with the novel pressures of the 1960s and 1970s. These included the rise of large-scale organized crime, and growing toleration of some illegal activities (like drug-taking or pornography), which increased their profitability and lessened the sense detectives had that conniving at them was harmful. The decline in public deference also made it much more likely that allegations against police would be believed.

The 1970s scandals fatally damaged the image of the police as disciplined law enforcers. While in the 1960 Royal Commission survey 46.9 per cent of the public did not believe bribe-taking occurred, the 1981 Policy Studies Institute study of Londoners found that only 14 per cent believed the police 'hardly ever' took bribes, a figure repeated in a later replication (Policy Studies Institute 1983, i: 249; Fitzgerald *et al.* 2002).

The rule of law?

The issue of police adherence to legality became acutely politicized in the 1970s. Civil libertarians had been arguing for years that the rights of suspects were routinely violated. Such claims were crystallized by the 1972 conviction of three teenage boys for the murder of Maxwell Confait. The verdict was eventually quashed by the Court of Appeal. An official inquiry under Sir Henry Fisher, a high court judge, found that the boys' rights had been violated, leading to their false confessions. Fisher suggested that reform of the 'Judges' Rules' (non-statutory directions for questioning) should be conducted in the light of a broader inquiry—'something like a Royal Commission'. The hint was taken up shortly afterwards when the prime minister, James Callaghan, announced the Royal Commission on Criminal Procedure (RCCP).

The 1981 RCCP report was eventually transmuted into the Police and Criminal Evidence Act 1984 (PACE). This purported to provide a balanced codification of police powers and citizens' safeguards, synthesizing the concerns of the 'law and order' and the civil liberties lobbies (Chapter 11).

Between 1989 and 1991 confidence in the police was further shaken by scandals revealing serious malpractice. In October 1989 the Court of Appeal released the 'Guildford Four', three men and a woman sentenced to life imprisonment in 1974 for the Guildford and Woolwich pub bombings. In 1990 the Court of Appeal exonerated the 'Maguire Seven', who had also been jailed in connection with the bombings. A further blow to confidence in the police was the March 1991 release of the 'Birmingham Six', who had been convicted of savage pub bombings in 1975. There was also continuing concern about a number of other miscarriages of justice, going as far back as the early 1950s (Woffinden 1989).

The anxiety produced by these revelations was enough to make the Home Secretary announce the establishment of a Royal Commission on Criminal Justice in 1991, chaired by Lord Runciman, the first Royal Commission in twelve years. The change in public views of the police was encapsulated by a *Guardian* cartoon: a man, late for a date, offers his girlfriend the excuse 'I asked a policeman the time, and he lied!'

The strategy of minimal force?

Was the traditional policy of 'winning by appearing to lose' abandoned? That was the question raised by a clear trend to harder-line policing of political and industrial conflict. The preparedness of the police to cope with public order problems began to be expanded and refined during the 1970s. The militarization of policing proceeded apace in the 1980s in the wake of more serious disorder, but since the early 1990s police around the world have been experimenting with more sophisticated strategies (Waddington 1994; Vogler 1991; Critcher and Waddington 1996; della Porta and Reiter 1998; della Porta *et al.* 2006; Waddington and Wright 2008; Waddington *et al.* 2009).

Without much public debate de facto 'third forces' emerged, specifically trained and readily mobilizable to cope with riots. The Metropolitan Police Special Patrol Group, formed in 1965 as a mobile reserve, developed a paramilitary role in dealing with public order and terrorism. After 1974 all forces formed Police Support Units (PSUs) specially trained for public order duties, including the use of shields, but normally engaged in ordinary policing at local level. They were readily mobilizable to deal with problems arising outside their own force under mutual aid arrangements.

These moves towards more militarized policing were the fruits of the establishment panic in 1972, after the Saltley coke depot had to be closed during picketing by miners. Saltley was seen as an abject defeat by many Conservatives and police officers. There was much debate about the need for a 'third force' specializing in riot control, along the line of the French CRS (Compagnies Républicaines de Sécurité). The police succeeded in scotching the idea, but in effect created 'third forces' within their own organizations.

In the 1984–5 miners' strike a massive, centrally coordinated police operation was directed by the National Reporting Centre, with much criticism of 'police-state' tactics, in a controversy that still rages (Reiner 1984; Fine and Millar 1985; Beckett and Hencke 2009; Granville Williams 2009; Milne 2014).

It is hard to remember the shock that greeted the deployment of police riot shields at Lewisham and Notting Hill in 1977, replacing the traditional protection of dustbin lids. Shields, strengthened helmets, and other protective equipment became regular sights. After the 1980 Bristol riots, and widespread damage and injuries in the 1981 Brixton, Toxteth, and other disorders, police preparation for riot control redoubled.

During the riots there was an evident intensification of police tactics, notably the first use of CS gas in riot control in mainland Britain. A deputation of senior English police officers visited Northern Ireland to see what lessons could be learned from RUC 'success', and the advice of the Hong Kong police was also sought.

In the end a balanced approach prevailed in Lord Scarman's inquiry into the Brixton riots (Scarman 1981). Nonetheless, serious urban riots occurred in 1985, in the West Midlands, Liverpool, Brixton, and the Broadwater Farm estate in north London. Most tragically there was the savage hacking to death of PC Keith Blakelock, the first Met police officer to be murdered in a riot since PC Culley in the 1833 Coldbath Fields case.

Serious public disorder occurred again in an industrial context at Wapping in 1986–7, during picketing by print workers outside the News International plant. Other apparently unjustified uses of tough public-order tactics occurred during the policing of hippie convoys converging on Stonehenge. During 1990 anti-poll-tax demonstrations were the source of severe public order clashes, especially following a rally in Trafalgar Square.

During the 1990s the greatest public order concerns were about disorder in a variety of leisure contexts. In 1988 ACPO had raised fears about growing disorder in rural areas caused by 'lager louts' with 'too much beer in their bellies and money in their pockets' (questioned by Home Office research, Tuck 1989). In 1989–90 there was media alarm about the spread of 'acid-house' parties. In 1991 riots occurred on the Blackbird Leys estate, Oxford, and Meadow Well estate, Tyneside, after police attempts to curb joy-riding (Campbell 1993).

In the mid-1990s there arose a variety of new forms of political protest, against specific issues such as live animal exports and the building of roads in rural areas. These united groups with long experience of the hard end of public order policing with middle-aged, middle-class people, including many women, who would traditionally have been stalwart police supporters. The combination created especially acute policing problems. Since the late 1990s there has been a resurgence of left-wing protest about financial globalization and its consequences of deepening inequality, including major clashes in the City of London in 1999, 2000, and 2009 (with counterparts in the USA and several other countries).

During the 1970s and 1980s the British police response to riots toughened, with resort to militaristic technology and weaponry. Darth Vader displaced Dixon in riot control. Similar developments towards 'militarised' policing have occurred around the world, with growing controversy (Kraska 2001, Vitale 2017, Bonner et al. 2018).

Apart from the growing use of riot control hardware, there was a rapid proliferation of firearms use by the police in Britain (Waddington and Wright 2008; Punch 2010). Although still unarmed (apart from the traditional truncheon) on routine patrol, the frequency with which firearms are issued to the police has escalated inexorably, as has the firepower of the guns used. The number of occasions when guns are fired by the police remains small by international standards, and the rules and accountability mechanisms have been tightened on numerous occasions, following a series of egregious wrongful shootings. The most notorious was the July 2005 killing of Jean Charles de Menezes, an innocent Brazilian electrician, in the wake of the London terrorist bombings. Whatever the justification in terms of the growing violence faced by police in public order and routine patrol work, the traditional unarmed image of the British bobby has been undermined.

Accountability?

As policing became more controversial in Britain so the old mystical accountability substitute of police identification with the public came under strain. The police were seen as unrepresentative in terms of race, gender, and culture. Throughout the 1980s radical critics sought to reform police governance to make policy-making accountable to the electoral process. Until recently all governments have wanted to maintain the constitutional status quo regarding police governance, while becoming concerned to render the police more accountable for the effective use of resources.

At the same time it was becoming increasingly evident that local accountability to police authorities has atrophied, replaced by a degree of central control amounting to a de facto national force. The perceived lack of adequate accountability was a major factor undermining legitimacy in the 1970s and 1980s.

Non-partisanship?

The spectacle of chief officers or the Police Federation preaching at the drop of a helmet about the sinking state of national moral fibre became familiar in the 1970s (Reiner 1980; Loader and Mulcahy 2003: chap. 7).

When, in 1965, the Police Federation held a Press conference to launch a pamphlet arguing for police pay rises to help the fight against crime, the authorities had been aghast. 'I never thought I would see the day when the representatives of law and order would be advocating anarchy' declared one member of the Police Council.

By 1980 the police, at all levels from chief constable down to the rank and file, seemed to set the terms of debate on law and order. This change was heralded by the Marksist revolution at Scotland Yard, when Sir Robert Mark delivered a controversial Dimbleby lecture on BBC television in 1972. In 1975, the Police Federation launched an unprecedented 'law-and-order' campaign to mobilize 'the silent majority' against the liberalizing trend in penal and social policy. During the 1979 general election strikingly similar pronouncements appeared from police spokesmen and Tory politicians, as part of what the media dubbed the 'great debate' on law and order. A fortnight before polling day, Robert Mark hit the headlines with a broadside comparing the relationship between the Labour Party and the trade unions to 'the way the National Socialist German Workers' Party achieved unrestricted control of the German state'. The Police Federation placed advertisements in national newspapers headed 'LAW AND ORDER', blaming Labour for rising crime. These proved to be an investment reaping handsome dividends. On the first working day after the Conservative victory, Federation leaders were summoned to Downing Street and told they would immediately receive the pay increase recommended by the Edmund-Davies committee.

The early 1980s were the high watermark of overt police lobbying for law and order (Savage *et al.* 2000: 50). During the late 1980s the love affair between the Tories and the police cooled as public expenditure cuts began to bite on the police, and they feared a hidden agenda of incipient privatization. For its part Labour tried hard to repair broken bridges, especially after Tony Blair used the influential soundbite 'Tough on crime, tough on the causes of crime' after 1992. Nonetheless, the years of partisanship had tarnished the sacred aura hitherto enjoyed by the British police of being, like the Queen, above party politics.

The service role?

The service role continued to be paid lip-service by chief constables. Indeed, a current of police thinking stressed that, contrary to the growing image of the police as primarily crime-fighters, much if not most uniformed policework consisted of service calls for help (Chapter 5). This approach, pioneered in the 1970s by the then chief constable of Devon and Cornwall's philosophy of community policing (Alderson 1979, 1984, 1998), subsequently became an influential movement among progressive police chiefs in the USA and elsewhere (Skolnick and Bayley 1986, 1988; Brogden and Nijhar 2005; Savage 2007: 55–9, 128–41).

After the 1981 *Scarman Report* endorsed a community policing philosophy it became the orthodox analysis of the police role for all chief constables (Reiner 1991: chap. 6). Declining public support in the late 1980s led to a redoubling of official efforts to define policing in service and consumerist terms (Squires 1998; Savage 2007: 136–41).

However, these efforts were largely overturned by the Conservative government's reform package launched in 1993, which explicitly sought to prioritize 'catching criminals' (White Paper on Police Reform). New Labour's Crime Reduction Programme continued this emphasis, albeit in a somewhat modulated form (Savage 2007: 185).

Preventive policing?

Peel's original conception of policing emphasized the bobby on the beat as the essential bedrock of the force. However, it was potent as symbol rather than practice. Despite the rhetoric, foot patrol was treated as a reserve from which high-flying specialists could be drawn, and a Siberia to which failed specialists could be banished.

Since the 1960s the meaning of crime prevention has transmuted from the 'scarecrow' function of regular uniform patrol into a notion of prevention as pre-emption (Crawford and Evans 2017). Partly this meant assiduously collecting and coordinating low-level information provided by local constables. With the growth in capacity of the Police National Computer this became more centralized and readily available, as well as acquiring an insidious status as 'hard data'.

The development of 'intelligence-led', risk-oriented, inter-agency, and 'partnership' policing methods accentuated the breadth and depth of pre-emptive surveillance and analysis around the world (Tilley 2008; Cope 2008; James 2013; Loftus *et al.* 2016: chaps 7, 9, 10).

The second meaning of pre-emption is the development of specialist crime prevention departments, providing advice to citizens on minimizing the risk of victimization. At first crime prevention departments were the Cinderellas of the service, low status, low budget, and low key. However, as crime prevention became increasingly central to the government's law-and-order policy in the 1980s so they blossomed into belles of the ball (Bottoms 1990; Reiner and Cross 1991: chap. 1). The impact of such vaunted crime prevention efforts as Neighbourhood Watch was mixed, however (Forrester *et al.* 1988; McConville and Shepherd 1992).

To some critics community policing was only a more covert, insidious means of penetrating communities to acquire information. What seems clear is that the pursuit of greater crime prevention effectiveness has meant a proliferation of proactive tactics and specialist plainclothes units, reversing the original Peelian strategy. These policies were themselves a response to the undermining of the eighth ingredient of legitimation.

Police effectiveness?

Police effectiveness is a notoriously slippery concept to define or measure. But the official statistics routinely produced by the Home Office recorded an inexorable rise in serious offences and decline in the clear-up rate, from the mid-1950s to the early 1990s (Reiner 2016b: chaps 5, 7).

The inadequacy of all these figures has long been well known (Reiner 2007: chap. 3; Maguire and McVie 2017). A rising crime rate may mean a greater propensity to report offences. The clear-up rate is affected by many determinants apart from detective effectiveness, including massaging the figures (Young 1991). Nonetheless, rising recorded crime was associated with a growing public fear that police effectiveness was declining, giving rise to a 'reassurance policing' agenda.

Police legitimacy was further undermined by their apparent inability to deal with crime in the suites as well as in the streets. As the salience of fraud problems grew in the 1980s, so there was increasing concern about police incompetence or partiality in this area, accentuated more recently by the 'credit crunch' and recession (Nelken 2012). In the 1980s the Home Office Research Unit produced a growing volume of evidence (paralleling earlier American findings) indicating that current methods of patrol and detection were of dubious effectiveness (Clarke and Hough 1984).

During the 1990s there was, however, a rebirth of political belief in the possibilities of crime control by the police, in particular using innovative methods, with some support from criminological researchers (Braga and Weisburd 2010). Whatever the outcome of these debates is, there can be no doubt that public concerns about apparently declining police effectiveness, and the law-and-order campaigns they stimulated, were a major factor in declining police legitimacy during the 1970s and 1980s.

The social context of declining police legitimacy

Police activity has always borne most heavily on the economically and socially marginal elements, whose lives are lived largely in streets and other public places. Such powerless groups have been named 'police property' (Cray 1972; Lee 1981). Police themselves recognize this, and their argot contains a variety of derogatory epithets for their regular clientele. In California they were 'assholes' (Van Maanen 1978), in Canada 'pukes' (Ericson 1982), in London 'slag' or 'scum' (Policy Studies Institute 1983, iv: 164–5), in Paris batardes, cocksuckers, or shitheads (Fassin 2013: 98).

Drawn mostly from the respectable working class, the police scorn those whose lifestyles deviate from their values. But, however conflict ridden, relations between the police and 'slag' are not usually politicized. Membership of the marginal strata is usually temporary (youths mature, the unemployed find jobs), so a sense of group identity is hard to develop. Moreover, police action against them has majority support, even (perhaps especially) from the respectable adult working class.

One crucial factor which politicized policing after the 1960s was the proliferation of social groups with a consciousness of antagonism towards the police. This was primarily the product of the emergence of more self-conscious youth cultures, the return of long-term unemployment, and militant industrial conflict in the 1970s and early 1980s.

A crucial change was the catastrophic deterioration of relations with black and minority ethnic communities. There is a long history of police prejudice against black people, in

Britain and many other countries. A vicious cycle developed between police stereotyping and black vulnerability to the situations that attract police attention (Chapter 6).

Research on police-public relations suggests that while these remain harmonious with the majority of the population, they tend to be tense and conflict ridden with the young, the unemployed, the economically marginal, and black people (Fitzgerald *et al.* 2002; Bowling *et al.* 2012; Phillips and Bowling 2017). It should be noted that there are signs that ethnic differences in trust in police are diminishing (Flatley 2016: Appendix table 1.02).

A crucial factor politicizing policing after the 1970s was a growth in the size of 'police property' groups. This resulted from increasing social inequality due to free-market policies (Currie 1998a, 1998b; Taylor 1999; Reiner 2007, 2016b), and a heightening of self-consciousness among targets of policing.

Policing de-legitimation reflected profound changes in the political economy of Western capitalism. Long-term structural unemployment (increasingly never-employment) re-emerged, leading to the *de-incorporation* of increasing sections of the young working class, especially among discriminated-against minorities, 'who are being defined out of the edifice of citizenship' (Dahrendorf 1985: 98). A new underclass formed not simply as a result of unemployment, but because of unemployment's apparent structural inevitability. The structurally generated formation of a completely marginalized segment of society underlay the huge growth since the 1970s in crime, disorder, and tensions around policing. Unemployment and inequality are not linked to crime or disorder in any straightforward, automatic way, but they are key sources of crime and disorder (Reiner 2007: chap. 4; 2016a: chaps 5, 7).

A further key shift feeding into political debate was a long-term cultural change in the opinion-forming middle class (Waddington 1982). The police lost the confidence of small but crucial sections of the 'talking classes', what may be described roughly as *Guardian*-reading circles. This developing gulf between the police and some educated middle-class opinion had a variety of roots, stretching back to the invention of the car (Weinberger 1995: chap. 4). But the most crucial developments were the growth of middle-class political protest from the early 1960s (CND, the anti-Vietnam War demonstrations, the student movement and counterculture, and the politicization of forms of marginal deviance which involve some middle-class people, notably drug-taking and homosexuality). This conflict with highly articulate and educated sections of the population was of enormous significance in converting policing into an overt political issue.

POLICING AS NECESSARY EVIL? PRAGMATIC POST-LEGITIMATION 1992–

The politics of policing since the 1990s has moved 'beyond legitimation'. This reflects the deeply embedded consensus on the politics of law and order that developed after New Labour's espousal of the rhetoric of toughness (Reiner 2007: chap. 5).

The Stephen Lawrence case, the main *cause célèbre* of the 1990s, illustrates this. It raised once again the vexed issues of police racism and discrimination, but these were manifest above all in the police failure to clear up the murder of a young black man, to deliver public protection from crime in an equitable and efficient way.

Policing has always been better interpreted dramaturgically than in terms of rational accomplishment of instrumental objectives (Manning 1997, 2003). The legitimatory performance played out in the first century and a half of the new police projected them as providing security and order by fair, legalistic, minimum force tactics. This covered up a backstage reality of widespread corruption and malpractice, but the front-of-house mythology projected the best police in the world.

The politicization of policing that developed from the 1960s to the early 1990s concerned principled disputes between fundamentally conflicting conceptions. These could be characterized somewhat simplistically in terms of contrasting crime control and due process models (Packer 1968; see also Chapter 2). On the one hand, a 'law-and-order' lobby regarded crime and disorder as out of control, and saw due process safeguards as 'handcuffs' on police. An opposing civil liberties lobby regarded adequate legal protections for suspected citizens as an important principle of the rule of law. This was associated with a social democratic analysis of crime and disorder stressing their deep social roots. Policing and punishment were short-term symptom relief not fundamental remedies (Reiner 2006). Whatever the virtues of this position, it proved an electoral albatross around Labour's neck in the 1980s as huge increases in crime and disorder fed public concerns for immediate crime suppression.

During the late 1980s Labour began to shed its electoral 'hostages to fortune' (Morgan and Smith 2017). A sharp break occurred when Tony Blair became Shadow Home Secretary in 1992, and sought to capture the law-and-order issue with the slogan 'tough on crime, tough on the causes of crime' (Newburn and Reiner 2007). It captured the mood of national soul-searching about crime and moral decline in the wake of the tragic 1993 murder of Liverpool toddler James Bulger. The political pay-off lurked in the subtext: a double-whammy of toughness locked into one short, sharp sentence.

The new cross-party consensus on the principles of law and order has been accompanied by sharp partisan conflict about delivery, with mutual attacks on the record and policies of the other, and much opportunistic borrowings and political cross-dressing. Recent quantitative survey data on public confidence on policing indicates increasing volatility and ambivalence. British Crime Survey ratings of the police as doing a good or excellent job declined from 64 per cent in 1996 to 48 per cent in 2004–5, but have since risen back to over 60 per cent. (Flatley 2016: figure 1.1).

Interpretations of policing in English culture encompass a variety of visions. These range from 'defenders of the faith' who cling to the Dixon ideal, through a complex array of less positive sensibilities: from 'the disenchanted', 'agnostics', and 'the hopeful' to the most alienated, the 'atheists' who have lost trust in the police as a source of security or justice (Loader and Mulcahy 2003: chap. 3). The massive social upheavals of recent decades have disturbed all perceptions and relations with policing, but diagnoses and prognoses differ considerably, and are ambivalent and volatile.

This is indicated too by changing mass-media representations of policing (see Chapter 10). These shifted from being almost entirely positive about police integrity and effectiveness in the two decades after the Second World War, through a phase of more critical images, to a complex and varied range from extremely hostile to laudatory (Reiner et al. 2000, 2001, 2003).

This new pragmatic and brittle politics of policing beyond legitimation can be analysed in terms of the same dimensions used to explain the rise and fall of legitimacy in the previous 150 years.

Policing policy and fragile re-legitimation

Bureaucratic organization?

There has been no recurrence of scandals on the scale of those of the 1980s, although corruption is a permanent danger (Punch 2009). There have been numerous *causes célèbres* involving what Sir Paul Condon, Metropolitan Police Commissioner in the 1990s, referred to as 'noble cause corruption'. However, they have not had the de-legitimating effects of the 1970s/1980s scandals, in part because they have been outweighed by anxieties about security.

The pluralization of policing—the proliferation of agencies apart from the Peelian police (notably private security), and internal diversification with greater specialization, civilianization, and a burgeoning 'extended police family'—complicate the image of police as a single omnibus bureaucracy (Chapter 7).

The police embodiment of impersonal bureaucratic state authority became a liability rather than a source of legitimation in a more individualistic neo-liberal culture. The prevailing narratives governing police reform shifted accordingly. There is an unfortunate Catch-22 for the police here. If they are caught out in rule-breaking malpractices this causes de-legitimating crises. But the notion of disciplined, bureaucratic rule-followers is problematically uncool in the free-wheeling consumerist culture of 'liquid modernity' (Bauman 2000). An ongoing attempt to square this circle is the 'professionalisation' agenda pursued in the UK and other jurisdictions (Brown 2014: Part V; Fleming 2015).

Rule of law?

The idea that police operations are governed by principles of due process legality was crucial to their legitimation. Until the 1970s the predominant rhetoric expressing this was the increasingly threadbare notion of the police as 'citizens in uniform', lacking legal powers beyond those of the ordinary citizen. The 1984 Police and Criminal Evidence Act (PACE), gave the police a battery of powers not available to ordinary citizens, based on a new legitimating principle: a 'fundamental balance' between investigative powers and safeguards for suspects (Chapter 11).

Since the hegemony of tough law-and-order politics in the 1990s, the old debates have shifted to another register. *Causes célèbres* about police malpractice, excessive force, and abuse of powers still occur. But the thrust of legal and policy development has been to enhance police power, watering down safeguards. In a context of heightened crisis about security and terrorism, this has happened with little questioning. What is evident is a new legitimatory rhetoric, the Dirty Harry discourse of the lesser evil, the need in emergencies to adopt tactics that would not normally be justified but which become routine.

This pervasive sense of crisis and exception was heightened by the terror attacks in many parts of the world in the twenty-first century. But it had already developed over the previous twenty years in relation to both traditional and new forms of crime. The sole exception to this trend was an attempt by the 2010–15 Coalition government to reduce the use of the internationally controversial stop and search power (Weber and Bowling 2014; Delsol and Shiner 2015; Bradford 2016). This achieved some success, at any rate until an increase in knife crime and homicide in 2018 that has seen government and police chiefs offering renewed support for the exercise of the powers. In the USA too, President Trump has urged police not to be over concerned with how they handle protestors or suspects, and these sentiments have been echoed by many other leaders.

Strategy of minimal force?

We have seen that a crucial aspect of the legitimation of the British police was the minimal force, 'win by appearing to lose', strategy. The militarization of public order tactics in the 1970s and 1980s was a focal point of de-legitimation. During the 1990s the issue of excessive use of force seemed to recede somewhat, but this was very much an illusion. In the background, social and policy developments were preparing the ground for the *causes célèbres* which have occurred in the twenty-first century, above all the tragic shooting of Jean Charles de Menezes in 2005 and the policing of protests like those at the 2009 London G20 or against fracking (Punch 2010; Gilmore *et al.* 2017; Jackson *et al.* 2018).

During the 1990s, with scarcely any public discussion or awareness, there was an increase in the deployment of (armed response vehicles) ARVs that permanently carried firearms, and a massive escalation in the firepower available to police (Roberts and Innes 2009). There has also been a growing deployment of 'non-lethal' weaponry such as tasers, indicating anticipation of higher levels of force in routine policing (Waddington and Wright 2008: 468–9).

In the public disorder context the militarization of police tactics appeared to abate in the 1990s. Confidence grew among the police in Britain and internationally that a new strategy of 'negotiated management' rather than 'escalated force', aiming at cooperation rather than confrontation with demonstrators (Waddington 1994; della Porta and Reiter 1998; della Porta *et al.* 2006), was proving successful at preventing violent conflict.

During the 1980s militaristic tactics had proved ineffective as well as de-legitimating, but they have returned during the twenty-first century. The 1990 poll tax riots 'prompted a minor revolution in police tactics that only came to public prominence a decade later' (Waddington and Wright 2008: 472). This was the pre-emptive containment of what were regarded as potentially disorderly crowds within tight static cordons—what has come to be known as 'kettling'—in a number of anti-globalization or climate change protests in London in the 2000s. The legality of this tactic, justified by the police as stemming from their common law powers to prevent a breach of the peace, was challenged as violating the right to liberty set out in the European Convention on Human Rights, Article 5. The House of Lords ruled that the tactic was lawful, provided it was used in good faith, was proportionate to the situation, and used for no longer than reasonably necessary (*Austin and another* v. *Commissioner of Police of the Metropolis* [2009] UKHL 5). This was upheld at the European Court of Human Rights in 2012, a judgment that has attracted much criticism (Christian 2012; Mansfield 2012).

However, the use of kettling at the April 2009 G20 protests arguably exceeded the conditions of legality. This controversial operation, which resulted in the tragic death of Ian Tomlinson, together with other cases of apparent brutality caught on video, was reviewed critically by a variety of official bodies (HMIC 2009; Mansfield 2013).

Further escalation of controversy about police use of force is likely. In addition to the continuing risk of terrorist incidents, the economic collapse of 2007–8 accentuated political conflicts and disorders already presaged by the anti-globalization protests of the last decade, most obviously the riots of 2011 (Briggs 2012; Winlow *et al.* 2015; Newburn 2015, 2016; Newburn *et al.* 2015).

While each incident sparks a storm of controversy, they do not seem to have the general de-legitimating effect of the 1970s/1980s militarization of policing. There is a pragmatic acceptance that tougher tactics—risking mistakes and malpractice—are necessitated by the problems the police face. This is illustrated by an Ipsos MORI survey on the policing of the G20 protests. Opinion was evenly divided over the overall handling of the protest: 51 per cent thought most or all police had handled it appropriately, with only 7 per cent saying most or all police had behaved inappropriately. The survey showed majority support for the use of force as justified not only to restrain or respond to violence, but to prevent disruption to transport and normal business (HMIC 2009: Annex E). This exemplifies a discourse of pragmatic, lesser evil legitimation.

Accountability?

During the 1980s, as neo-liberalism became hegemonic, the notion of accountability shifted from holding police power in check, to 'businesslike' accounting for efficient, effective, and economic policing (Chapter 11). The Conservative reforms heralded by the *Sheehy Report* and Police White Paper of 1993, partially realized in the 1994 Police and Magistrates' Courts Act, began in earnest the application of New Public Management to the police, extended by New Labour after 1997. Although the doctrine of constabulary independence remained intact as legal principle, the practice of policing became much more regulated by central government. 'Calculative and contractual' accountability (Reiner and Spencer 1993) penetrated police policy and practice in a way that no earlier model did. Similar developments have occurred in the USA and elsewhere, most famously in the NYPD Compstat model of constant answerability of police commanders for current crime trends (Zimring 2011; Roeder *et al.* 2015: 10), which has become influential throughout the world.

   This is the quintessence of pragmatic legitimation: the police are constantly on trial in terms of performance, and trust is always conditional.

   Since 2010 the Conservative dominated governments have pursued a dramatic transformation in police governance (Chapter 11), spearheaded by the 2012 Police Reform and Social Responsibility Act. This sought to reverse the long-standing centralizing trend by creating Police and Crime Commissioners in every provincial force area, elected locally every four years and given considerable powers. This was a remarkable *volte face* by the Conservatives, who had hitherto condemned such arrangements as politicizing the police (Jones *et al.* 2012; Reiner 2013, 2016a; Stenson and Silverstone 2014; Turner 2014, 2016; Lister and Rowe 2016).

Non-partisanship?

Policing is inherently political because it involves the exercise of power. But it is not necessarily *politicized* in the sense of being the subject of party political controversy (Reiner and O'Connor 2015). During the 1970s the police became politicized as the police became a Tory-leaning partisan political lobby. This alignment weakened in the 1990s, and in recent years there have been ever-more examples of political cross-dressing (Reiner 2016a).

   Strident accusations of politicizing the police have been hurled by Labour and the Conservatives at each other. In 2005 the Conservatives accused the Labour government of inducing police chiefs to lobby Parliament in support of proposals to extend detention limits for terror suspects to ninety days. Accusations of politicizing the police came from the Tories in 2008 over the arrest and detention of Damian Green, the Shadow Immigration Minister, during an investigation into leaked government documents. The resignation of Sir Ian Blair as Met Commissioner on 2 October 2008 prompted a storm of accusations that the new Conservative London Mayor Boris Johnson was politicizing the police.

These episodes indicate an orgy of political cross-dressing compared to the previous positions of the parties. Throughout the 1970s and 1980s Labour accused the Conservatives of politicizing the police for their own partisan advantage. Local democratic accountability was then seen as a left-Labour issue, opposed by the Conservatives. The ninety-day detention debate saw the Tories donning the civil libertarian mantle that had been one of Labour's electoral 'hostages to fortune' in the 1980s. The Conservatives have also flirted with another of old Labour's 'hostages to fortune', the social democratic root cause theory of crime, most prominently in David Cameron's short-lived 'hug-a-hoodie' phase in 2007–8.

In office after 2010 the Conservatives have reduced police autonomy and resources, in a way that Labour governments could never get away with (Reiner and O'Connor 2015). The dizzying policy and rhetorical cross-dressing, disguise the fundamental consensus on law-and-order principles since 1992. The police remain deeply embroiled in political controversy, but in pragmatic terms of who promotes their effectiveness best, not principled differences.

Service role?

The legitimation of the police was accomplished in part by encouraging them to perform services in addition to crime prevention. This was part of the ideal image of the British bobby, encapsulated by the *Dixon of Dock Green* mythology at the height of their legitimacy.

As police legitimacy began to wane, an increasingly influential response from police chiefs and policy-makers around the world has been the movement to reform forces on a 'community policing' model. This protean term clearly encompasses a variety of meanings, but paramount is the mood music of restoring friendly relations with the public, a 'cherry pie' promise (Brogden 1999) that renders it beyond principled critique (Klockars 1988).

The hegemony of the politics of law and order has transmuted the meaning of the service role. Instead of being a velvet glove of uncontentious friendly services legitimating the iron fist of coercive policing, now, as the title of an episode of *The Bill* once put it, 'force is part of the service'. In the pragmatic post-legitimation framework the service role has been assimilated into reassurance about crime and disorder reduction, rather than a balance against police force.

Preventive policing?

Crime prevention was the priority for the new police according to Peel's celebrated 1829 instructions. In practice this was narrowed to the scarecrow effect of uniform patrol. However, since the late 1980s prevention has transmuted into pre-emption, through problem-oriented and community policing, and intelligence-led targeting of 'hot spots' (James 2013, 2016; Bullock 2014; Ratcliffe 2016). It has also encouraged the spread of situational and physical security measures, notably CCTV, in which the UK became a world leader (Goold 2004, 2009; Norris and McCahill 2006). These have contributed to the reduction in recorded crime throughout the Western world since the mid-1990s (Reiner 2016b: 164–85).

Effectiveness?

The effectiveness of policing in controlling crime is hard to assess and remains much debated (Chapter 5). But the conjunction of the spread of the New Police in the second half of the nineteenth century with a long-term decline in crime statistics created a widespread perception of police as protectors against crime. This was a crucial element in their legitimation. Conversely, the remorseless rise of recorded crime from the mid-1950s until the early 1990s was an important element in declining public confidence.

The period since the early 1990s, in which the politics of tough law and order became embodied as a new cross-party conventional wisdom, is remarkable for the dissociation between different measures of crime and public perceptions. Comparing the police-recorded trend with that shown by the British Crime Survey (BCS) suggests a complex picture (Reiner 2007: chap. 3; 2016a: chaps 5, 7). Whereas in the first decade after the BCS began in 1981 the trend it portrayed confirmed the huge explosion of crime recorded by the police, after the early 1990s the series began to diverge. The BCS continued to chart a rise until 1995, but the police data fell from 1992 to 1997. As crime peaked in the early 1990s, insurance companies made claiming more onerous, discouraging reporting by victims, and more 'businesslike' managerial accountability for policing implicitly introduced incentives against recording. So police recorded less crime, although victimization was still rising. Home Secretary Michael Howard was certainly tough on the causes of recording crime, even if not on crime itself. After New Labour came to power in 1997 the two measures continued to diverge—but in the opposite direction. BCS recorded crime has fallen rapidly and is now below the level of the first BCS in 1981 (Flatley 2018: figure 1). Because of major counting rule changes, the police recorded statistics rose from 1998 up to 2004, since when they have declined again.

It seems clear that recorded crime has fallen substantially since the mid-1990s, although it seems to be picking up again in the UK, North America, and elsewhere as we approach 2020. But public perceptions about crime do not reflect this. The proportion of people interviewed by the BCS who think crime has risen nationally has fallen since 2009, but 60 per cent still believe crime is rising (Flatley 2018: figure 1). On the other hand, the proportion thinking crime has increased in their local area is generally substantially lower, and in line with measures of deprivation in specific areas which the survey considers 'an objective proxy measure of crime' (ibid.: 3). The mismatch between these images is probably because perceptions of national trends are mainly shaped by media focus on spectacular crimes whereas people are more aware of crime reductions in their own area (ibid.: figure 3).

There is a rational kernel to the public's failure to be reassured. The dramatic overall fall in crime statistics masks increases in some of the most alarming offences. Until the early 1970s annual recorded homicides remained between 300 and 400, but this doubled by 2007 (Flatley 2018: 30). Homicide then generally fell up to 2017, but increased sharply in 2018, sparking huge concern about knife crime in particular. There have also been increases in other crimes not well recorded by the crime surveys, notably domestic violence (Walby *et al.* 2016), and cybercrime (Reiner 2016b: 179–80). In so far as the decline in crime is the result of more effective security it is subject to a paradox: the very measures that contain victimization serve as constant reminders of risk (Zedner 2003: 165).

The New Labour government was reluctant to claim credit for its crime control success, partly because of concern that the tabloids, which routinely stoke fears about rising crime, would once more castigate Labour as out of touch and soft on security. A review by the Prime Minister's Strategy Unit concluded that 80 per cent of the crime reduction was due to economic factors, although this estimate is somehow omitted from the version of the report posted on the Cabinet website, which concentrated almost entirely on criminal justice solutions (Solomon *et al.* 2007). Thus New Labour had been successful in reducing crime, even with its very cautious approach to containing inequality and exclusion. But it was so locked into the politics of law and order that this was a success that dare not speak its name.

The last two decades have been extremely volatile in terms of the appearance of police effectiveness in crime control. As recorded crime increased, albeit largely for reasons beyond police control, pressure mounted on the police to actually deliver the security they had always claimed as their mission. Although the general trends in crime could be interpreted as evidence that New Labour largely succeeded (although other factors did most of the heavy lifting cf. Reiner 2016b: 164–85), febrile partisan competition about delivery places them on a tightrope, constantly exposed to the appearance of failure.

Social context of fragile re-legitimation

The vital precondition for police legitimation was the gradual incorporation of the working class, the main structurally rooted source of opposition to the new police, into citizenship—legal, political, and socio-economic (Marshall 1950; Reiner 2010a). Conversely, the de-legitimation of the police between the late 1960s and the early 1990s was only partly a consequence of shifts in policing. It was shaped primarily by deeper transformations in political economy and culture. The displacement of the post-Second World War Keynesian, welfare state consensus by neo-liberalism during the 1970s had profound reverberations for crime, criminal justice, and policing. The return of massive inequality and social exclusion drove crime up and re-politicized law and order.

The politics of policing became increasingly febrile and volatile. Principled debate about policing was attenuated. Their role as the front line of crime control became unquestioned. But partisan debate about tactics and who delivered policing most effectively became ever-more heated. The first decade of New Labour was a period of rising prosperity, relatively full employment (although with an ever-more divided dual labour market), some diminution of poverty although not inequality overall. This contributed to a considerable reduction of overall crime. But in the volatile party political competition about law and order the focus was on the aspects of crime that were *not* reducing, and on new threats, above all terrorism.

This was exacerbated considerably with the economic collapse since 2007. Sadly unemployment and long-term exclusion, poverty, inequality escalated, albeit without clearly driving up crime and disorder as they did in the 1980s. The police cannot long continue to contain rising social divisions and pressures, despite considerable advances in policing and community safety tactics, especially given the considerable cuts they have faced as part of Conservative austerity economics.

CONCLUSION

This chapter has analysed the construction of police legitimacy in the face of widespread opposition to the establishment of the New Police. It has also traced their subsequent de-legitimation up to the early 1990s. The embedding of a politics of tough law and order as the hegemonic discourse about crime control resulted in a decline of principled debate about policing, but a ferocious partisan competition about what works and who delivers best.

Throughout police history their legitimacy has been dependent fundamentally on wider trends in political economy and culture. The dominance of neo-liberalism since the 1970s has brought greater insecurity and anxiety, despite the apparent benefits in terms of economic growth and individual autonomy. The economic collapse precipitated by the credit crunch after 2007 has brought the dark side of the neo-liberal model to the fore, and confronts policing and criminal justice with massive new problems. The fragile and pragmatic legitimation of policing since 1992 is coming under enormous strain. Societies around the world are re-learning the old lesson that the police alone cannot be the basis of order and security.

PART III

SOCIAL RESEARCH ON CONTEMPORARY POLICING PRACTICE AND IMAGERY

5

THE POLICE ROLE, FUNCTION AND EFFECTS

INTRODUCTION

Conflicting political mythologies have obscured our understanding of the police role and its effects. The 'repressive state apparatus' myth, flourishing in the radical criminology of the 1970s and 1980s, depicted the police as an oppressive political force creating crime and criminals through labelling (Hall *et al.* 1978/2013; Scraton 1985, 1987). In the 1990s, the critical perspective disappeared from mainstream political discourse and its antithesis—the 'law-and-order' myth—dominated debate. This portrays the police as an effective force for the prevention and detection of crime and advocates police power as a panacea for crime control and public order (Jackall 2003). Recently there has been a resurgence of a critical perspective in police scholarship on both sides of the Atlantic (Vitale 2017, Bowling, Phillips, and Sheptycki 2012; Davis 2017). The research evidence shows policework is more complex and contradictory than these mythologies allow. The research evidence about police practice will be considered in this chapter in relation to three broad questions: what is the police role? what do the police actually do? and how well do they do it? (In Chapter 6, we ask how fair are the police?)

THE BREADTH OF THE POLICE ROLE

Empirical social research on the police began in the early 1960s. Social scientists began to ask questions about 'what the police actually did and how they spent their time' (Brodeur 2010: 150). The police were hotly debated in policy circles. This might well strike many people as an example of the intellectual and policy elites being out of touch, or worse still making work for themselves. Surely everyone knows what cops do—they cop robbers. After all, myriad TV shows have beamed this message into our homes nightly for more than half a century. This, however, is precisely why researchers have continued to probe the issue: the early research surprised those who carried it out by the clear finding that conventional mythology needed at least to be severely questioned and qualified, if not rejected altogether. Spoiler alert!—as will be shown in this chapter, research has shown conclusively, in many times and places, that the police spend far more time on tasks not clearly related to crime, and indeed the police catch a very small proportion of robbers or other criminals.

The history of policing shows that its architects were interested in much more than crime control and enforcement (see Chapter 2). The term police encompassed governance including reinforcing social norms, securing peace, good order, happiness, welfare, lighting, health, and hygiene. It remains the widest and most unfettered state power (Dubber 2005). A number of authors have pointed to the intangible 'everywhere and nowhere' and 'everything and nothing' qualities of policing that means that its scope and power defy limitation (Ryan 2013, Benjamin 2006; Dubber 2005). Egon Bittner, one of the most influential policing scholars of the mid-twentieth century, defined the role of the police as finding 'an unknown solution to an unknown problem' (Bittner 1967). According to him, the job of the police is to respond to *situations* definable as 'something-that-ought-not-be-to-happening-and-about-which-someone-had-better-do-something-now' (Bittner 1990: 249; Manning 2013).

Is the police role really that broad? Most discussions of the role of the police begin with patrolling neighbourhoods on foot or by car, rapid response to emergencies, and the investigation of crimes. Dig a little deeper, and myriad other roles are revealed: preparing criminal cases for prosecution, appearing in court, and holding arrestees in police cells; responding to terrorism; managing traffic; licensing firearms; controlling the vices of pornography, prostitution, and gambling; responding to sudden death; maintaining social order during elections and the detection of election malpractice; responding to people suffering mental health episodes in the community. How are we to make sense out of this bewildering diversity? Is it possible to divide these functions into neat categories? (See Table 5.1.) The breadth of this 'omnibus' role also means that the police officer is 'expected to achieve more than they can conceivably deliver' (Morgan and Newburn 1997:151). How does one distinguish between important 'core functions' and peripheral or ancillary tasks? There are certainly some common threads that unite this very wide spectrum of activities. However, some roles can only be achieved through negotiation, while others can arguably only be achieved through the use of force.

Table 5.1 The role of the public police

Functions	Mechanisms
Public reassurance	Visible patrol; contact with individuals and community organizations; effective crime investigation; and emergency service
Crime reduction	Visible patrol; targeted policing; proactive policing; effective crime investigation; and emergency service
Crime investigation	Reactive detective work to identify and arrest offenders and bring them to justice; proactive investigation
Emergency service	Rapid response to disputes, disturbances, accidents, and emergencies
Peacekeeping	Routine negotiation and problem solving in a range of neighbourhood disputes and disorders
Order maintenance	Controlling crowds at sporting events, entertainment venues, and demonstrations
State security	Protection of public figures (politicians, royal family, diplomats), state buildings, covert policing of dissident organizations
Road traffic control	Visible patrol (motorways), speed controls, rapid response to accidents and emergencies

THE POLICE ROLE: SEVEN ANSWERS IN SEARCH OF A QUESTION

Debate about the police role is concerned with what the police *could do*, what they *should do*, what they *actually do* in practice, and *how well* they do it. In its basic form this has taken two contrasting views. On one side, is the law-and-order view that the police are 'a force' which has the primary functions of crime control and criminal law enforcement. On the other, police are conceptualized as 'a service', calming a sea of social troubles. Since the 1960s this argument has been bolstered by the empirical discovery that, contrary to popular mythology, the police operate mainly not as crime-fighters or law-enforcers, but rather as providers of a range of services to members of the public, the variety of which defies description. Seldom considered is what these contrasting accounts of the police are supposed to be about. To what issues are the enquiries into the police 'role' meant to provide answers? The simple question 'what is the police role?' can refer to at least seven distinct conundrums:

(1) Original *historical* purpose: Why were the modern police set up in the first place? What was their original *raison d'être*?

(2) Contemporary *governmental authority*: What are the purposes or functions proposed in recent times by public authorities? What do contemporary policy statements mandate as the police role?

(3) *Populism*: What do public opinion surveys and other indicators suggest the public see as the police mission in principle?

(4) *Empirical study of policing in practice*: Why do people call the police? What is the demand for policing, as distinct from statements about the police role in the abstract? How do the police themselves view their role?

(5) *Police and crime control*: Given that crime control is a dominant modality in the police métier, to what extent are they successful or capable of achieving this?

(6) *Social functions of policing*: What are the broader social outcomes and effects of policework? Who benefits from these functions?

(7) *Conceptual analysis*: How can these six dimensions of debate about the police role be integrated theoretically? Is policing reducible to specifiable functions?

HISTORICAL CONCEPTIONS OF THE POLICE *RAISON D'ÊTRE*

The so-called Peelian Principles, supposedly hammered out by Peel, Rowan, and Mayne in the nineteenth century, continue to be regularly referenced in contemporary policy discussions (Emsley 2014). The 'nine principles' are arguably an invention of twenti-eth-century historians like Charles Reith (1940, 1956), embroidering Peel's brief initial 'instructions' to the Met's recruits (Lentz and Chaires 2007). The Peelian tradition sees the key roles of the police as the 'prevention of crime' and the preservation of 'public tranquility'. Public support is seen as essential for effective policing. Crime prevention and a broad service role are encouraged in order to facilitate policing by consent. Law enforcement and catching criminals are explicitly downplayed as evidence of failure in the primary police tasks of prevention and peacekeeping, and indeed are viewed as potentially undermining order by inflaming tensions. The fundamental shift these principles signalled was the establishment of the police as a specialist agency operating under representative democracy. This is underlined in the standard formulation of nine Peelian principles (crystallized by Reith 1940, 1956), still quoted on the British Home Office website as a continuing ideal:

1. To prevent crime and disorder, as an alternative to their repression by military force and severity of legal punishment.

2. To recognise always that the power of the police to fulfil their functions and duties is dependent on public approval of their existence, actions and behaviour and on their ability to secure and maintain public respect.

3. To recognise always that to secure and maintain the respect and approval of the public means also the securing of the willing co-operation of the public in the task of securing observance of laws.

4. To recognise always that the extent to which the co-operation of the public can be secured diminishes proportionately the necessity of the use of physical force and compulsion for achieving police objectives.

5. To seek and preserve public favour, not by pandering to public opinion; but by constantly demonstrating absolutely impartial service to law, in complete independence of policy, and without regard to the justice or injustice of the substance of individual laws, by ready offering of individual service and friendship to all members of the public without regard to their wealth or social standing, by ready exercise of courtesy and friendly good humour; and by ready offering of individual sacrifice in protecting and preserving life.

6. To use physical force only when the exercise of persuasion, advice and warning is found to be insufficient to obtain public co-operation to an extent necessary to secure observance of law or to restore order, and to use only the minimum degree of physical force which is necessary on any particular occasion for achieving a police objective.

7. To maintain at all times a relationship with the public that gives reality to the historic tradition that the police are the public and that the public are the police, the police being only members of the public who are paid to give full time attention to duties which are incumbent on every citizen in the interests of community welfare and existence.

8. To recognise always the need for strict adherence to police-executive functions, and to refrain from even seeming to usurp the powers of the judiciary of avenging individuals or the State, and of authoritatively judging guilt and punishing the guilty.

9. To recognise always that the test of police efficiency is the absence of crime and disorder, and not the visible evidence of police action in dealing with them.

Peelian Principles have continued to be influential, at least rhetorically, throughout Anglo-American police history (Kleinig 1996; Rowe 2014; Charman 2017). Lord Scarman's 1981 *Report on the Brixton Disorders*, to take an important example, was explicitly based on Mayne's 1829 formulation of the aims of police as: 'prevention of crime . . . protection of life and property, the preservation of public tranquillity'. It accepted Mayne's judgement that when these goals conflicted, discretion should be exercised, and strict law enforcement subordinated to safeguard public tranquillity. *Scarman* became Holy Writ for a generation of chief officers and policy-makers (Reiner 1991), and underlay the 1991 Operational Policing Review, an unprecedented cooperative venture between the representative bodies of all police ranks. It is echoed in the community policing philosophy that has been influential throughout the world (Kleinig 1996).

Despite the symbolic importance of the Peelian principles in policing, the actually existing British police tradition also incorporated other goals, such as a paramilitary riot control capacity. A key rationale for the creation of the Metropolitan Police was that the government should have an alternative to the military when responding to riotous political protest. In the first decade of their existence, the Metropolitan Police were dispatched regularly to provincial cities to quell public disorder, becoming 'something of a national riot squad' (Emsley 1983). The British police have always exhibited elements of military organization such as a parallel rank structure, military style uniforms, and of course one of the first commissioners of the Metropolitan Police—Lieutenant Colonel Sir Charles Rowan—was a former British Army officer. A late 1880s parliamentarian lamented that the police had become 'a quasi-military force, drilled, distributed and managed as soldiers . . . a cumbrous and badly-organised army' (Bailey 1981: 106). Nevertheless, the British police were generally successful in building a public image highlighting their civilian status (see Chapter 3).

While *The Scarman Report* is taken as the key restatement of Peelian policing and articulation of the 'community model' of the police (see Chapter 2), Scarman bemoaned the police lack of preparedness for disorder and recommended the development of the paramilitary policing function (Scarman 1981: paras 5.72–5.74). This was followed by the acquisition of flame-proof suits, NATO helmets, plastic bullets, CS gas, long shields, extendable truncheons, armoured vehicles, and a permanent paramilitary command and control training facility in West London known colloquially as 'riot city' (Waddington 1991). This form of policing does not quite square with Peelian principles because it permits repression by a (para)military force, casts sections of the public as enemies, negates the assumption of public cooperation, can justify the use of maximal force, and takes actions that judge guilt and inflict punishment such as baton strikes and the use of deadly force (Kraska 2001, 2007; Brown 2012; Balko 2014).

Similarly, although 'high policing' practices were eschewed by Peel, there was in fact widespread surveillance, intelligence gathering and infiltration of political movements, and close observation of ordinary criminality during the nineteenth century. A covert spy policing capacity was established in the formation of the Special Irish Branch in 1883 to deal with acts of terrorism targeted at the Houses of Parliament and railway stations (Ascoli 1979). Moreover, such secret intelligence has been described as 'the lifeblood of policing' and its use by the police 'as old as policing itself' (Gill 2000; HMIC 1997). The historical record shows that the police have run informers, worked undercover, and maintained card indexes and dossiers containing information organized by name and street address so as to keep tabs on local criminals (Gill 2000). The spy function of policing has always been downplayed historically and segmented organizationally through the creation of separate espionage institutions (MI5, MI6, GCHQ) at the national level whose distinctiveness is maintained by their lack of coercive law enforcement powers. Specialist police units based on the 'spy model' include the Special Demonstration Squad (1968) to infiltrate anti-war protest groups, the Illegal Immigration Intelligence Unit (1972), and the National Public Order Intelligence Unit (1999) to track environmental activists (Lewis and Evans 2014).

More generally, since the early 1990s police forces around the world have turned to the 'crime control model'; with the dominance of a tougher, more populist law-and-order conception of crime control, law enforcement is now a clear governmental priority. A renewed can-do confidence about policing has come to dominate policy throughout the Western world, bolstered by the ubiquitous fall of recorded crime rates from the mid-1990s until 2015–16. Tough and smart policing can and has cracked down on crime, claim police and policy-makers (Bratton 1998). Lip service continues to be paid to Peel's principles and their preventive priority, but this has been re-focused as 'putting the public in the driver's seat' in order to cut crime through 'common sense' policing (Home Office 2010: 3). As we have seen, this includes the incorporation of policing tactics based on espionage and militarization.

CONTEMPORARY GOVERNMENTAL AUTHORITY

We now turn to the functions advocated by contemporary public authorities and the policy statements about the police role. Since the 1970s, Anglo-American public and political debate on crime and justice has been dominated by the 'law-and-order' myth which portrays the police as an effective force for the prevention and detection of crime, and advocates police power as the panacea for law enforcement and public order problems (Reiner 2007: chap. 5; Rowe 2014; Morgan and Smith 2017). This has always been the primary representation of policing in mass news and entertainment media (Chapter 11), and in police subculture (see also Jewkes 2015). It was the position espoused by conservatives and the police in the late 1970s, at first controversially. Since the early 1990s, it has become the hegemonic, almost unquestioned perspective, as neo-liberalism became the embedded political consensus in most of the Western world. The erstwhile parties of the democratic left were born again as 'New', pushing out of mainstream debate the possibility of welfarist and Keynesian policies to tackle the root causes of crime and disorder in economy and culture. Rhetorically at least, a variety of 'third way' mythologies about policing also burgeoned in the 1990s, reflecting the broader quest for social policies 'beyond left and right' espoused by Blair's New Labour, Clintonian New Democrats, and other self-styled middle-way governments seeking to distance themselves from the truncheon-rattling rhetoric of 1980s Thatcherites and Reaganites.

'Community policing' remains a fashionable label internationally in police policy discussions, largely because of its apparently benign and uncontentious 'cherry pie' connotations (Brogden 1999; Ellison and Pino 2012; Manning 2010). Effective policework is possible only on the basis of public consent and cooperation. In some innocuous seeming rhetoric this proposition was combined with visions of policing as a social service, delivering good works to a harmonious community of satisfied customers, into a full-blown mythology. In so far as this idyll is not realized in today's harsh and conflict-ridden world, policy must be aimed at restoring it. Its apparent antithesis was 'zero tolerance' policing (Jones and Newburn 2006: chap. 5; Punch 2007). This was also a worldwide police slogan. A variety of community policing bridged a perceived gap between it, and the ZTP approach, euphemistically referred to as 'broken windows' policing (Kelling and Bratton 2015). In North America the 'weed and seed' analogy is popular, based on a marketing campaign for a mixture of weedkiller and fertilizer for gardeners keen on green grass. With 'weed and seed' policing, ZTP weeds out anti-social behaviour and community policing seeds safe and peaceful communities (Sheptycki 2018c).

The forensic version of 'third way' policing is the 'magic bullet' myth, epitomized by the flourishing *CSI* genre of scientific detection programmes (Byers and Johnson 2009).

Through the appliance of science, by research and analysis on policing problems, it is possible to develop tactics delivering precisely the right degree of force necessary for effective yet legitimate crime control and order maintenance (e.g. Sherman 1990). This view suggests that intelligently targeted policing can, using laser-like precision, excise crime and disorder with minimal negative side effects for civil liberties or social justice. At one level it is impossible to question the project, however, as with community policing, the questions are not over the desirability of ILP but its feasibility as a strategy for achieving public safety and security (Sheptycki 2017c; Gundhus et al. 2017).

To some extent, the complexity of the police role has been recognized by governmental authorities such as the UK College of Policing, the National Crime Agency, and Her Majesty's Inspectorate of Constabulary. The College of Policing is the professional body set up by the government in 2012 'to provide those working in policing with the skills and knowledge to prevent crime, protect the public and secure public trust'. The College's wide-ranging offer of standard-setting, a national policing curriculum, and standard operating practices acknowledges the breadth of the policing function. For example, police training in 'ensuring public safety' encompasses emergency first-responders' procedures in a wide variety of contexts involving interoperability with other emergency services, disaster victim identification, public order, firearms, roads policing and police driving, as well as first-aid and personal safety.

British government pronouncements about the purposes of policing embodied a substantial shift as neo-liberalism became firmly entrenched (Reiner 2007: chap. 5). Neo-liberal orthodoxy was made explicit in the Conservative government's 1993 *Police Reform* White Paper: 'The main job of the police is to catch criminals' (Home Office 1993: s. 2.2). The thief-taking priority was undercut by the very next sentence: 'In a typical day, however, only about 18 per cent of calls to the police are about crime.' In fact, a significant proportion of frontline policework involves people in mental and psychological states of distress. These people are another category of neo-liberalism's victims, as public funding for mental health services has been severely cut. On the grounds of public safety this leaves the police with a burden of responsibility. In the law-and-order perspective this is not an indication of effective public demand. Rather public demand is equated by governments with the populist views indicated in surveys. This was the explicit rationale for the new police governance arrangements introduced in 2012 by the British government, as expressed by the then Prime Minister David Cameron: 'People are going to be voting in their own law-and-order champion: one person who sets the budgets, sets the priorities; hires and fires the chief constable; bangs heads together to get things done . . . If you want more tough policing, you can get it' (Cameron 2012: 5).

At a more general level, there seems to be a consensus in governmental definitions of the goals of police: a core function of crime control with an ancillary public service role. However, there have been some important shifts in thinking, meaning that policing is 'being transformed and restructured in the modern world' (Bayley and Shearing 2001). There is extensive debate about the nature of this change and how it is to be understood and conceptualized (Bayley and Shearing 1996), but many scholars agree that far-reaching changes are under way. A key idea is that governmental authority is fragmenting *upwards* to transnational and global bodies (see Chapter 9), *downwards* to subnational bodies (see Chapter 11), and *sideways* to private, non-governmental bodies (see Chapter 8). These shifts, it is claimed, are bringing about changes in the organization and goals of policework, the rise of a proactive, risk-oriented outlook, and the establishment of a significantly more complex policing division of labour (see Chapter 8). The changing morphology of the state has led to the claim it is but one of many authorizing agencies or 'auspices' of policing alongside transnational agencies, private bodies, and 'responsibilized' citizens. This process of 'multilateralization' is such a substantial a shift away from the traditional state-centred view of policing that many authors now argue that we should now be talking about the 'governance of security' rather than policing (Johnston and Shearing 2003).

POPULIST CONCEPTIONS OF THE POLICE ROLE

What popular demand for policing is in the abstract can be probed by public opinion surveys and by content analysis of media representations. The latter offer a guide to what 'information' about policing people are exposed to, as surveys indicate that mass news and entertainment media are the principal source of 'knowledge' about policing (Fitzgerald *et al.* 2002: figure 6.1, p.78). The mass media frame public debate about policing, feeding into policy formulation and practice (Cavender 2004; Jewkes 2015; Hough and Roberts 2017; Greer and McLaughlin 2017). Content analyses show that media representations of policing and criminal justice follow a 'law of opposites' (Surette 2014). They greatly exaggerate both the prevalence of crime and its seriousness (Greer and Reiner 2012). This has always been the case but has become much more pronounced over time (Reiner 2016b: chap. 6). For many years, surveys suggested that popular views of the police role echo the crime control priorities of recent official statements, for example Home Affairs Select Committee Report, *New Landscape of Policing: Annex C* (House of Commons 2011; Greenhalgh and Gibbs 2014: chap.4; Muir 2017). Police officers themselves initially tend to be crime control and law enforcement oriented but with experience and training most police modify their views, coming to see public protection and service as central (Charman 2017). Although many sections of the media have a nuanced view of the police, there are many who reassert the 'law-and-order myth', for example the *Daily Telegraph* leader comment of 10 September 2018 declared that 'The public wants the police to be a force not a "service"—one that upholds law and order. It also expects the police to focus on preventing street violence and investigating offences like burglaries.'

The most recent public opinion surveys suggest a more nuanced view of the role of the police that recognizes the importance of emergency service alongside crime control. In a series of reports for HMIC, the social research organization MORI (2017, 2018) found that 'responding in person to emergencies' (67 per cent) was seen by the public as the first priority for the police time and resources nationally in 2017 compared with 'tackling crime of all types' (63 per cent) and 'countering terrorism and extremism' (56 per cent). Next in importance were 'providing local foot patrols' (37 per cent), responding to online crime (17 per cent), maintaining road safety (13 per cent), and responding in person to *non-emergencies* (MORI 2018: 200). The MORI surveys also suggest that that police are thought to have an important role in ensuring the safety of vulnerable people such as victims of stalking (70 per cent), missing people (60 per cent), and victims of domestic violence (48 per cent). We turn now to another source of information about the public demand for policing expressed by actual requests for service.

EMPIRICAL RESEARCH ON WHAT POLICE DO

The research dialectic began with the empirical 'discovery' that the police mainly operate not as crime-fighters or law-enforcers, but as providers of a range of services to the public. Banton (1964) was the first empirical study of the police in the UK and one of the first in the world. On the evidence from field diaries kept by a sample of Scottish policemen, observation, and interviews (both in Britain and in the USA) he concluded that the patrolling constable is primarily a 'peace officer' rather than a 'law officer' (Banton 1964: 127). In the USA, Cumming, Cumming, and Edell (1965) found in an analysis of phone calls by the public to a police department that over half involved demands for help or support in relation to personal and interpersonal problems, in which the police performed as 'philosopher, guide, and friend'. Although, half a century later, it seems unlikely that Cumming *et al*.'s formulation survives in a more complex and fractious world, the general pattern of policing as emergency order maintenance and problem solving has been confirmed by numerous subsequent studies in many different parts of the world (McCabe and Sutcliffe 1978; Morris and Heal 1981: chap. 3; Waddington 1993, 1999a: chap. 1; Bayley 1994; Morgan and Newburn 1997; Johnston 2000a: chap. 3; Skogan and Frydl 2004: 57–63). The late Jean-Paul Brodeur reviewed fifty-one studies conducted by a variety of methods in many jurisdictions and concluded that forty-six of these showed that crime constitutes under 50 per cent of policework and two-thirds found it to be less than 33 per cent (Brodeur 2010: 158–9).

The most recent analysis of national Command and Control data by the British College of Policing found that 83 per cent of all emergency calls to the police were to incidents unrelated to crime (College of Policing 2015: 9). In 2012–13, there were just under 20 million incidents recorded by the police, 38 per cent of which received an emergency response, 42 per cent were resolved over the phone, and the remainder received a scheduled visit. More than two million incidents of anti-social behaviour were recorded in 2012–13, 65 per cent of which were reports of non-criminal nuisance behaviour. There were also one million calls for domestic abuse-related incidents. Data from police services suggest, however, that the demand generated by 'public safety and welfare' incidents now leads the way (College of Policing 2015). Another area where forces are reporting increased levels of demand is responding to people with mental health problems, which requires not only attendance to a person in distress or causing disturbance to others, but also a growing number of people who are being detained in police cells under the Mental Health Act. Add to this demand the police being called out to most of the approximately 6,000 suicides that occur each year, reports of 280,000 missing persons, demands for child protection, and those associated with protective statutory requirements relating to dangerous people (e.g. Multi-Agency Public Protection Panels). Add in that the Civil Contingencies Act 2004 places a legal responsibility on the Police Service to provide an appropriate response to emergencies, meaning that they must be prepared to deal with a major accident or natural hazard which requires a national response such as health pandemic. The empirical effective demand for policing expressed in practice clearly contradicts the demand of the government that the police pursue 'just one objective—to cut crime' (May 2011). The police matter far 'beyond the myth of crime-fighting', although government policy sees its role as being to release *'the police's inner crime-fighter'* (Loader 2013: 43).

POLICE AND CRIME CONTROL

The rise and fall of crime

As we have seen, the idea of crime control has dominated both historical and contemporary discussions of what the police do. It has also been central to debates about *how well* the police do their job, to the extent that the police role and effectiveness has been understood largely, if not exclusively, in terms of recorded crime statistics. Relying on the rise and fall of recorded crime is problematic as a measure of actual offending rates and of police performance: definitions of crime change over time, as does public behaviour in reporting crime and police organizations in recording it; each change can have the effect of producing artificial changes in crime statistics (Reiner 2007: chap. 4; Reiner 2016b: 106–14). Nonetheless, crime data are widely used. Among these, it is widely agreed that recorded homicides have been fairly accurately recorded over a long period and provide a reasonable indicator of changing patterns of crime. Even when account has been taken of artefacts in crime statistics, there is the difficult question of cause and effect. It is extremely difficult to produce definitive evidence that isolates the impact of the police, or of a particular innovation in policing.

With these caveats in mind, it seems clear that British cities became significantly less violent, crime ridden, and disorderly during the course of the nineteenth and early twentieth century (Eisner 2003, 2014, 2015). This has been attributed to the advance of social pacification, the gradual reduction in the carrying of weapons, and other factors related to the 'civilizing process' that occurred over this period (Johnson and Monkkonen 1996; Elias 2000; Pinker 2011: 147–50). It seems plausible that the emergence of the police at this historical moment contributed to establishing a baseline of order and crime control by providing access to justice and social security (Levitt 2004; Zimring 2007). The gradual reduction in violent crime in most Western industrialized countries continued until the middle of the twentieth century (Eisner 2003; Pinker, 2011). The period immediately after the Second World War was characterized by relatively low rates of violent crime and public disorder, low levels of public anxiety about crime, and high levels of police legitimacy. For a brief period, it appeared that the police crime control mission had been accomplished and the British police were considered to be a successful public institution that was 'working well' (Banton 1964: iv).

From the late 1950s, however, recorded crime of all kinds, including homicide and other violent crime, burglary, robbery, and theft began to increase rapidly (Reiner 2007, 2016b). At the same time the conflict between police and people began to become more fractious, especially among more marginal social groups (Hall *et al.* 1978). Increasing crime was alarming to police chiefs, politicians and the general public, and this trend has continued in recent times (Rowe 2014; Jewkes 2015). The conviction that the police were able to control crime held fast even as crime rates rose, and many police administrators and Conservative politicians believed that all that was required was an increase in police power and resources. Police budgets increased to facilitate additional recruitment of police officers many of whom were deployed to specialist law enforcement functions (Audit Commission 1993; Maguire 2008; Brodeur 2010; Bacon 2016). The only opposition to the law-and-order lobby were the civil libertarians who argued that police effectiveness must not be bought at too high a price by the undermining of civil rights (Fielding 2005: chap. 6).

As crime rates continued to climb throughout the 1970s and 1980s, police research in the USA and Britain questioned the assumption that increased police power and resources could control crime at all (Clarke and Hough 1980, 1984; Morris and Heal 1981; Bayley 1994; Morgan and Newburn 1997). The first social scientific study to address the question of the relationship between police patrol strength and crime rates was the celebrated Kansas City preventive patrol experiment (Kelling *et al.* 1974). This found that doubling patrol strength or removing it altogether made no significant differences to crime rates, fear of crime, or satisfaction with the police. Although the study attracted some academic criticism and initial hostility from police chiefs (see Larson 1976; Skogan and Frydl 2004: 226), it came to be generally accepted as establishing that increasing motorized patrols did not, in itself, have an effect on crime rates (Clarke and Hough 1984). In an influential paper, the Audit Commission calculated that each patrolling officer typically covered an area containing: 18,000 inhabitants, 7,500 houses, twenty-three pubs, nine schools, 140 miles of pavement, eighty-five acres of parks or open space, and seventy-seven miles of road (Audit Commission 1996; Morgan and Newburn 1997: 126). The clear lesson was that the number of potential targets of crime, especially in urban areas, was simply too large to be covered effectively by police patrols of any feasible visibility and frequency (Clarke and Hough 1984). If car patrols have little 'scarecrow effect' and are unlikely to come across a crime in progress, perhaps a rapid response to emergency calls might have a crime control impact by apprehending criminals? But research again produced negative results: the overwhelming majority of 'crime-related' calls for service were discovered long after the event with the result that an on-scene arrest was made in only 3 per cent of cases (Pate *et al.* 1976; Clarke and Hough 1984; Skogan and Frydl 2004; see also Vidal and Kirchmaier (2018) who found, contrary to previous evidence, large and significant effects of rapid response).

The research evidence of the 1970s and 1980s ushered in a new cautionary attitude to the effectiveness of increased police spending, striking a harmonious note with the fiscal parsimony of the conservative regimes dominant in Britain and North America in the early 1980s (Reiner and Cross 1991: chap. 1). It also chimed in with the more general mood of 'nothing works' in criminal justice (Garland 2001: 61–3). A major shift in thinking about the crime control effect of the police occurred in the mid-1990s, stimulated by statistical evidence that recorded crime in the USA and UK had hit a peak and had started to fall. In the UK, crime of all types started to fall in 1993 and continued to do so every subsequent year until 2015. A broadly similar picture is true for the USA. The most celebrated crime drop of all was the 'New York miracle' that has acquired legendary status worldwide (Bowling 1999a; Karmen 2000; Blumstein 1999; Golub *et al.* 2004; MacDonald 2006; Zimring 2007, 2011; Pinker 2011). Particularly striking were the reductions in murder. From an all-time high of 2,262 in 1991, the murder count crashed by two-thirds to 767 within the six years to 1997 and continued to fall more or less every year, down to 292 in 2017. For comparison, London, which has a similar population, had 147 homicides in 1991 (the New York peak) and 130 in 2017. Unsurprisingly the police stepped in quickly to take credit, explaining the large increases in police resources, 'smarter management', and new crime control tactics as the reason for the drop (Dennis 1998; Silverman 1999, Bratton 1998). Within a relatively short period of time, the pessimism about the crime control effects of the police was replaced by wild optimism, causing the US magazine *Newsweek*, to declare 'the end of crime as we know it' (Bowling 1999a).

Zero Tolerance

Zero tolerance is the most celebrated crime control success story in recent history. Strict enforcement of what were sometimes referred to as 'quality of life offences' was based on the highly influential 'broken windows' hypothesis that serious crime flourishes where signs of disorder are left untended (Kelling and Wilson 1982). In the US magazine the *Atlantic Monthly* William Kelling and J. Q. Wilson argued that effective policing required the aggressive enforcement of the minor crimes and misdemeanours of disorderly people. These were 'not violent people, nor, necessarily, criminals', but rather the 'disreputable or obstreperous or unpredictable people: panhandlers, drunks, addicts, rowdy teenagers, prostitutes, loiterers, the mentally disturbed' many of whom would be ethnic minority citizens policed by mostly white police officers (Kelling and Wilson 1982: 29; Zimring 2007, 2011). In practical terms, zero tolerance policing meant relentless on-street interrogation and conducting personal searches on all suspicious people. Although the language of zero tolerance was new, the idea of aggressive patrol had been experimented with since the early 1970s with contradictory views on the results (Wilson and Boland 1978, 1981; Jacob and Rich 1981). Systematic research evidence, however, suggests that the crime drop had wider and multiple sources (Bowling 1999a; Silverman 1999; Karmen 2000; Zimring 2011). It is also clear that, like all aggressive policing tactics, 'quality of life policing' has the downside of exacerbating discrimination and alienating the people that it targets, being identified as the cause of the escalation of police violence across the USA (see McArdle and Erzen 2001; Golub *et al.* 2004; Jefferson 2015; Patton *et al.* 2016; Newberry 2017).

The language of zero tolerance was incorporated into the mainstream of the British policing lexicon in January 1997 when it was endorsed by Tony Blair, on the eve of New Labour's landslide election (Bowling 1999a; Punch 2009). Blair had, as Shadow Home Secretary, paved the way for the introduction of 'suspicionless searches' targeted at terrorism and serious violence in the 1994 Criminal Justice and Public Order Act. Between 2006 and 2009 there was a massive escalation of the use of the powers, rising to nearly 400,000 recorded searches per year at the peak of their use (Bowling and Marks 2017). The reasons for this escalation can be explained by a change in the interpretation of the laws by the police, which were in turn the result of the enthusiasm of the New Labour government for the extensive use of stop and search and a highly permissive operational policy (ibid.). The use of stop and search has been highly politicized, with arguments being made that it prevents crime through deterrence. Nevertheless stop and search has been viewed as having a negative impact on the individuals it is used against, and on wider police legitimacy.

In the earliest study of proactive enforcement, a quasi-experiment in San Diego, Boydstun (1975) found that when stop and searches were abandoned, no significant change in crime occurred across all sites. More recent research evidence bears out these early findings. (see McCandles *et al.* 2016; MacDonald *et al.* 2016; see also Smith *et al.* 2012; Rosenfeld and Fornango 2014). Weisburd used very finely grained analysis of crime data in New York in the context of hotspots policing and concluded that 'stop, question, frisk' had a small but statistically significant effect on crime but the size of the effect varied widely across different boroughs. Overall, their analysis suggested that 700,000 extra stops would reduce crime by 2 per cent. Tiratelli, Quinton, and Bradford (2018) examined the deterrent effect of stop and search based on ten years of data in London from 2004 to 2014. The authors examined the impact of both 'reasonable suspicion' and 'suspicionless searches' on those crimes susceptible to detection. Their overall finding was that stop and search has 'relatively little deterrent effect' (Tiratelli, Quinton, and Bradford 2018: 1225; see also Fagan 2016). They found 'no evidence for effects on robbery and theft, vehicle crime or criminal damage, and inconsistent evidence of very small effects on burglary, non-domestic violent crime and total crime; the only strong evidence was for effects on drug offences'.

Looking separately at suspicionless searches, Tiratelli *et al.* (2018) concluded that the sudden surge in usage had no effect on the underlying trend in violent crime. Tiratelli also suggests that stop and search 'may also play a structural role linked to the basic function of police as an institution of social ordering: a way for police to discipline and ascribe identity to the populations they police' (Tiratelli *et al.* 2018), particularly impacting on marginal groups (McAra and McVie 2005; Bradford and Loader 2016; Bradford 2016). The weight of evidence is that the power to stop and search cannot be justified—at least at the aggregate level—as a crime control tool. The evidence suggests that the idea that stop and search is a 'vital tool' in the crime-fighter's toolbox is a myth, but one that is held tightly by politicians, police leaders, the media, and the public because, as 'opposed to inaction [stop and search] is, if nothing else, a visible way of "doing something about crime"' (Tiratelli *et al.* 2018: 1227). If stop and search is to avoid damage to public trust and police legitimacy it should only be used for the investigation of specific crimes and limited to appropriate situations (Tiratelli *et al.* 2018; Bowling and Phillips 2007).

Clearing up crime

The investigative function has also been a key feature of the discussion of the police role in crime control. The police are the 'gatekeepers' of the criminal justice system, in that they are the main agency to which members of the public first report crime, and have specific obligations in terms of investigating crime, preparing cases for prosecution, and managing suspects held in custody (Skinns *et al.* 2017). The need to grade reported cases more formally according to their prospects of solvability became apparent during the 1980s as crime levels grew and so did the pressure on the police to enhance their appearance of efficiency, effectiveness, and economy. But first attempts to screen out cases according to explicit criteria of formality attracted condemnation when they were revealed to the public. However, as New Public Management (NPM), target specification, and monitoring intensified in the 1990s, more formalized systems came to be adopted, culminating in the 2000s when a formal operating system, the Volume Crime Management Model (VCMM) became standard, meaning that only leads with a reasonable chance of resulting in a positive outcome (i.e. arrest, prosecution) are followed up (O'Neill 2018).

The conventional method of evaluating criminal investigation work is the proportion of reported crimes where a suspect has been identified or the case is otherwise 'cleared up'. Before the Second World War the clear-up rate for recorded offences was usually over 50 per cent, but fell to 28 per cent by the end of the 2000s (Walker *et al.* 2009: 133–4). Since 2015, clear up rates have been replaced with data focusing more on specific outcomes. In 2018, 9 per cent of all crimes resulted in an offender being charged or summonsed, 1.8 per cent had a formal out of court disposal (such as a caution), and 2.6 per cent an informal warning or community resolution. Among those where there was no action, in just under half of cases (48 per cent) no suspect was identified, 20 per cent were closed because the victim did not support further action being taken, and in a further 9 per cent there were evidential difficulties (Home Office 2018: table 2.1). The proportion of cases resulting in an offender being charged varies widely for different crimes. It remains high for homicide (92 per cent), but is low for violence against the person (11 per cent), robbery (9 per cent), and for sexual offences (5 per cent) compared with 7 per cent for theft offences and 5.5 per cent for criminal damage (ibid.: table 2.2).

The clear-up rate is a notoriously problematic measure of detective effectiveness (Audit Commission 1990b; Gill 1987; Maguire 2007; Hough and Mayhew 1983; Reiner 2007: chap. 3; Walker et al. 2009: 24–42; Pogarsky and Laughran 2016; Nagin 2016). Studies of detective work show that only a relatively small number of major incident enquiries fit the model of 'classical' detection, starting from the crime itself and systematically investigating those with motive and opportunity to commit it (Maguire and Norris 1992; Ericson 1993; Innes 2003, 2007; Maguire 2008). A major finding of studies of the process by which detectives clear up crimes is that information is their lifeblood (Gill 2000; John and Maguire 2003, 2007; Maguire 2008). If adequate information is provided when officers arrive at a scene, to pinpoint the culprit fairly accurately, the crime will be resolved; if not, it is almost certain not to be (Chatterton 1976; Sanders 1977; Greenwood et al. 1977; Bottomley and Coleman 1981; Burrows and Tarling 1982; Maguire and Norris 1992; Innes 2003, 2007; Foster 2008). The crucial importance of initial information highlights not only the central role of the public in clearing up offences, but also the important part played by the uniformed branch. Most crimes are cleared up almost immediately, as a result of the offender still being at the scene when the police arrive or being named or fully and accurately described by victim or witnesses (Steer 1980).

Thus, only a small proportion of crimes are cleared up by investigative techniques bearing any resemblance to either the 'classical' or the 'bureaucratic' modes beloved by fiction. Most solved cases are essentially self-clearing. This does not mean that detectives are useless or inefficient (Morris and Heal 1981: 33; see also Maguire 2008: 440–1). There is also, of course, the relatively small but significant category of cases where the perpetrator is not initially known ('whodunits' in detectives' jargon) but which are nonetheless successfully cleared up by methods including the 'classical' and 'bureaucratic' modes and the construction and exploration of possible narratives explaining the crime (Innes 2003, 2007). However, the pressure on detectives to achieve more 'primary' clear-ups (not based on post-arrest or sentence interviewing) has led to increasing use of innovative methods which may themselves be ethically, legally, and practically problematic.

Proactive tactics also include covert methods such as undercover work, technological surveillance including video and audio recording, intercepting phone calls and internet communications, and running informers who are themselves offenders (Marx 1988, 1992; Audit Commission 1993; Greer 1995; Maguire and John 1995, 1996; Fijnaut and Marx 1995; Sheptycki 2000b; Norris and Armstrong 1999; Dunnighan and Norris 1999; Norris and Dunnighan 2000; Heaton 2000; Maguire 2000; Billingsley et al. 2000; Clark 2007; Sheptycki 2017c; Gill and Phythian 2018). There is scope for more effective management and coordination of the detective function (Maguire 2008), especially through 'case-screening' to distinguish crimes according to 'solvability' (and whether they should be allocated to CID or uniformed branches for investigation), more professional leadership of major enquiries (Smith and Flanagan 2000), and more effective proactive 'targeting' of some serious offences and offenders (Cope 2008). However, given the proliferation of recorded crimes and other demands for service relative to police resources (Audit Commission 1993; Morgan and Newburn 1997: 57), and the constraints on legitimate tactics in a liberal democracy (Weisburd *et al.* 1993), the prospects of successful investigation will always be limited.

Improvements in crime reduction and detection have also been claimed for proactive, problem-oriented, and intelligence-led approaches (Leigh *et al.* 1996; Maguire 2000, 2008; Williamson 2008; Tilley 2008; Cope 2008; Ratcliffe 2016; Brown *et al.*, 2018). The thinking behind these innovations is that traditional tactics fail because they spread scarce police resources too thinly across all victims, targets, and perpetrators of crime, whether in the form of preventive or detective activities. 'Smart' policing uses the analysis of crime and disorder patterns to target prevention and detection efforts at the most likely victims and offenders. While such approaches are likely to be more effective than traditional ones, there remains doubt about their efficacy in achieving substantial degrees of crime reduction (Jordan 1998). There is also considerable potential for unethical practices and encroachments on civil liberties, for example through intrusive forms of surveillance, and the abuse of informers and other undercover tactics (Marx 1988, 1992; Greer 1995; Fijnaut and Marx 1995; Norris and Armstrong 1999; Norris and Dunnighan 2000; Sheptycki 2000d, 2000c, 2017b; Billingsley *et al.* 2000; Neyroud and Beckley 2012; Goold 2004, 2009, 2016). Nonetheless, governments' search for 'magic bullets' has encouraged the proliferation of such approaches.

Evaluating crime reduction

A crucial difficulty in evaluating policing innovations is the absence of reliable and valid measures of police performance (Reiner 1998). One of the most methodologically self-conscious projects to evaluate policing initiatives concluded that measures of good practice could be developed meaningfully only in relation to specific areas of policework, not globally, and were inescapably political (Horton 1989). Nonetheless, since the 1980s successive governments' hunt for value for money in public services has led to the search for more adequate performance indicators in policing (Audit Commission 1990a, 1990b). HM Inspectorate of Constabulary in particular have developed an ever-more elaborate matrix of indicators for their annual assessments of forces (Bradley *et al.* 1986; Hough 1987; Weatheritt 1993; Butler 1992; Morgan and Newburn 1997; Savage *et al.* 2000: chap. 1; Savage 2007: chaps 3, 5). It is unlikely that these have overcome the intractable problems of measuring police effectiveness. The conclusion that we draw from the research is that there is little compelling evidence that policing has a significant impact on crime (see Table 5.2). It is not as simple as 'nothing works'; a fairer assessment is that some things work, in some places, when social and economic conditions are favourable (Sherman *et al.* 1997; Jordan 1998; Waddington 1999b: 4–12; Telep and Weisburd 2012: see table 4). The difficulty is disentangling the effect of 'good policework' with changes in the economic and social context. There is also evidence that policing, when carried out badly, is not merely ineffective, but is also counterproductive, potentially contributing to increases in crime and undermining security and legitimacy and engendering defiance (Tyler 1990).

Table 5.2 Police and crime control

Strategy	Underlying hypothesis	Effectiveness	Evidence
Increase police numbers	More police = less crime	Inconclusive	Kelling *et al.* (1974); Clarke and Hough (1984); Levitt (2004); Farrell (2013)
Random patrol	Deterrence through police omnipresence	Ineffective	Kelling *et al.* (1974); Sherman and Weisburd (1995); Audit Commission (1996); McGarrell *et al.* (2001); Telep and Weisburd (2012)
Mandatory arrest	More arrests = less crime	Effective in some contexts, ineffective in others; can result in defiance	Sirles, Lipchik, and Kowalski (1993); Sherman and Berk (1984); Maxwell *et al.* (2002); Dugan (2003); Iyengar (2009)
Community contact in general	More and better community contact = less crime	Inconclusive	Skolnick and Bayley (1988); Trojanowicz and Bucqueroux (1990); Fielding (1995); Bottoms and Tankebe (2012)
Contact with young people in particular	More and better contact with young people = less crime	Ineffective	Heal and Laycock (1987); Bernburg and Krohn (2003); Poyner (1993); Dodge *et al.* (2014); Vidal and Kirchmaier (2018)
Rapid response	The faster the response to incidents = less crime	Inconclusive	Pate *et al.* (1976); Coupe and Griffiths (1996); Sherman and Eck (2002)
Intelligence-led policing	Target prolific offences or offenders, increased arrest rate = less crime	Effective in some contexts	Maguire (2000); Innes (2000); Cope (2008); Ratcliffe (2016); Brown *et al.* (2018)
Directed patrol	Focus patrol on 'hot spots' and 'hot times' = less crime	Effective in some contexts	Sherman and Weisburd (1995); Frogner *et al.* (2013); Rosenfeld *et al.* (2014)
Target repeat victims	Protecting victims = less crime	Effective in some contexts	Forrester *et al.* (1988); Chenery *et al.* (1997); Farrell and Pease (2001); Stokes and Clare (2018)

Inter-agency working	Partnership between police and other agencies = less crime	Inconclusive	Liddle and Gelsthorpe (1994); Weatheritt (1986); Bowling (1999b: 101–45); Kemshall and Maguire (2001)
Problem-oriented policing	Analysis of crime patterns, addressing underlying causes through solving problems = less crime	Inconclusive	Goldstein (1990); Leigh *et al.* (1996); Laycock and Farrell (2003); Braga (2008, 2014); Eck and Spelman (2016)
Zero tolerance/ aggressive order maintenance	Crackdowns on minor offences lead to reductions in more serious offences	Inconclusive; risks public disorder	Bowling (1999b); Bratton (1998); Dennis (1998); Hopkins-Burke (1998); Jones and Newburn (2006); Jefferson (2015); Patton *et al.* (2016); Newberry (2017)
Proactive stop/ search	Increases in use of stop and search powers = decrease in crime	Inconclusive; risks public disorder	Boydstun (1975); Wilson and Boland (1978); Miller *et al.* (2000); Weber and Bowling (2014); Tiratelli *et al.* (2018)

The politics of the police shifted radically in the lead up to the 2010 General Election (Bowling and Marks 2017: 84). The Tory manifesto promised to roll back the Labour 'control state' and to curtail state intrusion into private life. It specifically promised to scrap the New Labour government's plans for ID cards and curtail DNA data retention. It accused Labour of creating the 'worst of all worlds—intrusive, ineffective and enormously expensive'. Shortly after the election, Theresa May, then Home Secretary, promised to abolish counter-terrorism suspicionless searches because they infringed the 'civil liberties of every one of us.'[1] Between 2009 and 2016 the use of suspicionless searches fell dramatically from 350,000 to under 1,000. The Conservative-Liberal coalition also began a programme of marked reductions to spending on the police as an important element of the policy of austerity. Having had decades of large increases in police spending from under £10 billion in the mid-2000s to nearly £14 billion in 2010, spending fell back to under £12 billion in 2014 before increasing again in 2015. In line with the spending patterns, the number of police officers in England and Wales rose steadily through the second half of the twentieth century from around 107,000 in the 1970s and reached a peak of 141,859 in 2009 (Reiner 2007: 134–5; Bullock 2008). Since then, police numbers have dropped quite sharply to 122,404 as of 31 March 2018, the fewest police officers since comparable records began in 1996 (House of Commons

---

[1] Home Office, 'Theresa May today tells Parliament that the government will change how stop and search powers are used under the Terrorism Act' (London: Home Office) 8 July 2010.

2018). For seven years after the 2007–8 financial crisis budgets tightened, the number of police fell, stop and search powers were severely curtailed; and recorded crime fell. Then in 2016, the picture changed again with a sharp increase in recorded crime that year which has been followed by further increases. In 2018 data showed striking increases in recorded crime (including a 16 per cent increase in knife crime, 12 per cent increase in homicide, 6 per cent increase in burglaries, and a 30 per cent increase in robberies). This prompted a rash of newspaper headlines such as 'Epidemic of violence', a 'Public health emergency' and claims that 'policing in the UK is on the critical list' (*Guardian*, 19 July 2018). The over-riding narrative was that the recent rise in crime had been caused by cuts in policing, reductions in stop and search, and by the impact of austerity on neighbourhood policing and broader social networks.

BROAD SOCIAL FUNCTIONS OF THE POLICE

In the wake of a growing crisis of legitimacy fanned by more violent forms of disorder in many countries, community policing became a new orthodoxy for a generation of progressive police administrators, chiefs, and commentators. The essence was that 'is' meant 'ought'. The police were de facto social workers, although not recognized as such; they were the 'secret social service' (Punch 1979b). But because this was covert and seldom articulated, there was a need for the police to be better trained and organized to cope with the work that anyway accounted for most of their activity. If the law-and-order panacea for police problems was bigger guns, the communitarian's was a sociology degree. Some argued that the mandate of crime prevention ought to mean more than the traditional techniques of patrol and detection. They should collaborate with other social service agencies and government to tackle the underlying social problems generating crime and disorder, rather than just suppressing the symptoms (Stephens and Becker 1994). In British police circles this view was championed above all by John Alderson, ex-chief constable of Devon and Cornwall, in his community policing philosophy (Alderson 1979 1984, 1998), and in the USA by former Chicago police administrator Professor Herman Goldstein (Goldstein 1979, 1990). This thinking was very influential in policy circles and among policy-oriented academics who carried out evaluations of the 'multi-agency approach' and 'coordinated crime prevention' in the late 1980s and early 1990s (Sampson *et al.* 1988/2017; Bowling and Saulsbury 1992; Bowling 1999b).

While this consensus was emerging at the top, there was a developing underswell of protest in the police rank and file. A plethora of research has shown that street-level police culture tends towards an action and crime-fighting orientation (Charman 2017). This was pithily summed up by one American patrolman: 'Every time you begin to do some real police work you get stuck with this stuff. I guess 90 per cent of all police work is bullshit' (Reiss 1971: 42; see also Rubin 1972, Kleinig 1996: 11). The 1990 *Operational Policing Review* survey of national samples of senior and rank-and-file police confirmed that this gulf still existed. However, the Conservative government's 1993–4 reform package, comprising a White Paper (Home Office 1993), the *Sheehy Report* (Sheehy 1993), and the Police and Magistrates' Courts Act 1994—explicitly sought to restructure the police on a 'businesslike' model aimed at the sole priority of 'catching criminals' (Savage 2007: chap. 3; McLaughlin 2007: 96–7, 182–7).

THE POLICE ROLE: CONCEPTUAL ISSUES

The force-service debate that has long bedevilled discussions of the police role rests on a false dichotomy: there is an excluded middle: first-aid order maintenance. Two cross-cutting dimensions underlie the distinctions between aspects of policework, generating four types of contrasting police action, not two (see Table 5.3):

(a) is there consensus or conflict between the civilians and the police in an interaction?

(b) does the police action invoke the legal powers of arrest, prosecution, and so on? Putting the two dimensions together yields a typology of four possible types of police intervention:

Table 5.3 Dimensions of policework

	Police do not use legal powers	Police use legal powers
Consensus	service	voluntary compliance
Conflict	order maintenance	law enforcement

The third cell in Table 5.3—law enforcement in a consensus situation—is a controversial area. If there is genuinely no conflict about desired outcomes between civilian and police participants in an interaction, there is no need for the invocation of legal powers, which are inherently coercive. However, police regularly detain individuals at police stations to 'assist with enquiries', without formally exercising their legal powers, claiming compliance has been 'voluntary'. There is room for much doubt about how often such compliance is genuinely voluntary. It is likely to be more often based on ignorance about rights, subtle coercion, and bluff by the police (McKenzie et al. 1990; Dixon 1997; Choongh 1997; Ericson 1982: 147–8).

An influential theory of the police role argues that it is best analysed not in terms of any of the social functions attributed to the police but to the special character of *the means* the police can bring to bear (Bittner 1970, 1974; Brodeur 2007, 2010; Reiner 2015). Echoing Weber's classic analysis of the state, Bittner starts by pointing out the bewildering variety of incidents to which the police are called by members of the public. The common feature explaining why the police are called lies not in the nature of the problems themselves, nor the functions that may be achieved, but the specialist resource helping them to deal with this sea of troubles—'the capacity for decisive action' (Bittner 1974: 35). 'The policeman, and the policeman alone, is equipped, entitled and required to deal with every exigency in which force may have to be used' (ibid.). Underlying the diversity of tasks, problems, situations, and means is the core capacity to use force if necessary (Brodeur 2010: 116–21; Klockars 1985).

The police are not, as is sometimes said, *monopolists* in the use of legal force. There are other occupations—such as psychiatric nurses, prison officers, and private security guards—who are specialists in the use of force and citizens have powers to use force if they can satisfy a court that their actions were necessary and proportionate to the danger they faced. Nor does it mean that the police typically (or even often) use coercion to resolve the troubles they deal with. The craft of good policework is to use the background possibility of legitimate force so skilfully that it never needs to be foregrounded (although of course excessive use of force has been problematic in many jurisdictions, cf. Belur 2010). Several observational studies have given impressive accounts of how competent patrol officers maintain peace in threatening situations, with their legal powers (including force) as a latent resource (Bittner 1967; Muir 1977; Kemp *et al.* 1992; Fassin 2013). The successful police officer draws on the authority of her office, as well as her personal and craft skills in handling people, rather than coercive power—although sometimes this will not be possible. These skills are not adequately recognized, rewarded, or understood, largely because popular and police preconceptions about the nature of the police task have precluded analysis of the craftsmanship involved in effective peacekeeping (Bittner 1983; Bayley and Bittner 1984; Norris and Norris 1993; Reiner 1998).

The notion of order maintenance is just as problematic in terms of social and political justice as the higher-profile mandates of law enforcement and crime control (Hall 1998). The observational studies that vividly depict many examples of good peacekeeping work fail to grapple with these problems adequately. For example, Chatterton (1983: 211–15) gives a detailed account of the calming down of a domestic dispute without the arrest of the husband, who had assaulted his wife. In Chatterton's analysis this was ultimately due to the officer exercising his sense of the justice of the man's position. As he described the case, an arrest accomplishing 'legal' justice would have been both unjust and troublesome to all concerned. This clearly raises the problem of whether we can rely on the personal sense of justice of patrol officers, and how its exercise can be made accountable. The typical handling of domestic 'disputes' as non-criminal, order-maintenance matters, rather than assaults, has been criticized effectively for many years by feminists, and has produced change in forces around the world. One common reaction has been the encouragement of mandatory arrest policies, shifting this large category of calls unequivocally into 'law enforcement'. There has been much debate about the effectiveness and desirability of such innovations (Sherman and Berk 1984; Edwards 1989; Sheptycki 1993; Sherman 1992b; Hoyle 1998; Chesney-Lind 2002; Maxwell *et al.* 2002; Skogan and Frydl 2004: 231–2; Heidensohn 2008: 661; Walby *et al.* 2016; Walby and Towers 2017). The antinomies of reconciling fairness, effectiveness, and accountability with police coercion are just as acute for order-maintenance work as for any other aspect of policework.

Nonetheless, that 'order maintenance' is the core of the police mandate is attested to in a variety of ways. In Britain it is reflected in the pattern of specific demands placed upon the police by calls for service. Most involve some element of conflict but do not relate unequivocally to a criminal offence. Second, it was a core mandate historically. The main *raison d'être* for the 'new police' was crime prevention by regular patrol (i.e. intervention in situations before crimes occurred) as well as order maintenance, particularly crowd control. The unique character of British policing lies partly in merging the tasks of law enforcement and order maintenance (including crowd and riot control) into the same organization, although in many other jurisdictions there are specialist riot control forces and behind all of these stands the military. Police seek to reproduce order in situations they define as disorderly. However, to say that the primary police role is order maintenance is not to give the police total responsibility for social order. The task is reducible to emergency maintenance of order, not the creation of its preconditions, as the broadest philosophies of community policing seek. 'The police are the social equivalent of the AA or RAC patrolmen, who intervene when things go unpredictably wrong and secure a provisional solution' (Waddington 1993: 34). In this analogy, they are neither service-station mechanics nor car-makers. But, like the AA, they have a role in advising on policy relevant to their duties and cooperating with other agencies.

The influential 'new left realist' school of criminologists in Britain argued for a 'minimalist' policing approach (Kinsey *et al.* 1986), and this has been echoed recently in a powerful critique of contemporary US policing (Vitale 2017). They argued that police intervention should be confined to cases where there was clear evidence of law-breaking, and then should take the form of the invocation of legal powers and criminal process. This aims to makes police fully 'accountable to the law'. However, the large bulk of calls for service are not unequivocally reports of crime. On a 'minimalist' strategy this would mean either not responding to such requests, or forcing the police response into a procrustean bed of legalism without discretion. Vitale argues rightly that the root causes of the problems the police deal with cannot be resolved by them, and that police intervention often exacerbates the issues (Vitale 2017). However, the left realists equally acknowledge that, in the absence of imminent fundamental social transformation, there remains a need for immediate response to the perceived harms that people call the police to handle.

An increasingly influential perspective on the police role has argued that the contemporary police task has shifted away from both crime control and order maintenance and is now geared instead towards 'risk management' (Ericson and Haggerty 1997; Johnston 2000a). Especially since the 2001 attacks on the Twin Towers and growing concern with the terrorist threat, policing has moved towards a 'high policing' model concerned primarily with protecting the overall political and social order rather than everyday 'low policing' of the streets (see Chapter 2). The police, it is said, have become knowledge workers, whose main function is to broker information about risks to public and private organizations concerned with the regulation and governance of people and territories. Ericson and Haggerty provide a rich account of policework involving the accumulation, analysis, and transmission of knowledge about risk to other institutions, and the impact of IT on this. Their data were derived from theoretical sampling of police with 'knowledge-work roles' (Ericson and Haggerty 1997: 128). Their work has to be set in the context of the broader police division of labour. They did not study the Guns and Gangs unit or the Public Order unit. They studied backroom knowledge workers of various sorts and frontline patrol to a certain extent. This concentration on what they regard as the prototypical aspects of policing is theoretically justifiable to allow analysis of police knowledge work. It does mean, however, that the material cannot itself establish empirically the extent to which this now characterizes policework in general. In any event, the police function of knowledge-brokering derives from their traditional patrolling and surveillance activities. It is this that gives them uniquely privileged access to risk knowledge. Order maintenance remains the core function of the police, and one that they are still primarily deployed towards.

Both the Bittnerian conception of policing as emergency order maintenance deploying the capacity for legitimate force, and Ericson and Haggerty's analysis of policing as risk information-brokering, agree that popular and political notions of the police as crime-fighters do not accord with what the police actually do. The central *raison d'être* of the new police was the prevention of crime, but in practice, once the resource of patrolling officers was established, the effective demand for them expressed by calls and other public-initiated contacts turned out to be other than crime related. What the police have in practice been called on to do the most—responding to people in trouble of diverse kinds of emergency—is castigated as 'fire-brigade' policing, and police reforms in Britian have been dedicated primarily to boosting their performance in reducing and clearing up crime (Reiner 2012c). Reducing the task of police to crime control comes at the expense of keeping the peace. It poses dangers, not least for the police themselves, for there are inherent limitations. As a society, we cannot arrest our way out of the crime problem. When crime, and only crime, is made central to the police métier, the police are dispatched in pursuit of a quixotic impossible dream.

CONCLUSION

The seemingly straightforward questions—'what should the police do?', 'what do they do in practice?', and 'how well do they do it?'—have been subject to intense debate. The answers depend on where the question is being asked as well as the political persuasion and theoretical perspective of the interlocutor. Moving from theory to practice, the research evidence shows that the police role cannot be reduced to a single task, goal, or function. In everyday practice, the police are expected to do a variety of things in their 'omnibus mandate'. Statements made by politicians, police chiefs, or pundits that there is one core function should be understood as disputed normative claims that reflect the politics of the police. Despite the fact that policing is extremely diverse in practice, contemporary discussion of the police role and effectiveness is dominated by the 'law-and-order' myth, which falsely portrays the police as an effective force for the prevention and detection of crime. Crime is shaped by many factors of which policing is only one aspect. Although it is impossible to calculate the overall impact of the police on crime levels, we can conceive of societies at particular times having long-run equilibrium levels of 'normal' crime, shaped by all these processes. Poor policing may result in higher, pathological crime levels, and police reform in such a context can appear to produce spectacular results by returning the level to its base of normality. Especially smart or tough policing may suppress official rates below the long-run norm. But these trends would fluctuate due to other factors, particularly political-economic ones. As the evidence of the rise and fall (and subsequent rise) in crime rates over the past hundred years suggests, neither more of the same nor any innovative tactics are likely to improve the police capacity for crime control to any substantial degree. Police have many indispensable functions: responding to a variety of troubles, including predatory and violent crimes, and symbolizing social concern for justice and for the plight of victims. But we must remember that all that is policing does not lie with the police. New thinking in the policing field means asking not 'what works?' but rather, 'what matters in policing?' (van Dijk, Hoogewoning, and Punch 2015; Sheptycki 2018c).

6

A FAIR COP? POLICING AND SOCIAL JUSTICE

INTRODUCTION

'It's a fair cop'—meaning 'you've caught me fair and square'—is an utterance with origins in the Victorian underworld that conveys an admission of guilt, and willingness to face the consequences because the arresting constable acted fairly (Partridge 1992). Fairness is an axiom of democratic policing (Jones *et al.* 1994; Skogan and Frydl 2004). Few would say that a person, or a particular group of people, should be treated unfairly; yet well-founded complaints of unfair policing abound. For example, women experiencing domestic violence and sexual assault complain that they are often not believed when they report cases, or that they are treated disrespectfully by the police who frequently fail to bring offenders to justice (Sheptycki 1993; Williams and Stanko 2015; Strang *et al.* 2017). Similar views are expressed by victims of racist violence (Bowling 1999b; Phillips and Bowling 2017). Black people, and other ethnic minority communities, allege that the police act oppressively in the use of their coercive powers (Institute of Race Relations 1979; Bowling, Parmar, and Phillips 2008). For example, the numbers of people of colour shot dead by the police or dying in police custody have been plausibly interpreted by some communities as suggesting their lives do not matter (Davis 2017; Vitale 2017; Camp and Heatherton 2016). The claim that the discriminatory use of stop and search is required to prevent crime, they contend, merely adds insult to injury (Bowling and Phillips 2007; Baumgartner, Epp, and Shoub 2018). When women, ethnic minorities, gay men, and lesbians join the police, they often complain that they have to put up with sexist, racist, and homophobic banter and barriers to promotion (Bowling and Sheptycki 2016b; Brown 2016; Brown *et al.* 2017; Prenzler and Sinclair 2013; Westmarland 2001a). How do we make sense of the contradiction between the claim that police forces provide equal protection to all and the claim that they are sometimes unfair and abusive?

This chapter examines the issue of fairness in policing with reference to issues of race and gender. In the next section we will get to grips with some definitions that set the terms of debate. Words like justice, fairness, and discrimination need to be defined in relation to each other, and in relation to policing. We then explore the historical and contemporary literature on how race and gender shape policework in order to reach a conclusion about whether or not the police are 'fair enough' (Bowling 2007).

CONCEPTUALIZING FAIRNESS, EQUALITY, AND JUSTICE IN POLICING

Fairness is synonymous with justice, impartiality, equity, legitimacy, lawfulness, reasonableness, honesty, fair dealing, and freedom from bias or injustice. In policing, fairness is used specifically to mean providing equality of service or actions that are not unduly favourable or unfavourable to anyone. A distinction can be made between *procedural fairness*—treating people with dignity and respect, according to established rules, listening to what they have to say, and explaining the reasons for their decisions—and *outcome fairness*—which means producing fair results or consequences (Hough, Jackson, and Bradford 2017). In criminal justice, the term is also used to refer to punitive or coercive interventions that are proportionate with the crime or injury inflicted or to the risk that a person poses to safety (Hudson 2003). Peter Manning usefully introduced ideas from the American liberal philosopher John Rawls into theories of democratic policing (Manning 2010). For Rawls (1971) justice comprises two principles—liberty and equality—both of which are essential for the police to work for the benefit of the least advantaged (Manning 2010: 248). The problem, according to Manning, is that the police métier too often 'envisions only the need to control, deter and punish' (ibid.: 105–6), yet policework cannot be reduced to coercion, authority, or threat. It represents the *unstated sociality of society*, tacitly binding people to each other in mutual obligation (ibid.: 54). As we have seen in Chapter 5, police neither create nor sustain social order, but react to episodes of breakdown, conflict, and distress which require temporary solutions to re-establish public safety and order. Manning argues that, in so doing, they should strive to minimize harm and to leave society no less troubled than before (ibid.: ix). He argues that police should, among other things, be constrained and procedurally fair in dealing with the public, reactive to citizen calls for service, fair in hiring and how police staff are treated, and should foster both individual and institutional accountability for action (ibid.: 65–8; see also Tyler 2011).

Ideas of justice, fairness, and equality lie at the heart of democratic policing (Sklansky 2008; Bradford and Quinton 2014). In most democracies, police officers swear an oath to serve society impartially. In England and Wales, police swear to perform their role of peacekeeping, crime prevention, and law enforcement with 'fairness, integrity, diligence and impartiality, upholding fundamental human rights and according equal respect to all people'. New Zealand police swear to carry out their function 'without favour or affection, malice or ill-will'. Such values are to be found in most Anglo-American police agencies and are built into departmental codes of ethics, guidelines, and policies. Nonetheless, there is a vein in the history of policing containing many examples of the police acting in partisan ways in support of particular social groups in society (Rowe 2014; Phillips and Bowling 2017). Because competing, contradictory, and confused use of key concepts continually vexes these debates, our first task is to pin down definitions of widely used terms.

PREJUDICE AND STEREOTYPING

Although the word prejudice is often taken to mean pre-judging a person, psychologists define it as 'a readiness to act, stemming from a negative feeling, often predicated upon a fixed over-generalisation or totally false belief and directed toward a group or individual members of that group' (Kleg 1993: 114; Bowling and Phillips 2002). Psychologists also distinguish prejudice (an attitude of mind) from discrimination (a form of behaviour). They contend that a prejudiced person does not always or necessarily discriminate, and discrimination is not necessarily the result of prejudice (Bowling and Phillips 2002). Social psychologists define attitudes, such as prejudice, as a state of mind which is organized and shaped through experience and exerts influence upon a person's responses to everyday situations (Allport 1935 cited by Kleg 1993: 118; Allport 1954). Attitudes, therefore, are not a form of behaviour *in themselves* but have a directive or dynamic influence on behaviour (see Etorno and Barrow 2017). There is good empirical evidence that people behave in ways that are consistent with the stereotypes they hold (Wheeler and Petty 2001). Prejudices can be positive, but the term usually has negative connotations. Examples include *ethnocentricity* (the belief that other groups are inferior to one's own), *overgeneralization* (beliefs about members of a group that are not true of all or most members), and *falsehood* (an entirely false attribution taken as characteristic of the entire group). Prejudice is also related closely with bias, the view that some types of people should have preferential treatment because of entitlement, regardless of merit or conduct.

Stereotyping is the application of a generalized 'mental picture' to all members of a group (Tajfel 1969). Stereotypes shape a person's perceived reality, based on information from experience together with ideas formed from cultural values, desires, and past experiences which stamp themselves on reality and transform reality to fit the stereotype (Kleg 1993: 137). Psychologists see stereotyping as a normal part of the mental process that 'fills in the gaps' between an observer's perception of information about the world and their *interpretation* of it, which can create highly distorted images of what is real (ibid.: 140). Stereotypes are an important aspect of prejudice because the process of categorizing people creates a *mindset* that can lead a person to select and interpret traits that members of the group *seem* to have in common but may, in fact, 'reside only in the mind of the perceiver' (ibid.: 147). Hall (1998) argue that stereotypes are diffused through every level of society and contribute to sustaining differences between 'us' and 'them'. They suggest that stereotyping is *structural*, persisting in the unconscious thoughts and long-term collective memory of groups, embedded in the culture and métier of police institutions and affecting routine police conduct.

DISCRIMINATION, DIFFERENTIATION, AND DISPROPORTIONALITY

Patterns in the exercise of police powers in relation to particular social groups that are, in some way, out of proportion when compared with a neutral criterion are referred to as *disproportionate* (Bowling and Phillips 2007). In public debates about policing, disproportionalities—such as an over-representation of black people in stop and search statistics when compared with their numbers in the general population—are sometimes taken as evidence of discrimination. Yet they are also often dismissed by police and political commentators as natural and inevitable, simply portraits of how things are, the result of some other psychological or social forces. For example, some commentators argue that although the police may use coercive force against black males more than against other groups, they contend that this is simply a reaction to the prob-lems and crime and disorder within black communities (Jackall 2003). How can this conundrum be understood? How do we distinguish that which is truly discriminatory from that which is merely different?

Discrimination refers to a pattern of the exercise of power or provision of service that results in unequal, unfavourable, and unjustifiable treatment based on a person's sex, gender, 'race', ethnicity, culture, religion, language, class, sexual orientation, age, physical disability, or any other improper ground (Bowling and Phillips 2002). It in-cludes refusal to offer employment, to provide a service, to use coercive powers in ways that disadvantage particular social groups, even when legally relevant variables are held constant. The law makes a distinction between direct and indirect discrimina-tion. We consider examples of *direct discrimination* later where formal policies that disadvantage particular groups are enshrined in law and enforced by police. One of the most explicit examples of this was the policing of South African apartheid where the police enforced laws that segregated black, white, and Asian populations, and pro-tected 'whites only areas' (Brewer 1994; Brogden and Shearing 1993; Marks 1999).

Sometimes discrimination persists even when laws are in place to prohibit discrimi-nation. This de facto discrimination is referred to as *indirect discrimination*, treatment that is formally considered 'equal' but disadvantages a particular group in its *actual effect* (Alexander 2012; Weitzer 2014; Etorno and Barrow 2017). The only justification for differential treatment is a normative one based on a legitimate reason (Baumgart-ner *et al.* 2018: 18). So, it is no defence to an allegation of discrimination to say that a black person was arrested because an officer believed he was more likely to com-mit crime, but it would be if there was an objectively reasonable basis for suspecting that he had actually committed a crime. Ignoring the motives or processes leading to discrimination may be desirable legally and morally. But in order to understand why discrimination occurs, and thus what policies might reduce or eliminate it, analysing the social and psychological sources of discrimination is important and it is to theories of discrimination that we now turn.

EXPLAINING DISCRIMINATION IN POLICING

INDIVIDUAL THEORIES

Individual or *categorical* discrimination refers to the ways in which police officers treat members of a group disadvantageously purely because they belong to that group, re-gardless of the relevance of this to any particular performance criteria (Banton 1983). It is the most straightforward, explicit, and direct form of discrimination and the way in which the problem has traditionally been understood in police services. The 'bad apple theory' contends that the cause of discrimination is the individual action of a small number of officers (Punch 2003). From this perspective, racism, sexism, and au-thoritarianism more generally, are personal attributes. An early study of the individual psychology of police officers found that they tended to be more authoritarian than similarly placed people in other professions (Colman and Gorman 1982). This work was influenced by Lord Scarman (1981/86: 105), who pointed to the 'ill-considered, immature and racially prejudiced actions of some officers in their dealings on the streets with young black people'. The 'bad apple theory' recognizes that there are prejudices against women, ethnic minorities and lesbian, gay, bisexual, and transgendered (LGBT) people in the general population and posits that because recruitment draws on a cross-section of society, the police will inevitably reflect the prejudices of wider society (Keith 1993). Scarman roundly rejected the idea that police prejudice was inevitable because officers represent a 'cross section of society'. The police occupy a unique status, he argued, and therefore 'the standards we apply to the police must be higher than the norms of behaviour prevalent in society as a whole.' (Scarman 1981/6:106; see also Punch, 2003).

CULTURAL THEORIES

The police service, like all organizations, has a distinctive range of occupational cultures marked by specific languages, rituals, values, norms, perspectives, and craft rules (see Chapter 9). These cultures change over time and differ among police forces, between 'rank and file', senior management, and specialisms (Stanko *et al.* 2012), but there are some 'core characteristics' including machismo, racism and sexism, conservatism, authoritarianism, suspiciousness, solidarity with other police, isolation from the public, and a sense of 'us against them'. The occupational culture is important to understanding the relationship between prejudice and discrimination because policing is characterized by wide discretion at the lowest ranks (Reiner 1992a; Wilson 1968). Although criminal procedure constrains police action it is permissive enough to grant 'considerable leeway for police culture to shape police practice in accordance with situational exigencies' (Reiner 1992a: 108; Bowling and Marks 2017). In practice, therefore, rank-and-file officers define police action on the street.

An important cultural characteristic is the prevalence of specific stereotypes and ways of classifying the public. Ethnic minorities, vagrants, alcoholics, unemployed, deviant youth, gays, sex workers, and political radicals have, historically, been seen as low status, powerless, and problematic by the police. Some police officers believe that the majority of the population have granted them permission to deal with such people as though they were 'police property' and turn a blind eye to how this is done (Lee 1981: 51–3; see also Bowling, Phillips, and Sheptycki 2012). Calls for service from these groups are seen by police officers as 'rubbish'—unworthy of attention, messy, intractable, or the complainant's own fault (Smith and Gray 1983; see also Reiner 1978a). Stereotypes are important because they are embedded, maintained, and transmitted within the culture of police organizations and circulate as the customary 'how-we-do-things-around-here' knowledge (Hall 1998). This is the 'habitus', the structuring of expected and acceptable behaviours in organizations such as the police (Chan 1996; Bourdieu 1984: 170; see also Mead 1934; Reiner 1991; Bowling 1999b; Phillips and Bowling 2017).

An important feature of the police organizational culture is *statistical discrimination* (Banton 1983), differential treatment of members of a group because of a stereotyped belief that they are more likely to have certain characteristics without reference to the specific behaviour of individual members. For example, a police constable quoted in a 1997 Home Office study said that 'if 99 per cent of people committing robberies are black—and in an area like this they are—then you would expect to find 99 per cent of the stop-searches to be of black people' (FitzGerald and Sibbitt 1997; see also Quinton *et al.* 2000; Bowling and Phillips 2007). Research based on interviews with police officers in 2003 indicated that stereotypes remained stable, with black males still described as typically uncooperative, confrontational, perpetrators of street crime (Delsol 2006). Such stereotypes are not a lawful basis for 'reasonable suspicion' but nonetheless statistical discrimination remains a tacit factor in stop and search practices in the USA, the UK, and elsewhere (Delsol and Shiner 2015; Weber and Bowling 2014; Bowling and Phillips 2007; Epp *et al.* 2014; Lerman and Weaver 2014; Baumgartner, Epp, and Shoub 2018).

INSTITUTIONAL THEORIES

Punch (2003) argues that the 'bad apple' thesis, emphasizing individual wrongdoing, should be replaced by the alternative metaphor of 'rotten orchards' to draw attention to system level institutional failure. Although the 1981 *Scarman Report* is taken by many as the classic defence against the allegation of institutional racism, the report actually suggests two contrasting definitions. First, discriminating knowingly, as a matter of policy and second, practices that are unwittingly discriminatory (1981/6: 28). Scarman adopted the narrow *de jure* definition of institutional racism and rejected the allegation. However, he did concede that the police were discriminatory in the second, de facto sense. The latter interpretation is the standard one used by most sociological analyses.

A decade later, the *Macpherson Report* on the Stephen Lawrence case adopted a wide and, arguably, amorphous definition of institutional racism:

> The collective failure of an organisation to provide an appropriate and professional service to people because of their colour, culture, or ethnic origin. It can be seen or detected in processes, attitudes and behaviour which amount to discrimination through unwitting prejudice, ignorance, thoughtlessness and racist stereotyping which disadvantages minority ethnic people. (Macpherson 1999: para. 34)

The inquiry considered evidence of various forms of indirect discrimination, concerning itself primarily with the experiences of black victims. The discriminatory use of powers against them as suspects, which had been the focus of most controversy until the Lawrence case, is swept into the broader range of discriminatory behaviour in the second sentence. Stress is on the *unconscious* processes that bring about the objectively identifiable outcome of discrimination. But the notion of 'collective failure of an organisation' runs together a variety of different ideas. Does it mean overtly discriminatory organizational policies, which Scarman rejected in the first instance? Or the concept as defined earlier—the unintended consequences of impartially framed policies? Or that enough officers act in a discriminatory manner, consciously or not, to label the whole organization as racist? Or is discrimination the result of a failure to train or discipline some members who are racist? The ambiguity accounts for the polarized response to the verdict. After varying degrees of soul-searching, most police leaders accepted Mapherson's conclusion and the need for radical change, but many officers resented the implication of collective guilt. Much hostility to the findings lingers, overtly or in the form of studied misunderstandings (Marlow and Loveday 2000;

Foster *et al.* 2005; McLaughlin 2007: chap. 6; Rowe 2007; Loftus 2007, 2008, 2009; Foster 2008). This is in part structured by vested interests, but it is also facilitated by the ambiguity of Macpherson's formulation, which lent itself to criticism even from sympathetic commentators (Singh 2000; Lea 2003; Souhami 2007; Stenson and Waddington 2007; Henry 2007: 80; Webster 2007; Phillips 2011). Against this it must be stressed that the finding of institutional racism was welcomed by most people from black and ethnic minority communities as an unequivocal vindication of the depth and range of their mistreatment by much policing over decades, as victims, as suspects, and as police officers.

Nonetheless, Scarman, who had to soft-peddle the terms in which he couched his criticism of the police (though not the substance), included crucial themes in his analysis that were absent from Macpherson. While Macpherson was certainly tough on the police, he was soft on the causes of racist policing. His focus is primarily on the police organization and the individuals within it. Scarman, however, located the sources of both the rioting and police racism in the wider structures of racism and disadvantage that generated them.

STRUCTURAL THEORIES

A broader perspective places discrimination in the context of the wider processes of social and economic exclusion (Bowling, Phillips, and Sheptycki 2012). For Susan Smith (1989:101), discrimination is a 'pervasive process sustained across a range of institutions' including employment, housing, education, health, social services, and the media that have procedures that 'combine to produce a mutually reinforcing' pattern of inequality. Organizations concerned with the allocation of power and resources develop conventions that distinguish 'the deserving from the undeserving and the reputable from the debased' (ibid.), in prioritizing those seeking access to goods and services provided by the police (see Bowling and Phillips 2007). These conventions tacitly or explicitly invoke attributes including those stemming from race and gender as criteria for exclusion or inclusion in the allocation of scarce resources (Smith 1989:102). This contention is related to the idea of *situational discrimination* which occurs when the socio-economic position of members of a group disproportionately shapes them as undeserving of police services or as legitimate targets of police suspicion. A classic early paper on the sociology of policing noted that legal powers are structured by the institution of privacy, which is itself related to inequality (Stinchcombe 1963). So, someone getting drunk or using drugs in their living room is unlikely to come to the attention of the police, but the same behaviour in the streets could end up in police custody. A controversial example is the concept of 'availability' for stop and search (Quinton, Miller, and Bland 2000; Stenson and Waddington 2007). Much of the disproportionate use of stop and search powers against young, black, and ethnic minority, less affluent men arises from the fact that they spend more of their time than other groups in the places and at times where stop and search is most widely used. The extent to which a social group is 'available' to come into contact with the police is shaped by structural factors such as unemployment or employment in occupations which require evening and night work, homelessness, or exclusion from school. From this perspective, disproportionate stop and search is the result of broader social and economic inequality (Bowling and Phillips 2007; Bowling, Sheptycki, and Phillips 2012; Phillips and Bowling 2017; Delsol and Shiner 2015; Wortley and Owusu-Bempah 2012).

HISTORIES OF INEQUALITY AND INJUSTICE IN POLICING

The history of policing takes on a particular hue when it is focused through the lens of fairness. In societies where distinctions in occupational class, caste, tribe, ethnicity, and race are imposed by law, the police have played an instrumental enforcement role. Best known are the 'peculiar institution' of chattel slavery (Turner *et al.* 2006), the system of 'Jim Crow' racial segregation in the USA (Alexander 2012), and the apartheid system in South Africa (Brogden and Shearing 1993; Brewer 1994). In such contexts, the role of the police has been explicitly to enforce laws that create and sustain the subordination of particular populations (Turner *et al.* 2006). Although most explicitly discriminatory laws have been abolished, a historical perspective is important to understand the contemporary legacy of these forms of policing. In Chapters 3 and 4 we discussed divergent perspectives on the history of policing and here we extend this analysis to focus on the inequality across social divisions such as social class, race, and ethnicity, gender and sexual orientation.

POLICING POVERTY

The conservative view is that problems of crime and disorder afflict all social classes and, as such, the creation of a public police force had the universal benefit of creating safer communities. Critics argue that laws concerned with policing marginal populations were designed to protect the interests of the ruling classes and served to uphold the industrial capitalist order (see Chapters 2 and 4). The new police acted, therefore, in ways that were detrimental to groups such as the very poor, vagrants, and migrants. Certain aspects of their behaviour—sleeping rough, begging, hawking their wares, soliciting customers, drinking, and gambling—were precisely the focus of police activity in the metropolis. The 1824 Vagrancy Act, enacted five years before the formation of the Metropolitan Police, provided wide powers for parish constables to control the behaviour of migrants travelling from Scotland, Ireland, and the English shires looking for work in London, many of whom were homeless. The Act was targeted at vagabonds; 'incorrigible rogues' and 'idle and disorderly people' such as beggars, peddlers, unlicensed traders, prostitutes, and reputed thieves. Lawrence (2017) shows that this Act was used through the nineteenth and twentieth centuries as a preventive power to punish and incapacitate people deemed to embody future crime threats (McCulloch and Wilson 2016: 1). Further legislation, such as the Habitual Criminals Act (1869) and the Prevention of Crimes Act (1871), added to police powers in terms of surveillance and prevention of 'known criminals', only losing ground when pre-emptive policing powers 'became entangled with debates about race relations in the 1970s' (Lawrence 2017: 513).

POLICING SLAVERY

It is frequently overlooked that the institutions of policing and slavery overlap historically. Slavery existed until 1833 in the British Empire, until 1848 in the French colonies
and until 1865 in the USA. Slave codes, established by colonial English law in Barba-
dos in 1661 and in force across North America and the Caribbean in the seventeenth
and eighteenth centuries, were used to keep iniquitous social relationships in place.
Although the focus of much of the scholarship in this area focuses on the antebellum
South, in fact northern states, including Connecticut and New York, had slavery laws
and the United States Congress also passed Fugitive Slave Laws in 1793 and 1850 sanctioning the detention and return of escaped slaves (Turner *et al.* 2006). These codes
were based on the principle that slaves were property rather than human beings and
were forbidden to read, write, assemble, bear arms, act in self-defence against violence,
or own property. The codes also prohibited slaves—at pain of corporal punishment or
death—from leaving their owner's property without permission unless accompanied
by an overseer. In many places slaves were required, as part of their labour, to move
between plantations and towns giving some degree of freedom of movement and also
justifying a system to maintain control. Slave patrols were a 'system of rural police'
(DuBois 1904) with the specific role of apprehending fugitive slaves and of protecting
white settlements from the threat of insurrections or crimes committed by slaves. A
number of authors argue that slave patrols, as a form of specialized police organization,
with a specific law enforcement function and accountability to local and to central
government, should be considered an important precursor to the modern police organizations (Walker 1992; Reichel 1988; Roth 2005; Turner *et al.* 2006; Vitale 2017). For
Turner *et al.* (2006: 186), 'similarities between the slave patrols and modern American
policing are too salient to dismiss or ignore. Hence, the slave patrol should be considered a forerunner of modern American law enforcement'.

POLICING RACIAL SEGREGATION

In the first half of the twentieth century, the US police played a crucial role in the
enforcement of segregationist Jim Crow laws (Alexander 2012; Vitale 2017). During
this period, a range of statutes formally segregated black and white populations in
areas of social life including marriage and sexual relationships, schools, public transport, public lavatories, hotels, theatres, and restaurants (Alexander 2012). The police
played a key role in enforcing segregation by arresting people who broke these laws,
or protested against them, and bringing offenders before the courts. As the twentieth century wore on, segregationist laws, and the policing required to enforce them,
were challenged by those most severely affected. From the late 1950s onwards, African
American people defied the law by refusing to move to 'coloured' sections of buses
and trains, from 'whites only' waiting rooms and restaurants, demonstrating in their
thousands against segregated schools and universities. In hundreds of famous cases,
including those involving Rosa Parks and Martin Luther King, state and county police
were on hand—often with dogs, fire hoses, whips, and clubs—to enforce segregation
laws (Bredhoff *et al.* 1999). The 1964 Civil Rights Act brought an end to this era and
by banning discrimination based on race, colour, religion, sex, or national origin, was
opposed by white communities—including some police chiefs.

POST-COLONIAL POLICING

Post-colonial policing refers to a pattern of policing in those countries that gained independence from colonial rule from Great Britain (and other imperial powers) in the
postwar period. In countries across Africa, the Caribbean, the Indian subcontinent,
South East Asia, Canada, and Australasia, the colonial model (see Chapter 3) shaped
policing practice (Chan 1996, 1997; Tankebe 2008; Marks 1999; 2000; Harriott 2000;
Bowling 2010). Colonial police forces were based on the idea of 'policing by strangers'
and often formally segregated, with 'native police' insulated from senior officers and
from the general population by being housed in barracks and encouraged to see the
general population as outsiders and enemies (Kappeler *et al.* 1994: 105–6; Brewer 1991,
1994). Post-colonial police forces tend, to this day, to be under direct central government control, are partisan in enforcing the rule of a specific political party or regime
and emphasize the use of force to control specific sections of the population using
coercion rather than consent, and with force used readily, sometimes as a first resort
(Brewer 1994).

POLICING RELIGIOUS CONFLICT

In the UK police services have played an active role in sustaining post-colonial religious conflict. It has long been recognized that the police force in Northern Ireland played a role in the development, and uneasy resolution of the Troubles with a
militaristic policing system (Ellison 2010; Mulcahy 2013). The Patten Commission
(1999), following the Good Friday Agreement, created a constitutional settlement
that brought peace to Northern Ireland. Patten (p. 2), acknowledged that views of
the Royal Ulster Constabulary (RUC) were polarized along religious lines, regarded
as 'custodians of nationhood' by unionists/Protestants and 'symbols of oppression' by
nationalists/Catholics (Ellison and Smyth 2000; Mulcahy 2013). It is not surprising,
therefore, that in post-conflict Northern Ireland the relationship between these communities and police forces is strained and often lacks trust (Goldsmith 2005). Patten's overarching recommendation was to move policing from a system reliant upon
coercion to one reliant upon consent (Mulcahy 2013; Tonge 2013). The RUC was
renamed the Police Service of Northern Ireland (PSNI) in 2001. Key to the reform
process was the recruitment of a more representative police force from the over-
whelmingly Protestant RUC, by introducing 50/50 recruitment strategies whereby
one Catholic and one Protestant applicant are chosen from a pool of qualified applicants. The recruitment strategies have been successful with Catholic officers now
representing 32 per cent of police in 2018 compared to 8 per cent in 1999 (PSNI
2018). Nonetheless, there is a long way to go in implementing all Patten's recommendations (Ellison 2007: 243) and there is a persistent 'relationship crisis' between
the PSNI and certain Catholic communities (Topping and Byrne 2012; Bradford *et
al.* 2018). This may be because transformational change is the result of collective and
individual memories of the officers within the organization that hinder positive pub-
lic-police relations to this day (Akgün *et al.* 2012; Murphy, Mcdowell, and Brainiff
2017). The PSNI, however, represents the closest thing to a blueprint for changing the
occupational cultures and structures of post-colonial police forces. The key is that

reform occurred alongside wider economic and social reforms (Bradford *et al.* 2018: 17; see also Hearty 2018; Hays 2012).

POLICING ETHNIC MINORITY COMMUNITIES

The policing of ethnic minority communities on the British mainland at the end of empire was fundamentally shaped by the police role in enforcing immigration law (Bowling, Phillips, and Sheptycki 2012). The so-called 'crimmigration control system' in the UK is primarily focused on the exclusion and control of migrants (Bowling and Westenra 2018a, 2018b; Bosworth *et al.* 2017; Bosworth *et al.* 2018). Internal controls, established by the 1914 Aliens Restriction Act and strengthened by the 1971 Immigration Act, empowered domestic constables to arrest people suspected of illegal entry, overstaying, or failure to observe rules attached to their entry permit (Gordon 1983: 15; Sivanandan 1982: 27). The 1965 Race Relations Act, and subsequent legislation, exempted the police from anti-discrimination law because the state required the police to enforce immigration law that was *designed to discriminate* against British commonwealth citizens of African, Caribbean, and Asian origin (Bowling and Iyer 2019). This gave impunity to the police to discriminate on the grounds of race, ethnic, and national origins until the Race Relations Amendment Act of 2000 (ibid.). The burden of immigration enforcement falls mainly on people from black and ethnic minority populations, even when nationality is taken into consideration (Bowling and Westenra 2018a). Simultaneously, migrants from former colonies—the so-called 'Windrush generation'—were barred from entering the police service despite no formal impediment to doing so since the 1948 British Nationality Act, while successive Chief Constables explicitly opposed the recruitment of black police officers (Whitfield 2004: 116).

LEARNING FROM POLICE HISTORY

These histories of inequality and injustice in policing illustrate the interactions between individual, cultural, institutional, and structural dimensions of discrimination. In all of these historical instances, it is the actions of individual police officers that have the effect of discriminating. In some cases, this was the reluctant enforcement of outmoded and unpopular laws, but quite often the police were enthusiastic proponents of iniquitous laws, holding fast to ideologies that cast the poor, women, ethnic and sexual minorities as inferior and held them to be legitimately subject to exclusion and separation. In this context, it is clear that class, race, and sex discrimination are not the result of a small number of men behaving badly within otherwise fair police forces. On the contrary, police organizations themselves were committed to discriminatory treatment that was often enshrined in laws and institutional policies and sustained by the police occupational culture. The historical evidence shows that discrimination was sustained over time at the intersection of unequal social structures and police organizational culture, executed through the actions of individual police officers. We now turn to the contemporary manifestations of unfairness, inequality, and injustice in policing.

CONTEMPORARY EVIDENCE OF FAIRNESS, EQUALITY, AND JUSTICE IN POLICING

From what has been written so far on this topic, it is clear that there is potential for discrimination and unfairness to afflict many aspects of policework. Entire books have been dedicated to exploring this subfield in the UK, the USA, and elsewhere (Vitale 2017). Rather than attempting the impossible task of examining the question of fairness in every aspect of policing, we focus here on three spheres of police activity where this has been a particularly salient issue and where the evidence is strong: the police response to women crime victims; the use of stop and search powers and deadly force against black people; and the experiences of people of colour, women, gay men, and lesbians as a minority within police forces.

TO PROTECT AND SERVE: VICTIMS' EXPERIENCE OF POLICING

The twin tropes of police 'force' and police 'service' have already been identified as a key problematic in theories of policing (see Chapter 1). The quality of service provided to crime victims is an important benchmark by which to judge fairness and equality in policing. A core police function is to respond rapidly to emergency calls for service, restore peace, and resolve conflict in disputes and disturbances, and to do something meaningful to help those who have been wounded or frightened. As discussed in Chapter 5, this complex emergency 'order maintenance' function of the police is crucial to the police mission to serve and to protect, and is intimately related to law enforcement and crime control, as well as an issue of distributive justice that is crucial to police legitimacy (Bottoms and Tankebe 2012, 2017). The key question of fairness in this context is: do the police respond equally well to all those who call for help?

Policing domestic violence

Calls to 'domestics' have always been a significant part of the police workload but have often been treated without recourse to criminal proceedings, even when evidence of assault is present (Hanmer et al. 1989; Sheptycki 1993). The Independent Police Complaints Commission's (IPCC) report into Cardiff police's failings in the Craig Thomas case, for example, revealed that the police failed to record the abuse despite multiple visits to Thomas's flat. Officers noted injury to Thomas's pregnant girlfriend's face but recorded 'no sign of a disturbance' (Olsen 2018). Responding to domestic violence was typically seen in traditional cop culture as messy, unproductive, and not 'real' policework (Reiner 1978a: 177, 214–15, 244–5; Young 1991: 315–16). In the US during the 1980s, mandatory arrest policies were introduced with the aim of shifting responsibility for filing complaints from the victim to the police (Li et al. 2015: 401). However, as survivors of domestic violence are usually closely tied to their abusers, the fear of legal action may deter women from reporting (Novisky and Peralta 2014). Although women experience violence from spouses, male acquaintances, and relatives more frequently than from a faceless assailant, the 'ideal victim' stereotype is someone who is abused by a stranger, vulnerable, respectable, blameless, and cooperative (Stanko and Heidensohn 1995). Those regarded as engaging in 'morally questionable' behaviour are seen as 'contributing to the victimization' and therefore less worthy of police attention

(Meyer 2015: 2). Victims of domestic violence tend not to get the support received by other violent crimes and victims are often blamed for staying with an abusive partner (Meyer 2015: 3).

This issue has been highly charged since the 1970s, and around the world police forces have attempted to improve their response with debatable results (Sheptycki 1993; Sherman 1992b; Hoyle 1998; Maxwell *et al.* 2002; Chesney-Lind 2002; Skogan and Frydl 2004: 231–2; Heidensohn 2008: 660–3). Seventy-seven women were killed by their partners or former partners in the UK between 2012 and 2013, while domestic violence accounted for 8 per cent of recorded crime and a third of recorded assaults with injury (HMIC 2014: 5). The Inspectorate concluded that although domestic violence was a priority on paper, in practice police leadership was lacking in this area and there were inadequate skills and knowledge to provide a decent service; the overall conclusion was that the police response to domestic abuse was 'not good enough' (ibid.: 6). In 2017, The Inspectorate reported progress: more officers allocated to domestic abuse cases, stronger partnerships with public services, and investment in training (HMICFRS 2017: 6). However, a 61 per cent increase in recorded domestic abuse since 2014 caused strain, and between 2012 and 2016 the proportion of unattended incidents increased from 5 per cent to 11 per cent (Agerholm 2017). Some forces downgraded 'the severity of calls from domestic abuse victims to justify a slower emergency response' and carried out risk-assessments over the phone rather than in person (HMICFRS 2017: 7).

Policing rape

Long standing concern remains about insensitive or even hostile treatment of rape victims. This was dramatically highlighted in 1982 by a celebrated episode of Roger Graef's TV documentary on the Thames Valley Police which showed a very disturbing interrogation of a rape victim (BBC 1, 18 January 1982). Recently, senior officers' failure to act on intelligence and evidence allowed serial sex offender John Worboys to avoid arrest repeatedly (Laville 2018). In 2018, the Supreme Court ruled in favour of two of Worboys' victims, ruling that the police had failed to investigate their allegations of rape in 2003 and 2007 effectively and breached Article 3 of the Human Rights Act against torture and inhuman or degrading treatment (Spurrier 2018). The victims' solicitor stated: 'It was not a lack of [police] resources that failed these women. It was a lack of belief [among police officers]' (Bowcott 2018). This case is significant as it found that the disregard for Worboys's victims constituted a dereliction of the duty of care and extended police liability for victimization following a failure to take action against a known offender.

In this case, as in many others, the police were influenced by 'real rape' myths and 'respectable woman' stereotypes, which determine how a case proceeds through the criminal justice system. A 'real rape' is perpetrated outdoors by a stranger using force, resisted by the victim and results in visible injuries (Hohl and Stanko 2015: 328). Victims who delay reporting, are unable to recollect the incident without inconsistencies, were affected by alcohol or mental health problems, all lack credibility in the eyes of the police. In reality, most rapes are committed by someone known to the victim, who will often not report the incident straight away and whose memory of the event may be impaired by trauma (ibid.). Significant efforts have been made to improve police handling of rape cases (Brown 2011; Hohl and Stanko 2015: 326), but the treatment of victims by police remains deeply problematic. Hohl and Stanko (2015: 325) found that cases were not prosecuted if there were inconsistencies in the evidence or in victims' recollection or if police opinion had cast doubt on the allegation. Victims are likely to become disengaged with the investigation and may withdraw their allegation if police officers express disbelief and disrespect or if the victims lose faith in the process (Hohl and Stanko 2015: 325). From 2017 to 2018, 5 per cent of sexual offence cases and 3 per cent of rape cases led to a charge or summons and one-third of cases closed because the victim did not support further police action (HOSB 2018: 15).

STOP AND SEARCH: POLICING FREEDOM OF MOVEMENT

The power to stop a person in the street, demand identity documents, or conduct a personal search, is controversial in public debates about equality and fairness in policing around the world (Weber and Bowling 2014; Delsol and Shiner 2015). Although sometimes thought to be 'minimally intrusive', in practice it is often experienced as a highly coercive infringement of liberty (Bowling and Marks 2015). The power can be used in a wide variety of public and private places. Once stopped by a police officer, the person may not leave the encounter and is, therefore, detained, is sometimes arrested for the duration of the stop, and may be subject to criminal charges if they refuse a search (Bowling and Phillips 2007). The stopped person may be subject to interrogation, vehicle and clothing searches, and can sometimes be handcuffed. The grounds for a stop can be extremely wide: to investigate crime, suspected possession of weapons or drugs, 'going equipped' to offend, to establish a person's identity, or even to collect intelligence or break up groups of young people (Choongh 1997; Bowling, Phillips, and Parmar 2008).

Some powers are defined tightly by reference to a legitimate aim such as to search for specific items in particular places. For example, the power to search a person at an airport is used by a private security officer who uses technical and human means to check whether a person is in possession of a weapon or other objects that could affect aircraft safety (see Chapter 7). Everyone is searched, in a closely defined location for a specific purpose. The power seems to be used with justification, and such searches are rarely the source of allegations of discrimination. In many places, stop and search is primarily understood to be an investigative power and governed by the test that stops are permitted only when the officer reasonably suspects a person of wrongdoing (Bowling and Marks 2017; Etorno and Barrow 2017). The problem with stop and search is that as officers rely on their perception of suspicious looking individuals, it is clear that because of stereotyping, marginalized groups are more likely to be affected (Weber and Bowling 2011; Bowling, Philips, and Sheptycki 2012).

Racial profiling

Controversy was sparked in the 1990s in the USA around what became known as 'racial profiling', a deeply entrenched police practice in which African Americans were more frequently stopped because of an explicit or implicit 'suspect profile' developed by police forces (Meeks 2000; Epp *et al.* 2014; Glaser 2015; White and Fradella 2016; Baumgartner *et al.* 2018). This general pattern is illustrated by a litany of disastrous stops and searches that have resulted in civil action against the police, having been filmed on smartphones and broadcast worldwide by media outlets (Bowling and Marks 2015; Jewkes 2015). Everywhere that evidence exists, it is minority communities who are affected most by stop and search practices.

In the UK there is evidence of both explicit targeting policy and ingrained police practices that amount to 'institutional racism' (Phillips and Bowling 2017). The research evidence in England and Wales shows consistently that people of Asian origin are twice as likely to be stopped than their white counterparts, and black people seven times as likely. In relation to suspicionless powers deployed in 'anticipation of violence', black people have been subject to searches at a rate sixty times greater than their white counterparts (Bowling and Phillips 2007). In Toronto, there is evidence of racial profiling specifically of people of colour (Wortley and Owusu-Bempah 2012; Sheptycki 2018c).

In New York, the data suggest that Blacks and Hispanics are racially-profiled, being nine times more likely to be subjected to 'stop and frisk' and use of force, despite the fact that white New Yorkers are more frequently in possession of contraband (Jones-Brown et al. 2010; Goel et al. 2016). Expatriate Mexican communities are targeted by local police in border states such as New Mexico (Provine and Sanchez 2012). In Paris, Blacks and Arabs are more likely to be the targets of stops. In Spain, Moroccans and Romanians are subjected to more intrusive measures such as searches by comparison with their ethnic Spanish counterparts (Open Society Justice Initiative 2006). Recent empirical work has documented racial profiling in Finland and Sweden (Keskinen et al. 2018; The Local 2013). In Hungary, the Roma minority are targets (Tóth and Kádár 2011). On the Moscow Metro, Non-Slavs were found to be twenty-two times more likely to be searched than Slavs (Open Society Justice Initiative 2006). In Japan, 'non-Japanese' South East Asians are the targets of stop, search, and questioning (Namba 2011). In South Africa (Marks 2011) and India (Belur 2011), the boundaries of suspicion may be subtler, less clearly aligned with racial or cultural categories, but economically marginal young people are specifically targeted. In Japan, Arizona, and Greece, policy-makers have declared 'war on illegal immigrants' with the effect of sanctioning the targeting of stop and question at people perceived to be non-nationals (Weber and Bowling 2014).

Extensive empirical data show that targeted stops unfold in a specific pattern that stems from and reproduces racial stereotypes with a far-reaching impact on police-public interactions and on the outlook and liberty of minority populations. Police stops are a great social unifier and divider (Epp et al. 2014: 156; Fassin 2013). On one side, is the majority community for whom police stops are an annoyance that yields, at worst, an expensive speeding ticket while reaffirming the driver's citizenship in a rule-bound society. On the other, are people from ethnic minority groups for whom police stops are the 'signal form of surveillance and legalized racial subordination' (Epp et al. 2014: 156). Epp et al. (2014) argue that the benefits of stop and search are modest and often greatly exaggerated, but have a substantial and largely unrecognized cost (see Chapter 5).

Unjustified stop and search undermines trust, discourages targeted groups from calling the police for help, and undermines informal social control. The core of the problem is not individual 'bad apples' but 'an institutionally supported practice celebrated by police professional associations, leaders and local departments' (Epp et al.

2014: 159). The research evidence shows that stop and search is experienced as legitimate when a good reason is given, when the officer behaves properly during the stop, and when the outcome was deserved. When stops are speculative and racially framed, they are experienced as a violation of rights, provoke feelings of indignation, and are judged as unfair (Tyler 1990). This practice conveys powerful messages about belonging, citizenship, race, and equality with far-reaching social consequences for the life chances of people of colour (Davis 2017; Bowling, Phillips, and Sheptycki 2012).

POLICE SHOOTINGS

There can surely be no more tragic and disturbing instance of unfairness and injustice than when a police officer kills an innocent person. Whether or not one subscribes to the view that police action provides public safety, it is vital to hold on to the principle of non-maleficence: *first, do no harm*. Police actions causing death are particularly troubling, above all to the families of the deceased, but also to wider society. Yet we should not be surprised that the police can cause serious injury. As we have argued previously, the police occupational life, its métier, is based on the possession of the power of coercion which, by definition, requires the deployment of physical force—restraint, constraint, compulsion, and even deadly violence—to exert control. Governments the world over issue police with weapons ranging in lethality from truncheons to machine guns. Injury, including fatality, is an inevitable consequence. Two key questions arise: what is the extent of police use of deadly or injurious force? On what criteria can such action be judged fair or unfair?

Official figures record that in 2017 a total of 283 people died during or after contact with the police in England and Wales, including four people who were shot dead (IOPC 2018). Although our focus here is on police shootings, the issue of deaths in police custody is a much wider one that concerns the use of force, and in particular, choke-holds that cause positional asphyxia and also the failure in the duty of care. From this perspective, the most recent figures are the worst on record. Focusing on police use of firearms, over the past two decades there has been an average of two fatal shootings by the police per year in England and Wales. Of course, when these do occur—for example the death of Mark Duggan in 2011—there is widespread public concern and, in that case, public protest and eventually rioting (Lewis *et al.* 2011). The annual total has never been more than six and in the years immediately after the 2011 riots (2012–14) not one person was shot dead by the police in England and Wales (ibid). Looking in more detail at the police shootings in 2017, in one episode armed officers from the Metropolitan Police and City of London police responded to an incident involving three men who drove a white van over London Bridge, hitting and injuring pedestrians. After crashing the van, the three men, armed with knives, ran through a pedestrian area stabbing and killing eight people. The men were wearing imitation 'suicide bombs' made from water bottles covered in black and silver duct tape, attached to a leather belt. Eight officers fired a total of forty-six bullets, killing all three men at the scene. Most people, if not all, would agree that these homicides were justifiable, under the circumstances, to prevent further loss of life. Indeed, the police were universally praised for the speed with which they were deployed and killed these assailants. Not all counter-terrorism operations using deadly force have been judged to be safe or fair, however. Jean Charles de Menezes, an innocent electrician was shot dead by the police at Stockwell underground station on 22 July 2015 because he was mistakenly suspected to be a suicide bomber (Punch 2010). Although an inquest exonerated the firearms officers and commanding officer, the Metropolitan Police was roundly criticized and found guilty of breaching health and safety law (ibid.).

The extent of police shootings in the USA makes for a very striking contrast with Britain (Camp and Heatherton 2016; Vitale 2017; Davis 2017). In the absence of official information, it was left to daily newspapers—*The Guardian* and the *Washington Post*—to document police shootings. From January 2015, these papers collected information on every fatal shooting by a police officer in the line of duty in the USA. The information, including the circumstances of the death, the race and gender of the deceased, whether the person was armed, and whether they were experiencing mental-health problems, was gathered through 'crowd sourcing', mining news reports, websites and social media, and monitoring independent databases such as *Killed by Police* and *Fatal Encounters*. Every year since 2015 around 1,000 civilians have been shot dead by US police officers in the line of duty (excluding people who died by suicides or drug overdoses in police custody, fatal shootings by off-duty officers, or police involved deaths other than gunshots). These independent records of police shootings were triggered by the deaths, in 2014, of Michael Brown in Ferguson, Missouri and Eric Garner in New York City. As the #BlackLivesMatter movement developed and protests spread across the USA, many activists sought to increase the focus on police accountability across the USA (Camp and Heatherton 2016; Vitale 2017). It became a public scandal that there was no reliable data even though the FBI had a mandate to record police involved deaths. In fact, only 1,100 of America's 18,000 police agencies reported what are termed 'justifiable homicides' to the FBI, with fewer than half of those subsequently uncovered making it into official records.

It is clear that US police kill far more people than in the UK, or indeed most other developed countries (there are also high levels in Columbia, Mexico, Jamaica, and Brazil). The reasons for this are complex. The US has a much higher rate of homicidal violence and a much higher rate of gun ownership (Squires 2014). Police officers therefore are much more likely to encounter people with guns and also to anticipate armed violence in routine public contacts. The deep public concern that has built up in recent years has focused most forcibly on the deaths of unarmed and innocent people, and in particular the disproportionate rate at which people of colour have been shot dead. Crucial here is the weakness of the law that permits the police to justify deadly force against unarmed people where there is no reasonable suspicion of them being armed. Indeed, analysis by *The Guardian* showed that not only were black people disproportionately shot by the police, but the disproportionality was particularly marked in the case of unarmed victims. Most cases of police shootings resulted in little or no action against the police, fuelling charges that the police have impunity. However, some of the more egregious cases have led to criminal actions against the police. In one extraordinary instance, Michael Slager, the police officer who shot Walter Scott, following a traffic stop on 4 April 2015 in North Charleston, South Carolina, pleaded guilty, was convicted of second-degree murder, and sentenced to a twenty-year jail term. The crucial evidence in this case was video footage filmed by a bystander that recorded Scott being shot repeatedly in the back while running away from officers.

POLICE STAFFING: RECRUITMENT, RETENTION, EXPERIENCES IN THE JOB

A very different perspective on fairness in policing can be found by looking *within* the police organization itself. David Sklansky (2008) argued that municipal police departments in the USA made successful efforts to increase racial and gender diversity, especially at senior levels of command, and that this has had a positive influence on police workplace democracy. Police forces the world over formally excluded women from the ranks throughout most of their history, and remained resistant to employing women for decades thereafter (Appier 1993; Heidensohn 1998; Brown 2000; Emsley 1996). There is a similar pattern in relation to the employment of black and ethnic minority police officers (Holdaway 2015) and in relation to gay and lesbian officers (Burke 1992; 1994). On one hand, this is an issue of equal opportunities in employment. It is a mark of a fair society that people should be employed on the basis of their ability and not excluded because of their gender, ethnicity, or sexual orientation. Beyond this, there is an argument that a police force that represents the demographic make-up of the society that it serves has the potential to increase police legitimacy and improve the fairness and effectiveness of police practices. The story of women's involvement in policing is well documented, and is one that speaks of a lack of equality in terms of recruitment and progression (see Brown 2016).

Women police officers

It is clear from a growing volume of evidence that women are discriminated against as police officers, in terms of career prospects as well as harassment in the job. Until the 1970s, discrimination within police forces was open and institutionalized in the existence of separate departments carrying out radically different functions (Brown 2016: 235). This followed from widespread resistance to the initial recruitment of policewomen in the early decades of the twentieth century, stemming from 'a struggle over the ownership of social control' and disagreement over 'who has a right to manage law and order' (Heidensohn 1992: 215; Silvestri 2007: 52; Brown 2016: 235). This explains the longstanding marginalization of groups outside the white, heteronormative male 'norm' in policing. Since the Sex Discrimination Act 1975, women have been formally integrated into the same units as male officers and their numbers have increased. In 1986, women in large and medium-sized police forces accounted for under 9 per cent of police officers, and minority women represented 4 per cent of all officers, low enough to warrant accusations that their presence was tokenistic (Martin 1989: 37; Guajardo 2016: 23). As of March 2017, there were 35,844 female police officers across the forty-three police forces in England and Wales, accounting for 29 per cent of all police officers (Hargreaves *et al.* 2017: 31). There is currently no police force in the world where women represent 50 per cent of the workforce (Van Ewijk 2012 in Silvestri *et al.* 2013: 62, 70). It has been argued that the under-representation of women and minority groups weakens the legitimacy of the police service (Silvestri *et al.* 2013: 70). However, there has been progress over the past decade; there are twice as many women in all the ranks now as there were a decade ago, including at the chief officer level (BBC Radio 4 2018). The police forces adopted comprehensive equal opportunities policies which, combined with the Human Rights Act, enabled women to challenge discrimination and abuse (Heidensohn 1998: 220).

Differential deployment continues to be a feature of working life for female officers, including those in senior positions, as certain specialist units are staffed almost entirely by one sex (Silvestri 2007: 52). Male squads include 'cars, guns, and horses', while units that deal with sexual offences and child protection are typically staffed by women (Westmarland 2017: 304). Women are called upon as 'gendered specialists' to deal with victims of rape and assault as they are seen as naturally more empathetic and their presence is needed to remove any items of women's clothing (ibid.: 306). As arrests may depend on strength, physical ability is regarded as an important marker of competence and the size and appearance of the body is significant in police culture (ibid.: 302). In the US, height and weight standards were dropped in the late 1970s as police management failed to show their value in determining effective police performance (Birzer and Craig 1996: 93). It has been argued that the physical ability tests that followed favoured men over women in a similar way to how height and weight standards served to exclude female applicants (ibid.: 93–4). Beliefs about the suitability of the strong, fit, male body for policework is indicative of the gendered outlook of police culture, and overlooks the fact that fit women trained in hand-to-hand combat are just as physically capable of performing police duties (Westmarland 2017: 305). The body and its functions have also been used to explain why there are few women firearms officers. It is not because the job is dangerous and needs 'bottle' but stems instead from the idea that women cannot manage prolonged periods in cold and uncomfortable conditions (ibid.: 311–12). It was not until 1995 that a woman attained the rank of chief constable in England (Brown 2000: 98), and in 2017, Cressida Dick became the first female head of the Metropolitan Police. It has been noted that women are typically given leadership positions in times of crisis (Silvestri *et al.* 2013: 62; Heidensohn 1992 in Brown 2016: 232). Indeed, upon her appointment, Dick faced a budget crisis and significant pressure to increase numbers of officers on the streets (Dodd 2017).

Black and ethnic minority police officers

Although people of colour migrated to Britain in significant numbers from the late 1940s, many with experience in the military and other uniformed services, the British police remained a completely white organization until police constable Norwell Robert's appointment to the London Metropolitan Police in 1967. As people from ethnic minority communities began to join the police service in the 1970s and 1980s, their treatment by their colleagues was often very hostile (Whitfield 2004). Smith and Gray's (1985) study of 'the police in action' documented the overt and often extreme racist language used by police officers. The centrality of racism in the subculture of the police that served to alienate, marginalize, and discriminate against minority ethnic officers in the early years persisted well into the 1990s. The overwhelming majority of black and Asian police officers interviewed by Holdaway (1993) reported that racist comments and jokes were routinely part of officers' conversations (see also Holdaway and Barron 1997). Even in the post-Macpherson policing climate, minority ethnic police officers referred to abuse by colleagues as a way of testing their commitment to the job (Cashmore 2002).

The recruitment of minority ethnic police officers was boosted by both the Scarman and Lawrence inquiries with the proportion rising from fewer than 1 per cent in the early 1980s, 2 per cent in 1988, and 4 per in 2007. In March 2018, 6 per cent of all police officers in England and Wales were from ethnic minority groups compared with 14 per cent of the general population. Although this represents very significant progress towards a more diverse police force, the retention rate for minority ethnic police officers is predictably lower than for white officers, promotion tends to be slower, and there is still a very clear under-representation at the senior ranks (Holdaway and Barron 1997). Recruitment has been accelerated by targets, positive action such as recruitment campaigns with the assistance of community organizations and contacts, running familiarization and access courses and placement schemes. Since the 1990s, many police forces have mentoring, informal networking, and welfare support as part of their retention policies and support groups and forums for minority officers have provided a safe space for discussions of occupational experiences, emotional assistance, advice, advocacy, and challenging institutional racism (Phillips 2005, 2007; Holdaway and O'Neill 2006).

LGBT police officers

The experience of LGBT police officers follows a similar pattern. Early research discovered that fear of prejudice and discrimination meant officers frequently lived 'double lives', not disclosing their sexual identity at work and hiding their profession to those in the 'gay scene' (Burke 1994: 219). Burke (1992: 32) argued that stereotypical ideas about homosexuals are antithetical to the machismo that is so strongly embraced within the force (see also Mennicke et al. 2016: 1). Gay men have been found to experience more barriers to equal opportunities than lesbian officers, particularly in the areas of work schedules, promotion, and postings (Colvin 2015). The 1999 *Macpherson Report* ushered in a new era that focused on recruiting minorities to increase diversity in the forces (Jones 2016), so that police departments would 'reflect the populations and communities they serve' and acknowledge minority interests (Mennicke et al. 2016: 2). This was accompanied by investment in the national Gay Police Association and local Gay Staff Networks and the instituting of LGBT liaison officers (Jones 2016). The 2010 Equality Act addressed discrimination based on sexual orientation, including in employment (Colvin 2015: 335). The decriminalization of same-sex sexual practices through the 2003 Sexual Offences Act in the UK and the Supreme Court case *Lawrence v. Texas* in the US, paved the way for significant changes in police relations with LGBT communities (Jones and Williams 2013: 188). Although the position has certainly improved in the last two decades, there remains evidence of continuing bias and discrimination (Williams and Robinson 2004; Colvin 2015; Jones and Williams 2013; Mennicke et al. 2016: 15).

Equal employment, equal justice?

The unequal employment and promotion of women, people of colour, and people of LGBT backgrounds is not only an issue of justice. A diverse police force is important, it is argued, to dilute the racism, machismo, and homophobia in police culture and to make policing more responsive to a diverse society. However, research evidence in the USA and Britain indicates that most women officers do not police differently from their male colleagues, but that they tend to be influenced by the traditional culture of masculinity (Heidensohn 1992, 1994; Westmarland 2001b, 2001b; Silvestri 2003, 2007; Skogan and Frydl 2004: 151–2). The picture is similar in relation to the policing styles of black and ethnic minority officers. A significant difference is that policewomen in the US are less likely to use excessive force than their male colleagues (Bergman *et al.* 2016: 591). The US National Centre of Women Police suggests that recruiting more women would be economically advantageous, as the average policewoman costs tax-payers between two and a half and five and a half times less than the average policeman on excessive force liability lawsuit payouts (Silvestri 2007: 43).

Other differences in women's approach to policework and their subsequent effect on policing may become apparent as the number of female officers increases (Brown 1997 in Silvestri 2007: 41). Guajardo (2016: 21) highlights the importance of increasing the number of women in supervisory and command positions, suggesting that their commitment to 'the equal employment and social equality of women in policing' could change employment policies and expand recruitment and promotion of policewomen. As Brown (1997) suggests, including groups previously excluded can have the effect of transforming the organization; just by 'being there', women and people of colour inevitably bring new and different perspectives and become catalysts for change within the organization. Silvestri (2007: 54) argues, however, that increasing diversity may be insufficient in changing the deep-rooted, gendered, and racialized assumptions in policing. Brown and Heidensohn (2000: 8) concur: increasing numbers alone may not be enough to transform the 'prevailing values and behaviours of the dominant (white male) group within the police' as wider changes within the criminal justice system and society in general are required. In order to make the link between representation and improvements in service delivery, policing needs to do more than simply accom-modate women and minority groups; it needs to make them a 'visible feature of the policing landscape' (Brown 1997).

CONCLUSION

The internal workings of the police service and the ways in which coercive and surveil-lant powers are deployed within the police métier reflect the law, politics, and culture of the societies that they serve. Ultimately, the twin tropes of police 'service' and police 'force' collide in the notion of democratic policing. Sometimes police force is a service but, like 'liberty' and 'security', the principles involved are discordant and cannot be perfectly reconciled. In highly authoritarian societies and those that are segregated along the lines of age, race, class, gender, and sexual orientation, the police are called upon by governments and more powerful social groups to reinforce boundaries of exclusion, belonging, and citizenship. South African police were instrumental in the enforcement of the laws of apartheid (Brewer 1994; Brogden and Shearing 1993) just as the police in the pre-civil rights USA played a vital role in enforcing segregation (Alexander 2012). The police in societies that condone violence against women fail to provide equal protection to victims of domestic and sexual violence. Although policing evolves with changes in social mores and values, patterns of inequality persist. Across the world, the already socially marginal are the focus of police attention as 'suspect populations' and conversely are not well served as victims; they tend to be over-policed and under-protected. The core argument of this book is that the police will exist in some form or another in any social order that has a complex division of labour; there-fore, questions of fairness and justice in policing cannot be avoided.

At least in democratic countries we expect the police to use their awesome powers for the good of the entire society, and yet they often act to exclude or oppress particular social groups. This, in our view, underlines the need for legal, political, and democratic means to ensure that the powers of coercion and surveillance are used for the general social good rather than for narrow sectional interests. Patterns of discrimination and the mental maps of the population found in police culture are isomorphic, bound up within the wider structure of race, gender, and class disadvantage that can also be found in the economy, education, employment, and housing (Bowling, Philips, and Sheptycki 2012; Alexander 2012; Eddo-Lodge 2017). These broader structural patterns are the common theme that link the exclusion of women, people of colour, and LGBT communities from police forces, with inequality of service provision and with the focus of street policing on marginalized communities. The exercise of coercive and intrusive police power has, through history, operated against the economically and socially marginal and has provided greater protection for the powerful. This remains true today. As we argue in the Conclusion (Chapter 12), attempts to improve the fairness of policing, as well as its effectiveness and legitimacy, are as much a matter of economic and social policy as they are of efforts to reform the laws that govern police powers, the occupational culture of policing, and the means through which the police are held democratically accountable to society as a whole.

7

BELOW, BEYOND, AND ABOVE THE POLICE: PLURALIZATION OF POLICING

INTRODUCTION

The task in this chapter is to overview the scholarly literature addressing plural policing and its meaning in terms of the politics of the police. Elsewhere in this book we have acknowledged the 'parallel universe' of transnational private policing and put any questions it might raise concerning these matters to one side. In this chapter we will look at the relationship between the police, politics, and law, taking into account the hybrid nature of the policing web where shifting legal distinctions between public and private are practically involved. The line between public and private law is an especially important feature of the opportunity structure of the policing web, and it requires consideration of the organizational forms of plural policing, their institutional practices, and the human interactions within and between them.

No discussion of the politics of the police would be complete without consideration of the role of force and the services that legitimate policework. Questions concerning the conceptual distinction between high and low policing are also critical. Pluralization entails recognition that changes in the application of force in policing and military contexts—due to technological innovation, technology transfer, and commonalities arising out of shared neo-liberal management strategies—have practical, political, and organizational effects. While some influential current theories suggest that private police are future oriented, leaning towards prevention and risk suppression, and public police are more inclined to retroactive law enforcement and a punishment mentality (Johnston and Shearing 2003), under conditions of global neo-liberalism such distinctions are increasingly dissolving (Bowling and Sheptycki 2012).

All of the above considerations have traditionally impinged on discussions about the appropriate relationship between 'the state' and 'society' and by extension 'the police' and 'the community', and more recently 'the global' and 'the local'. These neat dichotomies are disturbed by the hybrid nature of the plural policing web and the evidently fluid social situation of our times (Bauman 2000), but nonetheless continue to provide common reference points for theorists and practitioners interested in the politics of the police.

Of particular interest are certain technological transformations that have propelled the rise of so-called intelligence-led policing with big data—proactive and future oriented policing practices that contrast, complement, and connect with *post hoc* investigative work by police detectives. Inevitably in thinking about the politics of pluralized police, we shall have to consider the role of law in the politics of police accountability. But before we consider these points, it is first necessary to provide historical background and some sense of the language, debates, and key terms that have developed and transformed the conceptualization of plural policing.

HISTORICAL BACKGROUND

During the 1970s, and just as academic research on policing was beginning to achieve recognition as a distinct specialism in the social and human sciences, macro-level changes were taking place in political and economic policy that would have dramatic consequences for the politics of the police. These were largely unforeseeable for the pioneers of academic police research, and remain largely ignored in much routine 'scientific' police research today (e.g. Sherman 2013; Weisburd and Neyroud 2013). Around the time of the publication of Bittner's *The Functions of Policing in Modern Society* (1970) the predominant paradigmatic ways of thinking about the politics of the police were generally established. These were largely limited to empirical knowledge and theory about Anglo-American municipal policing paid through the public purse (e.g. Punch 1983).

In 1971 the RAND Corporation published a report that argued policing was a service which could be provided by either public or private agencies (Shearing 1992: 409). In 1976 a report commissioned by the US Law Enforcement Assistance Administration (LEAA) opened the way for a wider consideration of the role of private security in the policing sector (Joh 2004: 68). These reports were the harbinger of hybridized and plural institutional forms of policing, transgressing the line between public and private law, that were recognized in police scholarship only years later.

In the formative years of academic police research in the UK and North America only a few scholars recognized that, over the longer term, there had been shifts and oscillations in the balance between 'public' and 'private' policing under capitalist conditions, and that there was, indeed, often a practical interweaving of the two (Spitzer and Scull 1977; Marx 1987). A lesson articulated during this period was that, underneath the dominant discourse on the politics of the public police was a 'quiet revolution', and that new forms of private policing were in the ascendant (Shearing and Stenning 1979).

The landmark RAND and LEAA reports said to mark this shift were published around the time of the so-called 'Nixon Shock' that destroyed the Bretton-Woods system of international financial exchange in 1971. This historical date can be taken as the symbolic commencement of the neo-liberal turn against the Keynesian compromise that had sustained the political economies of the West since the end of the Second World War (Mann 2012: 129–40).

The neo-liberal turn became more visible during the years of Thatcher and Reagan but it was manifested differently across the many sovereign jurisdictions of the international system of states, a system that was held in stasis by Cold War tension until 1989. When the Cold War ended the global system rapidly transformed, raising acute questions about the fate of democracy under transnational conditions (Held

1991). The moral economy of neo-liberalism gradually made way for the emergence of 'aspirational policing' self-help, as both economically marginal communities and those with financial resources sought ways to preserve their own social orders and well-being (Fassin 2017).

This period coincided with the 'third wave' of democratization, commencing with the end of the Salazar dictatorship in Portugal in 1974 and expanding through southern Europe, South America, eastern Europe, South Asia and Africa throughout the 1980s and 1990s. The number of nominally democratic states went from approximately forty in the mid-1970s, to sixty-nine in 1989 and it reached a peak of 123 around 2005–6 (Bonner *et al.* 2018: 6). During this time the technological underpinnings of the 'global networked society' took shape (Castells 2011), atop of which emerged a global capitalist class (Sklair 2001; Harvey 2005b).

Concomitantly, while the number of formally designated democratic states rose, measures indicating the quality of human rights fell (Bowling and Sheptycki 2016b; Bonner *et al.* 2018: 11). This coincided with the escalation of police-military interaction in 'humanitarian assistance operations', which became an increasingly common feature of the international landscape (Goldsmith and Sheptycki 2007). It also coincided with a significant rise in 'international police co-operation' (Lemieux 2013). In short, from a global perspective a whole series of developments occurred that changed the shape of the political economy everywhere, and with that the social organization of the police changed as did the environments in which policing takes place. Borrowing the words of Clifford Shearing and David Bayley, the object of analysis became 'bigger than the breadbox of the police but smaller than the elephant of social control' (Bayley and Shearing 1996: 586).

The pluralization of policing gave rise to a number of competing theories and claims, and there emerged a complex language for talking about police governance and security (e.g. Button 2002; Johnston 2000a, 2000b; Johnston and Shearing 2003; Lippert and Walby 2014; Wood and Dupont 2006). However, systematic understanding of the political economy and relational effects of complex hybrid techno-policing networks on human security was largely absent (Manning 2014: 26).

The available literature concerning the changing morphology of policing is now very considerable, and it is quite possible to make sense of the wider politics of the police in the light of these developments without simply succumbing to a 'watershed syndrome' (Jones and Newburn 2002; Brodeur 2010: 260–3). The neo-liberal turn came amid a bewildering number of other social transformations that undoubtedly significantly affected the politics of the police, but there were also continuities. From the standpoint of the present, we can now look back and evaluate the pre-millennial claim that future generations would 'look back on our era as a time when one system of policing ended and another took its place' (Bayley and Shearing 1996: 92).

Efforts to describe 'postmodern' police have been hampered by the complexity of the phenomena under analysis (Murphy 1998; Reiner 1992b; Sheptycki 1995). The existing empirical literature on private and public policing now reveals that *in aggregate* there is practically no functional difference between the two, while 'the law recognizes a nearly absolute distinction' that separates them, a contradiction which results in a variety of paradoxes (Joh 2004: 49). Some theorists call it a 'police assemblage' (e.g. Fyfe, Grundhus, and Rønn 2017: 186–8), others 'the police extended family' (e.g. Crawford and Lister 2004), or the 'policing web' (Brodeur 2010), but regardless of terminology, plural policing extends across the legal dividing line between public and private institutions in complex ways (e.g. Wakefield 2005).

At a high enough level of abstraction, in theory we can hold the police métier—surveillance backed up by the possibility of coercive action—as a definitional constant, and examine similarities and differences as it is enacted from different institutional positions in plural policing (cf. Button 2016: 51–5, 87–95; Manning 2010: 118–20: 213–15; Rigakos 2002: 90; Wakefield 2012: 5–7). This is challenging because, from the point of view of social and political theory, the relationship of plural policing to public authority and civil society remains fraught with difficulties and ambiguities and is freighted with normative expectations (Hucklesby and Lister, 2018; Johnston and Shearing 2003; Loader and Walker 2007; Schuilenburg 2015; Wood and Dupont 2006).

THE TRANSFORMATIONS OF POLICE PLURALIZATION

Curiosity about the public-private distinction in policing extends back at least into the early 1970s (Jeffries *et al*. 1974; Kakalik and Wildhorn 1972), but the articles that most influenced thinking in this domain were probably Shearing and Stenning's essays 'From the Panopticon to Disney World' and 'Say Cheese! The Disney Order that is not so Mickey Mouse' (Shearing and Stenning 1985, 1987). In retrospect, the allure of Disney-policing seems misplaced. When John van Maanen (1991) undertook fieldwork behind the scenes in Disneyland he revealed a highly stratified, low-wage workforce, subject to a high degree of employer control and expectations of rigid conformity to workplace rules. In short, employee management in Disneyland perfectly instantiated neo-liberal philosophies of social control.

Not surprisingly, in the contemporary period the non-unionized contract workers at Disney often do not make enough money to be able to pay normal monthly expenses such as food and rent (Sanders 2018). From the point of view of those working in the 'happiest place on earth'—rather than that of the customer's experience—the social order of Disney is clearly oppressive (Velasco 2017). The trope of Disney that accompanied the discovery of 'mass private property' and the private guarding industry helped to set off a boom of research interest (Johnston 1992a, 1992b; Jones and Newburn 1999; Shearing and Stenning 1981; Shearing and Stenning 1987; South 1988).

THE TRANSFORMATION THESIS

By the 1990s a debate had crystallized about the extent to which the advent of private policing had ended 'the monopoly' of public police, 'fragmented policing', and otherwise 'transformed' the institutions of social control (Bayley and Shearing 1996; Cunningham *et al*. 1990; Jones and Newburn 1999). In the UK there was a concern that the transformations imagined by the advocates of the plural policing perspective were too sweeping and 'over globalized' (Jones and Newburn 2002: 132). A prevalent interest in England and Wales was to document the domestic situation, particularly with regard to the relative size of public and private sectors of policing and to gauge the extent to which it was part of a more global trend (e.g. Button 2007, 2016; Jones and Newburn 1998; Wakefield 2012; White 2010).

Brodeur surveyed the available international literature on the subject, remarking that it was a 'wilderness of numbers' (2010: 268). Nonetheless, he was able to conclude several things. First, that in only three countries—Canada, South Africa, and the USA—did private police agents clearly outnumber the public ones. Second, there was too much variation in the data and too many measurement problems to draw firm conclusions regarding European jurisdictions.

However, available statistics showed that the size of the public police sector was generally much larger than the private in all EU countries. Third, in every country reviewed, the trend was for the rate of growth to be faster in the private sector than the public. According to Brodeur, there remained large discrepancies between various developed countries with respect to the ratio of public to private police, and he concluded that 'the relative weakness of the numerical data should caution us against any dogmatic theoretical assertions' (Brodeur 2010: 275).

Brodeur also remarked that 'it is obvious that there will soon be more private security agents than public police in the United Kingdom' (ibid.: 275), and he wondered about the continuing impact of falling numbers of public police on counter-terrorism policing. On this point it is perhaps worth mentioning that in 2017 *The Guardian* reported that the number of police officers in England and Wales fell from a peak of 144,353 in 2009 to 122,859 in 2016, while the number of specialist armed police officers fell from a peak of 6,796 in 2010 to 5,639 in 2016 (Travis 2017).

While declining numbers of public police were increasingly in demand to undertake high policing type functions, Calum Macleod, Chair of the Police Federation of England and Wales, worried about the socially corrosive effects of the rising number of wealthy and privately policed community enclaves (Macleod 2018). Observing the rise to prominence of private security in upper-class neighbourhoods, John Harris opined:

> . . . in an age of marketised and consumerised everything, the point cries out to be made: true policing is not a matter of customer service. Its provision is universal not just in the sense that—in theory at least—we should all be protected by it but also in terms of its most basic operations . . . [police]work is not about seeing to individual complaints, nor being summoned to crime scenes and commencing investigations, but keeping a close eye on things that are ineffably social: from homelessness to drug abuse, to the serial failing of our threadbare system for treating mental health . . . as austerity carries on, how long can that hold? (Harris 2018)

Others made the point that historically 'the police' existed alongside a variety of 'secondary agents of social control', and that levels of crime or orderliness actually owed little to the police per se (Reiner 2015: 312).

The secondary agents of formal social control that British police were used to working alongside during the 'golden age of police legitimacy' included people in roles as various as park wardens, teachers, bus conductors, concierges and other kinds of private guardians (Jones and Newburn 2002: 140). Accordingly, in the UK the rise in numbers of people employed in the private security industry coincided with the diminution of those in positions of traditional secondary social control (while tertiary social control exercised within people's wider networks of association also deteriorated). The sanguine conclusion was that this pattern represented a formalization of social control, not the fragmentation of policing, and that the relative size of the public policing sector vis-à-vis secondary social control agents was not much changed (ibid.: 143).

THE POLICE AND SECURITY WEB

In terms of political economy, we would say that this is an effect of the neo-liberal 'hollowing out of the state', another step towards 'a dystopian vision in which the privileged float free, cocooned from the masses in security bubbles' (Reiner 2016a: 94). With respect to the pattern of pluralized policing in the UK, scholars argued that the police had always acted in the context of other control agents, but what changed from the 1970s onwards was that private security was increasingly corporatized in the 're-birth' of private policing (South 1989; Johnston 1992b).

Initially this was most visible in the changing landscape of the urban metropolis, where the advent of mass private property was accompanied by the novel presence of uniformed security guards, whose close semiotic resemblance to uniformed municipal police raised questions about 'policing for profit' (South 1988). Taking the long view, Zedner thought that the symbolic monopoly on policing asserted by what she called 'the modern criminal justice state' might have been a 'historical blip', a deviation from a longer-term pattern of multiple policing providers competing in markets for security (Zedner 2006).

A central strand of theoretical thinking regarding pluralized policing concerned the extent to which 'the state' had lost its monopoly claim on the use of force and the governance of security (Bayley and Shearing 1996). This thesis was contested (Jones and Newburn 2002; Loader and Walker 2007), but it was equally clear that the 'police division-of-labour' was more elaborate than the so-called 'Peelian model' allowed (Jones 2011; Newburn 2008/2011: 105). There is sometimes a tendency in this theorizing to reify notions such as 'the state' and 'the police' and to depict these institutions in rather monolithic terms, which belies what is actually known about the empirical complexity of either.

Anne Marie Slaughter, for example, looked at transnational relations not between states, but rather between states 'unbundled' into their constituent parts—regulatory agencies, municipal governments, law enforcement agencies, etc.—aiming to describe how these complex plural networks of actors comprise a 'transgovernmental order' (Slaughter 2004). This order operates alongside, and is interpenetrated by, the private transnational order of corporations and 'high net worth' individuals (Stalder 2006). Monolithic notions of 'the state' and 'society', 'the police' and 'community' need to be modified so as to properly describe such complex webs of social relations (Brodeur 2010: 255–308; Cooley 2005).

THE SEGMENTED POLICING WEB

Research on police organization has revealed 'the police' to consist in manifold discrete 'units' that are not always seamlessly integrated, coordinated or managed (de Lint et al. 2007; Giacomantonio 2015; Maguire 2003). Simply put, the police are not (and never have been) monolithic, and the internal order of these institutions is plural (Reiner 1978b: 70). Research concerning the inner workings of institutions in the public sphere reveals that they are multiplex, and scholars have shown how police institutions in particular have become even further internally segmented due to 'marketization', the adoption of 'new public management' and 'civilianization' (McLaughlin 2007: 96–7). Alongside this interest in the internal diversity of 'the police', research on plural policing emphasized the need to document the interactions of the police in 'community safety partnerships'. Empirical research mapped the complex operation of the extended 'policing family' (Crawford 2008/2011: 152–60), connections in the (de)regulated 'mixed economy' of policing (Crawford et al. 2005; White 2010, 2018), and the consequent 'securitization of society' (Schuilenburg 2015).

Neo-liberal concerns about the rising costs of policing dovetailed with promotion of the 'public safety and security web', and municipal police organizations were drawn into working with other agencies of governance in the context of 'community hubs' and other multi-agency community policing initiatives (Sampson et al. 1988/2017; Walters 1996/2017). Some argued that this was part of a pattern wherein police adapted to a situation 'in which they are no longer perceived as a monopoly provider' (Crawford 2008/2011: 175). Critical observers noted that, due to technical trends and developments in surveillance and big data analytics, this extension of plural policing could end up strengthening 'a more intelligence-driven paramilitary approach to community pacification' (Marquis 2016: 237). When exigencies arise and 'order' is threatened, the police métier will dominate any security partnership.

In a sense, much of the foundational research and theorizing about plural policing focused attention on low policing work, analogous to that of uniformed street-level policing among the general public (Brodeur 2010: 260–5). Research concerning private security guards is now quite comprehensive. The interface between public police and private security guards, the advent of 'mass private property', 'business improvement districts', and other kinds of privatized zones of consumption have significantly shaped the academic understanding of plural policing (e.g. Button 2016; Jones and Newburn 1998, 2002). Numerous studies have been undertaken of private guarding, surveillance, and investigation, and their relation to public police (e.g. Button 2016; Kempa, Stenning, and Wood 2004; Rigakos 2002; Wakefield 2012). Consequently, a much touted solution for bringing plural policing to account was the idea of democratically elected local municipal policing boards which would, in theory, be able to assume a meta-regulatory role in the governance of plural police (Jones 2011: 709–11; Loader 2013; Stenson and Silverstone 2014; Shearing 2006: 26–7).

The increasing visibility of 'self help' policing in poor and marginalized communities, which are often wracked by social conflict, has been idealized (Johnston and Shearing 2003: 151–60). What were once thought of as 'vigilante groups' have been radically re-conceptualized as a kind of 'community self-policing' (Bayley and Shearing 1996: 587; Kempa et al. 1999: 207–11). The rise of self-policing and conflict among the growing numbers of socially, economically, and politically excluded people have been depicted as an inevitable facet of pluralized policing. Critics argue that conceptualizing vigilante justice as policing promotes an epistemic murk that disempowers the police and serves to further de-legitimate them (Brodeur 2010: 323–6; Jauregui 2013).

ACCOUNTABILITY AND THE WEB OF PLURAL POLICE

Accountability remains a dominant and unresolved concern in theories of plural police. Shearing advocated a rhetorical move to get past the inflexibility of state bureaucracies, and achieve influence over plural police by promoting accountability through markets (Shearing 2001). According to him, the practical task was to construct a strategy:

> ... that moves beyond a dismissal of anything that bears a family resemblance to neo-liberal thinking to a more nuanced analysis that accepts the value of some neo-liberal premises while proposing alternative arrangements for realizing them, including (but not limited to) the reconstitution of market mechanisms (Shearing 2001: 270).

Drawing on his work with John Braithwaite, Scott Burris, and Peter Drahos, Shearing added a key set of descriptive terms to the language of plural police, elaborating the notion of 'security nodes' that has become widely influential. Nodal governance (as opposed to state governance) 'seeks to emphasize that networks are dependent on the mentalities, technologies, institutional arrangements and resources of nodes' (Shearing 2006: 26). These theories were propelled by a perceived need to move thinking about governance 'beyond the state'. Systems of private corporate governance thereby became a central concern (Braithwaite and Drahos 2000: 269; Johnston 2006).

Shearing advocated that democracies should mobilize and steer assemblages of security nodes via regulatory means 'at a distance'. He also raised the intriguing suggestion that state-organized policing might thereby be communalized, as security nodes generate new forms of 'indigenous sovereignty' that could elevate the position of politically and economically 'weak' social actors (Shearing 2006: 28–30; see also Wood 2006). He argued that 'no matter what governments say about their commitment to the provision of resources to the weak, they do not wish to trust the weak to direct their own affairs . . .' (Shearing 2006: 31).

Loader and Walker countered that in order for this to work theoretically in the sense of providing 'thick security' for all peoples, the state needed to be active so as to provide 'anchored pluralism' (Loader and Walker 2006: 194) They also emphasized the need for democratic pressures to 'civilize security' (Loader and Walker 2007: 246). Some sympathetic participants in these debates charged that the language of nodal security governance seemed rather vague, obscure, and overly optimistic (Schuilenburg 2015: 45–9). Pluralization could well result in a widening gap between the 'security rich', who live safe in 'security bubbles', and everybody else (Shearing 2006: 30; Sheptycki 1997). Nodal governance is contingent, relational, overlapping, and multi-site. Its complexity is difficult to map with precision, and at least one attempt to do so concluded that the prospects for bringing nodal governance to account by democratic means were weak: 'it is impossible to get a grip on the matter' (Schuilenburg 2015: 301).

TRANSFORMATIONS OF THE TRANSFORMATION THESIS

Initially much of the theorizing about plural police emphasized visible patrol (Brodeur 2010: 258–60; Rigakos 2002; Wakefield 2012). Gradually theoretical conceptions of plural policing outgrew the limitations of this initial formulation. Brodeur distinguished the following major categories of private security services: guarding and surveillance; investigation; expert consulting; technology and equipment servicing; armed transport; parapolicing; quality of life regulation and administration; and paramilitary services (Brodeur 2010: 279).

In extending thinking about plural policing beyond the uniformed-plainclothes dualism, Brodeur drew attention to connections between police and military institutions and private technology companies. This reinforced Johnston's earlier observations regarding the privatization of military and penal functions, and their connection with transnational private policing (Johnston 2000b, 2006). Analysis was also extended to the domain of high policing (Brodeur 2010: 329; O'Reilly and Ellison 2006).

Thinking in terms of political economy, rather than types of security function, there are four elements that can be distinguished and that have relevance in discussions about the politics of the police (Weiss 2018: 24). First there are the public-private partnerships, joint ventures, and other collaborative arrangements that facilitate the circulation of personnel and information between public and private spheres. Next is the interest group and corporate lobbying that has significantly shaped the provision of policing and security services. Third is the growing involvement of private telecommunications and social network technology companies providing privatized forms of surveillance to both corporate and state-based policing organizations. Lastly, transnational oligopolistic private security companies also impinge upon the politics of the police in complex ways.

More recently corporate in-house security has also been significantly opened up to academic enquiry and theorization (Walby and Lippert 2014). The concept of 'corporate policing' in this sense refers to 'in house security' that is neither contracted or purchased and is tied to a corporate model, regardless of whether the corporation is 'primarily public or private in character' (ibid.: 2). Compendious research on security reveals plural policing connections between law enforcement agencies, security-intelligence agencies, cybersecurity experts, the migration control industry, humanitarian assistance operations. This again raises questions about what it all means in terms of the prospects for global governance (Abrahamsen and Leander 2016).

The language of plural policing, which originally focused attention on security guards in shopping malls and Disneyland, was transformed over time and became more elaborate and historically informed (Hucklesby and Lister 2018). As research progressed the phenomena came to be seen as more broad-ranging, perhaps encompassing a politics of the police-industrial complex (Brodeur 2010: 302–5). Certainly global political and economic changes transformed the institutional basis of the social order, and the language of police pluralization also evolved. How then do we crystallize a relevant understanding of the politics of the police?

PLURAL POLICE AND THE LAW

The distinction between public and private law is important to the complex language of plural policing. In legal theory there has been considerable debate concerning the public-private distinction. In the civil law tradition, public law is defined as a body of autonomous rules entirely separate from private law. According to this theoretical viewpoint, state administration clearly has its own legal institutional basis besides that of private law. In the common law both public and private law are understood to be part of the same body of law (Harlow 1980; Horwitz 1982).

Despite any theoretical difficulties concerning the public-private distinction in jurisprudence, thinking in terms of the broader policing web requires acknowledgement of the importance of corporate and contract law, intellectual property law, banking and finance law, and other legal tools in the domain of private law, alongside other kinds typically associated with public police: constitutional, administrative, procedural, and criminal law. Increasingly there is a grey area between public and private forms of law and in the sphere of policing this provides cover in the evasion of attempts to achieve democratic political and legal accountability (Joh 2004, 2014; Marx 1987; O'Reilly 2010).

PLURAL POLICE AND PROCEDURAL JUSTICE

Elsewhere in this book (Chapter 11) we assess attempts to make the complex socio-legal world of public police more codified or 'constitutionalized'. The UK Police and Criminal Evidence Act (PACE 1984), for example, is a landmark attempt in common law jurisdictions to attain some degree of accountability for the public police via procedural means (Goldsmith and Lewis 2000; Skinns 2019). The procedural approach to police accountability concentrates attention on matters of 'fairness writ small'; that is on micro-social processes of procedural justice, rather than the larger socio-structural effects achieved by the diverse application of police power (Sklansky 1999: 1280).

Advocates of procedural justice make the distinction between 'distributive justice', which has to do with outcomes, and 'procedural justice' which is about process. They reason that people distinguish between the fairness of the procedures they undergo when interacting with police agents and the outcome they experience as a result. Advocates of procedural justice suggest that people may be upset by outcomes, such as an arrest, but not by the behaviour of the officer initiating and enacting the procedure. Research evidence suggests that procedural justice is crucial to trust and police legitimacy (Hough, Jackson, and Bradford 2010), and that police procedures shape social identity (Bradford, Murphy, and Jackson 2014).

Critics counter that, while officer demeanour matters, procedures cannot compensate when the political-economic order reproduced by police action is evidently unfair (Reiner 2007: 153). When distributive justice is not on offer, procedural justice is oppression with a veneer of good manners. Plural policing seems predicated on the lack of distributive justice.

A narrow view of police accountability is inadequate when considering the political effects of the plural policing web (Sheptycki 2002b). In contrast to the public police, private police are subject to far less regulation, and have access to legal tools that public police do not (Button 2016; Joh 2004: 60; Jones and Newburn 1998). Regulation of private policing in the USA remains resolutely laissez faire, and the passing of the UK Private Security Industry Act (2001) left the situation in Great Britain substantially the same, although different in the letter of the law (Button 2007).

PRIVILEGE AND PLURAL POLICE

The etymological roots of the English word 'privilege' lie in the Latinate words *privus* (meaning private) and *legis* (meaning law). Private police can be defined as referring to 'the various lawful forms of organized, for-profit personnel services whose primary objectives include the control of crime, the protection of property and life and the maintenance of order' (Joh 2004: 55). What counts as deviant, disorderly, or simply unwanted and therefore needs to be policed is defined by the clients' aims and preferences—that is their privilege (Button 2016). In concentrating attention on legally corporatized institutional forms, this definition of private police has the merit of leaving out mafia-like criminal extortion rackets antithetical to the presumed formal ends of plural police. This definition allows that, even under postmodern conditions, there remains such a thing as 'illegitimate protection' (Brodeur 2010: 333).

However, much of the thinking focuses attention on 'uniformed private police', possibly to the exclusion of other important nodes in the broader policing web which also exhibit bifurcation along similar lines. Private police can be found doing a variety of things: close-protection, investigation, intelligence gathering, patrolling, and public order maintenance to list some of the more obvious. The research literature on private police shows that they do substantially similar activities to public police, except the latter have the constraints and powers of public law while the former have the duties and privileges of private law. In general, private police do not invoke coercive powers not because they cannot, but rather because they need not.

The subtle controls that are at the forefront of private policework appear *de minimis* to observers on holiday in Disneyland because they do not usually involve overt coercive control (Shearing and Stenning 1985). Private police conduct pat-downs to check for weapons, question suspected persons and detain them, effectuating arrests when needed, and then pass them off to public police agents (Joh 2004). Private police also gather information and transform it into intelligence. Private police can also turn to private justice systems that offer distinct legal tools including banning, firing, and fining.

In the USA, given existing constitutional guidelines and case law, 'private security are still provided with a safe haven in the law of arrest, search and seizure' (Nemeth 2017: 89). That is to say they are not bound by the same due process restrictions as public agents. This is generally recognized to be the case in other jurisdictions (Brodeur 2010; Button 2016). Similarly with regard to the high/low distinction in policing, there is a complicated legal relationship at the interface of public and private institutions (O'Reilly 2015). Considering this, any information that comes into the hands of private police—through interviewing, surveillance, or non-warranted search and seizure, for example—can be transferred to public police agents for subsequent use via what has become known as the 'silver platter doctrine' (Joh 2004: 125).

This doctrine allows private police to collect evidence and information in ways proscribed to public police, and hand it to them 'on a silver platter' for possible use in court without being subject to the usual rules of exclusion or discovery (Beaton 2012: 595–7). This is easily facilitated in transnational contexts where plural police actors can 'jurisdiction shop' (Joubert and Bevers 1996; Bowling and Sheptycki 2012). In such instances the only remedy in law for private citizens is through tort law. However, such cases are 'strikingly rare and unsuccessful', as are attempts to mobilize tort law in cases involving misuse of force by private security agents (Beaton 2012: 597). In considering plural policing, the centrality of the public-private divide in law permits (and perhaps even encourages) exploitation of the full legal toolkit, including both public and private legal instruments (Joh 2004: 124–6).

Research in Canada documents the striking increase in intelligence and information sharing between and among commercial private policing firms and public police agencies (Lippert and O'Connor 2006). Three types of plural police information network have been discerned: ones that involve state-based agencies only; those exclusively involving private justice networks; or multilateralized networks which cross the line between the two.

Other research indicates substantial variation, asymmetry, and irrationality in networked information sharing processes generally (Delpeuch and Ross 2016). With reference to hybridized police information networks, Lippert and O'Connor (2006) demonstrated that private security actors are knowledge producers and brokers, who disseminate information to public police agencies in order to mobilize resources on behalf of their clients. They do so in a liminal grey area of legality. Lubbers' (2012) research revealed that private corporations—including McDonalds, Nestlé, and Shell—employ private security consultancies to undertake proactive surveillance on political activists in order to secure corporate interests and evade political, social, and legal accountability.

THE OPPORTUNITY STRUCTURES OF PLURAL POLICE

In 2008 the German retail supermarket chain Lidl was revealed to have engaged the services of a private security company to undertake surveillance on its employees, both on and off the job (Connolly 2008). This raised questions not only about employee expectations of privacy in the workplace, but also in the private sphere more generally (Wallach 2011). In 2013 it was revealed that parts of the Canadian security intelligence apparatus may have been involved in informal information sharing with private companies in Canada; corporations which were involved in resource extraction operations in Brazil. This resulted in questions concerning the possibility of state-based intelligence agencies undertaking international industrial espionage on behalf of private interests (Chase 2013).

In 2018, police in North America announced the resolution of a homicide cold-case involving two Canadian teenagers murdered in Seattle in 1987. The case was solved in part because, after DNA matching in official police data registers failed to produce any hits, police investigators compared the original crime-scene DNA against data obtained from a genealogy website owned and operated by a private company. Millions of people have sent their saliva to genealogy websites, most likely never suspecting that they were contributing to a databank that would be used for police investigative purposes (CP 2018). In 2019, one of the largest private DNA genetic testing companies in the USA issued a statement verifying a 'fresh agreement' with the FBI to allow the agency access to its databases (Song 2019).

Police body-camera-feeds attached to face-recognition software, processing images in real time and using 'black box' algorithmic profiling, can generate the legal basis of 'reasonable suspicion' and may thereby be used to justify the use of force (Friedersdorf 2016). However, it is impossible to find out how these 'black box' algorithms work because the proprietary software is protected behind the wall of private intellectual property rights (Joh 2017: 105–8).

In February of 2015 an armed security guard shot and killed two people in a Toronto fast food restaurant. Having sought advice from the Crown Prosecutor, and partly on the basis of (privately owned) CCTV evidence from the scene, city police declined to prosecute on the ground that there was little likelihood of a conviction. Subsequently, the CCTV video evidence used as the basis of the decision not to prosecute was held in evidence *sub judice* and could not be released to members of the public, including the victims who believed there had been a police cover-up. Later the private security company whose employee had shot the fatal rounds complained about lack of access to the CCTV data because they wanted to use it for training purposes. The public outcry concerning suspicions that police were colluding in the cover-up of a wrongful shooting death was assuaged when a private viewing of the footage was arranged for representatives of people who had been shot (Ross 2015).

All of these cases demonstrate the complex opportunity structure (and its hindrances) that the private-public legal distinction makes for in the context of the plural policing web, and the variety of legal and technological tools that need consideration in describing its operations. What makes these episodes interesting in terms of the politics of the police is that they manifest, in one way or another, the key elements of the police métier—surveillance and the capacity to orchestrate coercive measures. They also illustrate the complexity of bringing plural policing to democratic and legal account.

PLURAL POLICING AND THE MILITARY

There is a great deal of literature concerning the increasing interconnections between police and military (Kraska 2007), and sociologists have long noted that police operations have been organized around military techno-structures (Haggerty and Ericson 1999, 2004). Police and military surveillance capabilities and technologies exhibit increasing similarities (Doyle 2005). The nexus of police-military pluralization is facilitated by the evolution of a range of weaponry that lies between the destructiveness of battlefield weapons and the police officer's truncheon. These include noxious sprays, conducted energy weapons, energy rays, foam sprays, bean bag rounds, batons, and riot shields, varieties of which have been deployed by both police and military personnel (Brodeur 2010: 287; Wilkinson 2008).

Plural policing can also be seen in the convergence of police and military via peace-keeping and humanitarian assistance (Hönke and Müller 2016). On the frontiers of the global system, militarized plural policing structures have emerged to enforce monopoly control over the hinterland for the benefit of multinational corporations (Rodríguez and South 2016). Researchers question whether the police and military really are 'two worlds apart', or if there is a constabularization of the military along with a militarization of the civilian police (Easton *et al.* 2010). This aspect of police pluralization is particularly worrying because it blurs the boundary between peacekeeping and pacification, undermining the general consent of the citizenry not to violently resist policing (Brodeur 2010: 283–8, 350; Goldsmith, Wadham, and Halsey 2018; Maguire, Nix, and Campbell 2016).

PLURAL POLICE AND TECHNOLOGY

The influence of technology providers on police policy and practice is of consequence. Brodeur documented how Taser International marketed its conducted energy weapons products—the 'Taser Gun'—to police agencies around the world. He argued that claims that the weapons are 'less than lethal' are 'demonstrably mendacious' (Brodeur 2010: 286). We would point out that the introduction of these weapons in the context of neo-liberalism has had negative effects on the provision of police service, undermining public confidence in police.

For example, official figures revealed that in 2017 police in Regina, Saskatchewan deployed conducted energy weapons a total of eighteen times, seven of which were against persons suffering mental health crises (Saskatchewan Police Commission 2018). The rise in numbers of police occurrences involving people with mental health-related problems is the inevitable result of the ascendancy of the neo-liberal economic system and the embrace of economic austerity (Mukherjee and Harper 2018: 84–107). The negative effects of turning social responsibility for mental health into matters of 'law and order' and 'public safety' include the erosion of police legitimacy, partly because use-of-force technologies in the hands of police are inappropriate means to provide services to people in distress.

Taser International has achieved market dominance in the supply of police body-cameras, not by marketing the cameras themselves (which are essentially sold as loss-leaders) but by selling the cloud-management and analytical services necessary to cope with the truly gigantic volumes of data that the cameras produce (Joh 2017: 114). When it comes to policing localities and territories, the undue influence of corporations providing services and technologies to municipal police departments has been critically evaluated (Brodeur 2010: 283–8; Joh 2017; Sheptycki 2018a).

Brayne (2017) revealed that the LAPD's 'big data' surveillance and analytical technologies had been initially provided by a company called Palantir which started with venture capital provided by the CIA and originally had a host of customers in the realm of public police and law enforcement in the USA, including the FBI, CIA, ICE, LAPD, NYPD, NSA, and the DHS. Its existence was hardly known until the company took on a corporate security contract with J. P. Morgan, a major financial institution. The contract to provide cybersecurity services in the private corporate sector exposed Palantir to public scrutiny after it was revealed that J.P. Morgan's own senior executive had come under the surveillant eye of the company's contract security consultants who were using Palantir technology to covertly monitor employee activity. (Paretti 2017; Waldman, Chapman, and Robertson 2018). The growing and pervasive influence of private sector technology providers in reshaping the contours of public and private policing, and with it the territory being policed, is not yet well understood and is an important area for future enquiry.

PLURAL POLICE AND TERRITORY

The disaster response to Hurricane Katrina in 2005 included the presence of Blackwater International, a private security company (Deflem and Stuphin 2009). Katrina was a symbolic occasion in the pluralization of policing, where military personnel, police personnel, and private security providers were simultaneously deployed in a high-profile domestic situation. Large-scale security events represent temporary plural police arrangements to control territory in an intensive way (Whelan and Molnar 2019). The 2003 meetings for negotiating the neo-liberal Free Trade Area of the Americas (FTAA) treaty in Miami involved the deployment of approximately 2,500 riot control officers from more than three dozen US agencies (Maguire 2016: 83–4). The policing of the G20 meetings in Toronto in 2012 similarly involved large numbers of public police from multiple agencies as well as private security guards (Marquis 2016: 226–30).

Quite what this all means depends on the locality, and it is difficult to generalize. Plural policing is organized differently in Belgium (Devroe 2017; Easton and Dormaels 2017) than in Paris (de Maillard and Zagrodzki 2017; Mouhanna and Easton 2014). But these territories are close to economic centres of global neo-liberalism whereas on the edges of the system, in cities like Durban South Africa, the nexus of high-tech, militarized, plural policing has been described as 'twilight policing' (Diphoorn 2016).

Twilight Policing tries to capture three threads of thinking, the first having to do with the actuality of both public and private police acting in the capacity of armed response in public areas, the second with the punitive and exclusionary aims of these practices, and the third with the 'panoptic gaze of many masters' that plural police experience as part of their jobs (ibid.: 232). Perhaps Durban is more representative of the actuality of plural policing than that which can be found in the cities of the metropolitan centre.

At the edges of the international state system, in the frontier regions of Colombia, for example, a plural policing mixture of militarized state police and private security have 'become central to supporting the process of monopolization of land and resources by multinational companies' (Rodríguez and South 2016: 190). These trends are evident in Latin America, Africa and elsewhere in the global South, and need to be taken seriously in theoretical considerations of plural policing and transnational security governance (Beek *et al.* 2017; Bonner *et al.* 2018; Browne-Dianis and Sinha 2008; Diphoorn 2016; Jauregui 2016; Willis 2015).

Years after Hurricane Katrina devastated the city, it was revealed that the New Orleans Police Department used products supplied by Palantir (given under the guise of a private charitable donation to the municipality in order to escape local political accountability), as part of a predictive policing programme against serious crime (Winston 2018). A decade after Hurricane Katrina, the rebuilding of New Orleans had already provided opportunities for private developers to siphon off public resources, and exploit government agencies, to further their profiteering interests and accumulation agendas. It also facilitated the city's gentrification and the exclusion of many of the less economically advantaged people who used to live there (Brown-Dianis and Sinha 2008; Gotham 2012).

TRANSNATIONAL LOCALITIES OF PLURAL POLICING

Pluralized policing is sometimes obscure to those who experience it. Consider the contemporary international airport, which is a commonplace environment for most Europeans and many North Americans. These spaces are policed by multiple agencies, some under public auspices and others under private contract, and are practical examples of the nodal paradigm of security control at work (Leese 2015; Lippert and O'Connor 2003; Lippert and O'Connor 2006: 54). In such spaces there are flexible arrangements between multiple security service providers, who work together (and apart) to make 'security theatre' in the transportation hub (Tiessen 2011). It would be otiose to list the number and types of police agency present in the modern international airport or seaport. Suffice it to say they are multiple, and typically the police division of labour is split between public and private agents. Sometimes security actors in different parts of the police division of labour do go about their business in relative ignorance of work in other segments (cf. Jones and Newburn 1998, 179–81; Brodeur 2010: 299).

In their description of pluralized policing in the ports of Rotterdam and Antwerp, van Sluis *et al.* (2012) identify the 'fragmentation issue' as a problem in the provision of safety and security (van Sluis *et al.* 2012: 74). Paraphrasing somewhat, they describe nodal policing thus:

> The nodal orientation implies being directed towards flows and nodes in order to stop evil. Nodal security implies intensive control and monitoring of infrastructures and flows of people, goods and money that move along these infrastructures. Therefore controls are necessary at the nodes in networks, in order to limit the mobility of evil and to identify it in time, by removing anonymity and invisibility. (ibid: 74)

Behind the facade of security theatre that most travellers experience, at a deeper level of the nodal system of security governance so to speak, there is another network of plural police (Aas and Bosworth, 2013). Bowling and Westenra call this the 'crimmigration control industry', or 'system' (Bowling and Westenra 2018b). This is another parallel and pluralized control assemblage. Novel legal usage combining administrative immigration law and aspects of criminal law hybridizes into a powerful toolkit of 'crimmigration law' for controlling mass migration (Bowling 2013; Stumpf 2006).

Stumpf's socio-legal analysis shows the centrality of the state in drawing lines between 'members' and 'outsiders', in effect turning citizenship into a 'club good' (Crawford 2006). This reinforces in another way Brodeur's rule with respect to plural policing, that 'the higher the [perceived] stakes in the provision of security, the stronger the call to entrust the public police with the mission to provide it' (Brodeur 2010: 308). Private security personnel working on rather low wages are the frontline actors in the security theatre that holiday travellers experience, but their activities are 'underwritten' by state-based police agents (cf. ibid.: 297–300; Jones and Newburn 1998: 181).

In its most banal settings—places as diverse as international airports, Disneyland Paris, and university campuses—pluralized policing exists to 'select, eject and immobilize' (Weber and Bowling 2008). It has a twofold sense: it is negative in so far as it seeks to control, and it is positive in so far as it seeks to facilitate the flow of persons across a pluralized 'nodal' policing landscape (Bowling and Sheptycki 2014: 57). Increasingly, this model of policing is adapted to securing a global system of class privilege. Looked at in aggregate and from this abstract point of view, the pluralized nodal police penetrate deep into the fabric of society and, on the basis of *privus legis*, secure the particular interest against more general claims to the public good. This trend was certainly visible in developments at Los Angeles airport (LAX). In November 2015, it was announced that a new terminal would be built by a boutique security firm and, when it was opened two years later, it was touted as a private airport for the 1 per cent. (Carroll 2017).

PRIVATE HIGH POLICING

Private high policing can and should be studied as an object of enquiry in its own right (O'Reilly and Ellison 2006; O'Reilly 2010), not least because it 'enjoys a policing free ride and exercises, de facto and unaccountably, the powers legally granted to the public police' (Brodeur 2010: 329). In considering the upper echelons of the plural policing web, it is difficult (if not impossible) to discern the basis of maleficence and beneficence. These strata of the plural policing web are inhabited by a range of actors, some in the employ of state security services, euphemistically known as the 'Five Eyes' or 'the intelligence community' (Gill *et al.* 2007). These networks are 'securitizing policing', and the high end of the plural policing web is becoming increasingly expensive, as it expands intelligence activities into local municipal policing (Murphy 2007). Then there are private security contractors (many of whom are former members of the 'intelligence community'), and the 'boutique intelligence firms', along with private detective agencies and freelance covert operatives. Until very recently private high policing was not considered a mainstay of research on the plural policing web, but advances in theory and method have opened up this domain for further enquiry (O'Reilly 2015).

Taking up the sensitizing distinction between high and low police exposes what the practice and theories of pluralized nodal police successfully obscure. Plural policing is complex, hybrid, and multi-dimensional, and it does not lie along a neat continuum. The sensitizing distinction between high and low policing extends to another dimension which associates high policing with the *particular interest* and low policing with the *general interest*. With this in mind, we would argue that thinking about the political economy of the pluralized nodal policing web reveals a multi-dimensional and polycentric network of power serving the particular interests of what Sklair (2001) identified to be a 'transnational capitalist class'.

PLURAL POLICE AND SURVEILLANCE

Increasingly all elements of the plural policing web are managed according to the principles of pre-emption, precaution, and the concern to secure uncertainty (Ericson 2007; McCulloch and Wilson 2016). Policing on the basis of stochastic prediction has effects both at the level of the general population and with regard to individuals. It contributes to the erosion of the moral economy of policing and the further diminution of tertiary social control (Sanders and Sheptycki 2017).

Policing the global 'smart city' involves an array of technologies, orchestrated under a variety of auspices (Bowling and Sheptycki 2011). The proliferation of cameras, together with the interconnectivity of the internet via new social media has contributed to the conditions of 'ambient surveillance' (Stalcup and Hahn 2016). However, the plurality of policing actors operating under such conditions do not amount to 'big brother'. Rather, ambient surveillance is watchfulness by a multitude of them (Ericson and Haggerty 2005a). Present theories relating to plural policing surveillance demonstrate the degree of social control embedded in the surveillant assemblage, and are pessimistic that legal innovations can achieve democratic accountability (Ericson 2007; Ericson and Haggerty 2005b).

CONCLUSION: THE WATERSHED OF PLURAL POLICING?

During the era of Disneyland becoming 'the happiest place on earth' in the 1960s, the average fair-ground attraction employee could expect to earn a middle-class wage sufficient to purchase a home in nearby Anaheim, California. Subsequent to the neo-liberal turn, middle-class employees' lifestyles generally took a turn for the worse, and now workers at Disneyland struggle on the edge of homelessness (Martin 2018; Wasko 2001). This trajectory of decline had consequences within the institutions of policing and in the social world more generally. Policing Disneyland has been a persistent meme in the literature on private policing, and observing the continuities and changes in the Disney Corporation over the decades brings us back to a central question. To what extent does research and theorizing regarding pluralized policing over the past several decades reveal a genuine watershed in police systemic practice? Although there have been many changes, the totalitarian tendencies of Disney have troubled people since the 1930s (Shortsleeve 2004). Likewise there is both continuity and change in the twenty-first-century politics of the police.

Our analysis is predicated on holding the police métier as a definitional constant in order to appreciate the changing institutional forms by which it is practically enacted. To remind the reader, the defining features of the police métier involve the use of surveillance and coercion in the maintenance of some putative social order. Years ago Clifford Shearing argued that police processes of social control and social ordering involved 'subterranean mechanisms' in the reproduction of power (Shearing 1981b). Observing how public police draw distinctions between the deserving public and 'the scum' he averred that what he called 'liberal social control' was an institutional hypocrisy. At the macroscopic level liberal democracy promises legal equality, he argued, but subterranean processes in the maintenance of power ensure that social conflicts manifest at the micro-level become pretexts for social control, legitimating the policework necessary to reproduce capitalist relations of domination. *Plus ça change, plus c'est la même chose.*

In making the case for a revolution in policing, Shearing and Stenning argued that Disneyland exemplified a new paradigm, and they pointed to Huxley and Orwell thereby offering two contrasting images of social-control-dystopia (1985: 349). According to them, Orwell's 'Big Brother' epitomized the totalitarian state, whereas Huxley's *Brave New World* painted a picture of social control similar to Disneyland. They argued further that, generally speaking, social control had become more consensually based: that people were seduced into conformity rather than coerced into compliance. The existing literature reviewed here reveals that both Huxley's and Orwell's methods of policing dystopia are present on either side of the dividing line drawn on the basis of *privus legis*. Socio-legal analysis of the plural policing web reveals law as a set of legal tools with which agents on all sides work in order to engineer the institutional basis of their own action. This raises profound questions about the role of law in the account-ability of policing and the politics of the police (Chapter 11).

Readers will be concerned about the prospects for democratic political accountabil-ity of the plural police, which returns us to the introductory observation that, as the millennium turned, the number of nominally democratic countries in the world rose and the measurement indicators of human rights conditions fell. This is evidence of the degenerative effects of widening social inequality and it reinforces the sardonically critical point that, wherever it touches, the political outcome of neo-liberalism is the best democratic police money can buy (Reiner 2007: 2).

8

COP CULTURES

THE CONCEPT OF POLICE CULTURE

The origins of the idea of police culture[1] lie in a clutch of empirical studies in the 1960s and 1970s, widely regarded as the classics of the field (Reiner 2015). These were conducted by a variety of methods, but primarily involved in-depth ethnography. The theoretical and policy/political concerns of these works differed, and a number of them contained a comparative approach, analysing police in different jurisdictions and milieux within and between countries.

However, their very existence indicates one fundamental shared agenda. Before the emergence of empirical research on policing in the mid-twentieth century, police forces were tacitly assumed to be rule-bound, legalistic, bureaucratic organizations, in which top-down policies prevailed through a quasi-militaristic rank hierarchy and strict discipline code. This image was a deliberate creation of the founders of Anglo-American police institutions, intended to defuse widespread opposition to their creation by projecting them as bound by a universalistic and impartial rule of law.

In a wider politico-economic and cultural context of re-emerging conflicts and social divisions, challenges to that harmonious, rational-legal conception of policing developed in the late 1950s and 1960s. The shared ambition of empirical policing research, whatever its specific theoretical and political provenance, was to probe behind the mock-bureaucratic facade. In the language of legal realism, what was the law in action by contrast with the law in the books? How did the police think and behave behind the veil of legal rational discourse in which their practices were shrouded by court proceedings and official documents?

One of the key discoveries of early empirical research was the extent of discretion held by operational police officers, about whether and how to invoke legal powers and processes, and more broadly how to behave (or misbehave). Whether or not this was sanctioned *de jure*, police inevitably had considerable de facto discretion. The reasons range from pragmatic—above all that resources could never cover the vast array of offences police might uncover—to logical, the inescapable openness with which legal rules are interpreted in specific situations.

Perhaps over-reacting to an era in which 'the law' was often used as a synonym for police, early studies tended towards legal scepticism. Law was at best one factor shaping police practice, alongside a variety of social, political and economic processes that it was the project of empirical research to analyse.

---

[1] Some of this chapter is drawn from R. Reiner 'Is Police Culture Cultural?' (2017) *Policing* 11(3): 236–41.

In the array of possible explanations of police conduct and misconduct the ideas and perspectives—the world view—of rank-and-file police officers on the ground was seen as pivotal. This is the germ of the idea of police culture, but it was not formulated that way by any of the early studies now regarded as originators of the concept. The term 'culture' was hardly used by them, and figures at best as one of an array of words used to depict the beliefs and attitudes of police officers, including working personality, the patrol officer's view of his/her mandate, role conceptions, conceptual framework, orientations to work, manners and customs of the police, etc.

Even more significant than this verbal diversity, the perspectives or world views of officers were not seen as a unidirectional, primary cause of police practice. Rather they were seen as having an interactive, dialectical relationship of mutual interdependence with practice, with both poles shaped by wider institutional, political-economic, cultural, and social dynamics and structures. The probing of police perspectives and ideas was part of a much broader canvas analysing the nature, mandate, history, politico-economic, and social role of policing, and its interdependence with wider culture. Although often concerned about policy issues and debates, the classic studies were animated fundamentally by a variety of theoretical frames rather than immediate managerial utility.

Although the term itself was not used, the early studies did develop a framework for understanding the nature, functions, and origins of police perspectives and world views, the idea that has come to be crystallized under the label police culture. For the most part this was not spelled out explicitly, and there were considerable differences in overall theoretical, methodological, and political allegiances. Nonetheless, the general approach to what is now referred to as police culture was encapsulated in the chapter on the policeman's working personality in Jerome Skolnick's seminal *Justice Without Trial* (Skolnick 1966).

Skolnick's sketch has been widely celebrated and criticized from a variety of perspectives, and remains a pivotal reference point in discussions of police occupational culture. However, there are two crucial misinterpretations in much of this literature.

Skolnick's account of the police working personality (together with the work of other early researchers) is often criticized as ahistorical, based mainly if not solely on *patrol* officers, insufficiently critical and structural, monolithic and deterministic. Much of this critique stems from taking the working personality chapter out of context. It is intended as a synthesis of previous work on the police world view, and comes after an extended discussion of the problems and place of policing in democratic societies committed to principles of the rule of law. There is thus explicit acknowledgement of the variety of forms of policing in time and space, and the specificity of the socio-legal context being studied. The ethnographic fieldwork in *Justice Without Trial* focused on vice and other plain-clothes activities, not on patrol officers. Police practices are not portrayed as *determined* by their working personality, but as a subtle cat-and-mouse interplay between the tactics of suspects and cops, structured by wider socio-legal and political pressures.

The most problematic misinterpretation of Skolnick and the other classic first generation studies comes, however, from retrospectively representing them as primarily *cultural* analyses. It is important to distinguish various levels of explanation of the formation of police cultural perspectives. Most of the classic studies were ethnographies, and reflected a micro-level theorization, usually informed by symbolic interactionism. However, many also probed meso-level social sources, including the character of different organizations, communities, and legal accountability frameworks. But these are themselves structured at a macro-level by the overall political economy and culture of particular societies. Skolnick's ideal-typical working personality comprising suspiciousness, internal solidarity/external isolation, and conservatism, is shaped by the foundational elements of the police role in liberal democracies as legal authority, the consequent—but variable in intensity—dangers from symbolic assailants and accountability institutions, and politically and socially changeable pressures to produce results.

The social structural sources of police occupational perspectives is also evident, for example, in Banton's comparison of UK and US policing (Banton 1964), Bittner's consideration of the specificities of skid-row peacekeeping (Bittner 1967), Wilson's 'varieties of police behaviour' (Wilson 1968), Cain's rural-urban contrast (Cain 1973), Manning's study of Anglo-American policework (Manning 1997), Punch's analyses of small-town Essex versus the Amsterdam inner-city (Punch 1979a and 1979b), and Holdaway's rich ethnography (Holdaway 1983, 1989).

The culture of police is thus not a primary cause of police practice, for good, ill, or both. Cultural perspectives are mutually interdependent with practice, and structural pressures shape them both. How variable or constant particular facets of culture are depends on whether they are rooted in changeable or intrinsic elements of policing in various environments, both within and between police organizations. Skolnick's three shaping factors—the exercise of authority (legitimate power), danger (from those over whom power is exercised, *and* from those having authority over police), and pressure to produce results—differ across different environments.

Exercising power over populations is arguably fundamental to any policing mandate. In democratic societies a more or less successful governmental project is to render power into authority through legitimation strategies, such as accountability to the rule of law. The exercise of power creates primary dangers from those subject to it in any society. In democracies a secondary danger facing officers is sanctioning for breaches of legality. Both dangers vary in degree and kind in different jurisdictions. But the more or less constant elements of policing tend to generate an ideal-typical core pattern of cultural responses helping police to cope with their basic lot.

As Weber stressed, however, an ideal type is a pure conceptual model for illuminating reality, and is hardly ever actually embodied in particular cases. Partly this is because of detailed contextual differences, but fundamentally it is because of human subjectivity and a degree of autonomy in interpretation and action. Officers bring different personalities and initial orientations to situations, although the structural weight of the problems they face then tends to shape some commonalities in response.

The fate of this initial model of what has come to be known as police occupational culture has been subject to vicissitudes inherent in social scientific research, and in the structure and culture of academe. In a recent critique David Sklansky introduces the notion of 'cognitive burn-in', arguing that originally useful ideas get ossified into a fixed image, which impedes further development of insights and understanding. However, this tends to happen not so much with the original ideas themselves, as the version that is translated in simple form into textbooks, secondary treatments, and above all in policy debates. Sklansky's critique is levelled at the 'Police Subculture Schema': that 'police officers think alike; that they are paranoid, insular, and intolerant; that they intransigently oppose change; that they must be rigidly controlled from the outside, or at least from the top' (Sklansky 2007: 20).

This neatly sums up an interpretation of police culture now widely embedded not only in textbooks, but also more significantly in managerial and political debates about police reform. It is not, however, the analysis of police culture that can be found in the various classic ethnographies to which the concept can be traced. These studies recognized variations (within and between forces) right from the start. They saw culture not as free-floating ideas developed and transmitted by cultural processes alone. It is structurally rooted in the nature, stresses, and strains of policework in different contexts, interpreted variously by officers as they navigate the pressures and mandates of their roles.

Social science analyses have to grapple with perennial philosophical and theoretical antinomies that are never finally resolvable. In the case of studies of police culture these include determinism/autonomy; structure/action; social/individual; critique/ appreciation; materialism/idealism; macro/micro; realism/constructionism. These polarities can never be transcended, and are in inevitable tension. This was seen by all the classical theorists, including Marx and Weber (although in textbook caricature they are the quintessential one-sided materialist and idealist respectively). Both recognized that people make their own histories, albeit not under conditions of their own choosing; and that explanation had to be adequate at the level of meaning *and* of causal explanation. The history of social science, including the specific area of police culture studies, bounces between fresh attempts to suggest resolution through emphasizing what an earlier phase played down, and regularly relabelling old concepts to suggest progress.

The pressures and reward structures of academic life accentuate this mock progress by incentivizing neophilia. 'Originality' is the prime currency. This is embodied in the chronocentrism that pervades academic publications, where reference lists are dominated by the very recent, with a scattering of 'classics', but almost nothing between five and fifty years old (Rock 2005). There *is* an element of progress, to be sure, in terms of an accumulation of empirical knowledge, but not an ultimate resolution of fundamental epistemological and existential dilemmas in the quest to understand social phenomena.

The attitudes and perspectives of police officers, their cultures and subcultures, are relevant to understanding policing, but they shape practice only in interaction with a plethora of other factors, and not in a uni-directional way. In this there is nothing unique about policing.

All occupations have typical cultures. A reflexive study of police researchers by Al Reiss offers a particularly revealing example (Reiss 1968). Reiss was director of the largest-ever observational study of policing, conducted for the Presidential Commission on Law Enforcement established by Lyndon Johnson in 1965. Fieldwork was conducted by dozens of students who rode with police for hundreds of hours, producing a vast treasure trove of detailed observations of police-public encounters.

Reiss analysed the observers themselves, as a collateral by-product of their work with the police. Prior to their fieldwork, the students displayed the negative views of police that were standard in campus culture of the 1960s, seeing them as authoritarian and racist. Their observations did dutifully record many instances of the malpractices that underlay such critical views. However, after sharing the pressures of the encounters from the perspective of the patrol car, the students attenuated their condemnatory vilification of the cops. They continued to disapprove of the discriminatory and at times brutal practices they witnessed. However, they saw these as shaped—but not excused—by the pressures and problems of patrol work. They came to have an appreciation (though not an acceptance) of the police as fundamentally good people sometimes led to do bad things. Reiss demonstrated that the students' explanation of this related to their own disciplinary perspectives. Law students attributed the malpractices they encountered to bad laws administered by good cops, and saw legal reform as the solution. Management students put the blame on poor managerial practices. And the sociologists saw police wrongdoing as due to an unjust social system that generated the problems the cops had to deal with. In short, the students exhibited both an overall culture typical of their time and place, and subcultural twists on it that were related to their particular disciplinary orientations.

The main implication of the structural approach to the understanding of police culture that was implied by the classical studies is that there are limits to the reduction of police malpractices. This was true not only of individual level policies such as better selection, training, and ethics, or organizational/legal reforms such as more sophisticated discipline and accountability, but also meso-level reformulations of aims and methods like community or problem-oriented strategies transforming the field within which police culture is lived (Chan 1997).

To a large extent the structural sources of police attitudes and practices antithetical to liberal democratic values lie at a macro-level of constant and inevitable features of policing in particular political economies. The root is the fundamentally bifurcated mission of policing in deeply structurally unequal societies. Policing is concerned with the protection of order, but order has two faces: *general*—the universally beneficial achievement and safeguarding of social coordination and cooperation; and *particular*—the reproduction of the inequalities of power and privilege that characterizes all complex societies that have existed so far (see Chapters 1 and 5): 'parking tickets and class repression' (Marenin 1982).

This means that such blights as discrimination in police culture and practice can only be somewhat alleviated by reform policies. This is indicated empirically by a recent clutch of sophisticated and sensitive observational studies that indicate the continuing resilience of the perspectives found by the classic studies, despite decades of reform initiatives in many jurisdictions (Westmarland 2001a, 2017; Loftus 2009, 2010; Fassin 2013; Bacon 2016; Vitale 2017; Faull 2017a, 2017b, 2018). Fundamentally they can only be addressed by tackling the foundational injustices and inequalities in the societies being policed. In recent times, however, the inequalities exacerbated by the hegemony of neo-liberalism (Reiner 2007, 2016b) have intensified the pressures generating unequal policing, vitiating the effect of policies aiming to curb race, gender and other forms of discrimination and unjust policing.

The idea of 'cop culture' developed as a means of understanding police practices, although there is not a one-to-one correspondence between attitudes and behaviour (Waddington 1999b: chap. 4, 1999a). Many observational studies of policework have shown that officers regularly fail to enact in practice the attitudes they articulate in the canteen or in interviews, for example with regard to race (e.g. see Policy Studies Institute 1983: iv, chap. 4).

An important distinction must be made between 'cop culture'—the orientations implied and expressed by officers in the course of their work—and 'canteen culture'—the values and beliefs exhibited in off-duty socializing. The latter clearly has an important function of tension release, which is why it so often characterized by mordant gallows humour (Young 1995; Crank 2004: 322–3; Fassin 2013: 109, 203–9; Bacon 2016: 109).

There are many reasons why expressed attitudes may not be translated into action. They may not be genuine statements of belief but stated to please interviewers, to fit in with colleagues. or to let off steam. Even if they are truly and deeply held, there may be constraints against them being acted out. A racially prejudiced officer, for example, may not act in a discriminatory way because of fear of sanctions. Perspectives are complex and ambivalent, and vary in texture in different situations. An officer who expresses racist views in the canteen context may also be genuinely sympathetic to the plight of an ethnic minority victim and offer support. Conversely, officers who are not prejudiced may still act in discriminatory ways, as the now common concept of institutionalized racism implies. But while the link between ideas and action is far from straightforward, this does not mean that people's perspectives—complex, ambivalent, and fluid as they may be—bear *no* relation to their practices. After all, 'language is itself a form of practice' (Loftus 2007: 195). Interpreting actors' frames of reference and world views—their culture—is a useful element in understanding what they do, although it certainly cannot be the whole story. This is confirmed by research showing that officers holding perspectives closer to the 'ideal-type' of 'traditional' police culture are more likely to engage in violence, holding constant other relevant factors including situational ones such as the violence offered against the officer, and the policies and style of departmental management (Terrill *et al.* 2003).

The *Oxford English Dictionary* defines the 'anthropological' meaning of culture as 'the whole way of life of a society: its beliefs and ideas, its institutions and its systems, its laws and its customs'. Cultures are complex ensembles of values, attitudes, symbols, rules, recipes, and practices, emerging as people react to the exigencies and situations they confront, interpreted through the cognitive frames and orientations they carry with them from prior experiences.

Cultures are shaped, but not determined, by the structural pressures of actors' environments (what Chan (1997) following Bourdieu's usage calls the 'field', which shapes the "habitus"—the lived strategies or dispositions "triggered" by the encounter with a particular field'). Cultures develop as people respond in various meaningful ways to their predicament as constituted by the network of relations they find themselves in, which are in turn formed by different more macroscopic levels of structured action and institutions. Police officers interpret and act and interact in networks of relations structured by increasingly distant processes and institutions—their shifts, neighbourhoods, the police organizations with their internal division of labour. Each actor's responses shape the situations that others act within. In short, to paraphrase Marx: people create their own cultures, but not under conditions of their own choosing.

Police culture—like any other culture—is not monolithic, and is embodied in individuals who enjoy autonomy and creativity. There are particular variants— 'subcultures'—that can be discerned within police occupational culture, generated by distinct experiences associated with specific structural positions (ranks, specialisms, areas, etc.), or by special orientations officers bring with them from their past biographies and histories. In addition, cultures vary between forces, shaped by the differing patterns and problems of their environments, and the legacies of their histories. They will also change over time, as the structures generating them shift with developments in political economy and wider police cultural imaginaries.

Nonetheless, it will be argued that police forces in modern liberal democracies do face similar basic pressures that shape a distinctive and characteristic culture, discernible in many parts of the contemporary world, albeit with differing emphases across time and space, and with internal variations. This is because they face certain common problems arising from the bedrock elements of their role and the constraints of legality—although the precise intensity and form of these vary greatly. There are also deeply shared elements in the situation and exigencies facing all police, even in autocratic or totalitarian regimes that may generate some similarities in culture. These have not been researched for obvious reasons, but the plausibility of fiction featuring police protagonists in Nazi Germany and the USSR suggests that (e.g. *Fatherland*, and the novels of Philip Kerr and Stuart Kaminsky).

It is a commonplace of the now voluminous sociological literature on police operations and discretion that the rank-and-file officer is the primary determinant of policing where it really counts: on the street. As James Q. Wilson put it long ago, 'the police department has the special property . . . that within it discretion increases as one moves down the hierarchy' (Wilson 1968: 7). It has often been claimed that legal rules and departmental regulations are marginal to an account of how policework operates, and a tenet of the highly practical culture of policing is: 'You can't play it by the book.' The core laws enforced by the police often seem to be the 'Ways and Means Act' and 'contempt of cop'.

In the late 1970s this legal scepticism came under fire from a structuralist critique, pioneered by Doreen McBarnet (1978, 1979), which had a considerable influence over empirical studies in the 1980s (notably Shearing 1981a, 1981b; Ericson 1982, 1993; Grimshaw and Jefferson 1987; McConville *et al.* 1991). McBarnet argued that there was a gap between abstract rhetoric about the rule of law, and concrete legal rules (McBarnet 1981: 5). Purely cultural analysis makes the low-level operatives 'the "fall-guys" of the legal system taking the blame for any injustices' (ibid.: 156). Responsibility ought to be placed on 'the judicial and political elites' who make rules of sufficient elasticity to assimilate departures from idealized values of due process legality, which the law effectively condones or even demands.

McBarnet's structural critique does not displace the need for analysis of police culture and the situational pressures on officers' discretion. To say that the laws governing police behaviour are 'permissive' is only to suggest that they do not even purport to determine practical policing (contrary to legal ideology). That leaves leeway for police culture and the social and situational pressures on officers to shape police practice.

This means that the standard legalistic response to revelations of police malpractice—slap on a new rule—may be ineffective or even counter-productive. But legal rules may be inhibiting or become the 'blue-letter' law of police working practice rather than dead letters, depending on a variety of factors (Dixon 1997, 2008; Reiner and Leigh 1992). One of these is the culture of the police—the values, norms, perspectives, myths, and craft rules that inform their conduct. This is neither monolithic, universal, nor unchanging. There are differences of outlook within police forces, according to such individual variables as personality, gender, ethnicity, sexuality, generation, career trajectory, and structured variations according to rank, assignment, and specialization. The organizational styles and cultures of police forces vary between different places and periods (O'Neill *et al.* 2007). Informal rules are not clear-cut and articulated, but are embedded in specific practices and nuances, modulated by particular concrete situations and the interactional processes of each encounter.

Nonetheless, certain commonalities of the police outlook can be discerned in the reports of many studies in different social contexts. The very fact that these are observed at many times and places suggests that they are *not* a common culture that has been diffused and transmitted. Rather its themes and tropes are constantly reinvented and reproduced because they are rooted in constant problems that officers face in carrying out the role they are mandated to perform, at any rate in industrial capitalist societies with a liberal-democratic political ethos.

Cop culture offers a patterned set of understandings that helps officers to cope with the pressures and tensions confronting the police. Successive generations are socialized into it, but not as cultural dopes, passive or manipulated learners of didactic rules. The process of transmission is mediated by stories, legends, jokes, exploring models of good and bad conduct, which through metaphor enable conceptions of competent practice to be explored prefiguratively (Shearing and Ericson 1991). Elements of the culture survive because of their 'elective affinity', their psychological fit, with the demands of the rank-and-file cop condition, while other aspects change as the contexts and characteristics of officers develop.

COP CULTURE: THE CORE CHARACTERISTICS

The *locus classicus* for discussing the core police culture is Skolnick's (1966) account of the policeman's 'working personality'. What needs to be added to his discussion is the analysis of variations around his model, within and between police forces, and over time. Police cultures reflect and perpetuate the power differences within the social structure. The police officer is a microcosmic mediator of the relations of power in a society—a 'street corner politician' (Muir 1977). There is also the need to consider changes that have impacted on policing in the fifty plus years since his original analysis (Skolnick 2008 offers his own reflections on this).

Skolnick synthesized earlier sociological research with his own findings to construct a pioneering sketch of the police 'working personality' (Skolnick 1966: chap. 3). This referred not to an individual psychological phenomenon (as the term 'personality' misleadingly implies) but to a socially generated culture. It was a response to a unique combination of facets of the police role: 'two principal variables, danger and authority, which should be interpreted in the light of a "constant" pressure to appear efficient' (Skolnick 1966: 44).

The 'danger' in the police milieu is not adequately represented by quantitative estimates of the risk of physical injury, although these are not small. People in other occupations—say, steeplejacks, miners, deep-sea divers—may be exposed to higher risks of job-related disease or death. But the police role is unique in that its core tasks require officers to face situations where the risk lies in the unpredictable outcome of encounters with other people. The police confront the threat of sudden attack from 'symbolic assailants', not the more calculable risks of physical or environmental hazards. The extent of seriousness obviously varies. But the police officer faces, round every corner she turns or behind every door whose bell she rings, potential danger. Hence coping with violence is a recurring feature of police culture.

Danger is linked to authority, which is inherently part of the police milieu. It is because they represent authority that police officers face danger from those recalcitrant to its exercise. And the decline of deference in most societies since the mid-twentieth century, however desirable, has made police authority increasingly questioned. Danger and authority are thus interdependent elements in the police world, and cop culture develops adaptive rules, recipes, rhetoric, and rites to cope with those tensions.

Skolnick postulated a third environmental element producing cop culture: 'the pressure put upon individual policemen to "produce"—to be efficient rather than legal when the two norms are in conflict' (Skolnick 1966: 42, 231). Undoubtedly police officers experience external political pressure for 'results', more or less so at different times according to particular moral panics or crime trends. Under the pressure to get 'results' in the form of clear-ups, police may well feel impelled to stretch their powers and violate suspects' rights.

MISSION—ACTION—CYNICISM—PESSIMISM

A recurrent theme observed in studies of cop culture is a sense of mission: 'Down these mean streets a man must go, himself not mean, neither tarnished nor afraid' (Chandler 1944). Police officers are generally attracted to the job for non-instrumental reasons, although this does vary with labour market conditions (Reiner 1978a; Crank 2004; Charman 2017). Policing is regarded as not just a job but a way of life with a worthwhile purpose: the preservation of a valued way of life and the protection of the vulnerable against the predatory (Bacon 2016: 119–20).

The mission of policing is not regarded as irksome, but as fun, challenging, exciting, a game of wits and skill. Many commentators have stressed the hedonistic, action-centred aspects of cop culture (Holdaway 1977, 1983; Westmarland 2001a). The main substance to which the police are addicted is adrenalin (Graef 1989). But the thrills of the chase, the fight, the capture—the symbolic rare highlights of the work—are not merely a sport. They can be so delightedly engaged in because they are also seen as worthwhile.

This moralizing of the police mandate is in many respects misleading. It overlooks the mundane reality of everyday policing, which is often boring, messy, petty, trivial, and venal. It permits the elision of the universally approved elements of the police task, and the political role of policing in upholding a specific state and social order. The 'sacred canopy' (Manning 1997: 21) often drawn over policing can be a tool of the organization, protecting and advancing its interest in gaining resources, power, and autonomy. The myth of the 'thin blue line' is central to the police world view. Much police wrongdoing can be attributed to misguided pursuit of a 'noble cause', the Dirty Harry dilemma of achieving essential ends by tarnished means (Klockars 1980).

Nevertheless, police officers tend to acquire a set of views which have been described as 'cynical' (Niederhoffer 1967; Crank 2004; Charman 2017). Officers often develop a hard skin of bitterness, seeing all social trends in apocalyptic terms, with the police as a beleaguered minority about to be overrun by the forces of barbarism. This pessimistic outlook is only cynical in a sense—in the despair felt that the morality which the police officer adheres to is being eroded on all sides. It is not a Wildean cynicism which knows the price of everything and the value of nothing. Rather it resembles a Marxian account of commodity fetishism: price has sadly masked value. The hardboiled outlook of many police derives from the resilience of their sense of mission. Cynicism is the Janus face of commitment.

The salience of a sense of mission obviously varies between police officers. It was much more evident in the type Reiner labelled 'new centurions' (after the title of Joseph Wambaugh's 1971 police novel) than those the argot calls 'uniform-carriers', who shirk the work as much as possible (Reiner 1978a: chap. 12). Undoubtedly many police see their combat with 'villains' as a ritualized game, with 'winning' by an arrest giving personal satisfaction rather than any sense of public service.

Police culture typically reflects a subtle intermingling of themes of mission, hedonistic love of action, and pessimistic cynicism. Each feeds off and reinforces the others, leading to a pressure for 'results' which may strain against legalistic principles of due process. They are related to other facets of cop culture—suspicion, isolation/solidarity, conservatism.

SUSPICION

Suspicion has often been noted as a characteristic trait of police officers, responding to the danger, authority, and efficiency elements in the mission. Police develop fine-grained cognitive maps of the social world, so that they can readily predict and handle the behaviour of a wide range of others, in frequently fraught encounters, without losing authority (Rubinstein 1973: chaps 4–6; Holdaway 1983: chaps 6–7; Loftus 2009: 125; Cockcroft 2013: 25; Charman 2017: chap. 10).

Suspicion often leads to problematic stereotyping of likely offenders. These may become self-fulfilling prophecies as people with certain characteristics are disproportionately questioned or arrested, leading to a vicious cycle of deviance amplification.

The particular categories informing suspicion reflect the structure of power in society. This serves to reproduce that structure through a pattern of implicit—sometimes explicit—class, race, and gender discrimination.

ISOLATION/SOLIDARITY

Many commentators have observed the marked internal solidarity, coupled with social isolation, of many police officers (Clark 1965; Westley 1970: chap. 3; Reiner 1978a: 208–13; Crank 2004: section III; Loftus 2009: 117–21; Cockcroft 2013: 58).

A tendency to isolation stems from shift work, erratic hours, difficulty switching off from the tension engendered by the job, aspects of the discipline code, and the hostility or fear that citizens may exhibit to the police. Internal solidarity is a product not only of isolation, but also of the need to be able to rely on colleagues in a tight spot, and a protective armour shielding the force as a whole from public knowledge of infractions.

Many studies have suggested a powerful code enjoining officers to back each other up in the face of external investigation (Punch 1985, 2009; Skolnick and Fyfe 1993; Fassin 2013: 205–6; Bacon 2014: 117).

Despite the tendency towards solidarity there are many conflicts *inside* the police organization. Some are structured by the rank hierarchy and the force division of labour, say between uniform and detective branches (Bacon 2016: 237–43). Internal conflicts may often be overridden by the need to present a united front in the face of external attacks, but not always. The fundamental division between 'street cops' and 'management cops' can be reinforced in the face of external investigation (Ianni and Ianni 1983). The depth of the gulf relates to the different, often contradictory, functions of the two levels. 'Management' has to project an acceptable, legalistic, rational face of policing to the public. This may mean complicity with misconduct, hearing, seeing, and saying nothing. But when reform pressures become intense, 'management' may be forced into confrontation with the 'street'. Apparent conflict between 'street' and 'management' orientations may be functional for the organization itself. It allows presentational strategies by management in real ignorance of what these might cover up, while at the same time the sacrifice of some individuals as 'bent' ratifies the effectiveness of the disciplinary process as a whole.

Police perspectives on social divisions in the population clearly reflect the structure of power, filtered through the specific problems of policework (Reiner 1978a: chap. 11; Shearing 1981a; Lee 1981; Holdaway 1983: chap. 6; Loftus 2007, 2008, 2009; Fassin 2013: 42–53).

Many police subscribe to an ideal of egalitarianism (epitomized by remarks such as 'nothing would give me greater pleasure than being able to nick the Lord Mayor'). At the same time they are acutely aware of the status distinctions which do exist (and need to be finely tuned to them in giving and expecting the appropriate level of deference). The crucial divisions for the police do not readily fit a sociologist's categories of class or status, although they do often display contempt towards the undeserving poor (Loftus 2007; Fassin 2013: chap. 1; Vitale 2017: 50–4). They are police-relevant categories, generated by their power to cause problems, and their salience to the police value system. The fundamental division is between rough and respectable elements, those who challenge and those who accept the middle-class values of decency that most police revere. But finer distinctions within these categories can be generated by the police problematics.

'Good-class villains'

Pursuing professional or at least experienced criminals is seen as worthwhile, challenging, rewarding, often the *raison d'être* of policing, however infrequently the ordinary officer encounters such cases. While obviously wishing to evade arrest, they do not normally challenge the basic legitimacy of the police. Relations with them may well be amicable—indeed, this may be cultivated by both sides for favours—the thin end of the corruption wedge (Hobbs 1988).

'Police property'

'A category becomes police property when the dominant powers of society (in the economy, polity, etc.) leave the problems of social control of that category to the police'

(J. Lee 1981: 53–4). They are low-status, powerless groups whom the dominant majority see as problematic or distasteful. Examples at different times and places might be vagrants, skid-row alcoholics, drug addicts, the unemployed or casually employed residuum, youth adopting a deviant cultural style, ethnic minorities, gays, prostitutes, and radical political organizations. The prime function of the police has been to control and segregate such groups, and they are armed with a battery of permissive and discretionary laws for this purpose (Fassin 2013; Vitale 2017). In Britain and elsewhere these powers have been added to in recent years (Young 2008). The concern with 'police property' is not so much to enforce the law as to maintain order using the law as one resource among others. Stop and search (or frisk) has been a traditional and controversial tactic for doing this in jurisdictions around the world (Weber and Bowling 2011, 2014; Delsol and Shiner 2015; Bradford 2016; White and Fradella 2016; Newberry 2017).

A major pitfall for police is to mistake a member of a higher-status group for police property, a problem that has become accentuated for the police with the growth of respectable middle-class involvement in 'deviant' activities. The demonstrator or pot-smoker may turn out to be a university professor or lawyer.

'Rubbish'

'Rubbish' are people who make calls on the police which are seen as messy, intractable, unworthy of attention, or the complainant's own fault.

Domestic disputes are a common sort of call that has traditionally been regarded as 'rubbish' by many police officers. The tendency not to treat domestic violence seriously has generated reform attempts such as mandatory arrest policies in many countries, with disputed evidence of patchy improvement (Sherman 1992b; Sheptycki 1993; Hoyle 1998; Skogan and Frydl 2004: 231–2; Heidensohn 2008: 661; Gadd 2017). 'Rubbish' are essentially people from the 'police property' groups presenting themselves as victims or clients for service, as often happens.

'Challengers'

'Challengers' are defined by Holdaway (1983: 71–7) as those whose job routinely allows them to penetrate the secrecy of backstage policework, and gives them power and information with which they might challenge police control of their 'property'. Doctors, lawyers, journalists, and social workers are in this position (as are police researchers!). Efforts may be made to minimize their intrusion, and presentational skills used to colour what they see.

'Disarmers'

'"Disarmers" are members of groups who can weaken or neutralise police work' (Holdaway 1983: 77–81). They are groups who are hard to deal with as suspects, victims, witnesses, or in service work, because they are perceived as socially vulnerable and so allegations by them against the police may receive special sympathy, such as children or the elderly.

'Do-gooders'

'Do-gooders' include civil liberties or civil rights groups and activists who monitor the police and organize to limit abuses. Prime examples are Liberty (Moore 2017), the

American Civil Liberties Union (Walker 1999), the Canadian Civil Liberties Association, StopWatch, and Black Lives Matter (Lebron 2017).

Politicians

Politicians are often regarded suspiciously by police, seen as out of touch ivory-tower idealists or corrupt self-seekers. Unfortunately, however, they have the power to make law. The lawyers and judges involved in its administration tend to be made from the same cloth.

Running through the police perception of the social structure is a distinction between the powerless groups at the bottom of the social hierarchy who provide the 'rubbish' and the 'police property', and the respectable strata, each with distinct segments which in different ways threaten police interests. Police culture both reflects the wider power structure and reproduces it through its operations.

POLICE CONSERVATISM

What evidence we have of the political orientations of police officers suggests that they tend to be conservative, politically and morally. Partly this fits the nature of the job. The routine 'clients' of the police are drawn from the bottom layers of the social order.

Moreover, in their public order role, and even more so in the work of their specifically political 'high policing' sections, the police have been routinely pitted against organized labour and the left (Lipset 1969; Skolnick 1969; Bunyan 1977; Brodeur 1983, 1999, 2010: chap. 7; Morgan 1987; Weinberger 1991, 1995: chap. 9; Mazower 1997; Huggins 1998; Sheptycki 2007b; Hinton 2006; Fassin 2013; Deflem 2016; Albrecht and Kyed 2016; Bradford et al. 2016; Vitale 2017; Falker-Kantor 2018; Evans 2018a). Furthermore, police forces have usually been constructed as hierarchical, tightly disciplined organizations. Thus the police officer with a conservative outlook is more likely to fit in.

However, there are contradictory pressures at work. Fiscal and political prudence support pay and recruitment policies which mean that the bulk of officers have been drawn from the working class. The police are an employee group whose grievances over pay and conditions of work generate trade union organizations analogous to those of other workers, although police union militancy has often been a force for reaction (Reiner 1978a; Finnane 2002; Marks and Fleming 2006a, 2006b; Marks and Sklansky 2011). 'Deradicalization' of the policeman was not automatic, but had to be constructed (and continuously reconstructed), as Robinson (1978) cogently argued, and is sometimes challenged.

In the USA there has been copious historical evidence of police political support for the right and the far right (Skolnick 1966: 61; Lipset 1969). These attitudes have openly translated into political campaigning. Police associations on numerous occasions actively lobbied for reactionary political candidates, and in support of specific right-wing policies (Skolnick 1969: chap. 7; Bernstein et al. 1982). On the other hand, black and other police associations representing minorities have been a force for progressive reform (Holdaway 2009).

There is little hard evidence of British police officers' political views. An attempt to interview police in the 1970s about their political attitudes was prohibited by the Home Office, who claimed that it would impugn the traditional notion of the police

as outside any form of politics (Reiner 1978a: 11, 283). An unpublished 1977 disser-
tation by a police officer, who interviewed a sample of colleagues in a northern city
force using the questions Reiner had been prohibited from asking, found that 80 per
cent described themselves as Conservative—18 per cent of whom were to the right of
the party. More recently, a survey was conducted of 286 serving Metropolitan Police
officers which included questions on voting patterns and intentions (Scripture 1997).
This found that of those who had voted in the 1979, 1983, 1987, and 1992 general elections the overwhelming majority had supported the Conservatives (respectively 79 per
cent, 86 per cent, 74 per cent, and 74 per cent: ibid.: 172). However, only 44 per cent
intended to vote Conservative at the 1997 general election. This was probably a result
of police disenchantment with the Conservative government's 1993–4 reform package
aimed at subjecting the service to market disciplines (the *Sheehy Report* and the Police
and Magistrates' Courts Act 1994). Apart from specific party politics, the police have
tended to hold views on moral and social issues which are conservative (Skolnick 1966:
61; Reiner 1978a: chap. 11; J. Lee 1981).

Undoubtedly the very fact that some gay and lesbian police officers can now 'come
out' in some jurisdictions, and indeed form their own representative associations,
indicates a measure of progress in the last quarter of a century. However, they still
experience discrimination, and homophobia remains in police culture even if it is
expressed more covertly (Burke 1993; Jones and Williams 2013; Jones 2014, 2016;
https://www.lgbtpolice.uk/).

Although there is an obvious elective affinity for police officers between their role
as upholders of authority and conservative politics and morality, this is by no means
a constant. During the early and mid-1990s, as the Conservative government increasingly applied to the police its market-oriented approach to public services, so police
sympathy at all levels appeared to swing towards more radical views. This continued in
the heyday of New Labour, and has been consolidated by the post-2010 Conservative
government police reform programme (Reiner 2016a).

MACHISMO

The traditional police world is one of old-fashioned machismo (Graef 1989: chap. 6;
Young 1991: chap. 4; Westmarland 2001a, 2017; Silvestri 2017). Police officers are not
notorious for aversion to illicit heterosexual activities (Crank 2004: 191–5). Nor are
police abstemious from alcohol, despite common contempt for users of other drugs
(Bacon 2016: chap. 5).

It has always been tough for women police officers to gain acceptance. The establishment of employment for policewomen in the first place came only after a protracted
campaign (Jackson 2012). Despite formal integration, they continue to experience
discrimination (Heidensohn 1992, 1994, 2008: 646–56; Dunhill 1989; Brown 2003;
Brown and Heidensohn 2000, 2012; Westmarland 2001a; Silvestri 2003; Dick *et al.*
2014; Rabe-Hemp 2017). The difficulties women faced in achieving higher rank in
Britain were illustrated by the highly publicized action claiming sex discrimination
brought by Alison Halford, former assistant chief constable in Merseyside (Halford
1993). However, since then several women chief officers have been appointed, including Cressida Dick the Metropolitan Police Commissioner. The number of women

police has tripled since the early 1990s to nearly 36,000 in 2017—but this is still only 29 per cent (Hargreaves *et al.* 2017). Similar patterns and trends are found in the USA and other jurisdictions.

RACIAL PREJUDICE

Many American studies have demonstrated police suspiciousness, hostility, and prejudice towards blacks and other ethnic minorities (Crank 2004: chap. 18). Such prejudice has been diluted by the increasing recruitment of black and other ethnic minority officers in recent decades (Skogan and Frydl 2004: 312–14), although this has not significantly affected the practices of policing (ibid.: 147–52). The issue of racial bias and discrimination remains a hot issue in US policing, most recently in the ongoing controversies over racial profiling and police stops for the moving violation often characterized as D.W.B.: Driving While Black (Vitale 2017: 21–2). Ironically the Harvard Professor Henry Louis Gates who coined the phrase 'Driving While Black' in a 1995 article became the subject of headlines fourteen years later, when he was arrested on suspicion of breaking into his own house (ibid.: 3).

There is similar evidence of British police racial prejudice (Chapter 6). Up to the early 1970s arrest statistics indicated *under*-involvement of black people in crime compared to their proportion in the population. Nonetheless, studies in the 1960s to 1970s show a clear pattern of rank-and-file police prejudice, perceiving blacks as especially prone to violence or crime, and generally hard to handle (Lambert 1970; Cain 1973: 117–19; Reiner 1978a: 225–6).

Later work, conducted in a period during which black crime and especially mugging became heated political issues, confirms the evidence of prejudice (Holdaway 1983: 66–71, 1993; Policy Studies Institute 1983: iv, chap. 4; Reiner 1993; Whitfield 2004; Rowe 2004; Phillips and Bowling 2017: 198–202).

However, the extent to which racist views are expressed openly and virulently has generally lessened (Foster *et al.* 2005), although deeper prejudiced feelings remain in the culture of white officers, who resent some of the reform efforts (Loftus 2008, 2009, 2010; Foster 2008). The reduction of openly expressed prejudice is partly a result of changes in the demographic character of forces. These include more recruitment of ethnic minority officers (albeit still a disproportionately small number especially at more senior levels: Henry 2007: 92–9; Phillips and Bowling 2017), the influence of black and other minority police associations (Holdaway 2009), more officers with higher education (Lee and Punch 2006; Rogers and Frevel 2018), and a greater emphasis on multiculturalism in training and the official force ethos (Rowe 2007, 2014; Loftus 2009: chap. 2).

The extent of the change was vividly called into question, however, by the 2003 BBC documentary *The Secret Policeman*, which broadcast undercover film of a number of Greater Manchester Police recruits displaying virulent racial prejudice (McLaughlin 2007: chap. 6). Subsequent research documented more systematically the apparent failure of the post-Macpherson reforms to achieve more than cosmetic change (Souhami 2014). Chan's seminal Australian work on police culture was prompted by a media revelation of continuing racism in a 1992 documentary *Cop It Sweet* despite official reforms (Chan 1997, 2003: 54).

Police racial prejudice is in part a reflection of general societal prejudice. The consensus of social research (in Britain and the USA) suggests that, contrary to popular belief, police recruits do not have especially authoritarian or prejudiced personalities (Skolnick 1969: 252; Reiner 1978a: 157; Scripture 1997; Waddington 1999b: 102–4; Skogan and Frydl 2004: 128–30). Rather, they share the values of the social groups from which they are drawn—the lower middle and respectable working classes, which constitute the bulk of society. This is, of course, a double-edged finding, for even the 'normal' degree of authoritarianism is disturbing in an occupation which wields considerable power over minorities. As Stuart Hall commented trenchantly, chief constables would not state so cavalierly that the police force must contain its fair share of criminals (Hall 1979: 13).

What the research does reveal is that (although not necessarily sharply distinctive from the population norm) police recruits often manifest hostile attitudes to ethnic minorities. Such attitudes seem to be accentuated with work experience, after a temporary liberalizing effect during training (Fielding 1988), although more recent studies suggest this may not be as pronounced as in the past (Charman 2017). Unless the pressures generating traditional cultural attitudes alter as a result of more profound transformations in the social structural context of policework, reforms in the selection and training of individual officers cannot achieve much of substance (American and Australian experience confirms this; see Chan 1997, 2003; Skogan and Frydl 2004: 141–7).

Overall, it is necessary and sufficient to explain the police outlook on ethnic minorities (and other issues) by the police function, and the circumstances of policework, rather than by peculiarities of individual personality or socialization. The crucial source of police prejudice is societal racism, which places ethnic minorities disproportionately in those least privileged and powerful social strata, with exposed public on-the-street lifestyles, that are most prone to the limited kinds of crimes the police concentrate on. So they disproportionately become police 'property'. This structural feature of police-ethnic minority relations bolsters any prior prejudice police officers have.

PRAGMATISM

Some observers of police culture note a pragmatic, concrete, down-to-earth, anti-theoretical perspective. No doubt this is changing with the growing interconnections and partnerships between policing organizations and academe in many jurisdictions, as the number of officers with degrees and postgraduate qualifications multiples (Brown 1996; Engel and Henderson 2014; Bryant et al. 2014; Fleming 2015; van Dijk et al. 2015; Hallenberg and Cockroft 2017; Hesketh and Williams 2017; Rogers and Frevel 2018).

Although traditional barriers between police and academe have been crumbling around the world, it is possible the pragmatism of much of police culture may survive. Police officers are concerned to get from here to tomorrow (or the next hour) safely and with the least fuss and paperwork, which has made them reluctant in the past to contemplate innovation, experimentation, or research. This has changed in recent years with the impressive growth of a significant body of practice-oriented research, through think-tanks like the US and the British Police Foundations (www.policefoundation.org; www.police-foundation.org.uk) and police themselves, much of it stimulated by developments like intelligence-led policing (Cope 2008; James 2013, 2016).

Early in-house police research often tended to find 'foregone conclusions' (Weatheritt 1986). This is less true of current work, due in part to a significant influx of experienced civilian researchers into police research departments (Brown 1996), but resistance to analytic approaches continued (Cope 2004). The embedding of 'what works?' research into police policy-making around the world is accelerating (www.police.college.uk; https://www.campbellcollaboration.org/section on Crime and Justice), but some tension with the urgent timescales of fraught on-the-ground decision-making is likely to remain.

VARIATIONS IN COP CULTURE

Police culture is not monolithic, and there is both structured and individual diversity. The organizational division of labour is related to a variation in perspectives around the core elements of the culture (Chan 2003; Skogan and Frydl 2004: 130–3; Manning 2007; Ingram *et al.* 2013; Cockcroft 2013: chap. 4; van Hulst 2017; Charman 2017).

Muir's sensitive 1977 observation of twenty-eight American city police officers centred on the question: 'What makes a police officer good?' Muir highlighted how they dealt with handling coercive power. The good cop developed two virtues. 'Intellectually, he has to grasp the nature of human suffering. Morally, he has to resolve the contradiction of achieving just ends with coercive means' (Muir 1977: 3–4). Intellectual vision can be 'cynical', that is, based on a dualistic division of people into 'us' and 'them', fault-finding, and individualistic; or 'tragic', seeing mankind as of one unitary substance and moral value, seeing action as complexly produced by chance, will, and circumstance, and recognizing the important but fragile nature of social interdependence. Moral understanding may be 'integrated', that is, accommodating the exercise of coercion within an overall moral code; or 'conflictual' where it creates guilt because it is not related to basic moral principles. The two dimensions yield a fourfold typology of police officer. The 'avoider' (cynical perspective and conflicted morality) shirks duties; the 'reciprocator' (tragic perspective and conflicted morality) hesitates to use coercive power even when appropriate; the 'enforcer' (cynical perspective and integrated morality) acts in the heat of conflicts without understanding the need for restraint. The 'professional' (tragic perspective and integrated morality) is the 'good' cop. He or she is able to use violence where necessary in a principled way, but is adept at verbal and other skills that enable solutions to be resolved without coercive force wherever the opportunity exists.

Muir's four types were similar to those found in British research: the 'bobby', the ordinary copper applying the law with discretionary common sense to keep the peace; the 'uniform-carrier', the completely cynical, disillusioned time-server who'll 'never answer the phone if he can help it—it might be a job at the other end!'; the 'new centurion' (cf. Wambaugh 1971), dedicated to a crusade against crime and disorder, seeing crime control as the central function, and emphasizing the street cop as the repository of all truth, wisdom, and virtue; the 'professional' policeman, ambitious and career-conscious, with an appropriately balanced appreciation of the value of all aspects of policing from crime-fighting to sweeping the station floors, equipping him for the largely public relations functions of senior rank (Reiner 1978a: chap. 12).

Other studies have identified very similar perspectives (Broderick 1973; Walsh 1977; Shearing 1981a; M. Brown 1981; Paoline and Terrill 2013). All these studies distinguish: alienated cynics, managerial professionals, peacekeepers, and law-enforcers. These correspond with the basic organizational division of labour between management and rank and file, and between CID and uniform patrol. But they also stem from differing individual personalities, initial orientations to the job, and varying career ambitions and trajectories.

The culture of chief officers itself varies, with different perspectives related to the pattern of previous careers, the character of the force, and the experience of particular generations (Reiner 1991; Caless 2011; Roycroft 2017; Stevenson *et al.* 2017). Overall, British chief officers do not have fundamentally different cultural styles from the rank and file, having come from similar backgrounds and worked their way up the force hierarchy. However, they are more likely to espouse different policing philosophies, shaped by the need to accommodate pressures from governmental and social elites. In the 1980s the conventional wisdom of chief officers was moulded by the *Scarman Report*. During the 1990s, however, it increasingly adopted a managerialist, 'business-like' flavour, as the 'bureaucrat' became the 'business manager' (Savage *et al.* 2000: 86), in common with trends around the globe (Van Dijk *et al.* 2015; Caless and Tong 2017; Das and Marenin 2017).

The differing orientations are also related to demographic characteristics such as ethnic group and gender, and diversification in the demographic make-up of police forces around the world has led to hopes for benign cultural changes (Sklansky 2006). However, American work suggests there is no clear tendency for black officers to be different in work style from whites, or to be less punitive towards other blacks (Waddington 1999b: 111–12; Skogan and Frydl 2004: 148–50). It may be, though, that increasing the proportion of black officers changes the whole ethos of a department in ways which cannot be discerned in individual comparisons, in particular when organized into representative associations (Holdaway 2009).

Nor is there much evidence of differences in policing style between male and female officers, in particular because the pressures on women to adapt to the traditional ethos of masculinity seems to outweigh the counter-pressures coming from reform attempts to remodel policing (Heidensohn 1992, 1994, 2008; Skogan and Frydl 2004: 151–2; Dick *et al.* 2014). Again, though, it is plausible that raising the proportion of women in the department might dilute the masculine ethos. The recent increase in women at command levels may alter leadership styles and the organizational ethos, although the evidence so far is mixed (Brown 2003; Silvestri 2003, 2017). There is also growing evidence about variations in culture between proliferating specialist tasks in many jurisdictions, for example: drugs policing in the UK (Bacon 2016) and South Africa (Marks *et al.* 2017); border and migration policing in Australia (Weber 2013, Brewer 2014) and Norway (Gundhus 2017); domestic violence policing in Canada (Ballucci *et al.* 2017); community policing (Bullock 2013, 2014) and community support officers in the UK (O'Neill 2015); counter-terrorism policing in Australia (Sentas 2014).

VARIATIONS IN ORGANIZATIONAL CULTURE

Cultures vary not only within but also between forces. Research on differing department styles and reform attempts implies that there is some scope for change, although this is constrained by the social and political context in which the department is embedded (Chan 1997; Foster 2003; Faull 2017a and 2017b).

The *locus classicus* for considering differences in the styles of whole police organizations is J. Q. Wilson's (1968) study, *Varieties of Police Behaviour*. Wilson suggested that three departmental styles could be distinguished. The 'watchman' style emphasized order maintenance and the patrolman perspective. Bureaucratization, standardization, and professionalization were barely developed, and political influence was rife. Patrol officers had much discretion in handling their beats. The 'legalistic' style operated with a law enforcement approach, attempting to impose universalistic standards impartially on all communities. The organization was bureaucratic and professionalized. The 'service' style prioritized the consensual, helpful functions of the police. If it had to deal with law-breaking, it attempted to do so by cautioning, not prosecution. There is much stress on public relations and community involvement.

Although partly a product of departmental policy choices, the styles reflected social and political balances. 'Legalistic' departments replaced 'watchman' ones either after a corruption scandal bringing in a reform administration, or as a result of a slower process of change in the balance of power between class elements, elevating groups with an interest in rational universalistic authority as a framework for long-run planning. It could run into paradoxical difficulties if introduced in an adverse social context. For example, while less racially discriminatory, the 'legalistic' style enjoined higher levels of law enforcement, and might thus adopt aggressive methods of patrol which black people experienced as harassment. The 'service' style developed in middle-class suburban communities with a value consensus.

Subsequent American research on the effect on police practices of changes in organization and style suggests that these can have a significant impact on patterns of arrest, use of force, and other significant practices. However, the political economy, social structures, and political cultures of different areas seem to be the driving forces behind variations in police practices, rather than freely chosen organizational policies (Skogan and Frydl 2004: chap. 5).

Cain's (1973) British study of a rural and a city force indicated that country police were more closely integrated into their communities. City officers were much more closely interdependent with their police colleagues, and alienated from the populations they policed. This was probably a consequence of the different conditions of policing in rural and urban areas rather than a function of organizational styles readily open to policy change. Urban/rural differences in style are a frequently recurring motif (Shapland and Vagg 1988; Loftus 2009).

Jones and Levi (1983) collected data on police and public attitudes in two forces whose chief constables stood at opposite poles in the spectrum of police debate. Devon and Cornwall's John Alderson, was the foremost exponent of the 'community policing' philosophy, emphasizing the importance of a close, positive relationship between police and public as the essential precondition of effective policing. Manchester's James Anderton, by contrast, stood for a tough law-and-order approach. Jones and Levi found that on a variety of indicators the public in Devon and Cornwall had more favourable opinions of their police than people in Manchester. One common criticism levelled against Alderson's community policing policies was that, while they might be appropriate for tranquil rural counties, they would be impracticable in a city. Jones and Levi found, however, that the force contrast held true when Plymouth (the second largest city in the south-west) was compared to Wigan (a relatively small northern country town), although Plymouth did have the lowest levels of expressed public satisfaction in Devon and Cornwall. This suggests that, while it is indeed harder to cultivate positive police-public relations in cities, organizational culture and style are also important variables.

Some evidence of the possibility of successful change in police culture comes from an important ethnographic study (Foster 1989) comparing two inner-city London police stations. In one, substantial reforms in policing style and practices were introduced, altering the culture in the direction intended by the *Scarman Report*'s espousal of a community policing philosophy. The key ingredient of this achievement was the overall commitment and solid backing of the whole management hierarchy. In the other station, where this was lacking, traditional police culture remained resilient. A similar message of the possibilities of reform even in tough city areas is provided in a study of six innovative police chiefs in the USA, who set out to reorient their departments in a community policing direction (Skolnick and Bayley 1986). However, it is left somewhat unclear how far this translated successfully into sustained change in practices on the ground. Chan's (1997, 2003) influential accounts of attempts to change police culture by reforms in organization, recruitment, and training underlines the limited possibilities in the absence of fundamental transformation of the police role.

Altogether it seems that there are significant differences in the culture of policing between different jurisdictions. What is less clear is the extent to which the differences are the products of policy choices that can be made in areas with different social and political structures and cultural traditions. It is impossible to foreordain the degree of freedom facing reform strategies, although it is undoubtedly never very great.

Recent observational work has shown the survival of many of the facets of the culture described by earlier studies, despite massive police reform efforts and demographic changes in many countries. Westmarland (2001a) and Silvestri (2003, 2017) show the stubborn survival of the masculine ethos. Loftus's important recent ethnographic study of a British force finds many of the themes found in the classic research conducted decades ago still alive and kicking, despite the determined efforts of governments and police elites (Loftus 2007, 2008, 2009, 2010). It confirms the embeddedness of police culture in the deep structure of policing an unequal society, with policy reforms producing at best cosmetic alterations.

CONCLUSION

There seem to be certain commonalities in cop culture, as discovered by many studies in different places and periods. These arise from basic elements in the police role in liberal democracies: the fundamental remit to control crime and disorder in unequal, divided societies, while adhering to the rule of law. The salience of these pressures varies across time and space: it is greater in contemporary neo-liberalism than it was in the postwar heyday of social democracy. There are also structured variations within forces according to the internal division of labour, as well as individual differences of interpretation and style.

Police culture and its variations are reflections of the power structures of the societies policed. The social map of the police is differentiated according to the power of particular groups to cause problems for the police. It also reflects differential propensity to visibly commit the types of crime that the police and criminal justice system in practice deal with: street crimes involving an element of trespass on persons or property (Reiner 2007: chap. 2; Reiner 2016b).

The least powerful elements in society become police 'property'. The power structure of a community and the views of its elites are important sources of variation in policing styles. The different orientations within the police reflect the two ways police organizations have to face in a class-divided hierarchical social order: downwards by the rank and file, to the groups controlled with varying degrees of gusto or finesse; and upwards by the professional police chiefs, to the majority public and elite who want an acceptable gloss to be placed on what is done in their name.

Police culture is neither monolithic nor unchanging. But the predicament of the police in maintaining order and enforcing the law in liberal democracies generates a typical cultural pattern, albeit with variations around it. This may be finessed but is remarkably resilient, because it facilitates the accomplishment of policing in such societies. Officers vary in their responses, however, according to structural factors like their role in the organizational division of labour, their own demographic background, and their individual personalities and interpretations.

Nonetheless the nature of policework does seem to generate a recognizably similar basic culture. Fundamental change in this needs not just micro-level reforms aimed at individual officers (e.g. in selection and training), nor grand policy declarations and meso-level organizational and legal reformation. It requires reshaping the basic character of the police role, through wider transformation of the macro-structures of economic inequality and power.

9

THE POLITICS OF
GLOBAL POLICING

INTRODUCTION

The contemporary policing agenda is transnational as well as local. Dealing with cross-border criminality, disrupting organized crime and terrorism, managing mega-events, responding to transnational disasters, and searching for people missing overseas, today's varieties of policework mirror the transnational possibilities of everyday life and reflect the growth of global communications, culture, and the economy. The political responses to globalization have had a profound impact on the architecture and métier of policing, its organizational culture, priorities, and processes (Bowling and Sheptycki 2012; 2015a). This chapter explores the development of policing agencies that operate in regional and global arenas beyond the nation state, the role of foreign police agencies acting abroad, the emergence of the overseas liaison officer as a distinct policing specialism, and the impact of these developments on debates about national and local police capacity, accountability, and control.

THE SHIFTING CONTEXT

The simplistic functional explanation for the growth of transnational policing is that criminality is no longer constrained by national boundaries, and therefore global cops are required to catch global robbers (Aas, 2007; Bowling and Sheptycki 2012). The list of the specific crime types held to exemplify this trend is very long and includes smuggling drugs, guns, and tobacco; trafficking illicit products such as toxic waste, stolen artworks, antiquities, and endangered species; organized immigration crime, including people trafficking and what is now known as 'modern day slavery'; financial crimes such as fraud and money laundering; international terrorism, cybercrime, and online child exploitation and abuse. Given the global reach of criminality, so the argument goes, the long arm of the law should stretch well beyond local police force boundaries (Brown 2008).

There is a kernel of truth in this argument. The twenty-first-century world is more interconnected than any previous era, and this is evident in economic, political, and social spheres (Held and McGrew 2003; Stalder 2006). Intercontinental travel, for example, has increased exponentially. Between 1970 and 2016 air passenger transport increased twelve-fold from 310 million to 3.7 billion passengers, while freight carried by sea increased four-fold from 2.6 billion tonnes to 10.3 billion tonnes (ICAO 2017; UNCTAD 2017). The mobility of people and goods has implications for activities such as smuggling illicit goods such as drugs, fake pharmaceuticals, weapons, endangered wildlife, and toxic waste. Cybercrime, which is borderless, implicitly requires transnational collaboration, and has become a major preoccupation for the police (Wall 2007, 2011). Moreover, as world trade has become more extensive and society more 'wired', the economic philosophy of neo-liberalism has instilled more laissez faire forms of governance, and this has changed the opportunity structures for crime.

The revolution in information and communication technologies has also had a profound impact on the nature of criminal activities. This includes the banal point that the exponential growth of mobile telephone and computer networks enables a greater degree of communication and collaboration among groups involved in conventional organized criminal activity. It also extends to the emergence of entirely new forms of criminal behaviour. The fact that much of the business of banking and finance is now done via electronic devices means that the new crimes of hacking, spamming, and phishing account for a growing proportion of all criminal activity.

These points are undeniable, but do not make the argument that the recent expansion of global policing is simply a functional response to transnational organized crime any more persuasive (Bowling and Sheptycki 2012). For a start, transnational policing is nothing new (see Chapter 3). The arguments for international policing, which led to the creation of Interpol and a United Nations police capacity were first articulated in the nineteenth century (Deflem 2002). Moreover, European colonialism established strong links among police forces in far distant parts of the world (Brogden 1987; Anderson and Killingray 1991, 1992; Sinclair 2011, 2006; O'Reilly 2017), providing a template for contemporary transnational policing (Bowling 2010: 69–74; Bowling and Sheptycki 2012: 20–2).

In our view, transnational policing is better understood to be the result of changes in patterns of governance. Policing has developed in a number of stages. At the beginning of the modern period, policing was a matter of parochial governance, through the offices of the town or village constable and justice of the peace, and its focus was on local crime and disorder. This shifted in the nineteenth century as the police, along with other branches of government, became more important to the internal social order of the modern state competing in the international state system. After the Second World War, the transnationalization of policing intensified in step with the globalization of politics, the economy, and society. From this perspective, the development of global policing can be seen as a synecdoche of global governance; it is part of the emerging practices of the transnational state system and one of its defining features (Bowling and Sheptycki 2012; Sheptycki 2000b).

Our argument is not that the nation state has become irrelevant to the politics of the police. Far from it—police forces, with their varied uniforms, insignia, and traditions— are still potent symbols of nationhood. Rather, we contend that contemporary policing must be understood in the light of the development of the transnational state system that emerged in the second half of the twentieth century. This system of global governance is highly complex and constitutes regional and worldwide layers and networks that did not exist before the Second World War. Seen from an international relations perspective, the system consists of disaggregated states that are no longer seen as unitary 'billiard balls' but as governmental networks that link horizontally across borders (Slaughter 2004).

International organizations also play an important role in global governance, including the United Nations and its agencies, for instance the 1988 UN Office of Drugs and Crime and United Nations Police, financial regulatory bodies such as the World Bank and International Monetary Fund, the World Trade Organization and the World Customs Organization. Regional organizations such as the EU are also important to an understanding of supranational governance and, as we discuss later in this chapter, play a specific role in pan-continental policing. Non-state actors also play a pivotal role in global governance, including domestic and international non-governmental organizations as well as multinational corporations and financial institutions, which are arguably more important than many, if not all, governments in their control of the movement of vast quantities of capital.

Understanding globalization draws attention to the sense that many of the problems facing police organizations operating at any level stem from the consequences of the shifting flows of capital, employment opportunities, and people. Although debates about transnational policing equate the police role with crime control, there are a range transnational order maintenance and service functions. This is most obviously the case in relation to contributing to public order in post-conflict and disaster situations in weak and failing states, which has involved overseas policing since the 1960s (Greener 2012). During a major natural disaster, for example, police will be involved in maintaining order, evacuation, providing first aid, distributing water and food, and helping with disaster victim identification. The fact of extensive international travel and tourism, places obligations on the international community to ensure that global crises will often involve transnational cooperation. The 2004 Asian tsunami was probably the largest international police operation in history up to that point, with around 700 police officers and staff deployed from thirty countries and supported by Interpol. During a two-year period, police identified more than 3,000 victims, assisted with body recovery and repatriation, and investigated victims' last known movements. The police role in dealing with sudden death, which is commonplace in the domestic realm, is also an element of the role of international liaison officers (ILOs) who take responsibility for citizens of their countries who die overseas. Other transnational non-crime roles include the search for missing people, coordinated order maintenance during major sporting and cultural events, and managing international public protest (Bowling and Sheptycki 2012).

Situating policing in the development of broader political economy, there is evidence that globalization has exacerbated inequality and fuelled insecurity among the least powerful people in the world who are losing jobs, suffering income stagnation, experiencing shrinking welfare, and living more precarious lives. There is no denying that the widening, deepening, and speeding up of global interconnections has accelerated in the late modern age, and that this has implications for transnational policing.

Critics of the globalization thesis note, however, that human beings have communicated transnationally for centuries, at least since the establishment of ancient trade routes (Held and McGrew 2007). They also contend that globalization is neither inevitable nor on a one-way trajectory towards greater economic, political, and cultural integration. Rather, the process has been punctuated by global shocks such as the Great Depression of the 1930s, the Second Word War, and the financial crisis of 2007–8. In some respects—such as the rapid advance of technology and accelerating flows of information—globalization is marching forward, but there are also indications of opposition to globalization from the political left and right. In the

1990s, anti-globalization was identified with a youthful movement against corporate ruling elites. In recent years, however, President Trump's pledge to put 'America First', and the British referendum vote to leave the EU and 'take back control' from Brussels, are indications of a nativist and anti-elitist right-wing populism that is also hostile to globalization. At the same time, global trade is slowing, major powers are turning to economic protectionism and seeking to restrict international migration. Yet global problems persist: climate change, rising sea levels, pollution, and natural disasters require planetary thinking if they are to be solved. How the tension between globalization and anti-globalization plays out will shape the future politics of the police.

TRANSNATIONAL POLICING: AN EMERGING SUBFIELD

Academic interest in transnational policing only began in a concerted way in the UK and USA at the end of the 1980s (Anderson 1989; Nadelmann 1993; Benyon et al. 1993; Bowling and Sheptycki 2015a, 2015b; Sheptycki 1998a, 1998b, 1998c). This work revealed several important things. First, there had been a qualitative shift in policework whereby international police cooperation had become extensive and routine, thus establishing the conditions for a transnational professional community. This was true in Europe (Anderson et al. 1995; Deflem 2000, 2002; Fijnaut 1993, 2004; Nogala 2001; Pincen et al. 2014; Sheptycki 1995, 1998c, 2002a), the USA (Andreas and Nadelmann 2008), and in other regions (Bowling 2010; Ganapathy and Broadhurst 2008; Hufnagel 2013; Chappell and Hufnagel 2014). There was also the increasing global presence of international police missions, sometimes under the auspices of the United Nations and often with the substantial participation of non-state agencies (Goldsmith and Sheptycki 2007; Tanner and Dupont 2014). Research on police at air and seaports and the policing of human mobility revealed another aspect of transnational policing (Slater 2007; Weber and Bowling 2004, 2008; Bowling and Westenra 2018a).

Second, these shifts troubled notions of state sovereignty typically held by political scientists, because as policework transcended state boundaries, the locus of control and legality for their work also seemed to shift. Fairly early on it seemed possible to conclude that 'a gradual transfer of internal and external security control is taking place from the nation state to international institutions' (Anderson et al. 1995: 179). Observing the European situation, den Boer (2014) saw a 'reluctant dance' between the EU and domestic police agencies around the mutual desire for a collaborative response to transnational crime while being mindful of the imperatives of national sovereignty. The existing literature suggests that this complex dance is a global one (Body-Gendrot 2016; Bowling and Sheptycki 2012).

Research on the US police revealed a significant international presence (Nadelmann 1993). The dominance of the US law enforcement agenda and policing techniques are evident from the formulations of international agreements that have often been shaped by US officials. Such developments have led to expansion in the scope of criminal law towards US innovations such as asset forfeiture and counter-money laundering, as well as the use of methods such as undercover policing, the use of informers, and electronic surveillance. For Nadelmann, this process amounts to the promotion of US criminal justice norms in the transnational realm. According to him, the effect of this can be expressed in a word: Americanization. The linked processes of regularization, accommodation, and homogenization, has led foreign governments within the US sphere of influence to adapt to an American networked model of international policing. Nadelmann's work in this area demonstrates that overseas policing capacity tends to be enabled when it coincides with the perceived interests of powerful seigneurial states.

The transnational policing literature is now extensive. What might be called the 'globalization thesis' presents the challenge of how to depict the transnational police so as to include local community constables and international liaison officers, as well as all the other kinds of police agents (Bowling, 2009). The typology set out in Table 9.1 develops Mann's (1997) 'ideal type' socio-spatial networks of interaction, as one way to delineate the dimensions of transnational policing in different socio-spatial spheres. This typology focuses attention on state-based (public) police institutions, and 'private' policing is a conspicuous absence in the descriptive analysis that follows. We discussed plural and private policing in Chapter 7, but will return briefly to the matter when we consider issues relating to the political and legal accountability of transnational policing.

Table 9.1 A socio-spatial typology for transnational policing

Locus	Network	Examples
Global	Policing entities that have a global reach	Interpol; United Nations Police; International Criminal Court (Investigation Division); World Customs Organization (WCO); Financial Action Task Force (FATF); Francopol
International	International liaison officers posted overseas	1. National police officers posted within EU; 2. Europol Liaison Officers (seconded); 3. National police officers posted outside the EU; 4. Non-EU officers posted in EU countries (e.g. USA, Canada, South Korea, China); 5. Prosecutor liaison network; 6. Interpol liaison officers.
Regional (EU level)	EU specialized agencies	The European Police Office (Europol); European Border and Coast Guard Agency (Frontex)
	Information exchange	Schengen Information System (SIS); European Information Exchange Model (Prum Council Decision); Passenger Name Record; Data Retention
	Legal tools	European Arrest Warrant (EAW); European Investigation Order (EIO)
	Operational cooperation	EU Police Cycle for Serious and Organised Crime; Joint Investigation Teams; Cooperation between specialized units' networks of national special units; police and customs cooperation centres
	Training and support	European Union Agency for Law Enforcement Training (CEPOL); Europol Training; Internal Security Fund; Research and Innovation

(continued)

Table 9.1 (continued)

Locus	Network	Examples
Sub-regional (bilateral and multilateral agreements)	Cooperative collaboration where the relationship is structured around a specific geographical area between two or more countries	Benelux Working Group on the Administrative Approach to Organised Crime, Ramogepol (France, Monaco, Italy); NeBeDeAgPol (Netherlands, Belgium, Germany in the Meuse-Rhine Region)
National	National policing structures created to coordinate a national response and work with international partners, as well as civil agencies	UK National Crime Agency (NCA); USA Federal Bureau of Investigation (FBI); Drugs Enforcement Administration (DEA); German Bundeskriminalamt (BKA); French Police Nationale, Gendarmerie Nationale; etc.
Local	Local policing agencies and units transnationally linked	Interpol National Central Bureaux (NCBs) nested in domestic police forces' criminal investigation departments; drug squads; counter-terrorism; border agencies

Table 9.1 might give the impression of a hierarchy, but this is not the case. The interconnections across the putative levels of this system must be envisioned as a web. Nonetheless it is useful for the purposes of discussion to order our reading of the above table from bottom to top.

THE GLOBALIZATION OF LOCAL POLICING

At 4.15pm on Sunday 4 March 2018, a member of the public called the Wiltshire police to report that a middle-aged man and a young woman were slumped unconscious on a park bench in the centre of Salisbury, a medieval cathedral city in the south of England. The initial police response revealed that Mr Sergei Skripal, a former Russian double-agent, and his daughter, Yulia, had been poisoned by what was later discovered to be Novichok, a military-grade nerve agent. Within twenty-four hours, what started as a routine call to the local police had become a matter of national and international security. Overwhelmed by the scope and scale of the investigative task, Wiltshire's constabulary soon passed operational responsibility on to other parts of the British police network, notably to the counter-terrorism command of the London Metropolitan Police. Royal Marines and the RAF were also deployed. The secretive government Cobra emergency committee (a forum for collaboration among police, military, and the security and intelligence services MI5 and MI6) discussed the case. Subsequent investigation involved crime scene forensic analysts, chemical weapons inspectors, and detective work in the UK and Russia.[1] This is a rare, but not unique, example of the local impact

---

[1] The 2018 Novichok poisoning case took a tragic twist on 30 June when Dawn Sturgess sprayed on to her wrists what she thought was perfume from a bottle given to her by her partner, Charlie Rowley, who had found the bottle. The substance in the bottle turned out to be the same nerve agent. Both Rowley and his partner fell ill and Sturgess died on 8 July. In September 2018, two men, alleged to be active officers in the Russian military intelligence, were identified by the British authorities as having travelled to Salisbury to carry out the attack.

of transnational criminality. In 2006, Alexander Litvinenko, a former officer of the Russian Federal Security Service, was murdered by means of a cup of tea poisoned with the radioactive isotope polonium-2010, a crime which eventually implicated two Russian nationals linked to the security services there. These are dramatic instances of where 'high policing' impacts on city and country life. The bulk of everyday local–global police linkages among police officers are somewhat more mundane.

The 'paradigm example' of transnational policing concerns drug smuggling (Sheptycki 2002a). Police collect information and intelligence about smuggling routes and methods, the individuals and companies involved in transport, warehousing, trading, and distributing prohibited drugs in multiple jurisdictions, and try to coordinate operations and investigations (Bowling 2010). Starting in the late 1960s, police 'drugs squads' were created specifically to make links with other such squads, not least in 'source' and 'transit' countries. This process has been replicated with respect to people smuggling and human trafficking. Just as these illicit activities are local at all points, so too is transnational policing in the domain of drugs and people smuggling. Street dealing and sex work are linked in transnational commodity chains. But somewhere is a local operational, investigative, or intelligence police officer, perhaps in the Caribbean (Bowling 2010), linked through a network of communication, perhaps to police in the port of Antwerp in Belgium (van Sluis *et al.* 2012) and on further to the police of Paris (Mouhanna and Easton 2014), or maybe to Interpol NCBs located around the world (Stalcup 2013). On a day-to-day basis, drug squad commanders spend their time reviewing intelligence reports provided by local informers, communicating by phone or email with intelligence officers from other countries and preparing to interdict smuggling at ports, airports, and border crossings. This also requires extensive collaboration with officers from other agencies such as customs, immigration, and airport security.

NATIONAL POLICING HUBS

National-level policing capacity has also developed in many countries alongside the globalization of local policing, but it varies between jurisdictions (Bowling and Sheptycki 2012). Early attempts to document the variety of national police structures in the EU quickly established that they were moving targets for research (Benyon *et al.* 1993; den Boer 2002a, 2002b). The structures of national policing in Europe were, to varying extents and at different speeds, converging and gradually becoming more like each other (Lemieux 2013). France has three long-established national policing agencies—the Police Nationale, Gendarmerie, and Police Judiciare—directly controlled by the ministries of the interior, defence, and justice, respectively. Germany has a federal policing structure that devolves most policing to the *Lander*, while centralizing some high policing functions. Italy and Spain are again different. There has been a general trend in recent years in those countries where countrywide policing capacity did not exist, for the creation of national policing hubs. The Netherlands reorganized its police into an integrated national regional structure in 1993. Sweden created a National Criminal Intelligence Service in 1995, modelled on the British example, and Denmark did the same in 1998. Luxembourg merged its two national police forces into one in January 2000. In Belgium the *Gendarmerie*, Judicial Police, and Municipal Police, were integrated into one police force and rationalized into a federal structure in April 2001. Regional police networks based around major urban cores are overlaid with systems of specialized high policing (Deflem 2006; Devroe *et al.* 2017; Prins *et al.* 2012).

British policing has historically been geographically decentralized and locally accountable. Despite ongoing debate about the advantages and disadvantages of a fully national police structure, England and Wales retain forty-three separate police constabularies, while Northern Ireland (reformed in 2001) and Scotland (unified in 2013) each have one. There are also in the UK, nonetheless, a number of policing functions that have been centralized for many years, including the British Transport Police, Ministry of Defence police, and the Civil Nuclear Constabulary (Johnston 1992a, 1992b). More significantly, since the 1990s, there has been the gradual centralization of the police in the UK. Building on a network of nine Regional Crime Squads that were formed in the 1960s, the National Crime Squad (1998) and the National Criminal Intelligence Service (2001) were created as a means to coordinate a response to serious crimes that crossed constabulary boundaries. Most of these agencies were then amalgamated, together with the investigative and enforcement arms of the UK Customs and Excise and with the infusion of officers from the security and intelligence services (MI5, MI6, and GCHQ) to form the Serious Organised Crime Agency in 2005 (Bowling and Ross 2006). SOCA was subsequently reorganized and renamed the National Crime Agency in 2013. The policing response to terrorism is also centralized but nested within the London Metropolitan Police Service (James 2013).

The USA appears to have one of the most decentralized police systems in the world, with an estimated 14,000 police agencies country wide, from small county Sheriff's departments to large federal bureaucracies (Geller and Morris 1992). However, the police structure in the USA forms a highly complex and multilayered network of competing and cooperating interests (Willis 2014). From the early years of the twenty-first century, local, state, and federal police agencies in the USA have been coordinated regionally in 'fusion centers' (Peterson 2005). The national 'policing web' (Brodeur 2010) in the USA is far from the perfect bureaucratic 'iron cage' of rationality (Maguire 2014).

The impetus for nationalization comes from various sources. First, there is the belief that local police forces lack the capacity and expertise to deal with organized criminal activity, especially with transnational connections, which has been a catalyst for changing the structure of policing. It is common, for example, for national police forces to have dedicated units to respond to cybercrime, financial crime, online child exploitation, modern slavery, organized immigration crime, and so on. Second, centralized national hubs have been created as a means to respond to the rapid growth in demands from overseas police forces requesting information about suspects wanted for crimes committed overseas and requests for extradition. As the international demand has grown, national hubs have been the logical solution to coordinate the responses of large numbers of geographically and organizationally decentralized territorial police forces.

The creation of national hubs also intersects with the trend of integrating policing with other law enforcement agencies such as customs, immigration, intelligence, and security agencies. National-level policing also provides a crucial linkage with the international policing systems through its training, development, selection, and posting of officers overseas. While officers might once have anticipated spending their entire career focused on their local patch, with advanced telecommunications, ease of international travel for joint training, conferences, and operations, increasingly they are communicating, coordinating, and collaborating with counterparts from other countries. The typical career path would be to have some experience in a city or shire constabulary, or in a specialized domestic agency, before being appointed to a post in a national hub. Here, the officers would gain the skills and experience of a 'police diplomat'. There is no standard model for national policing hubs, but in all cases their role is to link domestic police agencies within a nation state, with police forces in other countries, and to global and regional policing organizations.

REGIONAL POLICING AGENCIES

Mirroring the development of regional economic arrangements, trading blocs, and political structures in various parts of the world, regional policing organizations such as Afripol, Ameripol, Asianapol, Europol, and Caripol have emerged in recent years. The rationale for the creation of such organizations reflects the previous discussion about domestic policing capacity, or lack of it. The development draws on broader political and economic arguments about the value of regional integration. In most instances, regional policing entities are designed to share information about criminal threats, to develop a strategic response, and bring police officers from different countries together to build strategic, tactical, and operational capacity, alongside objectives such as the building of trust and interoperability. Some regional entities also have shared databases, training programmes, and conferences, and in some instances, multinational joint investigation teams tasked with collaborative and coordinated operations.

The development of the EU can be regarded as one of the most advanced examples of an emerging system of supranational governance, in which the Member States' sovereignty is being pooled in certain spheres. The idea of European cooperation specifically in policing matters can be traced back to the nineteenth century congresses that eventually led to the creation of Interpol (see later). There were also numerous forms of bilateral police cooperation, exchange in practices, and the emergence of a professional culture. An interesting example is the French regional 'Brigades du Tigre' of mobile police which were established in 1907. Laurent López (2008) observes that Luxembourgish police officers performed placements of several months in the French units, with the aim of importing their competencies related to their research methods on criminals. Early multilateral cooperation instruments include the European Convention on Extradition signed in 1957 (Morán 2010). The Berne Club is another important development involving the directors of various European intelligence and security services meeting on an annual basis since 1968, and was the antecedent of the TREVI (Terrorism, Radicalism, Extremism and Violence International) group formed in 1975 (Sheptycki 1995, 1998c).

Today, transnational police cooperation is an integral part of the European enlargement agenda. According to the European Commission, the objective is to create a 'common security and justice area', strengthening regional cross-border cooperation between law enforcement agencies and judicial authorities in the fight against organized crime and corruption in Europe. This is to be achieved by 'networking, mutual legal assistance, transfer of proceedings, requests for extradition, joint investigation teams, [and] witness protection programmes' (Council of Europe 2016). Fijnaut contrasts multilateral with EU communitarian police cooperation, indicating the absence or presence of supranational elements to be found in the policing agencies (1991: 22). The distinction lies in decision-making procedures that derive from the composition of the governing bodies (Fijnaut 1991: 22). While the European Commission and the European Parliament play an important role in the 'community method', national governments have a greater say in multilateral agreements. The Schengen agreement and its implementation convention is an example of both categories at different points in time. At its birth in 1990, the agreement between France, Germany, Luxembourg, Belgium, and the Netherlands was of a multilateral nature, and then became part of the EU's legal framework with its authority extended to the other signatory states when it was integrated into the 1998 Amsterdam Treaty (Fijnaut 1991: 22; San Pedro 2006: 203).

Monica den Boer sketches the evolution of the European treaties that embedded existing police cooperation structures in the EU framework (den Boer 2014, 2015). The 1992 Maastricht Treaty was the 'first formal basis for police cooperation in the EU', but was widely criticized for its 'intricate hierarchical working structure, the lack of meaningful competences for EU institutions, the significant margin of discretion for the Member States, and the lowest common denominator decision-making process of the unanimity rule' (ibid.: 12). Nonetheless, Maastricht brought coherence to pan-European action and led to the creation of the European Drugs Unit in Strasbourg in 1993, that would eventually transmogrify into Europol (ibid.: 12). The influential 1997 Amsterdam Treaty led to a 'normative jump' in willingness among police officers, or at least police diplomats working in the interstices of the EU, to unify criteria and actions across Europe (Morán 2010: 269). It also gave more powers to Europol through the legislative instruments that guaranteed flexibility for Member States alongside a more binding path to implementation (den Boer 2014: 12). The 1999 Tampere decision of the European Council was also influential, concluding that mutual recognition would be the cornerstone of police and judicial cooperation. This signalled the political will that brought about the European Arrest Warrant and Investigation Order.

The development of the Schengen Information System (SIS) is key to understanding European police cooperation. Through the Amsterdam Treaty, the Schengen *acquis* was integrated into the institutional and judicial structure of the EU bringing crucial policing matters under European Community competence for the first time (den Boer 2014: 12). Within this framework, SIS aims to improve the cooperation of justice, police, and customs officials. Formally, the central organ, located in Strasbourg, receives information generated by each Schengen country and then, after verification, distributes it to a national hub in every Schengen Member State. The national hub is, in turn, connected to each policing and law enforcement agency in the system (San Pedro 2006: 206). The Amsterdam Treaty also saw the establishment of SIRENE offices in each country which are responsible for supplementary information exchange and coordination of activities connected to SIS alerts (Guille 2010: 60). In practice, this is a real-time system in which there is no central verification and validation is done by SIRENE officers in each state. Cooperation between states, linked to a specific SIS alert, may be one-to-one or one-to-many and involves coordination of cross-border policing. To enable prompt, confidential, and efficient follow-up of cases, communication is made through the exchange of standardized forms—providing additional information, validating alerts via a secure network.

The 2007 Lisbon Treaty made the most important change in European police cooperation (den Boer 2014: 13). This Treaty enabled the EU to establish minimum rules concerning the definition of criminal offences and sanctions in the case of serious crime with a cross-border dimension. In relation to criminal procedural law, the EU, after Lisbon (Article 82(2) TFEU), established minimum rules concerning mutual admissibility of evidence between Member States, the rights of individuals in criminal procedure, and the rights of the victims of crime (Hufnagel 2013: 38). It led to the creation of new intergovernmental bodies engaged in coordinating procedures, and a new Council Standing Committee on Internal Security (COSI), to 'facilitate, promote and strengthen coordination of operational actions between EU member states in the field of internal security . . . [concerning] police and customs cooperation, external border protection and judicial cooperation in criminal matters . . .' (European Commission, 2009: 3). It introduced the possibility of a European Public Prosecutor's Office. After Lisbon, EU institutions were provided with more powers in the area of police and justice cooperation in criminal matters, particularly the European Parliament and Court of Justice (den Boer 2014: 13), and established more effective mechanisms for cross-border policing (Hufnagel 2013: 39).

Europol is the most advanced and ambitious attempt at pan-continental police cooperation. Following ratification of the 1995 Europol Convention, the agency became operational in July 1999. It was fully integrated into the EU following a Council Decision in 2009. Europol is responsible for collecting and disseminating criminal intelligence, as well as law enforcement cooperation with the goal of responding to transnational organized crime and terrorism. It has specialist units including the European Serious and Organised Crime Centre, European Cybercrime Centre (established in 2013), and a European Counter Terrorism Centre (established in 2016). Sometimes characterized as the European FBI, the agency has no enforcement powers, but exists to enable cooperation among police agencies within the EU. The Tampere Programme of 2000 (den Boer 2014: 12) reinforced the powers of Europol, founded Eurojust, and opened the way for the creation of Joint Investigation Teams (JITs) and the European Police Academy (CEPOL) (ibid.: 13). Initiatives to simplify the mechanisms of enhanced cooperation came with the Nice Treaty in 2000. The powers of the Schengen agreement were extended in the internal security realm. This allowed, among other things, for the establishment of national biometric databases, holding DNA, fingerprints, and vehicle registration numbers to which other Member States can have access (den Boer 2010: 56).

Whereas some argue that the increased involvement of the European Parliament, and the European Court of Justice's enlarged powers, make EU policy-making and police cooperation more accountable and transparent (Mayoral 2011), others deem the changes brought by the Lisbon Treaty less favourable. They describe the OLP (ordinary legislative procedure) as a '"trialogue" . . . between the European Commission, Parliament and Council . . ., a series of informal working meetings [which] are a major transparency black hole where large concessions are won and lost with very little oversight and without public disclosure' (Dolan 2015). Essentially, the European Parliament serves only to rubber stamp the deals secured by a handful of negotiators from each institution, sidelining 99 per cent of MEPs in the process. There is still an extensive field of activity where European countries are not ready to synchronize their regulations on police cooperation, and wide variation in transnational policing practices across the continent. In short, we lack a supranational institutional framework to enable practice to be documented, examined, and held to account. Moreover, understanding transnational police cooperation requires a closer look at *informal* bilateral and multilateral practices (Hufnagel 2013: 236).

The preference for informal cooperation is one of the key findings from numerous case studies of transnational policing (Bigo 1998, Alain 2000; Bowling 2010; Sheptycki 2002a). Marc Alain's (2000: 247) analysis of cooperation practices in France, the Netherlands, Belgium, and Luxembourg, for example, demonstrates that formal channels and mechanisms of information exchange and communication have only partly achieved their intended goal, and are perceived as less efficient than informal practices by police officers. Herschinger and Jachtenfuchs (2012) challenge the antinomy between formal institutionalization and informality, arguing that they are not mutually exclusive. On the contrary, Anderson *et al.* (1995), Bigo (2000), Nogala (2001), and den Boer (2010) show that both formal and informal communication and cooperation coexist and develop simultaneously, and that the interplay of informality and institutionalization is not 'either-or' (Herschinger and Jachtenfuchs 2012: 505). Indeed, informal cooperation can function as an important prerequisite for formal institutionalization, and does not necessarily disappear once institutions have been created (ibid.). This is confirmed by Hufnagel's (2013: 243) analysis of cases of informal regional cooperation run by practitioners, that impacted significantly on the harmonized, institutionalized legal framework of the EU.

GLOBAL POLICING AGENCIES

Interpol declares itself to be 'the world's largest international police organization, the world's only global police organization, and the world's most effective international police body' (Cheah 2010a: 28; Sheptycki 2018b). It is without doubt the leading global policing brand (Sheptycki 2017a), and the second largest public international organization in the world. The seeds of the Interpol idea can be found in the latter part of the nineteenth century. These germinated at the first International Criminal Police Congress in Monaco in 1914 and came to fruition in the International Criminal Police Commission (ICPC) in 1929, based on an agreement among twenty-two European and US police chiefs and headquartered in Vienna. The Commission met annually in Vienna until 1938, on the eve of the Second World War, when the Nazis assumed control. In 1942 the ICPC fell completely under German control and relocated to Berlin (Anderson 1989: 41–2; Deflem 2002: 174–89). The postwar rebuilding was led by Belgium, and in 1946 the ICPC moved to a new headquarters in Paris. The name Interpol was formally adopted in 1956 as part of its modernized constitution, and the organization became autonomous by establishing a financial model based on collecting dues from member countries and relying on investments. The new constitution also established the political neutrality of Interpol by focusing its activity on 'ordinary law crime' in different countries in the spirit of the Universal Declaration of Human Rights. Intervention or activities of a 'political, military, religious or racial character' were forbidden (Sheptycki 2017b).

The structure of Interpol has remained stable despite a remarkable expansion in the size and function of the organization (Cheah 2010a). It currently has 192 member countries, each of which maintains a National Central Bureau (NCB) staffed by officers drawn from domestic police forces. The reference to member *countries* (rather than states) highlights the Interpol constitution (Sheptycki 2017d). Its members constitute 'any official police body whose functions come within the framework of activities of the organisation'. The organization is, therefore, unlike a true intergovernmental organization (IO). The United Nations, for example, is founded on an international convention between national governments. Interpol started out life as a non-governmental organization (NGO) in 1948. It has gradually achieved a special status as an IO although, in its actual functioning, it is a *transnational network* (Sheptycki 2017a: 74). This status is, in part, facilitated by the fact that its structure mirrors that of a typical IO (Sheptycki 2017a). That is, it has a permanent headquarters in the French city of Lyon; a decision-making body (the General Assembly); an administrative body (the General Secretariat); an Executive Committee for day-to-day running of the organization; and field offices in the form of the NCBs nested within each member police force (Sheptycki 2017a). The NCBs are bound by domestic laws, but act as an extension of Interpol through their activities in collecting information and communicating this to and from the central organs, tending to identify with the mission of the organization as they do so (Bowling 2010: 105–11; Sheptycki 2017a).

The autonomy of Interpol from the system of states and from the police organizations that make up its membership is crucial to its history and contemporary functioning. The attempts in the late nineteenth and early twentieth century to create a permanent international police agency foundered because of the reluctance on the part of national governments to do anything that would weaken or relinquish state sovereignty (Deflem 2002: 107). The key to the success of Interpol functioning is the ability of the police to gain independence from political centres, to present the problem of crime as an apolitical, technical matter that should be left to security experts, especially as it became transnational in nature, therefore requiring transnational communication, cooperation, and collaboration (ibid.).

The work of Interpol is organized around four core functions: (i) secure global communications; (ii) operational database and data-services; (iii) operational police support; (iv) training and development. The first two of these functions are concerned with collecting, storing, and sharing information. The infrastructure which is available at all times to its membership is its communications network—known as I-24/7—that connects all of the members with each other, and with headquarters and its centrally located databases. Many countries extend access to I-24/7 to other national law enforcement entities at strategic locations, such as border crossings, airports, and customs and immigration authorities. This gives frontline officers direct access to Interpol records of suspect names, lost and stolen travel documents, and stolen motor vehicles. The lost and stolen travel documents database is growing rapidly, from 55 million to 71 million between 2015 and 2016. In 2016, member countries undertook 1.7 billion searches to detect people attempting to travel with fraudulent or stolen documents (Interpol Annual report 2016).

Interpol circulates information among member countries through a system of notices, of which the Red Notice is the most significant. This advises the police receiving the notice that a person is wanted, and requests assistance in 'apprehending the wanted person on behalf of the requesting country' (Martha 2010, cited by Sheptycki 2017a). Before a Red Notice can be issued, requesting NCBs must ensure that the person sought is subject to criminal proceedings or has been convicted of a crime (with evidence of a domestic court order or arrest warrant), that extradition will be sought in the event that that person is arrested overseas, and that sufficient evidence has been provided. In 2016, nearly 13,000 Red Notices were circulated, a seventeen-fold increase from the 737 notices circulated in 1998 (Sheptycki 2017a: 78–9). The Red Notice cannot be construed as an international arrest warrant because receiving countries must work within their own legal framework and have discretion in how they decide to respond to the request. It does, nonetheless, provide prima facie evidence of wrongdoing that enables domestic police (or immigration) officers to use the power of arrest on behalf of a foreign government. In this respect Interpol harnesses national law and legal institutions to the global policing mission (Sheptycki 2017a: 70). It is true that 'the man from Interpol never arrested anyone' because the organization has no formal law enforcement powers (Sheptycki 2004a), but he (or she) has no more need to personally carry out an arrest than would a domestic chief constable.

In a world linked by instantaneous telecommunications, the coercive and intrusive powers of the police are able to travel through international boundaries largely unaffected by them and take effect at long distances from where the power was initially authorized (Bowling and Sheptycki 2012). The legality and rectitude of this process assumes that Red Notices are always based on accurate and reliable information, are transparent, fair, subject to proper oversight, and are free of corruption. Unfortunately, there is evidence that this is not always the case (Sheptycki 2017a: 81–2).

Beyond data processing and communications, Interpol has gradually expanded its operational and support services through its Command and Coordination Centre (CCC), which is the first point of contact for member countries requesting assistance with major incidents. In a crisis or emergency—such as an earthquake or terrorist attack—officers located in the CCC provide analytical and investigative support, including the deployment of specialized teams on the ground. In relation to mega-events, such as sporting events or international summits, the CCC can deploy officers to assist with security arrangements. Interpol also conducts research and development and has an extensive training capacity to develop skills for officers at headquarters, NCBs, and member police forces.

Interpol is a highly ambitious organization that has grown dramatically in geographical reach, resources, and power over the past two decades. It is well established as a worldwide hub for transnational police cooperation and it aims to lead global policing activities. Although the impact of Interpol in the day-to-day work of the British police is unlikely to be visible to any but the most acute observer, the Interpol NCB based in Manchester is an integral part of the contemporary policing scene. It acts as the UK link to international investigations and is home to the casework coordination and fugitives' units.

A key question raised by the rapid development of Interpol is what can authorize a policing capacity that transcends national frontiers and moves beyond the boundaries of traditional defined legal sovereignty? (Sheptycki 2017a: 68–9). Since legitimate authority depends on a democratic process to ensure that coercive and intrusive powers are deployed in the public interest, how far is Interpol structured to give life to that principle? The short answer is not very far (Sheptycki 2004a, 2017a). Although Interpol presents itself as an IO, all decisions within Interpol are made by 'high level' police officials and there is no external oversight (Sheptycki 2017a: 74). Although the NCBs are subject to domestic laws of the countries where they are based, they act effectively as an extension of the global reach of Interpol powers.

Despite Interpol's dominant position in public discussion of cross-border policing, there are numerous other agencies with a global policing function located within such organizations as the United Nations, International Criminal Court (Investigations Division), the World Customs Organization (Customs Enforcement Network) and the Financial Action Task Force, the inter-governmental organization concerned with money laundering, terrorist financing, and the integrity of the international financial system (Bowling and Sheptycki 2012). The most important of these is the United Nations Police, which coordinates ordinary law policing responses to work alongside military personnel in conflict, post-conflict, and other crisis situations (Hills 2009; Greener 2009, 2012). Wherever there is a UN mandate given by the Security Council, starting with Congo in 1960 and operational in places such as Haiti and Côte d'Ivoire in 2018, UN police officers—known as the 'blue berets'—are deployed as 'formed police units' or as individual police officers.

The scale and scope of UN policing has grown dramatically in the past decade with around 13,000 police from ninety countries deployed in eighteen UN peace missions. The role of the 'formed police unit' is to provide on the ground support, or stand in for domestic police who can sometimes be entirely non-existent. The mandate is to build, support, or 'act as substitute or partial substitute' for police forces in the ordinary policing functions of preventing and detecting crime, protecting life and property, and maintaining public order. The idea of an International Police Force (IPF) has been advocated since the interwar years (Davies 1930), and became a staple of discussions of global justice after the Second World War (Johansen and Mendlovitz 1980). The UN Police Division, as it exists today, with ambitious development plans and coordination with Interpol to 'develop a global policing doctrine', comes very close to the vision of a world police force first sketched out a century ago.

OVERSEAS LIAISON OFFICERS

Overseas liaison officers are crucial actors in the development and practice of transnational policing. For some decades, first in the USA and then on other continents, police officers have been specially selected from local or national police agencies and dispatched overseas. This may be for a short visit to one or more countries, or for a period of years working as an accredited 'police diplomat' in an embassy or high commission. In origins, the liaison officer represents an extension of domestic policing into the transnational realm; but in terms of contemporary practice, this person is a globally-mobile police officer. Having emerged in the latter part of the twentieth century, this specialism seems set to play a very significant role in the future of global policing. Didier Bigo's pioneering empirical and theoretical research on liaison officers shows that they play a key role in managing the flow of information between various police, gendarmes, and customs and immigration officers (Bigo 2000, 2014). Working in the spaces within and between police organizations, Bigo likens liaison officers to 'station-masters' directing and shunting information to where it is needed as quickly as possible. They are located in at least four positions: posted to other countries within a region (including specialist areas such as counter-terrorism); posted to countries outside the region; seconded to regional entities (such as Europol); or seconded to global agencies such as UNPOL or Interpol.

Sheptycki's analysis of police operational intelligence files, and observation of liaison officers' coordinating role in the work of police units, provides a grounded view of cooperation between France, Belgium, the Netherlands, and Great Britain in the English Channel Region (Sheptycki 1998c, 2001, 2002a, 2002b). The study of liaison officers in this region was undertaken under the auspices of a formal (although not Treaty-based) regional cooperation framework called the Cross Channel Intelligence Conference (CCIC). Sheptycki's work documents the beginning of the CCIC in 1968 and traces its development as a regional operational intelligence hub up to the end of the 1990s. It shows how advances in police communications technologies, from the telex machine to the mobile phone, facilitated the development of a transnational police network in the region. This research documents examples of long-term covert police drug investigations, and examples of the police service role. In the latter category are cases concerning animal and child welfare, and the repatriation of a dead body to the UK after it was found floating in international waters.

The number of liaison officers is growing all the time and developing from an ad hoc to a permanent presence on the global stage. In the year 2000, Bigo estimated that there were a few dozen overseas liaison officers in a small number of European countries and the USA. A decade later, Aydinli and Yon's (2011) survey identified 650 liaison officers deployed in fifty-four countries. Today there are certainly many more than this. There are at least 200 liaison officers located at Europol from forty countries based at its headquarters in The Hague. The FBI has at least 340 people assigned permanently overseas (Fowler 2008), the DEA has eighty-six foreign offices in sixty-seven countries, and the Treasury Department, State Department, Bureau of Alcohol Tobacco and Firearms (ATF), and the Federal Marshals Service all have liaison officers. The UK has at least 140, France 130, Canada thirty-five, Australia eighty, and South Africa thirty. The *China Daily* (28 September 2017) reported that Chinese police forces deploy sixty-three liaison officers to thirty-one countries overseas. The Nordic Liaison Officers network comprises police and customs officers who represent Sweden, Denmark, Finland, Iceland, and Norway in countries outside Scandinavia (Kleiven 2011; Courtin *et al.* 2002: 188). Initially focused on drug trafficking in production and transit countries, the network was extended to comprise generalist crime liaison officers concerned with child pornography, environmental crime, and human trafficking in the late 1990s (Kleiven 2011: 66–5). Conceiving of states as disaggregated institutions, with their various parts only loosely integrated, helps us to understand the autonomy of big city police forces—such as the NYPD or the London Metropolitan Police—who also post liaison officers abroad.

The liaison officers' role includes acting as first point of contact for visiting police officers, protecting the interests of nationals travelling overseas, exchanging information, investigating transnational criminal collaborations, identifying and repatriating fugitives. Block describes their function as being official representatives of their agencies as well as acting as *fixers*, facilitating requests to and from their home country for 'information, evidence, interrogations, searches, arrests and extraditions' (Block 2007: 374). They work across a web of local, national, and supranational security institutions, aiding judicial cooperation by preparing and supporting the execution of letters of request for evidence (*commissions rogatoire*), and assisting with extradition and rendition. They play a role in migration and visa matters, advice and capacity building, training and mentoring. An important element of the role is establishing trust among police officers from other jurisdictions. This requires the skilful use of formal and informal communication and collaboration to overcome procedural or bureaucratic problems. Although it may not have a 'grand rationale' (den Boer and Block 2013: 190), the liaison officer—especially when engaged in 'high policing'—is well established as having a privileged role in the transnational system.

Competition is an important dynamic in the work of liaison officers (Courtin *et al.* 2002: 188). In the context of eastern Europe, there is wide variation in the number of international liaison officers deployed in different countries. Compared to the German, French, and Scandinavian officers, the Dutch have fewer liaison officers dispatched to eastern European countries (ibid.: 188). In Sofia, the UK has only one customs officer who works with the local police and in Romania through policy advisers to the Ministry of the Interior (ibid.: 188). Galy observes that competition between liaison officers is always visible. The actors are respectful of national interests, and know how to work together coherently in the light of common European interests bearing in mind the strength of the US presence, with FBI offices in Warsaw and in Budapest and Sofia (Galy in ibid.: 188). European officers are aware of distinct national interests or differences in general, but that they can be overcome with regard to a greater common interest in the EU. This could point to a common culture and aim in European policing, which (in this case) competes with US police. Here again a balance of power is at play, and there is a visible struggle for greater cooperation to gain influence in policing.

Ludo Block, a former liaison officer, documents the daily practice of operational police cooperation between Europe and Russia (Block 2007: 367). Block suggests that Europol plays a less significant role in European relations with third countries than Interpol, which has not become redundant with the establishment of the former. Their coordinating and formalizing efforts testify to ambitious political goals. European policies have insufficient understanding of police reality (ibid.: 382). They have neither set up operational police collaboration nor have they designated a point of contact for Europol (ibid.: 373). The main vehicle for interaction between the EU Member States and Russia is still through bilateral relations among liaison officers, whose number is growing (ibid.: 373–4). The growth can partly be attributed to the general increase in liaison officers throughout Europe with as many as seven liaison officers being sent to one state (ibid.: 374).

Block provides a glimpse of the bilateral and multilateral agreements which supplement the liaison officer system, such as the Finnish-Russian border guard working group, the German-Russian working group on organized crime, and the multilateral Baltic Sea Task Force on organized crime. Golunov provides further examples referring to the Polish-Russian working group on coordination in the fight against trans-border crime and the Estonian-Russian collaboration (Golunov 2012:

130). There are numerous obstacles that shape the liaison officer's work including language barriers, bureaucratic hurdles, disparities in legal culture (e.g. prioritization of cases, differences in legal systems), competition among domestic agencies who are often under-resourced, dealing with corrupt officers and the political dependency of law enforcement agencies (Block 2012: 378–9).

There is now a solid body of work that has documented the roles and practices of liaison officers, sitting at the margins of domestic policing but increasingly central to transnational policing. There are clear affinities and rivalries among liaison officers, and numerous tensions as the motives of control, common to the occupational culture of police everywhere, collide with national and organizational identities (Bigo 2014). Although liaison officers come from a wide range of national and organizational backgrounds they share many similarities. They tend to be well educated, multilingual, urbane and cosmopolitan, and recognize each other as inhabitants of the small world of transnational policing. For some, the role offers the prospect of promotion while others find it frustrating. In common with domestic police, liaison officers value street experience, but are themselves 'knowledge workers' with skills in investigation and strategic analysis. There is a wide range of subcultural styles—including the technician, diplomat, entrepreneur, PR expert, legal ace, spy, field operator, and enforcer—which can be adapted to achieve shared goals in the 'transnational space between' (Bowling and Sheptycki 2012: 29–32, 78, 101–2).

The evidence suggests that horizontal trust-based relationships created among liaison officers enable transnational cooperation, in spite of differences based on divergent legel systems, nationality, gender, and ethnicity. This is because they achieve a depoliticized perspective in which the common enemy is the criminal (McKenzie 2018). Their work transcends allegiance to a specific police organization or nation state in order to build sufficient trust and commitment to effective cooperation. When national governments loosen direct control, Aydini and Yon argue, sub-state actors discover their potential to work efficiently by allowing a horizontal expansion of governance into the transnational space. This has been described elsewhere as the emerging transnational state system (Bowling and Sheptycki 2012). These 'transnational liasionships' are signs of a new form of public governance but leave open the question of how transnational governance can be held to account by the global commonwealth (Sheptycki 2002b).

CHALLENGES TO THE DOMESTIC POLITICS OF THE POLICE

The questions of accountability and national sovereignty can be answered theoretically by the contention that it is only permissible for police officers to use coercive and intrusive powers within their own geographical jurisdiction (Bowling and Sheptycki 2016b). The very definition of police power—the capacity to use legitimate coercive force within a given territory—implies jurisdictional exclusivity. And yet, it has been clear for decades that the domestic police forces have never really had a monopoly of policing power (see Chapters 1 and 7). Monica den Boer argues that there is an 'implementation gap': Member States 'have not embedded European police cooperation in their domestic systems . . . [and] remain caught between national sovereignty and solidarity' (den Boer 2014: 10). This makes the everyday reality of police cooperation a 'policy field far removed from supranational politics' (ibid.: 11). Deflem agrees, highlighting the 'remarkable persistence of nationality . . . in international police work' despite increasing transnational policing practices and the 'formation of multilateral cooperation initiatives' (2006: 339). Malcolm Anderson, writing about the emergence of transnational policing in the late 1980s and early 1990s, is critical of a central state model based on a strict adherence to the principle of national sovereignty in its purest form. The absolutist conception of state sovereignty, he argues, is anachronistic in the policing field because the speed of communication makes it impossible for states to maintain a monopoly of information (Anderson 1989; Anderson et al. 1995).

Where policing resources are fragmented, national authorities cannot dominate all external relations, and small and poor states in particular have difficulties exercising sovereignty. The polar alternative to the absolutist conception of sovereignty is the 'decentralized state' model. Here, officers in different countries communicate directly with one another, and informal contacts across frontiers become standard practice. This, Anderson predicted, would result in a free market in information, a reduction of nation state authority, and autonomy for the police working in the international domain. In Anderson's view, this 'represents an erosion of sovereignty and control, unacceptable to virtually all the advanced industrialized democracies' (Anderson 1989: 175). The decentralized model would have the virtue of ending clandestine or informal contacts, recognizing that technology facilitates direct communication that it is difficult to control using an authoritative set of rules.

Anderson (1989: 175–8) posed two intermediate models: (1) *qualified centralization* where national offices are normally in control but in exceptional circumstances (e.g. urgency) horizontal cooperation through ad hoc bilateral agreements is permitted. (2) *Qualified decentralization* allows direct communication but requires reporting of this to national offices. Anderson (1989: 178) foresaw a point at which police forces would become accustomed to direct communication with their counterparts; effective intervention by the national offices could become more and more difficult, thus eroding state sovereignty. This is in fact what has come to pass: officers are in constant contact with their counterparts and colleagues overseas, and in many cases, there is no requirement to report this to senior command. It is merely assumed that horizontal communication will stay at the officer-to-officer level to avoid compromising operations.

What of the use of coercive force beyond national boundaries? Research has documented instances where overseas police officers have carried out (or have attempted to carry out) arrests outside their jurisdiction without involving local police (Bowling 2010). The most blatant examples concern the high policing activities involved in the 'extraordinary rendition' of people suspected of involvement in terrorist activities. In these cases, domestic police and intelligence agencies have arrested people on 'watch lists', carried out interrogations and removed them to so called 'black sites' abroad. One of the most egregious was the case of Khalid El Masri, a German citizen who was abducted by the Macedonian police in 2003, handed over to the US Central Intelligence Agency and taken to the US 'Salt Pit'. There he was held for four months until the US government admitted that this was a case of mistaken identity and released him at night on a desolate road in Albania. In 2012, the European Court of Human Rights determined that El Masri had been detained unlawfully, tortured, and abused, and criticized the Macedonian police for collaborating with US secret programmes. In the US courts, the government claimed 'state secrets privilege' and the case was dismissed.

Police liaison officers do not have formal arrest powers, but they are able to achieve coercive outcomes through action that could be described as remote control or 'governing at a distance'. Through lawful routes, they can use available information and other resources to enable local police officers to undertake arrests on their behalf. Overseas liaison officers are experienced senior officers within their own organizations, who are perceived to outrank their counterparts in weaker states (Bowling 2010). Much of the formal relationship between the liaison officer and the local security authorities is at the commissioner level, and their operational work entails working with an assistant commissioner or senior superintendent. With liaison officers from powerful states based in various countries, the closeness of the working relationship permits more direct collaboration. There is a tension between the expectations of police officers working as representatives of sovereign nations, on the one hand, and police cultural autonomy and officer discretion on the other. Referring to developments in the dynamic European context, changes in national sovereignty, new actors in law enforcement and policing, as well as an increase in jurisdictional and investigation instruments, Bruggeman (2002b: 259) calls for a new system of accountability. While until now, the system of accountability has mainly been structured according to national borders, the fact that 'policing is no longer a set of practices embedded in the sovereign nation-state' (Sheptycki 2002: 323) necessitates an accountability structure which should apply to all forms of policing, including those carried out by intergovernmental and supranational law enforcement agencies (Bruggeman 2002: 259; Bowling 2010: 312–15; Bowling and Sheptycki 2012: 136). In Chapter 11 we return to the question of police accountability in the global age.

CONCLUSION

Globalization is reshaping the politics of the police. Although there have been international connections among police organizations since they emerged as an integral part of the machinery of government in the nineteenth century (see Chapter 3), a quantitative and qualitative shift is now under way. From the end of the twentieth century, the task of policing that had been seen for two hundred years as a domestic matter was transformed into a political and policy issue that was widely perceived as integral to global governance (Bowling and Sheptycki 2012). Henceforth, domestic police chiefs cannot afford to police their neighbourhoods without being 'indigenous-yet-globally-aware' (Cain 2000: 251).

This chapter has charted how the transnational turn is shaping policing in local, national, regional, and global spheres of activity. Global policing agencies emerged and gathered strength during the second half of the twentieth century. Although Interpol has nineteenth century roots and was formally established in 1923, it was decimated during the Second World War, and was rebuilt from the ground up in the postwar period to become today's leading global policing brand. The idea of an international police force also has old roots but only became a reality under the aegis of the United Nations in the 1960s; it too has grown into a powerful global policing entity. Every region of the world now has some form of pan-continental policing organization that provides coordination, cooperation, and collaboration across numerous policing agencies. Shared databases and common policing doctrine provide interoperability and joint investigation and enforcement activities across entire continental regions.

Debates about the case for and against national police forces have petered out in recent years, replaced with a diversity of pragmatic solutions to the increased demand for intelligence exchange and operational collaboration at the national level. In some instances—for example, Scotland and the Netherlands—the solution has been the creation of a national police force. While neither the UK nor the USA has a national police force, both have well-funded organizations that constitute the central authority for extradition requests, information repository, and expertise in such fields as transnational organized crime, cybercrime, money laundering, and counter-terrorism. National-level policing hubs provide a crucial linkage between thousands of local police forces and police entities operating in the global sphere.

The national policing architecture includes many other members of the wider policing family: most obviously siblings in immigration policing, border control, maritime, and customs; but also cousins in governmental agencies with powers of surveillance and coercion operating in financial regulation, tax and excise collection, health and safety and, environmental protection. Taken together, contemporary policing constitutes a complex 'patchwork quilt' of agencies that is stitched together by the efforts of transnational liaison officers (Sheptycki 1995: 613)

Like politics, however, policework is mostly a local matter. Despite the growth of global, regional, and national police agencies, the overwhelming majority of direct interaction between police and public is with uniformed officers in town and city streets and traffic police on the highways, and less frequently with plain-clothes detectives and other specialists. Behind this interaction, however, is a far-reaching change in the nature of policework. Today's street police, through the introduction of new information and communication technologies, are now able to check suspect identities using mobile fingerprint readers, facial recognition software, automatic vehicle number plate readers, and biometric means that link with domestic and international databases. Local policing has been transnationalized and global policing now reaches deep into local communities.

These developments raise profound new questions about the relationship between state and citizen. Observers are critical of the 'democratic deficit' at national and European levels (den Boer 2002a; Feys *et al.* 2018; Fijnaut 2002), with serious implications for local accountability (McLaughlin 1992) to which we return in Chapter 11. Local policing was proposed as the solution to the problems of burglary, theft, interpersonal violence, and social disorder in local communities; but what is the role of the domestic police officer when threats to life and property emanate from transnational organized crime groups and rogue states? Some parts of the world are made deeply insecure by political violence and international mafias. In many other locations, globalization has had the effect of increasing inequality, unemployment, and precariousness, undermining community safety.

In such circumstances, what kind of response can we expect from the local police, and from the newly created specialized agencies set up with the goal of keeping us safe? Moreover, are we content that the suitable foes of terrorists and transnational organized criminals are the main threats? Could global policing prioritize more pressing threats such as environmental destruction, global warming, or corporate crime? Perhaps worldwide policing could be better orientated towards a service role? Whatever its aims and objectives, how do we know whether or not international policing agencies are effective, efficient, and fair? On what criteria can we judge whether or not the billions of dollars spent on global policing is money well spent?

Transnational policing is growing in size, resources, and ambition. It is enabled by advances in technology, and by new laws and policies that are creating domestic and local linkages (Sheptycki 2017d). It is becoming more powerful and is now seen as indispensable to domestic and international security and order maintenance. Increasingly, local policework is shaped by global forces, linked via national policing hubs, into transnational databases and expertise. What are the implications of these changes for the fundamental questions of liberty, security, and accountability? As we have argued elsewhere in this book, the paradoxes of policing require a searching analysis of how power can be held to account, and through which democratic processes the police should be governed. This was never an easy question, even while policing was authorized and delivered in local communities by parish constables. Now that local policework is shaped, at least to some extent, by global forces, by what means can we be confident that coercive and intrusive powers are deployed for the social good?

10

POLICE AND MEDIA

INTRODUCTION

Debate is frequently split between claims that the media either fosters or debases police legitimacy. The intersection of police and media presents a critical juncture, but it is a challenging inter-disciplinary topic that is often under-theorized. The vast literature concerning the social effects of communications media technologies contains many perspectives. Greer has criticized criminologists for their 'parochialism', arguing that the common finding that media distort crime 'should be the starting point for a media criminology that seeks to interrogate, understand, and explain, rather than just repeatedly confirm what we already know' (Greer 2010: 3).

Any account of the police and the media which depends on this 'media criminology' point of view, is doubly handicapped, suffering from both a borrowed criminological parochialism, and a paucity of theoretical imagination regarding the inter-relations between police, media, and society. Policing is not merely crime control, and a purely criminological lens is inadequate for understanding police-media relations. In this chapter, we seek to understand media effects on the police métier, asking how theories about media, communications, and technology in society can help us better understand the politics of the police.

A central difficulty is defining the term 'media'. The term is often used in an overly broad manner, and is thereby rendered useless for analytical or theoretical purposes. The politics of the police loom large in news and entertainment media, but how to think about police-media relations and the conditions of democracy remains unsettled (Loader and Sparks 2011: 17; Mason 2003). If the doctrine of 'policing by consent' was hammered out by Peel, Rowan, Mayne, and others during the course of the nineteenth century, then it was a product of the age of print. Or perhaps it is a doctrine concocted in the mid-twentieth century by Charles Reith and others, in which case it was the product of the radio and cinema age.

As we explain elsewhere in this book, police legitimacy reached its apogee not not long after the Second World War. To what extent can the idea of policing by consent be achieved in a social order founded on increasingly technologically mediated communication? The condition of 'hyperreality', in which participants have no basis upon which to judge what is simulated and what is not, may well accurately describe a world where mediated communications have largely replaced face-to-face human interactions. That is, aside from the few remaining instances where people congregate together, but these are mediated by market exchange-relations in ersatz public space like Disneyland, university campuses, and international airports (Kumar 2005: 29-36; Postman 1985,

1992; Redhead 2008; Sheptycki 2013). It is necessary to step away from exclusive concern with the politics of the police *in* the media in order to understand also the political effects of media *on* policing.

A major issue has concerned the differentiation between 'folk devils' and what we are here calling 'suitable foes', since both terms are essentially contestable. At the level of connotative meaning the language of 'folk devils and moral panics' suggests a degree of scapegoating in the labelling process. The term 'suitable foe' connotes deviance widely considered totally unacceptable—a contemporary example might be the serial killer or the paedophile. Obviously the appropriateness of the designation of either a 'suitable foe' or a 'folk devil' will depend on audience and interpretation, and there is no hard and fast distinction between the two.

The 'social imaginary' (Taylor 2004) of police and crime is somewhat plastic, and influenced by the framing of police and the subjects of their enquiries in communications media. The police imaginary, as used here, refers simply to the cultural meanings of who the police are and what the police do. The stereotypes of policing are woven into the fabric of our collective imagination. The subjects of police enquires are not only framed within the media of mass communications, they are also framed by the information and communications media found in police organizations (Manning 1988). Some argue further that media technology purveyors have undue influence on police policies, procedures, and practices (Joh 2017). An important theoretical and political question therefore is: do police information systems contain data on suitable foes or folk devils? Are they a product, or productive of, the police imaginary?

Synthesizing for the sake of brevity, we can say that there are broadly three ways in which media can be defined and understood, and that are of relevance to the study of police. The first and most common way defines and understands the media in terms of its content and is often concerned, in one way or another, with questions regarding propaganda effects. The second way to theorize media is in terms of the instrumental relationship between people and media technologies, that is, as 'extensions of ourselves', and how new technologies change social organization. The third way to approach studying the media is in terms of political economy because, as common sense would put it, 'them that pays the piper calls the tune'.

The historical trajectory of technological innovation in communications media that took place during the course of the twentieth century decisively shaped the development of modern police and the politics of policing. The task of this chapter is to relate this process in the light of more general scholarship concerned with the social history of information technology and media (e.g. Bell 1973; Egerton 2007; Ellul 1964, 1965; Stuart 1996; Tye 1999; Winston 1986, 1998). The innovations in mass media and communications that we describe resulted in considerable social-organizational change, because they extended the temporal and spatial dimensions of human interaction. This has significance for democratic politics, but it has not revolutionized the social structure in terms of the dimensions of its stratification (Stalder 2006: 131–3). The shifting politics of police and policing over the past hundred or so years is part of a larger historical transformation brought on by continuous technological innovation and changes in media.

POLICE AND THIEVES—
FRAMING THE POLICE MÉTIER

The literature concerning crime, police, and media is voluminous (recent overviews include Greer 2010; Greer and Reiner 2012; Jewkes 2015). Everyone has their own favourite starting point for studying police *in* the media. In this section we seek to understand the professional police métier as projected by the media of mass news and entertainment since the mid-twentieth century. During the early part of this period, most means of mass communication were under fairly firm state regulatory control in North America, Great Britain, and elsewhere. Accompanying the neo-liberal turn since the 1970s, state regulation of mass media relaxed, and commercial news and entertainment enterprises expanded the space for media performance (Humphreys 1996).

The development of police professionalism in municipal American policing facilitated the movement of police to the centre stage of mass media entertainment. The stage was pre-set by Hollywood, an important example being the 1948 Academy Award winning film *The Naked City*, a film noir thriller which centred on a murder investigation by a team of police led by a veteran cop. An important move was made by Los Angeles Chief of Police William Parker, who facilitated access to police cases in the making of the popular radio show *Dragnet* in the 1940s. Parker was well known for his importation of military-style organizational principles (including media relations) into the notoriously violent and corrupt LAPD (Hays and Sjoquist 2005: 79; Punch 2009: 77). *Dragnet* enacted the cases of fictional Sergeant Joe Friday of the LAPD. After a successful television cross-over, it went on to become the most influential police procedural in TV history, spawning countless imitators. The Friday archetype is that of a professional insider, rational, calculating, scientific, a master of surveillance and investigation, a sure shot. Around this image all subsequent American police stereotypes revolve.

BOBBIES ON THE BOX: CONSTRUCTING THE DIXONIAN IDEAL

The British case of PC George Dixon was a rather different police archetype. Importantly, the image of the British bobby was the only national police symbol to emerge in Europe after the Second World War untainted by Nazism and Fascism. As an interesting aside, Jersey and the Channel Islands were occupied by the Nazis, who not only instituted work-camps with slave labour from occupied Poland, but also took the opportunity to produce propaganda photos of Nazi troops on British soil, some of which included photos of the occupiers alongside local bobbies. This little-known aspect of British Second World War history came to light when the actor John Nettles published a controversial book, *The Channel Islands at War* (Nettles 2012). Nettles was already famous as a television police detective, having played the lead role in *Bergerac* (1981–91), a police drama set on the Island of Jersey, and Detective Chief Inspector Tom Barnaby in *Midsomer Murders* (1997–2010). The controversy was that people did not necessarily enjoy a book that spoiled the pristine image of a Britain unsullied by Nazism.

Dixon of Dock Green was a comforting national symbol for a nation still suffering postwar austerity. Dixon personified the archetypal English bobby, the constable of good-hearted common sense both in and of the community. The Dixon persona was originally a product of Ealing Studios, which had spent the war years producing morale-boosting comedies and war 'documentaries'. His resurrection for the television series in 1955 happened as the studios were taken over by the BBC, a national broadcasting monopoly (which it would quickly lose to ITV). Although it was a very popular drama series, Dixon did not feature in lists of Top Twenty British television programmes till the 1980s. This was due to the intense competition between networks at a time in which game shows and light entertainment were more popular than drama.

We would emphasize that the police characters Friday and Dixon were the product of quasi-monopoly systems of media production and dissemination. As such the police métier is pictured in a socially integrative frame and projected by something close to a 'single channel' provider. The extent of the associated propaganda effects is contested but unarguably these images made a palpable cultural impression. Probably the consensus police image owed as much or more to social conditions, although that too is arguable. Emerging from the Second World War, while the US economy thrived Britain initially endured significant austerity, followed somewhat later by an economic boom. In both countries there were accompanying promises and assurances of the welfare state.

The conditions of production and consumption of police media representations have changed dramatically since the 1960s. By the end of the century the media had become a multi-channel 'virtual' free-for-all, including the new social spaces of the internet. It is important to remember that the manufacture of the Dixon, Friday, and other early policing stereotypes, were in conditions that are as close as it gets in the democratic countries of the West to production under a state-dominated propaganda model (Ellul 1965: 121–38; Herman and Chomsky 2002; Greer 2010: 32–41). The police are pictured unequivocally on the side of righteousness and justice, and the narratives construct the police role in morally clear terms (Allen *et al.* 1998; Reiner *et al.* 2003). The police are always successful and criminals are to be reviled.

The frame was dramatically altered in the late 1960s. In Britain, ITV was initially launched in 1955 as the first commercial channel, breaking the BBC monopoly (Humphreys 1996). By 1969, the year of the televised moon landings when both broadcasters in the UK began to transmit colour images to a mass audience for the first time, media communications had begun to diversify and become multi-channel.

Eugene McLaughlin records that 'despite all attempts to modernize and professionalize policing, the core British police identity remains profoundly dependent on a fictional image of the 'bobby on the beat' projected by Ealing Studios in 1950' (McLaughlin 2007: 24). He made this observation after recording the reminiscences of one police officer who had been present during the filming of *The Blue Lamp* who said 'we were told to co-operate with the film company as the Commissioner thought the film would be good propaganda for the service' (ibid.). Sir Harold Scott, the London Metropolitan Police Commissioner of the time, later revealed in his memoirs his encouragement for the making of *The Blue Lamp* and other quasi-fictions like the series *Fabian of Scotland Yard*.

THE VIEW FROM AMERICA

The situation in the USA was different from the beginning because television and radio were always multi-channel commercial ventures, albeit regulated by the US Federal Communications Commission (FCC) (Herman and McChesney 2004). In 1947 there were an estimated forty million radios in the USA, but only forty thousand televisions, two-thirds of which were in New York. With the first national television broadcasts in colour in the mid-1950s, the new medium began to significantly erode the size of cinema audiences. By the 1960s and 1970s the US national mass market for police and crime dramas served by both the movies and TV was enormous. The competition for market share between these two industries had consequences for the police and crime images they projected.

In the late 1960s the USA had become one nation united under television. That decade is legendary for media imagery of the American war in Vietnam, social conflict, and disintegration. As the century progressed there developed layer upon layer of media representations and styles projecting images of the police to a mass market of consumers interested largely in entertainment. In the USA, the number of cable television networks grew from twenty-eight in 1980 to seventy-nine in 1990, with over forty-five million subscribers. Having twenty-four hours and hundreds of channels to fill, television offered a torrential flow of viewing in which police were prominently featured.

At the end of the century, police 'reality television' programmes were highly popular. These used the conventions of documentary, 'fly-on-the-wall' and *cinéma vérité*, sometimes incorporating dramatic 're-enactments' or 'raw' police CCTV footage in order to create an ersatz appearance of unfiltered 'reality' (Doyle 2003; Fishman and Cavender 1998). Whether or not pluralized mass media project propaganda, the (hard to measure) social effects of the medium alarmed many (Reiner 1981a, 1994; Reiner, Livingstone, and Allen 2000, 2001, 2003).

Building on prior work, we suggest here that the postwar trajectory of the mass mediated police imaginary in North America and Great Britain can be seen as falling into three phases. The first period, in the immediate aftermath of the war, was one of recovery and rising economic affluence, reinforced by an active welfare state apparatus. There were only a few media channels. The second period, commenced around the time that the Beatles 'conquered America' in the mid-1960s and ended sometime around the establishment of MTV in NYC in 1981. It was one of perceived rising middle-class affluence, the multiplication of media channels, and the diversification of police and crime narratives. The third period, which extends into the twenty-first century, continues the trend of multiplying media channels, but in a climate of increasing economic turbulence and the financial undermining of middle-class lifestyles.

THE CRITICAL TURN IN CRIME AND MEDIA STUDIES

This timeline is punctuated by the neo-liberal turn that took place in the 1970s. This was heralded in more critical analyses of media-made criminality. Two studies exemplify this: *Folk Devils and Moral Panics* (Cohen 1972/2002) and *Policing the Crisis* (Hall *et al.* 1978/2013). These books presented a critique of media stereotypes of the police, and challenged existing orthodoxies regarding social order. *Folk Devils and Moral Panics* probed the societal reaction to 'primary deviance', charting 'deviance amplification' through the processes of 'secondary deviance', chiefly by looking at the medium of mass public news and entertainment. Cohen distilled a model that began with the identification of a population suitable for labelling as folk devils (Cohen 1972/2002:

199–200). Ensuing societal reaction to primary deviance creates self-fulfilling prophecies through the manufacture of culturally identifiable symbols, which structure future
situations and legitimize social control.

The police imaginary framed by news and entertainment more or less ensures continuing escalation. Mass media are understood to publicize events, leading to further
publicity-seeking behaviour by those who incorporate the folk devil label into their
self-identity. This triggers a contagion effect that justifies the mobilization of further efforts at control in an amplification spiral. The transmission of stereotypes about crime
and deviance through mass media works in this way because it emphasizes emotional
affect.

In general, the response of 'formal agents of social control'—i.e. 'the police'—is to
apply the narrow 'situational logic' of criminal law enforcement. These police control responses to moral panics may be experienced by sections of the affected public
as unfair and discriminatory. Over-dramatized and spurious reasoning, attributing
blameworthiness to officially labelled folk devils, makes police responses ineffectual
or iatrogenic. This summary is a highly condensed version of a subtle and nuanced
argument. Nonetheless, it indicates the basic template for a new way of thinking about
images of police and crime that began to emerge in the 1960s, one which inverted the
moral order of the earlier scripts (Cohen and Young 1973). Instead of imagining police
as modern, rational, humanistic, and out for common justice against 'suitable foes', the
new perspective aimed to develop an appreciative understanding of the 'folk devils'
who were targets of police attention.

In *Policing the Crisis*, the analysis was taken further. Whereas, in keeping with the
parameters of the labelling tradition, Cohen had largely eschewed references to political economy as a significant factor, Hall and his co-authors specifically identified the
political structure of capitalism as decisive to the trajectory of a crime panic, and central
in the process of criminal labelling. They argued that police and media over-reaction
sublimated an existing 'crisis of capitalism' through racial scapegoating. The media panic
thereby legitimated a shift to a more authoritarian state, and simultaneously split the
working class along racial and ethnic lines. Media presentations of police and crime
scripts are now commonly understood to be deeply encoded by power relations, especially racial and gendered ones (Hall 1973/1980; Brown and Heidensohn 2012).

Policing the Crisis was part of a much larger wave of research which argued that mass
communications broadcasting was structured by power relations between audience
and 'the media'. The real questions concerned the extent to which mass media could be
assessed as a means of ideological domination, by whom, and for what ends (Gurevitch
et al. 1982; Eick and Briken 2014). Political positions on these questions were clearly
distinguished between 'orthodox' and hegemonic on the one side, and 'revisionist' and
subversive on the other. Many studies argued that stereotypical and misleading por-
trayals of 'outsider' groups in media representations of political protest, youth gangs,
drug addicts, football hooligans, welfare scroungers, street criminals, gang members,
homosexuals, and 'others', deflected attention from wider concerns about the sources
of social conflict.

The observation that media presentations of police and crime are distortions
eventually established the blanket assumption that these images reinforce dominant
social and political norms or interests and everything became a 'social construction' (cf.
Hacking 2000).

FLUCTUATING TRENDS IN THE DIXONIAN MEDIA IDEAL

A narrative of changing police styles and legitimacy can been discerned in the time-line of the shifting TV police imaginary from the Second World War until 9/11 (Reiner 1994, 2008). The British trajectory starts with the iconic *Dixon of Dock Green* which ran on television from 1955 to 1976. This plodding image of the police was superseded by *Z-Cars* (1962–78), with its emphasis on the adventure-packed working life of two-man police car patrols in a fictional town somewhere near Liverpool, portraying a 'gritty realism' in contrast to the 'cosy' image of Dixon.

An archetypical 1970s series, *The Sweeney* was set in London. It emphasized fast-paced crime-fighting against serious robbers and criminals and spawned two feature films and many imitators. The shift was towards a more macho police style, emphasizing the car and other examples of police technology as symbolic markers of the police métier (Manning 2003, 2010). Even the theme music was thrilling. Frequently emulated, its influence continued into the 2000s with *Life on Mars*, a nostalgic back-to-the-future, somewhat tongue-in-cheek, police drama.

However, all was not well in the British police imaginary because the 'dividing line between overtly fictional crime stories and the presentation of crime news has become increasingly blurred' (Reiner 2016b: 134). Supposedly 'realistic' fictional images were mixed up in the media space alongside news reportage that, from the 1960s onwards, was increasingly negative for the police. The police imaginary framed in mass media is not easily separable into fact and fiction, as social scientists may conventionally suppose. Beginning slowly in the 1950s, a series of corruption scandals and stories of police wrongdoing began to appear in newspapers, and in 1969 *The Times* revealed evidence of widespread problems in the London Metropolitan Police. News of the 'firm within a firm'—organized corruption in certain units—blighted the mythology of the British detective.

As part of a strategy of reform intended to secure police independence from outside interference, London Metropolitan Police Commissioner Sir Robert Mark dealt with these not by shutting out the media, but by manipulating them skillfully through a policy of openness. Beginning with Mark's controversial Dimbleby lecture on BBC television in 1972, British police leadership at varying levels strayed increasingly into the public space of the news media. The Police Federation—collective voice of the British police rank and file—commenced a campaign in the press for 'law and order' in 1975. When G. F. Newman's four part 'quasi-documentary' drama series *Law and Order* was broadcast on BBC in 1978 it turned the phrase into one of criticism (Newman 1983; Turnbull 2014: 56–8). The depiction of a rough, violent, and corrupt police and prison system was deemed so shocking that the BBC Director General was summoned to the Home Office and the series was prohibited from subsequent broadcasting until 2009 (Gilbert 2009).

Throughout the 1970s, the British police were embroiled in a series of bad news stories. Roger Graef's documentary series about Thames Valley Police aired on BBC in 1982 in the cultural aftermath of the televised riots in Brixton and Toxteth in 1981. The third episode captured the crass and unkind grilling of a rape victim by a squad of CID men, and sparked great controversy. It was the first to use the fly-on-the-wall documentary technique in the police milieu, and the effects were disturbing. The series was subsequently archived and not publically broadcast, although scenes from the rape episode were reportedly used to spark discussion in sexual assault training at UK police colleges.

Graef followed up with a book entitled *Talking Blues: The Police in Their Own Words*, adopting an 'appreciative stance' on policework in the community for non-academic audiences (Graef 1989). In the middle years of the 1980s in Britain the community police ideal first embodied by Dixon staged a remarkable comeback in media representation with the long running series *The Bill* (1983–2010; cf. Colbran 2014). The keynotes of the community police story were an emphasis on generally harmonious relations within the organization, and a chiefly (although far from exclusively) non-crime focus for police in the external environment.

However, the channels of media transmission were multiplying as commercial satellite operators and later internet streaming increased the available media space. Contra-discourses proliferated in the multi-channel era, offering a complex representational array of the professional police métier in Britain. During the 1990s, for example, the format of police procedural drama was used to explore the themes of sexism in the police workplace in *Prime Suspect* (1991–6, 2003, 2006). Probably the most influential BBC police drama of this era was *Line of Duty* (2012–19), a procedural where the investigative quarry were 'bent coppers'.

In recent decades police dramatizations have been conflated in media space alongside mass news media projections of, *inter alia*: the violence of the 1984–5 Miners' Strike; police mis-management and lying following the Hillsborough disaster in 1989; the Poll-Tax riot in 1990; the heavy-handed police tactics used during the 1999 Carnival Against Capitalism in the City of London, and the 2001 May Day protests; and the death of Ian Tomlinson at the 2009 anti-globalization protests during the London G20 meeting.

The long-running media saga following the murder of black British teenager Stephen Lawrence in September 1993 came to a tentative conclusion only in 2012 with the conviction of two of the murderers. It exposed a view of the British police as racist, incompetent, and expensive. The brittle quality of police legitimacy and the 'corporate approach' to media relations adopted by the Association of Chief Police Officers (ACPO) suggested that media presentation had become much more unstable, complex, and contradictory than either the 'hegemonic' or the 'subversive' perspectives imply (McLaughlin 2007/2011: 152–62).

COPS, TV, THE MOVIES, AND THE SHIFTING AMERICAN POLICE IMAGINARY

The narrative trajectory played out differently in the North American media, on a much bigger scale with greater international ramifications. The American television police procedural initially framed the professional police métier, representing the protagonists as doing a job with vocational skill and dedication in the context of an efficiently run bureaucracy, aided by science. This formula was widely replicated in the USA, Great Britain, and elsewhere around the world. Titles in this genre include *Hawaii Five-O*, *Kojak*, and the popular *Crime Scene Investigation* (CSI) and *Law and Order* franchises.

The iconic 1968 film *Bullitt*, starring Steve McQueen, is notable for attention to procedural details like evidence processing and emergency room procedures, even if the film is mainly remembered for a car chase scene lasting ten minutes. This film injects the police procedural with a high-octane, hyper-masculine, 'let 'em have it' feel. McQueen modelled the character Lieutenant Frank Bullitt on the real life LAPD Inspector David Toschi, including his distinctive upside down 'quickdraw' underarm gun holster. Toschi later became famous for his role in the real-life Zodiac Serial Killer case (resurrected as an evil character giving the fictional cop *Dirty Harry* a 'suitable foe' to hunt in 1971). Dirty Harry was an enduring motif in police scholarship, cited as an ambivalent figure—a dirty cop on the side of right. The film, actually dedicated to the San Francisco Police Department, openly portrays police corruption and brutality (Klockars 1980).

The style was later replicated in the popular but less gritty 1970s television cop show *Starsky and Hutch*. In the make-believe TV world of American cops during this time, authority is accepted without undue deference or resentment, and professional pride and camaraderie hold the expert group together. Sometimes the bureaucratic environment is depicted as chaotic or difficult to manage, but more often it is one of unbelievably smooth-running efficiency. The external environment for police action is envisaged as safe and sound. Social life is punctuated by crime—usually homicide— and the task of the police procedural is to restore a sense of the normal social order of things by the end of the programme (allowing time for commercial breaks).

With the appliance of science, the television police procedurals unequivocally establish the guilt of obviously evil perpetrators, often without anything save the minimal use of force. Historical analysis of media content shows a massive increase in police use of force excesses over time as the external environment in which policing is depicted as taking place correspondingly became rougher (Reiner, Livingstone, and Allen 2000, 2003)

Although later procedurals upped the ante with muscle cars and bigger guns, on cinema and TV screens, the good guys and bad guys initially remained clearly demarcated. The purpose of the police procedural, as no doubt Chief William Parker— who purportedly originally coined the term 'thin blue line'—intended, is to represent the police as on the side of right (Shaw 1992).

When Sidney Poitier, in the character of the well-dressed, hip African-American big-city homicide investigator Virgil Tibbs, enters the town of Sparta Mississippi *In The Heat of the Night* (1968), the conventions of the police procedural are bent to the task of civil rights and anti-racism. This film broke American racial taboos—including a scene where Tibbs reacts to a slap in the face by an upper-class white racist with an impressive back-handed right swing. But it also showed the police solving a mystery using procedural and scientific means, and thereby upholding legal rights.

This pioneering portrayal of black police officers (Wilson and Henderson 2014) can be contrasted with the highly popular Andy Griffith Show (1960–8). Set in the rustic fictional town of Mayberry and chiefly concerned with the mundane life of its sheriff, the show was a gently humourous, bucolic fantasy of an all-white America. Mayberry later became an important cultural signifier, a stand-in for an American-style community policing lost to militarization (Kraska and Cubellis 1997).

From the late 1960s onwards, as television screens superseded cinema screens, new thematic fashions were established in police fiction. Television news increasingly featured police in conflict situations. Political tensions in the USA were marked by the assassinations of the Kennedys, Martin Luther King, and Malcolm X. There was a rise of popular movements: for civil rights, against the war in Vietnam, second wave feminism, Students for a Democratic Society, and the 'counter-culture'. In 1965 south-central Los Angeles erupted in a five-day conflagration—the Watts Riot—in which thirty-four people died, more than a thousand were hospitalized, and four thousand were arrested. This was the first of many American anti-police riots, all of which were given maximal television coverage. In 1970 the radical African America poet Gil Scott-Heron rapped: 'the revolution will not be televised'.

In this volatile climate the conditions of possibility for a new, more complex police imaginary began to crystallize. The 1967 landmark film *Bonnie and Clyde* is pivotal. The film itself was important in the establishment of the 'new' Hollywood, as cinema fought for audience share against television. Notable for one of the bloodiest death scenes in cinematic history, the plot romanticized the criminal lives of its protagonists. Bonnie and Clyde, played by Hollywood 'sex symbols' Faye Dunaway and Warren Beatty, are by turns comic, erotic and, sympathetic. They are sexy, anti-establishment underdogs, poor young white trash on the run and in love who happen to kill people and yet remain likeable (McDonagh 2004: 114). Conversely, Texas Ranger Frank Hamer is depicted as a cold hearted and vengeful bungler. A personification of the might of the state and the police, his blood-gushing ambush of the protagonists at the climax of the movie seems nearly as sadistic as the Mai Lai massacre which took place in the year of the film's release. *Bonnie and Clyde* was imaginatively interpreted by many as an allegorical critique of the American war in Vietnam (Boessenecker 2016).

Bonnie and Clyde offered an almost complete moral inversion of the police imaginary as depicted in an earlier time. The 1973 film *Serpico*—starring Al Pacino and based on the book *Serpico: The Cop who Defied the System* by Peter Maas—did not (quite). The real-life Frank Serpico was a whistle-blowing undercover NYPD police officer whose revelations stimulated the Knapp Commission into police corruption. Pacino played the character as a hip counter-culture participant with strong personal morals, adrift in a cop culture reeking with corruption. His human sense of honest decency simultaneously condemns the police, provides a brave model of non-conformity, and upholds the morality of legality.

Serpico is neatly contrasted with Clint Eastwood's *Dirty Harry* (1971) and Gene Hackman's 'Popeye' Doyle in *The French Connection* (1971). Dirty Harry and Popeye Doyle are tough cops out to do the right thing using unconventional and violent methods. They are justified in doing so because their suitable foes are respectively a psychotic serial killer and international heroin traffickers.

TV cop shows proliferated, such as *Hawaii Five-O*, the *Streets of San Francisco*, *Columbo*, but only *Baretta* (1975–8) stepped away from the procedural form. The TV character Tony Baretta was modelled on real-life Newark, New Jersey Vice Squad detective David Toma. The series depicted a police officer distinguished by his rule-breaking, tough, menacing, wily, and explosive persona. Lieutenant Dan Cooke, legendary press-relations officer for the LAPD appointed by Chief Parker, and an adviser to the TV programmes *Dragnet* and *Adam 12* among others, characterized Baretta as a 'murderer with a badge' (Stark 1988: 266).

American fictional police heroes have often been consciously modelled on 'real life' people, their careful crafting suggesting some behind the scenes awareness concerning the ideological importance of the police imaginary beyond merely making commercially successful shows (cf. Cashmore 2002). The American police procedural dramas *Hill Street Blues* (1981–7) and *NYPD Blue* (1995–2005) were originally inspired by the 1977 documentary *The Police Tapes* (which was filmed in a Bronx precinct). *Hill Street Blues* was not initially very popular, but it captured the same *zeitgeist* as James Q. Wilson and George Kelling, who published their famous essay 'Broken Windows' in the March 1982 issue of *The Atlantic* (Kelling and Wilson 1982).

These fictional programmes used hand-held cameras, fast pacing, multiple plotlines, and other documentary techniques to give a realistic feel to police melodrama. They projected a potent mix of themes and images generally sympathetic to the Sisyphean struggles of the bearers of the police métier (Turnbull 2014: 80). *Hill Street Blues* and its successors strongly conveyed the impression that the police could not repair social ills, and that the best they could do is maintain order (Gitlin 2000).

Fictional media representations of American policing, however realistic, were punctured by the real-life beating of Rodney King which was captured on video by a civilian observer of the occurrence, and given widespread media coverage (Jacobs 1996; Lawrence 2000). This was an important moment in police-media history, because it forced changes in the narrative construction of police use of force. The incident revealed how segmented the television viewing population was, with African Americans perceiving rather different messaging in police and crime drama (Manning 2003: 104).

The themes of social decay and growing social dissensus were further developed in *The Wire* (2002–8). This series exuded an even greater sense of social rot in American institutions, the police, the education system, and government generally (Turnbull 2014: 89–95). Significantly, it also highlighted the police use of covert techniques and electronic surveillance and, in the fifth season, the role of commercial print media—in the form of the fictionalized newspaper *The Baltimore Sun*. In the social imaginary constructed around the tropes of the police métier, not only were the police 'de-sacralized' (Loader and Mulcahy 2003) the entire edifice of governance of which police are a part lay in tatters.

MEDIA, CULTURE, AND POLICE— AMBIVALENCE AND SOCIAL DISSENSUS

However ambivalent the themes explored, and whether or not the police were heroes, anti-heroes or counter-culture heroes, what became normalized were 'crime control values'. Social research in the USA has long revealed public attitudes strongly in favour of tougher crime-fighting measures, more freedom for the police, and less government spending on the social causes of crime (Stark 1988: 268; Garland 2001). And there is evidence to suggest that watching police on TV impresses these views.

One 1980 survey revealed that crime show viewing had a small but persistent, measurable, and significant influence on perceptions. It found that such viewing promotes anxiety about victimization, ignorance of the procedural guarantees found in the US Constitution, and a rigid adherence to the dictates of authority. In contrast to the moral panics of the time about the socially harmful effects of violence in the media, the author of this study argued that, rather than threatening the social order, television could be a means of social control (Carlson 1985).

As the channels of mass media multiplied, the framing of the professional police protagonist became more complex, and the moral economy in which policing was imagined to take place became more ambiguous. The overall picture was one of social disintegration. Academics noted the rising fear of crime (Lee 2013) and—given that this diverged from the generally downward trend in a variety of formal measures of crime—this gave rise to a concern among professional police to manage the 'reassurance gap' (Reiner 2016b: 147–8). The launch of *Crime Watch UK* in 1984 combined aspects of 'reality television' and audience participation. Spawning many offshoots, the series laid claim to helping resolve many serious crimes over many decades of broadcast. Reality TV became a staple of late-night cable television, and it made real crime seem more pervasive than it was (Jewkes 2015).

There has been considerable debate about the extent of so-called 'media effects', with some arguing there is 'none discernible' to others arguing there is 'massive brainwashing' (Ditton *et al.* 2004; Chadee and Ditton 2005; Gauntlet 2005). Attempts at quantification often produced trivial results and weak conclusions (Greer: 4–5; 95–6; Livingstone 1996). McRobbie and Thornton (1995) argued that the standard academic template that focused on folk devils and moral panics no longer fit the conditions of a multi-mediated social world. The murder of *Crime Watch UK* presenter Jill Dando in April 1999 made reality crime programming seem all the more real, not least after an Institute of Crime Science was founded in her name at University College London on the second anniversary of her murder.

On the eve of 9/11 academics could no longer book-end the politics of the police between an orthodox and hegemonic view on the one side and a subversive and critical one on the other—not under postmodern conditions (Lea 1998; Perlmutter, 2000; Reiner 1999). 'There can be no effective symbol of a unitary order in a pluralistic and fragmented culture' (Reiner 1992b: 779). By the time of the publication of the third edition of *Folk Devils and Moral Panics* (2002) and the second edition of *Policing the Crisis* (2013), digital wireless communications and computing technology had progressed so far as to make analysis of daily newspaper content seem quaint and the vocabulary of crisis concerning the dangers of an emerging authoritarian populism seem prescient.

Many more cop shows can be cited. There are shows about the police in airports and traffic police, and shows that focus on police dogs, horses, or automobiles. All of them sustain an underlying cultural 'police fetishism'. Admirable, condemnable, or pitiable, shady, savvy, shifty, or slovenly, in the media imaginary the police protagonist has remained a necessary evil. Cops are 'the fire it takes to fight fire'. Sometimes caring and always controlling moral street-sweepers in an urban jungle, police symbolize the faltering and quixotic pursuit of order and security. They have been burdened with the responsibilities of ever-watchful guardianship, the bearers of legitimate force, which the patriarchal state has sought to monopolize.

In media space the police métier has been resilient, but the frame of meaning changed so that cultural stories of police and thieves came to reflect social disintegration (McLaughlin 2007: 113–14; Reiner 1994). And yet, as Raymond Chandler put it in *The Long Goodbye*, using cops to control the problems of the world is like taking aspirin to cure a brain tumour, but 'No way has yet been invented to say goodbye to them'.

POLICE AND SCREENS—REPRODUCING (DIS)ORDER IN THE SURVEILLANT ASSEMBLAGE

In this section we step away from narrowly focused considerations about police and crime as *content* in media space, and broaden our theoretical discussion of police and mediating technologies (de Pauw *et al.* 2011; Manning 1992, 2008). This is a necessary step in theorizing the police-media relationship if it is to account for the antinomies due to the surveillance power of new communications technologies and their implications for democratic policing by consent of the governed (Brodeur 2010: 38–9, 247–51).

In this section we want to focus attention on the instrumental uses of media technologies at the hands of police and other actors in the domain of policing. Police technological innovation is not a march of progress. Police media technologies have come between police and people, while both police and public are subject to intrusive supervision, oversight, and surveillance. The alienation that this technological sophistication engenders is conducive to police de-legitimation. The effects of intensified surveillance over human life may similarly distort social relationships and thereby undermine social consensus.

POLICE AND MEDIATING TECHNOLOGIES

The central symbolic motif of police professionalism in the later half of the twentieth century was the radio-dispatched patrol car (Manning 1988, 1992; Manning 2010: 70, 210–11; Walker 1984). In the period after the Second World War, police in North America and Great Britain sought to 'own the road', and key enabling technologies were communications media, particularly two-way radios (Manning and van Maanen 1978). The famed 1974 Kansas City Patrol Experiment—which aimed to measure the effectiveness of different methods of organizing police car patrol—therefore became the quintessential example symbolizing professional police research (Clarke and Hough 1980; Walker 1984). One repercussion of the spread of motorized, radio-dispatched police patrol was that it lessened opportunities for casual, non-conflictual interactions between police patrol officers and public, increasing the likelihood of police being involved in conflictual situations (Holdaway 1983; Punch 1983; Weatheritt 1986; Sheptycki 2018a). The radio-dispatched patrol car is one illustration of technological alienation. Not unlike the ubiquitous protective-vest and other paraphernalia that are now standard uniform for street-patrol officers, the radio-dispatched patrol car can be seen as something that gets in between the police and public.

The introduction of police communication dispatch systems occasioned the distinction between 'reactive' and 'proactive' police routines. This gave rise to subsequent efforts to measure efficiency, effectiveness, and the impact on police-public relations (Hough 2007a, 2007b; Reiss 1971; Smith and Gray 1985; Cordner *et al.* 1996; Fielding and Innes 2006; Manning 2010: 9–10, 220). With technological innovation, police managers intensified their control over front-line personnel. Police became subject to intense internal organizational surveillance (Ericson and Haggerty 1997: 348–9). COMPSTAT and other similar innovations in 'police intelligence analytics' subject police workers to 'management by numbers', prompting varying claims of success and scepticism (Brayne 2017; Chan and Moses 2017; Eterno and Silverman

2012; Fyfe Gundhus, and Rønn 2017; Haggerty and Ericson 2003; Harcourt 2001; Kelling and Coles 1998; Lum *et al.* 2016; Manning 2008; Joh 2014; Sanders and Condon 2017; Sanders and Sheptycki 2017; Sheptycki 2017c; Weisburd *et al.* 2003).

Police institutions increasingly depend on gathering intelligence and gleaning information by mediated means. Police organization is based on data analytics and stochastic prediction and, as much as these measures might indicate any actual increase in unsafety, the resulting perceptions of an increasingly risky and threatening environment can be read as symptoms of alienation between police and public.

We fully acknowledge the significant variability and unevenness in these technological innovations across jurisdictions and organizations (Darroch and Mazerolle 2012; Dupont 2001; Hughes and Jackson 2004; Monahan 2010). Yet there does seem to be a discernible pattern. The adaptation of new technologies in policing mediates *between* police and public. No longer 'low visibility decision-makers in the criminal justice system' (Goldstein 1960), police patrol officers are now on directed patrol as determined by algorithmic design (Sanders and Sheptycki 2017).

The contemporary patrol officer's primary visual engagement with the external environment is mediated by a squad car's windscreen and by the on-board computer screen. Even the foot or bicycle patrol officer—a chief symbolic representation of the community-policing ideal—is primarily attuned to the two-way radio, smartphone, and other systems that process and serve up formal police knowledge of 'the community'. In a hyper-mediated condition like this uncertainty reigns. In the backstage areas of police organizations, projected onto screens are the panic scenes of which they are part authors, and over which they have the 'impossible mandate' to ensure order and security (Manning 2003).

POLICE, NEW DIGITAL MEDIA, AND ILLUSIONS OF CONTROL

However, there may also be an illusion of control. Whereas, at one time police officers would have to engage with members of the public in order to ascertain details of personal identification, with 'real-time intelligence'—based on widespread CCTV surveillance, social media scraping, officer body-worn cameras, face-recognition, and data-matching analytics—officers on the street may soon be able to identify persons' threat levels and risk profiles *prior to* engagement with them. Indeed, in some places they already do (Brayne 2017; Ferguson 2017; Joh 2014).

Computer screens, television screens, and presentation screens project a variety of visual representations of the police métier to its practitioners in their everyday work environment. These help to organize police knowledge work and give it the appearance of scientific rationality, but they do not overcome the alienation between police and public. They further instill it.

According to van Dijck and Poell (2013), new social media has a distinct logic as platforms such as Instagram, Twitter, Facebook, YouTube, and others have penetrated the mechanics of everyday life changing informal socializing, institutional structures, and professional routines. Social media have 'changed the rules of social interaction' through the imposition of social media logic and this has had consequences for, among many other things, the politics of law and order.

The research concern is to map the complex connections between platforms, the users that employ them, technologies that drive them, economic structures that scaffold them, and institutional bodies that incorporate them. The public is panicked, and criminological research has largely been concerned to uncover the extent to which the activities of urban rioters or criminals have been facilitated by these media (Lewis *et al.* 2011; Yar 2012). The police profess a need to understand how new social media affect rioters and gang members, while learning to use those same platforms as a means of surveillance and control (Brayne 2017). When police and public view each other through the screens of new social media, they see themselves in a black mirror. Screen-age paranoia is a characteristic feature of contemporary alienation.

Police have long been subject to internal organizational surveillance. In the recent past they have also become increasingly subject to surveillance by citizens. Due to the increasing power and omnipresence of surveillance technologies, the relationship between police and people is changing in important ways. Panoptic power, the ability of the few to oversee the many, gave obvious advantages to control agents like the police. Synoptic power, the ability of the many to undertake surveillance of the few, in a sense democratized surveillance power. Souveillance allows for the routine visual recording of activity by a participant, and may be undertaken both by the police officer with a body-worn camera and a civilian with a smartphone. Police and people have become the subjects of ambient surveillance, where all human subjects are always already under the gaze of technology (Bradshaw 2013; Diphoorn 2016; Doyle *et al.* 2013; Goldsmith 2015; Hampson and Jardine 2017; Mathiesen 1997; Sandhu 2016; Stalcup and Hahn 2016). Some argue that this has had devastating consequences for police legitimacy, others that it is a step towards democratically 'policing the police'.

The shooting death of Sammy Yatim by a Toronto Police constable in July 2013 offers a case in point. Greatly condensing for simplicity's sake, the occurrence led to murder charges being laid against an officer who used deadly force 'in the line of duty'. Such charges would certainly not have been laid but for the widespread availability of video footage of the incident captured by independent witnesses and other non-police sources and posted on the internet. The shooting of Yatim and the trial of his killer are similar to the 1991 Rodney King incident but 'because of the widespread proliferation of mobile technologies capable of recording everyday social life and the multitude of social media platforms' its effects were intensified (Schneider 2016: 120). These developments in media technology have spawned a number of civilian police 'watchdog' organizations such as CopWatch (www.copwatch.org) and the Network for the Elimination of Police Violence (http://nevp.org).

POLICE-MEDIA AS INSTITUTIONALIZED RELATIONS

In earlier sections of this chapter we have looked at two aspects of media theory relevant to the politics of the police. First we looked at media as a container of encoded discourse, a figurative 'public space' of political and cultural articulation, discussion, and debate. We examined evidence from media content analysis relevant to the narrative rise and fall of police political legitimacy. Then we examined some salient social and organizational effects of media tools in the hands of agents in the sphere of policing, concluding that alienation between police and public is partly attributable to technological advances.

There is a third sense in which it is worth thinking about media and society, and that is in terms of political economy. Media theory that analyses content can be usefully supplemented by examining the institutional conditions of content production (e.g. Ericson 1989; Ericson *et al.* 1991; Colbran 2014). A further step must be taken, explaining how the conditions of media production and consumption are shaped by the political and economic configuration of institutional forces surrounding them (Herman and Chomsky 2002; Reiner 2016b). If it 'is no longer clear what the boundaries of political discourse are when presidents and actors switch roles yet play the same character' (Altheide 2004: 293), then the way to crack the code of the police social imaginary is not only by analysis of its contents, formulae, and techniques. We must also attend to the structured institutional arrangements in which they take place.

In this section we look at transnational corporate control and ownership of the technological means of media production and dissemination, and connect this theoretically with commercialization of police information and control technologies. Corporate exploitation of the commercial potential of media technologies has affected the politics of the police as a result of both.

CORPORATE MEDIA AND DEMOCRATIC PLURALISM

At the turn of the millennium, advances in communications technologies included global satellite broadcasting owned and operated by transnational media conglomerates (Arsenault and Castells 2008a, 2008b; Stalder 2006). This raised questions about threats to democratic pluralism due to political influence by corporate media. Prior to 9/11 there was already a discernible and rapid growth in the power of these conglomerates, resulting from neo-liberal market policies that facilitated deregulation and convergence of global media and telecommunications systems.

This was accompanied by the rise of the commercialized internet. The most salient feature of this process was the implantation, consolidation, and concentration of advertisement-dependent media. This development was paralleled by a perceived weakening 'public sphere'; that is, the diminution of media space unaffected by commercial influence. More worrying, this oligopolistic concentration of ownership concerns 'persuasive technologies'. These are machines that influence human behaviour. The potential totalitarian tendencies of new social media are not easily swept aside by voluntarist notions of corporate ethics (Eyal 2014; Fogg 2003; Schneider 2016; Williams 2018).

The trend to media oligopoly was first observable in the USA, and rippled out to impinge upon most other countries and regions around the world (Humphreys 1996; Herman and McChesney 2004). The digitization of cultural production and dissemination took place under conditions of globalized neo-liberal de-regulation. Media content was increasingly shaped by interlocking ownership, globalized, concentrated, and organized through networks of production and dissemination. Local influences and global forces now shape the content of communications networks connected by a variety of information technologies. Corporate media are driven by neo-liberal logic, intent upon the commodification of mediated culture and the subordination of all forms of communication to profit-making and the marketplace (Arsenault and Castells 2008a; 2008b). How does this impinge on police in the news?

POLICE AND THE 'INSIDE SCOOP'

Drawing on Ericson (1989) we can distinguish two journalistic-media archetypes who operate either in the 'front regions' where the drama of police-public relations is enacted—the domain of censorship and publicity—or those of the 'back region' of institutional life—the domain of secrecy and confidentiality. The latter Ericson identified as the 'inner circle' type, who cultivate their insider status so as to authentically publicize a world view commensurate with the police métier. The other type inhabit the 'outer circle', and Ericson associates them with 'quality' media outlets. They tend to look at the politics of the police from the point of view of procedural justice, civil liberties, and other substantive social and political concerns not necessarily in tune with the police métier and, oftentimes, in direct opposition to it. In relation to the 'outer circle' type, the police are 'involved in a perpetual dance of secrecy and revelation, constantly forced to refine their accountability to achieve accountability in public culture' (Ericson 1989: 224). On the other hand, media types who have the inside scoop, routinely reproduce 'the performative and promotional character of police news releases' (ibid.). Identifying these relations take us part way to understanding the causes of police media representation (Reiner 2016b: 133–5).

Abstracting and synthesizing what we know about globalized corporate news media and the manufacture of the police imaginary, we can come to some theoretical conclusions. In terms of the contemporary politics of the police as manufactured by institutionalized media corporations, we can say that critical or 'quality' outlets are minority providers. For majority providers, there is an extended filtration process in both news and entertainment mass media production that shapes and censors the manufacture of the police imaginary.

Adapting Herman's and Chomsky's (2002) five filters of corporate media bias, we would first say that the police métier strives to make 'suitable foes'—e.g. 'transnational criminals' and 'terrorists'—which serve to naturalize it, and give it a normative justification. Insider journalists must unfailingly adopt this stance, because not to do so would cut them off from their sources. Next we note how the complex politics of policing are projected in the media, and the competing claims and counter-claims made by various parties: think-tanks, police associations, civil society groups, social activists, victims advocates, scientific experts, celebrities, celebrity intellectuals, and the 'lonely prophets' of the academy.

In the flak of the media storm that surrounds the politics of the police are various enforcers who patrol the boundaries of meaning in the police imaginary, and some-times flood the airwaves with disinformation. 'Quality' news by investigative journal-ists melds into the background of this information wash. This helps explain why the increase of white-collar crime stories in news and entertainment media over recent years has been so easily absorbed in the medium of publicity (Levi 2006; Reiner 2016b: 89–93). The superabundance of narratives of bad government and bad policing, along-side the plethora of state-crime and corruption stories and all the other 'bad news', is interpretable as further media evidence of state rot, conducive to neo-liberal ideology justifying further hollowing out of the social welfare state. Add to this the power of advertisers to shape media content so as not to be in conflict with their own interests, or the image-making needs of global media conglomerates (which define the basis of social order the police métier is designed to uphold), and the description of police-media as institutionalized relations is nearly complete.

UNDER THE INFLUENCE—POLICE AND CORPORATE MEDIA

To this must be added an awareness of the manufacture of entertainment concerning police and thieves, and the commercial pressures that motivate those processes. These issues were touched upon previously when we looked at the development of movies and television cop shows. Media industries manufacture publicity, transfer meanings, shape opinions, change attitudes, and influence interactions within social groups, thereby lending meaning to the social structure in which this all takes place. News and entertainment media shape cognitive habits.

Police power depends upon the general consent of the public, otherwise it degenerates into military occupation (Brodeur 2010: 322), and so the politics of the police inevitably involves engaging in 'a battle over the minds of the people' (Castells 2007: 239; Castells, 2009/2013). The police are everywhere engaged in mediated politics. This is played out globally in a segmented, customized mass media market, under the hegemony of a select number of transnational media conglomerates capable of exercising undue influence on democratic processes of governance.

As we have already shown, the cognitive habits of police on the job are shaped by the information and communications media at their disposal. The police métier combines the power of coercion and the power of surveillance, and its application is intended to reproduce the existing social order. Increasingly police practice is dependent on sophisticated technological wizardry.

Social media are new forms of communication by which people link up in the global networked society. These were initially thought to have provided 'horizontal' modes of organization capable of countering the hegemony of the neo-liberal project (Bradshaw 2013; Castells 2007; Loader and Mercea 2011; Schneider 2016). This belief could be sustained until very recently because the technological infrastructure for police information management was believed to be crippled by 'data smog' (Brodeur 2010: 250), and suffering from fundamental 'organization pathologies' as a result (Sheptycki 2004b).

New developments in police-media technology seem to have begun to solve the problems of information overload, converting new social media into a means of mass surveillance (Brayne 2017; Chan and Moses 2017; de Pauw et al. 2011; Ferguson 2017; Fyfe, Gundhus, and Rønn 2017; Joh 2017). Looked at from the point of view of the politics of the police, the relationships between power and counter-power in communications media—between police and public—are skewed. The synoptic power of the public to 'police the police' seems puny in comparison with the combined powers of the police métier. Moreover, recent revelations about the ability to manipulate emotions, perceptions and attitudes through new social media raise fundamental questions regarding the changing capacities of high policing in the global networked society that have scarcely been asked (Morozov 2011, 2013; Hampson and Jardine 2017; Sheptycki 2013, 2017b). The undue influence of corporate media and technology companies on police policy and practice further shapes the politics of the police in non-democratic ways (Joh 2017).

An obvious problem arises out of this because the results seem to perpetuate social disintegration and dissensus. This makes the task of policing more conflictual and difficult, eroding the doctrine of democratic policing by consent of the governed. It is, however, entirely in keeping with the moral economy of neo-liberalism based on narcissistic and competitive individualism (Reiner 2016b: 86). Perhaps the mediatized catharsis of the 'carnival of crime' (Presdee 2000) is a necessary social-psychological projection, an adaptation to the hegemony of the neo-liberal politics of policing, and 'reading' media events like riots merely another moment in the ongoing mediatization of policing (Lewis *et al.* 2011). Taking into account the political economy of the institutional nexus in which media content is manufactured, identifies in another way the influence of a global elite class and the social order which the police métier strives to enforce (Harvey 2005b: 148, 157).

CONCLUDING THOUGHTS ON POLICE AND MEDIA

Until now the standard approach to theorizing the police-media relation mainly focused on the contents of mass news and entertainment media. We have attempted to synthesize a broader account of police and media which brings into view not only an understanding of content, but also how different kinds of media technologies function as tools in the hands of a variety of different kinds of institutional actors who interact, often in conflict, sometimes in cooperation and, in the contemporary period, always firmly embedded in neo-liberal market conditions.

Much of the controversy concerning police and media has been described as happening between two poles of argument—the orthodox/hegemonic and the revisionist/subversive—but 'postmodern conditions' of social fragmentation associated with the end of the millennium troubled this binary. Underlying a great deal of thinking about the police and media has been an assumption that these processes ought to be socially integrative, in order to create the best conditions for policing by consent of the governed. What our analysis reveals is that social conflict and dissensus are quite functional for a neo-liberal order, in which security has become a commodity along with everything else. The evident social disintegration symptomatic of an over-mediatized—even 'hyperreal'—society is hardly disfunctional to market relations.

We shall return to these points elsewhere in the book, but for now we can conclude that broadening our understanding of police and media helps us to understand even better why it is that the 'rich get richer and the poor get the blame' (Reiner 2016b: 102–3). It remains to be seen if new media relations can turn competitive individualism upside down and help to constitute a new kind of reciprocal individualism conducive to social democracy (Reiner 2011). We would hope that a critical appreciation of police-media relations helps to inform a fundamental challenge to the continuation of police complicity in the as yet ongoing attempt to manufacture consent for transnational neo-liberalism.

PART IV

LAW AND POLITICS

PART IV

LAW AND POLITICS

11
POLICE POWERS AND ACCOUNTABILITY

INTRODUCTION

The legal powers of the police are arguably their defining feature. As discussed in Chapter 1, the most persuasive approach to defining the police was formulated in the 1970s by Egon Bittner. Police are 'equipped, entitled and required to deal with every exigency in which force may have to be used' (Bittner 1974: 35). In a sympathetic critique of this 'police-use-of-force' paradigm, Jean-Paul Brodeur developed the concept in a variety of ways (Brodeur 2010: chap. 4). Crucially he built upon a common observation about, and indeed tenet of, effective policing. The use of force must be minimized to be legitimate, deployed only when absolutely necessary, and calibrated proportionately to the threat that justifies it. Identifying the police primarily through the use of legitimate force is misleading in that it postulates as their essence a capacity that is seldom actually resorted to and it neglects the power of surveillance. What marks the police out on a more regular basis is their endowment with a battery of special legal powers beyond those of the ordinary citizen, supposedly to enable them to maintain order and enforce substantive criminal law. The strongest of these legal powers is the ability to deprive people of their liberty, by arrest and detention, but extends to other forms of coercive and intrusive powers. In what purport to be democratic societies the use of these powers is subject to legal constraints formulated as safeguards for citizens from unwarranted or unfair intrusions into their liberty.

The topic of this chapter goes to the very heart of key issues concerning human rights, effective democratic government, and social justice. It concerns a conundrum: how can an institution endowed with special coercive powers be rendered accountable to the legal and political processes that established it. This is an especially poignant issue for societies that claim the mantle 'democratic'. How is it possible that 'the people', nominally the ultimate rulers and beneficiaries in democracies, can be both subject to and masters of police power?

The chapter will consider the politics of policing, law, and democratic accountability. First, we will briefly analyse the idea of 'democracy', an issue since ancient times. It has become especially vexed in the twenty-first century states that have long prided themselves on exemplifying or at least approximating to that ideal. Second, we will consider the special issues of police powers and accountability in a democracy. Third, we review the attempts to reconcile police power and democratic accountability in contemporary democracies characterized by a patchwork quilt of domestic, transnational, public, and private policing agencies.

DEMOCRACY: AN ESSENTIALLY CONTESTED CONCEPT

'Democratic Policing' is a motherhood-and-apple-pie ideal that is never explicitly re-jected (Manning 2010). But what does it mean? Is it achievable in principle or practice? Are we moving closer to or further from its realization? Both 'democracy' and 'polic-ing' are essentially contested concepts, and the relationship between them is fraught *a fortiori*. How can the exercise of power to regulate conflict and maintain order accord with equal liberty, power, and welfare? Is policing per se antithetical to democracy? A seminal philosophical paper introduced the notion of 'essentially contested concepts' over six decades ago (Gallie 1953). These were 'concepts the proper use of which in-evitably involves endless disputes about their proper uses on the part of their users' (ibid.: 169). Four conditions characterized these concepts. They were: 'appraisive' (i.e. inextricably involving value judgements), 'internally complex', 'variously describable', and 'open' (they altered unpredictably with changing circumstances). Gallie gave 'de-mocracy' as a 'live example' (ibid. 183–7; the others were 'religion', 'art', and 'social justice'). Democracy was '*The* appraisive political concept par excellence in modern times' (ibid.). It subsumed various complex meanings: majority choice of government, equal opportunity to acquire responsible leadership positions, citizen participation, or self-government. Its fundamental meaning was vague:

> . . . certain political aspirations which have been embodied in countless slave, peasant, national and middle-class revolts and revolutions, as well as in scores of national consti-tutions and party records and programmes. These aspirations are evidently centred in a demand for increased equality.

Interpretations of democracy are contested between changing cultures and values, and by conflicting interests and perspectives. Today, the notion of democracy as for-mally free and fair elections is paramount. The fear of democratic theorists that voting may produce a 'tyranny of the majority' is generally downplayed nowadays. Nonethe-less some protection of minority rights is widely seen as essential by many, as is the 'rule of law'. But neglected in contemporary discussion is the idea that democracy is an expression of aspirations for equality, or at any rate a rejection of gross inequality (Gallie 1953).

As the earlier chapters have shown, police and policing are also *conceptually* con-tested. This is in large part because they are inherently bound up with social conflict, and the exercise of power (ultimately force) for some interests over others. Repro-ducing inequality is central to policing, not deviant (see Chapter 6). As Engels (1844: 234–5) dryly observed: 'Because the English Bourgeois finds himself reproduced in his law . . . the policeman's truncheon has for him a wonderfully soothing power. But for the workingman quite otherwise!' There is some ambiguity in this, because police simultaneously protect the universal interest in the coordination of complex societies. There is thus an inherent tension between policing, and egalitarian aspira-tions of democracy and rule of law (Bowling and Sheptycki 2015b). As seen in earlier chapters, police face an uphill struggle for legitimacy, with the general population, and *a fortiori* with the 'usual suspects' or 'police property' who bear the brunt of coercive powers.

POLICE ACCOUNTABILITY: ITS SPECIAL PROBLEMS

The ancient pedigree of the problem of police accountability is often underlined by citing Juvenal's question: '*Quis custodiet ipsos custodes*—who will guard the guards themselves'? This was not originally a reference to a conundrum of statecraft, but to the predicament of a husband worried about his wife's fidelity, and more particularly the fidelity of those entrusted with safeguarding it (from Juvenal's Satire VI). Relying on any agents to deal with deviance or preserve peace leads to a potentially infinite regress. Who or what protects against the guards' deviance or unreliability? And then how is that line of security itself secured, and so on. There are special problems, both practical and principled, in rendering *police* accountable, in addition to those involved in achieving the accountability of any organization or agents.

A well-established argument is that one of the special practical problems for police accountability is the 'low visibility' of everyday policework, and the considerable discretion this gives cops and constables (Goldstein 1960). Low visibility stems in part from the practical exigencies of policework, which is necessarily conducted mostly out on the streets, beyond the gaze of supervisors. The history of police management can be told in terms of an arms race between successive techniques of supervisory control and new rank-and-file strategies of evasion (Rubinstein 1973). In recent decades this has intensified with the increasing use of high-tech methods of recording police operations, including the automatic recording of all telephone calls to the police, tape recording of suspect interviews, installation of video cameras in police custody areas, satellite tracking of all police vehicles, and mobile phones to the introduction of body-worn video cameras (see Chapter 10).

A new twist in this tale is the proliferation of citizen recording technology since the 1990s, especially as mobile phones with cameras became ubiquitous. Many notorious cases of police abuse have thus been caught on video, from the beating of Rodney King in Los Angeles in 1991, to British cases such as the death of Ian Tomlinson during the London 2009 G20 protests after he was struck by a police officer (Lawrence 2000; Goldsmith 2010, 2015; Greer and McLaughlin 2012). In the Tomlinson case, the Independent Office of Police Conduct collected evidence from 220 cameras. Video evidence from citizen's smartphones and police dashboard cameras has been highly significant in a number of recent cases in the USA (see Chapter 5). This profound shift has been analysed as 'synopticon' (Mathiesen 1997) or 'sousveillance' (Mann *et al.* 2003): the capacity of the masses to parallel the gaze of the powerful, partially countering the top-down surveillance of the 'panopticon'. There can be no doubt that such developments have brought to light police malpractice that would otherwise have remained hidden, creating an impression of greater police wrongdoing, and hence accentuating the search for further technological ways to penetrate everyday policing. An illustration of the power of new technologies to make policing visible can be found in the investigative practice of Forensic Architecture which has used a wide range of analytical and visualization techniques to hold the police to account for serious wrongdoing in many places, including Germany, Israel, Palestine, and Mexico (Weizman 2017). Although it is likely that the police will find ways to subvert the ways that these new visual technologies are turning the surveillant gaze back on power, it seems clear that a major shift is taking place that has been characterized as the 'new visibility' of policing (Goldsmith 2010; Brown 2016; Sandhu 2016).

The physical 'low visibility' of many police actions is bolstered by the socially contingent fact that most street encounters are with relatively powerless groups, with low-status in the politics of creditability in a hierarchical society. Their accounts are liable to be rejected in favour of police officers' versions of events in any adjudicating forum, although with declining deference since the 1960s, 'police property' groups have gained greater 'voice' to some extent (Box and Russell 1975; Lee 1981). This is also true of video evidence. For example, Lawrence's (2000) analysis of the beating of Rodney King by the LAPD showed that what appeared to some as incontrovertible video evidence of police brutality was interpreted in completely different ways by different audiences according to their preconception. In this sense, low visibility renders the formally lowest ranks of the police 'street-corner' politicians, making effective policy decisions in practice. This frustrates the nominal control of those higher ranked in the organization, and *a fortiori* of external agents of accountability (Muir 1977; Punch 1983). Furthermore, the craft of policing also inculcates greater ability to avoid discovery of police wrongdoing: detectives learn skills of covering as well as uncovering deviance. A crucial factor aiding this is the 'blue curtain' of silence against prying governors, bolstered by the solidarity developed by doing a sometimes dangerous and frequently controversial job (Punch 2009).

Even more fundamental problems of governance are due to the very nature of policing, as indicated by ongoing debates about what their role is or should be (see Chapter 5). Policing is 'dirty work' (Everett Hughes 1961); the 'fire to fight fire' (Brodeur 2010: 107); a necessary evil not an unequivocal good. Policing is 'a mechanism for the distribution of non-negotiable coercive force' that is 'situationally justified' (Bittner 1970: 131). This immediately triggers the query: justified by and to whom, by what principles of justice? Whose law, what order? As argued earlier, policing is Janus faced, simultaneously reproducing 'general' order (the universally beneficial protection of the prerequisites of cooperation and coexistence) and 'particular' order (a structure of power and privileges that oppresses as well as serves). In core policing contexts there is always an explicit or implicit conflict of viewpoints and interests. 'You're right from your side, I'm right from mine' as Bob Dylan taught.

Thus, special riddles of police accountability arise in principle and practice. Other public service bureaucracies have to meet two dimensions of accountability: effectiveness and fairness. How can we ensure effective health, education, and so on? To what extent is policing a public good (Loader and Walker 2007; Bowling 2007)? And is this 'good' fairly distributed? But a third dimension makes defining, let alone delivering or regulating, 'good' policing a deeper riddle (Morrell and Bradford 2019). Policing inherently involves intervening in conflicts, so 'good' service to some means 'bad' outcomes for others (Bowling 2007). Policing itself, and hence any processes of accountability, are clogged by the fallout from socio-economic and power inequalities, shaping what counts as 'crime' or 'disorder' (Reiner 2011), and what police responses are considered to be 'good enough' (Bowling 2007).

There is also a semantic dimension to the conundrums of police accountability. Accountability is a weasel word, implying a desirable state of affairs but without clear and agreed meaning. The *Oxford English Dictionary* offers a number of different (albeit related) definitions, with two fundamental versions: (i) the obligation to give reports (often in the form of numerical statements of receipts and expenditure); and (ii) the duty to 'settle' these, a responsibility to meet the expectations of those to whom account is given. These variants underlie the two models of police accountability that were distinguished by Geoffrey Marshall in his classic analysis: 'explanatory and co-operative' as distinct from 'subordinate and obedient' (Marshall 1978). In the former model, accountability is merely the obligation to tell stories, to give 'an account' in the form of reports to the relevant authorities, but without any corresponding requirement to take account of their responses. In the latter model, accountability entails control: the police, like other public services, should be governed by democratically elected authorities, compliant with egalitarian principles of justice such as those articulated by John Rawls (Manning 2010). The conflict between these models of accountability has been perennial throughout police history in nominally democratic societies. The ultimate question is whether policing can comply with democratic values in a fundamentally unequal society?

POLICE ACCOUNTABILITY: A CHIMERICAL PURSUIT?

The historical chapters of this volume (found in Part II) outlined the variety of routes by which contemporary policing developed. Four main ideal-type trajectories can be distinguished: common law, civil law, ex-colonial, and settler-colonial. The exemplars of the common law trajectory are Great Britain and the USA. Western European countries primarily have civil law systems, but with many distinct past and contemporary differences. Ex-colonial systems are ones that attained independence relatively recently (in the second half of the twentieth century), with legal systems based on those imposed by the dominant power and attempts at subsequent reform. Settler colonial systems attained independence in the later nineteenth or early twentieth centuries, and power lies primarily in the hands of the descendants of settlers rather than indigenous populations. These are broad distinctions, and, as with ideal types generally, it is arguable how concrete cases fit in. The USA, for example, arose from colonial settlers who came to dominate (indeed largely exterminate) the indigenous population. However, it has for the main part of the two and a half centuries since independence operated versions of common law, albeit with traces of both civil and frontier law values.

These various types of legal system have considerable implications for patterns of police powers and accountability. All systems give the police special powers backed by the potential for legitimate force. At a very high level of abstraction they also charge them with functions that can be expressed in similar terms, notably the maintenance and reproduction of social order. However, at a more concrete level order is defined in quite different ways. In regimes *without* democratic pretensions (e.g. those with absolutist or colonial rulers) order is specified by and benefits the governing elite, with at most the vaguest lip service to general interests. In states with democratic aspirations, by contrast, government is meant to be *of the people*, but also *for* and *by* them, at least in some sense.

As discussed in Chapter 2, there is tension between crime control and due process values (Packer 1968). A bifurcation between powers enabling police activity, and safeguards intended to protect suspect citizens' rights, is universally found in contemporary Western democracies. The legitimation of special police powers was, however, a site of considerable controversy in the common law jurisdictions that saw themselves as democratic when police were initially formed. The legitimation of the British police in the nineteenth century was partly based on minimizing their legal powers (Chapter 4). This developed into the myth of the constable as the 'citizen in uniform':

> The policeman, in the view of the common law, is only a person paid to perform, as a matter of duty, acts which if he were so minded he might have done voluntarily . . . Indeed a policeman possesses few powers not enjoyed by the ordinary citizen (Royal Commission on Police Powers and Procedure 1929: 6; Royal Commission on the Police 1962: 11).

For a century and a half, the quaintly antique yet stirring ideal of the 'citizen in uniform' sought to legitimate the British police. Since the embroilment of the police in a storm of controversies after the 1960s, two successive revolutions have occurred in the legitimation of police powers. The 1984 Police and Criminal Evidence Act (PACE) replaced the 'citizen in uniform' myth with the principle of 'fundamental balance' between police powers and suspects' safeguards (controversially formulated by the Royal Commission on Criminal Procedure (1981)). A little more than a decade later, this itself came to be superseded by a proliferation of police powers, largely without balancing safeguards and indeed some whittling away of the PACE safeguards. This has been legitimated by 'Dirty Harry' rhetoric, a supposed need to *rebalance* the system in the interests of victims, because of a persisting state of emergency posed by crime, antisocial behaviour, and latterly, terrorism (despite a simultaneous decline in recorded crime). This was accompanied by a castigation of 'traditional' principles (barely twenty-five years old!) as standing in the way of modernization. Similar developments have occurred in most Western polities.

The shift in legitimatory myths reveals dramatic transformations in the politics of policing and security, and involves deep issues of principle about the relationship between state and citizens in a democratic society (Loader and Walker 2007). But in terms of policing practice, public policy debates about police powers commonly involve two fallacious assumptions. These are shared by the otherwise opposed law-and-order and civil liberties lobbies. Both emphasize law enforcement as the central police function, and adopt the rational deterrence model of classical criminology, albeit at different stages of the argument. In this sense both fail to take on board the implications of social research on the police, discussed in Chapters 5 to 8. Neither has adequately considered or explained the fundamental question 'What are police powers for?'

If pushed on the issue, both camps would say the police are primarily concerned with preventing and detecting crime. The historical and sociological evidence indicates that crime-fighting has never been, and cannot be the prime activity of the police, despite the mythology of media images, cop culture, and, in recent years, government policy (see Chapter 5). The core mandate of policing, historically and in terms of concrete demands placed upon the police, is the more diffuse one of order maintenance. Only if this is recognized can the problems of police powers and accountability really be confronted in all their complexity. The vaguely defined 'public order' offences like breach of the peace or anti-social behaviour (which appear to be a scandalous embarrassment from either a crime control or due process approach) speak to the very heart of the police role.

Given this, the implicit goal of many civil libertarian critiques—a precisely and un-ambiguously defined set of criminal offences and police powers to deal with them—becomes an unattainable chimera. Indeed, an influential theoretical analysis of the concept of 'the police power' sees it as a survival in modern times of ancient untram-melled powers exercised by patriarchal rulers (Dubber 2005). Its origins are said to lie in the discretionary and virtually limitless patriarchal power of the householder over his household. This contrasts with liberal ideas of law developing in modern societies that stress its rule-bound, principled, and democratic character. Certainly, as discussed in Chapters 1 to 4, in early modern times the conceptualization and the practices of police were wide-ranging and amorphous, encompassing all aspects of domestic urban governance. During the eighteenth and nineteenth centuries policing came to be narrowed down to the mandates of law enforcement, public order, and se-curity that are now seen as its *raison d'être*. In US constitutional jurisprudence, police power does not specifically refer to the right of government to create police forces. The 'police power' is also used at the basis for enacting laws regulating such areas as land use, fire and building codes, commerce, traffic, schooling, and sanitation—as well as crime and disorder.

Increasing police powers is often seen as a panacea for security. The Conservative government in 1984 advocated PACE as its 'main current policy initiative in the field of police powers to combat crime' (Home Office Working Paper *Criminal Justice* 1984). The law-and-order model errs in postulating the rational deterrent model with regard to policing crime (more police power + greater deterrence = less crime). But the civil liberties lobby adopt the same erroneous recipe for policing the police. For years it has been the refrain of radical and liberal criminologists that policing and penal policy have a limited, primarily symbolic role in restraining deviance. This analysis should ex-tend to police wrongdoing. The main way that the sanctions and enforcement machin-ery proposed by a rational deterrence model can be effective is by the impact they have on the cultural controls in a community, including the police. This moral economy is the immediate bedrock of law-abidingness or deviation, dialectically interdependent with a society's political economy, social patterns, and history (Reiner 2007: chap. 4).

What needs more precise analysis is the relationship between formal rules of law and police conduct. How does black-letter law 'in the books' relate to 'blue-letter' law in action (Reiner and Leigh 1992; Bowling and Sheptycki 2015b), shaped by police culture, the situational exigencies and organizational sanctions of policing, and the broader moral and political economies in which they are embedded? There are two competing views on this in the research literature. Interactionists largely assume that formal rules are primarily presentational (Holdaway 1979, 1983, 1989; Chatterton 1983, 1995; Punch 1979a; Fielding 1989). They are the terms in which conduct has to be justified, but which do not really affect practice. It is the police subculture that is the key to understanding police actions. This culturalist perspective sometimes amounted to an extreme rule scepticism. 'Sociologists of the police have tended to treat the notion of legality as unproblematic, not because they assume the police operate according to these principles, but rather because they assume the opposite, that they are largely ir-relevant in practice' (McBarnet 1979: 25).

But interactionist studies themselves point to some impact of formal rules, for ex-ample in emphasizing rank-and-file solidarity aimed at shielding deviant practices from the senior ranks, and the need always to have a good story to 'cover your ass'. Rank-and-file subcultural autonomy is limited to a degree by formal controls, but how much, when, and in what way? Police subcultures are by no means radically distinct or deviant in values from either legal or popular morality. The police are broadly representative of the population, as is their culture (Waddington 1999a, 1999b; Foster 2003: 198–9). While there is some tolerance for rule-bending as 'noble cause corruption' in police culture, that does not mean carte blanche for gross abuse.

The danger of police subcultural notions of justice becomes acute, however, when there is moral conflict, confusion, or change in a society, and police ethics are at odds with those of their 'clients'. When the police deal with those regarded as 'alien', disreputable, and 'police property', the constraints of traditional communal morality are not an adequate protective guide or check. The problem in contemporary liberal democracies is less how to protect the majority, the 'public', from police oppression, than how to protect vulnerable minorities (see Chapter 6). The rules of criminal procedure are dangerously stretched in relation to suspects drawn from relatively vulnerable and powerless social groups, but these constitute the vast majority of cases. 'Democratic controls' through the electoral process are not much help here. What has to be achieved is the incorporation within operative police subcultures of working procedures and norms embodying universal respect for the rights even of weak or unpopular minorities, which the rhetoric of legality purports to represent (Goldsmith 1990). The task of reform is neither just laying down the law, nor achieving majority control. It is probing what policy changes can achieve their desired objectives, bearing in mind the refracting effects of rank-and-file subculture, and the situational exigencies structuring policework and culture (Chan 1997; Dixon 1997; Foster 2003).

The second strand in research literature on the police is a structuralist one. It argues that the source of police deviance is not primarily rank-and-file subcultural autonomy. The problem is the tacit encouragement, by senior officers, judges, and the state elite, of deviations from the ideal of legality. This is accomplished through a permissive structure of vaguely stated legal rules, and the accommodation of case law to police practices (McBarnet 1979, 1981; Brogden 1982; Jefferson and Grimshaw 1984; Grimshaw and Jefferson 1987; McConville et al. 1991). This structuralist case needs qualification in terms of specifying which rules, in which circumstances, are bent, and in what ways. (Dixon 1997; Cape and Young 2008). Indeed, there is good evidence that changes in formal rules—through legislation, judicial interpretation, or official police force policies—can bring about quite marked changes in police operational practices (Bowling and Marks 2017).

A prime problem in controlling police deviation from legality is the pervasiveness of conflicts of evidence about whether malpractice has occurred. In such arguments the suspect is usually at a structural disadvantage, which is why complaints against the police are so seldom upheld (Smith 2001, 2004, 2005, 2009). A key aspect of the PACE project was a variety of tactics, from tape recording to CCTV, aimed at opening up the visibility of routine policing (Newburn and Hayman 2001). Much of the criticism of PACE and other extensions of formal police powers rests upon an assumed 'law of inevitable increment: whatever powers the police have they will exceed by a given margin' (Reiner 1981b: 38). But police abuse will not necessarily burst the seams of whatever rules are laid down. It is based on pressure to achieve specific results, using

record-keeping monitored by internal discipline, ran through all the main sections of PACE. It can be seen in the provisions on powers to arrest suspects, to enter and search their premises and seize evidence, and to detain them for questioning.

In addition, some general safeguards were introduced. Perhaps the most significant was the possible exclusion of evidence obtained in violation of PACE procedures. A general discretion was provided for judges to exclude evidence if it appears that 'the circumstances in which the evidence was obtained' would have 'an adverse effect on the fairness of the proceedings' (s 78). This rather loose discretion fell far short of the tough exclusionary rule found in some other jurisdictions, notably the US in the days of the Warren-led Supreme Court. However, one of the surprises following PACE was a tougher attitude adopted by the judiciary towards police breaches of the Codes (Feldman 1990).

In the decade following the implementation of PACE there was a plethora of empirical evaluations of its core aspects, largely sponsored by the Home Office. This represented an impressively 'reflexive' approach to policy, embodying a dialectic of scandal, reform, research, and further reform. Since then such research has not taken place on anything like the same scale, largely because of the new era of tough law-and-order politics.

Evaluative empirical research suggests a more complex picture than was implied by the polarized polemics that attended the birth pangs of PACE. Routine practice has incorporated many of the procedures of the Codes of Practice. On the other hand, much is ritualistic and presentational, affecting little of substance in the experience of suspects. Empirical research suggests some improvements in the protection of suspects since PACE, but also failures (Research up to 1997 is summarized in: Dixon 1997, and previous editions of this book. More recent studies include: Newburn *et al.* 2004; Delsol and Shiner 2006, 2015; Bowling and Phillips 2007; Henry 2007; Cape and Young 2008; Pleasance *et al.* 2011; Hodgson 2011; Kemp 2014; Young 2016; Skinns 2012, 2019; Skinns *et al.* 2017; Bradford 2016).

On the plus side, empirical research suggests that:

(i) Suspects are almost invariably informed of their rights on reception at the police station.

(ii) As a result, the proportion receiving legal advice increased between two and four times.

(iii) The special extended powers (such as denial of the right to see a solicitor) available for 'serious arrestable offences' were obtained relatively rarely.

(iv) The extent of the use of dubious 'tactics' to extract incriminating statements by interrogation declined. Police and the Home Office have worked to develop more effective and ethical interviewing techniques.

(v) Tape recording of interviews reduced arguments in court about what occurred in them, and is now welcomed by police who were long opposed to it.

(vi) The average period of detention in police stations for all cases remained roughly the same in the early years of PACE, about six hours and forty minutes, despite the formal extension of the legal length of detention. However, it has increased subsequently, to about nine to ten hours.

(vii)   The PCA's supervision of the police investigation of complaints could be vigorous and active. The PCA was superseded by the IPCC in 2004 with full
investigative powers in serious cases. Following reforms in the Policing and
Crime Act 2017, the IPCC became the Independent Office for Police Conduct
(IOPC) in 2018.

There is also much evidence from the same research, however, which paints a more
negative picture:

(i)   Detention is authorized almost automatically and invariably.

(ii)   The information to suspects about their rights is often given in a ritualistic and
meaningless way. This may explain why the majority of suspects do not take
them up. It has been claimed also that 'ploys' are frequently used to dissuade
suspects from taking up their rights.

(iii)   Relatively few offenders ever exercised their right of silence, in part or completely. The proportion has declined substantially (but hardly surprisingly)
since the Criminal Justice and Public Order Act 1994 permitted adverse inferences to be drawn.

(iv)   Later stages in the detention process (such as reviews, or regulating access
to suspects by investigating officers) are less punctiliously followed than the
reception rituals.

(v)   PACE procedures can frequently be sidestepped by securing 'voluntary' compliance with police requests. This was how police operated before PACE con-
ferred on them clear statutory powers, as the euphemism familiar to Agatha
Christie readers, 'assisting with enquiries', indicates.

(vi)   After PACE bedded in, the use of 'tactics' in interrogation increased once
more, compared to its virtual elimination immediately after the Act.

(vii)   The provision of 'appropriate adults' to assist vulnerable suspects remains inadequate.

(viii) However adequate PCA supervision of complaints investigations may have
been, public confidence and complainant satisfaction remained low, as it is
with the its successor bodies.

(ix)   Consultative committees impress police views on the public rather than vice
versa, and act as a legitimating device more than a means of accountability.

(x)   The socially discriminatory pattern of use of police powers remains as marked
as before. The burden of police powers still falls disproportionately on the
young, economically marginal, ethnic minority males, who are the overwhelming majority of those stop/searched, arrested, detained, strip-searched.

PACE: GLASS HALF FULL OR HALF EMPTY?

The resilience of the social pattern of policing in the face of PACE is due to the unchanging role of the police, primarily as regulators of public space and those who live their
lives there. PACE could do little to alter the impact of this on the culture and organization of policing, and after the late 1990s policy tilted towards unbalanced extensions

of police power. Nonetheless the Act *has* impacted on police practices, albeit unevenly and patchily. Recent comparative research suggests it protects suspects better than the uncodified legal regulation in other common law countries (Skinns 2019), and in the EU mainly civil law jurisdictions have moved towards similar safeguards (Hodgson 2011). PACE's modest degree of success was due in part to the symbolic consequences of the codified legislation, which carried more weight with police at all levels than the previous Judges' Rules. It was also because of a variety of changes making punishment of breaches more likely. These included the tougher line taken by the courts, and the deterrent value of internal disciplinary sanctions.

Of particular importance has been a variety of devices which began to open up the 'low visibility' backstage areas of routine policing. Key examples are the recording requirements; Independent Custody Visitors who make spot-checks on people detained in police custody; enhanced access to solicitors (severely threatened in recent years by cuts in legal aid); and the introduction of CCTV in police stations. The legislation has achieved far more than its civil libertarian critics initially expected, if far less than they would have wished.

Deterrence, symbolism, and enhanced training are all important in understanding how PACE affected police culture and practice. If powers are precisely rather than permissively formulated, procedures to render their use more visible are constructed, and supervisors and courts determined to police the police, change *can* occur in line with the law. Thus, the booking-in procedures, which are precise, relatively visible to supervisors, and clearly enjoined in training, are religiously followed. However, the danger of precisely formulated rules is also evident here. They can be satisfied by ritualistic observance with little meaning, defeating their intended objectives.

In short, PACE accomplished significant constitutional and control functions, transforming police practices in large part. Key changes occurred in the informal culture of the police, their practical working rules. These were affected through symbolism, training, organization, and discipline. Police culture is primarily a function of the structurally determined social role of the police, however, which has not altered in any fundamental way. Policing in a hierarchical and divided society can never be even in its impact, and the socially discriminatory use of police powers continues (see Chapter 6).

Legal regulation alone will always be inadequate to secure legitimacy and genuine consent. After the 1990s, however, the hegemonic politics of tough law and order shifted policy away from concern with achieving 'fundamental balance' between powers and safeguards, towards the continuing enhancement of powers without corresponding safeguards, and indeed with some attrition of PACE protections. This unbalancing purported to be justified by a rhetoric of re-balancing powers in favour of victims, exceptional emergencies requiring tougher policing, and a modernization of procedures not fit for purpose in the twenty-first century. Tony Blair, launching the Home Office Five Year Strategy for Criminal Justice on 19 July 2004, boasted that 'We asked the police what powers they wanted and gave them to them' in order to 'rebalance the system radically in favour of the victim . . . our first duty is to the law-abiding citizen'. Contrary to this modernizing discourse, the state of police powers was not a hoary Victorian relic, but scarcely thirty years old. Never trust any policing procedures over thirty seems to be the watchword of the 1960s generation in office.

POLICE POWERS SINCE PACE

Since the early 1990s shift in the politics of law and order (Reiner 2007: chap. 5) crime control values have overwhelmed due process. A paradoxical feature of the all-pervasive law-and-order climate is that even some changes seeking to render the police exercise of powers more accountable have the unintended consequence of legitimizing and enhancing them. An example is the creeping de facto recognition of a power to 'stop and question' out of the *Macpherson Report*'s attempt to regulate the practice, which had no clear legal basis (Young 2016). The *Macpherson Report* was rightly concerned that the pattern of 'stop and question' seemed as racially discriminatory as the exercise of stop and search powers. It recommended that police be required to record all stops with the PACE recording requirements, and forces began to speak of a power to 'stop and account'. The 2008 Report of the *Independent Review of Policing* by Sir Ronnie Flanagan proposed as part of an attack on 'unnecessary bureaucracy' that stop and account recording should be drastically simplified. So, an attempt to regulate a *sub rosa* procedure culminated in de facto recognition of a power never actually granted by legislation or case law, with reporting requirements that have been cut as bureaucratic impediments to crime control.

A stream of legislation in the 1990s/2000s extended police powers (albeit with some extensions of citizens' rights by the Human Rights Act 1998, and the creation of the IPCC by the Police Reform Act (PRA) 2002):

- The Criminal Justice and Public Order Act 1994 permitted adverse inferences to be drawn from the accused's silence. Section 60 of the CJPOA introduced a stop and search power that could be operated without the reasonable suspicion required by PACE, if an inspector or higher-rank officer reasonably believes an area is likely to experience serious violence.

- The Crime and Disorder Act 1998 established an ambitious Crime Reduction Programme. It significantly expanded police powers, empowering chief officers to apply for Anti-Social Behaviour Orders (ASBOs), and to make local child curfew orders.

- The Regulation of Investigatory Powers Act 2000 extended powers and procedures to enable and regulate interception of communications, covert and intrusive surveillance, and covert intelligence operations.

- The Terrorism Act 2000 extended stop and search powers without the PACE's reasonable suspicion requirement. Section 44 gave an assistant chief officer power to designate an area for extended powers if 'expedient for the prevention of acts of terrorism', subject to confirmation by the Home Secretary. In designated areas, a constable can stop and search any vehicle or person without requiring reasonable suspicion. This has frequently been used against people where there is no suspected connection with terrorism, as in the 2006 *Gillan* case, in which the House of Lords upheld the legality of the search of peaceful protestors going to demonstrate at an arms fair. (In 2010 the European Court of Human Rights ruled s 44 powers as incompatible with the UK Human Rights Act. The government repealed the power and replaced it with a much more tightly circumscribed s 47A which has been very little used in mainland Britain.)

- The Criminal Justice and Police Act 2001 extended powers to control public alcohol consumption and to protect witnesses. But its most significant contribution was the introduction of on the spot penalties for certain listed offences, Penalty Notices for Disorder (PNDs). Originally directed mainly at 'safety' offences such as false alarms and drink-related disorder, the scope of PNDs was extended repeatedly (Young 2008: 166–71). They contribute to a growing battery of powers available to the police for regulating their 'property' on the streets without needing to overcome significant evidentiary hurdles.

Alongside this expansion of high discretion, hard-to-regulate powers, there was a continuing erosion of PACE safeguards. This was signalled clearly by Home Office Reviews of PACE instituted in 2002 and 2007 (Zander 2007), with the remit: 'To ensure that the legislation remains a useful tool supporting the police and providing them with the powers they need to combat crime.' Many suggestions have now been implemented in legislation:

- The Criminal Justice Act 2003 extended detention up to thirty-six hours for all arrestable offences not just the most serious ones, and empowered stop and search for criminal damage.
- The Serious Organised Crime and Police Act 2005 allowed for civilian custody officers. It creates a power of arrest for *all* offences, not just arrestable offences or those satisfying the necessity criteria of PACE s 25. It enhanced powers to search premises, and authorized police officers to take fingerprints or foot impressions on the street. Community support officers (CSOs) were given more powers, e.g. of search. A power was given for police to impose conditions on demonstrations near Parliament.

The clear trend from 1993 to 2010 was to extend police powers, without specific safeguards. This was confirmed by House of Lords' judgments in several cases: *Clingham* (2003) on ASBOs, *Gillan* (2006) on stop and search under the Terrorism Act 2000, *Austin (FC) and another v. Commissioner of Police of the Metropolis* (2009) on policing public order, legitimizing the controversial 'kettling' tactic subject to proportionality and necessity criteria. This suggests a rather different judicial attitude than in the early days of PACE, sensitive to the climate of exceptionalism and emergency. In sum, the period of legitimation of police powers by the principle of fundamental balance between powers and safeguards, supposedly enshrined in PACE 1984, lasted scarcely two decades. It was displaced by a rhetoric of modernization to rebalance in favour of victims, supposedly justified by a new era of exceptional insecurity and threat.

The politics of policing changed sharply from 2010 onwards, first brought about by the uneasy coalition government formed between the Conservative party and Liberal Democrats. Theresa May (then Home Secretary), began a campaign of police reform that aimed to scale back the police powers on the street, which had grown significantly under New Labour. The scrapping of the national ID card scheme, which would have transformed the police-public relationship by giving power to police potentially to demand identity documents, was a clear indication that the extension of police powers was being brought to a halt. This was followed by the abolition of s 44 stop and search powers by which officers were entitled to stop and search under the Terrorism Act 2000 without suspicion, and a radical reduction in suspicionless stop and search powers under s 60 Criminal Justice and Public Order Act 1994 (Bowling and Marks 2017; see also Chapter 5). In 2012, the Protection of Freedoms Act abolished the permanent retention of fingerprint and DNA records and established the independent office of the Biometrics Commissioner. In many ways the Conservative-led governments of post-2010 have adopted liberal attitudes and policies to the matter of police powers. More consistent with the extension of police powers argument are the extension of the Regulation of Investigatory Powers 2000 in the Investigatory Powers Act 2016. The key extension of power here concerns itself with the bulk acquisition of data, and is an issue pertaining to the accountability of 'high policing'. The Counter Terrorism and Security Act 2015 extended police powers by allowing access to internet communication services and extends a range of powers available to police officers at borders, including the temporary seizure of passports.

CONTROLLING THE CONTROLLERS: DEVELOPMENTS IN POLICE ACCOUNTABILITY

The basic objectives and rules of criminal procedure in democracies are framed by legislatures enacting substantive and procedural law. The issue of accountability is the question of how to keep police practice, in particular the operation of discretion, within that broad framework. This itself resolves into three analytically distinct functions:

- 'judicial': determining whether specific police actions have breached legal or procedural rules;
- quasi-'legislative': setting priorities in the allocation of resources between different legitimate policing duties;
- 'executive': managing performance in as efficient and effective a way as possible.

There are debates reflecting differing conceptions of who should have the ultimate power of decision when there is a conflict of viewpoints over the goals and means of policing, over what range of issues accountability operates, and by what political conceptions of justice should policing arrangements be evaluated (Reiner and Spencer 1993; Stenning 1995; Walker 2000; Manning 2010; Jones et al. 2012; Stenson and Silverstone 2014; Barton and Johns 2014; Lister and Rowe 2016).

A central role is played in official ideological claims about democratic policing by the notion of police accountability to law. The precise mechanisms vary between places and times, but all contemporary jurisdictions claiming the mantle democratic subject police to some judicial oversight. This is most direct in civil law inquisitorial models, where serious criminal investigation by police is under the supervision of prosecuting authorities or magistrates. There are four main ways in which courts regulate police conduct in common law systems: (i) police officers may be prosecuted for crimes, for example arising out of serious allegations of criminal misconduct; (ii) civil actions may be brought against police officers for damages in cases of wrongful arrest, trespass, assault, or for negligent performance of their duties; (iii) judges have discretion to exclude evidence obtained in violation of due process of law, as embodied primarily in PACE and its accompanying Codes; (iv) judicial review of police policy decisions may be sought, if they are claimed to be *ultra vires*. In practice none of these has operated very effectively. Police officers are rarely prosecuted for crimes arising out of wrongful performance of their duties (Dixon and Smith 1998; Smith 2001).

THE COMPLAINTS SYSTEM AND CIVIL ACTIONS

In Britain a statutory system for handling complaints against the police began with the Police Act 1964. From the start it was subject to severe criticism for relying entirely on internal police investigation and adjudication, which has been an issue around the world (Goldsmith 1991, Goldsmith and Lewis 2000). In the early 1980s pressure mounted for a more vigorous and independent scrutiny of allegations of serious police misconduct. In response PACE instituted the Police Complaints Authority, which was required to supervise the investigation of complaints alleging death or serious injury. By the late 1990s pressure for a fundamental overhaul of the system had mounted to a crescendo, following several years of gradual reform. In 1998 the Police (Northern Ireland) Act established a fully independent ombudsman to investigate and adjudicate complaints against the police (s 51), and it became fully operational in 2001 (Mulcahy 2013).

The 2002 Police Reform Act established the Independent Police Complaints Commission (IPCC), with the responsibility of investigating serious complaints against the police in England and Wales. The IPCC investigates all cases involving death, serious injury, assault, or corruption, and was given the power to take over the investigation of cases involving major matters of public interest. IPCC investigators are drawn from a variety of backgrounds involving suitable skills, including former police officers but also such occupations as financial services analysis, customs and excise, and social work. The Policing and Crime Act 2017 brought about further reform to the police complaints system, replacing the IPCC with the Independent Office for Police Conduct (IOPC) which has independent investigatory powers. The Act also places an emphasis on more independent end-to-end inspections of police services by Her Majesty's Inspectorate of Constabularies (HMIC). It makes provision for the Police Federation of England and Wales to be subject to the Freedom of Information Act 2000.

It is too early to know the effect of the IOPC but the results of having a completely independent system may not be as dramatic as many hoped. The low rates of clear-up of complaints against the police were not due mainly to cover-ups by police investigators, and the focus of debate on the issue of *who* investigates neglects more fundamental questions such as what are the functions of the system and how can complainants' interests be foregrounded (Smith 2004, 2005, 2009). A key problem is the 'low visibility' of the operational situations that give rise to most complaints. Frequently they turn on conflicts of testimony between complainants and police officers, with no independent evidence. Irrespective of who does the investigating and adjudicating many are unlikely to be sustained, leaving many complainants with a sense of grievance. This problem has bedevilled attempts to establish complaints systems in all jurisdictions (Goldsmith 1991; Goldsmith and Lewis 2000).

THE GOVERNANCE OF THE POLICE

Some of the most contentious issues of police accountability arise in relation to the quasi-legislative and executive functions of determining the priorities and efficiency of policing policy. To what extent, if any, should this be determined by political authorities? On the one hand, it can be argued that in societies purporting to be democratic, decisions about policing, like other policy areas, should be made by elected governmental bodies. On the other hand, it can be argued that police decisions are more like legal issues, impacting on the liberties and rights of particular individuals and groups. Thus, there are special dangers if they are made in partisan political ways. Rather, like judgments in court, they should be the province of independent office holders with a duty to be impartial in determining cases.

A common attempt to cut this Gordian knot is to argue that policy issues can and should be distinguished from decisions about individual cases. The problem with this argument is that many if not all general policies—for example, to deploy stringent stop and search tactics in areas with recorded crime above specified levels—structure decisions in particular cases. Conversely, the sum total of decisions by individual operational officers constitute de facto general policies, which is why police are often called 'street-level politicians'. If, for example, they are unconsciously affected by stereotypes about the criminal propensities of certain groups these can result in unwittingly discriminatory policies (and *a fortiori* if this is deliberate targeting). The issue of whether democratically elected political authorities or police professionals should be in the driving seat of police policy is a chestnut that has been resolved with varying results in different times and places (Bayley and Stenning 2016). So too is the question of how relations between political and professional authorities should be constituted. How much independence, if any, should professionals have, and how are they to be accountable to democratic processes?

A second perennial tension in police governance is the balance between local, regional, and national power. Different jurisdictions have drawn the balance variously, and there are considerable changes over time (ibid.: chap. 5). In general, this is dependent on the geographical and governmental complexity of different systems, and particular cultural and political histories, as well as the extent of social inequality, diversity, and conflict. Police systems vary from fundamentally centralized national forces (albeit with some internal localization and specialization, e.g. New Zealand, and in the last few years Scotland and the Netherlands), through hybrid combinations of national and local police bodies (like Canada, or France and several other western European forces), to highly diversified tapestries of local, regional, and national bodies with complex inter-relationships (like the USA and England and Wales since 2012).

THE GOVERNANCE OF DOMESTIC POLICING IN BRITAIN: A CASE STUDY

The labelling of this section is problematic. The British Isles have altered in political structure since the development of modern police in the early nineteenth century, and further change is imminent. The British police tradition (and Sir Robert Peel) spawned both archetypal *soi disant* democratic constabularies spreading out from the London

Metropolitan Police (the Met) in 1829, and colonial forces beginning in Ireland (Brogden 1987; Palmer 1988; and see also Chapter 3). After the Republic of Ireland won independence in 1922, Northern Ireland was policed by the Royal Ulster Constabulary which carried the taint of partisanship on behalf of the Protestant majority (see Chapter 6). The 1998 Good Friday Agreement led to the *Patten Report* which recommended a set of reforms to make policing more democratic. The RUC was replaced by the Police Service of Northern Ireland in 2001, which is accountable to a Policing Board (Ellison and Smyth 2000; Mulcahy 2013; Topping 2016). Scotland has always had a distinct legal and policing system from the rest of the UK. In 2013 its eight regional forces were merged into Police Scotland, a national organization accountable to a Scottish Police Authority and Inspectorate of Constabulary (Fyfe 2014).

The UK thus has three distinct police systems, with a complex backstory. The focus here will be on police governance in England and Wales. Since the 1970s this has encompassed forty-three forces, two of which are in London and have distinct accountability structures. The largest force, the London Met, was historically accountable to the Home Secretary only. However, in 2000 a Metropolitan Police Authority was established along the lines of the Police Authorities in the forty-one provincial forces, subjecting the Met to a similar tripartite governance structure. This changed again in 2012, when the MPA was replaced by the Mayor's Office for Policing and Crime, as part of the major shake-up of police organization flowing from the Police Reform and Social Responsibility Act 2011.

The 2011 transformation of governance is the greatest in the nearly two hundred years of British police history. It is so momentous that we shall follow the usage of a valuable recent comparative study by two doyens of police scholarship and distinguish 'Old' and 'New' Britain (Bayley and Stenning 2016). The 'Old' system itself went through various changes that will be reviewed briefly (it is covered in more detail in earlier editions). The urban police forces that were set up in the nineteenth century outside London were under the control of elected Watch Committees. County forces were governed by magistrates, with an admixture of elected members of the Standing Joint Committees established after 1888. Although there is some controversy among historians about this, Watch Committees did issue instructions about operational matters. This changed crucially in the late 1920s as an explicit legal doctrine of 'constabulary independence' developed, above all in the 1930 case of *Fisher* v. *Oldham*. This held that constables exercised independent law enforcement powers vested in them by the Crown, and were not subject to instructions about these from any elected or other authority. The emergence of the strong constabulary independence doctrine was arguably in response to the advent of the universal franchise, heralding the risk of radical Labour control of some local authorities (Lustgarten 1986).

Signs of new legitimation problems developed in the late 1950s (see Chapter 4), leading to the Royal Commission on Police 1960–2. Its recommendations about accountability were embodied in the Police Act 1964. This consolidated the tripartite governance structure outside London, with the three poles of the chief constable, a local police authority (two-thirds of the members were elected councillors, with one third magistrates), and the Home Secretary. The constabulary independence doctrine survived the statutory changes, as was confirmed by several court cases. But as a series of conflicts demonstrated, especially those related to the 1984–5 Miners' Strike, local police authorities had very circumscribed powers. There was a clear trend towards increasing central influence, arguably control, from the Home Office (Reiner 1991).

During the 1980s there were growing indications of a transformation of police governance, in line with New Public Management models importing private business principles into the public sector, under the mantra 'economy, efficiency, effectiveness'. The 1994 Police and Magistrates Courts Act was a highpoint of this process. It restricted the elected element of police authorities, and added central government appointed members who were intended to bring an element of business experience. The specified function of police authorities was subtly altered from the 1964 Act. The 1994 Act changed this from maintenance of an 'adequate and efficient' force to 'efficient and effective'. The precise scope of this responsibility remains as gnomic as in the 1964 version, but the symbolism is obvious. The prime motif of the newfangled police authorities was as local watchdogs of the managerialist, value-for-money, private enterprise ethos underpinning the whole reform package (Savage 2007: 173–83).

The intention was to make police authorities more 'businesslike', but the business was that of central government rather than the local electorate. The Home Secretary decided the codes of practice for police authorities, set national objectives and performance targets which local plans must take into account, determined the central government grant to police forces which covered most of their expenditure, and directed police authorities about the minimum amount of their budgetary contribution and other matters. Constabulary independence was preserved in principle but rendered somewhat illusory in the context of the other elements of the government's police reform package. The Sheehy Inquiry into Police Responsibilities and Rewards, which reported in the same week of June 1993 as the Police Reform White Paper, recommended that all police officers should be appointed on short-term contracts with performance-related pay. This was adopted for senior officers, but not all ranks. Without abandoning the constabulary independence doctrine in any formal way, the Home Secretary could colour constables' use of discretion by setting and assessing the criteria for performance that determine pay and job security.

The police were no longer accountable in the gentlemanly 'explanatory and co-operative' style that characterized the 1964 Police Act, but nor were they under the 'subordinate and obedient' style of accountability to democratically elected local authorities demanded by radical critics (Marshall 1978). Instead they were subject to a new market-style discipline, which can be called 'calculative and contractual' (Reiner and Spencer 1993). In the fashionable terminology of New Public Management, the government would be 'steering' but not 'rowing' (Osborne and Gaebler 1992). While not concerned directly with the details of policing, central government could in practice penetrate the parts of policing that they could not reach hitherto, the day-to-day operation of discretion. This would be accomplished by attaching offers that could not be refused to the attainment of the targets specified in policing plans. The centralized and New Public Management governance structure and style were backed by reforms strengthening the conduits linking the Home Office and local forces, notably HM Inspectorate of Constabulary and the Association of Chief Police Officers (Savage 2007).

These changes in governance to a 'calculative and contractual' model were enhanced during the New Labour years up to 2010. However, they were upended by a yet more dramatic transformation under the Conservative led governments since 2010. The flagship Police Reform and Social Responsibility Act 2011 introduced a radically new model based on elected Police and Crime Commissioners (PCCs) in charge of local policing. The other elements of the governance structure remain the Home Secretary and the Chief Constables, but inaugurate a new entity: the Police and Crime Panels. The latter are selected in a similar way to the old police authorities, but with an explicitly advisory rather than even a nominally powerful role (Lister 2013, 2014). Constabulary independence is formally retained, through a tenuous operational/policy distinction elaborated in the 2011 Policing Protocol Order. But with PCCs having formidable powers to set objectives and budgets, hire and fire chief officers, what is really reproduced is the neo-liberal 'calculative and contractual' mode of shaping 'independence', albeit at local rather than national level (Turner 2014). And the driving agenda remains crime control. The concerns about malpractice and discrimination which drove the old agenda of accountability receive no mention. The purpose of electoral input is to keep policing tough and on its toes. As then Prime Minister David Cameron put it: 'People are going to be voting in their own law-and-order champion: one person who sets the budgets, sets the priorities; hires and fires the chief constable; bangs heads together to get things done . . . If you want more tough policing, you can get it'.

The PCC system is an unprecedented innovation in public administration, in the UK or elsewhere. It is fundamentally different from the governance arrangements for other public services in the UK:

> What is new about PCCs is that their remit covers a specific and narrow field. By creating PCCs, Parliament gives birth to a multitude of dogs that didn't bark. Where is the directly elected commissioner for primary schools, for example? For health services? For children's services? To pose the question is to show that this new structure directs attention to one specific field of policy at the expense of others. (Jones *et al.* 2012: 232)

The novel structure reflects the view that crime is an exceptionally tough and threatening problem, unrelated to any other social, economic, or cultural processes, and needs its own tough and smart specialists to tackle it and to bring retributive justice to victims. Together with the growth of police powers outlined earlier, it is a quintessential embodiment of the politics of law and order that has become hegemonic over the last four decades.

GOVERNING HIGH POLICING

Discussions about the accountability of policing have, historically, focused largely on the low policing functions of patrol and reactive investigation and paid much less attention to the question of how high policing techniques—use of undercover police, civilian informers, and technical surveillance devices—are to be held accountable. These functions are often hidden, operating in a realm deliberately cloaked from the gaze of citizens, which in liberal democracies at least are involved in holding the police to account (Gill and Phythian 2018). As Gill argues (2014: 18), 'the context of secrecy may provide the cover for authoritarianism and corruption'. Whether or not police agents are visible—an issue touched upon earlier in this chapter—is often considered key to holding these agencies to account. High policing functions, such as surveillance, informant handling, and covert information gathering, are, by definition, performed in secret and will often fall beyond the reach of the domestic accountability structures explained earlier. The task of holding secret policing to account is extremely challenging (Gill 2014). Public police intelligence gathering in England and Wales began with the establishment of Special Branch in 1883. Gill and Phythian suggest that intelligence gathering units, such as Special Branch, occupy a unique status within UK police forces; while 'they are part of their parent police force in terms of budget and recruitment, their day-to-day activities are determined mainly by current MI5 priorities' (Gill and Phythian 2018: 48–9). Much controversy exists in relation to the operation of intelligence units because they often monitor the actions of individuals that are not engaging in criminality, but in legal activities such as peaceful protest. A review of Special Branches by Her Majesty's Inspectorate of Constabulary (HMIC) in 2002 resulted in the creation of a specific agency to oversee national coordination of regional Special Branches.

The aim of Special Branch and other forms of high policing is to use subversion tactics of investigation in order to protect the state from acts of terror or politically fuelled violence. With this aim in mind, Gill and Phythian ask a key question—how democratic can intelligence gathering be? (Gill and Phythian 2018: 154–82). The recent 'spycop' scandal that uncovered a thirty-seven-year campaign by undercover police infiltrating the Socialist Workers party from 1970 until 2007 (Evans 2018b), highlights the politicized nature of much of the high policing function. The Special Demonstration Squad (SDS) was an undercover unit operating from 1968 until 2008, with the aim of gathering intelligence about political groups and reporting back to Special Branch. A public inquiry established in 2014 and headed by Sir John Mitting, has uncovered a long history of police 'spies' infiltrating extreme left- and right-wing groups. However the inquiry has run into criticism for being too slow—the final report will not be published until 2023 at the earliest (Evans 2018a). So far, however, it has shed light on a range of unethical behaviours, including the deception of women into intimate relations as a tactic, resulting in the birth of a number of children.

The SDS and subsequent Inquiry is evidence of Gill and Phythian's argument that secrecy may provide the cover for abuses of power. This is a major challenge in terms of accountability. The 'spycop' scandal creates much distrust given that the SDS was interested in gathering intelligence on organizations that threatened the status quo, raising the question of whether high policing can ever be made democratically accountable. Much has changed, of course, since the abandoning of the SDS, but if the public Inquiry into its practices is one form of accountability, then critics have argued that it is not adequate nor proportionate to the harm that has been caused to victims of state subversion tactics. Much of the contemporary focus of high policing centres on the issue of terrorism. This was highlighted by the creation of the Counter Terrorism Command within the Metropolitan Police in 2006, which resulted from a merging of the Anti-Terrorist Branch and Special Branch. There is also evidence, however, that covert policing techniques are widely and increasingly used in everyday operational policing (Loftus and Goold 2012, Loftus 2019)

The issue of accountability in high policing is further complicated by the complexity of security and intelligence networks consisting of a multitude of state and non-state actors (Benner et al. 2005). The issues of transnational accountability have already been discussed in Chapter 9 and are returned to below. A challenge for oversight is the development of networks that cross the boundaries of organizational and jurisdictional within nations, involve foreign agencies and private sector organizations and NGOs (Gill and

Phythian 2018: 176–82). As discussed later, the pluralization of policing has resulted in regulatory authorities such as the Security Industry Authority (SIA), and their remit is meant to extend to some high policing functions such as surveillance. However, private investigators engaging in spying on individuals do not fall under this authority and as such remain unaccountable. Bayley and Shearing (2001) argue that if the 'public interest' is to be defended, then the responsibility of regulating high policing performed by non-state actors must lie with the state, regardless of how effective the state is at realizing this aim. Gill and Phythian (2018) point to the difficulty of achieving accountability in networks where power dynamics are not as easily definable as in traditional bureaucracies. Sheptycki (2004b), however, argues in favour of the development of network intelligence 'cells' which would be organized in a way that would ignore unhelpful hierarchy structures, and ensure that intelligence is shared so that it can be audited at every step with reference to an agreed standard such as human rights. This solution seems unlikely to ever gain traction because of the enormous effort that would be needed in terms of implementation. Furthermore, O'Reilly and Ellison (2006: 652) argue that the pluralization of high policing in states such as the USA has served to 'stymie' accountability 'through absorbing the "corporate veil", "commercial confidentiality", and the inapplicability of Freedom of Information legislation into their security activities'. The complex policing 'web' may, therefore, well be the result of purposeful action by the state to shift the responsibility of high policing onto private companies that are able to hide behind the complexities of corporate structures.

GOVERNING PLURAL POLICING

Plural policing, the mixed economy of public and private provision, and the outsourcing of services and operations that were hitherto performed by public police, raises knotty accountability issues (see Chapter 7). There are numerous private policing functions performed by a variety of actors such as security guards and bouncers. The most evident form of pluralized policing, which is now widely accepted, is the role of the uniformed private security guard (Jones and Newburn 1998; Wakefield 2003). Private security guards do not possess the powers of a police constable, but in many ways their uniforms and civic function embodies that of the bobby on the beat. As such, Stenning (2000) argues that far from being limited in the powers that they possess, private security officers are authorized to exercise a great deal of coercive power. It is not uncommon for security guards to subject members of the public to bag searches when an alarm has been triggered, but it may surprise some to find that there is no legal grounding by which a security guard can do so without the consent of the individual (Button 2007). As already discussed, the private security industry relies heavily on legislation that affords ordinary citizens powers in circumstances where crimes may have been committed.

As discussed earlier, the power to use reasonable force is afforded to all citizens, and it is this that provides the legal grounding for a number of functions that private security officers perform (Wakefield 2003). Legal powers that are solely afforded to private security companies include the power to remove someone from private property, and the power to search someone without consent after an arrest has been made (Button 2007). Holding the 'policing web' to account is a complex matter

(Sheptycki 2002b; Brodeur 2010; Stenning 2009; Lister and Jones 2016). Nevertheless, attempts to regulate private policing have been made. The Security Industry Authority (SIA) was created as a result of the Private Security Industry Act (2001), with the aim of regulating private security by barring those with criminal convictions from working in the industry (Lister and Jones 2016). The SIA assesses private security companies independently, and regulates the provision of security guards, bouncers, close protection operatives, transit of cash and valuables, and public space surveillance using CCTV. White (2010) suggests that the SIA is not comprehensive enough and does not hold to account all private security workers such as security systems installers and in-house guards. However, he also notes that the general consensus is that the SIA had succeeded in its aims of reducing criminality and raising standards within the profession (White 2013).

Lister and Jones (2016) build on the work of Jones *et al.* (1996) in suggesting that there are a number of criteria by which plural policing could be held democratically to account. These include 'equity, delivery of service, responsiveness, distribution of power, information, redress and participation' (Lister and Jones 2016: 199). In certain aspects such as the distribution of power, plural policing has the advantage over that of public policing because power is distributed across a number of agencies rather than being under the power of a single state agent. Nevertheless, 'for-profit' policing will always face the criticism of being more partisan than public policing, with the concern being that private policing agents will be more inclined to follow the directives of their paymasters (Zedner 2009). Loader (2000) suggested that one way of solving the accountability of plural policing dilemma is to create Policing Commissions that would regulate the entire policing sector with a mixture of elected and appointed representatives. This would, in theory, ensure that marginal groups are represented, and could be a robust, fair, and democratic way of holding plural policing to account (Lister and Jones 2016). Crawford *et al.* (2005) support Loader's suggestion and argue that extending the remit of Police and Crime Commissioners (PCCs) to private sector organizations could be one way of implementing such an accountability mechanism. An issue with this approach is how successful this model of governance proves to be in its current form, and that as Loader (2013) points out, by definition the PCC is a 'Police' commissioner, and not a 'Policing' commissioner (see Lister and Jones 2016).

GOVERNING GLOBAL POLICING

Globalization has reshaped the politics of policing at all levels (see Chapter 9). Local police officers often call on assistance from national, regional, and global agencies and vice versa. Policework, on the ground, regularly involves intelligence sharing and cross-border cooperation among officers from different countries, joint investigative teams, and the pursuit of fugitives overseas, as well as involvement in extradition, rendition, and removal. The result is that police powers of surveillance and coercion now travel, increasingly unhindered, across national boundaries. Malcolm Anderson, one of the first scholars to comment on this development, argued that effective transnational police cooperation requires 'a commitment to a robust supranational system of accountability' to ensure its long-term popular legitimacy (Anderson *et al.* 1995: 287–9). The question of how, and to whom, transnational policing practices can be held accountable continues to be a puzzle.

Police agencies operating above the nation state do not stand up well on the criteria of transparency, accountability, and democratic control. Interpol has no system of external accountability and is, in effect, accountable only to itself (Sheptycki 2004a). It has a Commission to control the data held in its files but falls far short of generally accepted standards for international governmental organizations (IGOs) (Cheah 2010b). The *Global Accountability Report* places Interpol at the bottom of the accountability league for IGOs because it lacks transparency and is closed to scrutiny by civil society (Lloyd *et al.* 2007). The best developed regional policing entities—Europol and Frontex—fare little better. The growth in legal powers afforded to the various forms of transnational policing across Europe has not been accompanied by the development of comprehensive accountability mechanisms, which are in any case difficult to implement at the international level (den Boer 2010: 43–4; Hufnagel 2013: 38). Pandit (2012: 397) argues that EU police institutions demonstrate 'poor democratic legitimacy, weak parliamentary political accountability and insufficient legal safeguards'.

It can be argued that despite the changes wrought by globalization, police action—however authorized—must be accountable to *domestic* legal and political institutions. The action of overseas officers in Britain, for example, is regulated by the Crime (International Cooperation) Act 2003, s 83 of which allows foreign police to undertake surveillance for no more than five hours, and only if the surveillance started overseas and an authorization under the Regulation of Investigatory Powers Act is requested immediately. International Liaison Officers (ILOs) are technically accountable for any enforcement actions to the police authorities in the country to which they are posted. In most instances, however, ILOs work seamlessly behind the scenes and it is, therefore, unnecessary for an ILO to take independent enforcement action (Bowling 2010). Intelligence gathered at home or received from a foreign source can be passed directly to where it is needed for local police, customs, or immigration officers to act upon. There may or may not be a paper trail to allow transparency in intelligence sharing. Extensive empirical research shows that transnational police officers prefer informal procedures and personal contacts to what they perceive as complicated, time-consuming, and ineffective formal cooperation agreements (den Boer 2010). They see accountability and control measures as an obstruction to efficient information exchange and try to avoid official channels (Bigo 2000; Alain 2000; Dolan 2015). A deeply impregnated work culture and wide discretion makes it difficult to formalize practices and it is almost impossible to require police officers to disclose their informal networks of contacts.

Bigo's (2006) examination of European fusion centres—in which police, customs, and immigration officers from various countries are co-located in border regions—suggests that these have become 'security archipelagos' that are independent of the requirements of national sovereignty. This is consistent with Sheptycki's (2009: 283) observation that in transnational systems the: 'State *qua* state is no longer the structural keystone'. Instead, the world system is polycentric with non-state, supra-state, and sub-state actors playing roles in the governance of security that are equal to, or greater than those played by state actors (Sheptycki 2008b). When officers from different countries work together, they break down the myth of national sovereignty, challenging the Weberian view of the state monopoly of legitimate force within a bounded territory. Globalization challenges state sovereignty 'from below' by non-state transnational actors and 'from above' by actors whose first allegiance lies with a foreign state. Similarly,

Anne-Marie Slaughter's (2004) view of the late modern state as disaggregated requires an analysis of transnational networks of actors that form horizontal and vertical connections between multiple institutional sites of power, who interact with other actors in the global system. In her view, 'we need global rules without centralized power but with government actors who can be held to account through a variety of political mechanisms' (Slaughter 2004: 10). Applying this idea to policing is consistent with den Boer *et al.*'s (den Boer *et al.* 2008: 109) argument for a comprehensive framework that attends to democratic, legal, and social legitimacy for transnational policing. Democratic legitimacy is indicated by parliamentary scrutiny and control of matters such as appointments, policy plans, and budgets. Legal legitimacy derives from the formal adoption of binding legal instruments, clear organizational jurisdiction and mandate, and the existence of robust procedural safeguards and complaint mechanisms. Social legitimacy depends on transparency through public reporting, independent monitoring, and the consultation of citizens (ibid.).

Reflecting on the globalization of police power, Bowling and Sheptycki (2012) argue for an approach to police accountability that holds coercive and intrusive police powers to account 'from above' and 'from below'. Ensuring the accountability of global and regional policing agencies and cross-border joint operations requires a *supranational* regulatory system, though whether this can be provided by existing international governmental agencies is an open question (Bowling and Sheptycki 2016a). Equally important are bottom-up accountability mechanisms rooted in an active and globally-connected civil society (Bowling and Sheptycki 2016b; Bowling 2010: 311–15). The work of such organizations as Human Rights Watch, Amnesty International, the Small Arms Survey, Fair Trials Abroad, The Vera Institute, the Open Society Institute, and Forensic Architecture have made the local impact of transnational policing vividly transparent. Good global policing would have accountability running through its 'entire blood stream' (Patten 1999). It would have a strong 'constabulary ethic' (Sheptycki 2007a) imbued with the principles of responsiveness to the global commonwealth, adherence to international human rights norms, and the values of 'human security' and internal democracy to ensure that police organizations reflect the communities that they serve.

CONCLUSION: DEMOCRACY IN ONE INSTITUTION?

The case for the 2011–12 revolution in domestic police governance in England and Wales rested primarily on the claim, articulated explicitly by the then Home Secretary Theresa May, that they brought democracy to policing. This identifies democracy entirely with voting. Elected PCCs give a vestige of democratic political rights. But this must be set in a broader context whereby the massive widening of inequality due to neo-liberalism makes all electoral processes an increasingly empty shell. 'Democracy' everywhere has become a facade for plutocracy. Elected governments have largely lost the capacity to shape the policies that most affect people's everyday lives, which are dominated by apparently impersonal economic forces over which 'TINA' (there is no alternative) rules.

The pluralization of policing brought about by transnational police organizations, secret intelligence agencies, and private corporations underlines the point. To stave off the crisis of legitimation posed by realization that people's aspirations built up over the postwar decades of increasing welfare can no longer be met, governments have resorted to 'buying time' through financialization, a series of devices for borrowing from the future (Streeck 2017b). This larger crisis of 'post-democracy' (Crouch 2004) is reflected in the police context. Successive reform initiatives to achieve substantively as well as procedurally just outcomes (from Scarman to Macpherson and beyond) have changed at most some superficial aspects of verbal style, leaving the underlying inequalities in treatment intact. In the absence of wider social justice, indeed with spiralling injustice, this can only grow ever worse. The quest for socialism in one country was abortive, and so too is the pursuit of democracy in one institution. These issues will be considered further in the Conclusion, looking at the future of policing.

12

CONCLUSION: HISTORIES OF THE FUTURE

WHITHER POLICING?

The task of the concluding chapter is to pull together the implications of the earlier chapters of this book for an assessment of where policing is heading, and what is to be done to achieve greater effectiveness, fairness, and justice. Crystal ball gazing is always hazardous, but in previous editions it was possible to extrapolate a little from analysis of the past and present. In the first quarter of the twenty-first century, however, the world has been subject to global shock waves unprecedented in the lifetimes of most readers. The most dramatic are the effects of the financial and economic crisis still reverberating since 2007, and the political upsets of 2016, notably the Brexit vote in the UK and the election of Trump in the USA, events that were unanticipated by most social analysts and commentators.

Because policing is at the cutting edge of social conflicts, it is like the 'canary in a coalmine', an indicator and early warning of adverse conditions or trouble ahead. So, it has been apparent throughout successive editions of this volume since 1985 that major changes were under way in the politics of policing. The fundamental thesis of this book is that not all that is policing lies in the police. So, to understand police and policing it is necessary to examine the broader political and moral economy of any society. Policing is shaped by deep currents, flowing from the past and bearing it to an unfathomable future. The previous chapters have analysed the historical development and research evidence about the operations and problems of policing in a variety of social contexts. In the next section we assess critically some major attempts to characterize contemporary policing transformation, before offering our own concluding reflections.

THEORIZING POLICING: THE TRANSFORMATION THESIS

Twenty years ago, Bayley and Shearing (1996: 585) made an exceptionally bold claim: 'Future generations will look back on our era as a time when one system of policing ended and another took its place'. This pioneering critique, known as the 'transformation thesis' (Jones and Newburn 2002), broadened into the claim that a new theoretical paradigm is needed to make sense of these developments, replacing the concepts of police and policing altogether by a framework based on 'the governance of security'

(Johnston and Shearing 2003). Clifford Shearing and a number of associates, argued explicitly for a complete paradigm shift, from 'policing' to 'security governance'. Another radical critique advocated a 'new police science', spearheaded by Markus Dubber's acclaimed historical analysis of the 'police power' (Dubber 2005; Dubber and Valverde 2006; Loader and Zedner 2007). Developed without reference to Shearing *et al.*, this has a common inspiration in Foucault's ideas about governmentality. Richard Ericson and Kevin Haggerty's influential account of policing the 'risk society' is a third important theoretical strand, largely incorporated into the wider paradigm shift theses (Ericson and Haggerty 1997; Johnston 2000a, 2000b). Other 'new policing' theses (McLaughlin 2007) include a variety of discussions about the impact of post or late modernity on policing (Reiner 1992b; Sheptycki 1995, 1998a; McLaughlin and Murji 1999; Waters 2007), and O'Malley's claim that policing is now 'post-Keynesian' (O'Malley and Palmer 1996; O'Malley 1997).

The transformation thesis rested on two elements: 'policing is no longer monopolized by the public police . . . created by government', and 'the public police are going through . . . an identity crisis' (Bayley and Shearing 1996: 585). The 'new police science' and the security governance perspective both reject 'mainstream criminological discourse', said to be 'still preoccupied with issues relating to the administration of security and justice by states' (Johnston and Shearing 2003: 10). Similarly, the 'new police science' castigates 'the trap of twentieth century criminology, which tries to think of policing in isolation from other practices of power' (Neocleous 2006: 19). In an otherwise sophisticated analysis, Neocleous repeats a familiar caricature of the field as a 'backwater of a very narrowly conceived "police studies" . . ., reduced to the study of crime and law enforcement . . . [eschewing] any attempt to make sense of the concept itself or to explore the possible diversity of police powers in terms of either their historical origins or political diversity' (ibid.: 17). The main thrust was to relocate the idea of police within a framework of political economy and governance, harking back to the eighteenth-century 'police science' that preceded the coming of the modern police. We are entirely in sympathy with the call for a political economy of policing. As we have demonstrated in this book, valuable empirical research findings and a theoretical framework can be found within police research. In their wholesale rejection of the sociology of policing, the theoretical critiques first articulated in the 1990s threw the baby out with the bathwater. The trends targeted by the 'new theorists' are occurring, but their diagnoses and prescriptions are wide of the mark. Moreover, it is now clear, twenty years on, that reports of the death of an old policing system, and the arrival of an entirely new one, were exaggerated, inaccurate, and incomplete.

THEORIES OF POLICING: THE ANALYTIC DIMENSIONS

A theory of policing has to tackle a number of related questions, as we suggested in Chapter 1. Theorizations of policing should include analysis of the following eight dimensions:

(1) What is policing?

(2) Who is involved in policing?

(3) What do they actually do?

(4) What are the means and powers of policing?

(5) What social functions do they achieve?

(6) How does policing impact on different groups?

(7) By whom are the police themselves policed, by what means, and to what ends?

(8) How can the developing purposes and practices of policing be understood?

Answers to these questions are of course diverse, complex, and evolving. Nonetheless they can be represented as discussed in the following sections.

WHAT IS POLICING?

As we explain in Chapter 9, the main plank of the transformation thesis is the supposed end of the state monopoly of policing, that is, its principal concern is *who* does policing. The seminal texts are surprisingly coy about the prior theoretical issue of defining policing, although they are clear—but wrong—about what policing *was* prior to the so-called transformation. Defining the specificity of policing is problematic, as seen earlier. Most common attempts to define policing are functional—what policing achieves, or rather, is supposed to achieve. This is largely true of the new theories which remain firmly focused on crime control, order maintenance, and public safety. The reconceptualization of policing as security governance did not change this much. When Johnston and Shearing (2003: 9) wrote about the governance of security they referred to 'programmes for promoting peace in the face of threats (either realized or anticipated) that arise from collective life rather than from non-human sources . . . that have their origin in human intentions and actions'. Such functional definitions of policing are problematic because they don't fit with what police (public or private) actually do or can do. Police are called upon to deal with many tasks other than crime or conflict, and they can make little contribution to crime control or social peace—however effective they are (see Chapter 5).

It is the 'elephant' of social control rather than the 'breadbox' of policing agencies which accomplishes the functions attributed to policing (in so far as they are met at all). This is because the sources of order lie outside the ambit of the police, in the culture and the political and moral economy of a society. To the extent that these provide most people with meaningful and rewarding lives, conflict, crime, and disorder will be relatively infrequent. Subtle, informal social controls embedded in other institutions do the heavy work of policing. The 'breadbox' of overt policing agencies is important in its impact on many people's lives, but its contribution to overall social order and peace is largely symbolic rather than instrumental (Manning 1997, 2003).

Functionalist definitions also sanitize a key aspect of policing—that it deals with conflict and hence has a perpetual Janus face, helping some by controlling others. Thus, one party's functional policing may be another's repression. The order that the police are charged to protect always has this double aspect. *General* order, the requirements of any coordinated and complex civilization, is conceptually distinct from but inextricably intertwined with *particular* order—specific patterns of inequality and dominance. Policing deals simultaneously with 'parking tickets and class repression' (Marenin

1982). This is glossed over by talking, as the above definitions do, of 'society', as opposed to dominant social powers authorizing policing. A more satisfactory analysis suggests that tactics or capacities rather than functions constitute the distinctive character of policing (Klockars 1985), as Egon Bittner argued some forty years ago, and as was elaborated in Chapter 1. The distinctiveness of the police lies not in their performance of a specific social function, but in being the specialist repositories for the state's symbolic monopolization of legitimate force in its territory.

WHAT AGENCIES AND AGENTS ARE INVOLVED IN POLICING?

As discussed in Chapters 7 and 9, many other agents and agencies apart from the police can and do perform policing tasks. Despite the pluralization of policing, it is still the state agency with the omnibus mandate of order maintenance that is popularly understood by the label—deliberately capitalized—The Police. The question is whether the new theories are correct in asserting that the shift away from state policing towards private forms amounts to a fundamental and qualitative transformation. Although empirically the personnel employed by private security have indeed grown to be more numerous than public constabularies in some countries, they were already close during the supposed heyday of state policing just after the Second World War. Moreover, part of the increase in private security employment statistics occurred as corporations substituted contract for in-house employees with partial security functions. Jones and Newburn showed that the growth of private security in Britain represented an formalization of social control, as the number of employees with *secondary* but substantial security functions—such as bus and rail conductors and inspectors, park-keepers, roundsmen, etc.—declined (Jones and Newburn 2002: table 41.1). Although the mushrooming of private security performing an increasing array of functions, and the internal diversification of state policing, were significant developments, in our view, they do not amount to a qualitatively new model of policing requiring an entirely new paradigm.

The state has never had a monopoly of security arrangements (Zedner 2006), even though in stable liberal democracies it has claimed control over *legitimate* force. There is no evidence, however, that this domination of *legitimacy* is under challenge as a result of pluralization, although police legitimacy has undoubtedly become more tenuous since the late 1960s in many jurisdictions (Chapter 4). The new theorists claim that the status and image of private security have been transformed, in addition to the latter's quantitative proliferation (Bayley and Shearing 1996, in Newburn 2005: 716–17). While they are certainly more in demand, however, it is far from clear that they are viewed by the mass of the public as, in any sense, equivalent to The Police. Since the Second World War, when the transformation theorists claimed that the public police monopoly came under increasing challenge, police heroes have come to the fore in popular culture (Allen *et al.* 1998). On the other hand, private detectives scarcely appear except as residual and unheroic characters, unlike their heyday in the early twentieth century when Sherlock Holmes, Poirot, Philip Marlowe, *et al.* captured the police cultural imaginary (Chapter 10). Although for primarily economic reasons it has been government policy in many jurisdictions to develop civilianization and auxiliaries, these do not threaten the hold over the mainstream 'sworn' constables in the public imagination. While there has undoubtedly been a pluralization of policing in recent decades, in neither substance nor symbolism does it amount to qualitative transformation.

The emphasis on privatization as the key to understanding the transformation in policing ignores a number of important aspects of the diversity in the past and present provision of policing. First, there are a plethora of public policing agencies—including the police forces of the ministries of defence and environment, each of the armed forces, Airports, Harbours, and Docks Police, British Transport Police, Civil Nuclear Constabulary—that have been largely ignored by police researchers, as well as the numerous other law enforcement agencies that work alongside them, such as borders and internal immigration police, customs, and financial regulatory agencies (see Chapter 5). The diversity of these agencies is documented in the *Police and Constabulary Almanac* (published annually since 1909). Second, policing is organized at national and continental levels with numerous institutions such as the National Crime Agency and Europol that have been created to work alongside local city and county constabularies (see Chapter 9). Third, policing is a transnational enterprise; communication, coordination, and cooperation with officers from overseas was a feature of the birth of policing and continues to this day (Chapter 9). Policing practices and models (Chapter 3) have been shared internationally since the nineteenth century, facilitated by conferences, exchanges, and overseas postings. The most obvious example of the transnational policing network was during the colonial period when British Colonies around the world were connected with the metropolis like spokes on a wheel. Today, many thousands of police officers 'network' in global and regional police organizations (such as Interpol and Europol) and as liaison officers. As Sheptycki (1995) observed more than twenty years ago, policing comprises agencies of different sizes and shapes, working and overlapping at different geographical levels like a 'patchwork quilt'. As Rosa Luxemburg said a century ago, the police force is the only one true international.

Fourth, alongside the diversity in organizational structure, there are distinct police specialisms that require disaggregation, and in particular units engaged in paramilitary 'low policing' of public order and the 'high policing' intelligence-gathering. The latter role is particularly important in relation to understanding the British police. The conventional view is that 'spy policing' was not part of the British tradition. However, secret intelligence gathering, surveillance, undercover, recruiting and handling informers has been part of British policing since the nineteenth century (as depicted vividly in Mike Leigh's 2018 film *Peterloo*), and is today an integral and even 'normal' aspect of operational practice (Loftus 2019). The sociology of policing has yet to fully explore low visibility decisions in police intelligence and information processes. Understanding contemporary policing requires a fuller account of information communication technologies in creating databases, networks, information sharing, and connecting across organizational and geographical boundaries. None of these elements in this account of the plurality and diversity are new to policing: the currents of militarization, privatization, technologization, securitization and intelligencization have ebbed and flowed across the global policing field for two centuries. We are not arguing that nothing changes, but simply that it is incorrect to see any of these changes as a qualitative break. This is because qualitative breaks do not occur because of policing.

Policing has always contained a variety of potential organizational forms and tactics which come to the fore or ebb away with much wider social currents.

There remain a number of institutions with a complex division of labour but which, by means of their capacity for surveillance and to organize coercive force, maintain the designation The Police. The first quarter of the twenty-first century has proven to be one of rapid and deep social transformation. In a sea of troubles, it is understandable that a more complex view of the policing 'web', 'assemblage', or 'family' might be sought as a way of navigating a course through uncertainty. However, in order not to get lost in the theoretical margins of security governance it remains useful to focus on the agents and agencies who participate directly in the police division of labour. The sociological study of The Police remains a vital resource to understand the politics of a society more generally.

WHAT DO POLICE ACTUALLY DO?

One of the earliest findings of sociological research on policing, replicated time and time again over more than fifty years, is that—contrary to popular images—most policework does not involve crime or law enforcement (see Chapter 5). Police routinely under-enforce the law, using their discretion to deal with incidents in a variety of 'peacekeeping' ways, even if an offence may have been committed. Discretion may be operated in discriminatory or other controversial ways, but it is inevitable and necessary, because of the limited capacity of the criminal justice system. Calls to the police for help only involve clear references to crime in a minority of cases, although the exact proportion varies between places, over time, and according to different definitions and research methodologies. Nonetheless, most policing does not involve use of law enforcement powers. The police may be the normal gateway to the criminal justice process, but it is a gate that they open relatively seldom.

Altogether the police are marginal to the control of crime and the maintenance of order, and always have been. Only a tiny fraction of crimes come to their attention or are recorded by them, and the overwhelming majority of these are not cleared up (apart from serious violent offences such as homicide). This does not mean that the police do not play a useful role in managing the crimes they deal with, nor that they could not boost their performance by exploring new tactics—as they have done in recent years. But seeing the police as major players in crime control gives them an 'impossible mandate', and their primary contribution remains symbolic not instrumental. The basic reason for this is the huge array of potential offences and offenders relative to any conceivable resources for policing (Chapter 5). The toughest zero-tolerance or the smartest intelligence-led approaches cannot do more than chip away at the edges of this mass of potential targets. Moreover, attempts at crime control through aggressive law enforcement or covert policing sometimes cause lasting social harms through abuse of power, undermining trust and confidence in government as well as unjustified loss of liberty and physical injury.

The marginality of crime to policing and policing to crime was a staple conclusion of the sociology of the police and confirmed by earlier studies (Ericson 1982; Shearing 1984; Bayley 1985, 1994). So it is somewhat disconcerting to find statements like: 'The risk-communication view of policing we are advancing here obviously decenters the criminal law and criminal justice aspects of police work' (Ericson and Haggerty 2002, in Newburn 2005: 553)—as if it had formerly been central. Or 'Police are no longer the primary crime-deterrent presence in society' (Bayley and Shearing 1996, in Newburn 2005: 717)—as if they ever had been, outside media mythology and police hucksterism. The transformation thesis juxtaposed contemporary policing with a depiction of the past in terms of its mythical representation rather than reality. The focus on 'crime control' is also problematic because it obscures the importance of the so-called 'fire-brigade policing' role in emergency order maintenance (Reiner 2012c). People call The Police because they are the agency of last resort in an extraordinarily wide range of instances including road accidents and disasters, disputes and disturbances, and to human beings facing mental disorder, suicide risk, or sudden death (Chapter 5). Taking a broader geographical and historical view of policing shows that at many times and places, the police remit was conceived as being wider still, concerned with the general welfare of the people with a substantive mandate including dealing with vagrancy, begging, sanitation, street lighting, licensing, and public health (Chapter 3).

WHAT ARE THE MEANS AND POWERS OF POLICING?

Bayley and Shearing claimed that the change to a pluralized marketplace of contemporary policing was linked to a welcome shift in style, effectiveness, programmes, and practices. 'It seems reasonable to conclude . . . that pluralizing has made communities safer'. Their argument was partly quantitative: pluralization has created a huge expansion of private security personnel, public police auxiliaries, and a 'responsibilized' citizenry (Bayley and Shearing 1996: 592) which, due to numbers alone, would enhance public safety in itself. This claim was made despite the large volume of previous research questioning the impact on crime of increasing public police numbers, through their deterrent or other effects (see Chapter 5). But the main argument was that pluralization qualitatively improved policing because of differences in technique and style between private and public police. Whereas state policing embodied a 'punishment mentality and coercive technologies', corporate security rested on 'the risk paradigm' (Johnston and Shearing 2003). Furthermore:

> . . . private police emphasise the logic of security, while public police emphasise the logic of justice. The major purpose of private security, therefore, is to reduce the risk of crime by taking preventive actions; the major purpose of the public police is to deter crime by catching and punishing criminals. (Bayley and Shearing 1996: 592)

The supposedly more effective, efficient, and benign private corporate style is also seen as a model that is positively transforming public police, through reforms of internal governance under the influence of the 'New Public Management' (NPM) and innovative operating strategies such as community, risk, and problem-oriented policing (O'Malley 1997; Johnston 2000a: chaps 4, 5, 10; McLaughlin 2007: chap. 4). The paradox, they claimed, was that Anglo-American public policing was originally established after 1829 on a Peelian model with an explicit preventive, forward-looking philosophy. Over time this is said to have degenerated into a reactive, coercive, punitive justice mentality (Johnston and Shearing 2003: 15) that would benefit from restoring the private model that Peelian policing supposedly displaced.

This analysis mischaracterized the techniques, programmes, and resources of both old and new policing. As argued earlier, the portrait of policing in the past as primarily concerned with crime is flatly contradicted by the evidence. Although the defining feature of state policing is the symbolic monopolization of legitimate force, the tendency of police was to minimize actual use of force (Brodeur 2010: chap. 4) for principled and pragmatic reasons, although the *abuse* of force—particularly against those marginal and powerless groups that have aptly been called 'police property' (Lee 1981)—has been a perennial problem (Bonner *et al.* 2018). Nonetheless the predominant Anglo-American police style has included peacekeeping and the provision of a 'secret' social service (Marquis 1992; Punch 1979b).

The prevailing analysis emphasized that the police were *not* themselves responsible for the impossible mandate of containing crime and disorder (Chapter 5). Security and order maintenance depended on a complex network of informal social, economic, and cultural controls of which the police were only one part, primarily important symbolically rather than instrumentally (Banton 1964; Loader 1997; Loader and Mulcahy 2003). This is uncannily prescient of the image of 'nodal governance'—'that . . . the police constitute one node amongst many nodes engaged in governance of security' (Shearing 2007: 252), postulated as a rebuttal of the old idea that 'policing belongs to the police' (ibid.). The new theorists promote this as the image of the *future*, although their notion of nodal governance is seen as a network of explicit security providers, not general processes conducive to social peace such as full employment, stable families, and communities with cultural capital. But the idea of the police as one source of security among many was a well-trodden theme of the sociology of policing from its beginnings; only the terminology of nodes is new.

Private police and indeed police auxiliaries (such as Police Community Support Officers in the UK) generally lack the special police powers and weaponry available to public police (Stenning 2000; Button 2007), although this is gradually changing (Crawford 2006: 114–17; Diphoorn, 2016). But this does not mean that their capacity to control the areas they are responsible for is based on a superior mentality of risk analysis and intelligent problem solving. Certainly, the calibre of security officers in terms of selection and training is far below that of the public police (Michael 2002; Button 2007, 2008: chap. 4). Against this, however, corporate security has enormous advantages stemming from the powers of private property ownership, as well as a much narrower remit to police privilege (Joh 2004).

Shearing and Stenning (1983, 1987) were the first to illuminate social control in 'mass private property', areas which are legally private but function as public spaces accessible to many people, such as shopping malls, 'gated' residential estates, entertainment complexes, theme parks and, industrial estates. They show that the extent of crime and disorder in such places is generally low (perhaps because it is not reported to the police) and that internal peace results largely from exclusionary tactics that depend ultimately on coercion. The key point is that the owners of mass private property, and the security officers who are their agents, enjoy the power to exclude without the legal hurdle of reasonable suspicion (Chapter 9). As a condition of entry, they can require searches and checks that are more intrusive and discriminatory than those carried out by public police on the streets, without even the minimal accountability to law that circumscribes the latter. Potential sources of trouble and conflict can be swept out—possibly onto the public streets (a burgle-my-neighbour tactic; enhanced private security may reduce public safety). The nodal theorists themselves speak of such areas as 'security bubbles'. But depending on the powers of property and purse, the bubbles vary in scope and desirability. They are positional goods, stretching from champagne bubbles to toxic-waste bubbles.

Shearing and Stenning's celebrated analysis of Disney World as the future of security shows the importance of exclusion in safeguarding tranquility in that hedonistic idyll (Chapter 9). Exclusion derives from the cost of entry, physical seclusion, myriad devices inscribed into architecture and routines, and when these fail, guards in Mickey Mouse costumes are there to expel deviants. The example of 'Club Med' holiday resorts shows that the security of such enclaves is a 'club good' depending on barring all but a privileged few (Johnston and Shearing 2003: 9). The cliché of the 'iron fist in the velvet glove' pertains to private security just as much as to public policing and the mentalities and practices are similar. This is even more obvious in the use of private security in 'high policing' (Brodeur 2010; O'Reilly 2015; Wadham and Goldsmith 2018). The 'success' of corporate security derives from its power to coerce compliance as a condition of being in the bubble, and its narrow remit—to maximize profit—rather than working for the public good (Walby and Lippert 2014). The excluded are of no concern to them, unlike the way they are, at least in principle, for public police.

The ongoing development of the means and powers of policing should also be seen in the context of currents, other than privatization, that are shaping the modern world. The same logic of exclusion that shapes the controls of access into security bubbles is also highly influential in the policing of global flows of people (see Chapter 9). Information and communication technologies—cameras, biometrics, databases, and computer networks—play a key role in social sorting and the physical mechanisms of surveillance and access control. As local police organizations become more closely aligned and integrated with regional and global policing networks, social exclusion of 'suitable foes' is writ-large on a transnational scale, with major implications for social justice (Bowling, Phillips, and Sheptycki 2012). The securitizing logic also makes for important connections, especially in the area of 'high policing' across the public and private sectors, so that the two are not readily distinguishable. When public police use technical surveillance devices, run undercover operations, recruit and handle informers, the boundaries between public and private action become almost irretrievably blurred. Understanding the means and powers of globally networked policing requires an analysis of public and private law as a tool in the hands of knowing social actors (Bowling and Sheptycki 2015c).

WHAT SOCIAL FUNCTIONS DO POLICE ACHIEVE?

To Bayley and Shearing the bottom line is plain: 'Both quantitatively and qualitatively . . . the pluralising of policing should increase public safety' (1996, in Newburn 2005: 721). This is 'police fetishism', based on a myth constructed over two centuries by a complex of cultural processes, including endless media reproduction of storylines depicting heroic police as 'the thin blue line' battling to protect order and justice (Chapter 10). But as indicated earlier, public peace and security are a function of deeper processes in political economy and culture. This does not mean, however, that strategic changes in police tactics cannot have a crime-reducing effect, and there are many such claims. Most notably, the police have, of course, popularly been credited with the huge drop in crime in New York City in the 1990s, not least because they have not been shy to claim the credit. There has, however, been much debate about the precise contribution made by policing to the crime drop of the 1990s (see Chapter 5). Many analysts point out that the timing of the drop did not tally with the policing changes, that substantial (although smaller) crime reductions were achieved in many parts of the USA and the rest of the world without similar policing tactics, and that other economic, social, and criminal justice changes played a larger part (Reiner 2016b: chap. 7).

The crucial problem with the quintessential policing tactics of 'random' uniform patrol and after-the-event investigation is that they are spread too thinly over the multitude of potential victims and offenders. The innovative tactics that have produced some improvements in police performance are directed at remedying this. 'Smart', intelligence-led analysis helps to identify and target crime hotspots and prolific offenders. 'Problem solving' may identify and remove (or displace) some risks. 'Community policing' may improve the flow of information and public cooperation. 'Zero-tolerance' order maintenance blitzes can create false impressions of police omnipresence that may deter potential offenders and reassure others.

All these are examples of the kind of risk-oriented strategies attributed to the influence of the commercial private security industry: 'Through community policing and order-maintenance policing, the public police are developing strategies . . . similar to the practices readily accepted by commercial and informal communities from private police' (Bayley and Shearing 1996: 593). But they are more plausibly interpreted as formalizations of tactics that were deeply engrained in traditional public policing. Cultivating public cooperation was central to the Peelian model, because of the deep and wide hostility to the creation of the new police in 1829 (see Chapter 4). Community policing was a bid to recapture the popular support threatened by social and economic change in the later twentieth century. The only sense in which it was inspired by private sector examples is that it had parallels with the heritage industry developing in the same period as a response to similar stresses. The consumerist phase of policing came to its height in the early 1990s as 'businesslike' management began to be the new gospel and even prisoners were rebranded as 'customers'. It was modelled on private sector PR but had scant positive effects. Exemplified in studies of criminal investigation, the careful cultivation and use of information was a staple tool long before the creation of the Peelian new police (e.g. Styles 1983). Appraising situations and people to assess risk and danger was a noted trope of traditional police culture (see Chapter 8). These are not aspects of a new risk-oriented, actuarial mentality, although they are of course greatly enhanced by recent technological developments.

What has undoubtedly been imported from private sector models, largely at the behest of neo-liberal governments, is what has become know as the 'New Public Management' (NPM). This focuses on central government 'ruling at a distance', 'steering' the local 'rowers' through target setting, performance measurement, league tables, competition, 'best value', and other market style sanctions. Enthusiasm for these tactics among private police theorists stems from the neo-liberal belief that private enterprise and markets work best (Johnston and Shearing 2003; McLaughlin 2007: 96–7, 182–7). But such faith is largely *a priori* and even market-oriented think-tanks have seen the danger—captured in the phrase 'what gets measured gets done'—that perverse incentives direct police activity away from the important but difficult to the trivial but achievable (Cooley 2005).

The claim that pluralization enhances policing is a category error. It presupposes that policing is best thought of in terms of the achievement of macro-functions such as crime control, law enforcement, maintaining public order, and security. The problems are not only the thorny practical ones of measuring the achievement of such functions and identifying the policing contribution towards this. As suggested earlier, function-alism misidentifies the bulk of policing activity which is an emergency response to a myriad problems for which policing can at best provide only an interim solution. To adopt a medical metaphor, police are analogous to paramedics or accident and emer-gency doctors, delivering first-aid relief but generally unable to cure the basic prob-lems. Their contribution may have been enhanced by the kind of partnerships with other local agencies that are mandated by the British Crime and Disorder Act 1998, which Johnston and Shearing (2003) celebrate rightly in principle as an illustration of the nodal-governance mentality (see also McLaughlin 2007: 126–30). But it is unlikely to be able to tackle the root causes of most problems, which lie outside the locality and require central government or even transnational support. This is a major lacuna of the nodal vision, indicating a necessary role for the state (Goldsmith 2003; Marks and Goldsmith 2006; Zedner 2009: 161–7).

Policing cannot be seen primarily as satisfying grand social functions but rather as a Sisyphean labour of continuous partial emergency alleviation of recurring problems, posing thorny problems of assessment (Reiner 1998). The statistical measures of per-formance that are the stock-in-trade of 'businesslike' models may be useful diagnostic tools, prompting questions about comparative results and reflexive analysis of why one sector's results are less favourable than a comparator's. But used as sanctions they are likely to lead to dissimulation of practices, distortion of statistics, and counter-produc-tive diversion of activity to the measurable and easily achievable. Although policing can bring short-term balm to desperate suffering, to believe it capable of achieving the grand functions of order and security is a dangerous category error. This is particu-larly pertinent in a world that is polarized politically and socially and where the police appear on the front line of conflict along the lines of class, gender, race, and nation (Chapter 6).

HOW DOES POLICING IMPACT ON DIFFERENT GROUPS?

Policing is regularly blighted by inequality, injustice, and discrimination. Groups that are low in power and status, such as the poor and unemployed, ethnic minori-ties, young people (especially if they are 'underclass'), often become 'police property' disproportionately likely to be treated as suspects at each stage of the criminal justice process (see Chapter 6). This arises for a variety of reasons. Volume crime such as property offences, violence, and disorder in public space, are the kinds of activity that the police in practice focus on. These are instances more likely to involve young, poor men and certain ethnic minority groups who are disproportionately poor. Such groups spend more time in public spaces and lack the wherewithal to enter mass private prop-erty citadels of consumption so they are more 'available' to become targets of police suspicion (Waddington *et al.* 2004). They are likely to fit stereotypes of suspiciousness, and have less power to challenge coercive police actions. These same groups are also disproportionately likely to be victimized by crime, and tend to receive less satisfactory police treatment. They are also less often recruited into the police, and have suffered career discrimination.

Discrimination and disparity are perennial problems of policing, violating the public service mandate of the police and the principle of equality before the law. The revelation of discrimination sometimes creates a major scandal, setting in train efforts to reform the police (see Chapter 5). This is in sharp contrast to private policing. Inequality of treatment is a barnacle on the boat of so-called public service policing. But it is the hull of the corporate policing vessel. Private security firms have duties to their shareholders, and to those they contract to provide services to (Joh 2004). The consequences of their activities to other parties—those they police, and the public at large—are not even a formal concern. As Zedner argues cogently:

> Although the practice of state policing never fulfilled its collectivist pretensions, it did profess, at least, to provide a public service available to all. . . . Private providers make no such claim but avowedly seek to protect the partisan interests (whether individual, communal or commercial) of those who pay. No surprise here: it is central to the logic of market societies that goods be distributed not according to need, but to the ability of the consumer to buy. (Zedner 2006: 92)

Shearing and Stenning (1983) show how mass private property has grown to create a 'new feudalism' of security fortresses separated sharply from their surroundings. At first, this analysis of growing social division had sinister and critical tones, but as the transformation thesis developed it came to be represented positively as 'nodal governance', with the private sector and its actuarial mentality of risk prevention supposedly setting an example to the public police. Theorists of private policing recognized the equity problem and explore the possibilities of levelling up security provision. They saw difficulties in increasing the provision of police to poorer areas, or by communal self-help alone (Bayley and Shearing 1996). So, their main hope was 'to enable poor people to participate in markets for security' by vouchers or block grants. 'In effect, communities would be given security budgets that they could spend on various mixtures of public and private policing' (ibid.: 730–1). This presupposed that the problems could be met by policing, and that pluralization would improve its efficacy—both questionable propositions. It also raised the issue of how the redistributive security budget was to gain political acceptance:

> Distributional problems between rich and poor might still arise, of course, particularly if the rich refused to pay. All policies that have any prospect of mitigating the growing class differences in public safety depend on the affluent segments of our societies recognising that security is indivisible. The well-to-do are paying for crime now; but they have not learned that they will save more by levelling up security than by ghettoising it. (ibid.: 730)

Achieving this consensus in support of redistribution is a formidable challenge. But as safety depends on much wider social and economic justice tackling the 'root causes' of threat, the task is the even more daunting one of constructing a consensus for a broad alleviation of inequality. The theorists who subscribe to the transformation thesis offer idealistic and inspirational examples of successful efforts to organize security in poor communities such as the South African township Zwelethemba (Johnston and Shearing 2003: 151–60). But these are dependent on outside financial and other support (Marks and Goldsmith 2006; T. Jones 2007: 858–60). The state remains the necessary 'anchor' for security (Loader and Walker 2006, 2007) if there is any hope to avert stark polarization between safe and dreadful enclosures. Here again, seeing the problem of justice and fairness in global context draws attention to the role of transnational policing in guarding the boundaries of the privileged global North. Neo-liberalism and authoritarianism are barriers to the pursuit of economic equality and are driving the construction of longer, stronger and taller physical fences as well as metaphorical barriers between people. Developments in information communication and crime control technologies further strengthen practices of exclusion. The result is a world with difference entrenched ever-more deeply within and between societies, polarized between a 'gilded but insecure elite and a threatening temporarily subjugated mass' (Reiner 2010a: 258). If justice is to be achieved in the context of a new cosmopolitan reality, a radical shift in global political economy is required (Bowling, Phillips, and Sheptycki 2012). Any theory of policing that puts blind faith in neo-liberalism and market solutions without closely examining their inherent perils is fundamentally flawed. A lesson of policing history, this book suggests, is that democratic policing can be approximated to only in a context of social, not just liberal—and certainly not neo-liberal—democracy.

BY WHOM AND HOW ARE THE POLICE THEMSELVES POLICED?

The issue of police accountability has, if anything, become more vexed in recent years (see Chapter 11). One of the reasons is the Janus face of policing discussed earlier: the problem of accountability has a double aspect—achieving effective and efficient service delivery, but also minimizing abuse and injustice in the use of coercive powers. In the last two decades, with the dominance of the politics of law and order, the issue of accountability has shifted strongly towards emphasizing effective delivery of security, with lower priority given to equity or the control of malpractice or indeed to general questions of transparency, answerability, and democratic control. Crime control has been declared as the overriding objective of policing, and a 'calculative and contractual' structure of monitoring and incentives is intended to achieve this.

The transformation thesis asserts that pluralization is making policing more accountable and responsive. Private security, in this analysis, is inherently accountable because of the contractual relationships between client and security firm, which provide sanctions for performance failure. As far as the public sector is concerned, they welcome a more businesslike structure of accountability (Johnston and Shearing 2003: 26). The brave new 'rule at a distance' world is contrasted with a supposed sclerotic old regime of state centralized command and control. The latter is inefficient because of the Hayekian problem: 'top-down government does not permit entrepreneurship because those "at the top of the pyramid" do not have "enough information to make informed decisions" [Osborne and Gaebler 1992: 15] about how to govern locally' (Shearing 2006: 23). Such problems supposedly do not apply to the corporate sector, which is imagined as vibrant, responsive, and efficient due to market incentives. This formulation misrepresents the past and current pattern of police governance. In

Anglo-American policing it was never the case that the state 'rowed'. The British legal doctrine of constabulary independence explicitly sought to shield police officers from direct instruction by government, central or local, although the operation of this in practice has been problematic. In the USA until relatively recently, the federal government role in local and state law policing was minimal. So Anglo-American policing has traditionally been governed 'at a distance' by the state (unless it is tautologically equated with it).

As shown in earlier chapters of this book, legal and state regulation of private security is weak and patchy, and there have long been calls for its enhancement. It has been argued that 'Private police are more responsive than public police to the "bottom line" of safety. If safety is not increased, private police can be fired' (Bayley and Shearing 1996, in Newburn 2005: 721). How effective private security is in satisfying its customers is no doubt variable, and in principle it should be acceptable to say *caveat emptor*. But they have no responsibilities for *public* security apart from their own limited 'nodes'. It is hard to see how pluralization has enhanced accountability, in the sense of responsiveness to general public concerns about safety or justice. The fact that policing networks tend to crisscross organizational, geographical, and jurisdictional boundaries means engaging in a debate about how accountability mechanisms can capture the full diversity of the policing function in its high/low, domestic/transnational, public/private forms (see Chapter 11).

HOW CAN THE DEVELOPING PURPOSES AND PRACTICES OF POLICING BE UNDERSTOOD?

The transformation thesis was primarily presented as a description of trends and an analysis of their 'progressive' potential. The main explanatory theme was implicitly 'truth will out': the new trends emerged because they solve manifest problems with the old policing arrangements. Johnston and Shearing (2003: 67) assert that 'Peel's aspiration to ensure prevention through the certainty of detection and punishment has remained unrealized during the two centuries since the inception of the new police . . . For example, during most of the postwar period, steadily rising rates of crime have exposed the limits of the Peelian project'. These claims distort the history of policing in a number of ways. Crime rates fell steadily after the 1850s as the Peelian police were rolled out across England and Wales, remaining low until the First World War (Chapter 4). It is doubtful that the falling crime rates were primarily due to the policing changes (Chapter 5). A much greater role was played by the long-term process of converting the 'dangerous classes' into the solid working class by incorporating them into the civil, political, and economic rights of citizenship. But if falling crime rates were largely a political conjuring trick to promote the bobbies, it worked, and the myth of Scotland Yard's prowess ('always getting their man') became an international symbol of successful policing.

Although crime rates rose in the 1920s and 1930s, they declined again in the first postwar decade, and the myth of the bobby as an important aspect of British national pride reached its zenith in the 1940s and 1950s. Recorded crime rates did begin to increase almost continuously after the mid-1950s until the mid-1990s, but the increase up to 1980 was largely a statistical illusion, as more property crime was reported to the police by victims due to the spread of household insurance. The real explosion in crime came in the 1980s and early 1990s, when the British Crime Surveys confirmed the police-recorded trend (Reiner 2016b: chap. 5). The police certainly got some of the blame for this—but as unfairly as the credit they had received for the earlier fall. The main factor in the crime explosion was the advent of neo-liberal economic policy, with its effects of precipitously increasing inequality, long-term unemployment, and social exclusion, and a culture of ever-expanding consumer aspirations and egoism (Reiner 2007: chap. 4; Hall *et al.* 2008). Faced with these huge crime increases, swamping their resources, the police were able to detect only a diminishing proportion of offences, further undermining public confidence in them.

Then, in the mid-1990s, across the USA and UK recorded crime and that measured by surveys began a period of falling crime that was sustained until around 2015. To the surprise of many people, the fall in crime was not halted by the 2007–8 financial crisis and subsequent 'credit crunch', especially after the election of the 2010 Conservative-Liberal Democrat coalition government implemented economic policies defined by austerity. Real terms spending on police fell by 17 per cent, police numbers by 14 per cent, and with it rates of recorded stop and search, arrests, and prosecutions. In 2014, the then Home Secretary Theresa May declared triumphantly, 'Police reform is working and crime is falling . . . we have achieved something no modern government has achieved before. We have proved that, through reform, it is possible to do more with less.' Then, from around 2015, after nearly two decades of falling crime, there have been sharp increases in knife crime, robbery, and homicide. Unsurprisingly, perhaps, many commentators—including senior police officers—now attribute rising crime to the impact of austerity in terms of police capacity but also the impact on other areas of the public sector such as mental health provision and social care. Additionally, there are anxieties about the capacity to respond to a terrorist attack, or the 'growing threats' of cybercrime, serious organized crime, and money laundering at a time when police resources have been cut significantly. Fights over priorities for scarce resources seem likely to intensify in the future.

The shifts in statistical crime trends and the changing public standing of the police had little to do with the supposed failures of the Peelian model. The real driver was the 'hollowing out of the state', a phenomenon shaped by broad transnational processes in culture, economy, and society (Sheptycki 1995). Transformation theorists evidently saw neo-liberalism as bearing the seeds of a solution contained in a rational set of programmes and ideas, curiously abstracted from its material effects and origins (Harvey 2005a; Mirowski and Plehwe 2009; Stedman Jones 2012; Davies 2016; Cahill and Konings 2017; Streeck 2017b; Bullough 2018; Shaxson 2018). Neo-liberal rhetoric was presented as if it corresponded to practice (e.g. O'Malley 1997, in Newburn 2005: 701–12), ignoring the (by now) clear deleterious effects. There is an acceptance of neo-liberal claims about the pathologies of state institutions, but no recognition of the pathologies of the market.

Johnston and Shearing's critique of the state was presented as rooted in the radical criminologies that flourished in the 1960s and early 1970s:

> Three decades ago cutting-edge criminological theory grappled with 'the problem of the state'. . . . the state was considered to *be* 'the problem', its capitalist character rendering it structurally incapable of representing general 'public interests' over particular private ones. (Johnston and Shearing 2003: 33–4)

They then reflected on the 'strange paradox' that 'many of today's theorists' bemoan 'how neoliberalism has disaggregated the state apparatus' (ibid.). There is no paradox here. The nub of the critique of the state it that it was captured by the interests of capital, and the problem was how to make it deliver on its promise to represent the public good. As Tawney put it over eighty years ago, the question is 'who owns and controls the State' (Tawney 1935: 165). 'The reality behind the decorous drapery of political democracy', he argued is 'the economic power wielded by a few thousand—or . . . a few hundred thousand—bankers, industrialists, and landowners' (ibid.: 60). The 'state' stands for a more or less loosely coupled set of sites for struggle over direction and control. To be sure the struggle is stacked currently in favour of 'the 1 per cent', but there have been eras (e.g. the pre-First World War decade when the seeds of the welfare state were planted, the post-Second World War Keynesian consensus) when states have operated more in the general interest.

To espouse neo-liberalism—'capitalism unleashed' (Glyn 2006)—as an escape from the ideological hegemony of the state, is to jump from the frying pan into the fire. The claim that there are 'possibilities for disaggregating neo-liberal strategies and practices, and rendering their often highly innovative developments available for appropriation and development by a "progressive" postwelfare politics' (O'Malley 1997, in Newburn 2005: 712) simply overlooks the inherent dysfunctions of markets. Markets have many unwelcome economic consequences, unless states take countervailing measures: growing inequalities of power and wealth; allocation of resources tilted towards the desires of the rich (the democracy of the market is not one person one vote, but one pound one vote); insecurities caused by vicissitudes of health, age, natural disasters; and, as we have relearned since 2007–8, wild macroeconomic fluctuations (Reiner 2007: 1–11). Market-dominated societies are associated with further social, ethical, political, and cultural problems: the financialization of all values, anomie produced by the stimulation of desires and aspirations beyond the possibility of achievement, egoism, corruption of democracy by the influence of affluence over the best politicians money can buy (Gilens 2014; Palast 2016), and authoritarianism as the 'strong state' seeks to suppress resistance to the pathologies of the 'free market' (Polanyi 1944; Gamble 1994; Winlow et al. 2015).

Specifically relevant to policing, there is now a host of research evidence showing that neo-liberalism—as contrasted with social democracy—is associated with higher risks of serious violent crime, and more punitive cultures and penal practices, because of its economic, social, and cultural pathologies (Hall and Winlow 2003, 2015; Dorling 2004; Cavadino and Dignan 2006; Reiner 2007, 2016a; Lacey 2008; Hall et al. 2008; Hall and McLean 2009; Wilkinson and Pickett 2009, 2018; Gilligan 2011; Cooper and Whyte 2017).

The main explanatory deficit of the 'new' policing theories of the 1990s and 2000s is a bracketing-out of the significance of political and moral economy in shaping the context and problems that police organizations, cultures, and officers face. Explanations of changing programmes and practices, and their impacts—intended and unintended—require a multilayered political/moral economy of the macro-, intermediate, and immediate social processes and contexts that shape policing (Reiner 2017; Rogan 2018).

Analysing the historical roots of policing transformations through the lens of political and moral economy suggests a very different diagnosis. The pluralization of policing is a symptom of, not a solution to, the current predicament. As elaborated in Chapters 3 and 4, the Peelian police were established in Britain (and the USA) in the early nineteenth century against wide and deep hostility, especially from the then politically, socially, and economically excluded masses. The big job facing the early police leaders was to gain public consent, and somewhat different strategies were followed in Britain and the USA (Miller 1999). The British route was a set of organizational policies seeking to represent the police as disciplined, apolitical, minimally armed 'citizens in uniform', enforcing an impartial law, as well as providing emergency social services. These tactics ultimately succeeded in winning a fragile legitimation of the police, but only because the policies were developed in a benign context of the general march of social, political, and economic citizenship (as classically spelled out by Marshall 1950). This reduced the extent of crime and disorder confronting the police, allowing them to consolidate the image of operating with minimum force, and creating space for the service role to be emphasized.

Police legitimacy was gradually undermined after the late 1960s, but not because of defects in the policing model. The ultimate source was economic neo-liberalism, initially heralded by the 1971 'Nixon shock' in the USA when the convertibility of the dollar to gold was abandoned. This effectively ended the Bretton Woods system, established after the Second World War to regulate international finance, which was the bedrock of the Keynesian consensus and *Les Trente Glorieuses* of unprecedented growth in mass prosperity. Neo-liberalism set in train massive economic and social dislocation (especially large-scale long-term unemployment, inequality, and social exclusion) and an increasingly anomic and egoistic culture. During the 1980s it generated a crime explosion and public disorder on a scale not seen for a century. Mediated by the unintended reversal of the policing policies that had achieved legitimation, the result was a decline in public confidence in the police.

How to deal with this was politically controversial in the 1970s and 1980s, and there appeared sharp politicization of the issue of law and order (Downes and Morgan 2007; Reiner 2007: chap. 5). In the UK, the Tories espoused a tough new law-and-order rhetoric, while Labour clung to a social democratic analysis of the roots of crime and disorder. This changed in 1992 when the then Shadow Home Secretary Tony Blair's celebrated slogan 'tough on crime, tough on the causes of crime' heralded New Labour's conversion to the law-and-order approach, the first of several 'Clause 4' moments signifying its embrace of neo-liberalism. For the British police this meant calling a bluff that had been successful for 150 years. The police had been symbolically acclaimed as guardians of the public against threats of crime and disorder, but the real work was done by an array of economic, social, and cultural processes which incorporated most of society into a common status of citizenship, and held tensions at bay. When neo-liberalism unravelled this complex of subtle, hidden, inclusionary controls, the thin blue line turned out to be an imaginary line in the sand. As researchers had suggested all along, the police alone could not have much impact on crime and disorder. But the newly ascendant and unquestioned politics of law and order demanded that they do just that. Meanwhile, as ever, those with the motive and means to do so built their exclusive bubbles of security.

Transformation of policing stems neither from the inherent deficiencies of old state policing, nor the technical superiority of a new corporate mentality of pluralism, combining private security and an NPM-invigorated public sector. It results from the destabilizing and criminogenic effects of neo-liberalism, which is the problem, not the solution. There have been many valuable analyses of the legal, constitutional, procedural, and organizational requirements for democratic and legitimate policing (see Chapter 11). British policing history suggests that a further ingredient is needed: social democracy. The organizational elements of the legitimation of the police only succeeded because of the wider transformation of British society that culminated in the postwar Keynesian and welfare state settlement, incorporating all sections of society into a common status of citizenship. The political triumph of neo-liberalism since the 1970s, and the ensuing 'death of the social' (Rose 1996), eroded these conditions of peace and security.

ALL TO PLAY FOR? PERIODIZING THE POLITICS OF THE POLICE

A clock striking thirteen reveals not only the wrong time but that the clock's fundamental mechanism is faulty. The financial crisis of 2007–8 made many doubt the deregulated system that had developed over the previous three decades. The emergency measures taken by central banks rescued the financial institutions that had been the immediate sources of the crisis. But most people were subject to draconian cutbacks in the public sector and welfare, befuddled by a narrative that placed the blame on excessive government spending. Socialism for banks, austerity for the people. Thus, a zombie neo-liberalism stumbled on, still dominating the world in practice, but with its brain and heart cut out. Although some politicians and analysts had initially thought the crisis could be a social democratic moment, this never materialized. As so many times before, the political right, and the corporate power it represented, seized the day after the crisis, before the left was anywhere near getting its act together (Klein 2008; Mirowski 2014). The political shocks of 2016, summed up by a broad swathe of left-liberal opinion as a surge of populism, fuelled by the left-behind victims of economic neo-liberalism, created a chaos of possibilities. Diagnoses were plentiful, solutions scarce (Tooze 2018; Skidelsky 2018). Yeats' century old words—'The best lack all conviction, while the worst are full of passionate intensity'—never seemed more apposite: Only time will tell if reinvigorated democratic socialist voices across the world (e.g. Jeremy Corbyn in the UK, Bernie Sanders in the USA, and others elsewhere), can dent the dominance of right-wing rhetoric calling to 'take back control', and to 'make America great again' (Panich and Godin 2018).

The various versions of the 'transformation thesis' discussed earlier were formulated some time ago and now we can place them better in an overall context of political-economic development. It is universally recognized that capitalism is subject to periodic cycles of prosperity and recession, despite the recurring hubris of economists and politicians claiming to have found the Holy Grail ending boom and bust. What remains vigorously contested is how to mitigate, let alone eliminate, these cycles. More controversial still is the view, proposed by a variety of political economists over the last 150 years, that there are also longer-term fluctuations in economic development. These are commonly referred to as 'Kondratieff waves', after the Soviet economist who proposed the existence of cycles lasting around fifty years (Hobsbawm 1995: 87). However, many other political economists—Marxist, liberal, and conservative—have analysed long cycles or stages in the history of capitalism, notably Marx, Keynes, Schumpeter,

Polanyi, Wallerstein, Mandel, Minsky, and Arrighi. Synthesizing these periodizations very roughly suggests the following stages:

- **A) 18th century–1979**: Capitalist industrialization, followed by gradual incorporation of whole societies into Marshallian citizenship, divisible into three sub-phases:

    1) Harsh 'primitive' accumulation, eighteenth–early nineteenth century;

    2) Liberal-democratic incorporation spreading civil rights in the eighteenth century, then political rights from the 1830s;

    3) Social Democratic incorporation 1945–1970s, extending economic and social rights to the whole population.

- **B) Neo-liberal Counter-Revolution 1979–2008**. Reassertion of free market utopian ideals necessitating the hollowing out of the state in two broad phases:

    1) 1979–1992: Contested neo-liberalism;

    2) 1992–2008: Hegemonic neo-liberalism as erstwhile political opponents (Labour, Democrats, etc.) are converted.

- **C) 2008–2016 'Zombie' neo-liberalism**. Seemingly permanent economic crisis fatally challenges the intellectual basis of neo-liberalism (seen as largely based on 'borrowed time' Streeck 2014). But it remains the dominant form of economic structure and policy ('austerity'), primarily challenged only rhetorically.

- **D) 2016– The Road to Where?**

    Political earthquakes in the USA and UK, and elsewhere, reveal the fatal flaws of neo-liberalism. They are widely seen as threatening the survival of liberal democratic capitalism. But what comes after is deeply contested, analytically and in political practice.

This periodization broadly fits the development of policing as traced in Chapters 3 and 4. The birth of professional policing during the travails of early capitalist industrialization; police legitimation as inequality is attenuated by the spread of citizenship, and Keynesian welfarism; renewed police politicization as neo-liberalism once again deepens social divisions; a fragile re-legitimation amid social dissensus and cultural fragmentation as neo-liberalism becomes embedded. But what will follow the rapidly and massively widening economic, social, and cultural chasms as neo-liberalism decays? Governmental and police elites are resorting to accentuated high policing, with sophisticated ever higher-tech intelligence gathering and analysis, and militaristic responses to disorder. They are 'able to scale up the enforcement and scale down the due process'. Can these keep the lid on increasing tensions and differences? Even if administrative criminology offers an evidence-based lidology, trying to find out which lid works best? Nobody really knows. But the earlier historical legitimation of police suggests that even wise police strategies can be effective only with a wider context of declining inequality and greater social integration. As the T-shirts of Black Lives Matter protestors declare: 'No Justice, No Peace'.

BIBLIOGRAPHY AND REFERENCES

AAS, K. F. (2007). *Globalization and Crime*. London: Sage.

AAS, K. F. and BOSWORTH, M. (eds) (2013). *The Borders of Punishment: Migration, Citizenship, and Social Exclusion*. Oxford: Oxford University Press.

ABRAHAMSEN, R. and LEANDER, A. (eds) (2016). *Routledge Handbook of Private Security Studies*. London: Routledge.

AEPLI, P., RIBAUX, O., and SUMMERFIELD, E. (2011). *Decision Making in Policing: Operations and Management*. Paris: EPFL Press.

AGERHOLM, H. (2017). 'Police Failing to Attend One in Nine Domestic Violence Incidents, Figures Show'. *The Independent*, 10 December.

AGOZINO, B. (2003). *Counter-Colonial Criminology: A Critique of Imperialist Reason*. London: Pluto Press.

AGOZINO, B. (2004). 'Crime, Criminology and Post-Colonial Theory: Criminological Reflections on West Africa', in J. SHEPTYCKI and A. WARDAK (eds), *Transnational and Comparative Criminology*. London: Taylor & Francis.

AKGÜN, A. E., KESKIN, H., and BYRNE, J. (2012). 'Organizational Emotional Memory'. *Management Decision*, 50(1): 95–114.

ALAIN, M. (2000). 'Les heurts et les bonheurs de la coopération policière internationale en Europe, entre la myopie des bureau-crates et la sclérose culturelle policière'. *Déviance et société*, 24(3): 237–53. doi: 10.3406/ds.2000.1728.

ALBRECHT, P. and KYED, H. M. (eds) (2016). *Policing and the Politics of Order-Making*. London: Routledge.

ALDERSON, J. (1979). *Policing Freedom*. Plymouth: Macdonald & Evans.

ALDERSON, J. (1984). *Law and Disorder*. London: Hamish Hamilton.

ALDERSON, J. (1998). *Principled Policing*. Winchester: Waterside Press.

ALEXANDER, M. (2012). *The New Jim Crow*. New York: The New York Press.

ALLEN, J., LIVINGSTONE, S., and REINER, R. (1998). 'True Lies: Changing Images of Crime in British Postwar Cinema'. *European Journal of Communication*, 13(1): 53–75.

ALLPORT, G. (1935). 'Attitudes', in C. MURCHINSON (ed.), *A Handbook of Social Psychology*. Worcester, MA: Clark University Press.

ALLPORT, G. (1954). *The Nature of Prejudice*. Reading, MA: Addison-Wesley.

ALPERT, G. P. and DUNHAM, R. D. (2004). *Understanding Police Use of Force: Officers, Suspects and Reciprocity*. Cambridge: Cambridge University Press.

ALTBEKER, A. (2005). *The Dirty Work of Democracy: A Year on the Streets with the SAP*. Capetown: Johnathan Ball Publishers.

ALTHEIDE, D. L. (2004). 'Media Logic and Political Communication'. *Political Communication*, 21(3): 293–96.

AMATRUDO, A. (2009). *Criminology and Political Theory*. London: Sage.

AMICELLE, A., CÔTÉ-BOUCER, K., DUPONT, B., MULONE, M., SHEARING, C., and TANNER, S. (eds) (2017). 'Criminology in the Face of Flows: Reflections on Contemporary Policing and Security'. *Global Crime*, 18(3) Numéro special.

ANDERSON, D. M. and KILLINGRAY, D. (eds) (1991). *Policing the Empire: Government, Authority and Control, 1830–1940*. Manchester: Manchester University Press.

ANDERSON, D. M. and KILLINGRAY, D. (eds) (1992). *Policing and Decolonisation:*

Politics, Nationalism and the Police, 1917–65. Manchester: Manchester University Press.

ANDERSON, M. (1989). *Policing the World: Interpol and the Politics of International Police Co-operation.* Oxford: Clarendon.

ANDERSON, M. (2011). *In Thrall to Political Change: Police and Gendarmerie in France.* Oxford: Oxford University Press.

ANDERSON, M., DEN BOER, M., CULLEN, P., GILMORE, W., RAAB, C., and WALKER, N. (1995). *Policing the European Union.* Oxford: Oxford University Press.

ANDREAS, P. and NADELMANN, E. (2008). *Policing the Globe: Criminalization and Crime Control in International Relations.* Oxford: Oxford University Press.

ANSARI, A. (2003). *Modern Iran since 1921: The Pahlavis and After.* London: Longman.

APPIER, J. (1993). 'Preventive Justice: The Campaign for Women Police, 1910–1940'. *Women & Criminal Justice,* 4(1): 3–36.

ARMITAGE, G. (1932). *The History of the Bow Street Runners.* London: Wishart & Co.

ARNOLD, E. A. (1979). *Fouché, Napoleon and the General Police.* Washington, DC: University Press of America.

ARSENAULT, A. H. and CASTELLS, M. (2008a). 'The Structure and Dynamics of Global Multi-Media Business Networks'. *International Journal of Communication,* 2: 707–48.

ARSENAULT, A. H. and CASTELLS, M. (2008b). 'Switching Power: Rupert Murdoch and the Global Business of Media Politics: A Sociological Analysis'. *International Sociology,* 23(4): 488–513.

ASCOLI, D. (1979). *The Queen's Peace: The Origins and Development of the Metropolitan Police 1829–1979.* London: Hamish Hamilton.

ASHWORTH, A. and ZEDNER, L. (2014). *Preventive Justice.* Oxford: Oxford University Press.

AUDIT COMMISSION (1990a). *Effective Policing: Performance Review in Police Forces.* London: HMSO.

AUDIT COMMISSION (1990b). *Footing the Bill: Financing Provincial Police Forces.* London: HMSO.

AUDIT COMMISSION (1993). *Helping with Inquiries: Tackling Crime Effectively.* London: HMSO.

AUDIT COMMISSION (1996). *Streetwise: Effective Police Patrol.* London: HMSO.

AXTMANN, R. (1992). '"Police" and the Formation of the Modern State. Legal and Ideological Assumptions on State Capacity in the Austrian Lands of the Habsburg Empire, 1500–1800'. *German History,* 10: 39–61.

AYDINLI, E. and YON, H. (2011). 'Transgovernmentalism Meets Security: Police Liaison Officers, Terrorism and Statist Transnationalism'. *Governance,* 24(1): 55–84.

BACON, M. (2014). 'Police Culture and the New Policing Context', in J. BROWN (ed.), *The Future of Policing.* London: Routledge.

BACON, M. (2016). *Taking Care of Business: Police Detectives, Drug Law Enforcement and Proactive Investigation.* Oxford: Oxford University Press.

BAILEY, V. (1981). 'The Metropolitan Police, the Home Office and the Threat of Outcast London', in V. BAILEY (ed.), *Policing and Punishment in Nineteenth Century England.* London: Croom Helm.

BAKKEN, B. (2000). *The Exemplary Society: Human Improvement, Social Control and the Dangers of Modernity in China.* New York: Oxford University Press.

BAKKEN, B. (2005). *Crime, Punishment and Policing in China.* Lanham, MD: Rowman and Littlefield.

BALKO, R. (2014). *Rise of the Warrior Cop: The Militarization of America's Police Forces.* New York: Public Affairs.

BALL, J., CHESTER, L., and PERROTT, R. (1979). *Cops and Robbers.* Harmondsworth: Penguin Books.

BALL, K., HAGGERTY K. D., and LYON, D. (2012). *The Routledge Handbook of Surveillance Studies.* London: Routledge.

BALLUCCI, D., GILL, C., and CAMPBELL, M. A. (2017). 'The Power of Attitude: The Role of Police Culture and Receptivity of Risk Assessment Tools in IPV Calls'. *Policing*, 11(3): 242–57.

BANTON, M. (1964). *The Policeman in the Community*. London: Tavistock.

BANTON, M. (1983). 'Categorical and Statistical Discrimination'. *Ethnic and Racial Studies* 6(3): 269–83.

BARTON, A. and JOHNS, N. (2014). 'Engaging the Citizen', in J. BROWN (ed.), *The Future of Policing*. London: Routledge.

Bauman, Z. (2000). *Liquid Modernity* Cambridge: Polity. Ben's.

BAUMAN, Z. (2005). 'The Demons of an Open Society'. Ralph Miliband Lecture, 20 November. London: LSE.

BAUMAN, Z. (2013). *Liquid Times: Living in an Age of Uncertainty*. London: John Wiley.

BAUMAN, Z. and LYON, D. (2007). *Liquid Surveillance*. Cambridge: Polity Press.

BAUMGARTNER, F., EPP, D., and SHOUB, K. (2018). *Suspect Citizens: What 20 Million Traffic Stops Tell Us about Policing and Race*. Cambridge: Cambridge University Press.

BAYER, M. D. (2010). *The Blue Planet: Informal International Police Networks and National Intelligence*. Washington, DC: US Government Printing Office.

BAYLEY, D. H. (1975). 'The Police and Political Development in Europe', in C. TILLY (ed.), *The Formation of National States in Western Europe*. Princeton, NJ: Princeton University Press.

BAYLEY, D. (1976). *Forces of Order: Police Behaviour in Japan and the United States*. Berkeley, CA: University of California Press.

BAYLEY, D. H. (1985). *Patterns of Policing*. New Brunswick, NJ: Rutgers University Press.

BAYLEY, D. H. (1991). *Forces of Order: Police Behavior in Japan and the United States* (2nd edn). Berkeley, CA: University of California Press.

BAYLEY, D. H. (1992). 'Police Function, Structure, and Control in Western Europe and North America: Comparative and Historical Studies', in E. H. MONKKONEN (ed.), *Crime and Justice in American History, Vol. 5: Policing and Control*. Munich: K. G. Saur.

BAYLEY, D. H. (1994). *Police for the Future*. New York: Oxford University Press.

BAYLEY, D. H. (1998). *What Works in Policing?* New York: Oxford University Press.

BAYLEY, D. H. (2006). *Changing the Guard: Developing Democratic Police Abroad*. Oxford: Oxford University Press.

BAYLEY, D. and BITTNER, E. (1984). 'Learning the Skills of Policing'. *Law and Contemporary Problems*, 47: 35–60.

BAYLEY, D. and SHEARING, C. (1996). 'The Future of Policing'. *Law and Society Review*, 30(3): 586–606.

BAYLEY, D. H. and SHEARING, C. (2001). *The New Structure of Policing: Description, Conceptualization and Research Agenda*. Washington, DC: National Institute of Justice.

BAYLEY, D. and STENNING, P. (2016). *Governing Police: Experience in Six Democracies*. London: CRC Press/Taylor and Francis.

BBC Radio 4 (2018). 'A life's work: Female Police Officers'. First broadcast, Wednesday 25 July 2018. https://www.bbc.co.uk/programmes/b0bbq3vp

BEATON, S. J. (2012). 'Counterparts in Modern Policing: The Influence of Corporate Investigators on the Public Police and a Call for the Broadening of the State Action Doctrine'. *Touro Law Review*, 26(2): 593–618.

BEATTIE, J. (2006). 'Early Detection: The Bow Street Runners', in C. EMSLEY and H. SHPAYER-MAKOV (eds), *Police Detectives in History 1750–1950*. London: Longman.

BEATTIE, J. (2007). 'Sir John Fielding and Public Justice: The Bow Street Magistrates' Court, 1754–1780'. *Law and History Review*, 25(1): 61–100.

BECKER, H. (1963). *Outsiders: Studies in the Sociology of Deviance*. New York: Free Press.

BECKER, H. (1967). 'Whose Side Are We On?'. *Social Problems*, 14(3): 239–47.

BECKETT, F. and HENCKE, D. (2009). *Marching to the Fault Line: The 1984 Miners' Strike and the Death of Industrial Britain*. London: Constable and Robinson.

BEEK, J., GÖPFERT, M., OWEN, O., and STEINBERG, J. (eds) (2017). *Police in Africa: A Street Level View*. Oxford: Oxford University Press.

BEETHAM, D. (1991). *The Legitimation of Power*. London: Macmillan.

BELL, D. J. (1973). *The Coming of Post-Industrial Society: A Venture in Social Forecasting*, New York: Basic Books.

BELUR, J. (2010). *Permission to Shoot? Police Use of Deadly Force in Democracies*. Berlin: Springer.

BELUR, J. (2011). 'Police Stop and Search in India: Mumbai Nakabandi'. *Policing and Society*, 21(4): 420–31.

BENJAMIN, W. (1996). *Selected Writings*. Cambridge, MA: Harvard University Press.

BENJAMIN, W. (2006). 'Critique of Violence', in W. BENJAMIN (ed.), *One-Way Street*. London: Verso.

BENNER, T., WOLFGANG, R., and JAN, W. (2005). 'Multisectoral Networks in Global Governance: Towards a Pluralistic System of Accountability', in D. HELD and M. KOENIG-ARCHIBUGI (eds), *Global Governance and Public Accountability*. Oxford: Blackwell.

BENYON, J., TURNBULL, L., WILLIS, A., and BECK, A. (1993). *Police Cooperation in Europe: An Investigation*. Leicester: University of Leicester Centre for the Study of Public Order.

BERGMAN, M. E., WALKER, J. M., and JEAN, V. A. (2016). 'A Simple Solution to Policing Problems: Women!'. *Industrial and Organizational Psychology*, 9(3): 590–7.

BERNBURG, J. G. and KROHN, M. D. (2003). 'Labeling, Life Chances, and Adult Crime: The Direct and Indirect Effects of Official Intervention in Adolescence on Crime in Early Adulthood'. *Criminology*, 41(4): 1287–318.

BERNSTEIN, S., BIGELOW, B., COOPER, L., CURRIE, E., FRAPPIER, J., HARRING, S., KLARE, M., POYNER, P., RAY, G., SCHAUFFLER, R., SCRUGGS, J., STEIN, N., THAYER, M., and TRUJILLO, L. (1982). *The Iron Fist and the Velvet Glove: An Analysis of the US Police* (3rd edn). Berkeley, CA: Centre for Research on Criminal Justice.

BIGO, D. (1998). 'Frontiers and Security in the European Union: The Illusion of Migration Control', in M. ANDERSON and E. BORT (eds), *The Frontiers of Europe*. London: Pinter.

BIGO, D. (2000). 'Liaison Officers in Europe', in J. SHEPTYCKI (ed.), *Issues in Transnational Policing*. London: Routledge.

BIGO, D. (2001). 'Internal and External Security(ies): The *Möbius Ribbon*', in M. JACOBSON, D. ALBERT, and Y. LAPID (eds), *Identities, Borders, Orders: Rethinking International Relations Theory*. Minneapolis, MN: University of Minnesota Press.

BIGO, D. (2006). 'Internal and External Aspects of Security'. *European Security*, 15(4): 385–404.

BIGO, D. (2014). 'The Insecurity Practices of the Three Universes of EU Border Control: Military/Navy—Border Guards/Police—Database Analysts'. *Security Dialogue*, 45(3): 209–25.

BILLINGSLEY, R., NEMITZ, T., and BEAN, P. (2000). *Informers: Policing, Policy Practice*. Cullhompton: Willan.

BIRZER, M. L., and CRAIG, D. E. (1996). 'Gender Differences in Police Physical Ability Test Performance'. *American Journal of Police*, 15(2): 93–108.

BITTNER, E. (1967). 'The Police on Skid Row', *American Sociological Review*, 32(5): 699–715.

BITTNER, E. (1970). *The Functions of the Police in Modern Society*. Chevy Chase, MD: National Institute of Mental Health.

BITTNER, E. (1974). 'Florence Nightingale in Pursuit of Willie Sutton: A Theory of the Police', in H. JACOB (ed.), *The Potential for Reform of Criminal Justice*. Beverly Hills, CA: Sage.

BITTNER, E. (1980). *The Functions of Policing in Modern Society: A Review of Background Factors, Current Practices and Possible Role Models*. Cambridge MA: Oelgeschlager, Gunn and Hain, Publishers.

BITTNER, E. (1983). 'Legality and Workmanship', in M. PUNCH (ed.), *Control in the Police Organization*. Cambridge, MA: MIT Press.

BITTNER, E. (1990). *Aspects of Police Work*. Boston, MA: Northeastern University Press [p. 249 cited by Blanes i Vidal, J. and Kirchmaier, T. (2017). 'The Effect of Police Response Time on Crime Clearance Rates'. *The Review of Economic Studies*, 85(2): 855–91].

BLACK, D. (1976). *The Behavior of Law*. New York: Academic Press.

BLACK, D. (1980). *The Manners and Customs of the Police*. New York: Academic Press.

BLAKE, H. (2010). 'Terrorists Could Use Exploding Breast Implants to Blow Up Jet' *The Daily Telegraph*, 24 March.

BLOCK, L. (2007). 'International Policing in Russia: Police Co-operation Between the European Union Member States and the Russian Federation'. *Policing and Society*, 17(5): 367–87.

BLOCK, L. (2012). 'EU Joint Investigation Teams: Political Ambitions and Police Practices' in S. HUFNAGEL, S. BRONITT, and C. HARFIELD (eds), *Cross-Border Law Enforcement Regional Law Enforcement Cooperation—European, Australian and Asia-Pacific Perspectives*. Routledge: London.

BLUMSTEIN, A. (1999). 'Measuring What Matters in Policing', in R. LANGWORTHY (ed.), *Measuring What Matters: Proceedings from the Policing Research Institute Meetings*. Washington, DC: National Institute of Justice.

BODY-GENDROT, S. (2016). *Public Disorder and Globalization*. London and New York: Routledge.

BOESSENECKER, J. (2016). *Texas Ranger: The Epic Life of Frank Hamer, the Man who Killed Bonnie and Clyde*. London: St Martin's Press.

BONNER, M. D., GUILLERMINA, S., KUBAL, M. R., and KEMPA, M. (2018). *Police Abuse in Contemporary Democracies*. London: Palgrave Macmillan.

BOOT, M. (2002). *The Savage Wars of Peace: Small Wars and the Rise of American Power*. New York: Basic Books.

BOSWORTH, M., FRANKO, K., and PICKERING, S. (2017). 'Punishment, Globalisation and Migration Control: "Get them the hell out of here"'. *Punishment and Society* 20(1): 34–53.

BOSWORTH, M., PARMAR, A., and VAZQUEZ, Y. (eds) (2018). *Race, Criminal Justice and Immigration Control: Enforcing the Boundaries of Belonging*. Oxford: Oxford University Press.

BOTTOMLEY, A. K. and COLEMAN, C. (1981). *Understanding Crime Rates*. Farnborough: Gower.

BOTTOMS, A. E. (1990). 'Crime Prevention Facing the 1990s'. *Policing and Society*, 1(1): 3–22.

BOTTOMS, A. E. and STEVENSON, S. (1990). 'The Politics of the Police 1958–1970', in R. MORGAN (ed.), *Policing, Organised Crime and Crime Prevention*. British Criminology Conference Papers 4. Bristol: Bristol University, Centre for Criminal Justice..

BOTTOMS, A. E. and TANKEBE, J. (2012). 'Beyond Procedural Justice: A Dialogic Approach to Legitimacy in Criminal Justice'. *Journal of Criminal Law and Criminology*, 102: 119–70.

BOTTOMS, A. E. and TANKEBE, J. (2017). 'Police Legitimacy and the Authority of the State', in A. DU BOIS-PEDAIN, M. ULVÄNG, and P. ASP, *Criminal Law and the Authority of the State*. Oxford: Hart.

BOURDIEU, P. (1984). *Distinction: A Social Critique of the Judgement of Taste*. London: Routledge.

BOWCOTT, O. (2018). 'John Worboys' Victims Win Human Rights Case against Police'. *The Guardian*, 21 February.

BOWLING, B. (1999a). 'The Rise and Fall of New York Murder'. *British Journal of Criminology*, 39(4): 531–54.

BOWLING, B. (1999b). *Violent Racism: Victimisation, Policing and Social Context*. Revised Edition. Oxford: Oxford University Press.

BOWLING. B. (2007). 'Fair and Effective Police Methods: Towards "Good Enough" Policing'. *Scandinavian Studies in Criminology and Crime Prevention*, 8(S1): 17–23.

BOWLING, B. (2009). 'Transnational Policing: The Globalisation Thesis, a Typology and a Research Agenda'. *Policing*, 3(2): 1–12.

BOWLING, B. (2010). *Policing the Caribbean*. Oxford: Oxford University Press.

BOWLING, B. (2013). 'Epilogue: The Borders of Punishment: Towards a Criminology of Mobility', in A. K. FRANKO and M. BOSWORTH (eds), *The Borders of Punishment: Migration, Citizenship, and Social Exclusion*. Oxford: Oxford University Press.

BOWLING, B. and IYER, S. (2019) 'Race, Law and the Police: Fifty Years of Anti-Discrimination Law and Policing'. *Policing and Society*. (forthcoming).

BOWLING, B. and MARKS, E. (2015). 'Stop and Search: Towards a Transnational and Comparative Perspective', in R. DELSOL and M. SHINER (eds), *Stop and Search. The Anatomy of a Police Power*. London: Palgrave Macmillan.

BOWLING, B. and MARKS, E. (2017). 'The Rise and Fall of Suspicionless Searches'. *King's Law Journal*, 28(1): 62–88.

BOWLING, B. and PHILLIPS, C. (2002). *Racism, Crime and Justice*. London: Pearson.

BOWLING, B. and PHILLIPS, C. (2007). 'Disproportionate and Discriminatory: Reviewing the Evidence on Police Stop and Search'. *Modern Law Review*, 70(6): 936–61.

BOWLING, B. and ROSS, J. (2006). 'The Serious Organised Crime Agency: Should We be Afraid?', *Criminal Law Review*, (December): 1019–34.

BOWLING, B. and SAULSBURY, W. (1992). *A Multiagency Approach to Racial Harassment*. Home Office Research Bulletin, 32. London: Home Office.

BOWLING, B. and SHEPTYCKI, J. (2011). 'Policing Globopolis'. *Social Justice: Special Double Issue Policing in Crisis*, 38(1–2): 184–202.

BOWLING, B. and SHEPTYCKI, J. (2012). *Global Policing*. London: Sage.

BOWLING, B. and SHEPTYCKI, J. (2014). 'Global Policing, Mobility and Social Control', in S. PICKERING and J. HAM (eds), *The Routledge Handbook on Crime and International Migration*, London: Routledge.

BOWLING, B. and SHEPTYCKI, J. (2015a). *Global Policing and Transnational Law Enforcement* (Volumes 1–4). London: Sage.

BOWLING, B. and SHEPTYCKI, J. (2015b). 'Global Policing and Transnational Rule with Law'. *Transnational Legal Theory*, 6(1): 141–73.

BOWLING, B. and SHEPTYCKI, J. (2015c). 'Talking to the Man—Some Gendered Reflections on the Relationship between the Global System and Policing Subculture(s)'. *European Journal of Policing Studies*, 3(2): 116–34.

BOWLING, B. and SHEPTYCKI, J. (2016a). 'Reflections on Political Accountability for Global Policing', in M. ROWE and S. LISTER (eds), *Police Accountability*. London: Routledge.

BOWLING, B. and SHEPTYCKI, J. (2016b). 'Transnational Policing and the End Times of Human Rights', in L. WEBER, E. FISHWICH, and M. MARMO (eds),

Routledge Handbook of Criminology and Human Rights. London: Taylor & Francis.

BOWLING, B. and WESTENRA, S. (2018a). 'Racism, Immigration and Policing', in M. BOSWORTH, A. PARMAR, and Y. VÁZQUEZ (eds), *Race, Criminal Justice and Migration Control: Enforcing the Boundaries of Belonging*. Oxford: Oxford University Press.

BOWLING, B. and WESTENRA, S. (2018b). 'A Really Hostile Environment: Adiaphorisation, Global Policing and the Crimmigration Control System'. *Theoretical Criminology*, https://doi. org/10.1177/1362480618774034.

BOWLING, B., PARMAR, A., and PHILLIPS, C. (2008). 'Policing Ethnic Minority Communities', in T. NEWBURN (ed.), *Handbook of Policing*. Cullompton: Willan.

BOWLING, B., PHILLIPS, C., and SHEPTYCKI, J. (2012). '"Race", Political Economy and the Coercive State', in T. NEWBURN and J. PEAY (eds), *Policing: Politics, Culture and Control*. Portland, OR: Hart.

BOX, S. and RUSSELL, K. (1975). 'The Politics of Discreditability'. *Sociological Review*, 23(2): 315–46.

BOYDSTUN, J. (1975). *The San Diego Field Interrogation Experiment*. Washington, DC: Police Foundation.

BRADFORD, B. (2016). *Stop and Search and Police Legitimacy*. Abingdon: Routledge.

BRADFORD, B. and LOADER, I. (2016). 'Police, Crime and Order: The Case of Stop and Search', in B. BRADFORD, B. JAUREGUI, I. LOADER, and J. STEINBERG (eds), *The Sage Handbook of Global Policing*. London: Sage.

BRADFORD, B. and QUINTON, P. (2014). Self-legitimacy, Police Culture and Support for Democratic Policing in an English Constabulary. *British Journal of Criminology*, 54: 1023–46.

BRADFORD, B., JAUREGUI, B., LOADER, I., and STEINBERG, J. (eds) (2016). *The Sage Handbook of Global Policing*. London: Sage.

BRADFORD, B., MURPHY, K., and JACKSON, J. (2014). 'Officers as Mirrors: Policing,

Procedural Justice and the (Re)Production of Social Identity'. *British Journal of Criminology*, 54(4): 527–50.

BRADFORD, B., TOPPING, J., MARTIN, R., and JACKSON, J. (2018). 'Can Diversity Promote Trust? Neighbourhood Context and Trust in the Police in Northern Ireland'. *Policing and Society*, 1–20, https://doi.org/10.1080/ 10439463.2018.1479409.

BRADLEY, D., WALKER, N., and WILKIE, R. (1986). *Managing the Police*. Brighton: Wheatsheaf.

BRADSHAW, E. A. (2013). 'This is What a Police State Looks Like: Sousveillance, Direct Action and the Anti-corporate Globalization Movement'. *Critical Criminology*, 21(4): 447–61.

BRAGA, A. A. (2008). *Problem-oriented Policing and Crime Prevention*. Monsey, NY: Willow Tree Press.

BRAGA, A. A. (2014). 'Problem-oriented Policing'. *Encyclopedia of Criminology and Criminal Justice*, 3989–4000.

BRAGA, A.A. and WEISBURD, D. (2010). *Policing Problem Places*. Oxford: Oxford University Press.

BRAITHWAITE, J. and DRAHOS, P. (2000). *Global Business Regulation*. Cambridge: Cambridge University Press.

BRATTON, W. (1998). 'Crime is Down: Blame the Police', in N. DENNIS (ed.), *Zero Tolerance: Policing a Free Society* (2nd edn). London: Institute of Economic Affairs.

BRAYNE, S. (2017). 'Big Data Surveillance: The Case of Policing'. *American Sociological Review*, 82(5): 977–1008.

BREDHOFF, S., WYNELL, S., and POTTER, L. A. (1999). 'The Arrest Records of Rosa Parks'. *Social Education*, (May/June) 63(4): 207–11.

BREWER, J. D. (1991). 'Policing in Divided Societies: Theorising a Type of Policing'. *Policing and Society*, 1(3): 179–91.

BREWER, J. D. (1994). *Black and Blue: Policing in South Africa*. Oxford: Oxford University Press.

BREWER, R. (2014). *Policing the Waterfront*. Oxford: Oxford University Press.

BRIGGS, D. (2012). *The English Riots of 2011*. Hook: Waterside Press.

BRODERICK, J. (1973) *Policing in a Time of Change*. Morristown: General Learning.

BRODEUR, J.-P. (1983). 'High and Low Policing: Remarks About the Policing of Political Activities'. *Social Problems*, 30(5): 507–20.

BRODEUR, J.-P. (ed.) (1998). *How to Recognize Good Policing: Problems and Issues*. Thousand Oaks, CA: Sage.

BRODEUR, J.-P. (1999). 'Cops and Spooks: The Uneasy Partnership'. *Police Practice and Research*, 1(3): 1–25.

BRODEUR, J.-P. (2007). 'An Encounter with Egon Bittner'. *Crime, Law and Social Change*, 48(1): 105–32.

BRODEUR, J.-P. (2007). 'High and Low Policing in Post-9/11 Times', 25–37.

BRODEUR, J.-P. (2010). *The Policing Web*. Oxford: Oxford University Press.

BROGDEN, M. (1982). *The Police: Autonomy and Consent*. London and New York: Academic Press.

BROGDEN, M. (1987). 'The Emergence of the Police: The Colonial Dimension'. *British Journal of Criminology*, 27(1): 4–14.

BROGDEN, M. (1991). *On the Mersey Beat: An Oral History of Policing Liverpool between the Wars*. Oxford: Oxford University Press.

BROGDEN, M. (1999). 'Community Policing as Cherry Pie', in R. MAWBY (ed.), *Policing across the World*. London: UCL Press.

BROGDEN, M. and NIJHAR, P. (2005). *Community Policing*. Cullompton: Willan.

BROGDEN, M. and SHEARING, C. (1993). *Policing for a New South Africa*. London: Routledge.

BROGDEN, M., FIELDING, N., WADDINGTON, P. A. J., and REINER, R. (1986). 'Review Symposium: The Politics of the Police'. *British Journal of Criminology*, 26(1): 94–105.

BROWN, D. (1997). *PACE Ten Years On: A Review of the Research*. Home Office Research Study 155. London: Home Office.

BROWN, G. R. (2016). 'The Blue Line on Thin Ice: Police use of Force Modifications in the Era of Cameraphones and YouTube'. *British Journal of Criminology*. 56: 293–312.

BROWN, J. (1996). 'Police Research: Some Critical Issues', in F. LEISHMAN, B. LOVEDAY, and S. SAVAGE (eds), *Core Issues in Policing*. London: Longman.

BROWN, J. (2000). 'Discriminatory Experiences of Women Police. A Comparison of Officers Serving in England and Wales, Scotland, Northern Ireland and the Republic of Ireland'. *International Journal of the Sociology of Law*, 28(2): 91–111.

BROWN, J. (2003). 'Women Leaders: A Catalyst for Change', in R. ADLAM and P. VILLIERS (eds), *Leadership in the Twenty-first Century*. Winchester: Waterside.

BROWN, J. (2011). 'We Mind and We Care but Have Things Changed? Assessment of Progress in the Reporting, Investigating and Prosecution of Allegations of Rape'. *Journal of Sexual Aggression*, 17(3): 263–72.

BROWN, J. (ed.) (2014). *The Future of Policing*. London and New York: Routledge.

BROWN, J. (2016). 'Revisiting the Classics: Women in Control? The Role of Women in Law Enforcement: Frances Heidensohn'. *Policing and Society*, 26(2): 230–7.

BROWN, J. and HEIDENSOHN, F. (2000). *Gender and Policing: Comparative Perspectives*. London: Macmillan Press.

BROWN, J. and HEIDENSOHN, F. (2012). 'From Juliet to Jane: Women Police in TV Cop Shows, Reality, Rank and Careers', in T. NEWBURN and J. PEAY (eds), *Policing: Politics, Culture and Control*. Oxford: Hart.

BROWN, J., BELUR, J., TOMPSON, L., MCDOWALL, A., HUNTER, G., and MAY, T. (2018). 'Extending the Remit of Evidence-based Policing'. *International Journal of Police Science & Management*, 20(1): 38–51.

BROWN, J., GOUSETI, I., and FIFE-SCHAW, C. (2017). 'Sexual Harassment Experienced by Police Staff Serving in England, Wales and Scotland: A Descriptive Exploration of Incidence, Antecedents and Harm'. *The Police Journal: Theory, Practice and Principles*, 91(4): 356–74.

BROWN, L. P. (2012). *Policing in the 21st century: Community Policing*. Bloomington, IN: AuthorHouse.

BROWN, M. (1981). *Working the Street*. New York: Russell Sage.

BROWN, R. M. (1969). 'The American Vigilante Tradition', in H. D. GRAHAM and T. R. GURR (eds), *Violence in America: Historical and Contemporary Perspectives*. Washington, DC: Staff Report to the National Commission on the Causes of Violence.

BROWN, S. (ed.) (2008). *Combating International Crime: The Longer Arm of the Law*. London: Routledge.

BROWNE-DIANIS, J. and SINHA, A. (2008). 'Exiling the Poor: The Clash of Redevelopment and Fair Housing in Post-Katrina New Orleans'. *Howard Law Journal*, 51(3): 481–508.

BRUGGEMAN, W. (2002). 'Policing an Accountability in a Dynamic European Context'. *Policing and Society*, 12: 259–73.

BRUNGER, M., TONG, S., and MARTIN, D. (eds) (2016). *Introduction to Policing Research*. Abingdon: Routledge.

BRYANT, R., COCKROFT, T., TONG, S., and WOOD, D. (2014). 'Police Training and Education: Past, Present and Future', in J. BROWN (ed.), *The Future of Policing*. London: Routledge.

BULLOCK, K. (2013). 'Community, Intelligence-led Policing and Crime Control'. *Policing and Society*, 23(2): 125–44.

BULLOCK, K. (2014). *Citizens, Community and Crime Control*. London: Palgrave Macmillan.

BULLOCK, K. and MILLIE, A. (eds) (2017). *The Special Constabulary*. London: Routledge.

BULLOCK, S. (2008). *Police Service Strength England and Wales*. London: Home Office.

BULLOUGH, O. (2018). *Moneyland*. London: Profile Books.

BUNYAN, T. (1977). *The Political Police in Britain*. London: Quartet Books.

BURKE, M. E. (1992). 'Cop Culture and Homosexuality'. *The Police Journal: Theory, Practice and Principles*, 65(1): 30–9.

BURKE, M. E. (1993). *Coming Out of the Blue*. London: Cassell.

BURKE, M. E. (1994). 'Prejudice and Discrimination: The Case of the Gay Police Officer'. *The Police Journal: Theory, Practice and Principles*, 67(3): 219–29.

BURROWS, J. and TARLING, R. (1982). *Clearing up Crime*. Home Office Research Unit. London: Home Office.

BUTLER, A. J. (1992). *Police Management* (2nd edn). Aldershot: Dartmouth.

BUTTON, M. (2002). *Private Policing*. Cullompton: Willan Press.

BUTTON, M. (2007). 'Assessing the Regulation of Private Security across Europe'. *European Journal of Criminology*, 4(1): 109–28.

BUTTON, M. (2008). *Doing Security*. London: Macmillan.

BUTTON, M. (2016). *Security Officers and Policing: Powers, Culture and Control in the Governance of Private Space*. London: Routledge.

BYERS, M. and JOHNSON, C. (2009). *The CSI Effect*. Lanham, MD: Lexington.

CAHILL, D. and KONINGS, M. (2017). *Neoliberalism*. Cambridge: Polity Press.

CAIN, M. (1973). *Society and the Policeman's Role*. London: Routledge & Kegan Paul.

CAIN, M. (2000). 'Orientalism, Occidentalism and the Sociology of Crime'. *British Journal of Criminology*, 40: 239–60.

CALESS, B. (2011). *Policing at the Top*. Bristol: Policy Press.

CALESS, B. and TONG, S. (2017). *Leading Policing in Europe*. Bristol: Policy Press.

CAMERON, D. (2012). *Speech to Centre for Social Justice*, 22 October, www.gov.uk/government/speeches/crime-and-justice-speech.pdf.

CAMERON, I. A. (1977). 'The Police of Eighteenth-Century France'. *European Studies Review*, 7: 47–75.

CAMERON, I. A. (1981). *Crime and Repression in the Auvergne and the Guyenne 1720–1790*. Cambridge: Cambridge University Press.

CAMP, J. and HEATHERTON, C. (eds) (2016). *Policing the Planet: Why the Policing Crisis Led to Black Lives Matter*. London: Verso.

CAMPBELL, B. (1993). *Goliath: Britain's Dangerous Places*. London: Methuen.

CANADIAN PRESS (CP) (2018). 'New DNA Analysis Could Solve 30-year-old Murders of Victoria Couple'. *Globe and Mail*, 10 April.

CAPE, E., and YOUNG, R. (eds) (2008). *Regulating Policing: The Police and Criminal Evidence Act 1984—Past, Present and Future*. Oxford: Hart.

CARLSON, J. M. (1985). *Prime Time Law Enforcement—Crime Show Viewing and Attitudes toward the Criminal Justice System*. Westport. CT: Praeger.

CARROLL, R. (2017). 'At LAX's New Private Terminal, the Rich are Pampered while the Normal People Suffer'. *The Guardian*, 16 May.

CASHMORE, E. (2002). *And Then There Was Television*. London: Routledge.

CASSAN, D. (2010). 'Police Socialisation in France and in England: How Do They Stand towards the Community Policing Model?'. *Cahiers Politiestudies: Journal of Police Studies*, (2010-13) 16: 243–60.

CASTELLS, M. (1996/2000). *The Information Age: Economy, Society and Culture* 1996–8, 2000–4 editions. Oxford: Blackwell: Vol. 1 *The Rise of the Network Society* (1996, 2nd edn 2000); Vol. 2 *The Power of Identity* (1997, 2nd edn 2004); Vol. 3, *End of the Millenium* (1998, 2nd edn 2000), 1996–2004.

CASTELLS, M. (2007) 'Communication, Power and Counter-power in the Networked Society'. *International Journal of Communication*, 1: 238–66.

CASTELLS, M. (2009/2013). *Communication Power*. Oxford: Oxford University Press.

CASTELLS, M. (2011). *The Rise of the Network Society*. Oxford: Wiley.

CAVADINO, M. and DIGNAN, J. (2006). *Penal Systems: A Comparative Approach*. London: Sage.

CAVENDER, G. (2004). 'Media and Crime Policy'. *Punishment and Society*, 6(3): 335–48.

CEREZALES, D. P. (2013). 'The Military and the (Colonial) Policing of Mainland Portugal 1850–1910', in C. O'REILLY (ed.), *Colonial Policing and the Transnational Legacy: The Global Dynamics of Policing Across the Lusophone Community*. Farnham: Ashgate.

CHADEE, D. and DITTON J. (2005). 'Fear of Crime and the Media: Assessing the Lack of Relationship'. *Crime, Media and Culture*, 1(3): 322–32.

CHAN, J. (1996). 'Changing Police Culture'. *British Journal of Criminology*, 36(1): 109–34.

CHAN, J. (1997). *Changing Police Culture: Policing in a Multicultural Society*. Cambridge: Cambridge University Press.

CHAN, J. (2003). *Fair Cop: Learning the Art of Policing*. Toronto: University of Toronto Press.

CHAN, J. and MOSES, L. B. (2017). 'Making Sense of Big Data for Security'. *The British Journal of Criminology*, 57(2): 299–319.

CHANDLER, R. (1944). 'The Simple Art of Murder'. *Atlantic Monthly*, December.

CHAPMAN, B. (1970). *Police State*. London: Macmillan.

CHAPPELL, D. and HUFNAGEL, S. (eds) (2014). *Contemporary Perspectives on the Detection, Investigation and Prosecution of Art Crime: Australasian, European and North American Perspectives*. Aldershot: Ashgate.

CHARMAN, S. (2017). *Police Socialisation, Identity and Culture: Becoming Blue*. New York: Springer International.

CHASE, S. (2013). 'CSEC Defends Practices in Wake of Brazilian Spy Reports'. *The Globe and Mail*, 9 October.

CHATTERTON, M. (1976). 'Police in Social Control', in J. KING (ed.), *Control Without Custody*. Cropwood Papers No. 7. Cambridge: Institute of Criminology.

CHATTERTON, M. (1979). 'The Supervision of Patrol Work under the Fixed Points System', in S. HOLDAWAY (ed.), *The British Police*. London: Edward Arnold.

CHATTERTON, M. (1983). 'Police Work and Assault Charges', in M. PUNCH (ed.), *Control in the Police Organization*. Cambridge, MA: MIT Press.

CHATTERTON, M. (1995). 'The Cultural Craft of Policing—Its Past and Future Relevance'. *Policing and Society*, 5(2): 97–108.

CHEAH, W. L (2010a). 'Mapping Interpol's Evolution: Functional Expansion and the Move towards Legalization', *Policing: A Journal of Policy and Practice* Vol. 4.1, 2010, pp 28–37.

CHEAH, W. L. (2010b). 'Policing Interpol: The Commission for the Control of Interpol's Files and the Right to Remedy'. *International Organizations Law Review*, 7: 375–404.

CHENERY S., HOLT, J., and PEASE, K. (1997). *Biting Back II: Reducing Repeat Victimisation in Huddersfield*, Crime Detection and Prevention Series Paper 82. London: Home Office.

CHESNEY-LIND, M. (2002). 'Criminalising Victimisation: The Unintended Consequences of Pro-arrest Policies for Girls and Women'. *Criminology and Public Policy*, 2(1): 81–90.

CHEVIGNY, P. (1995). *The Edge of the Knife: Police Violence in the Americas*. New York: New Press.

CHIBNALL, S. (1977). *Law and Order News*. London: Tavistock.

CHOONGH, S. (1997). *Policing as Social Discipline*. Oxford: Oxford University Press.

CHRISTIAN, L. (1983). *Policing by Coercion*. London: GLC Police Committee and Pluto Press.

CHRISTIAN, L. (2012). 'This Judgment in Favour of Kettling is a Missed Opportunity'. *The Guardian*, 15 March.

CLARK, D. (2007). 'Covert Surveillance and Informant Handling', in T. NEWBURN, T. WILLIAMSON, and A. WRIGHT (eds), *Handbook of Criminal Investigation*. Cullompton: Willan.

CLARK, J. P. (1965). 'Isolation of the Police: A Comparison of the British and American Situations'. *Journal of Criminal Law, Criminology and Police Science*, 56(3): 307–19.

CLARKE, R. and HOUGH, M. (1980). *The Effectiveness of Policing*. Farnborough: Gower.

CLARKE, R., and HOUGH, M. (1984). *Crime and Police Effectiveness*. Home Office Research Unit. London: Home Office.

COCKCROFT, T. (2013). *Police Culture: Themes and Concepts*. London: Routledge.

COHEN, P. (1979). 'Policing the Working Class City', in B. FINE, R. KINSEY, J. LEA, S. PICCIOTTO, and J. YOUNG (eds), *Capitalism and the Rule of Law*. London: Hutchinson.

COHEN, S. (1972). *Folk Devils and Moral Panics* (3rd edn). London: Routledge.

COHEN, S. (1985). *Visions of Social Control*. Cambridge: Polity Press.

COHEN, S. (1997). 'The Revenge of the Null Hypothesis: Evaluating Crime Control Policies'. *Critical Criminologist*, 8: 21–5.

COHEN, S. and YOUNG, J. (1973). *The Manufacture of News: A Reader*. London: Sage.

COLBRAN, M. (2014). *Media Representations of Police and Crime*. London: Palgrave.

COLE, B. A. (1999). 'Post Colonial Systems', in R. MAWBY (ed.), *Policing Across the World: Issues for the Twenty-first Century*. London: Routledge.

COLLEGE OF POLICING (2015). 'College of Policing Analysis: Estimating Demand on the Police Service', January. London.

COLMAN, A., and GORMAN, L. (1982). 'Conservatism, Dogmatism and Authoritarianism in British Police Officers'. *Sociology*, 16(1): 1–11.

COLVIN, R. (2015). 'Shared Workplace Experiences of Lesbian and Gay Police Officers in the United Kingdom', *Policing*, 38(2): 333–49.

CONNOLLY, K. (2008). 'German Supermarket Chain Lidl Accused of Snooping on Staff' *The Guardian*, 27 March.

COOLEY, D. (ed.) (2005). *Reimagining Policing in Canada*. Toronto: University of Toronto Press.

COOPER, V. and WHYTE, D. (eds) (2017). *The Violence of Austerity*. London: Pluto Press.

COPE, N. (2004). 'Intelligence Led Policing or Policing Led Intelligence? Integrating Volume Crime Analysis into Policing'. *British Journal of Criminology*, 44(2): 188–203.

COPE, N. (2008). '"Interpretation for Action?": Definitions and Potential of Crime Analysis for Policing', in T. NEWBURN (ed.), *Handbook of Policing*. Cullompton: Willan.

CORDNER G. W., GAINES, L. K., and KAPPELER, V. E. (1996). *Police Operations and Evaluation*, Cincinnati, OH: Anderson Publishing.

CORREIA, D. and WALL, T. (2018). *Police: A Field Guide*. London: Verso.

COTTERRELL, R. (1989). *The Politics of Jurisprudence: A Critical Introduction to Legal Philosophy*. London: Butterworths.

COTTERRELL, R. (1992). *The Sociology of Law* (2nd edn). London: Butterworths.

COUNCIL OF EUROPE. (2016). *European Committee on Crime Problems: Action Plan on Transnational Organised Crime*.

COUPE, T. and GRIFFITHS, M. (1996). *Solving Residential Burglary*, Crime Detection and Prevention Series, Paper 77. Home Office Police Research Group. London: Home Office.

COURTIN, Y., DEUNET, P., GILBERT, G., and WILLEM, J.-J. (2002). 'La coopération au jour le jour'. *Les Cahiers de la Sécurité Intérieure—Dossier spécial : 'Polices post-communistes—Une transformation inachevée ?*. 41(3): 175–89.

COX, B., SHIRLEY, J., and SHORT, M. (1977). *The Fall of Scotland Yard*. Harmondsworth: Penguin.

CRANK, J. P. (2004). *Understanding Police Culture* (2nd edn). Cincinatti, OH: Anderson Publishing.

CRAWFORD, A. (2006). 'Policing and Security as "Club Goods": The New Enclosures', in J. WOOD and B. DUPONT (eds), *Democracy, Society and the Governance of Security*. Cambridge: Cambridge University Press.

CRAWFORD, A. (2008/2011). 'Plural Policing in the UK: Policing Beyond the Police', in T. NEWBURN (ed.), *Handbook of Policing* (2nd edn). London: Routledge.

CRAWFORD, A. and EVANS, K. (2017). 'Crime prevention and community safety' in A. Liebling, S. MARUNA and L. McARA (eds) *Oxford Handbook of Criminology* (6th edn). Oxford: Oxford University Press.

CRAWFORD, A. and LISTER, S. (2004). *The Extended Policing Family: Visible Patrols in Residential Areas*. York: Joseph Rowntree Foundation.

CRAWFORD, A., LISTER, S., BLACKBURN, S., and BURNETT, J. (2005). *Plural Policing: The Mixed Economy of Visible Patrols in England and Wales*. Bristol: Policy Press.

CRAY, E. (1972). *The Enemy in the Streets*. New York: Anchor.

CRITCHER, C. and WADDINGTON, D. (eds) (1996). *Policing Public Order: Theoretical and Practical Issues*. Aldershot: Avebury.

CRITCHLEY, T. A. (1970). *The Conquest of Violence*. London: Constable.

CRITCHLEY, T. A. (1978). *A History of Police in England and Wales* (2nd edn). London: Constable [1st edn, 1967].

CROUCH, C. (2004). *Post-democracy*. Malden, MA: Polity Press.

CROWTHER, C. (2000a). 'Thinking about the "Underclass": Towards a Political Economy of Policing'. *Theoretical Criminology*, 4(2): 149–68.

CROWTHER, C. (2000b). *Policing Urban Poverty*. London: Macmillan.

CUMMING, E., CUMMING, I., and EDELL, L. (1965). 'The Policeman as Philosopher, Guide and Friend'. *Social Problems*, 12(3): 276–86.

CUNNINGHAM, W. C., STRAUCHS, J. J., and VAN METER, C. W. (1990). *Private Security Trends 1970–2000: The Hallcrest Report II*. Boston: Butterworths.

CURRIE, E. (1998a). 'Crime and Market Society: Lessons from the United States', in P. WALTON and J. YOUNG (eds), *The New Criminology Revisited*. London: Macmillan.

CURRIE, E. (1998b). *Crime and Punishment in America*. New York: Holt.

CURTO, JOSÉ (2004) *Enslaving Spirits: The Portuguese-Brazilian alcohol trade at Luanda and its Hinterland 1550–1830*. Leiden: Brill Publishers.

CURTO, JOSÉ and LOVEJOY, P. E. (2004). *Enslaving Connections: Changing Cultures of Africa and Brazil during the Era of Slavery*. Amherst, NY: Humanity Books.

DAHRENDORF, R. (1985). *Law and Order*. London: Sweet & Maxwell.

DALEY, H. (1986). *This Small Cloud*. London: Weidenfeld.

DALY, J. (2018). *Crime and Punishment in Russia: A Comparative History*. London: Bloomsbury.

DANIELS, R. J., TREBILCOCK, M. J., and CARSON, L. D. (2011). 'Commitments to Legality in Former British Colonies'. *American Journal of Comparative Law*, 59(1): 111–78.

DARROCH, S. and MAZEROLLE, L. (2012). 'Intelligence-led Policing: A Comparative Analysis of Organizational Factors Influencing Innovation Uptake'. *Police Quarterly*, 16: 3–27.

DAS, D. and MARENIN, O. (2017). *Trends in Policing: Interviews with Police Leaders Across the Globe*. London: CRC Press.

DAVIES, L. D. (1930). *The Problem of the Twentieth Century: A Study in International Relationships*. London: E. Benn Publishers.

DAVIES, W. (2016). *The Limits of Neoliberalism*. London: Sage.

DAVIS, A. J. (ed.) (2017). *Policing the Black Man: Arrest, Prosecution and Imprisonment*. New York: Vintage.

DAVIS, J. (1984). 'A Poor Man's System of Justice: The London Police Courts in the Second Half of the 19th Century'. *Historical Journal*, 27(2): 309–35.

DAVIS, M. (1990). *City of Quartz*. London: Vintage.

DE LINT, W., O'CONNOR, D., and COTTER, R. (2007). 'Controlling the Flow: Security, Exclusivity and Criminal Intelligence in Ontario'. *International Journal of the Sociology of Law*, 35(1): 41–58.

DE MAILLARD, J. and ZAGRODZKI, M. (2017). 'Plural Policing in Paris: Variations and Pitfalls of Cooperation between National and Municipal Police Forces'. *Policing and Society*, 27(1): 54–67.

DE PAUW, E., PONSARS, P., VAN DER VIJVER, K., BRUGGERMAN, W., and DEELMAN, P. (eds) (2011). 'Technology-Led Policing'. *Journal of Police Studies*, 3(2). Antwerpen-Apeldoorn-Portland: Maklu.

DEFLEM, M. (1994). 'Law Enforcement in Colonial Africa: A Comparative Analysis of Imperial Policing in Nyasaland, the Gold Coast and Kenya'. *Police Studies*, 17(1): 45–65.

DEFLEM, M. (2000). 'Bureaucratization and Social Control: Historical Foundations of International Police Cooperation', *Law and Society Review*, 34(3): 739–78.

DEFLEM, M. (2002). *Policing World Society: Historical Foundations of International Police Co-operation*. Oxford: Clarendon.

DEFLEM, M. (2006). 'Europol and the Policing of International Terrorism: Counter-terrorism in a Global Perspective'. *Justice Quarterly*, 23(3): 336–59.

DEFLEM, M. (ed.) (2016). *The Politics of Policing: Between Force and Legitimacy*. Bingley: Emerald.

DEFLEM, M. and STUPHIN, S. (2009). 'Policing Katrina: Managing Law Enforcement in New Orleans'. *Policing*, 3(1): 41–9.

DELLA PORTA, D., and REITER, H. (eds) (1998). *Policing Protest*. Minneapolis, MN: University of Minnesota Press.

DELLA PORTA, D., PETERSON, A., and REITER, H. (eds) (2006). *The Policing of Transnational Protest*. Aldershot: Ashgate.

DELPEUCH, T. and ROSS, J. E. (2016). *Comparing the Democratic Governance of Police Intelligence*. Northampton, MA: Edward Elgar.

DELSOL, R (2006). *Institutional Racism, the Police and Stop and Search: A Comparative Study of Stop and Search at a Local Level in the UK and USA*, PhD Thesis: University of Warwick.

DELSOL, R., and SHINER, M. (2006). 'Regulating Stop and Search: A Challenge for Police and Community Relations in England and Wales'. *Critical Criminology*, 14(3): 241–63.

DELSOL, R. and SHINER, M. (eds) (2015). *Stop and Search. The Anatomy of a Police Power*. Basingstoke: Palgrave Macmillan.

DEN BOER, M. (2002a) *Organized Crime: A Catalyst in the Europeanisation of National Police and Prosecution Agencies?* Maastricht: European Institute of Public Administration.

DEN BOER, M. (2002b). 'Towards an Accountability Regime for an Emerging European Police Governance'. *Policing and Society*, 12(2): 275–90.

DEN BOER, M. (2010). 'Towards a Governance Model of Police Cooperation in Europe: The Twist between Networks and Bureaucracies', in F. LEMIEUX (ed.), *International Police Cooperation: Emerging Issues, Theory and Practice*. Portland, OR: Willan.

DEN BOER, M. and BLOCK, L. (2013). *Liaison Officers: essential actors in transnational policing*. Den Haag: Eleven International Publishing.

DEN BOER, M. (2014). 'Police, Policy and Politics in Brussels: Scenarios for the Shift from Sovereignty to Solidarity', in C. KAUNERT, J. OCCHIPINTI, and S. LEONARD (eds), *Supranational Governance of Europe's Area of Freedom, Security and Justice*. London: Routledge.

DEN BOER, M. (2015) 'Police Cooperation: A Reluctant Dance with the Supranational EU Institutions', in F. TRAUNER and A. R. SERVENT (eds), *Policy Change in the Area of Freedom, Security and Justice: How EU Institutions Matter*. London: Routledge.

DEN BOER, M., HILLEBRAND, C., and NÖLKE A. (2008). 'Legitimacy under Pressure: The European Web of Counter-Terrorism Networks'. *Journal of Common Market Studies*, 46(1): 101–24.

DENNIS, N. (ed.) (1998). *Zero Tolerance : Policing a Free Society*. London : Institute of Economic Affairs.

DEVROE, E. (2017). 'Bringing Politics Back into the Study of Policing? A Case Study on the Policing of Social Disorder in Belgium'. *Policing and Society*, 27(1): 82–103.

DEVROE, E., EDWARDS, A., and PONSAERS, P. (eds) (2017). *Policing European Metropolises: The Politics of Security in City-Regions*. London: Taylor & Francis.

DEVROE, E., PONSAARS, P., MOOR, L. G., GREENE, J., SKINNS, L., BISSCHOP, L., VERHAGE, A., and BACON, M. (eds) (2012). 'Tides and Currents in Police Theories'. *Journal of Police Studies*, 25. Antwerpen-Apeldoorn-Portland: Maklu.

DICK, P., SIVESTRI, M., and WESTMARLAND, L. (2014). 'Women Police: Potential and Possibilities for Reform', in J. BROWN (ed.), *The Future of Policing*. London: Routledge.

DILLON, M. (2012). *China: A Modern History*. New York: I. B. Taurus.

DIPHOORN, T. G. (2016). *Twilight Policing: Private Security and Violence in Urban South Africa*. Oakland, CA: University of California Press.

DITTON, J., CHADEE, D., FARRALL, S., GILCHRIST, E., and BANNISTER, J. (2004). 'From Imitation to Intimidation: A Note on the Curious and Changing Relationship between the Media, Crime and Fear of Crime'. *British Journal of Criminology*, 44(4): 595–610.

DIXON, B. and SMITH, G. (1998). 'Laying Down the Law: The Police, the Courts and

Legal Accountability'. *International Journal of the Sociology of Law*, 26: 419–35.

DIXON, D. (1997). *Law in Policing*. Oxford: Oxford University Press.

DIXON, D. (2008). 'Authorise and Regulate: A Comparative Perspective on the Rise and Fall of a Regulatory Strategy', in E. CAPE and R. YOUNG (eds), *Regulating Policing*. Oxford: Hart.

DODD, V. (2017). 'Cressida Dick Appointed First Female Met Police Commissioner'. *The Guardian*, 22 February.

DODGE, K. A., BIERMAN, K. L., COIE, J. D., GREENBERG, M. T., LOCHMAN, J. E., MCMAHON, R. J., PINDERHUGHES, E. E., and CONDUCT PROBLEMS PREVENTION RESEARCH GROUP (2014). 'Impact of Early Intervention on Psychopathology, Crime, and Well-being at Age 25'. *American Journal of Psychiatry*, 172(1): 59–70.

DODSWORTH, F. M. (2007). 'Police and Prevention of Crime: Commerce, Temptation and the Corruption of the Body Politic, from Fielding to Colquhoun'. *British Journal of Criminology*, 47(3): 439–54.

DOLAN, C. (2015). 'Trialogues: What goes on behind closed doors?'. *EurActiv*. https://Www.Euractiv.Com/Section/Eu-Priorities-2020/Opinion/Trialogues-What-Goes-On-Behind-Closed-Doors/.

DORLING, D. (2004). 'Prime Suspect: Murder in Britain', in P. HILLYARD, C. PANTAZIS, S. TOMBS, and D. GORDON (eds), *Beyond Criminology*. London: Pluto Press.

DOUGLAS, M. (1999). 'Four Cultures: The Evolution of a Parsimonious Model'. *GeoJournal*, 47(3): 411–15.

DOWNES, D. and MORGAN, R. (2007). 'No Turning Back: The Politics of Law and Order into the Millennium', in M. MAGUIRE, R. MORGAN, and R. REINER (eds), *The Oxford Handbook of Criminology* (4th edn). Oxford: Oxford University Press.

DOWNES, D., ROCK, P., and MCLAUGHLIN, E. (2016). *Understanding Deviance: A Guide to the Sociology of Crime and Rule Breaking* (7th edn). Oxford: Oxford University Press.

DOYLE, A. (2003). *Arresting Images: Crime and Policing in Front of the Television Camera*. Toronto: University of Toronto Press.

DOYLE, A. (2005). 'Surveillance and Military Transformation: Organizational Trends in Twenty-First Century Armed Services', in R. V. ERICSON and K. D. HAGGERTY (eds), *The New Politics of Surveillance and Visibility*. Toronto: University of Toronto Press.

DOYLE, A., LIPPERT, R., and LYON, D. (2013). *Eyes Are Everywhere: The Global Growth of Camera Surveillance*. London: Routledge.

DUBBER, M. (2005). *The Police Power: Patriarchy and the Foundations of American Government*. New York: Columbia University Press.

DUBBER, M. and VALVERDE, M. (eds) (2006). *The New Police Science*. Stanford, CA: Stanford University Press.

DUBOIS, W. E. B. (1904). *Some Notes on Negro Crime, Particularly in Georgia*. Atlanta, GA: Atlanta University Press [reprinted in DUBOIS, W. E. B. (ed.) (1968). *Atlanta University Publications*, Vol. II. New York: Octagon Books].

DUGAN, L. (2003). 'Domestic Violence Legislation: Exploring its Impact on the Likelihood of Domestic Violence, Police Involvement, and Arrest'. *Criminology and Public Policy*, 2(2), 283–312.

DUNHAM, R. G. and ALPERT, G. P. (2015). *Critical Issues in Policing: Contemporary Readings* (7th edn). Long Grove, IL: Waveland Press.

DUNHILL, C. (ed.) (1989). *The Boys in Blue: Women's Challenge to Policing*. London: Virago.

DUNNAGE, J. (1997). *The Italian Police and the Rise of Fascism: A Case Study of the Province of Bologna 1897–1925*, Westport, CT: Praeger.

DUNNIGHAN, C. and NORRIS, C. (1999). 'The Detective, the Snout and the Audit Commission: The Real Cost of Using Informants'. *Howard Journal of Criminal Justice*, 38(1): 67–86.

Dupont, B. (2001). 'Technological Errors of the Past in Perspective', in M. Enders and B. Dupont (eds), *Policing the Lucky Country*, Annandale, NSW: Hawkins Press.

Easton, M. and Dormaels, A. (2017). 'Reflections on the Triple Helix as a Vehicle to Stimulate Innovation in Technology and Security: A Belgian Case Study' *International Journal of Comparative and Applied Criminal Justice*, http://hdl.handle.net/1854/LU-8514073.

Easton, M., den Boer, M., Janssens, J., Moelker, R., and Vander Beken, T. (2010). *Blurring Military and Police Roles*, The Hague: Eleven Publishers (Het Groene Gras).

Eck, J. and Spelman, W. (2016). *Problem Oriented Policing*. Washington, DC: National Institute of Justice.

Eddo-Lodge, R. (2017). *Why I'm No Longer Talking to White People about Race*. London: Bloomsbury.

Edwards, S. (1989). *Policing 'Domestic' Violence*. London: Sage.

Egerton, D. (2007). *The Shock of the Old: Technology and Global History since 1900*. London: Profile Books.

Eick, V. and Briken, K. (2014). *Urban (In) Security: Policing the Neoliberal Crisis*. Ottawa: Red Quill Books.

Eisner, M. (2001). 'Modernisation, Self-control and Lethal Violence: The Long-term Dynamics of European Homicide Rates in Theoretical Perspective'. *British Journal of Criminology*, 41: 618–38.

Eisner, M. (2003). 'Long-term Historical Trends In Violent Crime'. *Crime and Justice*, 30: 83–142.

Eisner, M. (2014). 'From Swords to Words: Does Macro-Level Change in Self-Control Predict Long-Term Variation in Levels of Homicide?'. *Crime and Justice*, 43(1): 65–134.

Eisner, M. (2015). 'Holding Violence Down'. *New Scientist*, 225(3007): 26–7.

Elias, N. (2000). *The Civilizing Process: Sociogenetic and Psychogenetic Investigations*. Cambridge: Blackwell.

Ellis, T., Hamai, K., and Williamson, T. (2008). 'Japanese Community Policing Under the Microscope', in T. Williamson (ed.), *The Handbook of Knowledge-Based Policing: Current Conceptions and Future Directions*. Chichester, West Sussex: Wiley.

Ellison, G. (2007). 'A Blueprint for Democratic Policing Anywhere in the World?: Police Reform, Political Transition, and Conflict Resolution in Northern Ireland'. *Police Quarterly*, 10(3): 243–69.

Ellison, G. (2010). 'Police Community Relations in Northern Ireland in the Post-Patten Era: Towards an Ecological Analysis', in J. Doyle (ed.), *Policing the Narrow Ground: Lessons from the Transformation of Policing in Northern Ireland*. Dublin: Royal Irish Academy.

Ellison, G. and O'Reilly, C. (2006). 'Eye Spy Private High: Re-conceptualizing High Policing Theory', *British Journal of Criminology*, 46(4): 641–60.

Ellison, G. and Pino, N. (2012). *Globalization, Police Reform and Development: Doing it the Western Way*. London: Palgrave Macmillan.

Ellison, G. and Smyth, J. (2000). *The Crowned Harp: Policing Northern Ireland*. London: Pluto Press.

Ellul, J. (1964). *The Technological Society*. New York: Alfred A. Knopf.

Ellul, J. (1965). *Propaganda: The Formations of Men's Attitudes*. New York: Alfred A. Knopf.

Emsley, C. (1983). *Policing and Its Context 1750–1870*. London: Macmillan.

Emsley, C. (1996). *The English Police: A Political and Social History* (2nd edn). London: Longman.

Emsley, C. (1999). 'A Typology of Nineteenth-century Police', *Crime, Histoire & Sociétés/Crime History & Societies*, 3(1): 29–44.

EMSLEY, C. (2007). *Crime, Police, and Penal Policy: European Experiences 1750–1940*. Oxford: Oxford University Press.

EMSLEY, C. (2011). *Theories and Origins of the Modern Police*, Farnham: Ashgate.

EMSLEY, C. (2014). 'Policing the Empire: Some Thoughts on Models and Types' *Crime, Histoire & Sociétés/Crime History & Societies*, 18(2): 5–25.

EMSLEY, C. and SHPAYER-MAKOV, H. (2006). *Police Detectives in History, 1750–1950*. Aldershot: Ashgate.

ENGEL, R. and HENDERSON, S. (2014). 'Beyond Rhetoric: Establishing Police-Academic Partnerships That Work', in J. BROWN (ed.), *The Future of Policing*. London: Routledge.

Engels, F. (1844). *The Condition of the Working Class in England*, republished by Oxford University Press 2009.

EPP, C. R., MAYNARD-MOODY, R., and HAIDER-MARKEL, D. (2014). *Pulled Over: How Police Stops Define Race and Citizenship*. Chicago, IL: University of Chicago Press.

ERICSON, R. V. (1981). *Making Crime: A Study of Detective Work*. Toronto: Butterworths.

ERICSON, R. V. (1982). *Reproducing Order: A Study of Police Patrol Work*. Toronto: University of Toronto Press.

ERICSON, R. V. (1983). *The Constitution of Legal Inequality: The 1983 John Porter Memorial Lecture*. Ottawa: Carleton University Press.

ERICSON, R. V. (1989). 'Patrolling the Facts: Secrecy and Publicity in Police Work'. *British Journal of Sociology*, 40(2): 205–26.

ERICSON, R. V. (1993). *Making Crime: A Study of Detective Work* (2nd edn). Toronto: University of Toronto Press.

ERICSON, R. V. (1994). 'The Division of Expert Knowledge In Policing and Security'. *British Journal of Sociology*, 45(2): 149–75.

ERICSON, R. V. (2007). *Crime in an Insecure World*. Cambridge: Polity Press.

ERICSON, R. V. and HAGGERTY, K. D. (1997). *Policing the Risk Society*. Oxford: Clarendon.

ERICSON, R. and HAGGERTY, K. (2002). 'The Policing of Risk', in T. NEWBURN (ed.), *Policing—Key Readings* (2005). Cullompton: Willan. (2005),

ERICSON, R. V. and HAGGERTY, K. D. (eds) (2005a), *The New Politics of Surveillance and Visibility*. Toronto: University of Toronto Press.

ERICSON, R. V. and HAGGERTY, K. D. (2005b). 'The Surveillant Assemblage', *British Journal of Sociology*, 51(4): 605–22.

ERICSON, R. V. and SHEARING, C.D. (1986). 'The Scientification of Police Work', in G. BÖHME and N. STEHR (eds), *The Knowledge Society*. Dordrecht, Kluwer.

ERICSON, R. V., BARANEK, P. M., and CHAN, J. B. (1991). *Representing Order: Crime, Law, and Justice in the News Media*. Milton Keynes: Open University Press.

ETORNO, J. A. and BARROW, C. S. (2017). 'Causes, Theories and Solutions' in J. D. WARD (ed.), *Policing and Race in America: Economic, Political and Social Dynamics*. Lanham, MD: Lexington Books.

ETERNO, J. A. and SILVERMAN, E. B. (2012). *The Crime Numbers Game: Management by Manipulation*. Boca Raton, FL: CRC Press.

EUROPEAN COMMISSION (2009). *The Lisbon Treaty's impact on the Justice and Home Affairs (JHA) Council*, https://www.con-silium.europa.eu/uedocs/cms_data/docs/pressdata/en/ec/111615.pdf.

EVANS, R. (2018a). 'Undercover Policing Inquiry: Victims Launch Legal Action'. *The Guardian*, 15 July.

EVANS, R. (2018b). 'Police Spies Infiltrated UK Leftwing Groups For Decades'. *The Guardian*, 15 October.

EYAL, N. (with Ryan Hoover) (2014). *Hooked: How to Build Habit-forming Products*. New York: Penguin.

FAGAN, J. (2016). 'Terry's Original Sin', *University of Chicago Legal Forum*, 43–97.

FALKER-KANTOR, M. (2018). *Policing Los Angeles*. Chapel Hill, NC: University of North Carolina Press.

FARRELL, G. (2013). 'Five Tests for a Theory of the Crime Drop'. *Crime Science*, 2(5): 1–8.

FARRELL, G. and PEASE, K. (2001). *Repeat Victimization*. Monsey, NY: Criminal Justice Press.

FASSIN, D. (2013). *Enforcing Order: An Ethnography of Urban Policing*. Cambridge: Polity Press.

FASSIN, D. (2017). *Writing the World of Policing: The Difference Ethnography Makes*. Chicago, IL: University of Chicago Press.

FAULL, A. (2017a). 'Police Culture and Personal Identity in South Africa'. *Policing*, 11(3): 332–45.

FAULL, A. (2017b). *Police Work and Identity: A South African Ethnography*. Abingdon: Routledge.

FAULL, A. (2018). *Police Work and Identity*. London: Routledge.

FEELEY, M. M. (2001). 'Three Voices of Socio-Legal Studies'. *Israel Law Review*, 35(2–3): 175–204.

FELDMAN, D. (1990). 'Regulating Treatment of Suspects in Police Stations: Judicial Interpretations of Detention Provisions in the Police and Criminal Evidence Act 1984'. *Criminal Law Review*, 452–71.

FERGUSON, A. G. (2017). *The Rise of Big Data Policing: Surveillance, Race and the Future of Law Enforcement*. New York: New York University Press.

FEYS, Y., VERHAGE, A., and BOELS, D. (2018). 'A State-of-the-art Review on Police Accountability: What Do We Know from Empirical Studies?'. *International Journal of Police Science & Management*, https://doi.org/10.1177/1461355718786297.

FIELD, J. (1981). 'Police, Power and Community in a Provincial English Town: Portsmouth 1815–75', in V. BAILEY (ed.), *Policing and Punishment in 19th Century Britain*. London: Croom Helm.

FIELDING, N. (1988). *Joining Forces*. London: Routledge.

FIELDING, N. (1989). 'Police Culture and Police Practice', in M. WEATHERITT (ed.), *Police Research: Some Future Prospects*. Aldershot: Avebury.

FIELDING, N. (1995). *Community Policing*. Oxford: Oxford University Press.

FIELDING, N. (2002). 'Theorising Community Policing'. *British Journal of Criminology*, 42(1): 147–63.

FIELDING, N. (2005). *The Police and Social Conflict*. (2nd edn). London: Routledge.

FIELDING, N. and INNES, M. (2006). 'Reassurance Policing, Community Policing and Measuring Police Performance'. *Policing and Society*, 16(2): 127–45.

FIELDING, N. (2018). Professionalizing the Police: *The Unfulfilled Promise of Police Training* Oxford: Clarendon.

FIJNAUT, C. (1991). 'Europeanisation or Americanisation of the Police in Europe?'. *Proceedings European Police Summer-Course*, 2: 19–27. Apeldoorn: Nederlandse Politie.

FIJNAUT, C. (1993). 'The "Communitization" of Police Cooperation in Western Europe', in H. G. SCHERMERS, C. FLINTERMAN, and A. KELLERMAN (eds), *Free Movement of Persons in Europe: Legal Problems and Experiences*. Dordrecht: Nijhoff.

FIJNAUT, C. (ed.) (2002). 'Special Issue of Policing and Society on Police Accountability in Europe', *Policing and Society* 12(4).

FIJNAUT, C. (2004). 'Police Cooperation and the Area of Freedom, Security and Justice', in N. WALKER (ed.), *Europe's Area of Freedom, Security and Justice*. Oxford: Oxford University Press.

FIJNAUT, C. and MARX, G. (eds) (1995). *Undercover: Police Surveillance in Comparative Perspective*. The Hague: Kluwer Law International.

FINE, B. and MILLAR, R. (eds) (1985). *Policing the Miners' Strike*. London: Lawrence & Wishart.

FINNANE, M. (1994). *Police and Government: Histories of Policing in Australia*. Melbourne: Oxford University Press.

FINNANE, M. (2002). *When Police Unionise: The Politics of Law and Order in Australia*. Annandale, NSW: Federation Press.

FISHMAN, M. and CAVENDER, G. (1998). *Entertaining Crime: Television Reality Programs*, New York: Aldine de Gruyter.

FITZGERALD, M. and SIBBITT, R. (1997). *Ethnic Monitoring in Police Forces: A Beginning*, Home Office Research Study 173, Home Office Research and Statistics Directorate, 36. London: Home Office.

FITZGERALD, M., HOUGH, M., JOSEPH, I., and QURESHI, T. (2002). *Policing For London*. Cullompton: Willan.

FLATLEY, J. (2016). *Crime in England and Wales*. London: Office for National Statistics.

FLATLEY, J. (2018). *Crime in England and Wales*. London: Office for National Statistics.

FLEMING, J. (ed.) (2015). *Police Leadership*. Oxford: Oxford University Press.

FOGG, B. J. (2003). *Persuasive Technology: Using Computers to Change What We Think And Do*. San Francisco, CA: Morgan Kaufmann Publishers.

FORD, L. (2010). *Settler Sovereignty— Jurisdiction and Indigenous People in America and Australia 1788–1836*, Cambridge, MA: Harvard University Press.

FORRESTER, D., CHATTERTON, M., and PEASE, K. (1988). *The Kirkholt Burglary Prevention Project*. Crime Prevention Unit Paper 13. London: Home Office.

FORSELL, N. (1928/2018). *Fouché, the Man Napoleon Feared*, trans from Swedish by A. Harwell, New York: Frederick A. Stokes & Co [Reprint published by Forgotten Books].

FOSDICK, R. (1915). *European Police Systems*. New York: Century Books.

FOSDICK, R. (1920). *American Police Systems*. New York: Century Books.

FOSTER, J. (1989). 'Two Stations: An Ethnographic Study of Policing in the Inner City', in D. DOWNES (ed.), *Crime and the City*. London: Macmillan.

FOSTER, J. (2003). 'Police Cultures', in T. NEWBURN (ed.), *Handbook of Policing*. Cullompton: Willan.

FOSTER, J. (2008). '"It might have been incompetent, but it wasn't racist": Murder Detectives' Perceptions of the Lawrence Inquiry and its Impact on Homicide Investigation in London'. *Policing and Society*, 18(2), 89–112.

FOSTER, J., NEWBURN, T., and SOUHAMI, A. (2005). *Assessing the Impact of the Stephen Lawrence Enquiry*. London: Home Office.

FOUCAULT, M. (1994). 'The Political Technology of Individuals', in P. RABINOW (ed.), *Power*. London: Penguin.

FOWLER, S. (2008). 'Legal Attachés and Liaison: The FBI', in S. BROWN (ed.), *Combating International Crime: The Longer Arm of the Law*. London: Routledge-Cavendish.

FRANTZ, J. B. (1969). 'The Frontier Tradition: An Invitation to Violence', in H. D. GRAHAM and T. R. GURR (eds), *Violence in America: Historical and Contemporary Perspectives*. Washington, DC: Staff Report to the National Commission on the Causes of Violence.

FRIEDERSDORF, C. (2016). 'A Police Department's Secret Formula for Judging Danger'. *The Atlantic*, 13 January.

FROGNER, L., ANDERSHED, H., LINDBERG, O., and JOHANSSON, M. (2013). 'Directed Patrol for Preventing City Centre Street Violence in Sweden—a Hot Spot Policing Intervention'. *European Journal on Criminal Policy and Research*, 19(4): 333–50.

FUKUYAMA, F. (2012). *The Origins of Political Order: From Pre-human Times to the French Revolution*. New York: Farrar, Straus and Giroux.

FYFE, N. R. (2014). 'A Different and Divergent Trajectory? Reforming the Structure, Governance and Narrative of Policing in Scotland', in J. BROWN (ed.), *The Future of Policing*. London: Routledge.

FYFE, N. R., GUNDHUS H. O. I., and RØNN, K. V. (2017). *Moral Issues in Intelligence-led Policing*. London: Routledge.

GADD, D. (2017). 'Domestic Violence' in A. LIEBLING, S. MARUNA, and L. McARA (eds), *The Oxford Handbook of Criminology* (6th edn). Oxford: Oxford University Press.

GALLIE, W. B. (1953). *Essentially Contested Concepts*. Oxford: Blackwell.

GAMBLE, A. (1994). *The Free Economy and the Strong State*. London: Macmillan.

GANAPATHY, N. and BROADHURST, R. (eds) (2008). 'Organized Crime in Asia'. *Special Issue of the Asian Journal of Criminology*, 3(1).

GARLAND, D. (1996). 'The Limits of the Sovereign State: Strategies of Crime Control in Contemporary Societies'. *British Journal of Criminology*, 36(4): 1–27.

GARLAND, D. (1997). '"Governmentality" and the Problem of Crime: Foucault, Criminology, and Sociology'. *Theoretical Criminology*, 1(2): 173–214.

GARLAND, D. (2001). *The Culture of Control*. Oxford: Oxford University Press.

GARRIOTT, W. (ed.) (2013). *Policing and Contemporary Governance: The Anthropology of Police in Practice*. New York: Palgrave Macmillan.

GATRELL, V. (1980). 'The Decline of Theft and Violence in Victorian and Edwardian England', in V. GATRELL, B. LENMAN, and G. PARKER (eds), *Crime and the Law*. London: Europa.

GATRELL, V. (1990). 'Crime, Authority and the Policeman-State 1750–1950', in F. M. THOMPSON (ed.), *The Cambridge Social History of Britain*. Cambridge: Cambridge University Press.

GATRELL, V. (1994). *The Hanging Tree*. Oxford: Oxford University Press.

GAUNTLETT, D. (2005). *Moving Experiences Second Edition: Media Effects and Beyond*. Bloomington, IN: Indiana University Press.

GEARY, R. (1985). *Policing Industrial Disputes*. Cambridge: Cambridge University Press.

GELLER, W. A. and MORRIS, N. (1992). 'Relations between Federal and Local Police', in M. TONRY (ed.), *Modern Policing: Crime and Justice and Review of the Research, Vol. 15*, Chicago, IL: University of Chicago Press.

GIACOMANTONIO, C. (2014). 'A Typology of Police Organizational Boundaries'. *Policing and Society*, 24(5): 545–64.

GIACOMANTONIO, C. (2015). *Policing Integration: The Sociology of Police Co-ordination Work*. London: Palgrave Macmillan.

GIDDENS, A. (1986). *The Constitution of Society: Outline of the Theory of Structuration*. Berkeley and Los Angeles, CA: University of California Press.

GILBERT, G. (2009). 'The Cop Drama that Rewrote TV History'. *The Independent*, 24 March.

GILENS, M. (2014). *Affluence and Influence*. Princeton, NJ: Princeton University Press.

GILL, P. (1987). 'Clearing Up Crime: The Big "Con"'. *Journal of Law and Society*, 14(2): 254–65.

GILL, P. (1994). *Policing Politics: Security Intelligence and the Liberal Democratic State*. London: Frank Cass.

GILL, P. (1998). 'Making Sense of Police Intelligence? The Use of a Cybernetic Model in Analysis Information and Power in Police Intelligence Processes'. *Policing and Society*, 8: 289–314.

GILL, P. (2000). *Rounding Up the Usual Suspects: Developments in Contemporary Law Enforcement Intelligence*. Aldershot: Ashgate.

GILL, P. (2014). 'Thinking about Intelligence Within, Without, and Beyond the State'. *All Azimuth*, 3(2): 5–20.

GILL, P. and PHYTHIAN, M. (2018). *Intelligence in an Insecure World* (3rd edn). Cambridge: Polity Press.

GILL, P., MARRIN, S., and PHYTHIAN, M. (2007). *Intelligence Theory: Key Questions and Debates*. London: Routledge.

GILLIGAN, J. (2011). *Why Some Politicians are More Dangerous than Others*. Cambridge: Polity Press.

GILLING, D. (2007). *Crime Prevention and Community Safety*. Cullompton: Willan.

GILMORE, J., JACKSON, W., and MONK, H. (2017). '"That is not facilitating peaceful protest. That is dismantling the protest": Anti-fracking Protesters' Experiences of Dialogue Policing and Mass Arrest'. *Policing and Society*. doi: 10.1080/10439463.2017.1319365.

GITLIN, T. (2000). *Inside Prime Time*. Berkeley and Los Angeles, CA: University of California Press.

GLASER, J. (2015). *Suspect Race: Causes and Consequences of Racial Profiling*. Oxford: Oxford University Press.

GLYN, A. (2006). *Capitalism Unleashed*. Oxford: Oxford University Press.

GODFREY, B. S. and DUNSTALL, G. (2012). *Crime and Empire 1840–1940, Criminal Justice in a Local and Global Context*. London and New York: Taylor & Francis.

GOEL, S., RAO, J., and SHROFF, R. (2016). 'Precinct or Prejudice? Understanding Racial Disparities in New York City's Stop-and-Frisk Policy'. *The Annals of Applied Statistics*, 10(1): 365–94.

GOLDSMITH, A. (1990). 'Taking Police Culture Seriously: Police Discretion and the Limits of Law'. *Policing and Society*, 1(2): 91–114.

GOLDSMITH, A. (ed.) (1991). *Complaints Against the Police: The Trend to External Review*. Oxford: Oxford University Press.

GOLDSMITH, A. (2003). 'Policing Weak States: Citizen Safety and State Responsibility'. *Policing and Society*, 13(1): 3–21.

GOLDSMITH, A. (2005). 'Police Reform and the Problem of Trust'. *Theoretical Criminology*, 9(4): 443–70.

GOLDSMITH, A. (2010). 'Policing's New Visibility'. *British Journal of Criminology*, 50(5): 914–34.

GOLDSMITH, A. (2015). 'Disgracebook Policing: Social Media and the Rise of Police Indiscretion'. *Policing and Society*, 25(3): 249–67.

GOLDSMITH, A. and LEWIS, C. (2000). *Civilian Oversight of Policing: Governance, Democracy and Human Rights*, Oxford: Hart.

GOLDSMITH, A. and SHEPTYCKI, J. (2007). *Crafting Transnational Policing: Police Capacity Building and Global Policing Reform*. Oxford: Hart.

GOLDSMITH, A., WADHAM, B., and HALSEY, M. (2018). *Criminologies of the Miltary: Militarism, National Security and Justice*. Oxford: Hart.

GOLDSTEIN, A. S. and GOLDSTEIN, J. (eds) (1971). *Crime, Law and Society*. New York: The Free Press.

GOLDSTEIN, H. (1979). 'Policing: A Problem-Oriented Approach'. *Crime and Delinquency*, 25(2): 236–58.

GOLDSTEIN, H. (1990). *Problem-Oriented Policing*. New York: McGraw-Hill.

GOLDSTEIN, J. (1960). 'Police Discretion not to Invoke the Criminal Process: Low Visibility Decisions in the Administration of Justice'. *Yale Law Journal*, 69: 543–94.

GOLKAR, S. (2011). 'Liberation or Suppression Technologies? The Internet, the Green Movement and the Regime in Iran'. *International Journal of Emerging Technologies and Society*, 9(1): 50–70.

GOLUB, A., JOHNSON, B. D., TAYLOR, A., and ETERNO, J. A. (2004). '"Does Quality-of-Life Policing Widen the Net?" A Partial Analysis'. *Justice Research and Policy*, 6(1): 1–22.

GOLUNOV, S. (2012). *EU-Russian Border Security: Challenges, (Mis)perceptions, and Responses*. London: Routledge.

GOOLD, B. (2004). *CCTV and Policing.* Oxford: Oxford University Press.

GOOLD, B. (2009). *Surveillance.* London: Routledge.

GOOLD, B. J. (2016). 'Policing and Human Rights', in B. BRADFORD, B. JAUREGUI, I. LOADER, and J. STEINBERG (eds), *The SAGE Handbook of Global Policing.* Thousand Oaks, CA: Sage.

GORDON, P. (1983). *White Law.* London: Pluto Press.

GOTHAM, K. F. (2012). 'Disaster Inc.: Privatization and Post-Katrina Re-building in New Orleans'. *Perspectives on Politics,* 10(3): 633–46.

GRAEF, R. (1989). *Talking Blues: The Police in Their Own Words.* London: Collins.

GRAHAM, H. D. and GURR, T. R. (1969). *Violence in America: Historical and Comparative Perspectives.* Washington, DC: Report to the National Commission on the Causes and Prevention of Violence.

GRAHAM, R. (1980). *Iran: The Illusion of Power.* New York: St Martin's Press.

GRAVELLE, J. and ROGERS, C. (2014). *Researching the Police in the 21st Century.* London: Palgrave.

GREEN, P. and WARD, T. (2004). *State Crime: Governments, Violence and Corruption.* London: Pluto Press.

GREENER, B. K. (2009). 'UNPOL: UN Police as Peacekeepers'. *Policing and Society,* 19(2). 106–18.

GREENER, B. K. (2012). 'International Policing and International Relations'. *International Relations,* 26(2). 181–98.

GREENHALGH, S. and GIBBS, B. (2014). *The Police Mission in the Twenty-First Century: Rebalancing the Role of the First Public Service.* London: Reform.

GREENWOOD, P., CHAIKEN, J., and PETERSILIA, J. (1977). *The Criminal Investigation Process.* Lexington, MA: D. C. Heath.

GREER, C. (2010). *Crime and Media: A Reader.* London: Routledge.

GREER, C. and McLAUGHLIN, E. (2012). '"This is not justice": Ian Tomlinson, Institutional Failure and the Press Politics of Outrage'. *British Journal of Criminology,* 52(2): 274–93.

GREER, C. and McLAUGHLIN, E. (2017). 'News Power, Crime and Media Justice', in A. LIEBLING, S. MARUNA, and L. McARA (eds), *The Oxford Handbook of Criminology* (6th edn). Oxford: Oxford University Press.

GREER, C. and REINER, R. (2012). 'Mediated Mayhem: Media, Crime and Criminal Justice', in M. MAGUIRE, R. MORGAN, and R. REINER (eds), *The Oxford Handbook of Criminology* (5th edn), Oxford: Oxford University Press.

GREER, S. (1995). *Supergrasses: A Study in Anti-Terrorist Law Enforcement in Northern Ireland.* Oxford: Oxford University Press.

GRIMSHAW, R. and JEFFERSON, T. (1987). *Interpreting Policework.* London: Allen & Unwin.

GUAJARDO, S. A. (2016). 'Women in Policing: A Longitudinal Assessment of Female Officers in Supervisory Positions in the New York City Police Department'. *Women and Criminal Justice,* 26(1): 20–36.

GUILLE, L. (2010). 'The Proliferation of Parallel Tracks in Police and Judicial Cooperation in Europe: The current Chaos', in A. VERHAEGE, A. J. TERPSTRA, P. DEELMA, E. MUYLAERT, and P. VAN PARYS (eds), 'Policing In Europe'. *Journal of Police Studies.* 3(16): 57–74. Antwerpen-Apeldoorn-Portland: Maklu.

GUNDHUS, H.O. (2017). 'Discretion as an Obstacle'. *Policing,* 11(3): 258–72.

GUREVITCH, M., BENNETT, T., CURRAN, J., and WOOLLACOTT, J. (eds) (1982). *Culture, Society and the Media.* London: Methuen.

GURR, T. R., GRABOSKY, P. N., and HULA, R. C. (1977). *The Politics of Crime and Conflict: A Comparative History of Four Cities.* Beverly Hills, CA/London: Sage.

HACKING, I. (2000). *The Social Construction of What?* Cambridge, MA: Harvard University Press.

HAGGERTY, K. D. and ERICSON, R. V. (1999). 'The Militarization of Policing in the Information Age'. *Journal of Political and Military Sociology*, (Winter) 27: 233–55.

HAGGERTY, K. D. and ERICSON, R. V. (2003). 'The Surveillant Assemblage'. *British Journal of Sociology*, 51(4): 605–22.

HAGGERTY, K. D. and ERICSON, R. V. (2004). 'The Military Technostructures of Policing', in P. B. KRASKA (ed.), *Militarizing the American Criminal Justice System: The Changing Roles of the Military and the Police*. Boston, MA: Northeastern University Press.

HALFORD, A. (1993). *No Way Up the Greasy Pole*. London: Constable.

HALL, P. T. (1998). 'Policing Order: Assessments of Effectiveness and Efficiency'. *Policing and Society*, 8(3): 225–52.

HALL, STEVE and MCLEAN, C. (2009). 'A Tale of Two Capitalisms: Preliminary Spatial and Historical Comparisons of Homicide'. *Theoretical Criminology*, 13(3): 313–39.

HALL, STEVE, and WINLOW, S. (2003). 'Rehabilitating Leviathan: Reflections on the State, Economic Regulation and Violence Reduction'. *Theoretical Criminology*, 7(2): 139–62.

HALL, STEVE and WINLOW, S. (2015). *Revitalising Criminological Theory*. London: Routledge.

HALL, STEVE, WINLOW, S., and ANCRUM, C. (2008). *Criminal Identities and Consumer Culture*. Cullompton: Willan.

HALL, STUART (1973–80). 'Encoding and Decoding', in *Culture, Media, Language Working Papers in Cultural Studies. 1972–1979*, Center for Contemporary Cultural Studies, London: Routledge.

HALL, STUART (1979). *Drifting into a Law and Order Society*. London: Cobden Trust.

HALL, STUART, CRITCHER, C., JEFFERSON, T., CLARKE, J., and ROBERTS, B. (1978/2013). *Policing the Crisis: Mugging, the State, and Law and Order* (2nd edn). London: Palgrave-Macmillan.

HALLENBERG, K. and COCKROFT, T. (2017). 'From Indifference to Hostility: Police Officers, Organisational Responses and the Symbolic Value of "In-Service" Higher Education in Policing'. *Policing* 11(3): 273–88.

HAMPSON, F. O. and JARDINE, E. (2017). *Look Who's Watching: Surveillance, Treachery and Trust On-line*. Montreal and Kingston: McGill-Queen's University Press.

HANMER, J., RADFORD, J., and STANKO, E.A. (1989). *Women, Violence and Policing: International Perspectives*. London: Routledge.

HARCOURT, B. (2001). *Illusion of Order: The False Promise of Broken Windows Policing*. Cambridge, MA: Harvard University Press.

HARGREAVES, J., HUSBAND, H., and LINEHAN, C. (2017). 'Police Workforce, England and Wales, 31 March 2017'. London: Home Office.

HARLOW, C. (1980). '"Public" and "Private" Law: Definition without Distinction'. *Modern Law Review*, 43(3): 241–65.

HARRIOTT, A. (2000). *Police and Crime Control in Jamaica: Problems in Reforming Ex-Colonial Constabularies*. Kingston, Jamaica: University of the West Indies Press.

HARRIS, J. (2018). 'The Growth of Private Policing is Eroding Justice For All'. *The Guardian*, 10 September.

HARRIS, R. (1988). *Language, Saussure and Wittgenstein: How to Play Games with Words*. London and New York: Routledge.

HARVEY, D. (2005a). *A Brief History of Neo-liberalism*. Oxford: Oxford University Press.

HARVEY, D. (2005b). 'Neo-Liberalism as Creative Destruction'. *Geografiska Annaler, Series B Human Geography*, 88(2): 145–58.

HAY, D. (ed.) (1975). *Albion's Fatal Tree*. Harmondsworth: Penguin.

HAYS, R. (2012). 'Policing in Northern Ireland: Community Control, Community Policing, and the Search for Legitimacy'. *Urban Affairs Review*, 49(4): 557–92.

HAYS, T. G. and SJOQUIST, A. W. (2005). *Los Angeles Police Department*. Arcadia Publishing and the Los Angles Police Historical Society.

HEAL, K. and LAYCOCK, G. (1987). *Preventing Juvenile Crime: The Staffordshire Experience*, Crime Prevention Unit Paper 8. London: Home Office.

HEARTY, K. (2018). 'Discourses of Political Policing in Post-Patten Northern Ireland'. *Critical Criminology*, 26(1), 129–43.

HEATON, R. (2000). 'The Prospects for Intelligence-led Policing: Some Historical and Quantitative Considerations'. *Policing and Society*, 9(4): 337–56.

HEIDENSOHN, F. (1992). *Women in Control— The Role of Women in Law Enforcement*. Oxford: Oxford University Press.

HEIDENSOHN, F. (1994). '"We can handle it out here". Women Police Officers in Britain and the USA and the Policing of Public Order'. *Policing and Society*, 4(4): 293–303.

HEIDENSOHN, F. (1998). 'Comparative Models of Policing and the Role of Women Officers'. *International Journal of Police Science and Management*, 1(3): 215–26.

HEIDENSOHN, F. (2008). 'Gender and Policing', in T. NEWBURN (ed.), *Handbook of Policing*. Cullompton: Willan.

HELD, D. (1991). 'Democracy, the Nation State and the Global System'. *Economy and Society*, 20(2): 138–72.

HELD, D. and MCGREW, A. (2003). *The Global Transformations Reader: An Introduction to the Globalization Debate* (2nd edn). Oxford: Polity Press.

HELD, D. and MCGREW, A. G. (eds) (2007). *Globalization Theory: Approaches and Controversies*. Cambridge: Polity Press.

HENRY, A. (2007). 'Policing and Ethnic Minorities', in A. HENRY and D. J. SMITH (eds), *Transformations of Policing*. Aldershot: Ashgate.

HENRY, A. and SMITH, D. J. (2017). *Transformations in Policing*. London: Routledge.

HERMAN, E. S. and CHOMSKY, N. (2002). *Manufacturing Consent: The Political Economy of the Mass Media*, New York: Pantheon.

HERMAN, E. S. and MCCHESNEY, R. W. (2004). *The Global Media: The Missionaries of the New Global Capitalism*. London and New York: Continuum.

HERSCHINGER, E. and JACHTENFUCHS, M. (2012). 'Informell oder institutionalisiert? Die Internationalisierung der inneren Sicherheit'. *Politische Vierteljahresschrift*, 53(3): 493–514. doi: 10.5771/0032-3470-2012-3-493.

HESKETH, I. and WILLIAMS, E. (2017). 'A New Canteen Culture'. *Policing*, 11(3): 346–55.

HILL, R. S. (1995). *The Iron Hand in the Velvet Glove: The Modernization of Policing in New Zealand 1886-1917*. Palmerston North: Dunmore Press.

HILLS, A. (2000). *Policing Africa: Internal Security and the Limits of Liberalization*. New York: Lynne Rienner.

HILLS, A. (2009). 'The Possibility of Transnational Policing'. *Policing and Society*, 19(3): 300–17.

HINTON, M. (2006). *The State in the Streets: Police and Politics in Argentina and Brazil*. Boulder, CO: Rienner.

HINTON, M., and NEWBURN, T. (eds) (2008). *Policing Developing Democracies*. London: Routledge.

HMIC (1997). *Policing with Intelligence*. London: Her Majesty's Inspectorate of Constabulary.

HMIC (2009). *Adapting to Protest*. London: Her Majesty's Inspectorate of Constabulary.

HMIC (2014). *Everyone's Business: Improving the Police Response to Domestic Violence*. London: Her Majesty's Inspectorate of Constabulary.

HMICFRS (2017). 'A Progress Report on the Police Response to Domestic Abuse'. London: Her Majesty's Inspectorate for the Constabulary and Fire & Rescue Services.

HOBBS, D. (1988). *Doing the Business: Entrepreneurship, the Working Class and*

Detectives in the East End of London. Oxford: Oxford University Press.

HOBDEN, S. and HOBSON, J. M. (eds) (2002). *Historical Sociology of International Relations.* Cambridge: Cambridge University Press.

HOBSBAWM, E. (1959). *Primitive Rebels.* Manchester: Manchester University Press.

HOBSBAWM, E. (1988). *The Age of Revolution 1789–1848.* London: Little Brown.

HOBSBAWM, E. (1995). *The Age of Extremes.* London: Abacus.

HODGSON, J. (2011). 'Safeguarding Suspects' Rights in Europe'. *New Criminal Law Review*, 14(2): 611–65.

HOHL, K., and STANKO, E. A. (2015). 'Complaints of Rape and the Criminal Justice System: Fresh Evidence on the Attrition Problem in England and Wales'. *European Journal of Criminology*, 12(3): 324–41.

HOLDAWAY, S. (1977). 'Changes in Urban Policing'. *British Journal of Sociology*, 28(2): 119–37.

HOLDAWAY, S. (ed.) (1979). *The British Police.* London: Edward Arnold.

HOLDAWAY, S. (1983). *Inside the British Police.* Oxford: Basil Blackwell.

HOLDAWAY, S. (1989). 'Discovering Structure: Studies of the British Police Occupational Culture', in M. WEATHERITT (ed.), *Police Research: Some Future Prospects.* Aldershot: Avebury.

HOLDAWAY, S. (1993). *The Resignation of Black and Asian Officers from the Police Service.* A Report to the Home Office. London: Home Office.

HOLDAWAY, S. (2009). *Black Police Associations.* Oxford: Oxford University Press.

HOLDAWAY, S. (2015). 'What Do We Know? Lessons from the History of Race Relations within Constabularies'. *Policing* 9(1): 5–14.

HOLDAWAY, S. and BARRON, A. M. (1997). *Resigners? The Experience of Black and Asian Police Officers.* Basingstoke: Macmillan.

HOLDAWAY, S. and O'NEILL, M. (2006). 'Institutional Racism after Macpherson: An Analysis of Police Views'. *Policing and Society*, 16(4): 349–69.

HOME OFFICE (1993). *Police Reform: A Police Service for the Twenty-First Century.* Cm. 2281. London: HMSO.

HOME OFFICE (2010). *Policing in the 21st Century: Reconnecting Police and the People.* London: Home Office.

HOME OFFICE (2018). *Crime Outcomes in England and Wales: Year Ending March 2018*: Statistical Bulletin HOSB 10/18. London: Home Office.

HÖNKE, J. and MÜLLER, M.-M. (2016). *The Global Making of Policing: Post-Colonial Perspectives.* London: Routledge.

HOOGENBOOM, B. (1991). 'Grey Policing: A Theoretical Framework'. *Policing and Society*, 2(1): 17–30.

HOOGENBOOM, B. (2010). *The Governance of Policing and Security.* London: Palgrave Macmillan.

HOPE, T. (2004). 'Pretend It Works: Evidence and Governance in the Evaluation of the Reducing Burglary Initiative'. *Criminal Justice*, 4(3): 287–308.

HOPKIN, J. (2012). 'Clientalism, Corruption and Political Cartels: Informal Governance in Southern Europe', in T. CHRISTIANSEN and C. NEUHOLD (eds), *International Handbook on Informal Governance.* Cheltenham: Edward Elgar.

HOPKINS-BURKE, R. (ed.) (1998). *Zero Tolerance Policing.* Leicester: Perpetuity Press.

HÖRQVIST, M. (2016). 'Riots in the Welfare State: The Contours of a Modern Day Moral Economy'. *European Journal of Criminology*, 13(5): 573–89.

HORTON, C. (1989). 'Good Practice and Evaluative Policing', in R. MORGAN and D. SMITH (eds), *Coming to Terms with Policing.* London: Routledge.

HORWITZ, M. J. (1982). 'The History of the Public/Private Distinction'. *University of Pennsylvania Law Review*, 130(6): 1423–8.

HOSB (Home Office Statistical Bulletin) (2018). 'Crime Outcomes in England and Wales: Year Ending March 2018'. London: Home Office.

HOUGH, M. (1987). 'Thinking about Effectiveness'. *British Journal of Criminology*, 27(1): 70–9.

HOUGH, M. (2003). 'Modernization and Public Opinion: Some Criminal Justice Paradoxes'. *Contemporary Politics*, 9: 143–55.

HOUGH, M. (2007a). 'Policing London, Twenty Years On', in A. HENRY and D. J. SMITH (eds), *Transformations of Policing*. Aldershot: Avebury.

HOUGH, M. (2007b). 'Policing, New Public Management and Legitimacy in Britain', in T. TYLER (ed.), *Legitimacy and Criminal Justice*. New York: Russell Sage Foundation Press.

HOUGH, M. and MAYHEW, P. (1983). *The British Crime Survey: first report*. Home Office Research Study 76. London: HMSO.

HOUGH, M. and ROBERTS, J. (2017). 'Public Opinion, Crime, and Criminal Justice', in A. LIEBLING, S. MARUNA, and L. McARA (eds), *The Oxford Handbook of Criminology* (6th edn). Oxford: Oxford University Press.

HOUGH, M., JACKSON, J., and BRADFORD, B. (2010). 'Procedural Justice, Trust and Legitimacy'. *Policing*, 4(3): 203–10.

HOUGH, M., JACKSON, J., and BRADFORD, B. (2017). 'Policing, Procedural Justice and Prevention', in N. TILLEY and A. SIDEBOTTOM (eds), *The Handbook of Crime Prevention and Community Safety*. London: Taylor & Francis.

HOUSE OF COMMONS (2011). *New Landscape of Policing*. London: Home Affairs Select Committee Fourteenth Report.

HOUSE OF COMMONS (2018). *Police Service Strength*. House of Commons Briefing Paper No 634 October 2018 by Graham Allen and Yago Zayed. London: House of Commons Library.

HOYLE, C. (1998). *Negotiating Domestic Violence: Police, Criminal Justice and Victims*. Oxford: Oxford University Press.

HUCKLESBY, A. and LISTER, S. (2018). *The Private Sector and Criminal Justice*. London: Palgrave Macmillan.

HUDSON, B. (2003). *Understanding Justice*. Buckingham: Open University Press.

HUFNAGEL, S. (2013). *Policing Cooperation Across Borders: Comparative Perspectives on Law Enforcement within the EU and Australia*. Farnham and Burlington, VT: Ashgate.

HUGGINS, M. (1998). *Political Policing*. Durham, NC: Duke University Press.

HUGHES, E. C. (1961). 'Good People and Dirty Work'. *Social Problems*, 10(1): 3–11.

HUGHES, V. and JACKSON, P. (2004). 'The Influence of Technical, Social and Structural Factors on the Effective use of Information in a Policing Environment'. *The Electronic Journal of Knowledge Management*, 2(1): 65–76.

HUMPHREYS, P. (1996). *Mass Media and Media Policy in Western Europe*. Manchester: Manchester University Press.

IANNI, E. R., and IANNI, R. (1983). 'Street Cops and Management Cops: The Two Cultures of Policing', in M. PUNCH (ed.), *Control in the Police Organization*. Cambridge, MA: MIT Press.

ICAO INTERNATIONAL CIVIL AVIATION AUTHORITY STATISTICS (2017). World Air Transport Statistics.

IGNATIEFF, M. (1979). 'Police and People: The Birth of Mr Peel's Blue Locusts'. *New Society*, 49(882): 443–5.

INGRAM, J., PAOLINE, E., and TERRILL, W. (2013). 'A Multilevel Framework for Understanding Police Culture'. *Criminology*, 51(2): 365–97.

INNES, M. (2000). '"Professionalizing" the Role of the Police Informant: The British Experience'. *Policing and Society*, 9(4): 357–83.

INNES, M. (2003). *Investigating Murder: Detective Work and the Police Response to Criminal Homicide*. Oxford: Oxford University Press.

INNES, M. (2007). 'The Reassurance Function'. *Policing*, 1(2): 132–41.

INNES, M. and SHEPTYCKI, J. (2004). 'From Detection to Disruption: Intelligence and the Changing Logic of Police Crime Control in the United Kingdom'. *International Criminal Justice Review*, 14: 1–24. doi:10.1177/105756770401400101.

INSTITUTE OF RACE RELATIONS (1979). 'Police Against Black People: Evidence submitted to the Royal Commission on Criminal Procedure', Race and Class pamphlet No. 6.

Interpol (2016). *Annual Report* 2016. Lyon: Interpol.

IOPC (2018). *Annual Report and Statement of Accounts 2017/18*. London: House of Commons.

ISENBERG, N. (2016). *White Trash: The 400-Year Untold History of Class in America*. New York: Viking Press.

IYENGAR, R. (2009). 'Does the Certainty of Arrest Reduce Domestic Violence? Evidence from Mandatory and Recommended Arrest Laws'. *Journal of Public Economics*, 93(1–2), 85–98.

JACKALL, R. (1997). *Wild Cowboys, Urban Marauders and the Forces of Order*. Cambridge, MA: Harvard University Press.

JACKALL, R. (2003). 'Review Essay/What Kind of Order?'. *Criminal Justice Ethics*, 22(2): 54–66.

JACKALL, R. (2005). *Street Stories: The World of Police Detectives*. Cambridge, MA: Harvard University Press.

JACKSON, L. (2012). *Women Police*. Manchester: Manchester University Press.

JACKSON, J., BRADFORD, B., STANKO, B., and HOHL, K. (2014). *Just Authority? Public Trust and Police Legitimacy*. London: Routledge.

JACKSON, W., GILMORE, J., and MONK, H. (2018). 'Policing Unacceptable Protest in England and Wales: A Case Study of the Policing of Anti-Fracking Protests'. *Critical Social Policy*, 39(1): 23–43.

JACOB, H. and RICH, M. J. (1981). 'The Effects of the Police on Crime: A Second Look'. *Law and Society Review*, 15(1): 109–22.

JACOBS, R. N. (1996). 'The Construction of Meaning: Civil Society and Crisis: Culture, Discourse and the Rodney King Beating'. *American Journal of Sociology*, 101(5): 1238–72.

JAMES, A. (2013). *Examining Intelligence-led Policing: Developments in Research, Policy and Practice*. London: Palgrave.

JAMES, A. (2016). *Understanding Police Intelligence Work*. Bristol: Policy Press.

JASCHKE, H., BJØRGO, T., DEL BARRIO, R. F., KWANTEN, C., MAWBY, R., and PAGON, M. (2007). *Perspectives of Police Science in Europe—Final Report*, Budapest, Hungary: CEPOL, European Police College.

JAUREGUI, B. J. (2013). 'Beating, Beacons and Big Men: Police Disempowerment and Delegitimation in India'. *Law and Social Inquiry*, 38(3): 643–69.

JAUREGUI, B. J. (2016). *Provisional Authority: Police, Order, and Security in India*. Chicago, IL: University of Chicago Press.

JEFFERSON, B. J. (2015). 'Zero Tolerance for Zero Tolerance?: Analyzing how Zero Tolerance Discourse Mediates Police Accountability Activism'. *City, Culture and Society*, 6(1): 9–17.

JEFFERSON, T. (1990). *The Case against Paramilitary Policing*. Milton Keynes: Open University Press.

JEFFERSON, T., and GRIMSHAW, R. (1984). *Controlling the Constable: Police Accountability in England and Wales*. London: Muller.

JEFFRIES, F., ARTHURS, S., CHEARING, C. D., and STENNING, P. C. (eds) (1974). *Private Policing and Security in Canada: A Workshop Report*, held 16–17 October 1973, Toronto: Center of Criminology.

JEWKES, Y. (2015). *Media and Crime*. London: Sage.

JOBARD, F. and DE MAILLARD, J. (2015). *Sociologie de la police: Politiques, organisations, réformes*. Paris, A. Colin.

JOCHELSON, R., GACEK, J., MENZIE, L., KRAMAR, K., and DOERKSEN, M. (2017). *Criminal Law and Precrime: Legal Studies in Canadian Punishment and Surveillance in Anticipation of Criminal Guilt*. London: Taylor & Francis.

JOH, E. E. (2004). 'The Paradox of Private Policing'. *Journal of Criminal Law and Criminology*, 95(1): 49–132.

JOH, E. E. (2014). 'Policing by Numbers: Big Data and the Fourth Amendment'. *Washington Law Review*, 89(1): 35–68.

JOH, E. E. (2017). 'The Undue Influence of Surveillance Technology Companies on Policing'. *New York University Law Review*, 92: 101–30.

JOHANSEN, R. C. and MENDLOVITZ, S. H. (1980). 'The Role of Enforcement of Law in the Establishment of a New International Order: A Proposal for a Transnational Police Force'. *Alternatives: Global, Local, Political*, 6: 307–37.

JOHN, T. and MAGUIRE, M. (2003). 'Rolling Out the National Intelligence Model: Key Challenges', in K. BULLOCK and N. TILLEY (eds), *Essays in Problem-Oriented Policing*. Cullompton: Willan.

JOHN, T. and MAGUIRE, M. (2007). 'Criminal Intelligence and the National Intelligence Model', in T. NEWBURN, T. WILLIAMSON, and A. WRIGHT (eds), *Handbook of Criminal Investigation*. Cullompton: Willan.

JOHNSON, E. A. and MONKKONEN, E. H. (1996). *The Civilization of Crime: Violence in Town and Country since the Middle Ages*. Urbana, IL: University of Illinois Press.

JOHNSON, P. (1991). *Birth of the Modern*, London: George Weidenfeld & Nicholson.

JOHNSTON, L. (1992a). 'The Politics of Private Policing'. *The Political Quarterly*, 63(3): 341–9.

JOHNSTON, L. (1992b). *The Rebirth of Private Policing*. London: Routledge.

JOHNSTON, L. (1996). 'What is Vigilantism?'. *British Journal of Criminology*, 36(2): 220–36.

JOHNSTON, L. (2000a). *Policing Britain: Risk, Security and Governance*. London: Longman.

JOHNSTON, L. (2000b). 'Transnational Private Policing: The Impact of Global Commercial Security', in J. SHEPTYCKI (ed.), *Issues in Transnational Policing*. London: Routledge.

JOHNSTON, L. (2006). 'Transnational Security Governance', in J. WOOD and B. DUPONT (eds), *Democracy, Society and the Governance of Security*. Cambridge: Cambridge University Press.

JOHNSTON, L. and SHEARING, C. (2003). *Governing Security: Explorations in Policing and Justice*. London: Routledge.

JOIREMAN, S. F. (2001). 'Inherited Legal Systems and Effective Rule of Law: Africa and the Colonial Legacy'. *Journal of Modern African Studies*, 39(4): 571–96.

JONES, C. (2004). 'Crime and Justice in China: 1949–99', in J. SHEPTYCKI and A. WARDAK (eds), *Transnational and Comparative Criminology*. London: Routledge.

JONES, M. (2014). 'A Diversity Stone Left Unturned? Exploring the Occupational Complexities Surrounding Lesbian, Gay and Bisexual Police Officers', in J. BROWN (ed.), *The Future of Policing*. London: Routledge.

JONES, M. (2016). 'Researching Sexuality and Policing: Reflections from the Field', in M. BRUNGER, S. TONG, and D. MARTIN (eds), *Introduction to Policing Research: Taking Lessons from Practice*. Oxford and New York: Routledge.

JONES, M. and WILLIAMS, M. L. (2013). 'Twenty Years On: Lesbian, Gay and Bisexual Police Officers' Experiences of Workplace Discrimination in England and Wales'. *Policing and Society*, 25(2): 188–211.

JONES, S. and LEVI, M. (1983). 'The Police and the Majority: The Neglect of the Obvious'. *Police Journal*, 56(4): 351–64.

JONES, T. (2007). 'The Governance of Security' in M. Maguire, R.Morgan and R.Reiner (eds.) *The Oxford Handbook of Criminology* (4th edn). Oxford: Oxford University Press.

JONES, T. (2011). 'The Accountability of Policing', in T. NEWBURN (ed.), *Handbook of Policing* (2nd edn). London: Routledge.

JONES, T. and NEWBURN, T. (1998). *Private Security and Public Policing*. Oxford: Clarendon.

JONES, T. and NEWBURN, T. (1999). 'Urban Change and Policing: Mass Private Property Re-considered'. *European Journal on Criminal Policy and Research*, 7(2): 225–44.

JONES, T. and NEWBURN, T. (2002). 'The Transformation of Policing: Understanding Current Trends in Policing Systems'. *British Journal of Criminology*, 42(1): 129–46.

JONES, T. and NEWBURN, T. (eds) (2006). *Plural Policing: A Comparative Perspective*. London: Routledge.

JONES, T., NEWBURN, T., and REINER, R. (2017). 'Policing and the Police', in A. LIEBLING, S. MARUNA, and L. MCARA (eds), *The Oxford Handbook of Criminology* (6th edn). Oxford: Oxford University Press.

JONES, T., NEWBURN, T., and SMITH, D. J. (1994). *Democracy and Policing*. PSI Research Report: 784. London: Policy Studies Institute.

JONES, T., NEWBURN, T., and SMITH, D. J. (1996). 'Policing and the Idea of Democracy'. *British Journal of Criminology*, 36(2): 182–98.

JONES, T., NEWBURN, T., and SMITH, D. (2012). 'Policing and Crime Commissioners', in T. NEWBURN and J. PEAY (eds), *Policing: Politics, Culture and Control*. Oxford: Hart.

JONES-BROWN, D., GILL, J., and TRONE, J. (2010). *Stop, Question and Frisk Policing Practices in New York City: A Primer*. Center on Race, Crime and Justice: John J. College of Criminal Justice.

JORDAN, P. (1998). 'Effective Policing Strategies for Reducing Crime' in P. Nuttall, P. Goldblatt and C. Lewis (eds.) *Reducing Offending* London: Home Office Research Study 187.

JOUBERT, C. and BEVERS, H. (1996). *Schengen Investigated: A Comparative Interpretation of the Schengen Provisions on International Police Cooperation in the Light of the European Convention on Human Rights*. The Hague: Kluwer.

KAIMING, S. (1985). *1840–1983 Modern China: A Topical History*. Bejing: New World Press.

KAKALIK, J. S. and WILDHORN, S. (1972). 'Private Police in the United States', RAND Report, 4 Volumes. Washington, DC: US Department of Justice.

KAPLAN, D. E. and DUBRO, A. (2012). *Yakuza: Japan's Criminal Underworld*. Berkeley, CA: University of California Press.

KAPPELER, V., SLUDER, R., and ALPERT, G. (1994). *Forces of Deviance: Understanding the Dark Side of Policing*. Prospect Heights, IL: Waveland Press.

KARMEN, A. (2000). *New York Murder Mystery*. New York: New York University Press.

KEITH, M. (1993). *Race Riots and Policing: Lore and Disorder in a Multi-Racist Society*. London: UCL Press.

KEITH, R. and LIN, Z. (2005). *New Crime in China: Public Order and Human Rights*. London: Routledge.

KELLING G. L. and WILSON, J. Q. (1982). 'Broken Windows: The Police and Neighbourhood Safety'. *The Atlantic*, March.

KELLING, G. *et al.* (1974). *The Kansas City Preventive Patrol Experiment*. Washington, DC: Police Foundation.

KELLING, G. and BRATTON, W. (2015). 'Why We Need Broken Windows Policing' *City Journal* (Winter).

KELLING, G. and COLES, C. (1998). *Fixing Broken Windows: Restoring Order and Reducing Crime in Our Communities*. New York: Free Press.

KEMP, C., NORRIS, C., and FIELDING, N. (1992). *Negotiating Nothing: Police Decision-Making in Disputes*. Aldershot: Avebury.

KEMP, V. (2014). 'PACE, Performance Targets and Legal Protections'. *Criminal Law Review*, 4: 278–97.

KEMPA, M., CARRIER, R., WOOD, J., and SHEARING, C. (1999). 'Reflections of the Evolving Concept of "Private Policing"'. *European Journal on Criminal Policy and Research*, 7(2): 197–223.

KEMPA, M., STENNING, P., and WOOD, J. (2004). 'Policing Communal Spaces: A Reconfiguration of the "Mass Private Property" Hypothesis'. *British Journal of Criminology*, 44(4): 562–81.

KEMSHALL, H. and MAGUIRE, M. (2001). 'Public Protection, Partnership and Risk Penality: The Multi-Agency Risk Management of Sexual and Violent Offenders'. *Punishment & Society*, 3(2): 237–64.

KESKINEN, S., ALEMANJI, A., HIMANEN, M., KIVIJÄRVI, A., OSAZEE, U., PÖYHÖLÄ, N., and ROUSKU, U. (2018). *The Stopped: Ethnic Profiling in Finland*. Helsinki: University of Helskini.

KHALIFEH, H., JOHNSON, S., HOWARD, L. M., BORSCHMANN, R., OSBORN, D., DEAN, K., HART, C., HOGG, J. and MORAN, P. (2015). 'Violent and Non-Violent Crime against Adults with Severe Mental Illness'. *British Journal of Psychiatry*, 206(4): 275–82.

KING, P. (2006). *Crime and Law in England 1750–1850. Remaking Justice from the Margins*. Cambridge: Cambridge University Press.

KINSEY, R., LEA, J., and YOUNG, J. (1986). *Losing the Fight against Crime*. Oxford: Blackwell.

KLEG, M. (1993). *Hate Prejudice and Racism*. Albany, NY: State University of New York Press.

KLEIN, J. (2001). 'Blue-Collar Job, Blue Collar Career: Policemen's Perplexing Struggle for a Voice in Birmingham, Liverpool, and Manchester, 1900–1919'. *Crime, History and Societies*, 6(1): 5–29.

KLEIN, N. (2008). *The Shock Doctrine*. London: Penguin.

KLEINIG, J. (1996). *The Ethics of Policing*. Cambridge: Cambridge University Press.

KLEIVEN, M. E. (2011). 'Nordic Police Cooperation', in S. BRONITT, C. HARFIELD, and S. HUFNAGEL (eds), *Cross-border Law Enforcement: Regional Law Enforcement Cooperation—European, Australian and Asia-Pacific Perspectives*. London: Routledge.

KLOCKARS, C. B. (1980). 'The Dirty Harry Problem'. *Annals of the American Academy of Political and Social Sciences*, 352: 33–47.

KLOCKARS, C. B. (1985). *The Idea of Police*. Beverly Hills, CA: Sage.

KLOCKARS, C. B. (1988). 'The Rhetoric of Community Policing', in J. R. GREENE and S. D. MASTROFSKI (eds), *Community Policing: Rhetoric or Reality?* New York: Praeger.

KRASKA, P. (ed.) (2001). *Militarizing the American Criminal Justice System: The Changing Roles of the Armed Forces and the Police*. Chicago, IL: Northeastern University Press.

KRASKA, P. (2007). 'Militarization and Policing—Its Relevance to 21st Century Police'. *Policing*, 1(4): 501–13.

KRASKA, P. B. and CUBELLIS, L. J. (1997). 'Militarizing Mayberry and Beyond: Making Sense of American Paramilitary Policing'. *Justice Quarterly*, 14(4): 607–29.

KUMAR, K. (2005). *From Post-Industrial to Post-Modern Society: New Theories of the Contemporary World*. Oxford: Basil Blackwell.

LACEY, N. (2008). *The Prisoners' Dilemma: Political Economy and Punishment in Contemporary Democracies*. Cambridge: Cambridge University Press.

LAMBERT, J. (1970). *Crime, Police and Race Relations*. Oxford: Oxford University Press.

LANDAU, T. (1996). 'Policing and Security in Four Remote Aboriginal Communities: A Challenge to Coercive Models of Police Work'. *Canadian Journal of Criminology*, 38(1): 1–32.

LANE, R. (1992). 'Urban Police and Crime in Nineteenth Century America', in M. TONRY and N. MORRIS (eds), *Modern Policing*. Chicago, IL: University of Chicago Press.

LARSON, R. (1976). 'What Happened to Patrol Operations in Kansas City?'. *Journal of Criminal Justice*, 3(4): 267–97.

LAURIE, P. (1970). *Scotland Yard*. London: Penguin.

LAVILLE, S. (2018). 'Serial Sex Attacker Kirk Reid to be Considered for Release from Jail'. *The Guardian*, 17 January.

LAWRENCE, P. (2000). 'Images of Poverty and Crime. Police Memoirs in England and France at the End of the Nineteenth Century'. *Crime, History and Societies*, 4(1): 63–82.

LAWRENCE, P. (2003). '"Scoundrels and Scallywags, and some honest men . . ." Memoirs and the Self-Image of French and English Policemen, c.1870–1939', in C. EMSLEY, B. GODFREY, and G. DUNSTALL (eds), *Comparative Histories of Crime*. Cullompton: Willan.

LAWRENCE, P. (2017). 'The Vagrancy Act (1824) and the Persistence of Pre-emptive Policing in England since 1750'. *British Journal of Criminology*, 57(3): 513–31.

LAWRENCE, R. (2000). *The Politics of Force: Media and the Construction of Police Brutality*. Berkeley, CA: University of California Press.

LAYCOCK, G. and FARRELL, G. (2003). 'Repeat Victimization: Lessons for Implementing Problem-Oriented Policing', in J. KNUTSSON (ed.), Problem-oriented Policing: From Innovation to Mainstream. *Crime Prevention Studies*, 15: 213–37.

LEA, J. (1998). 'Criminology and Postmodernity', in P. WALTON and J. YOUNG (eds), *The New Criminology Revisited*. London: Palgrave Macmillan.

LEA, J. (2003). 'Institutional Racism in Policing: The Macpherson Report and its Consequences', in R. MATTHEWS and J. YOUNG (eds), *The New Politics of Crime and Justice*. Cullompton: Willan.

LEA, J., and YOUNG, J. (1984). *What is to be Done about Law and Order?* Harmondsworth: Penguin.

LEBRON, C. (2017). *The Making of Black Lives Matter*. New York: Oxford University Press.

LEE, J. A. (1981). 'Some Structural Aspects of Police Deviance in Relations with Minority Groups', in C. SHEARING (ed.), *Organizational Police Deviance*. Toronto: Butterworth.

LEE, MELVILLE. (1901). *A History of Police in England*. London: Methuen.

LEE, MURRAY. (2013). *Inventing Fear of Crime: Criminology and the Politics of Anxiety*. London: Routledge.

LEE, MAGGY and PUNCH, M. (2006). *Policing by Degrees*. Groningen: Hondsrug Pers.

LEESE, M. (2015). 'Governing Airport Security between the Market and the Public Good'. *Criminology and Criminal Justice*, 16(2): 158–75.

LEIGH, A., READ, T., and TILLEY, N. (1996). *Problem-Oriented Policing: Brit Pop*. Police Research Group Paper 75. London: Home Office.

LEISHMAN, F., and MASON, P. (2003). *Policing and the Media: Facts, Fictions and Factions*. Cullompton: Willan.

LEMIEUX, F. (2013). *International Police Co-operation: Emerging Issues, Theory and Practice*. London: Routledge.

LENTZ, S. A. and CHAIRES, R. H. (2007). 'The Invention of Peel's Principles: A Study of Policing "Textbook" History'. *Journal of Criminal Justice*, 35(1): 69–79.

LEON, C. (2017). 'Special Constables and the Birth of "Regular" Policing' and 'From Special Constables to Special Constabularies', in K. BULLOCK and A. MILLIE (eds), *The Special Constabulary*. London: Routledge.

LERMAN, A. and WEAVER, V. (2014). *Arresting Citizenship: The Democratic Consequences of American Crime Control*. Chicago, IL: University of Chicago Press.

LEVI, M. (2006). 'The Media Construction of Financial White-Collar Crimes'. *British Journal of Criminology*, 46(6): 1037–57.

LEVIN, S. (2018). 'Tech firms make millions from Trump's anti-immigrant agenda, report finds'. *The Guardian*, 23 October 2018.

LEVITT, S. D. (2004). 'Understanding Why Crime Fell in the 1990s: Four Factors that Explain the Decline and Six that Do Not'. *Journal of Economic Perspectives*, 18(1): 163–90.

LEVY, R. and HAGAN, J. (2006). 'International Police' in M. D. DUBBER and M. VALVERDE (eds), *The New Police Science: The Police Power in Domestic and International Law*. Stanford, CA: Stanford University Press.

LEWIS, P. and EVANS, R. (2014). *Undercover: The True Story of Britain's Secret Police*. London: Guardian Faber Publishing.

LEWIS, P., NEWBURN, T., TAYLOR, M., MCGILLVRAY, C., GREENHILL, A., FRAYMAN, H., and PROCTOR, R. (2011). *Reading the Riots: Investigating England's Summer of Disorder*. London: The London School of Economics and Political Science and *The Guardian*.

LI, S., LEVICK, A., EICHMAN, A., and CHANG, J. C. (2015). 'Women's Perspectives on the Context of Violence and Role of Police in their Intimate Partner Violence Arrest Experiences'. *Journal of Interpersonal Violence*, 30(3): 400–19.

LIANG, H. (1992). *The Rise of Modern Police and the European State System from Metternich to the Second World War*. Cambridge: Cambridge University Press.

LIDDLE, A. M. and GELSTHORPE, L. R. (1994). *Crime Prevention and Inter-Agency Co-operation*. Home Office Police Research Group. London: Home Office.

LIN, Z. (2007). *Policing the Wild North West: A Sociological Study of the Provincial Police in Alberta and Saskatchewan 1905–32*. Calgary: University of Calgary Press.

LINEBAUGH, P. (2006). *The London Hanged: Crime and Civil Society in the Eighteenth Century* (2nd edn). London: Allen Lane.

LIPPERT, R. and O'CONNOR, D. (2003). 'Security Assemblages: Airport Security, Flexible Work, and Liberal Governance'. *Alternatives*, 28(3): 331–58.

LIPPERT, R. and O'CONNOR, D. (2006). 'Security Intelligence Networks and the Transformation of Contract Private Security'. *Policing and Society*, 16(1): 50–66.

LIPPERT, R. K. and WALBY, K. (2014). *Policing Cities: Urban Securitization and Regulation in a Twenty-First Century World*. London: Routledge.

LIPSET, S. M. (1969). 'Why Cops Hate Liberals, and Vice Versa'. *Atlantic Monthly*, March, 76–83.

LISTER, S. (2013). 'The New Politics of the Police: Police and Crime Commissioners and the "Operational Independence" of the Police'. *Policing*, 7(3): 239–47.

LISTER, S. (2014). 'Scrutinising the Role of the Police and Crime Panel in the New Era of Police Governance in England and Wales'. *Safer Communities*, 14(1): 22–31.

LISTER, S. and JONES, T. (2016). 'Plural Policing and the Challenge of Democratic Accountability', in S. LISTER and M. ROWE (eds), *Accountability of Policing*. London: Routledge.

LISTER, S. and ROWE, M. (eds) (2016). *Accountability of Policing*. London: Routledge.

LIVINGSTONE, S. (1996). 'On the Continuing Problem of Media Effects', in J. CURRAN and M. GUREVICH (eds), *Mass Media and Society*. London: Edward Arnold.

LLOYD, R., OATHAM, J., and HAMMER, M. (2007). *2007 Global Accountability Report*. London: One World Trust.

LOADER, B. and MERCEA, D. (2011). 'Networking Democracy? Social Media Innovations and Participatory Politics'. *Special Issue of Information Communication and Society*, 14(6).

LOADER, I. (1997). 'Policing and the Social: Questions of Symbolic Power'. *British Journal of Sociology*, 48(1): 1–18.

LOADER, I. (2000). 'Plural Policing and Democratic Governance'. *Social and Legal Studies*, 9(3): 323–45.

LOADER, I. (2013). 'Why Do the Police Matter? Beyond the Myth of Crime-Fighting', in J. BROWN (ed.), *The Future of Policing*. London: Routledge.

LOADER, I. and MULCAHY, A. (2003). *Policing and the Condition of England*. Oxford: Oxford University Press.

LOADER, I. and SPARKS, R. (2011). *Public Criminology?*. London: Routledge.

LOADER, I. and WALKER, N. (2006). 'Necessary Virtues: The Legitimate Place of the State in the Production of Security', in J. WOOD and B. DUPONT (eds), *Democracy, Society and the Governance of Security*. Cambridge: Cambridge University Press.

LOADER, I. and WALKER, N. (2007). *Civilizing Security*. Cambridge: Cambridge University Press.

LOADER, I. and ZEDNER, L. (2007). 'Police Beyond Law?'. *New Criminal Law Review*, 10(1): 142–52.

LOFTUS, B. (2007). 'Policing the "Irrelevant": Class, Diversity and Contemporary Police Culture', in M. O'NEILL, M. MARKS, and A.-M. SINGH (eds), *Police Occupational Culture*. Oxford: JAI Press.

LOFTUS, B. (2008). 'Dominant Culture Interrupted: Recognition, Resentment and the Politics of Change in an English Police Force'. *British Journal of Criminology*, 48(6): 778–97.

LOFTUS, B. (2009). *Police Culture in a Changing World*. Oxford: Oxford University Press.

LOFTUS, B. (2010). 'Police Occupational Culture: Classic Themes, Altered Times'. *Policing and Society*, 20(1): 1–20.

LOFTUS, B. (2019). 'Normalising the Exceptional: Covert Surveillance and the Subterranean World of Policing' (forthcoming).

LOFTUS, B. and GOOLD, B. J. (2012). 'Covert Surveillance and the Invisibilities of Policing'. *Criminology and Criminal Justice*, 12(3): 275–88.

LOFTUS, B., GOOLD, B., and MAC GIOLLABHUI, S. (2016). 'From a Visible Spectacle to an Invisible Presence: The Working Culture of Covert Policing'. *British Journal of Criminology*, 56(4): 629–45.

LÓPEZ, L. (2008). 'Des gendarmes Luxembourgeois chez les Brigades du Tigre: Les prémices de la coopération policière transfrontalière en Europe Occidentale'. *Revue De La Gendarmerie Nationale*, 226: 116–25.

LOVEDAY, B. (2006). *Size Isn't Everything: Restructuring Policing in England and Wales*. London: Policy Exchange.

LUBBERS, E. (2012). *Secret Manoeuvres in the Dark: Corporate Spying on Activists*. London: Pluto Press.

LUM C., KOPER, C. S., and WILLIS, J. (2016). 'Understanding the Limits of Technology's Impact on Police Effectiveness'. *Police Quarterly*, 20(2): 135–63.

LUSTGARTEN, L. (1986). *The Governance of the Police*. London: Sweet & Maxwell.

McARA, L. and McVIE, S. (2005). 'The Usual Suspects? Street Life, Young People and the Police'. *Criminal Justice*, 5(1): 5–36.

McARDLE, A., and ERZEN, T. (eds) (2001). *Zero Tolerance: Quality of Life and the New Police Brutality in New York City*. New York: New York University Press.

McBARNET, D. (1978). 'The Police and the State', in G. LITTLEJOHN, B. SMART, J. WAKEFORD, and N. YUVAL-DAVIS (eds), *Power and the State*. London: Croom Helm.

McBARNET, D. (1979). 'Arrest: The Legal Context of Policing', in S. HOLDAWAY (ed.), *The British Police*. London: Edward Arnold.

McBARNET, D. (1981). *Conviction*. London: Macmillan.

McCABE, S. and SUTCLIFFE, F. (1978). *Defining Crime: A Study of Police Decisions*. Oxford: Oxford Centre for Criminological Research.

McCANDLESS, R., FEIST, A., ALLAN, J., and MORGAN, N. (2016). 'Do Initiatives Involving Substantial Increases in Stop and Search Reduce Crime? Assessing the Impact of Operation BLUNT 2'. London: Home Office.

McCONVILLE, M. (2011). *Criminal Justice in China*. Cheltenham: Edward Elgar.

McCONVILLE, M. and SHEPHERD, D. (1992). *Watching Police, Watching Communities*. London: Routledge.

McConville, M., Sanders, A., and Leng, R. (1991). *The Case for the Prosecution: Police Suspects and the Construction of Criminality*. London: Routledge.

McCoy, A. W. (2009). *Policing America's Empire: The United States, the Philippines and the Rise of the Surveillance State*. Madison, WI: University of Wisconsin Press.

McCue, C. (2014). *Data Mining and Predictive Analysis: Intelligence Gathering and Crime Analysis* (2nd edn). Amsterdam: Elsevier.

McCulloch, J. (2001). *Blue Army: Paramilitary Policing in Australia*. Melbourne: Melbourne University Press.

McCulloch, J. and Wilson, D. (2016). *Pre-crime: Pre-emption, Precaution and the Future*. London: Routledge.

McDonagh, M. (2004). 'The Exploitation Generation or: How Marginal Movies Came in from the Cold', in A. H. T. Elsaesser and N. King (eds), *The Last Great American Picture Show: New Hollywood Cinema in the 1970s*. Amsterdam: Amsterdam University Press.

MacDonald, H. (2006). New York Cops: Still the Finest. *City Journal*, 16.

MacDonald, J., Fagan, J., and Geller, A. (2016). 'The Effects of Local Police Surges on Crime and Arrests in New York City'. *PLoS ONE*, 11: 1–13.

McGarrell, E. F., Chermak, S., Weiss, A., and Wilson J. (2001). 'Reducing Firearms Violence through Directed Police Patrol'. *Criminology and Public Policy*, 1: 119–48.

Machold, R. (2018). 'Reconsidering the Laboratory Thesis: Israel/Palestine and the Geopolitics of Representation'. *Political Geography*, 65: 88–97.

McKenzie, I., Morgan, R., and Reiner, R. (1990). 'Helping the Police with Their Inquiries: The Necessity Principle and Voluntary Attendance at the Police Station'. *Criminal Law Review*, January: 22–33.

McKenzie, M. (2018). *Common Enemies; Crime, Policy, and Politics in Australia-Indonesia Relations*, Oxford: Clarendon.

McLaughlin, E. (1992). 'The Democratic Deficit: European Unity and the Accountability of the British Police'. *British Journal of Criminology*, 32(4): 473–87.

McLaughlin, E. (2005). 'From Reel to Ideal: *The Blue Lamp* and the Popular Construction of the English "Bobby"'. *Crime Media Culture*, 1(1): 11–30.

McLaughlin, E. (2007/2011). *The New Policing*. London and Thousand Oaks, CA: Sage.

McLaughlin, E. and Murji, K. (1999). 'The Postmodern Condition of the Police'. *Liverpool Law Review*, 21: 217–40.

Macleod, C. (2018). 'A Private Police Force is Not the Answer to the UK Policing Crisis, Better Funding Is'. *The Guardian*, 12 February.

McMullan, J. (1996). 'The New Improved Monied Police: Reform, Crime Control, and the Commodification of Policing in London'. *British Journal of Criminology*, 36(1): 85–108.

McMullan, J. (1998). 'Social Surveillance and the Rise of the "Police Machine"'. *Theoretical Criminology*, 2(1): 93–117.

McNee, D. (1979). 'The Queen's Police Keepeth the Peace'. *The Guardian*, 25 September.

Macpherson, W. (1999). *The Stephen Lawrence Inquiry*. London: HMSO.

McRobbie, A. and Thornton, S. (1995). 'Rethinking "Moral Panic" for Multi-Mediated Social Worlds'. *British Journal of Sociology*, 46(4): 559–74.

Magone, J. M. (2003). *The Politics of Southern Europe: Integration into the European Union*. Westport, CT: Praeger.

Maguire, E. R. (2003). *Organizational Structure in American Police Agencies: Context, Complexity and Control*. Albany, NY: State University of New York Press.

Maguire, E. R. (2014). 'Police Organizations and the Iron Cage of Rationality', in M. D. Reisig and R. J. Kane (eds), *The Oxford*

Handbook of Police and Policing. Oxford: Oxford University Press.

MAGUIRE, E. R. (2016). 'New Directions in Protest Policing'. *Saint Louis University Public Law Review*, 35: 67–108.

MAGUIRE, E. R., NIX, J., and CAMPBELL, B. (2016). 'A War on Cops?—The Effects of Ferguson on the Number of U.S. Police Officers Murdered in the Line of Duty'. *Justice Quarterly*, 34(5): 739–58.

MAGUIRE, M. (2000). 'Policing by Risks and Targets: Some Dimensions and Implications of Intelligence-led Social Control'. *Policing and Society*, 9(4): 315–37.

MAGUIRE, M. (2004). 'The Crime Reduction Programme: Reflections on the Vision and the Reality'. *Criminal Justice*, 4(3): 213–38.

MAGUIRE, M. (2007). 'Crime Data and Statistics', in M. MAGUIRE, R. MORGAN, and R. REINER (eds), *The Oxford Handbook of Criminology* (4th edn). Oxford: Oxford University Press.

MAGUIRE, M. (2008). 'Criminal Investigation and Crime Control', in T. NEWBURN (ed.), *Handbook of Policing* (2nd edn). Cullompton: Willan.

MAGUIRE, M. and FUSSEY, P. (2016). 'Sensing Evil; Counterterrorism, Techno-science and the Cultural Reproduction of Security'. *Focaal*, 2016(75): 31–44.

MAGUIRE, M., and JOHN, T. (1995). *Intelligence, Surveillance and Informants: Integrated Approaches*. Crime Detection and Prevention Series Paper 64. London: Home Office.

MAGUIRE, M. and JOHN, T. (1996). 'Covert and Deceptive Policing in England and Wales: Issues in Regulation and Practice'. *European Journal of Crime, Criminal Law and Criminal Justice*, 4(3): 316–34.

MAGUIRE, M. and McVIE, S. (2017). 'Crime Data and Criminal Statistics: A Critical Reflection', in A. LIEBLING, S. MARUNA, and L. McARA (eds), *The Oxford Handbook of Criminology* (6th edn). Oxford: Oxford University Press.

MAGUIRE, M. and NORRIS, C. (1992). *The Conduct and Supervision of Criminal Investigations*, Royal Commission on Criminal Justice Research Report 5. London: HMSO.

MAITLAND, R. (1885). *Justice and Police*. London: Macmillan.

MANN, M. (1993). *The Sources of Social Power, Vol. 2: The Rise of Classes and Nation-States, 1760–1914*. Cambridge: Cambridge University Press.

MANN, M. (1997). 'Has Globalization Ended the Rise and Rise of the Nation-State?'. *Review of International Political Economy*, 4(2): 472–96.

MANN, M. (2012). *The Sources of Social Power, Vol. 3: Global Empires and Revolution, 1890–1945*. Cambridge: Cambridge University Press.

MANN, S., NOLAN, J., and WELLMAN, B. (2003). 'Sousveillance: Inventing and Using Wearable Computing Devices for Data Collection in Surveillance Environments'. *Surveillance & Society*, 1(3): 331–55.

MANNING, P. (1979). 'The Social Control of Police Work', in S. HOLDAWAY (ed.), *The British Police*. London: Edward Arnold.

MANNING, P. (1988). *Symbolic Communication: Signifying Calls and the Police Response*, Cambridge, MA: MIT Press.

MANNING, P. (1992). 'Information Technologies and the Police', in M. TONRY (ed.), *Crime and Justice: A Review of the Research*. Chicago, IL: University of Chicago Press.

MANNING, P. (1997). *Police Work* (2nd edn). Prospect Heights, IL: Waveland Press.

MANNING, P. (2003). *Policing Contingencies*. Chicago, IL: Chicago University Press.

MANNING, P. (2007). 'A Dialectic of Organisational and Occupational Culture', in M. O'NEILL, M. MARKS, and A.-M. SINGH (eds), *Police Occupational Culture*. Oxford: JAI Press.

MANNING, P. (2008). *The Technology of Policing: Crime Mapping, Information Technology and the Rationality of Crime Control*, New York: New York University Press.

MANNING, P. (2010). *Democratic Policing in a Changing World*. London: Routledge.

MANNING, P. (2013). 'The Work of Egon Bittner'. *Ethnographic Studies*, 13: 51–66.

MANNING, P. (2014). 'Privatizing and Changes in the Policing Web' in J. M. BROWN (ed.), *The Future of Policing*. London: Routledge.

MANNING, P. and VAN MAANEN, J. (eds) (1978). *Policing: A View from the Street*. Santa Monica, CA: Goodyear Press.

MANNING, P. and REDLINGER, J. (1977). 'Invitational Edges of Corruption', in P. ROCK (ed.), *Politics and Drugs*. Rutgers, NJ: Dutton.

MANSFIELD, M. (2012). 'Our Right to Protest is Under Attack'. *The Guardian*, 1 May.

MANSFIELD, M. (2013). 'A Dangerous Use of Police Force to Quell Protest'. *The Guardian*, 10 March.

MARENIN, O. (1982). 'Parking Tickets and Class Repression: The Concept of Policing in Critical Theories of Criminal Justice'. *Contemporary Crises*, 6(2): 241–66.

MARK, R. (1978). *In the Office of Constable*. London: Collins.

MARKS, M. (1999). 'Changing Dilemmas and Dilemmas of Change: Transforming the Public Order Police Unit in Durban'. *Policing and Society*, 9(2): 157–79.

MARKS, M. (2000). 'Transforming Police Organisations from Within: Police Dissident Groupings in South Africa'. *British Journal of Criminology*, 40: 557–73.

MARKS, M. (2005). *Transforming the Robocops: Changing Police in South Africa*. Durban: University of Kwazulu-Natal Press.

MARKS, M. (2011). 'The Fantastical World of South Africa's Roadblocks: The Dilemmas of a Ubiquitous Police Strategy'. *Policing and Society*, 21(4): 408–19.

MARKS, M. and FLEMING, J. (2006a). 'The Right to Unionise, the Right to Bargain and the Right to Democratic Policing'. *The Annals*, 605(1): 178–99.

MARKS, M. and FLEMING, J. (2006b). 'The Untold Story: The Regulation of Police Labour Rights and the Quest for Police Democratisation'. *Police Practice and Research*, 7(4): 309–22.

MARKS, M. and GOLDSMITH, A. (2006). 'The State, the People and Democratic Policing: The Case of South Africa', in J. WOOD and B. DUPONT (eds), *Democracy, Society and the Governance of Security*. Cambridge: Cambridge University Press.

MARKS, M. and SKLANSKY, D. (eds) (2011). *Police Reform from the Bottom Up*. London: Routledge.

MARKS, M., HOWELL, S., and SHELLY, S. (2017). 'The Fluidity of "Police Culture"'. *Policing*, 11(3): 318–31.

MARLOW, A. and LOVEDAY, B. (eds) (2000). *After Macpherson*. Lyme Regis: Russell House.

MARQUIS, G. (1992). 'The Police as a Social Service in Early Twentieth-Century Toronto'. *Histoire sociale—Social History*, XXV: 335–58.

MARQUIS, G. (2016). *The Vigilant Eye: Policing Canada from 1867 to 9/11*. Ocean Vista, Nova Scotia: Fernwood Publishing.

MARSHALL, G. (1965). *Police and Government*. London: Methuen.

MARSHALL, G. (1978). 'Police Accountability Revisited', in D. BUTLER and A. H. HALSEY (eds), *Policy and Politics*. London: Macmillan.

MARSHALL, T. H. (1950). *Citizenship and Social Class*. Cambridge: Cambridge University Press.

MARTHA, R. S. (2010). *The Legal Foundations of Interpol*. Oxford: Hart.

MARTIN, H. (2018). 'Three-quarters of Disneyland Employees can't afford Basic Living Expenses'. *Los Angles Times*, 1 March.

MARTIN, S. E. (1989). 'Women on the Move?'. *Women & Criminal Justice*, 1(1): 21–40.

MARX, G. (1987). 'The Interweaving of Public and Private Police in Undercover Work', in C. D. SHEARING and P. C. STENNING (eds), *Private Policing*. Newbury Park, CA: Sage.

Marx, G. (1988). *Undercover: Police Surveillance in America*. Berkeley, CA: University of California Press.

Marx, G. (1992). 'Under-the-covers Undercover Investigations: Some Reflections on the State's use of Sex and Deception in Law Enforcement'. *Criminal Justice Ethics*, 11(1): 13–24.

Mason, P. (2003/2013). *Criminal Visions: Media Representations of Crime and Justice*. London: Routledge.

Mathiesen, T. (1997). 'The Viewer Society: Michel Foucault's "Panopticon" Revisited'. *Theoretical Criminology*, 1(2): 215–34.

Mawby, R. C. and Wright, A. (2008). 'Models of Policing', in T. Newburn (ed.), *Handbook of Policing* (2nd edn). London: Routledge.

Mawby, R. I. (1991). *Comparative Policing Issues*. London: Unwin.

Mawby, R. I. (ed.) (1999). *Policing across the World: Issues for the Twenty-First Century*. London: UCL Press.

Maxwell, C., Garner, J., and Fagan, J. (2002). 'The Preventive Effect of Arrest on Intimate Partner Violence: Research, Policy and Theory'. *Criminology and Public Policy*, 2(1): 51–80.

Mayoral, J. A. (2011). 'Democratic Improvements in the European Union under the Lisbon Treaty: Institutional Changes regarding Democratic Government in the EU'. Robert Schuman Centre for Advanced Studies, European University Institute, February.

Mazower, M. (ed.) (1997). *The Policing of Politics in the Twentieth Century*. Providence, RI: Berghahn Books.

Mead, G. (1934). *Mind, Self and Society*. Chicago, IL: University of Chicago Press.

Meeks, K. (2000). *Driving While Black: Highways, Shopping Malls, Taxicabs, Sidewalks*. London: Penguin Random House.

Mennicke, A., Gromer, J., Oehme, K., and MacConnie, L. (2016). 'Workplace Experiences of Gay and Lesbian Criminal Justice Officers in the United States: A Qualitative Investigation of Officers Attending a LGBT Law Enforcement Conference'. *Policing and Society*, 28(6): 712–29.

Meyer, S. (2015). 'Still Blaming the Victim of Intimate Partner Violence? Women's Narratives of Victim Desistance and Redemption when Seeking Support'. *Theoretical Criminology*, 20(1): 75–90.

Michael, D. (2002). *A Sense of Security? The Ideology and Accountability of Private Security Officers*, PhD Thesis: London School of Economics.

Miller, J., Bland, N., and Quinton, P. (2000). *The Impact of Stops and Searches on Crime and the Community*. London: Home Office.

Miller, W. (1999). *Cops and Bobbies* (2nd edn). Columbus, OH: Ohio State University Press.

Millie, A., and Herrington, V. (2005). 'Bridging the Gap: Understanding Reassurance Policing'. *Howard Journal*, 44(1): 41–56.

Milne, S. (2014). *The Enemy Within: Thatcher's Secret War Against the Miners* (4th edn). London: Verso.

Mirowski, P. and Plehwe, D. (2009). *The Road from Mont Pelerin: The Making of the Neoliberal Thought Collective*. Cambridge, MA: Harvard University Press.

Mirowski, P. (2014). *Never Let a Serious Crisis Go to Waste: How Neoliberalism Survived the Financial Meltdown*. London: Verso.

Miyazawa, S. (1992). *Policing in Japan: A Study in Making Crime*. New York: University of New York Press.

Moe, N. J. (2006). *The View from Vesuvius: Italian Culture and the Southern Question*. Oakland, CA: University of California Press.

Monahan, T. (2010). 'The Future of Security? Surveillance Operations at Homeland Security Fusion Centers'. *Social Justice*, 37(2–3): 84–98.

Monjardet, D. (1996). *Ce que fait la police: sociologie de la force publique*. Paris: La Découverte.

MONKKONEN, E. H. (1981). *Police in Urban America 1860–1920*. Cambridge: Cambridge University Press.

MONKKONEN, E. H. (1992). 'History of Urban Police', in M. TONRY and N. MORRIS (eds), *Modern Policing: Crime and Justice: A Review of the Research, Vol. 15*. Chicago, IL: University of Chicago Press.

MOORE, C. (2017). *Civil Liberties and Human Rights in Twentieth-Century Britain*. Cambridge: Cambridge University Press.

MORABITO, M. S. (2014). 'Policing Vulnerable Populations', in M. D. REISIG and R. J. KANE (eds), *The Oxford Handbook of Police and Policing*. Oxford: Oxford University Press.

MORÁN, S. B. (2010). 'La Unión Europea y la creación de un espacio de seguridad y justicia—Visión histórica de la lucha contra el terrorismo internacional en Europa'. *Anuario Español de Derecho Internacional*, 26: 251–84.

MORGAN, J. (1987). *Conflict and Order: The Police and Labour Disputes in England and Wales 1900–1939*. Oxford: Oxford University Press.

MORGAN, R. and NEWBURN, T. (1997). *The Future of Policing*. Oxford: Oxford University Press.

MORGAN, R. and SMITH, D. (2017). 'Delivering More with Less: Austerity and the Politics of Law and Order', in A. LIEBLING, S. MARUNA, and L. MCARA (eds), *The Oxford Handbook of Criminology* (6th edn). Oxford: Oxford University Press.

MORI (2017). *Public Views of Policing in England and Wales 2016/17*. London: Ipsos MORI.

MORI (2018). *Public Views of Policing in England and Wales 2017/18*. London: Ipsos MORI.

MOROZOV, E. (2011). *The Net Delusion: The Dark Side of Internet Freedom*. New York: Public Affairs.

MOROZOV, E. (2013) *To Save Everything, Click Here: The Folly of Technological Solutionism*. New York: Public Affairs.

MORRELL, K. and BRADFORD, B. (2019). *Policing and Public Management*. London: Routledge.

MORRIS, P. and HEAL, K. (1981). *Crime Control and the Police*. Home Office Research Unit. London: Home Office.

MORRIS, R. M. (2001). '"Lies, Damned Lies and Criminal Statistics": Reinterpreting the Criminal Statistics in England and Wales'. *Crime, History and Societies*, 5: 111–27.

MOSKOS, P. (2008). *Cop in the Hood: My Year Policing Baltimore's Eastern District*. Princeton, NJ: Princeton University Press.

MOUHANNA, C. (2008). 'The Failure of "Ilotage" and "Police de Proximité" Systems to Withstand "Law and Order" Rhetoric in Contemporary France', in T. WILLIAMSON (ed.), *The Handbook of Knowledge-Based Policing*. Chichester: Wiley.

MOUHANNA, C. (2009). 'French Police and Urban Riots: Is the National Police Force Part of the Solution or Part of the Problem?', in D. WADDINGTON, F. JOBARD, and M. KING (eds), *Rioting in the UK and France: A Comparative Analysis*. Cullompton: Willan.

MOUHANNA, C. and EASTON, M. (2014). 'Policing Paris: "out of" or "still in" Napoleonic Time?'. *European Journal of Police Studies*, 2(1): 94–109.

MUIR, R. (2017). 'What Do We Want the Police to Do?', 25 October. London: Police Foundation.

MUIR, W. K. (1977). *Police: Streetcorner Politicians*. Chicago, IL: University of Chicago Press.

MUKHERJEE, A. and HARPER, T. (2018). *Excessive Force: The Fight to Reform City Policing*. Madeira Park, BC: Douglas & McIntyre.

MULCAHY, A. (2013). *Policing Northern Ireland: Conflict, Legitimacy and Reform*. Cullompton: Willan.

MULLINS, C. M. and ROTHE, D. (2008). *Blood, Power and Bedlam: Violations of International Criminal Law in*

Post-Colonial Africa—Vol. 2 of New Perspectives in Criminology. New York: Peter Lang.

MURPHY, C. (1998). 'Policing Postmodern Canada'. *Canadian Journal of Law and Society*, 13(2): 1–25.

MURPHY, C. (2007). '"Securitizing" Canadian Policing: A New Paradigm for the Post 9/11 Security State?'. *Canadian Journal of Sociology*, 32(4): 449–75.

MURPHY, J., MCDOWELL, S., and BRANIFF, M. (2017). 'Historical Dialogue and Memory in Policing Change: The Case of the Police in Northern Ireland'. *Memory Studies*, 10(4), 406–22.

NADELMANN, E. (1990). 'Global Prohibition Regimes: The Evolution of Norms in International Society'. *International Organization*, 44(4): 479–526.

NADELMANN, E. (1993). *Cops Across Borders: The Internationalization of US Law Enforcement*. University Park, PA: Pennsylvania State University Press.

NAGIN, D. S. (2016). 'What We've Got Here is Failure to Communicate'. *Criminology and Public Policy*, 15: 753–65.

NAMBA, M. (2011) '"War on Illegal Immigrants" National Narratives, and Globalisation: Japanese Policy and Practice of Stop and Question in Global Perspective'. *Policing and Society*, 21(4): 432–43.

NEAL, D. (1991). *The Rule of Law in a Penal Colony: Law and Power in Early New South Wales*. Sydney: Cambridge University Press.

Nelken, D. (2012) 'White-collar and corporate crime' in M.Maguire, R.Morgan and R.Reiner (eds). The Oxford Handbook of Criminology 5th.ed. Oxford: Oxford University Press.

NEMETH, C. P. (2017). *Private Security and the Law* (5th edn). London: Taylor & Francis.

NEOCLEOUS, M. (1998). 'Policing and pin-making: Adam Smith, police and the state of prosperity'. *Policing and Society* 8(4): 425-49.

NEOCLEOUS, M. (2000). *The Fabrication of Social Order: A Critical Theory of Police Power*. London: Pluto Press.

NEOCLEOUS, M. (2006). 'Theoretical Foundations of the "New Police Science"', in M. DUBBER and M. VALVERDE (eds), *The New Police Science*. Stanford, CA: Stanford University Press.

NETTLES, J. (2012). *Jewels and Jackboots: Hitler's British Isles, the German Occupation of the British Channel Islands 1940–1945*. St Helens: Channel Islands Publishing.

NEWBERRY J. (2017). 'Broken Windows or Breaking Communities', in *Racial Profiling and the NYPD*. New York: Palgrave Macmillan.

NEWBURN, T. (ed.) (2005). *Policing—Key Readings*. Cullompton: Willan.

NEWBURN, T. (2008/2011). 'Policing Since 1945', in T. NEWBURN (ed.), *Handbook of Policing* (2nd edn). London: Routledge.

NEWBURN, T. (2015). 'The 2011 England Riots in Recent Historical Perspective'. *British Journal of Criminology*, 55(1): 39–64.

NEWBURN, T. (2016). 'The 2011 England Riots in European Context: A Framework for Understanding the "Life-cycle of Riots"'. *European Journal of Criminology*, 13(5). doi: 10.1177/1477370816633726.

NEWBURN, T. and HAYMAN, S. (2001). *Policing, CCTV and Social Control: Police Surveillance of Suspects in Custody*. Cullompton: Willan.

NEWBURN, T. and REINER, R. (2007). 'Crime and Penal Policy', in A. SELDON (ed.), *Blair's Britain*. Cambridge: Cambridge University Press.

NEWBURN, T., COOPER, K., DEACON, R., and DISKI, R. (2015). 'Shopping for Free? Looting, Consumerism and the 2011 Riots'. *British Journal of Criminology*, 55(5). doi: 10.1093/bjc/azv007.

NEWBURN, T., SHINER, M., and HAYMAN, S. (2004). 'Race, Crime and Injustice?: Strip Search and the Treatment of Suspects in Custody'. *British Journal of Criminology*, 44(5): 677–94.

NEWBURN, T., WILLIAMSON, T., and WRIGHT, A. (eds) (2007). *Handbook of Criminal Investigation*. Cullompton: Willan.

NEWMAN, G. F. (1983). *Law and Order*. London: Granada.

NEYROUD, P. W. (2016). 'The Ethics of Learning by Testing: The Police, Professionalism and Researching the Police', in M. COWBURN, L. GELSTHORPE, and A. WAHIDIN (eds), Research Ethics in Criminology—Dilemmas, Issues and Solutions. London: Routledge.

NEYROUD, P. and BECKLEY, A. (2012). *Policing, Ethics and Human Rights*. Cullompton: Willan.

NIEDERHOFFER, A. (1967). *Behind the Shield*. New York: Doubleday.

NOGALA, D. (2001). 'Policing across a Dimorphous Border: Challenge and Innovation at the French-German Border'. *European Journal of Crime, Criminal Law and Criminal Justice*, 9(2): 130–43.

NOGALA, D., FEHERVARY, J., JASCHKE, H.-G., DEN BOER, M. (eds) (2017). 'Police Science and Police Practice in Europe'. *European Police Science and Research Bulletin*. Budapest: CEPOL.

NORRIS, C. and ARMSTRONG, G. (1999). *The Maximum Surveillance Society: The Rise of CCTV*. West Sussex: Berg.

NORRIS, C. and DUNNIGHAN, C. (2000). 'Subterranean Blues: Conflict as an Unintended Consequence of the Police Use of Informers'. *Policing and Society*, 9(4): 385–412.

NORRIS, C., and McCAHILL, M. (2006). 'CCTV: Beyond Penal Modernism?'. *British Journal of Criminology*, 46(1): 97–118.

NORRIS, C., and NORRIS, N. (1993). 'Defining Good Policing: The Instrumental and Moral in Approaches to Good Practice and Competence'. *Policing and Society*, 3(3): 205–22.

NORRIS, J. J. (2016). 'Entrapment and Terrorism on the Left: An Analysis of Post 9/11 Cases'. *New Criminal Law Review*, 19(2): 236–78.

NOVISKY, M. A., and PERALTA, R. L. (2014). 'When Women Tell: Intimate Partner Violence and the Factors Related to Police Notification'. *Violence Against Women*, 21(1): 65–86.

O'DONNELL, G. (2010). *Democracy, Agency and the State: Theory with Comparative Intent*. Oxford: Oxford University Press.

O'MALLEY, P. (1997). 'Policing, Post-Modernism and Political Rationality'. *Social and Legal Studies*, 6(3): 363–81 [as reprinted in T. NEWBURN (ed.), *Policing—Key Readings*. Cullompton: Willan 2005].

O'MALLEY, P. (1999). '"Social Justice" after the "Death of the Social"'. *Social Justice*, 26(2): 327–56.

O'MALLEY, P. and PALMER, D. (1996). 'Post-Keynesian Policing'. *Economy and Society*, 25(2): 137–55.

O'NEILL, M. (2015). 'Police Community Support Officers in England'. *Policing and Society*, 27(1): 21–39.

O'NEILL, M. (2018). *Key Challenges in Criminal Investigation*. Bristol: Policy Press.

O'NEILL, M., MARKS, M., and SINGH, A.-M. (eds) (2007). *Police Occupational Culture: New Debates and Directions*. Oxford: JAI Press.

O'REILLY, C. (2010). 'The Transnational Security Industry: A Case of State-Corporate Symbiosis'. *Theoretical Criminology*, 14(2): 183–210.

O'REILLY, C. (2015). 'The Pluralization of High Policing: Convergence and Divergence at the Public-Private Interface'. *British Journal of Criminology*, 55(4): 688–710.

O'REILLY, C. (ed.) (2017). *Colonial Policing and the Transnational Legacy: The Global Dynamics of Policing across the Lusophone Community*. London: Routledge.

O'REILLY, C. and ELLISON, G. (2006). '"Eye Spy Private High": Reconceptualizing High Policing Theory'. *British Journal of Criminology*, 46(4): 641–60.

OLDFIELD, J.R. (1998). *Popular Politics and British Anti-Slavery: The Mobilization of Public Opinion Against the Slave Trade 1787–1807*. London: Routledge.

OLSEN, M. B. (2018). 'Victim of "Worst Domestic Violence Case Ever" Says Police Did Nothing to Help'. *Metro*, 7 January.

OPEN SOCIETY JUSTICE INITIATIVE (2006). *I Can Stop and Search Whoever I Want: Ethnic Profiling by Police in Bulgaria, Hungary and Spain*. New York: Open Society Institute.

OSBORNE, D. and GAEBLER, T. (1992). *Reinventing Government*. New York: Addison-Wesley.

PACE (1984). *The Police and Criminal Evidence Act 1984* London: HMSO.

PACKER, H. L. (1968). *The Limits of the Criminal Sanction*. Stanford, CA: Stanford University Press and Oxford University Press.

PACKER, H. L. (1968/1971). 'Two Models of Criminal Process', in A. S. GOLDSTEIN and J. GOLDSTEIN (eds), *Crime, Law and Society*, New York: The Free Press.

PALAST, G. (2016). *The Best Democracy Money Can Buy*. New York: Seven Stories Press.

PALMER, S. H. (1988). *Police and Protest in England and Ireland 1780–1850*. Cambridge: Cambridge University Press.

PANDIT, N. (2012). 'Policing the EU's External Border: Legitimacy and Accountability under Scrutiny'. *ERA Forum*, 13(3): 397–410. doi: 10.1007/s12027-012-0273-9.

PANICH, L. and GODIN, S. (2018). *The Socialist Challenge Today*. London: Merlin.

PAOLINE, E. and TERRILL, W. (2013). *Police Culture*. Durham, NC: Carolina Academic Press.

PARETTI, J. (2017). 'Palantir: The "Special Ops" Tech Giant that Wields as much Real-World Power as Google'. *The Guardian*, 30 July.

PARTRIDGE, E. (1992). *A Dictionary of Catch Phrases: American & British from the Sixteenth Century to the Present Day*. London: Scarborough House.

PASQUINO, P. (1991). 'Theatrum Politicum: The Genealogy of Capital—Police and the State of Prosperity', in G. BURCHELL, C. GORDON, and P. MILLER (eds), *The Foucault Effect: Studies in Governmentality*. Hemel Hempstead: Harvester Wheatsheaf [originally in *Ideology and Consciousness*, 4(1) (1978): 41–54].

PATE, T., FERRARA, A., BOWERS, R., and LORENCE, J. (1976). *Police Response Time, its Determinants and Effects*. Washington, DC: Police Foundation.

PATTEN, C. (1999). *A New Beginning: Policing Northern Ireland*. The Report of the Independent Commission on Policing for Northern Ireland, Copyright Unit. Norwich: HMSO.

PATTON, D. U., LEONARD, P., CAHILL, L., MACBETH, J., CROSBY, S., and BRUNTON, D. W. (2016). '"Police took my homie I dedicate my life 2 his revenge": Twitter Tensions between Gang-Involved Youth and Police in Chicago'. *Journal of Human Behavior in the Social Environment*, 26(3–4): 310–24.

PEARSON, G. (1983). *Hooligan*. London: Macmillan.

PERLMUTTER, D. D. (2000). *Policing the Media: Street Cops and Public Perceptions of Law*. London: Sage.

PETERSON, M. (2005). *Intelligence-led Policing: The New Intelligence Architecture*. September, NCJ 210681. Washington, DC: National Institute of Justice.

PHILLIPS, C. (2005). 'Facing Inwards and Outwards?: Institutional Racism, Race Equality and the Role of Black and Asian Professional Associations'. *Criminology and Criminal Justice*, 5(4): 357–77.

PHILLIPS, C. (2007). 'The Re-Emergence of the "Black Spectre": Minority Professional Associations in the Post-Macpherson Era'. *Ethnic and Racial Studies*, 30(3): 375–96.

PHILLIPS, C. (2011). 'Institutional Racism and Ethnic Inequalities: An Expanded Multilevel Framework'. *Journal of Social Policy*, 40(1): 173–92.

PHILLIPS, C. and BOWLING, B. (2017). 'Ethnicities, Racism, Crime, and Criminal Justice', in A. LIEBLING, S. MARUNA, and

L. McAra (eds), *The Oxford Handbook of Criminology* (6th edn). Oxford: Oxford University Press.

Philips, D. (1980). 'A New Engine of Power and Authority: The Institutionalisation of Law Enforcement in England 1780–1830', in V. Gatrell, B. Lenman, and G. Parker (eds), *Crime and the Law*. London: Europa.

Philips, D., and Storch, R. (1999). *Policing Provincial England, 1829–1856*. Leicester: Leicester University Press.

Phythian, M. (ed.) (2013). *Understanding the Intelligence Cycle*. London: Routledge.

Pincen, S. *et al.* (2014). 'Establishing Cross-border Co-operation between Professional Organizations: Police, Fire Brigades and Emergency Health Services in Dutch Border Regions'. *European Urban and Regional Studies*, 21: 1–16.

Pinker, S. (2011). *The Better Angels of our Nature*. London: Penguin Books.

Pleasance, P., Kemp, V., and Balmer N. (2011). 'The Justice Lottery? Police Station Advice 25 Years On from PACE'. *Criminal Law Review*, 1: 3–18.

Pogarsky, G. and Loughran, T. A. (2016). 'The Policy-to-Perceptions Link in Deterrence: Time to Retire the Clearance Rate'. *Criminology and Public Policy*, 15(3): 777–90.

Polanyi, K. (1944). *The Great Transformation*. Boston, MA: Beacon.

Policy Studies Institute (1983). *Police and People in London*: i, D. J. Smith, *A Survey of Londoners*; ii, S. Small, *A Group of Young Black People*; iii, D. J. Smith, *A Survey of Police Officers*; iv, D. J. Smith and J. Gray, *The Police in Action*. London: PSI.

Porter, B. (1987). *The Origins of the Vigilante State*. London: Macmillan.

Postman, N. (1985). *Amusing Ourselves to Death: Public Discourse in the Age of Show Business*. New York: Basic Books.

Postman, N. (1992). *Technopoly: The Surrender of Culture to Technology*, New York: Alfred A. Knopf.

Poyner, B. (1993). 'What Works in Crime Prevention: An Overview of Evaluations'. *Crime Prevention Studies*, 1: 7–34.

Pratt, J. (2014). 'Civilizing and Decivilizing Characteristics of the Contemporary Penal Field', in T. Landini and F. Dépelteau (eds), *Norbert Elias and Empirical Research*. London: Palgrave Macmillan.

Prenzler, T. and Sinclair, G. (2013). 'The Status of Women Police Officers: An International Review'. *International Journal of Law, Crime and Justice*, 41(2): 115–31.

Presdee, M. (2000). *Cultural Criminology and the Carnival of Crime*. London: Routledge.

Prins, R., Cachet, L., Ponsaers, P., and Hughes, G. (2012). 'Fragmentation and Interconnection in Public Safety Governance in the Netherlands, Belgium and England', in M. Fenger and V. Bekkers (eds), *Beyond Fragmentation and Interconnectivity, Innovation and the Public Sector*. Amsterdam: IOS Publishing.

Provine, D. M. and Sanchez, G. (2012). 'Suspecting Immigrants: Exploring the Links between Racialized Anxieties and Expanded Police Powers in Arizona'. *Policing and Society*, 21(4): 468–79.

PSNI (2018) *Workforce Composition Statistics*. Belfast: Police Service of Northern Ireland https://www.psni.police.uk/inside-psni/Statistics/workforce-composition-statistics/.

Patten, C. (1999). *A New Beginning: Policing Northern Ireland*. The Report of the Independent Commission on Policing for Northern Ireland, Copyright Unit. Norwich: HMSO.

Punch, M. (1979a). *Policing the Inner City*. London: Macmillan.

Punch, M. (1979b). 'The Secret Social Service', in S. Holdaway (ed.), *The British Police*. London: Edward Arnold.

Punch, M. (ed.) (1983). *Control in the Police Organization*. Cambridge, MA: MIT Press.

Punch, M. (1985). *Conduct Unbecoming: The Social Construction of Police Deviance and Control*. London: Tavistock.

Punch, M. (2003). Rotten Orchards: 'Pestilence', Police Misconduct and System Failure. *Policing and Society*, 13(2): 171–96.

Punch, M. (2007). *Zero Tolerance Policing*. Bristol: Policy Press.

PUNCH, M. (2009). *Police Corruption: Deviance, Accountability and Reform in Policing*. Cullompton: Willan.

PUNCH, M. (2010). *Shoot to Kill: Police Accountability, Firearms and Fatal Force*. Bristol: Policy Press.

PUNCH, M. and NAYLOR, T. (1973). 'The Police: A Social Service'. *New Society*, 24.

QUINTON, P., BLAND, N., and MILLER, J. (2000). *Police Stops, Decision-making and Practice*, Police Research Series 130, Policing and Reducing Crime Unit, 38. London: Home Office.

RABE-HEMP, C. (2017). *Thriving in an All-Boys Club: Women Police and Their Fight For Equality*. Lanham, MD: Rowman and Littlefield.

RADZINOWICZ, L. (1956). *A History of the English Criminal Law and its Administration from 1750, Vol 3: Cross Currents in the Movement for the Reform of the Police*. London: Stevens & Sons.

RAEFF, M. (1975). 'The Well-ordered Police State and the Development of Modernity in Seventeenth and Eighteenth-Century Europe: An Attempt at a Comparative Approach'. *American Historical Review*, 80(5): 1221–43.

RAEFF, M. (1983). *The Well-Ordered Police State: Social and Institutional Change through Law in the Germanies and Russia 1600–1800*. New Haven, CT: Yale University Press.

RATCLIFFE, J. (2009). *Strategic Thinking in Criminal Intelligence* (2nd edn). Annandale, NSW: The Federation Press.

RATCLIFFE, J. (2016). *Intelligence-led Policing*. London: Routledge.

RATCLIFFE, J. (2018). *Reducing Crime*. London: Routledge.

RAWLINGS, P. (2008). 'Policing Before the Police', in T. NEWBURN (ed.), *Handbook of Policing* (2nd edn). Cullompton: Willan.

RAWLS, J (1971). *A Theory of Justice*. Cambridge, MA: Harvard University Press.

REDHEAD, S. (ed.) (2008). *The Jean Baudrillard Reader*. New York: Columbia University Press.

REICHEL, P. L. (1988). 'Southern Slave Patrols as a Transitional Police Type'. *American Journal of Police*, 7: 51–77.

REIMAN, J. (2004). *The Rich Get Rich and the Poor Get Prison: Ideology, Class and Criminal Justice* (7th edn). Boston, MA: Allyn and Bacon.

REINER, R. (1978a). *The Blue-Coated Worker*. Cambridge: Cambridge University Press.

REINER, R. (1978b). 'The Police, Class and Politics'. *Marxism Today*, March, 69–80.

REINER, R. (1980). 'Fuzzy Thoughts: The Police and Law and Order Politics'. *Sociological Review*, (March) 28(2): 377–413.

REINER, R. (1981a). 'Keystone to Kojak: the Hollywood Cop', in P. DAVIES and B. NEVE (eds), *Politics, Society and Cinema in America*. Manchester: Manchester University Press.

REINER, R. (1981b). 'The Politics of Police Power', in *Politics and Power 4: Law, Politics and Justice*. London: Routledge.

REINER, R. (1984). 'Is Britain Turning into a Police State?'. *New Society*, 2 August.

REINER, R. (1985). *The Politics of the Police*. Brighton: Harvester Wheatsheaf.

REINER, R. (1988). 'British Criminology and the State'. *British Journal of Criminology*, 29(1): 138–58.

REINER, R. (1989). 'The Politics of Police Research', in M. WEATHERITT (ed.), *Police Research: Some Future Prospects*. Aldershot: Avebury.

REINER, R. (1991). *Chief Constables: Bobbies, Bosses or Bureaucrats*. Oxford: Clarendon.

REINER, R. (1992a). 'Police Research in the United Kingdom: A Critical Review', in N. MORRIS and M. TONRY (eds), *Modern Policing*. Chicago, IL: Chicago University Press.

REINER, R. (1992b). 'Policing a Postmodern Society'. *Modern Law Review*, 55(6): 761–81.

REINER, R. (1993). 'Race, Crime and Justice', in L. GELSTHORPE and W. McWILLIAMS (eds), *Minority Ethnic Groups and the Criminal Justice System*. Cambridge University: Institute of Criminology.

REINER, R. (1994). 'The Dialectics of Dixon: The Changing Image of the TV Cop' in M. Stephens and S. Becker (eds.) *Police Force, Police Service* London: Macmillan 48) Tilly Charles and Wood, Lesley J. (2013) *Social Movements 1768-2012* (3rd edn). London: Routledge.

REINER, R. (1998). 'Process or Product? Problems of Assessing Individual Police Performance', in J.-P. BRODEUR (ed.), *How to Recognize Good Policing*. Thousand Oaks, CA: Sage.

REINER, R. (1999). 'Order and Discipline', in I. HOLLIDAY, A. GAMBLE, and G. PARRY (eds), *Fundamentals in British Politics*. London: Macmillan.

REINER, R. (2007). 'Media Made Criminality: The Representations of Crime in the Mass Media', in M. MAGUIRE, R. MORGAN, and R. REINER (eds), *The Oxford Handbook of Criminology* (4th edn). Oxford: Clarendon.

REINER, R. (2006). 'Beyond Risk: A Lament for Social Democratic Criminology', in T. NEWBURN and P. ROCK (eds), *The Politics of Crime Control*. Oxford: Oxford University Press.

REINER, R. (2007). *Law and Order: An Honest Citizen's Guide to Crime and Control*. Cambridge: Polity Press.

REINER, R. (2008). 'Policing and the Media', in T. NEWBURN (ed.), *Handbook of Policing* (2nd edn). Cullompton: Willan.

REINER, R. (2010a). 'Citizenship, Crime, Criminalization: Marshalling a Social Democratic Perspective'. *New Criminal Law Review*, 13(2): 241–61.

REINER, R. (2010b). 'New Theories of Policing: A Social Democratic Critique', in D. DOWNES, D. HOBBS, and T. NEWBURN (eds), *The Eternal Recurrence of Crime and Control: Essays in Honour of Paul Rock*. Oxford: Clarendon.

REINER, R. (2010c). *The Politics of the Police* 4th ed. Oxford: Oxford University Press.

REINER, R. (2011). *Policing, Popular Culture and Political Economy: Towards a Social Democratic Criminology*. London: Ashgate.

REINER, R. (2012a). 'Policing and Social Democracy: Resuscitating a Lost Perspective', *Cahiers Politiestudies Jaargang* 2012-4, No. 25: 91–114.

REINER, R. (2012b). 'What's left? The Prospect for Social Democratic Criminology', *Crime, Media and Culture* Vol. 8, No.2: 135

REINER, R. (2012C). *In Praise of Fire Brigade Policing: Contra Common Sense Conceptions of the Police Role*. London: Howard League.

REINER, R. (2013). 'Who Governs? Democracy, Plutocracy, Science and Prophecy in Policing'. *Criminology and Criminal Justice*, 13: 161–80.

REINER, R. (2015). 'Revisiting the Classics: Three Seminal Founders of the Study of Policing: Michael Banton, Jerome Skolnick and Egon Bittner'. *Policing and Society*, 25(3): 308–27.

REINER, R. (2016a). 'Conservatives and the Constabulary in Great Britain: Cross-Dressing Conundrums', in M. DEFLEM (ed.), *The Politics of Policing: Between Force and Legitimacy, Sociology of Crime, Law and Deviance, Vol. 21*. Bingley: Emerald Group.

REINER, R. (2016b). *Crime: The Mystery of the Common-Sense Concept*. Cambridge: Polity Press.

REINER, R. (2017). 'Political Economy, Crime, and Criminal Justice', in A. LIEBLING, S. MARUNA, and L. McARA (eds), *The Oxford Handbook of Criminology* (6th edn). Oxford: Oxford University Press.

REINER, R. and CROSS, M. (eds) (1991). *Beyond Law and Order: Criminal Justice Policy and Politics into the 1990s*. London: Macmillan.

REINER, R. and LEIGH, L. (1992). 'Police Power', in G. CHAMBERS and C. McCRUDDEN (eds), *Individual Rights in the UK since 1945*. Oxford: Oxford University Press.

REINER, R. and NEWBURN, T. (2007). 'Police Research', in R. KING and E. WINCUP (eds), *Doing Research on Crime and Justice* (2nd edn). Oxford: Oxford University Press.

REINER, R. and O'CONNOR, D. (2015). 'Politics and Policing: The Terrible Twins', in J. FLEMING (ed.), *Police Leadership*. Oxford: Oxford University Press.

REINER, R. and SPENCER, S. (eds) (1993). *Accountable Policing: Effectiveness, Empowerment and Equity*. London: Institute for Public Policy Research.

REINER, R., LIVINGSTONE, S., and ALLEN, J. (2000). 'No More Happy Endings? The Media and Popular Concern about Crime since the Second World War', in T. HOPE and R. SPARKS (eds), *Crime, Risk and Insecurity*. London: Routledge.

REINER, R., LIVINGSTONE, S., and ALLEN, J. (2001). 'Casino Culture: The Media and Crime in a Winner-Loser Society', in K. STENSON and R. SULLIVAN (eds), *Crime and Risk Society*. Cullompton: Willan.

REINER, R., LIVINGSTONE, S., and ALLEN, J. (2003). 'From Law and Order to Lynch Mobs: Crime News since the Second World War', in P. MASON (ed.), *Criminal Visions*. London: Routledge.

REISIG, M. D. and KANE, R. J. (eds) (2014). *The Oxford Handbook of Police and Policing*. Oxford: Oxford University Press.

REISS, A. J., JR (1968). 'Stuff and Nonsense about Social Surveys and Observation' in H. BECKER, B. GREER, D. RIESMAN, and R. WEISS (eds), *Institutions and the Person*. Chicago, IL: Aldine.

REISS, A. J., JR (1971). *The Police and the Public*. New Haven, CT: Yale University Press.

REITH, C. (1938). *The Police Idea*. Oxford: Oxford University Press.

REITH, C. (1940). *Police Principles and the Problem of War*. Oxford: Oxford University Press.

REITH, C. (1943). *British Police and the Democratic Ideal*. Oxford: Oxford University Press.

REITH, C. (1948). *A Short History of the Police*. Oxford: Oxford University Press.

REITH, C. (1956). *A New Study of Police History*. London: Oliver & Boyd.

REUSS-IANNI, E. (1983). *The Two Cultures of Policing: Street Cops and Management Cops*. New Brunswick, NJ: Transaction Books.

RICHARDS, J. (2008). *The Secret War: A True History of Queensland's Native Police*. Brisbane: University of Queensland Press.

RIGAKOS, G. (2002). *The New Parapolice: Risks, Markets and Commodified Social Control*. Toronto: University of Toronto Press.

ROADER, O., EISEN, L.-B., and BOWLING, J. (2015). *What Caused the Crime Decline?*. New York: Brennan Center for Justice, New York University.

ROBERTS, C. and INNES, M. (2009). 'The "Death" of Dixon? Policing Gun Crime and the End of the Generalist Police Constable in England and Wales'. *Criminology and Criminal Justice*, 9(3): 337–57.

ROBINSON, C. (1978). 'The Deradicalisation of the Policeman'. *Crime and Delinquency*, 24(2): 129–51.

ROBINSON, C. (1979). 'Ideology as History'. *Police Studies*, (Summer) 2(2): 35–49.

ROBINSON, C. and SCAGLION, R. (1987). 'The Origins and Evolution of the Police Function in Society: Notes towards A Theory'. *Law and Society Review*, 21(1): 109–53.

ROBINSON, C., SCAGLION, R., and OLIVERO, J. M. (1994). *Police in Contradiction: The Evolution of the Police Function in Society*. Westport, CT: Greenwood.

ROBINSON, G. T. (1967). *Rural Russia under the Old Regime*. Berkeley, CA: University of California Press.

ROBISHEAUX, E. (1973). 'The "Private Army" of the Tax Farms: The Men and Their Origins'. *Histoire Sociale/Social History*, 12: 256–69.

ROCK, P. (2005). 'Chronocentrism and British Criminology'. *British Journal of Sociology*, 56(3): 473–791.

RODRÍGUEZ GOYES, D. and SOUTH, N. (2016). 'The Injustices of Policing, Law and Multinational Monopolization in the Privatization of Natural Diversity: Cases from Colombia and Latin America', in D. RODRÍGUEZ GOYES, H. MOL, A. BRISMAM, and N. SOUTH (eds), *Environmental Crime In Latin America*. London: Palgrave Studies in Green Criminology.

ROEDER, O., LAUREN-BROOKE EISEN and BOWLING, J. (2015). *What Caused the Crime Decline?* New York University: Brennan Center for Justic.

ROGAN, T. (2018). *The Moral Economists*. Princeton, NJ: Princeton University Press.

ROGERS, C. and FREVEL, B. (eds) (2018). *Higher Education and Police: An International View*. London: Springer.

ROLPH, C. H. (ed.) (1962). *The Police and the Public*. London: Heinemann.

RØNN, K. V. (2012). '"Democratizing Strategic Intelligence?" On the Feasibility of an Objective, Decision-making Framework when Assessing Threats and Harms or Organized Crime'. *Policing*, 7(1): 53–62.

ROSE, N. (1996). 'The Death of the Social? Refiguring the Territory of Government'. *Economy and Society*, 25(3): 321–56.

ROSENFELD, R. and FORNANGO, R. (2014). 'The Impact of Police Stops on Precinct Robbery and Burglary Rates in New York City, 2003–2010'. *Justice Quarterly*, 31: 96–122.

ROSENFELD, R., DECKARD, M. J., and BLACKBURN, E. (2014). 'The Effects of Directed Patrol and Self-initiated Enforcement on Firearm Violence: A Randomized Controlled Study of Hot Spot Policing'. *Criminology*, 52(3), 428–49.

ROSS, J. I. (2017). *Controlling State Crime*. London: Routledge.

ROSS, S. (2015). 'Security Firms want more Information from Toronto McDonald's Shooting'. *Globe and Mail*, 17 July.

ROTH, M. P. (2005). *Crime and Punishment: A History of the Criminal Justice System*. Belmont, CA: Thomson/Wadsworth.

ROWE, M. (2004). *Policing, Race and Racism*. London: Routledge.

ROWE, M. (ed.) (2007). *Policing beyond Macpherson*. Cullompton: Willan.

ROWE, M. (2014). *Introduction to Policing*. London: Sage.

ROWE, M. (2018). 'Visible Policing: The Affective Properties of Police Buildings, Images and Material Culture'. *ESRC Project Proposal. Swindon*: Economic Research Council.

ROYAL COMMISSION ON CRIMINAL PROCEDURE (1981). *Report and Law and Procedure*. Cmnd. 8092. London: HMSO.

ROYAL COMMISSION ON POLICE POWERS AND PROCEDURE (1929). *Report*. Cmnd. 3297. London: HMSO.

ROYAL COMMISSION ON THE POLICE (1962). *Final Report*. Cmnd. 1728. London: HMSO.

ROYCROFT, M. (2017). *Police Chiefs in the UK*. London: Palgrave Macmillan.

RUBIN, J. (1972). 'Police Identity and the Police Role' in R. F. STEADMAN (ed.), *The Police and the Community*. Baltimore, MD: John Hopkins Press.

RUBINSTEIN, J. (1973). *City Police*. New York: Ballantine.

RYAN, B. (2013). 'Reasonable Force: The Emergence of Global Policing Power'. *Review of International Studies*, 39(2): 435–57.

SAMPSON, A., STUBBS, P., SMITH, D., PEARSON G., and BLAGG, H. (1988/2017). 'Crime, Localities and the Multi-Agency Approach', in T. HOPE (ed.), *Perspectives on Crime Reduction*. London: Routledge.

SAN PEDRO, J. G. (2006). La Cooperación policial en la Unión Europea. *Revista de Derecho de la Unión Europea*, n 10–1.

SANDERS, B. (2018). 'Disneyland Workers Face Ruthless Exploitation. Their Fight is Our Fight'. *The Guardian*, 7 June.

SANDERS, C. B. and CONDON, C. (2017). 'Crime Analysis and Cognitive Effects: The Practice of Policing Through Flows of Data'. *Global Crime*, 18(3): 237–55.

SANDERS, C. B. and HENDERSON, S. (2013). 'Police "Empires" and Information Technologies: Uncovering Material and Organizational Barriers to Information Sharing in Canadian Police Services'. *Policing and Society*, 23(2): 243–60.

SANDERS, C. B. and SHEPTYCKI, J. (2017). 'Policing, Crime and "Big Data": Towards a Critique of the Moral Economy of Stochastic Governance'. *Crime, Law and Social Change*, 68(1–2): 1–15, https://doi.org/10.1007/s10611-016-9678-7.

SANDERS, C. B., CHRISTENSEN, T., and WESTON, C. (2015). 'Constructing Crime in a Database: Big Data and the Mangle of Social Problems Work'. *Qualitative Sociology Review*, 11(2): 180–95.

SANDERS, W. (1977). *Detective Work*. Glencoe, MN: Free Press.

SANDHU, A. (2016). 'Camera Friendly Policing: How Police Respond to Cameras and Photographers'. *Surveillance and Society*, 14(1): 78–89.

SASKATCHEWAN POLICE COMMISSION, (2018). *Annual Report 2017–18*, Saskatchewan Police College, University of Regina.

SAVAGE, S. (2007). *Police Reform*. Oxford: Oxford University Press.

SAVAGE, S., CHARMAN, S., and COPE, S. (2000). *Policing and the Power of Persuasion*. London: Blackstone.

SCARMAN, LORD (1981). *The Scarman Report: The Brixton Disorders*. Cmnd 8427. London: HMSO.

SCHNEIDER, C. (2016). *Policing and Social Media: Social Control in an Era of New Media*. Lanham, MD: Lexington Books.

SCHUILENBURG, M. (2015). *The Securitization of Society: Crime, Risk And Social Order*. New York: New York University Press.

SCHWARTZ, R. D. and MILLER, J. C. (1964). 'Legal Evolution and Societal Complexity'. *American Journal of Sociology*, 70(1): 159–69.

SCRATON, P. (1985). *The State of the Police*. London: Pluto.

SCRATON, P. (ed.) (1987). *Law, Order and the Authoritarian State*. Milton Keynes: Open University Press.

SCRIPTURE, A. (1997). 'The Sources of Police Culture: Demographic or Environmental Variables?'. *Policing and Society*, 7(3): 163–76.

SEIGEL, M. (2018). *Violence Work: State Power and the Limits of Police*. Durham, NC: Duke University Press.

SENTAS, V. (2014). *Traces of Terror*. Oxford: Oxford University Press.

SHAPLAND, J. and VAGG, J. (1988). *Policing by the Public*. London: Routledge.

SHAW, D. (1992). 'Chief Parker Molded LAPD Image—Then Came the '60s: The Media and the LAPD From Coziness to Conflict'. *Los Angeles Times*, 25 May.

SHAW, M. and WILLIAMSON, W. (1972). 'Public Attitudes to the Police'. *Criminologist*, 7(26): 18–33..

SHAXSON, N. (2018). *The Finance Curse*. London: Bodley Head.

SHEARING, C. (ed.) (1981a). *Organisational Police Deviance*. Toronto: Butterworth.

SHEARING C. (1981b). 'Subterranean Processes in the Maintenance of Power'. *The Canadian Journal of Sociology and Anthropology*, 18(3): 283–98.

SHEARING, C. (1984). *Dial-A-Cop: A Study of Police Mobilisation*. Toronto: University of Toronto Centre of Criminology.

SHEARING, C. (1992). 'The Relation between Public and Private Policing', in M. TONRY and N. MORRIS (eds), *Modern Policing*. Chicago, IL: Chicago University Press.

SHEARING, C. (2001). 'A Nodal Conception of Governance: Thoughts on a Police Commission'. *Policing and Society*, 11(3–4): 259–72.

SHEARING, C. (2006). 'Reflections on the Refusal to Acknowledge Private Governments', in J. WOOD and B. DUPONT (eds), *Democracy, Society and the Governance of Security*. Cambridge: Cambridge University Press.

SHEARING, C. (2007). 'Policing Our Future', in A. HENRY and D. J. SMITH (eds), *Transformations of Policing*. Aldershot: Ashgate.

SHEARING, C. and ERICSON, R. (1991). 'Culture as Figurative Action'. *British Journal of Sociology*, 42(4): 481–506.

SHEARING, C. and STENNING P. C. (1979). 'The Quiet Revolution: The Nature, Development and General Legal Implications of Private Policing in Canada'. *Criminal Law Quarterly*, 22: 220–48.

SHEARING, C., and STENNING, P. C. (1981). 'Modern Private Security: Its growth and implications *Crime and Justice*, 193-246.

SHEARING, C., and STENNING, P. C, (1983). 'Private Security: Implications for Social Control'. *Social Problems*, 30(5): 493–506.

SHEARING, C. and STENNING, P. C. (1985). 'From Panopticon to Disney World: The Development of Discipline', in *Perspectives in Criminal Law: Essays in Honour of John L.L. Edwards*. Toronto: Toronto University Press.

SHEARING, C. and STENNING, P.C. (1987). 'Say "Cheese!": The Disney Order that is Not so Mickey Mouse', in C.D. SHEARING and P.C. STENNING (eds), *Private Policing*. Newbury Park, CA: Sage.

SHEEHY, P. (1993). *Report of the Inquiry into Police Responsibilities and Rewards*, 2 vols. Cm. 2280. London: HMSO.

SHEPTYCKI, J. (1993). *Innovations in Policing Domestic Violence*. Aldershot: Avebury.

SHEPTYCKI, J. (1995). 'Transnational Policing and the Makings of a Postmodern State'. *British Journal of Criminology*, (Autumn) 35(4): 613–35.

SHEPTYCKI, J. (1997). 'Insecurity, Risk Suppression and Segregation: Some Reflections on Policing in the Transnational Age', *Theoretical Criminology*, 1(3): 303–16.

SHEPTYCKI, J. (1998a). 'Policing, Postmodernism and Transnationalisation'.

British Journal of Criminology, 38(3): 485–503.

SHEPTYCKI, J. (1998b). 'The Global Cops Cometh'. *British Journal of Sociology*, 49(1): 57–74.

SHEPTYCKI, J. (1998c) 'Police Co-operation in the English Channel Region, 1968–1996'. *European Journal of Crime, Criminal Law and Criminal Justice*, 7(3): 216–36.

SHEPTYCKI, J. (2000a). 'The "Drug War": Learning from the Paradigm Example of Transnational Policing', in J. SHEPTYCKI (ed.), *Issues in Transnational Policing*. London: Routledge.

SHEPTYCKI, J. (ed.) (2000b). *Issues in Transnational Policing*. London: Routledge.

SHEPTYCKI, J. (2000c). 'Policing and Human Rights: An Introduction'. *Policing and Society*, 10(1): 1–10.

SHEPTYCKI, J. (2000d). 'Surveillance, Closed Circuit Television and Social Control'. *Policing and Society*, 9(4): 429–34.

SHEPTYCKI, J. (2001). 'Patrolling the New European (In)security Field: Organisational Dilemmas and Operational Solutions for Policing the Internal Borders of Europe'. *European Journal of Crime, Criminal Law and Criminal Justice*, 10(2): 144–58.

Sheptycki, J. (2002a). *In Search of Transnational Policing*. Aldershot: Ashgate.

SHEPTYCKI, J. (2002b). 'Accountability across the Policing Field: Towards a General Cartography of Accountability for Post-Modern Policing'. *Policing and Society*, 12(4): 323–38.

SHEPTYCKI, J. (2004a). 'The Accountability of Transnational Policing Institutions: The Strange Case of Interpol'. *Canadian Journal of Law and Society*, 19(1): 107–34.

SHEPTYCKI, J. (2004b). 'Organizational Pathologies in Police Intelligence Systems: Some Contributions to the Lexicon of Intelligence-led Policing'. *European Journal of Criminology*, 1(3): 307–32.

SHEPTYCKI, J. (2007a). 'The Constabulary Ethic and the Transnational Condition', in A. GOLDSMITH and J. SHEPTYCKI (eds), *Crafting Transnational Policing, Police Capacity Building and Global Policing Reform.* Oxford: Hart.

SHEPTYCKI, J. (2007b). 'High Policing in the Security Control Society'. *Policing*, 1(1): 70–9.

SHEPTYCKI, J. (2007c). 'Police Ethnography in the House of Serious and Organised Crime', in A. HENRY and D. J. SMITH (eds), *Transformations of Policing.* Aldershot: Ashgate.

SHEPTYCKI, J. (2008a). 'Policing, Intelligence Theory and the New Human Security Paradigm: Some Lessons from the Field', in P. GILL, S. MARRIN, and M. PHYTHIAN (eds), *Intelligence Theory: Key Questions and Debates.* London: Routledge.

SHEPTYCKI, J. (2008b). 'Transnationalization, Orientalism and Crime'. *Asian Journal of Criminology*, 3(1): 13–35.

SHEPTYCKI, J. (2009). 'Policing, Intelligence Theory and the New Human Security Paradigm: Some Lessons from the Field', in P. GILL, S. MARRIN, and M. PHYTHIAN (eds), *Intelligence Theory: Key Questions and Debates.* London: Routledge.

SHEPTYCKI, J. (2013). 'Technocrime, Criminology and Marshall McLuhan: Towards an Inventory of Criminological Effects', in S. LEMAN-LANGLOIS (ed.), *Technocrime, Policing and Surveillance.* London: Routledge.

SHEPTYCKI, J. (2017a). 'Brand Interpol', in S. HUFNAGEL and C. MCCARTNEY (eds), *Trust in International Police and Justice Cooperation.* Oxford: Hart.

SHEPTYCKI, J. (2017b). 'Liquid Modernity and the Police Métier: Thinking About Information Flows in Police Organisation'. *Global Crime*, 18(3): 286–302.

SHEPTYCKI, J. (2017c). 'The Police Intelligence Division-of-Labour'. *Policing and Society*, 27(6): 620–35.

SHEPTYCKI, J. (2017d). 'Technopoly and Policing Practice: Critical Reflections on Innovations in Police Control Technology',

Presentation to the 2017 CEPOL Research and Science Conference, Budapest, Hungary, 28–30 November.

SHEPTYCKI, J. (2018a). 'Technopoly and Policing Practice'. *European Law Enforcement Bulletin*, (SCE 4), https://bulletin.cepol.europa.eu/index.php/bulletin/article/view/362.

SHEPTYCKI, J. (2018b) 'Transnational Organization, Transnational Law and the Ambiguity of Interpol: Thinking about the Quasi-Legal Status of the Interpol Red Notice in a Global Context', in N. BOISTER and M. CHRISTENSEN (eds), *The Structure of Transnational Criminal Law.* The Hague: Brill Research Perspectives in International Law.

SHEPTYCKI, J. (2018c). 'What is Police Research Good For?—Reflections on the Moral Economy of Police Research'. *European Journal of Policing Studies*, 5(3): 16–35.

SHERMAN, L. (1978). *Scandal and Reform: Controlling Police Corruption.* Berkeley, CA: University of California Press.

SHERMAN, L. (1990). 'Police Crackdowns: Initial and Residual Deterrence', in M. TONRY (ed.), *Crime and Justice, Vol. 12.* Chicago, IL: University of Chicago Press.

SHERMAN, L. (1992a). 'Attacking Crime: Police and Crime Control', in M. TONRY and N. MORRIS (eds), *Modern Policing.* Chicago, IL: Chicago University Press.

SHERMAN, L. (1992b). *Policing Domestic Violence.* New York: Free Press.

SHERMAN, L. (2011/2015). 'Professional Policing and Liberal Democracy', in J. SHEPTYCKI (ed.), *Transnational Crime, Vol. 4: Transnational Crime Issues and Control Responses.* London: Routledge.

SHERMAN, L. (2013). 'The Rise of Evidence-based Policing: Targeting, Testing and Tracking'. *Crime and Justice*, 42(1): 377–451.

SHERMAN, L. and BERK, R. A. (1984). 'The Specific Deterrence Effects of Arrest for Domestic Violence'. *American Sociological Review*, 49: 261–72.

SHERMAN, L. and ECK, J. E. (2002). 'Policing for Crime Prevention'. *Evidence-based Crime Prevention*, 295.

SHERMAN L. and WEISBURD, D. A. (1995). 'General Deterrent Effects of Police Patrol in Crime 'Hot Spots': A Randomized, Controlled Trial'. *Justice Quarterly*, 12: 625–48.

SHERMAN, L., GOTTFREDSON, D., MacKENZIE, D., ECK, J., REUTER, P., and BUSHWAY, S. (1997). *Preventing Crime: What Works, What Doesn't, What's Promising*. Report to the U.S. Congress. Washington, DC: U.S. Dept. of Justice.

SHORTSLEEVE, K. (2004). 'The Wonderful World of the Depression: Disney, Despotism and the 1930s. Or, Why Disney Scares Us'. *The Lion and the Unicorn*, 28(1): 1–30

SHPAYER-MAKOV, H. (2002). *The Making of a Policeman: A Social History of a Labour Force in Metropolitan London 1829-1914*. Aldershot: Ashgate.

SHUBERT, A. (2003). *A Social History of Modern Spain*. London: Routledge.

SILBERMAN, C. E. (1978). *Criminal Violence, Criminal Justice*. New York: Random House.

SILVER, A. (1967). 'The Demand for Order in Civil Society', in D. BORDUA (ed.), *The Police*. New York: Wiley.

SILVER, A. (1971). 'Social and Ideological Bases of British Élite Reactions to Domestic Crises'. *Politics in Society*, 1(2): 179–201.

SILVERMAN, E. (1999). *NYPD Battles Crime*. Boston, MA: Northeastern University Press.

SILVESTRI, M. (2003). *Women in Charge: Policing, Gender and Leadership*. Cullompton: Willan.

SILVESTRI, M. (2007). '"Doing" Police Leadership: Enter the "New Smart Macho"'. *Policing and Society*, 17(1): 38–58.

SILVESTRI, M. (2017). 'Police Culture and Gender'. *Policing*, 11(3): 289–300.

SILVESTRI, M., TONG, S., and BROWN, J. (2013). 'Gender and Police Leadership: Time for a Paradigm Shift?'. *International Journal of Police Science and Management*, 15(1): 61–73.

SINCLAIR, G. (2006). *End of the Line: Colonial Policing and the Imperial Endgame, 1945–80*. Manchester: Manchester University Press.

SINCLAIR, G. (ed.) (2011). *Globalising British Policing. The History of Policing, 4*. Farnham: Ashgate.

SINGH, G. (2000). 'The Concept and Context of Institutional Racism', in A. MARLOW and B. LOVEDAY (eds), *After Macpherson*. Lyme Regis: Russell House.

SIRLES, E. A., LIPCHICK, E., and KOWALSKI, K. (1993). 'A Consumer's Perspective on Domestic Violence Interventions'. *Journal of Family Violence*, 8(3): 267–76.

SIVANANDAN, A. (1982). *A Different Hunger: Writings on Black Resistance*. London: Pluto Press.

SKIDELSKY, R. (2018). *Money and Government*. London: Allen Lane.

SKINNS, L. (2012). *Police Custody*. Abingdon: Willan.

SKINNS, L. (2019). *Police Powers and Citizens' Rights: Discretionary Decision-Making in Police Detention*. London: Routledge.

SKINNS, L., WOOFF, A., and SPRAWSON, A. (2017). 'Preliminary Findings on Police Custody Delivery in the Twenty-First Century: Is it "Good' Enough?"'. *Policing and Society*, 27(4): 358–71.

SKLAIR, L. (2001). *The Transnational Capitalist Class*. Oxford: Basil Blackwell.

SKLANSKY, D. (1999). 'The Private Police'. *UCLA Law Review*, 46(4): 1165–287.

SKLANSKY, D. (2006). 'Not Your Father's Police Department: Making Sense of the New Demographics of Law Enforcement'. *Journal of Criminal Law and Criminology*, 96(3): 1209–43.

SKLANSKY, D. (2007). 'Police Reform, Occupational Culture, and Cognitive Burn-In', in M. O'NEILL, M. MARKS, and A.-M. SINGH (eds), *Police Occupational Culture*. Oxford: JAI Press.

SKLANSKY, D. (2008). *Democracy and the Police*. Stanford, CA: Stanford University Press.

SKOGAN, W. (ed.) (2004). 'To Better Serve and Protect: Improving Police Practices'. *Special Issue, The Annals*, 593.

SKOGAN, W. (2006). *Police and Community in Chicago: A Tale of Three Cities*. Oxford: Oxford University Press.

SKOGAN, W. G. and FRYDL, K. (2004). *Fairness and Effectiveness in Policing: The Evidence*. Washington, DC: National Academies Press.

SKOLNICK, J. (1966). *Justice Without Trial*. New York: Wiley.

SKOLNICK, J. (1969). *The Politics of Protest*. New York: Bantam.

SKOLNICK, J. (2008). 'Enduring Issues of Police Culture and Demographics'. *Policing and Society*, 18(1): 35–45.

SKOLNICK, J. and BAYLEY, D. B. (1986). *The New Blue Line*. New York: Free Press.

SKOLNICK, J. and BAYLEY, D. B. (1988). *Community Policing: Issues and Practices around the World*. Washington, DC: National Institute of Justice.

SKOLNICK, J. and FYFE, J. (1993). *Above the Law: Police and the Excessive Use of Force*. New York: Free Press.

SLADE, G. and LIGHT, M. (2015). 'Crime and Criminal Justice after Communism: Why the Post-Soviet Region?'. *Theoretical Criminology*, 19(2): 147–58.

SLATER, M. (2007). 'Governmentalities of an Airport: Heterotopia and Confession'. *International Political Sociology*, 1: 49–66

SLAUGHTER, A.-M. (2004). *A New World Order*. Princeton, NJ: Princeton University Press.

SMITH, D. J. (1997). 'Case Construction and the Goals of the Criminal Process'. *British Journal of Criminology*, 37(3): 319–46.

SMITH, D. J. (2007a). 'New Challenges to Police Legitimacy', in A. HENRY and D. SMITH (eds), *Transformations of Policing*. Aldershot: Ashgate.

SMITH, D. J. (2007b). 'The Foundations of Legitimacy', in T. TYLER (ed.), *Legitimacy and Criminal Justice*. New York: Russell Sage.

SMITH, D. J. and GRAY, J. (1983). *The Police in Action*. London: Policy Studies Institute.

SMITH, D. J. and GRAY, J. (1985). *The Police and People in London*. London: Gower & the Policy Studies Institute.

SMITH, D., PURTELL, R., and GUERRERO, S. (2012). 'Is Stop, Question and Frisk an Effective Tool in the Fight Against Crime?', Paper presented at the Annual Research Conference of the Association of Public Policy and Management: Baltimore, Maryland.

SMITH, G. (2001). 'Police Complaints and Criminal Prosecutions'. *Modern Law Review*, 64(3): 372–92.

SMITH, G. (2004). 'Rethinking Police Complaints'. *British Journal of Criminology*, 44(1): 15–33.

SMITH, G. (2005). 'A Most Enduring Problem: Police Complaints Reform in England and Wales'. *Journal of Social Policy*, 35(1): 121–41.

SMITH, G. (2009). 'Why Don't More People Complain against the Police?'. *European Journal of Criminology*, 6(3): 249–66.

SMITH, N. and FLANAGAN, C. (2000). *The Effective Detective: Identifying the Skills of an Effective SIO*. London: Home Office.

SMITH, S. J. (1989). *The Politics of Race and Residence: Citizenship, Segregation and White Supremacy in Britain*. Oxford: Polity Press.

SOLOMON, E., EADES, C., and GARSIDE, R. (2007). *Ten Years of Criminal Justice under Labour*. London: Centre for Crime and Justice Studies.

SONG, V. (2019). 'FamilyTree DNA Hands the FBI Access to its Database'. Gizmodo, 1 February, https://gizmodo.com/family-treedna-hands-the-fbi-access-to-its-database-1832259369.

SOUHAMI, A. (2007). 'Understanding Institutional Racism: The Stephen

Lawrence Inquiry and the Police Service Reaction', in M. Rowe (ed.), *Policing Beyond Macpherson*. Cullompton: Willan.

Souhami, A. (2014). 'Institutional Racism and Police Reform: An Empirical Critique'. *Policing and Society* 24(1): 1–21.

South, N. (1988). *Policing for Profit: The Private Security Sector*. London: Sage.

South, N. (1989). 'Reconstructing Policing: Differentiation and Contradiction in Post-War Private and Public Policing', in R. Matthews (ed.), *Privatizing Criminal Justice*. London: Sage.

Spitzer, S. and Scull, A. (1977). 'Privatisation and Social Control'. *Social Problems*, 25.

Spurrier, M. (2018). 'After Worboys, the Met will have to Take Rape Victims Seriously'. *The Guardian*, 21 February.

Squires, P. (1998). 'Cops and Customers?: Consumerism and the Demand for Police Services'. *Policing and Society*, 8(2): 169–88.

Squires, P. (2014). *Gun Crime in Global Contexts*. London: Routledge.

Stalcup, M. (2013). 'Interpol and the Emergence of Global Policing', in W. Garriott (ed.), *Policing and Contemporary Governance: The Anthropology of Police in Practice*. New York: Palgrave Macmillan.

Stalcup, M. and Hahn, C. (2016). 'Cops, Cameras and the Policing of Ethics'. *Theoretical Criminology*, 20(4): 482–501.

Stalder, F. (2006). *Manuel Castells: The Theory of the Network Society*. Cambridge: Polity Press.

Stanislas, P. (ed.) (2015). *International Perspectives on Police Education and Training*. Abingdon: Routledge.

Stanko, B. and Heidensohn, F. (1995). 'Gender and Crime'. *Criminal Justice Matters*, 19(1): 3–5.

Stanko, E., Jackson, J., Bradford, B., and Hohl, K. (2012). 'A Golden Thread, a Presence amongst Uniforms, and a Good Deal of Data: Studying Public Confidence in the London Metropolitan Police'. *Policing and Society*, 22(3): 317–31.

Stark, S. D. (1988). 'Perry Mason Meets Sonny Crockett: The History of Lawyers and the Police as Television Heroes'. *University of Miami Law Review*, 42: 229–83.

Stead, J. (1957). *The Police of Paris*. London: Staples Press.

Stead, J. (1983). *The Police of France*. New York: Macmillan.

Stead, P. (ed.) (1977). *Pioneers in Policing*. Montclair, NJ: Patterson Smith.

Stedman Jones, D. (2012). *Masters of the Universe: Hayek, Friedman and the Birth of Neoliberal Politics*. Princeton, NJ: Princeton University Press.

Steedman, C. (1984). *Policing the Victorian Community*. London: Routledge.

Steer, D. (1980). *Uncovering Crime*. Royal Commission on Criminal Procedure, Research Study 7. London: HMSO.

Stenning, P. (ed.) (1995). *Accountability in Criminal Justice*. Toronto: University of Toronto Press.

Stenning, P. (2000). 'Powers and accountability of the Private Police'. *European Journal of Criminal Policy and Research*, 8(3): 325–52.

Stenning, P. (2009). 'Governance and Accountability in a Plural Policing Environment—The Story So Far'. *Policing*, 3(1): 22–33.

Stenning, P., Birkbeck, C., Adang, O., Baker, D., and Feltes, T. (2009). 'Researching the Use of Force: The Background to the International Project'. *Crime, Law and Social Change*, 52(2): 95–110.

Stenson, K. and Silverstone, D. (2014). 'Making Police Accountable', in J. Brown (ed.), *The Future of Policing*. London: Routledge.

Stenson, K. and Waddington, P. A. J. (2007). 'Macpherson, Police Stops and

Institutionalised Racism', in M. Rowe (ed.), *Policing Beyond Macpherson*. Cullompton: Willan.

Stephens, M. and Becker, S. (1994). *Police Force, Police Service*. London: Macmillan.

Stevenson, K., Cox, D., and Channing, I. (eds) (2017). *Leading the Police*. London: Routledge.

Stinchcombe, A. (1963). 'Institutions of Privacy in the Determination of Police Administrative Practice'. *American Journal of Sociology*, 69(2): 150–60.

Stokes, N. and Clare, J. (2018). 'Preventing Near-Repeat Residential Burglary through Cocooning: Post Hoc Evaluation of a Targeted Police-led Pilot Intervention'. *Security Journal*, 1–18.

Storch, R. (1975). 'The Plague of Blue Locusts: Police Reform and Popular Resistance in Northern England 1840–57'. *International Review of Social History*, 20: 61–90.

Storch, R. (1976). 'The Policeman as Domestic Missionary'. *Journal of Social History*, (Summer) 9(4): 481–509.

Strang, H., Sherman, L., Ariel, B., Chilton, S., Braddock, R., Rowlinson, T., Cornelius, N., Jarman, R., and Weinborn, C. (2017). 'Reducing the Harm of Intimate Partner Violence: Randomised Controlled Trial of the Hampshire Constabulary CARA Experiment'. *Cambridge Journal of Evidence-Based Policing*, 1: 160–73.

Streeck, W. (2014). *Buying Time*. London: Verso.

Streeck, W. (2017a). 'Between Charity and Justice: Remarks on the Social Construction of Immigration Policy in Rich Democracies'. DaWS working paper series.

Streeck, W. (2017b). *How Will Capitalism End?*. London: Verso.

Stuart, E. (1996). *PR! A Social History of Spin*. New York: Basic Books.

Stumpf, J. (2006). 'The Crimmigration Crisis: Immigrants, Crime and Sovereign Power'. *American University Law Review*, 56(2): 367–419.

Styles, J. (1983). 'Sir John Fielding and the Problem of Criminal Investigation in 18th-century England'. *Transactions of the Royal Historical Society*, 33: 127–49.

Surette, R. (2014). *Media, Crime and Criminal Justice* (4th edn). Belmont, CA: Wadsworth.

Tajfel, H. (1969). 'Cognitive Aspects of Prejudice'. *Journal of Social Issues*, 25(4): 79–97.

Tankebe, J. (2008). 'Colonialism, Legitimation and Policing in Ghana'. *International Journal of Law, Crime and Justice*, 36: 67–84.

Tanner, S. and Dupont, B. (2014). 'Police Work in International Peace Operation Environments: A Perspective from Canadian Police Officers in the MINUSTAH'. *Policing and Society*, 24: 1–18.

Tawney, R. H. (1935/1981). *The Attack and other Papers*. Nottingham: Spokesman.

Taylor, C. (2004). *Modern Social Imaginaries*. Durham, NC: Duke University Press.

Taylor, H. (1998a). 'The Politics of the Rising Crime Statistics of England and Wales 1914–1960'. *Crime, History and Societies*, 2(1): 5–28.

Taylor, H. (1998b). 'Rising Crime: The Political Economy of Criminal Statistics since the 1850s'. *Economic History Review*, 51: 569–90.

Taylor, H. (1999). 'Forging the Job: A Crisis of "Modernisation" or Redundancy for the Police in England and Wales 1900–39'. *British Journal of Criminology*, 39(1): 113–35.

Taylor, I. (1999). *Crime in Context: A Critical Criminology of Market Societies*. Cambridge: Polity Press.

Telep, C. W. and Weisburd, D. (2012). 'What is Known about the Effectiveness of Police Practices in Reducing Crime and Disorder?'. *Police Quarterly*, 15(4): 331–57.

TERRILL, W., PAOLINE, E., and MANNING, P. (2003). 'Police Culture and Coercion'. *Criminology*, 41(4): 1003–34.

The Local (2013). 'No probe into Stockholm police's 'racial profiling'. https://www.thelocal.se/20130506/47748

THOMAS, J. E. (1996/2014). *Modern Japan: A Social History since 1868*. London Routledge [first published 1996, Addison Wesley Longman].

THOMPSON, E. P. (1971). 'The Moral Economy of the English Crowd'. *Past and Present*, 50(1): 76–136.

THOMPSON, E. P. (1975). *Whigs and Hunters*. London: Penguin.

THOMSON, D. (1957/1990). *Europe Since Napoleon*. London: Penguin Books.

TIESSEN, M. (2011). 'Being Watched Watching Watchers Watch: Determining the Digitized Future while Profitably Modulating Preemption (at the Airport)'. *Surveillance and Society*, 9(1–2): 167–84.

TILLEY, N. (2008). 'Modern Approaches to Policing: Community, Problem-Oriented and Intelligence-Led', in T. NEWBURN (ed.), *Handbook of Policing* (2nd edn). Cullompton: Willan.

TILLEY, N. and SIDEBOTTOM, A. (2017). *The Handbook of Crime Prevention and Community Safety* (2nd edn). London: Routledge.

TILLY, C. (ed.) (1975). *The Formation of National States in Western Europe*. Princeton, NJ: Princeton University Press.

TILLY, C. (1985). 'War Making and State Making as Organized Crime', in P. EVANS, D. RUESCHEMEYER, and T. SKOCPOL (eds), *Bringing the State Back In*. Cambridge: Cambridge University Press.

TIPTON, E. K. (1990). *The Japanese Police State: The Tokkô in Interwar Japan*, London: Athlone Press.

TIRATELLI, M., QUINTON, P., and BRADFORD, B. (2018). 'Does Stop and Search Deter Crime? Evidence from Ten Years of London-wide Data'. *British Journal of Criminology*, 58(5): 1212–31.

TOBIAS, J. J. (1972). 'Police and the Public in the UK'. *Journal of Contemporary History*, 7(1): 201–20.

TONGE, J. (2013). *Northern Ireland: Conflict and Change*. Routledge: London.

TONRY, M. (2014). *Why Crime Rates Fall and Why They Don't*. Chicago: Chicago University Press.

TOOZE, A. (2018). *Crashed: How a Decade of Financial Crisis Changed the World*. London: Allen Lane.

TOPPING, J. (2016). 'Accountability, Policing, and the Police Service of Northern Ireland', in S. LISTER and M. ROWE (eds), *Accountability of Policing*. London: Routledge.

TOPPING, J. and BYRNE, J. (2012). Paramilitary Punishments in Belfast: Policing Beneath the Peace. *Behavioral Sciences of Terrorism and Political Aggression*, 4(1), 41–59.

TORPEY, J. (2000). *The Invention of the Passport: Surveillance, Citizenship and the State*. Cambridge: Cambridge University Press.

TÓTH, B. and KÁDÁR, A. (2011). 'Ethnic Profiling in ID Checks by the Hungarian Police'. *Policing and Society*, 21(4): 383–94.

TRAVERS, M. and MANZO, J. (1997). *Law in Action: Ethnomethodological and Conversation Analytic Approaches to Law*. Milton Park: Ashgate.

TRAVIS, A. (2017). 'Simple Numbers Tell Story of Police Cuts under Theresa May'. *The Guardian*, 5 June.

TREVASKES, S. (2007). 'Severe and Swift Justice in China'. *British Journal of Criminology*, 47(1): 23–41.

TRINDADE, L. (2013). *The Making of Modern Portugal*. Cambridge: Cambridge Scholars Publishing.

TROJANOWICZ, R. and BACQUEROUX, B. (1990). *Community Policing: A Contemporary Perspective*. Cincinnati, OH: Anderson Publishing.

TUCK, M. (1989). *Drinking and Disorder: A Study of Non-Metropolitan Violence*. Home

Office Research and Planning Unit Study 108. London: HMSO.

Turnbull, S. (2014). *TV Crime Drama*. Edinburgh: Edinburgh University Press.

Turner, K. B., Giacopassi, D., and Vandiver, M. (2006). 'Ignoring the Past: Coverage of Slavery and Slave Patrols in Criminal Justice Texts'. *Journal of Criminal Justice Education*, 17(1): 181–95.

Turner, L. (2014). 'PCCs, Neo-Liberal Hegemony and Democratic Policing'. *Safer Communities* 13(1): 13–21.

Turner, L. (2016). 'Democracy (Re)imagined: Some Proposals for Democratic Policing', in S. Farrall, B. Goldson, I. Loader, and A. Dockley (eds), *Justice and Penal Reform: Re-shaping the Penal Landscape*. Abingdon: Routledge.

Tye, L. (1999). *The Father of Spin: Edward L. Bernays and the Birth of Public Relations*. New York: Random House.

Tyler, T. R. (1990). *Why People Obey the Law*. Woodstock: Princeton University Press.

Tyler, T. R. (2004). 'Enhancing Police Legitimacy'. *The Annals*, 593: 84–99.

Tyler, T. R. (2011). 'Trust and Legitimacy: Policing in the USA and Europe'. *European Journal of Criminology*, 8: 254–66.

UNCTAD (2017). United Nations Conference on Trade and Development, handbook of statistics. Fact Sheet 13, Word Seaborne Trade.

Ungar, M. (2011). Policing Democracy: Overcoming Obstacles to Citizen Security in Latin America, Baltimore: Johns Hopkins University Press.

Vagg, J. (1995). 'Rough Seas?: Contemporary Piracy in South East Asia'. *British Journal of Criminology*, 35(1): 63–80.

Van Dijck, J. and Poell, T. (2013). 'Understanding Social Media Logic'. *Media and Communication*, 1(1): 2–14.

Van Dijk, A., Hoogewoning, F., and Punch, M. (2015). *What Matters in Policing?* Bristol: Policy Press.

Van Ewijk, A. R. (2012). 'Diversity within Police Forces in Europe: A Case for the Comprehensive Review'. *Policing*, 6(1): 76–92.

Van Hulst, M. (2017). 'Backstage Storytelling and Leadership'. *Policing*, 11(3): 356–68.

Van Maanen, J. (1978). 'Watching the Watchers', in P. K. Manning and J. Van Maanen (eds), *Policing*. Santa Monica, CA: Goodyear.

Van Maanen, J. (1991). 'The Smile Factory', in D. M. Newman and J. O'Brien (eds), *Sociology: Exploring the Architecture of Everyday Life Readings*. London: Sage.

van Sluis, A., Marks, P., Gilleir, F., and Easton, M. (2012). 'Nodal Security in the Ports of Rotterdam and Antwerp', in H. J. M. Fender, V. J. J. M. Bekkers, and M. Fenger (eds), *Beyond Fragmentation and Interconnectivity: Public Governance and the Search for Connective Capacity*. Amsterdam, ISO Press.

Velasco, P. (2017). 'Cinderella is Homeless, Ariel Can't Afford to Live on Land: Disney under Fire for Pay', *The Guardian*, 17 July.

Veracini, L. (2010). *Settler Colonialism: A Theoretical Overview*. Basingstoke: Palgrave Macmillan.

Vestby, A. (2018). 'Policy-making without Politics: Overstating Objectivity in Intelligence-led Policing', in N. R. Fyfe, H. O. I. Gundhus, and K. V. Rønn (eds), *Moral Issues in Intelligence-led Policing*. London and New York: Routledge.

Vidal, J. and Kirchmaier, T. (2018). 'The Effect of Police Response Time on Crime Clearance Rates'. *Review of Economic Studies*, 85(2): 855–91.

Vitale, A. (2017). *The End of Policing*. London: Verso.

Vogler, R. (1991). *Reading the Riot Act*. Milton Keynes: Open University Press.

Waddington, D. (2007). *Policing Public Disorder*. Cullompton: Willan.

Waddington, D., Jobard, F., and King, M. (eds) (2009). *Rioting in the UK and France: A Comparative Analysis*. Cullompton: Willan.

Waddington, P. A. J. (1982). 'Why the "Opinion Makers" No Longer Support the Police'. *Police*, December.

WADDINGTON, P. A. J. (1991). *The Strong Arm of the Law*. Oxford: Oxford University Press.

WADDINGTON, P. A. J. (1993). *Calling the Police*. Aldershot: Avebury.

WADDINGTON, P. A. J. (1994). *Liberty and Order: Public Order Policing in a Capital City*. London: UCL Press.

WADDINGTON, P. A. J. (1999a). 'Police (Canteen). Sub-Culture: An Appreciation'. *British Journal of Criminology*, 39(2): 286–308.

WADDINGTON, P. A. J. (1999b). *Policing Citizens: Authority and Rights*. London: UCL Press.

WADDINGTON, P. A. J. and WRIGHT, M. (2008). 'Police Use of Force, Firearms and Riot-Control', in T. NEWBURN (ed.), *Handbook of Policing* (2nd edn). Cullompton: Willan.

WADDINGTON, P. A. J., STENSON, K., and DON, D. (2004). 'In Proportion: Race and Police Stop and Search'. *British Journal of Criminology*, 44(6): 889–914.

WADHAM, B. and GOLDSMITH, A. (2018). *Criminologies of the Military*. London: Hart.

WAKEFIELD, A. (2003). *Selling Security: The Private Policing of Public Space*. Cullompton: Willan.

WAKEFIELD, A. (2005). 'The Public Surveillance Functions of Private Police'. *Surveillance and Society*, 24(4): 529–45.

WAKEFIELD, A. (2012). *Selling Security*. London: Routledge.

WALBY, K. and LIPPERT, R. (2014). *Corporate Security in the 21st Century: Theory and Practice in International Perspective*. Houndsmills, Basingstoke: Palgrave Macmillan.

WALBY, S. and TOWERS, J. (2017). 'Measuring Violence to End Violence: Mainstreaming Gender'. *Journal of Gender-Based Violence*, 1(1): 11–31.

WALBY, S., TOWERS, J., and FRANCIS, B. (2016). 'Is Violent Crime Increasing or Decreasing? A New Methodology to Measure Repeat Attacks Making Visible the Significance of Gender and Domestic Relations'. *British Journal of Criminology*, 56(6): 1203–34.

WALDMAN, P., CHAPMAN, L., and ROBERTSON, J. (2018). 'Peter Thiel's Data-Mining Company is Using War on Terror Tools to Track American Citizens. The Scary Thing? Palantir is Desperate for New Customers'. *Bloomberg*, 19 April.

WALKER, A., FLATLEY, J., KERSHAW, C., and MOON, D. (2009). *Crime in England and Wales 2008/9*. Home Office Statistical Bulletin 11/09 Vol. 1. London: Home Office.

WALKER, N. (2000). *Policing in a Changing Constitutional Order*. London: Sweet & Maxwell.

WALKER, N. (2012). 'The Pattern of Transnational Policing', in TIM NEWBURN (ed.), *The Handbook of Policing* (2nd edn). London: Routledge.

WALKER, S. (1984). '"Broken Windows" and Fractured History: The Use and Misuse of History in Recent Police Patrol Analysis'. *Justice Quarterly*, 1(1): 75–90.

WALKER, S. (1992). *The Police in America: An Introduction* (2nd edn). New York: McGraw-Hill.

WALKER, S. (1999). *In Defense of American Liberties*. Carbondale, IL: Southern Illinois University Press.

WALL, D. (1998). *The Chief Constables of England and Wales*. Aldershot: Avebury.

WALL, D. (2007). *Cybercrime—The Transformation of Crime in the Information Age*. Cambridge: Polity Press.

WALL, D. (2011). 'Policing Cybercrimes: Situating the Public Police in Networks of Security within Cyberspace'. *Police Practice and Research*, 8(2): 185–205.

WALLACH, S. (2011). 'The Medusa Stare: Surveillance and Monitoring of Employees and the Right to Privacy'. *International Journal of Comparative Labour Law and Industrial Relations*, 27: 189–219.

WALSH, J. L. (1977). 'Career Styles and Police Behaviour', in D. H. BAYLEY (ed.), *Police and Society*. Beverly Hills, CA: Sage.

WALTERS, R. (1996/2017). 'The Dream of Multi-Agency Crime Prevention: Pitfalls in Policy and Practice', in T. HOPE (ed.), *Perspectives on Crime Reduction*. London: Routledge.

WAMBAUGH, J. (1971). *The New Centurions*. London: Sphere/New York: Dell.

WARDAK, A. and SHEPTYCKI, J. (2005). *Transnational and Comparative Criminology*. London: Routledge.

WASKO, J. (2001). *Understanding Disney: The Manufacture of Fantasy*. Cambridge: Polity Press.

WATERS, I. (2007). 'Policing, Modernity and Postmodernity'. *Policing and Society*, 17(3): 257–78.

WATTS-MILLER, W. (1987). 'Party Politics, Class Interest and Reform of the Police 1829–56'. *Police Studies*, 10(1): 42–60.

WEATHERITT, M. (1986). *Innovations in Policing*. London: Croom Helm.

WEATHERITT, M. (1993). 'Measuring Police Performance: Accounting or Accountability?', in R. REINER and S. SPENCER (eds), *Accountable Policing: Empowerment, Effectiveness and Equity*. London: Institute for Public Policy Research.

WEBER, L. (2013). *Policing Non-Citizens*. London: Routledge.

WEBER, L. and BOWLING B. (2004). 'Policing Migration: A Framework for Investigating the Regulation of Global Mobility'. *Policing and Society*, 14(3): 195–212.

WEBER, L. and BOWLING, B. (2008). 'Valiant Beggars and Global Vagabonds: Select, Eject, Immobilize'. *Theoretical Criminology*, 12(3): 355–75.

WEBER, L. and BOWLING, B. (2011). 'Stop and Search in Global Context'. *Policing and Society*, 21(4), 353–56.

WEBER, L. and BOWLING, B. (eds) (2014). *Stop and Search: Police Power in Global Context*. London: Taylor & Francis.

WEBSTER, C. (2007). *Understanding Race and Crime*. Maidenhead: Open University Press.

WEINBERGER, B. (1991). *Keeping the Peace? Policing Strikes in Britain 1906–1926*. Oxford: Berg.

WEINBERGER, B. (1995). *The Best Police in the World*. London: Scolar Press.

WEISBURD, D. and NEYROUD, P. (2013). 'Police Science: Toward a New Paradigm'. *Australasian Policing*, 5(2): 13–21.

WEISBURD, D., MASTROFSKI, S. D., MCNALLY, A. M., GREENSPAN, R., and WILLIS, J. J. (2003). 'Reforming to Preserve: Compstat and Strategic Problem Solving in American Policing'. *Criminology and Public Policy*, 2(3): 421–56.

WEISBURD, D., UCHIDA, C., and GREEN, L. (eds) (1993). *Police Innovation and Control of Police*. New York: Springer.

WEISS, R. P. (2018). 'Vanishing Boundaries of Control: Implications for Security and Sovereignty of the Changing Nature and Global Expansion of Neoliberal Criminal Justice Provision', in A. HUCKLESBY and S. LISTER (eds), *The Private Sector and Criminal Justice*. London: Palgrave Macmillan.

WEITZER, R. (2014). 'The Puzzling Neglect of Hispanic Americans in Research on Police-Citizen Relations'. *Ethnic and Racial Studies*, 37(11): 1995–2013.

WEIZMAN, E. (2012). *The Worst of All Possible Evils: Humanitarian Violence from Arendt to Gaza*. London: Verso.

WEIZMAN, E. (2017). *Forensic Architecture: Violence at the Threshold of Detectability*. New York: Zone Books.

WESTLEY, W. (1970). *Violence and the Police*. Cambridge, MA: MIT Press.

WESTMARLAND, L. (2001a). *Gender and Policing: Sex, Power and Police Culture*. Cullompton: Willan.

WESTMARLAND, L. (2001b). 'Blowing the Whistle on Police Violence: Gender, Ethnography and Ethics'. *British Journal of Criminology*, 41(3): 523–35.

WESTMARLAND, L. (2017). 'Putting their Bodies on the Line: Police Culture and Gendered Physicality'. *Policing*, 11(3): 301–17.

WHEELER, S. C. and PETTY, R. E. (2001). 'The Effects of Stereotype Activation on Behaviour'. *Psychological Bulletin*, 127(6): 797–826.

WHELAN, C. and MOLNAR, A. (2019). 'Policing Political Mega-events through "Hard" and "Soft" Tactics: Reflections on Local and Organizational Tensions in Public Order Policing'. *Policing and Society* Vol. 29 No. 1: 85–99.

WHITAKER, B. (1964). *The Police*. London: Penguin.

WHITE, A. (2010). *The Politics of Private Security: Regulation, Reform and Re-Legitimation*. Basingstoke: Palgrave Macmillan.

WHITE, A. (2013). 'The Impact of the Private Security Industry Act 2001'. *Security Journal*, 28(4): 425–42.

WHITE, A. (2018). 'Just Another Industry? (De)Regulation, Public Expectations and Private Security', in A. HUCKLESBY and S. LISTER (eds), *The Private Sector and Criminal Justice*. London: Palgrave Macmillan.

WHITE, M. and FRADELLA, H. (2016). *Stop and Frisk*. New York: New York University Press.

WHITFIELD, J. (2004). *Unhappy Dialogue: The Metropolitan Police and Black Londoners in Post-War Britain*. Cullompton: Willan.

WILKINSON, A. (2008). 'Non-Lethal Force: Looking for Ways to Stop Violent Criminals without Killing Them'. *The New Yorker*, 2 June.

WILKINSON, R. and PICKETT, K. (2009). *The Spirit Level: Why More Equal Societies Almost Always Do Better*. London: Allen Lane.

WILKINSON, R. and PICKETT, K. (2018). *The Inner Level*. London: Allen Lane.

WILLIAMS, E. and STANKO, B. (2015). 'Researching Sexual Violence', in M.

BRUNGER, S. TONG, and D. MARTIN (eds), *Introduction to Policing Research: Taking Lessons from Practice*. London: Routledge.

WILLIAMS, G. (2009). *Shafted: The Media, the Miners' Strike and the Aftermath*. London: Campaign for Press and Broadcasting Freedom.

WILLIAMS, J. (2018). *Stand Out of Our Light: Freedom and Resistance in the Attention Economy*. Cambridge: Cambridge University Press.

WILLIAMS, M., and ROBINSON, A. (2004). 'Problems and Prospects with Policing the Lesbian, Gay and Bisexual Community in Wales'. *Policing and Society*, 14(3): 213–32.

WILLIAMSON, T. (ed.) (2008). *The Handbook of Knowledge-Based Policing*. Chichester: Wiley.

WILLIS, G. D. (2015). *The Killing Consensus: Police, Organized Crime and the Regulation of Life and Death in Urban Brazil*. Oakland, CA: University of California Press.

WILLIS, J. J. (2014). 'A Recent History of the Police', in M. D. REISIG and R. J. KANE (eds), *The Oxford Handbook of Police and Policing*. Oxford: Oxford University Press.

WILSON, F. T. and HENDERSON, H. (2014). 'The Criminological Cultivation of African American Municipal Police Officers: Sambo or Sellout'. *Race and Justice*, 4(1): 45–67.

WILSON, J. Q. (1968). *Varieties of Police Behavior*. Cambridge, MA: Harvard University Press.

WILSON, J. Q. (1975). *Thinking about Crime*. New York: Vintage.

WILSON, J. Q. and BOLAND, B. (1978). 'The Effect of the Police on Crime'. *Law and Society Review*, 12(3): 367.

WILSON, J. Q. and BOLAND, B. (1981). 'The Effect of the Police on Crime: A Response to Jacob and Rich'. *Law and Society Review*, 16(1): 163–70.

WILSON, J. Q., and KELLING, G. (1982). 'Broken Windows'. *Atlantic Monthly*, March: 29–38.

WINLOW, S., HALL, S., TREADWELL, J., and BRIGGS, D. (2015). *Riots and Political Protest*. London: Routledge.

WINSTON, A. (2018). 'Palantir has Secretly been Using New Orleans to test its Predictive Policing Technology'. *The Verge*, 27 February.

WINSTON, B. (1986). *Misunderstanding Media*. Cambridge MA: Harvard University Press.

WINSTON, B. (1998). *Media, Technology and Society A History: From the Telegraph to the Internet*. London: Routledge.

WOFFINDEN, B. (1989). *Miscarriages of Justice* London: Coronet.

WOOD, J. (2006). 'Research and Innovation in the Field of Security: A Nodal Governance View', in J. WOOD and B. DUPONT (eds), *Democracy, Society and the Governance of Security*. Cambridge: Cambridge University Press.

WOOD, J. and DUPONT, B. (eds) (2006). *Democracy, Society and the Governance of Security*. Cambridge: Cambridge University Press.

WOOD, L. (2014). *Crisis and Control: The Militarization of Protest Policing*. London: Pluto Press.

WORTLEY, S. and OWUSU-BEMPAH, A. (2012). 'The Usual Suspects: Police Stop and Search in Canada'. *Policing and Society*, 21(4): 395–407.

YAR, M. (2012). 'Crime, Media and the Will to Representation: Reconsidering Representations in the New Media Age'. *Crime, Media and Culture*, 8(3): 245–60.

YOUNG, J. (1999). *The Exclusive Society*. London: Macmillan.

YOUNG, J. (2007). *The Vertigo of Later Modernity*. London: Sage.

YOUNG, J. (2011). *The Criminological Imagination*. Cambridge: Polity Press.

YOUNG, M. (1991). *An Inside Job: Policing and Police Culture in Britain*. Oxford: Oxford University Press.

YOUNG, M. (1993). *In the Sticks: An Anthropologist in a Shire Force*. Oxford: Oxford University Press.

YOUNG, M. (1995). 'Black Humour—Making Light of Death'. *Policing and Society*, 5(2): 151–68.

YOUNG, R. (2008). 'Street Policing After PACE: The Drift to Summary Justice', in E. CAPE and R. YOUNG (eds), *Regulating Policing*. Oxford: Hart.

YOUNG, R. (2016). 'The Rise and Fall of Stop and Account', in S. LISTER and M. ROWE (eds), *Accountability of Policing*. London: Routledge.

ZAMANI, A. and JORDAN, C. (1989). 'Law Enforcement in the Islamic Republic of Iran and the Socialist Peoples' Libyan Arab Jamahiriya'. *Police Studies*, 12: 39–50.

ZANDER, M. (2007). *Response to Home Office Consultation on the Future of PACE*. London: LSE.

ZEDNER, L. (2003). 'Too Much Security?'. *International Journal of the Sociology of Law*, 31(1): 155–84.

ZEDNER, L. (2006). 'Policing Before and After the Police: The Historical Antecedents of Contemporary Crime Control'. *British Journal of Criminology*, 46(1): 78–96.

ZEDNER, L. (2007). 'Precrime and Postcriminology?'. *Theoretical Criminology*, 11(2): 261–81.

ZEDNER, L. (2009). *Security*. London: Routledge.

ZIMRING, F. (2007). *The Great American Crime Decline*. Oxford: Oxford University Press.

ZIMRING, F. E. (2011). *The City that Became Safe: New York's Lessons for Urban Crime and its Control*. Oxford: Oxford University Press.

SUBJECT INDEX

NAME INDEX